Sicily

F. Mannino/LARA PESSINA

Travel Publications

38 Clarendon Road – WATFORD Herts WD1 1 SX – U.K.
☎ (01923) 415 000
www.ViaMichelin.com
TheGreenGuide-uk@uk.michelin.com

Manufacture française des pneumatiques Michelin
Société en commandite par actions au capital de 304 000 000 EUR
Place des Carmes-Déchaux – 63 Clermont-Ferrand (France)
R.C.S. Clermont-Fd B 855 200 507

No part of this publication may be reproduced in any form
without the prior permission of the publisher.

© Michelin et Cie, Propriétaires-éditeurs, 2001
Dépôt légal Août 2001 – ISBN 2-06-000079-3 – ISSN 0763-1383
Printed in France 07-01/2.1

Typesetting: NORD COMPO, Villeneuve-d'Ascq
Printing & binding: AUBIN, Ligugé

Cover design: Carré Noir, Paris 17ᵉ arr.

THE GREEN GUIDE:
The Spirit of Discovery

The exhilaration of new horizons,
the fun of seeing the world,
the excitement of discovery: this is
what we seek to share with you.
To help you make the most of your
travel experience, we offer first-hand
knowledge and turn a discerning eye
on places to visit.
This wealth of information gives
you the expertise to plan your own
enriching adventure. With THE
GREEN GUIDE showing you the way,
you can explore new destinations
with confidence or rediscover old
ones.
Leisure time spent with THE GREEN
GUIDE is also a time for refreshing
your spirit, enjoying yourself, and
taking advantage of our selection
of fine restaurants, hotels and other
places for relaxing.
So turn the page and open a window
on the world. Join THE GREEN
GUIDE in the spirit of discovery.

Contents

Manuela Magni/MICHELIN

Sicilian puppet

Prickly pears

Sights 98

Admission times and charges 354

Index 372

Traditional Sicilian cart

Sicily's emblem, the Trinacria

5

Maps and plans

COMPANION PUBLICATIONS

Michelin map 432 Sicilia

– covers the island of Sicily and includes an alphabetical index of towns, as well as maps of Agrigento, Catania, Messina, Palermo and Siracusa. Scale 1:400 000.

Travelling to Sicily

Michelin map 988 Italia

– a practical map which provides the visitor with a complete picture of Italy's road network. Scale 1:1 000 000.

Michelin Road Atlas Italia

– a useful, spiral-bound atlas with an alphabetical index of 70 towns and cities. Scale 1:300 000.

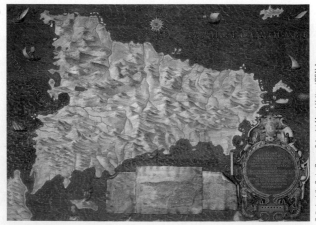

Galleria delle Carte Geografiche dei Musei Vaticani/SCALA

LIST OF MAPS AND PLANS

Map of touring programmes

Plans of archaeological sites

Plans of churches

Using this guide

● The summary maps at the front of this guide are designed to assist at the planning stage of your holiday: the **map of principal sights** is followed by a **map of touring programmes**, with a few suggested itineraries. The **map of places to stay** indicates the main spas, seaside resorts and winter sports resorts, marked by symbols of fountains, suns or snowflakes respectively.

● The **Practical Information** section at the front of the guide provides a wealth of practical tips and suggestions on travelling to and around Sicily, as well as a calendar of traditional events and information on books and films.

● The **Introduction** gives interesting background information on the history, art, culture, natural landscapes, regional specialities and arts and crafts of the island.

● The central section of the guide describes the **Sights** of Sicily, listed in alphabetical order, and includes suggested itineraries and information on surrounding areas. The clock symbol ⊙, placed after sight names, indicates that opening hours and prices for that sight are included in the **Admission times and charges** section at the back of the guide. The pink boxes in the guide contain anecdotes, legends and unusual facts, while the blue boxes give practical information.

● The new **Directory** sections, marked by a marbled blue margin, feature a selection of hotels and restaurants to cater for all budgets and tastes, as well as some practical information. Addresses include family-run *pensioni*, elegant restaurants, typical *trattorie*, traditional cafés, wine bars, ice-cream parlours and *pasticcerie*.

● We greatly appreciate comments and suggestions from our readers. Contact us at:

Michelin Travel Publications, 38 Clarendon Road,
Watford, Herts WD 1 1SX, England.
☎ 01923 415 000
Fax 01923 415 250
TheGreenGuide-uk@uk.michelin.com
www.ViaMichelin.com

G. Guittot/DIAF

Key

	Sight	Seaside Resort	Winter Sports Resort	Spa
Worth a journey	★★★	☆☆☆	�֍✸✸	♧♧♧
Worth a detour	★★	☆☆	✸✸	♧♧
Interesting	★	☆	✸	♧

Tourism

⊘	Admission Times and Charges listed at the end of the guide	►►	Visit if time permits
◉➡	Sightseeing route with departure point indicated	AZ B	Map co-ordinates locating sights
♟♦♟♦	Ecclesiastical building	🄱	Tourist information
✡ ☪	Synagogue – Mosque	⨯ ⁂	Historic house, castle – Ruins
▣ ▥	Building (with main entrance)	ᴗ ✿	Dam – Factory or power station
▪	Statue, small building	☆ ∩	Fort – Cave
✝	Wayside cross	⊓	Prehistoric site
◎	Fountain	▼ Ⱳ	Viewing table – View
●━▪◼━■►	Fortified walls – Tower – Gate	▲	Miscellaneous sight

Recreation

🏇	Racecourse	🚶	Waymarked footpath
⛸	Skating rink	◆	Outdoor leisure park/centre
≋ ▣	Outdoor, indoor swimming pool	🎿	Theme/Amusement park
⚓	Marina, moorings	🐃	Wildlife/Safari park, zoo
⛺	Mountain refuge hut	⊛	Gardens, park, arboretum
□▪■▪□	Overhead cable-car	◔	Aviary, bird sanctuary
🚂	Tourist or steam railway		

Additional symbols

═ ═	Motorway (unclassified)	⊖ ⊙	Post office – Telephone centre
❶ ❶	Junction: complete, limited	✉	Covered market
⊨═	Pedestrian street	·×·	Barracks
ɪ═══ɪ	Unsuitable for traffic, street subject to restrictions	△	Swing bridge
▥▥ ----	Steps – Footpath	ᴗ ✕	Quarry – Mine
🚆 🚌	Railway – Coach station	Ⓑ Ⓕ	Ferry (river and lake crossings)
□+++++□	Funicular – Rack-railway	⛴	Ferry services: Passengers and cars
━ ⬤	Tram – Metro, Underground	⛴	Foot passengers only
Bert (R.)...	Main shopping street	③	Access route number common to MICHELIN maps and town plans

Abbreviations and special symbols

H	Town hall (Municipio)	**T**	Theatre (Teatro)
J	Law courts (Palazzo di Giustizia)	**U**	University (Università)
M	Museum (Museo)	◈	Gendarmerie (carabinieri)
P	Local authority offices (Prefettura)	⛪	Temple, Greek and Roman ruins
POL.	Police station (Polizia, -in large towns: Questura)	🏖	Beach

9

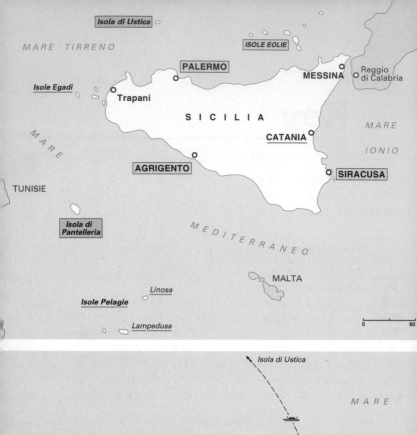

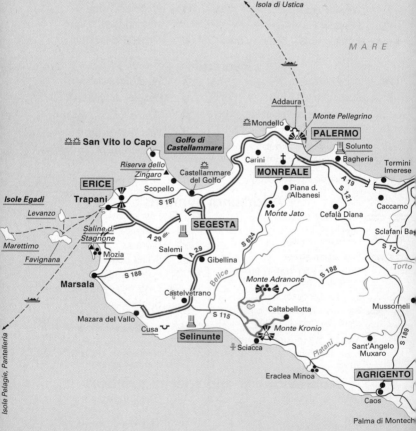

Principal sights

The names of towns or sights described in the guide appear in black on the maps; consult the index for the page number.

Seaside resorts ⚲, spas ♨ and winter resorts ❋ are classified according to the quality and range of facilities offered.

Worth a journey ★★★	⚲⚲⚲ ♨♨♨ ❋❋❋
Worth a detour ★★	⚲⚲ ♨♨ ❋❋
Interesting ★	⚲ ♨ ❋

Itinerary described in this guide: look up one of the sites in the index at the back of the guide to find the page where the tour is described.

STROMBOLI

Panarea

Salina

Filicudi

ISOLE EOLIE

Alicudi

Lipari

VULCANO

Capo di Milazzo

C. Peloro

S 113 d.

TIRRENO

Milazzo

Golfo di Patti

MESSINA

M. Antennammare

Capo Calavà

Tindari

Farmacia di Roccavaldina

Reggio di Calabria

Capo d'Orlando

A 20

Castroreale

Villa Romana di Terme Vigliatore

San Marco d'Alunzio

San Salvatore di Fitalia

Savoca

Pollina

Santo Stefano di Camastra

Novara di Sicilia

Sant' Alessio Siculo

falù

Halæsa

San Fratello

Montalbano Elicona

Castel Mula

Forza d'Agrò

A 20

Castelbuono

Mistretta

Nebrodi

Gole dell'Alcantara

TAORMINA

ollesano

Fiumara d'Arte

San Mauro Castelverde

Madonie

Cesarò

S 120

Randazzo

Linguaglossa ❋

Giardini Naxos ⚲⚲

Naxos

MARE

S 120

Gangi

Nicosia

S 284

ETNA

A 18

S 114

Sperlinga

S 117

Nicolosi ❋

Acireale ♨

A 19

Leonforte

Agira

Simeto

Adrano

Aci Trezza

Faraglioni dei Ciclopi

Calascibetta

Aci Castello

Enna

A 19

Dittaino

A 19

CATANIA

IONIO

S 121

Morgantina

S 417

Caltanissetta

Piazza Armerina

Militello in Val di Catania

S 194

Megara Hyblaea

VILLA ROMANA DEL CASALE

Leontinoi

Thapsos

Eurialo

S 123

S 626

Mazzarino

Pantalica

Anapo

SIRACUSA

Caltagirone

Licodia Eubea

Gli Iblei

Palazzolo Acreide

Fonte Ciane

S 115

Acate o Dirillo

S 514

Chiaramonte Gulfi

Cava Grande

Gela

Comiso

Ragusa

Noto

Eloro

Camarina

Donnafugata

Modica

Ispica

S 115

Riserva Naturale di Vendicari

Scicli

Marina di Ragusa

Touring programmes

ETNA ★★★   Region described in the guide
accompanied by a detailed map.

★★★   ❋❋❋   ♯♯♯   ♨♨♨
★★   = ❋❋   = ♯♯   = ♨♨
★   ❋   ♯   ♨

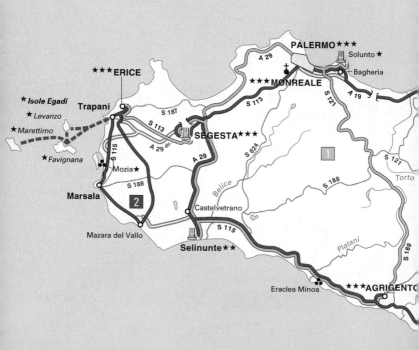

Isola di Ustica

MARE

PALERMO★★★
Solunto ★
★★★ MONREALE
Bagheria
A 29
A 19
S 121
S 113

★★★ ERICE
★ Isole Egadi
★ Levanzo
★ Marettimo
Trapani
★ Favignana
Mozia ★
S 187
S 113
A 29 dir.
A 29
SEGESTA ★★★
S 624
S 115
S 188
Marsala
2
Castelvetrano
S 188
S 121
Torto
Belice
Mazara del Vallo
S 115
Selinunte ★★
Platani
S 189
Eraclea Minoa
★★★ AGRIGENTO

MARE   MEDITERRANEO

0 ———————————— 40 km

1	Archaeological sites and antiquities: 500 km/310 mi (9 days including 3 in Palermo and 2 in Agrigento)
2	Saltworks and tuna fisheries: 150 km/90mi (8 days including 4 in the Egadi Islands)
3	Reach for the heights: 250 km/155mi (5 days)
4	Baroque Sicily - demise and revival in 1693: 350 km/220mi (9 days including 3 in Siracusa)
5	The Demone Valley: 400 km/250mi (10 days including 4 in the Aeolian Islands)
6	Grand Tour of Sicily: 850 km/530mi (15 days)

STROMBOLI ★★★

Panarea

ISOLE EOLIE ★★★

★Lipari

★★★ VULCANO

TIRRENO

Milazzo   S 113   A 20   MESSINA

★Tindari

Capo d'Orlando   Patti   Reggio di Calabria

S 116

5

Cefalù ★★   S 113   A 20   Randazzo   TAORMINA ★★★

6   Linguaglossa   MARE

S 120

Petralia   Gangi   Nicosia   ETNA ★★★

S 120   S 117   Acireale

3   Leonforte   S 121   Aci Trezza

A 19   Simeto

altanissetta   Enna★   Dittaino   A 19   CATANIA★   IONIO

S 121

S 117b.

Pietraperzia   Piazza Armerina   S 417

S 626   SIRACUSA ★★★

S 123   **VILLA ROMANA DEL CASALE ★★★**   Grammichele   **4**   Anapo

S 115   Caltagirone ★   S 194

Acate o Dirillo   S 514   Ragusa ★   S 115

Ispica ★   Noto ★★

★Modica

Scicli

Places to stay

- Seaside resort
- Spa
- Winter sports resort

Seaside resorts ⚓ , spas ♨
and winter resorts ❄ are classified
according to the quality and range
of facilities offered.

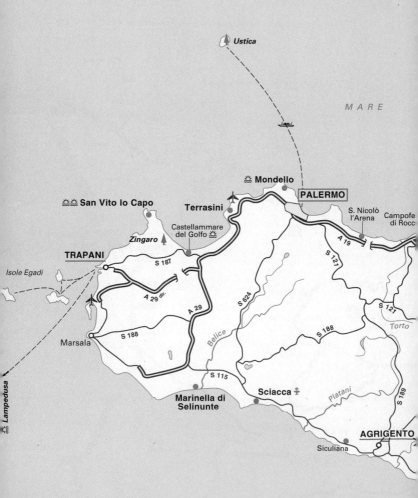

STROMBOLI

ISOLE EOLIE

Lipari

♨ Porto di Levante

T I R R E N O

MESSINA

Milazzo

Reggio di
Calabria

Gioiosa Marea   Oliveri

♨ **Capo d'Orlando**

**Castroreale
Terme** ♨

**S. Agata
di Militello**

A 20

Novara di
Sicilia

**Sant' Alessio
Siculo** ♨

EFALÙ

Pollina

Madonie

♠ *Nebrodi*

Mistretta

Linguaglossa ✳

TAORMINA

Castelbuono

Cesarò

**GIARDINI
NAXOS** ♨♨

Isnello

**Piano
Zucchi**

Geraci Siculo

♠ *Etna*

△
ETNA

MARE

esano

Petralia Soprana

S 120

S 117

Simeto

S 120

S 284

Nicolosi ✳

Acireale ♨

A 19

S 121

S 121

ENNA

Dittaino

A 19

CATANIA

I O N I O

640

S 417

S 6 26

S 123

S 19A

S 115

S 115

SIRACUSA

Salso

Acate o Dirillo

S 514

Fontane Bianche

Gela

RAGUSA

Noto Marina

♠ *Vendicari*

♨ **Marina di Ragusa**

Anapo

Practical
Information

Planning your trip

PASSPORTS AND VISAS

British visitors travelling to Italy must be in possession of a valid national passport. Citizens of other European Union countries only need a national identity card. In case of loss or theft report to the embassy or consulate and the local police.

Entry visas are required by Australian, New Zealand, Canadian and US citizens (if their intended stay exceeds three months). Apply to the Italian Consulate (visa issued same day; delay if submitted by mail). US citizens may find the booklet **Your Trip Abroad** useful for information on visa requirements, customs regulations, medical care, etc when travelling in Europe – available from the Superintendent of Documents, PO Box 371954, Pittsburgh, PA 15250-7954, ☎ (202) 512 1800; Fax (202) 512 2250; www.access.gpo.gov

CUSTOMS

As of 30 June 1999, those travelling between countries within the European Union can no longer purchase "duty-free" goods. For further information, there is a free leaflet, **Duty Paid**, available from HM Customs and Excise, Finchley Excise Advice Centre, Berkeley House, 304 Regents Park Road, London N3 2JY, ☎ (020) 7865 4400. The US Customs Service offers a free publication **Know Before You Go** for US citizens, ☎ (202) 927 6724; www.customs.gov

HEALTH

British citizens should apply for **Form E 111**, issued by the Post Office, which entitles the holder to urgent treatment for accident or unexpected illness in EU countries. This form should be presented to the relevant medical services prior to receiving treatment. For further information in the UK, contact the Department of Health and Social Security ☎ (0191) 218 7777. Visitors are strongly advised to take out additional travel insurance to cover against any expenses not covered by form E 111, as well as lost luggage, theft, cancellation, delayed departure etc.

Non-EU travellers are advised to check with their insurance companies about taking out supplementary medical insurance with specific overseas coverage.

DRIVING DOCUMENTS

Drivers must have a valid national or international **driving licence**, the vehicle's current **registration certificate** and a **green card** for insurance.

PETS (CATS AND DOGS)

A general health certificate and proof of rabies vaccination should be obtained from your local vet before departure.

BY AIR

Several international airlines fly into Palermo, Catania and Reggio Calabria, especially during the summer season when additional charter flights are laid on. For further details consult your local travel agents.

The three leading Italian companies providing air services to Sicily are Alitalia, Air Sicilia and Meridiana.

Alitalia: 4 Portman Square, Marble Arch, London W1H 9PS; ☎ (020) 7486 8432; Fax (020) 7486 8431; www.alitalia.co.uk Reservations can also be made (by telephone only) on ☎ 08705 448 259.

4-5 Dawson Street, Dublin 2; ☎ (01) 677 5171; Fax (01) 677 3373.

666 Fifth Avenue, New York, NY 10103; ☎ (212) 903 3300; toll-free 1 800 223 5730 (reservations from within the USA); Fax (212) 903 3350; www.alitaliausa.com

Viale Marchetti 111, 00148 Rome; ☎ 06 65 621; www.alitalia.com

Air Sicilia: the headquarters of Air Sicilia is in Palermo, at 9 via Pasubio; ☎ 091 626 12 22 or 800 412 411 (toll-free number from within Italy).

Air Sicilia offices are located at the airports of Palermo ☎ 091 21 85 13; Lampedusa ☎ 0922 97 19 96; Pantelleria ☎ 0923 91 22 13; and Trapani ☎ 0923 84 14 23.

Meridiana: operate flights from London Gatwick via Florence to Palermo, and from Heathrow via Rome and Milan (connecting with other internal services) to Catania and Reggio Calabria.

Sales offices in London (☎ 020 7839 2222), Los Angeles (☎ 310 216 5777), New York (☎ 201 228 5200) and Miami (☎ 954 447 4390), toll-free from the United States ☎ 1 800 275 5566.

Travelling in Sicily

BY AIR

Airports – Sicily's two main airports are Punta Raisi (now re-named **Falcone e Borsellino** after the two judges killed in a terrorist attack nearby) in Palermo and **Fontanarossa** close to the sprawling city of Catania on the east coast; the latter is well located for visitors intending to stay around Taormina and Siracusa, Ragusa and Gela, or even for the hinterland (Piazza Armerina).

There is also an airport in **Reggio Calabria**, which although on the Italian peninsula, lies close to the Straits of Messina.

Other Sicilian airports are located at **Trapani**, where the services are neither regular nor frequent, and on the islands of **Pantelleria** and **Lampedusa**, which are extremely important for people only interested in these two islands. During the summer, there are direct flights to and from some of the larger Italian cities. For detailed information, see the relevant section *(see PANTELLERIA and LAMPEDUSA)*.

BY CAR

Until the bridge over the Straits becomes a reality, the link between Sicily and the rest of Italy is provided by ferries and hydrofoils between Reggio Calabria or Villa San Giovanni and Messina.

Ferrovie dello Stato (Italian state railways) provide a car-ferry service, but only from **Villa San Giovanni** (☎ 0965 75 60 99). The time of the crossing depends on the type of ferry (whether it is transporting only cars or also train carriages), and varies between 25-45min. A ferry service is also operated by Società Caronte Shipping, ☎ 0965 75 14 13. Because of the frequent service (every 30min), booking is not necessary. Just turn up at the dock.

From **Reggio Calabria**, there are also services for foot-passengers only, both by ferry (Stazione Ferrovie dello Stato, ☎ 0965 00 35 25) and hydrofoil (Aliscafi SNAV, ☎ 0965 29 568). *For connections between Palermo and the Italian mainland, see p 258.*

Travelling by car is certainly one of the best ways of covering the island for people who intend to visit not only the main towns and cities, but also the smaller, more remote centres. However, this clearly does not apply once your destination has been reached: Palermo traffic is so heavy and chaotic that you would be well advised to leave your car somewhere safe and rely on public transport to get around, or walk. The motorways *(autostrade)* in Sicily do not cover the whole island. Tolls must be paid on the sections between Messina and Furiano (A 20), Catania and Messina (A 18) and Cefalù and Buonfornello (A 20). However, the others are all free of charge. Otherwise, towns are normally connected by good roads with fast-flowing traffic. The only "problems" you are likely to encounter are on roads to small mountain towns and villages, where the views are marvellous but the roads tend to be winding and therefore slower to use.

Maritime connections

Accident or breakdown – A **road-rescue** service is provided by the ACI (Automobile Club Italia).
For information ☏ 06 44 77 (24-hour service).
For the emergency service ☏ 116 (24-hour service).

Maps – The **Michelin Map 432** covers Sicily (scale 1:400 000). A practical alternative is the spiral-bound **Michelin Tourist & Motoring Atlas Italy** (scale: 1:300 000).

Car rental – The major car-hire companies are represented in most of the larger cities and at the main airports. Some tour operators offer fly-and-drive packages.

BY TRAIN

The train operates via the Straits of Messina, with coaches being loaded directly onto the ferry at Villa San Giovanni. Ticket prices are all inclusive. For information, apply to the Ferrovie dello Stato (Italian State Railways).

General information

BEACHES

At the seaside there are supervised beaches where a fee is charged for umbrellas, chairs and sunbeds; other beaches, which are free of charge, may be less well-maintained.

CHURCHES

Churches are usually open in the morning, close at lunchtime, often until 5pm or 6pm, and then stay open until 7pm or 8pm.
Visitors should be appropriately dressed: long trousers for men; no bare shoulders or very short skirts for women; those who do not observe this convention may be refused entry by the Verger or others in authority.
As many of the works of art are positioned high up, it is a good idea to take binoculars. Small change (100L, 200L and 500L coins) is useful for activating light time-switches.

CURRENCY AND CHANGING MONEY

The unit of currency is the lira which is issued in notes (100 000L, 50 000L, 20 000L, 10 000L, 5 000L, 2 000L and 1 000L) and in coins (1 000L, 500L, 200L, 100L and 50L). Brass telephone tokens known as *gettone* are also legal tender (200L). Banks are usually open Monday to Friday, 8.30am to 1.30pm and 3pm to 4pm. They are closed on Saturdays, Sundays and public holidays.
Foreign currency may be changed at banks, hotels, post offices (no travellers cheques), bureaux de change, at railway stations and airports. Commission is always charged.

CREDIT CARDS

Payment by credit card is widespread in shops, hotels and restaurants but rare at petrol stations. **The Red Guide Italia** and the **The Red Guide Europe** indicate which credit cards are accepted at hotels and restaurants.

ELECTRICITY

The voltage is 220AC, 50Hz; the sockets are for two-pin plugs – so do not forget to take an adaptor for hairdryers etc.

HOLIDAYS

Public holidays *(giorni festivi)* include Saturdays and Sundays.

January: 1 (New Year) and 6 (Epiphany)

Easter: Sunday and Monday *(lunedi dell'Angelo)*

April: 25 (St Mark's day and liberation in 1945)

May: 1

August: 15 (The Assumption – *Ferragosto*)

November: 1

December: 8 (Immaculate Conception), 25 and 26 (Christmas and St Steven's day).

A working day is *un giorno feriale.*

MUSEUMS

Most museums do not open on Mondays; on other days many close at 2pm and the ticket offices at 1.30pm. It is advisable to check opening times before visiting as these are subject to change.

In many museums bags must be left in the cloakroom. Flash photography is usually not permitted.

PHARMACIES

A pharmacy *(farmacia)* is identified by a red and white cross. When it is closed it will advertise the names of the pharmacy on duty and a list of doctors.

SHOPPING

Most shops are open from Mondays to Saturdays, 8am to 1pm and 3.30pm to 7.30pm.

Italian **sizes** are not the same as other European sizes: for women an English 12 in clothes corresponds to an Italian size 44 and an English 5 in shoes corresponds to an Italian size 37; for men an English 40 in clothes corresponds to an Italian size 50, an English 15 in collar size to an Italian size 38, and an English size 8 in shoes corresponds to an Italian size 42.

Italian **videos** tend to be recorded on the PAL system.

TIME DIFFERENCES

The time in Italy is usually one hour ahead of the United Kingdom and changes during the last weekend in March and October between Summer Time *(ora legale)* and Winter Time *(ora solare)*.

TELEPHONE

The state telecommunication system is run by **TELECOM ITALIA.** Telephone **bureaux** have public booths where the customer pays for units used *(scatti)* at the counter after the call. Public **call boxes**, operated by phone cards and/or coins or tokens are to be found along the street and in most bars. Phone cards are sold in denominations of 5 000L, 10 000L or 15 000L *(schede da cinque, dieci, quindici mille lire)* and are available from post offices and tobacconists (*Tabaccaio* sign bearing a white T on a black background). Reduced rates for national calls apply after 6.30pm and between 10pm and 8am for international calls.

Dialling codes – For calls to other towns in Italy, dial the area code and the correspondent's number.

For international calls dial 00 followed by the country code: **61** for **Australia**; **1** for **Canada**; **353** for **Ireland**; **64** for **New Zealand**; **44** for the **UK**; **1** for the **USA**.

For calls from the UK to Italy dial **00 39**, followed by the area code, including the first 0, and the correspondent's number.

Operator service – **12** (national directory enquiries); **15** (assisted operator service, eg reverse charge call); **176** (information in foreign languages).

Accommodation

HOTELS

The **Directory** sections in the main text of the guide list a selection of hotels chosen for their value for money, location or character, including historic hotels, old converted buildings, such as *bagli* (fortified buildings) and convents. Hotels are sub-divided into three categories, each based on the price of a double room:
– **Budget**: Under 150 000L.
– **Moderate**: Between 150 000L and 300 000L.
– **Expensive**: Comfort and charm for a memorable stay – with prices to match!
For a more exhaustive list of hotels consult **The Red Guide Italia**.
Visitors are advised to book in advance during the high season (July and August) when prices are significantly higher than at other times of the year; it is worth remembering that good service and value for money are often easier to find a few miles from the historic centre of towns. It is also advisable to check when making a reservation whether or not the hotel accepts credit cards.

CAMP SITES

The guide *Campeggi e villaggi in Italia* published annually by the TCI, in collaboration with Federcampeggio, provides details on the camping facilities available nationwide, including Sicily. Information can also be obtained from the **Federazione Italiana del Campeggio e del Caravanning** (via Vittorio Emanuele II 11, 50041 Calenzano (FI), ☎ 055 88 23 91, Fax 055 88 25 918) which also has illustrated information on the various camp sites.
Information on particularly attractive or well-located camp sites is given in the **Directory** sections in the main text of the guide.

AGRITURISMO

This option offers a special kind of holiday: it involves staying in a rural setting, often in close contact with a working farm or land-holding. In most cases, the farm owners provide accommodation and hospitality and the chance to taste the specialities produced on the farm. For the names and details of *agriturismi* in Sicily, consult the *Turismo Verde in Sicilia* guide promoted by the **Consorzio Villaggio Globale** (an offshoot of the Italian Farming Confederation) ☎ 091 30 81 51, *Vacanze e Natura*, compiled by the **Associazione Terranostra** (Rome) ☎ 06 46 82 370, *Agriturismo e Vacanze Verdi*, compiled by the **Associazione Agriturist** (Rome) ☎ 06 68 52 342, *Guida all'Agriturismo* by Demetra and *Vacanze Verdi* edited by Edagricole. For the more intrepid, the *Guida del Turismo alternativo* (*Sicilia occidentale* and *Sicilia orientale*) is available from bookshops and newsagents, or can be requested directly from the Sicilian Tourist Service, which provides an information and booking service ☎ 091 54 35 06.
For further information, contact *Turismo Verde*, via Flaminia 56, Rome, ☎ 06 36 00 02 94. Information on particularly attractive or well-located accommodation is given in the **Directory** sections in the main text of the guide.

BED AND BREAKFAST

The bed and breakfast formula is becoming increasingly popular in Italy, allowing visitors to overnight in high quality accommodation, often in rural areas. For further information, contact **Bed & Breakfast Italia**, Palazzo Sforza Cesarini, corso Vittorio Emanuele II 282, 00186 Rome, ☎ 06 68 78 618, Fax 06 68 78 619; www.bbitalia.it/, or **Dolce Casa**, via Messina 15, 20154 Milan, ☎ 02 33 11 814, Fax 02 33 13 009; www.touritel.com/dolcecasa

CONVENTS AND MONASTERIES

A number of religious orders provide simple and reasonably priced accommodation for visitors, mainly in the major cities. The only disadvantage is the curfew, which is usually around 10.30-11pm. For information, contact the relevant tourist office or the archidiocese.

RESTAURANTS

The **Directory** sections (marked by a blue margin) list a choice of typical local restaurants and *trattorie*, chosen for their unusual character, attractive atmosphere or excellent local cuisine. For a more exhaustive list of restaurants consult the current edition of **The Red Guide Italia** *(see p 94 for information on Sicilian regional specialities)*.

Useful addresses

ITALIAN EMBASSIES AND CONSULATES

To obtain further information, contact the nearest Italian embassy or consulate:

Embassies

14 Three Kings Yard, London W1Y 2EH; ☎ (020) 7312 2200, Fax (020) 7312 2230; emblondon@embitaly.org.uk; www.embitaly.org.uk

1601 Fuller Street, NW Washington, DC 20009; ☎ (202) 328 5500, Fax (202) 462 3605; www.italyemb.org

275 Slater Street, 21st floor, Ottawa, Ontario, K1P 5H9; ☎ (613) 232 2401/2/3, Fax (613) 233 1484; italcomm@trytel.com

Consulates

38 Eaton Place, London SW1X 8AN; ☎ (020) 7235 9371, Fax (020) 7823 1609.

Rodwell Tower, 111 Piccadilly, Manchester M1 2HY; ☎ (0161) 236 9024, Fax (0161) 236 5574; passaporti@italconsulman.demon.co.uk

32 Melville Street, Edinburgh EH3 7HA; ☎ (0131) 226 3631, Fax (0131) 226 6260; consedimb@consedimb.demon.co.uk

690 Park Avenue, New York, NY 10021; ☎ (212) 737 9100, Fax (212) 249 4945; italconsny@aol.com; www.italconsulnyc.org

3489 Drummond Street, Montreal, Quebec, H3G 1X6; ☎ (514) 849 8351/2/3/4, Fax (514) 499 9471; consitmtl@cyberglobe.net

136 Beverley Street, Toronto, Ontario, M5T 1Y5; ☎ (416) 977 1566 (from Canada and USA); (416) 977 2569 (from other countries); Fax (416) 977 1119; consolato.it@toronto.italconsulate.org www.toronto.italconsulate.org

FOREIGN EMBASSIES AND CONSULATES IN ITALY

Australia – Via Alessandria 215, 00198 Rome; ☎ 06 85 27 21; www.australian embassy.it

Canada – Via GB Rossi 27, 00161 Rome; ☎ 06 44 59 81; rome@dfait-maeci.gc.ca

Ireland – Piazza di Campitolli 3, 00100 Rome; ☎ 06 69 79 121, Fax 06 67 92 354.

UK – Via XX Settembre 80a, 00187 Rome ☎ 06 48 25 441 or 06 48 25 551, Fax 06 48 73 324; www.ukinitalia.it
Via Cavour 121, Palermo ☎ 091 32 64 12 or 091 58 25 33, Fax 091 58 42 40.

USA – Via Veneto 119a, 00187 Rome ☎ 06 46 741, Fax 06 48 82 672; www.usis.it
Via Vaccarini 1, 90143 Palermo ☎ 091 30 58 57, Fax 091 62 56 026.

ITALIAN STATE TOURIST BOARD

The **Ente Nazionale Italiano per il Turismo** (ENIT) has offices at home and abroad – for local tourist information services see below:

UK – 1 Princes Street, London W1R 8AY; ☎ (020) 7408 1254; Fax (020) 7493 6695; enitlond@globalnet.co.uk; www.enit.it *(office open Mon to Fri, 9am-5pm)*.

USA – Suite 1565, 630 Fifth Avenue, New York, NY 10111; ☎ (212) 245 5095; (212) 245 4822 (brochure line); enitny@italiantourism.com For Los Angeles, ☎ (310) 820 0098 (brochure line).

Canada – Italian Government Travel Office, 1 Place Ville Marie, Suite 1914, Montreal, Quebec, H3B 2C3; ☎ (514) 866 7667/8 (information office); (514) 392 1429 (brochure line); initaly@ican.net

Regional tourist information office addresses and telephone numbers are given in the **Admission times and charges** section of this guide.

Useful telephone numbers

Directory enquiries: 12 (free of charge from call phones or if the number requested does not yet feature in the list of subscribers)
Call collect: 15
Carabinieri: 112 (only to be used in an emergency)
Police, Red Cross, Ambulance: 113
Fire brigade: 115
Vehicle recovery service (ACI): 116

Leisure activities

"Per montagne e per valloni colle nevi e i sollioni...
– Through mountains and valleys, in the snows and the summer heat"

Marriage of Figaro by Da Ponte

Sicily can be explored on foot, on horseback, underwater, by canoe, in a sailing-boat, even by bicycle. The scope is endless for anyone with a love of the great outdoors. An excellent tool for getting organised, offering a host of good suggestions, is the **Guida per il turismo alternativo**, divided into two volumes, one covering the east and the other the west of the island. It is available from newsagents and book-shops, or can be ordered through ☎ 091 54 35 06.

Below are listed the organisations and associations where information about specific activities can be obtained.

Canoeing and kayaking – Comitato Regionale Canoa-Cayak, via Vittorio Emanuele traversa 6/2, 98030 Giardini Naxos. ☎/Fax: 0942 510 00.

Touring by bike – Comitato Regionale della Federazione Ciclistica Italiana, Settore Cicloturismo, c/o Velodromo Paolo Borsellino, via Lanza di Scalea, 90146 Palermo; ☎/Fax 091 67 18 711.

Walking and mountaineering – Recently a number of parks and nature reserves have been created in Sicily, providing comprehensive networks of footpaths in order to keep visitors away from vulnerable tracts of land; they also often provide guides for visitors. Not far from Palermo there is the **Riserva Naturale dello Zingaro** *(see p 136)* with particularly good walking between Scopello and San Vito lo Capo.

In the hinterland between Palermo and Messina, the **Parco dei Nebrodi** and **Parco delle Madonie** *(see MADONIE e NEBRODI)* offer plenty of scope for walking for all levels of ability. Another very popular area for walking and studying botany is the **Parco dell'Etna** *(see ETNA)* where there are ranges of interesting hiking routes and nature trails. Apply to the associations mentioned above (particularly if intending to climb to the craters) and make allowances for taking a guide – a wise investment for peace of mind. For information, illustrated material and local guides for low-level paths, enquire at the park headquarters (Ente Parco) located at via Etnea 107, **Nicolosi** ☎ 095 91 45 88, Fax 095 91 47 38 (Monday to Friday, 9am-1pm, and 3.30pm-6.30pm Wednesday).

For studying botany and bird watching, the following nature reserves are recommended:
– **Riserva Naturale orientata del Simeto** (visitors centre on SS114 between Catania and Syracuse, in the direction of Syracuse, at Ponte Primosole): open 9am-1pm and 2pm-6.30pm (4pm in winter).
– **Riserva Fiumefreddo** (visitor centre c/o Masseria Belfiore in via Marina at Fiumefreddo, *see p 190*): open 9am-1pm and 2pm-6.30pm (4pm in winter).
– **Cava Grande di Cassibile** *(see NOTO)*, a deep gorge carved out by the River Cassibile.
– **Anapo Valley**, a quarry about 13km/8mi long (although people wishing to walk only part of the route may take advantage of the minibus service provided by the Corpo Forestale, *see PANTALICA)*.
– **Riserva Naturale Orientata di Vendicari** *(see VENDICARI)*, a marsh with an extremely rich eco-system, option of guided tours.
– **Riserva Naturale della Foce dell'Irminio** (Province of Ragusa), Provincia Regionale di Ragusa, viale del Fante 2, 97100 Ragusa. ☎ 0932 67 51 11.
– **Oasi di Torresalsa** (near Siculiana) run by the WWF, via E Albanese 98, 90139 Palermo. ☎ 091 58 30 40.
– **Riserva delle Maccalube** at Aragona (Province of Agrigento), Legambiente, via S La Rosa 53, 92021 Aragona. ☎ 0922 69 92 10.
– **Riserva Naturale Orientata Monte Pellegrino**, run by Rangers d'Italia, viale Diana, Giusino, Palermo. ☎ 091 67 16 066.
– **Riserva del Bosco della Ficuzza e della Rocca Busambra** *(see p 296)*.

For information about the above reserves and others in the process of being created, contact the **Assessorato Regionale Territorio e Ambiente**, ☎ 091 40 95 44.

For details of more arduous walking, hostelling and cross-country hiking, contact: **CAI** (Club Alpino Italiano), via G Natoli 20, 98100 Messina, ☎ 090 69 31 96.

Pot-holing – The **Federazione Speleologica Regionale Siciliana**, which has its main office in Palermo, is an umbrella organisation for the various pot-holing associations. For further information, contact the president of the organisation, Dott. Ruggeri, ☎ 0932 62 16 99. There are some cave-systems classed as natural reserves maintained by the CAI *(for address, see above)* and by Legambiente, Comitato Regionale, via Agrigento 67, Palermo ☎ 091 30 16 63.

The main options are listed below:
– **Riserva Grotta di Carburangeli** at Carini (Province of Palermo). Legambiente organises guided tours of the cave. Corso Umberto I 64, Carini, ☎ 091 86 69 797.
– **Riserva Grotta di Santa Ninfa** (Province of Trapani). Legambiente organises guided tours of the cave. Via S. Anna 101, Santa Ninfa, ☎ 0924 62 376.
– **Riserva Naturale Grotta Conza** (Province of Palermo). CAI Sicilia, via Roma 443, Palermo, ☎ 091 32 26 89.

– **Riserva Naturale Monte Conca** (Province of Caltanissetta). CAI, corso Pietro Nenni 4, Milena, ☎ 0934 93 32 54.

– **Riserva Naturale Grotta di Entella** at Contessa Entellina (Province of Palermo). CAI, ☎ 091 84 65 70.

For information on these and other reserves in the process of being created, contact the **Assessorato Regionale Territorio e Ambiente**, ☎ 091 40 95 44.

Winter sports – The best place for skiing in Sicily is Mount Etna. There are two main centres: Nicolosi and Linguaglossa. For detailed information about the facilities, contact the Pro Loco of the individual towns *(addresses and contact numbers listed in the section on ETNA)*.

Scuba-diving and other underwater activities – Much of the Sicilian coastline is fringed by fascinating underwater seascapes. The most exotic havens are the islands offshore where the water is particularly clear and the sea-life especially varied. On Ustica, the **Riserva Naturale Marina** *(see USTICA)* organises sea-watching and diving trips, special scuba-diving courses and the opportunity of exploring underwater archaeology and photography. For further information, contact the **Federazione Italiana Pesca Sportiva Attività Subacquea, Comitato Regionale Sicilia**, via Terrasanta 93, Palermo, ☎ 091 30 23 02.

Sailing – For details of yacht-charters contact specialist tour operators in your home country or the **Federazione Italiana Vela**, via E Albanese 7, Palermo ☎ 091 34 28 20.

Boating around the Egadi Islands

25

Alternative options – Both the **World Wide Fund for Nature (WWF)** and Legambiente, another conservation organisation, oversee holiday camps and animal recovery centres. The **WWF** operate three recovery centres for wild animals at Alcamo, Enna and Messina, a centre for domestic breeds in danger of extinction (the Sicilian hen, Agrigento goat and ass of Pantelleria) at Alcamo, as well as various recovery centres for wild turtles. In addition to these, they organise a series of summer camps each year. To receive further information contact the Sicilian regional office: Delegazione Sicilia della WWF at via E Albanese 98, Palermo ☎ 091 58 30 40.
Legambiente (☎ 091 30 16 63) organise a summer camp on Lampedusa (to help protect the loggerhead turtles) and another on Pantelleria.

Books, films and the Internet

RECOMMENDED READING

Fiction

The Leopard – Giuseppe Lampedusa (Harvill Press 1996)
Little Novels of Sicily – Giovanni Verga, DH Lawrence (Steerforth Press 2000)
Sometimes the Soul: Two Novellas of Sicily – Gioia Timpanelli (WW Norton & Co 1998)
"Cavalleria Rusticana" and Other Stories – Giovanni Verga, H McWilliam (Trans) (Penguin Books 1999)
Short Sicilian Novels – Giovanni Verga (Dedalus Ltd 1994)
The House by the Medlar Tree – Giovanni Verga (University of California Press 1983)
Il Giorno Della Civetta – Leonardo Sciascia, G Slowey (Ed) (St Martin's Press 1998)

Biography

Italian Journey – JW Goethe (Penguin Books 1970)
The Sicilian – M Puzo (Arrow 2000)
The Honoured Society – N Lewis (Eland Books 1984)
The Happy Ant-heap – N Lewis (Jonathan Cape 1998)
The Dark Princes of Palermo – N Lewis (Jonathan Cape 2000)
I Came, I Saw: an Autobiography – N Lewis (Picador 1996)
On Persephone's Island: A Sicilian Journal (Vintage Departures) – Mary Taylor Simeti (Vintage Books 1995)
Sicilian Lives – D Dolci (Writers and Readers 1982)

Reference

The Greek Myths – R Graves (Penguin Books 1984)
Metamorphoses – Ovid, EJ Kenney (Ed), AD Melville (Trans) (Oxford Paperbacks 1998)
Odes – Pindar (Penguin Books 1901)
The Odyssey – Homer, R Fagles (Trans), B Knox (Intro) (Penguin Books 1997)
The Aeneid – Virgil, D West (Trans) (Penguin Books 1991)
The Normans in Sicily – John Julius Norwich (Penguin Books 1992)
The Sicilian Vespers – S Runciman (Cambridge University Press 1992)
The Norman Kingdom of Sicily – D Matthew (Cambridge University Press 1992)
The Golden Honeycomb – V Cronin, W Forman (Harvill Press 1992)
Walking in Sicily – Gillian Price (Cicerone Press 2000)
In Sicily – Norman Lewis (Jonathan Cape 2000)
The Honoured Society – Norman Lewis (Eland Books 1984)

FILMS

1948	*La Terra Trema* (The Earth Trembles) by Luchino Visconti, based on *I Malavoglia* by G Verga, tells the story of a family of fishermen from Aci Trezza.
1950	*Stromboli* by Roberto Rossellini.
1959	*L'Avventura* (The Adventure) by Michelangelo Antonioni.
1972	*The Godfather* by Francis Ford Coppola, the first of a series of three films, *The Godfather Trilogy*.
1987	*Il Siciliano* (The Sicilian) by Michael Cimino.

1989	*Cinema Paradiso* by Giuseppe Tornatore.
1989	*Mery per sempre* (Mary For Ever) by Marco Risi, set in Palermo prison.
1994	*Caro Diario* (Dear Diary) by Nanni Moretti, the second episode of which is set in the Aeolian Islands.
1995	*Il Postino* (The Postman) by Massimo Troisi, set in Salina.
1995	*Mighty Aphrodite* by Woody Allen, in which the Greek choir sings in the theatre at Taormina.

WEB SITES

SICILY IN GENERAL

Regione Sicilia: www.sicily.infcom.it

Regione Sicilia: www.regione.sicilia.it (Sicily's official web site)

Sicilia in Tour: www.sicilia.com (art, history, local events and wine routes)

Omaggio alla poesia siciliana: www.cys.it/poesie (poetry in dialect recited by the authors)

Sicilia e le sue tradizioni: www.videobank.it/sicily (information on Sicily's traditional carts and puppets)

Enna: www.deltaenna.it

Etna On Line: /etna.masterweb.it/index.htm

PROVINCES AND TOWNS

Agrigento: www.mediatel.it/comune.agrigento

Agrigento e provincia: www.mediatel.it/provincia.agrigento/hometur.html

Bagheria: www.datastudio.it/comune/guttuso.htm

Catania: www.apt-catania.com

Cefalù: www.kefa.it/cefalu

Messina: www.meonline.it (also supplies information about the Aeolian Islands)

Palermo: www.comune.palermo.it/index.htm

Palermo e provincia: www.aapit.pa.it

Ragusa e provincia: www.ibla.net

Trapani: www.assoi.com/comunetp/index1.htm

Calendar of events

This section does not include all the traditional festivals that take place on the island, which are particularly numerous around Easter and Carnival. For a complete list, contact the APT (tourist information office) of the town or area you plan to visit.

6 January
Piana degli Albanesi............. *Festa della Teofania* – Greek-Orthodox Epiphany.

20 January
Acireale.................................. *Festa di San Sebastiano* (St Sebastian): the litter bearing the statue of the saint is carried out of the church dedicated to the saint and through the streets of the little town in a frantic race.

3 February
Salemi.................................... *Festa dei Pani di San Biagio* – Festival of St Blaise held in the Rabato district of the town. Small decorative loaves of bread are baked for the occasion.

1-15 February
Agrigento.............................. *Sagra del mandorlo in fiore* (Almond-blossom Festival) and International Folklore Festival.

5 February
Catania .... *Festa di Sant'Agata*.

Week of carnival, culminating in Martedì Grasso (Shrove Tuesday).
Acireale.................................. Carnival celebrations with processions of allegorical floats.

Sciacca .... Carnival celebrations with processions of allegorical floats.

Termini Imerese .... Processions of allegorical floats through the town.

Saturday preceding 19 March
Scicli .... *Cavalcata di San Giuseppe.*

19 March
Salemi.................................... Festa di San Giuseppe (St Joseph's day) – *Cene di San Giuseppe*, special dinners and votive loaves of bread.

Easter
Alcamo................................... *Procession of the dead Christ and Our Lady of Sorrows* on Good Friday.

Caltanissetta......................... Procession of 16 groups of statues.

Castelvetrano........................ Good Friday procession. Easter Sunday morning: Festa dell'Aurora, celebrated since 1860.

Enna .... Procession of the Confraternities on Good Friday.

Erice .... *Processione dei Misteri* on Good Friday.

Marsala.................................. Holy Week procession.

Messina .... *Processione delle Varette*, with the 14 Stations of the Cross on Good Friday.

Piana degli Albanesi............. During Holy Week, the inhabitants walk about in traditional costumes embroidered with gold and silver thread. On Good Friday, choral concert given by the Simenon Kremate choir and the Enkomia procession takes place. On Easter Sunday, white doves are released, sprigs of rosemary are thrown about and red-painted eggs are exchanged.

Prizzi .... Easter Sunday morning: *U n'contru – U ballu di diavula.*

Ragusa................................... Good Friday: *Processione e fiaccolata dei Misteri.* Candle-lit procession. In Ibla, re-enactment of the martyrdom of St George.

Scicli .... Procession of the Resurrected Christ, called *U gioia.*

Trapani .... *Processione dei Misteri* held on Good Friday afternoon and Saturday morning.

April-May
Taormina .... *Festa del costume e del carretto siciliano.* Festival of traditional Sicilian carts and local costume.

T. Spagone/LARA PESSINA

A. Pitrone/LARA PESSINA

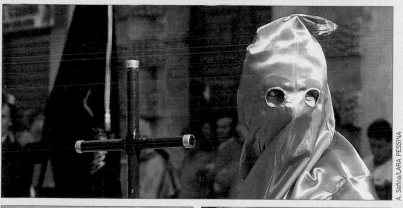

A. Safina/LARA PESSINA

N. Reitano/LARA PESSINA

25 April
Vizzini .... Festa di San Marco; Festa della Liberazione *Sagra della Ricotta.*

Third Sunday in May
Noto.. *Primavera barocca* and the *Infiorata.*

Last Saturday in May
Scicli .... *Festa di Maria Santissima delle Milizie.*

Last Sunday in May
Ragusa................................... Re-enactment of the martyrdom of St George ending with grand firework display.

May-June, years ending in even number
Siracusa .... Performances of classical drama at the Greek theatre.

June-December
Gibellina................................ *Orestiadi*, theatre, music and film festival.

July-August
Taormina .... *Taormina arte*, theatre, music, film and dance festival.
Tindari .... Season of prose readings in the Greek theatre.

July-August, years ending in odd number
Segesta .... Performances of classical drama at the Greek theatre.

14-15 July
Palermo .... *"U fistinu"*, festival in honour of the city's patron saint, Santa Rosalia.

24-25 July
Caltagirone .... *Festa di San Giacomo* with the *Luminaria*: 4 000 candles flicker up and down the steps of Santa Maria del Monte.

End July
Marsala.................................. *Marsala Doc Jazz Festival.*

2-6 August
Cefalù .... *Festa del Santo Salvatore* and the *'nntinna 'a mari*, which involves volunteers crawling along a long horizontal pole suspended above water to reach the statue of the Saviour at the tip (held at 5pm on 6 August).

12-14 August
Piazza Armerina .... *Palio dei Normanni.* Re-enactment of the legendary arrival of Roger d'Atavilla in the town, followed by jousting and a procession in which the statue of the Madonna and Child with two angels, kept in the cathedral, is carried through the streets to be presented to the town by the Count.

14 August
Messina .... *Passeggiata dei Giganti* (the giants being the Moor Grifone and Mata, a native of Messina and the legendary founder of the town).
Cefalù .... *Madonna della Luce.* Procession of boats from Kalura to the old harbour and back.

21-24 August
Lipari...................................... *Festa di San Bartolomeo* with offshore firework display.

Early September
Erice .... Medieval and Renaissance music performed in the town's churches.

2 September
Piana degli Albanesi............. *Festa della Madonna Odigitria.* Festival of Piana's patron saint, with horse races and a parade in traditional costume.

7-8 September
Mistretta .... *Madonna della Luce* with procession of the two giants Kronos and Mytia.

Militello in Val di Catania .... *Sagra della Mostarda*.

Monreale .... Festival of sacred music.

Palermo .... *Festa dei Morti*, during which children receive gifts and sweets from their ancestors.

Calatagirone .... Exhibition of terracotta Nativity figures.

Palermo .... *Festival di Morgana* (held at the Museo Internazionale delle Marionette), a gathering of puppeteers and show-business people from all over the world.

Glossary

Basic vocabulary

si/no – yes/no
per favore – please
grazie – thank you
buongiorno – good morning
buona sera – good afternoon
buona notte – good night
arrivederci – goodbye
scusi – excuse me
piccolo/un po – small/a little
grande – large/big
meno – less

molto – much
più – more
basta! – enough
quando? – when?
perché? – why
con/senza – with/without
l'aeroporto – the airport
la stazione – the station
un biglietto – a ticket
una scheda per il telefono – a telephone card

Numbers and numerals

1 – uno
2 – due
3 – tre
4 – quattro
5 – cinque
6 – sei
7 – sette
8 – otto
9 – nove
10 – dieci
11 – undici
12 – dodici
13 – tredici
14 – quattordici
15 – quindici

16 – sedici
17 – diciassette
18 – diciotto
19 – diciannove
20 – venti
30 – trenta
40 – quaranta
50 – cinquanta
60 – sessanta
70 – settanta
80 – ottanta
90 – novanta
100 – cento
1000 – mille
2000 – due mila

Time, days of the week and seasons

1.00 – l'una
1.15 – una e un quarto – one fifteen
1.30 – un 'ora e mezzo – one thirty
1.45 – l'una e quaranta cinque – one forty-five
mattina – morning
pomeriggio – afternoon
sera – evening
ieri – yesterday
oggi – today
domani – tomorrow
una settimana – a week

lunedì – Monday
martedì – Tuesday
mercoledì – Wednesday
giovedì – Thursday
venerdì – Friday
sabato – Saturday
domenica – Sunday
inverno – winter
primavera – spring
estate – summer
autunno – autumn/fall

Food and drink

un piatto – a plate
un coltello – a knife
una forchetta – a fork
un cucchiaio – a spoon
il cibo – food
un piatto vegetariano
– a vegetarian dish
un bicchiere – a glass
acqua minerale (gassata)
– (fizzy) mineral water
vino rosso – red wine
vino bianco – white wine
una birra (alla spina) – a beer (on tap)
carne – meat
manzo/vitello – beef/veal

maiale – pork
agnello – lamb
prosciutto cotto (crudo) – ham cooked (cured)
pollo – chicken
pesce – fish (pesca – peach)
uova – eggs (uva – grapes)
verdura – green vegetables
burro – butter
formaggio – cheese
un dolce – a dessert
frutta – fruit
zucchero – sugar
sale/pepe – salt/pepper
senape – mustard
olio/aceto – oil/vinegar

Shopping

un negozio – a shop
la posta – a post office
francobolli – stamps
macellaio – a butcher's
farmacia – a chemist's
sciroppo per la tosse – cough mixture
pastiglie per la gola – throat pastilles
cerotto – sticking plaster
scottato dal sole – sun burn

mal di pancia – stomach-ache
mal di testa – headache
punture di zanzara/ape/vespa
– mosquito bites/bee- /wasp-sting
il panificio – a baker's
pane (integrale) – bread (wholemeal)
un supermercato – a supermarket
un giornale – a newspaper
pescivendolo – a fishmonger

Sightseeing and orientation

si puo visitare? – can one visit?
chiuso/aperto – closed/open
destra/sinistra – right/left
nord/sud – north/south
est/ovest – east/west
la strada per ...? – the road for ...?
una vista – a view
al primo piano – on the first floor
tirare – pull
spingere – push

bussare – ring (the bell)
le luci – lights
le scale – stairs
l'ascensore – lift
i bagni per uomo/donna
– WC facilities men's/ladies
una camera singola/doppia/matrimoniale
– a single room, with twln beds, double bed
con doccia/con bagno – with shower/bath
un giorno/una notte – one day/night

Urban sites

la città – the town
una chiesa – a church
il duomo – the cathedral
una cappella – a chapel
il chiostro – the cloisters
la navata – the nave
il coro – the choir or chancel
il transetto – the transept
la cripta – the crypt
un palazzo – a town house or mansion
una casa – a house
un castello – a castle
un monastero/convento – an abbey/monastery
un cortile – a courtyard
un museo – a museum

una torre – a tower
un campanile – a belfry
una piazza – a square
un giardino – a garden
un parco – a park
una via/strada – a street/road
un ponte – a bridge
un molo – a pier or jetty
un cimitero – a cemetery
una barca – a boat
un motoscafo – a motor boat
la spiaggia – the beach
il mare – the sea
pericolo – danger
vietato – prohibited or forbidden

Natural sites

il fiume – the river
un lago – a lake

un belvedere – a viewpoint
un bosco – a wood

On the road

l'autostrada – a motorway/highway
la patente – a driving licence
un garage – a garage (for repairs)
nel parcheggio – in the car-park
benzina – petrol (UK)/gas (US)

una gomma – a tyre
le luci – headlights
il parabrezza – the windscreen
il motore – the engine

Useful phrases

Parla l'inglese? – Do you speak English?
Non capisco. – I do not understand.
Parli piano per favore. – Please speak slowly.
Dove sono i bagni? – Where are the toilets?
Dove...? – Where's ...?
A che ora parte il treno/l'autobus/l'aerio ...? – At what time does the train/bus/plane leave?
A che ora arriva il treno ...? – At what time does the train ... arrive?
Quanto costa? – What does it cost?
Dove posso comprare un giornale inglese? – Where can I buy an English news-paper in?
Dove posso cambiare i miei soldi? – Where can I change my money?
Entra! – Come in!
Posso pagare con una carta di credito? – May I pay with a credit card?

Introduction

Landscape

Sicily is the largest island of the Mediterranean (25 709km²/992sq mi). The widest and southernmost region of Italy, it is separated from the Italian Peninsula by the Straits of Messina – a mere three kilometres at the widest point – and from Africa about 140km/87mi away, by the Sicily Canal. The island is more or less triangular in shape, its long sides fronting onto the Tyrrhenian Sea in the north and the Sicily Canal in the south while the short side coasts the Ionian Sea to the east. The region of Sicily includes many minor islands: off the northern coast, in the Tyrrhenian Sea, the **Aeolian** or **Lipari** Islands (north-east) and **Ustica** (north-west); the **Egadi** lie to the west close to the Trapanese Coast; the **Pelagian** and **Pantelleria** Islands nestle south, in the Sicily Canal.

COASTAL REGIONS

The Sicilian coastline stretches over some 1 000km/621mi. The northern or Tyrrhenian flank extends from Cape Peloro, near Messina, to Cape Lilibeo in the vicinity of Marsala: here the rocks are uniformly high and protrude jaggedly into the sea.

This leaves the short distance between Trapani and Marsala on the western coast. Here, the landscape suddenly changes into what in contrast with the high rocky northern edge, seems rather flat and uninteresting. The southern coast of Sicily main tains this same make-up along its length as far as Capo Passero, the far south-western spur of the island. Small creeks interrupt the otherwise streamlined profile of the shoreline which accommodates a few of the main resorts like Mazzara del Vallo, Sciacca and Gela, set in the broad bay with the same name between Licata and Marina di Ragusa.

The eastern coast facing onto the Ionian Sea, running northwards, begins low-lying, shaped into a succession of three broad sweeps: the Gulf of Noto, the Gulf of Augusta and the great Gulf of Catania, which provides Sicily's largest plain with a sea front. North of Catania, the shoreline to Messina consists once more of high cliffs broken by a series of craggy inlets. As Etna's tall black lava flows give way to the Peloritani Mountain limestone, huge steep cliffs plunge down to the sea, endowing the landscape with matchless beauty as at Taormina and Arcireale.

UPLANDS AND LOWLAND PLAINS

The Sicilian land-mass is predominantly hilly (62 % of the surface area); 24 % is mountainous with the remainder (14 %) classified as plain or low-land. The highest outcrop is **Etna**, a volcanic mass with an altitude of 3 323m/10 902ft *(see below, VOLCANIC PHENOMENON)*. This mountain typifies the Sicilian landscape dominating, as it does, the skyline from almost every raised viewpoint on the island.

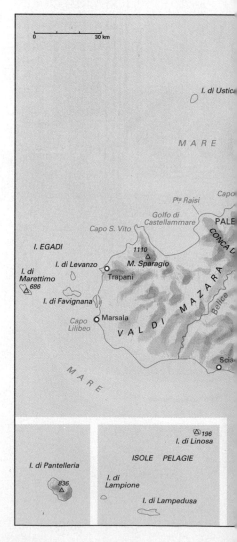

North of Etna, separated from the Alcantara Valley, rises the precipitous heights of Sicily's principal mountain range which run some 200km/ 124mi parallel to the Tyrrhenian Coast. This chain of peaks comprises, even from a geological point of view, a natural extension of the Calabrian Apennines, hence its name **Appennino Siculo**. These fall into three distinctive sections. The western portion constitutes the **Monti Peloritani** which lie between Messina and Patti; the highest peak is Montagna Grande (1 374m/4 507ft). This relief does not rise to any great altitude: in contrast with a steeply angular and craggy profile, its lower slopes have been eroded by powerful streams heavy with rocks and pebbles discarded along the narrow coastal shelf or plain. The northern range extends westwards with the **Monti Nebrodi** or *Caronie*: these have gentler slopes and rounded, densely wooded summits; the highest point being marked Monte Soro (1 847m/6 060ft). Next in line, west of the Nebrodi, come the **Madonie**: these do not extend very far but do include several high peaks. This group includes **Pizzo Carbonara** (1 977m/6 486ft), the second highest mountain point on the island. On the western flank of the Madonie, the high relief is interrupted by Torto Valley, after which it loses its momentum *(see also MADONIE e NEBRODI)*. The vast area between Termini Imerese and the Trapanese consists of a gently undulating landscape of hills and broad depressions. This is rudely broken by three minor massifs – the **Monti Termini Imerese**, **Monti di Palermo** and **Monti di Trapani** – that have geological rather than orographic (physical geography of mountains) affinities with the northern range.

To the south, the high relief gives way to a vast open region of arid upland (often called the **solfiferi** or solfataras after the high levels of sulphur deposits in the area) which stretches from Marsala to Caltanissetta with the exception of the Sicani Mountains north-east of Sciacca and of the **Monti Erei** to the east of Caltanissetta. In the south-western corner of the island rise the massive calcareous (limestone) **Monti Iblei** which rise to 1 000m/3 280ft.

The largest expanse of lowland plain in Sicily is the **Piana di Catania** which extends from the southern lower slopes of Etna to the foothills of the Iblei range. Criss-crossed by large rivers, the plain is renowned as being especially fertile and is intensively farmed (citrus, fruit and market gardening). Other areas of open lowland, although not as extensive, include the plain of Palermo known as the **Conca d'Oro** (golden horn of plenty), the plain of Milazzo which shelters behind its very own promontory, the areas between Trapani and Marsala, and, finally, that south-east of Gela.

RIVERS AND LAKES

The island's water-distribution network is not very developed because of low rainfall. Along the Tyrrhenian coast, the rivers, although numerous, rise in the mountains nearby and drain quickly and furiously into the sea. The most significant are the **River Torto** which rises in the Lecara Mountains before making its way through the Termini Imerese region, and the **River Oreto** which flows across the Conca d'Oro.

The tributary rivers of the Sicily Canal are more important by far not only because they are sustained by a more extensive system of sunken wells and natural springs but also because they are required to maintain a constant flow of water, however sluggishly, to the waterway. The main rivers from west to east, are the **Belice**, the **Platani** which flows in the vicinity of Eraclea Minoa, and the **Salso** or Imera Meridionale which rises in the Madonie and runs down to the Sicily Sea.

On the western side of the island, going northwards, there are several substantial but slow-moving rivers such as the **Tellaro**, the **Anapo** which drains the area around Siracusa, and the historical **Ciane** which stems from the springs with the same name. Next comes the most important water network of the island which comprises the **Gornalunga**, the **Dittaino**, and the **Simeto** whose source nestles among the southern slopes of the Nebrodi Mountains and collects the water from Etna's southern and western flanks. The importance given to these rivers depends upon them supplying sufficient volumes of water to sustain a rational system of irrigation across the fertile plain of Catania, before petering out. North of Etna the **Alcàntara** traces its way through the volcano's northern slopes hollowing out its famous gorge *(see Gole dell'ALCANTARA)*. Finally, many seasonal torrents wash down from the Peloritana upland range after the snow-melt betraying all the same characteristics as those rushing into the Tyrrhenian Sea.

Sicily is deprived of any natural lake of any size; however, there are a number of man-made reservoirs in among the mountains.

Frequently punctuating the coastline are many brackish ponds called *bivieri* or *pantani* which form behind the dunes along the shore. A few of these may be observed at the far end of the southernmost tip of the island or near Capo Peloro. Many, however, have recently been drained to allow the wider area around them to be cultivated.

CLIMATE

The diversity offered by Sicily's landscape provides the conditions for a broad range of weather conditions across the island. In general terms, the climate enjoyed by the northern and eastern coasts and the minor islands is mild in winter and hot in summer, giving an annual average temperature of 18°C. The southern coast and the immediate hinterland for the most part are subjected to winds from the African continent; these can bring especially torrid conditions in summer. The inland mountainous areas are blessed with more consistent patterns in weather although temperatures can soar to great heights, and frequent rainfall, turning to snow in winter, is to be expected.

SICILIAN FLORA

The mild climate enjoyed by the island of Sicily nurtures a fairly typical range of Mediterranean flora, certainly in the coastal regions and low-lying flatlands. Much of the coastline has been cultivated for centuries, but pockets of indigenous vegetation thrive in less accessible corners. The most common species include **myrtle** *(Myrtus)*, **strawberry tree** *(Arbutus)*, **lentisk** *(Pistacia lentiscus)* and **tree spurge** *(Euphorbia dendroides)* – a many-branched bush which grows to a height of 1.5m/4.9ft by producing thick reddish stems that only issue leaves towards the end of the summer, to coincide with the first rains. It is widespread throughout western Sicily. In springtime, large stretches of sun-drenched calcareous hillsides are set ablaze by yellow flowering, sweet-smelling **broom** bushes *(Ginestra cinera)*, the spineless genus which grows to 2m/6.5ft in height, and which was used traditionally to make brooms for sweeping floors. These species alternate with such imports as the evergreen, river-bed loving **oleander** *(Nerium)*; the **carob tree** *(Ceratonia)* that produces toffee-brown bean-pods, populating the landscape around Ragusa; the formally erect gum or **eucalyptus** with its weeping branches and aromatic leaves; the tall pyramidal **maritime pine** *(Pinus pinaster)* producing large cones which is often planted to reclaim sand-dunes or for extracting timber and turpentine; and the majestic **stone or umbrella pine** *(Pinus pinea)* that produces delicious pine nuts *(pinoli* in Italian; *pignons* in French; used for making *pesto* sauce). The Umbrella pine is thought to have been imported from Syria by the Romans and introduced throughout the Mediterranean basin. The **bastard olive** *(Olea oleaster)* grows everywhere; interestingly, this spiny shrub produces rather mean, less fleshy fruits than its cultivated cousin even though this wild form was probably the original species grafted by the Syrians to produce the variety cultivated for its fruit and oil. Large tracts of land are devoted to groves of **olive-trees** *(Olea)* that assume contorted shapes with age, **citrus trees** (lemons; sweet, blood and Seville oranges; mandarins), and, of course, numerous **vineyards**.

In the more arid areas thorny plants are common, such as various varieties of thistle *(Silybum)*, **palms** and **dwarf palms** – a perennial typical of the Zingaro area (so much so that it has been chosen as the symbol of the nature reserve). A broad range of succulent plants encompass the huge **agave** or **century plant** with its long triangular fleshy leaves edged with a yellow border which produces a tall pale yellow flower before it dies (some taking up to 10 years to reach flowering size), **cactuses** and the ubiquitous **prickly pears** *(Opuntia* – known locally as *Fico d'India)* which generate flat green fleshy panels instead of branches and garishly yellow flowers that transform themselves into bright pinky-red fruit in summer and autumn.

The first signs of spring, heralded by meadows of wild garlic and garishly yellow oxalis at ground level, stir the **almond trees** (especially around Agrigento) into injecting delicate clouds of white blossom into the landscape; there follows the fluffly yellow **mimosa** and the sweet-smelling crisp white **orange-blossom**. Soon the pinks and reds of the **oleanders** and **hibiscus** mark the advent of summer; they are joined by the garishly purple, puce and magenta **bougainvillaeas** and the intensely perfumed **jasmine** which

B. Kaufmann

Prickly pear

Caper

Bitter orange

blinks open its starry flowers all over the main island – but most especially throughout the small offshore archipelagos (Pantelleria, Aeolian Islands). Through the summer, issuing from the apparently arid stone walls, there tumbles forth a cascade of round-leafed **caper plants** from which are plucked the buds long before those exquisite pinkish-white flowers are allowed to flourish.

In and among the hills and mountains, the most common trees are the evergreen **holm oak** *(Quercus ilex)* which produces small acorns favoured by pigs and wild-boar; the **beech** *(Fagaceae)* which thrives at higher altitudes and turns into burnished yellows and browns with the advent of winter; and the cultivated wise and wondrous **sweet chestnuts** and **conifers** of different kinds.

Economy

The long periods of foreign domination not only left their mark on the art, culture and literature of Sicily, but also on its economy.

The Greek era brought great splendour to the island in terms of art and architecture, but it was also a time of successful cultivation and economic prosperity. Plants imported by the Greeks from their homelands still grown on the island today include the sweet and juicy water-melon, the almond-trees which blossom in spring and of course the great swathes of olive trees and vineyards. The Romans, who settled in Sicily in the 3C BC, left a far fainter mark on the countryside: the longest lasting phenomenon was the large estate holding, which, in years to come, was to cause many problems and major economic dichotomies between the social classes.

It was the Arabs in the 9C who prompted a new Golden Age and revived an economic prosperity that reached new heights. They nurtured the fertile land blessed with a mild climate, vesting it with new crops like the carob tree, the fragrant Seville orange and its cousin the lemon, sugar cane, cotton, sumac, the date-palm and the mulberry: the very plants and trees that still form a vital part of Sicilian life, and populate the bitter-sweet and very Mediterranean impressions given to visitors.

The successive sovereigns, save for a period of Norman Swabian rule (during which the indigo plant was introduced), precipitated a slow economic decline. The island's natural vegetation and forests were plundered and impoverished, the population was exploited beyond its means and inhibited from cultivating the land. In short, the island was prevented from developing in the right direction and attaining its enormous potential.

MODERN ECONOMY

Agriculture – Agriculture is still the prime activity in Sicily (generating in excess of 6000 billion Lire and providing employment for the majority of the local population), although competition from other Mediterranean countries and difficulties implementing improved irrigation systems are gradually eroding its importance. The Sicilian hinterland is still farmed using antiquated methods geared mainly to cultivating wheat: a somewhat unprofitable activity, but one which occupies vast tracts of arid land. The coastal regions, on the other hand, are much more fertile and better equipped with efficient, hi-tech irrigation systems that ensure better productivity and more profitable crops. The main crops (almost one-third of the area farmed) are wheat and other cereals. The cultivation of citrus fruits, olives, vines and fruit-trees is much more profitable especially where Sicily's famous liqueur wines like Marsala, Passito di Pantelleria and Malvasia di Lipari are concerned. The cash crops that generate the highest returns include vegetables and pulses which are grown in coastal areas on the east of the island. One hundred percent of Italian cotton is grown in Sicily.

Fishing – Fishing continues to be a mainstay of the Sicilian economy, especially in the areas around Trapani where the tuna-fishing industry continues to thrive, and Messina where large quantities of swordfish are netted. Today Sicily is running a rigorous programme for restocking the hitherto widely and indiscriminately exploited waters offshore by rationalising fishing quotas. In the first instance, fishing is being developed in tandem with tourism: one project centred around Trapani involves restoring and regenerating the once famous tuna fisheries by converting them into visitor attractions and facilities. At Capo Granitola and Bonagia two are already up and running. But the most exciting project which will finally enable the fishing industry to extricate itself from its predicament is to trade the fish quotas via a computer network connecting the fishing fleet with the markets through a real-time stock-exchange.

Industry – Sicily is one of the three regions in Italy (together with Sardinia and Tuscany) to be blessed with substantial natural mineral reserves. For many centuries, Sicily benefited from large-scale sulphur extraction to such an extent as to reign supreme over other world producers. In the last 60 years, however, the region has proved unable

---

Sicilian wine

The wine industry accounts for a cultivated area of 150 000ha/370 658 acres, generating 9 million hectolitres of grape juice and 1 000 000 billion Lire a year. A total of 400 000 people are employed in this sector, making it one of the most important agricultural interests.

There exist various initiatives linking wine, tourism and art, including *Le strade del vino*: seven wine and gastronomy routes including wine-tastings at wineries and the chance to appreciate the full artistic, cultural and traditional heritage of the island. For additional information, contact the **Istituto Regionale della Vite e del Vino** in Palermo: ☎ 091 62 78 111; www.infcom.it/irvv

LARA PESSINA

to modernise its mining techniques sufficiently; this in turn has meant that the product is no longer as financially viable and cannot compete with producers in the United States and Mexico who have implemented state-of-the-art methods of extraction and operate even more economically. The collapse of the sulphur market was partly offset by the discovery, in the early 1950s, of fossil fuels (oil and gas). Since the first well came on line in 1957, the oil, petrochemical and thermo-electrical industries have developed considerably. The discovery in recent years of potassium salts in the hinterland has given the chemical industry a further boost. The metallurgical and engineering industries are still fairly limited. In addition to the above industries, the food sector can boast a buoyant market in wine, olive-oil, pasta, pickled vegetables and canned fish.

Tourism – Despite being endowed with an abundance of natural and artistic wonders, colourful traditions and folkloric festivals, the one industry that the island would like to exploit above all other, tourism, is failing to develop fast enough. Such fundamental problems as a shortage of beds and lack of infrastructure and a sparse and inefficient public transport system are crippling the evolution of tourism. Until the region confronts these basic issues and invests money in a modern co-ordinated system able to deal with the ever-growing numbers of visitors, the region with the wealthiest artistic heritage and the richest natural resources of all Italy will continue to lie beyond the reach of the main market.

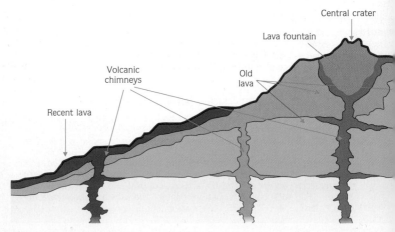

Central crater

Lava fountain

Volcanic chimneys

Old lava

Recent lava

Volcanic phenomenon

Sicily has been shaken by its volcanoes since the island was formed and continues to witness the most compelling manifestations of such activity today. Just as every continental land-mass in the earth's configuration presents its own particular make-up in terms of relief and geology, so the Sicilian volcanoes have their own pattern of activity and their own peculiar family of extrusive igneous rocks (basalts, granites, rhyolites). Put another way, the analysis of the lava released by the group of three volcanic hotspots (Mount Etna, Aeolian Islands and Sicily Canal), coupled with the study of the frequency and regularity of the eruptions, confirms the magma as issuing from a highly localised area of fusion deep below the earth's solid mantle. This, in turn, sheds valuable light on the geodynamism of the planet as a whole, and explains in part how rigid tectonic plates, forced apart, can precipitate a chain of volcanoes.

Volcanic activity – Volcanoes occur in subduction zones where one plate is forced beneath another; this movement may force magma and gas to rise under pressure through the earth's crust until they are released onto the earth's surface and into the atmosphere; the resulting volcanic eruptions have been categorised relative to their cause and effect. Traditionally, the four types of explosion are the Plinian, Hawaiian, Strombolian and Vulcanian. The two latter types take their name from the Sicilian volcanoes where the phenomena was first observed.

The *Strombolian phenomenon*, peculiar to the volcano on Stromboli, is characterised by phases of persistent, moderate, explosions followed by intermittent periods of idleness. Such eruptions, caused by a large build-up of gas being suddenly released like a pressure cooker, have been known to project tall fountains of lava, attaining in some cases several hundred metres; they also provoke shred-like lava-slag and pumice rubble to be violently ejected. This is then followed by longer periods of heavy and smooth molten lava flow.

Vulcanian eruptions, as first observed on the island of Vulcano in 1888, result in outpourings of lava and pyroclastics, accompanied by discharges of ash and scoria. This phenomenon is also described as hydrovolcanic because the highly explosive effect is caused by an interaction of molten magma with trapped water deep within the earth's crust.

Volcanic fall-out – During volcanic eruptions three types of matter are ejected: lava, pyroclastics and gas (including smoke, steam and chemical vapours).

Lava consists of melt or magma with solid crystal particles suspended within it. As these particles are borne down the sides of the volcano, they rise towards the surface, cooling and hardening into complex structures with distinctive topologies. Depending on their viscosity and the nature of the lava in which they set, they are separated out as pegmatite (coarsely crystalline) or phenocryst (large or conspicuous crystal in porphyritic rock) formations. **Fluid lava** collects into smooth flows that wrinkle around the obstacles that snag its course, cooling quickly into glassy smooth stone like obsidian. In contrast to this, **viscous lava** is uneven: it travels overground with difficulty; heavy scoria causes it to break up into blocks. Both types of lava flow can be seen on the slopes of Mount Etna. Examples of lava tunnel are also in evidence there: these consist of underground conduits of molten lava which form pipe-like outer crusts; as the melt contained within continues to flow away it leaves a tubular cavity behind. In the final cooling stage the lava may contract into columnar formations with a polyhedral cross-section: this phenomena may be seen around Etna, in the gorges of the Alcantara *(see Gole dell'ALCANTARA)* and at the Faraglioni dei Ciclopi *(see ACI CASTELLO)*.

By-products of explosive eruptions are generally classified as **pyroclastics** and include xenoliths, crystals and juvenile rocks: **xenoliths** are splinters of pre-existing rock that are collected from the immediate environment; **crystals** consist of solidified (often into glassy) particles suspended in the magma/granite; **juvenile** formations or tuff (consolidated volcanic fragments and solidified magma) include various types of ash, lapilli and volcanic bombs depending on size. When molten, the two latter categories contain high percentages of vapour; depending on how the lava cools, the gases are released at variable rates and in different quantities. Should the volcanic discharge cool rapidly, it will solidify into a dense formation like obsidian or lava glass; should it cool slowly over a long period

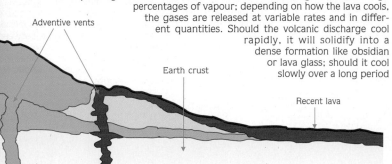

Adventive vents

Earth crust

Recent lava

of time, trapped gases can bubble out so imparting to the stone a distinctive sponge-like appearance as in pumice and scoria. Pyroclastics conform to three main types depending on the way they are deposited, be it by fall-out, flow or surge. **Fall-out material** lands on the ground with considerable impact, having been propelled through the atmosphere like a ballistic missile. Material ejected with an **outpouring of lava** might be suspended in a dense cloud of vapour at extreme temperatures before running down the slopes of the volcano at high speeds: once arrested, these flows can precipitate ignimbrites (the type of rock which covered, for example, the remains of Pompeii). **Pyroclastic surges** emit material suspended in turbulent clouds of vapour under high pressure: this form of volcanic explosion occurs principally when magma comes into contact with underground water.

Great quantities of **volcanic vapour** are released during eruptions, indeed, sometimes this is the only form of material emitted: both Etna and Vulcano, for example, have intensively active vents or fumeroles through which hot gases are expelled. The main constituents of volcanic vapour are aqueous (and highly acidic) compounds of the base elements carbon, hydrogen and sulphur. Fumeroles and thermal springs (therapeutic mud) are the outward effects of magma cooling at depth.

VOLCANIC AREAS OF SICILY

Aeolian Islands – The Aeolian fault stretches in an arc over some 200km/124mi in the southern Tyrrhenian Sea; it comprises eight separate islands (seven Aeolian proper plus Ustica) and a large number of submerged volcanoes. **Lipari** is the most complex in geological terms, having been formed in several successive stages. The earliest consequences affected the north-western part of the island, where Monte Sant'Angelo erupted some 50 000 years ago. More recent volcanic activity increased the height of Monte Giardina and Monte Guardia as large volumes of pumice and fall-out pyroplastic debris were deposited. The most recent phase in the landscape's evolution occurred during our own era (6C-7C AD), forming the pumice cone of Monte Pilato and the flows of obsidian known as Rocche Rosse and Forgia Vecchia.

The first evidence of volcanic activity on **Vulcano** is to be found in the Caldera del Piano, within which the Fossa (or Gran Cratere) and Vulcanello were formed. **Stromboli** is defined by a series of volcanic outcrops layered one on top of the other over the past 100 000 years. Today the active craters, which vary in number and position, emerge at about 700m/2 296ft up the Sciara del Fuoco, an impressive slope between two ridges – Filo del Fuoco and Filo di Baraona. At a distance of 1.5km/0.9mi off the north-eastern coast of Stromboli sits **Strombolicchio**: the outcrop which stands over 40m/131ft high is all that remains of the main core of the volcano that erupted during the earliest phase in the island's creation.

Mount Etna – Etna is Europe's largest active volcano, rising to a height of over 3 300m/10 826ft from a base diameter of about 40km/25mi. Volcanic activity started 600 000 years ago following movement between the tectonic plates: this released magma up through the ocean floor into the area now occupied by Acicastello, and provoked surges of lava and vapour which settled in the vicinity of modern-day Paternò. During the past 100 000 years, the thrust of subsequent volcanic activity has shifted westwards, resulting in a chain of at least six volcanic outcrops of alkaline sodium-rich lava rock. The mountain's present profile is largely the result of an explosion c 14 000 years ago in which the Cratere Ellittico (or elliptical crater) came into being. The summit of Etna comprises four active craters (Cratere di Sud-Est, Bocca Nuova, Voragine, Crateredi Nord-Est); in addition there are three principal radial fissures and many (approximately 250) irregular secondary craters. Historically, the activity has manifested itself as a continuous release of vapour vented through the top craters – in accordance with Strombolian and Plinian patterns; the most violent eruptions to be documented occurred in 122 BC. The most significant outpourings of lava have been released even in the most recent times, through the secondary craters.

Sicily Canal – The Sicily Canal harbours two volcanic islands (Pantelleria and Linosa) and a large number of submarine outcrops. The region's volcanic activity is caused by a rift between the continental shelves of Sicily and Tunisia. The most recent signs were registered in 1831 following the emergence of the island of Giulia, currently below sea level, 50km/31mi north-east of Pantelleria, and in 1891, on the seabed approximately 7km/4mi north-west of Pantelleria. Pantelleria began life sometime between 325 000 and 15 000 years ago with an initial series of eruptions during which the crater La Vecchia was formed; a second phase, 50 000 years ago, resulted in the island being covered with ignimbrites deposited by the Tufo Verde. Given its distinctive appearance, the rock on Pantelleria is described as "pantellerite".

Historical table and notes

Pre-Hellenistic Sicily

14C BC: The Mediterranean is crucial to the history of man: people flock to its coasts "like frogs around a pond", according to Plato. Sicily lies in the centre of this sea and thus became a natural intersection of many cultures and civilisations. In Antiquity, it attracted navigators from the East: it is very probable that some of the episodes of the Odyssey, that great collection of sea-faring sagas, took place in a Sicily transfigured by myth and poetry. The Greek historian Dionysius of Halicarnassus tells of how ancient expeditions embarked in the East setting their sails on course for the Italian peninsula and Sicily. Archaeology provides more concrete proof of this. In fact, evidence of visitations made by the Mycenaeans has been found at Thapsos and Panarea (pottery incised with Linear B script, the Mycenaean syllabic alphabet) – from which it may be assumed that the island acted as a trading post for the Mycenaean fleets.

1270-650 BC	Late Bronze Age: significant finds retrieved from the necropolis at Pantalica (5000 tombs) and from the one at Cassibile. The arrival of the Greeks seems to have brought with it the use of iron and a higher level of material civilisation.

The Athenian historian Thucydides (Vol VI, Chapters 1-5) provides us with information about ancient Sicily. In addition to telling us about the history of Greek colonisation, he also talks about the non-Greek, indigenous peoples of the island: the Siculi, who inhabited eastern and central-southern Sicily, and the Sicani who lived in the western part of the island. The former resided in the area between Syracuse and Gela, the area around the lake that was sacred to the Pàlici gods (Lake Naftia, near modern Palagonia) and the town of Morgantina. The origins of the Siculi should, perhaps, be traced back to the Italian peninsula, given that many pointers indicate an association with the Apennine culture on the mainland. The Sicani seem not to conform with Indo-European people, but rather to be of Iberian origin; the affinity of their name with that of the Siculi has not yet been satisfactorily explained.

The people of the Elimi, the founders of Erice (Eryx) and Segesta, seem to belong to the ancient family of Mediterranean and pre-Indo European peoples. Various pieces of evidence suggest contact with the East (like the cult of Aphrodite Ericina) and a rapid Hellenisation of this people (the Doric temple at Segesta).

Phoenicians from Carthage settled at Solunto, Panormus (modern Palermo) and Mozia (Motya) in the north-western part of the island, where the foundations of Lilybaeum (modern Marsala), an impregnable stronghold and the fulcrum of Carthaginian military power, was later to be laid.

Sikelía: Sicily under the Greeks

1050 BC	Dawn of the Iron Age in Greece.
775	Establishment of the trading colony of Pithecusa on Ischia; this date heralds the first Hellenistic settlements in mainland Italy.
c 735	The first Hellenistic settlement, Naxos, is founded in Sicily, a strategic move that would secure control over the trade routes operating through the Straits of Messina. In 734 the Corinthians lay the foundations of Syracuse (Siracusa).
728-700	The Chalcidians found Catana, Leontinoi and Zancle (now Messina); the Megarians found Megara Hyblaea (727).
688	Colonists from Rhodes and Crete found Gela; the same city that seized Akragas (Agrigento) in 580.
598	Foundation of Camarina.
491	Gelon becomes the tyrant of Gela. In 488, he wins the chariot race at Olympia, thus winning great prestige among the Greeks.
480-479	The Greeks in Sicily face hostility from the Carthaginians and the Etruscans, probably in reaction to the increased threat from Persia against the Greek homeland.
485	Gelon becomes tyrant of Syracuse.
480	Battle of Himera: the Syracusans defeat the Carthaginian onslaught.
474	Hieron, tyrant of Syracuse, wins a decisive naval victory at Cumae over the Etruscans. Catania, on the Ionian coast, is occupied by Dorian colonists and subjugated to the rule of Hieron's son.
465	The tyrant Thrasybulus is expelled and Syracuse is ruled by a moderate democracy.
453	The rebellion of Ducetius results in all the Siculi towns being brought into one confederation. The uprising is quelled in 450.
415	The Athenian fleet, marshalled by Nicias and Alcibiades, sets out to wage war on the enemy, Syracuse.

414	Siege of Syracuse. The Spartan Gylippus comes to the town's rescue.
413	The Athenian hold over Sicily is broken. During the war, Athens loses 50 000 men (including 12 000 ordinary citizens) and more than 200 triremes.
409	The Carthaginians attack and destroy Selinunte and Himera.
406	The general Dionysius I seizes power in Syracuse. Over the ensuing years he secures a vast dominion including a large portion of southern Italy and the Adriatic coast (he conquers Croton and founds Ancona).
392	Peace between the Carthaginians and Dionysius I.
367	Death of Dionysius I.
347	Dionysius II, exiled previously by Dion, a family relative and fellow adherent of Plato, returns to Syracuse.
344	The motherland of Corinth sends 700 soldiers to Syracuse led by Timoleon, who defeats the Carthaginians at the battle of River Crimisus (341).
316	Agathocles, a man of modest origins, heads a revolt against the barons and seizes power in Syracuse.
310	The Carthaginians defeat Agathocles at Ecnomus. Soon after, he lands in Africa at the head of 14 000 men bent on avenging Carthage.
289	Death of Agathocles. In the same year, the Mamertini, mercenaries of Campanian origin, seize Messina.
280	Pyrrhus in Italy. Between 278 and 275, he tries in vain to unite Sicily.
269	Hieron II, formerly one of Pyrrhus' officers, declares himself *basileus* (king) of Syracuse after a victory over the Mamertini.
264-241	First Punic War.

Coins

Sicily under the Romans

Ruled by a praetor and two quaestors, Sicily was evidently of prime importance to Rome: the tribute levied has been calculated as around two million *modii*; this was paid according to methods devised by Hieron II (hence the law *lex hieronica*) and probably satisfied one-fifth of the total financial requirement of the city of Rome.

Despite suffering two devastating slave rebellions and reeling from the disastrous outcome of Syracuse's revolt – which resulted in the town being sacked – the island continued to be of economic importance. Sicily possessed a good number of large estates, which, in turn, provided the Roman aristocracy with elegant residences; in many cases these villas became centres of literary patronage and recreation for the ennobled Romans.

227 BC	Sicily is made a Roman province.
218-201	Second Punic War. In 211, after a long siege, Consul Marcellus sacks Syracuse which was rebelling against Rome.
149-146	Third Punic War and final destruction of Carthage.
138-131	First slave revolt in Sicily led by the Syrian slave Eunus.
104-99	Second slave revolt led by the slave Trifon.
70	Verres, the praetor in Sicily, is accused by several Sicilian towns of embezzlement. Their legal defence is conducted by Cicero.
48	Battle of Pharsalus: Caesar's troops defeat Pompey's.
44	Pompey's son, Sextus Pompeius, controls Sardinia, Corsica and Sicily with his fleets. In 36 BC he is defeated by Vipsanius Agrippa, one of Octavian's admirals.
31	Battle of Actium.
2C AD	Spread of Christianity on the island.
468	Gaiseric, King of the Vandals in Africa, conquers the island.

Sicily in the Middle Ages

The island was also to flourish in the Middle Ages, both on account of its sustained economic importance and because of the cultural dynamism perpetrated by the meeting and exchange of many different and colourful civilisations, as had been the case in Antiquity. In particular, the island was to benefit from almost two centuries of Muslim domination before submitting to Norman rule and becoming the focus of imperial ambitions harboured by the Hohenstaufens. The evolution of a magnificent and highly original Arab-Norman style of architecture, the continued flowering of a uniquely Sicilian literary tradition and a predilection for scholarship (it was in Sicily that a selection of Plato's *Dialogues* were first translated in the 11C) combined to give medieval Sicily an autonomous culture that has proved to be vital to the understanding of European history as a whole.

AD 491	Theodoric's Ostrogoths assume control of the island: its administration is re-organised according to Imperial standards. The Roman Church extends its land holding.
535	Belisarius, a general in Justinian's army, annexes Sicily to the Eastern Roman Empire at the start of the Gothic-Byzantine war. On a cultural level, Sicily, where Greek and Latin was still commonly spoken, draws closer to the Byzantine East.
652	First Arab incursions on the island: numerous Saracen fleets set out from the fortified camp of Kairouan (in Tunisia).
663	For political reasons, the Byzantine *basileus*, Constans II, takes up residence in Sicily.
725	Iconoclastic crisis: Sicily remains faithful to the cult of images. In 732, the Sicilian Church comes under the Patriarchate of Constantinople.
827	The Arabs land at Mazara. The invaders (mostly Berbers and Persians) conquer Palermo (831) which they then make their capital.
842-59	Messina, Modica, Ragusa and Enna fall: the Byzantine army is put to flight, the last indigenous Christians to resist are quashed. Only the north-eastern part of the Island resists effectively, with Byzantine assistance.
878	Syracuse, the ancient capital, is taken by storm and destroyed.
902	Fall of Taormina, the last Byzantine stronghold in Sicily.
948-1040	The island is ruled by the Emirs of the Kalbite dynasty. Of Arab origin, they are loyal to the Caliphs of Egypt.

The arrival of the Arabs split the political and economic status quo in Sicily: while a profitable period of collaboration between the indigenous people and invaders in the western part of the island was enjoyed, the area around Syracuse never fully conceded to the Arab dominion, even if their arrival sealed the demise of the decadent ancient metropolis and of eastern Sicily where the Greek language and culture continued to be implemented. The north-eastern part of the island, which maintained its Christian solidarity, offered fierce resistance.

Palermo came to symbolise Arab-Sicilian civilisation: densely populated (estimated at 300 000 inhabitants) and wealthy, bands of sprawling suburbs and small farm-holdings surrounded the ancient city centre; some 300 mosques and as many *madrasa* (Koranic schools) were instituted. The Emir was advised by an influential assembly *(giama'a)* drawn from members of the local aristocracy. The region of Palermo best epitomised the economic success of the Arab domination: land was divided into small plots, thus benefiting the new rulers; intensive and more sophisticated farming methods were imposed (these were often further improved by networks of irrigation channels) and new cash-crops were introduced such as cotton, linen, flax, sugar cane, rice, citrus fruits, henna, nuts and dates.

Besides the affluence generated by the new materialism, culture flourished, encouraged by links with Islam from around the Mediterranean (Andalucia in the case of literature, Maghreb and Egypt in the case of science). The perfect expression of this cross-fertilisation is the splendid Arabic literature that emerged from the court at Palermo. Poetry, in particular, was highly regarded and therefore encouraged. Ibn Hamdis, in his melancholy farewell to his beloved Sicily now in Norman hands, wrote:

"a land to which the dove lent its collar,
clothed by the peacock from its many-coloured mantle of feathers".

AD 1061	The Normans land in Sicily. During the next 30 years, Christianity struggles to re-affirm itself across the island and drive out the Arabs. Despite this, Islamic culture continues to prosper until the beginning of the 13C.

Sicily under the Normans

The Normans, the so-called "men of the north", having set out from their homes in Scandinavia, had settled in what is now Normandy by 911. Subsequently, groups of Norman mercenaries were engaged in the southern Italian peninsula to settle the disputes that raged between the Roman popes, Lombard dukes of Benevento and Salerno, Arabs in Sicily, and Byzantines in Apulia and Calabria. Through the Treaty of Melfi (1059), the Normans not only obtained for themselves the privilege of being recognised as vassals of the pope, they also secured feudal rights over southern Italy. One mercenary among them belonging to the Altavilla (or Hauteville) family, a certain Robert Guiscard ("the Sly"), having acquired the title of Duke of Apulia, promptly subdued Bari and Salerno. One of his brothers, Roger, set about conquering Sicily, marching into Palermo in 1072. The last Arab stronghold, Noto, did not capitulate until 1091 when Roger was awarded the coveted title of Papal Legate, making him the direct representative of the Holy See on the island.

| 1130 | **Roger II** succeeds his father Roger I in 1101; the title of King of Sicily and Duke of Campania is conferred upon him by the anti-Pope Anacletus II; this position is sanctioned nine years later by Innocent II. |

Roger II extended his kingdom as far as Tronto, thereby adding Capua, Amalfi and Naples; he maintained his capital at Palermo. Having claimed all rights to the land, Roger proceeded to assign territory to his followers in return for their support. Meanwhile, the feudal system was spreading through Sicily. A key element in the organisation of the Kingdom of Sicily was its complex structure of administration left over from the Byzantine and Arab dominion: in simple terms, the king was assisted by six officials and by magistrates posted throughout the provinces (*iusticiarii* and *connestabuli*). There was also a financial administration (*dohana* in Arabic) and a system of self-government for the Arab community in Palermo, ruled by a *qadì*.

In ecclesiastical circles, special prerogatives were given to the Norman sovereigns nominated as Papal Legates by Pope Urban II: their prime objective was to eradicate Islam and to resist corruption from the (Greco-Byzantine) Eastern Church. Meanwhile, the Arab influence persisted at Roger's court at Palermo: there, the geographer **al-Idrisi** constructed a large silver planisphere and wrote his geographical treatise which was significantly entitled *Kitab-Rugiar*, or *The Book of Roger*.

1147	Incursions by the Norman fleet in the Byzantine Empire: Corfu, Thessalonika and Thebes are sacked; numerous craftsmen skilled in working with silk are deported to Sicily.
1154	William I succeeds Roger. While engaged in conflict with Frederick Barbarossa, he must also confront a rebellion from his barons, which he succeeds in quelling in 1156.
1166	William II is crowned king. By supporting the Pope and the northern towns in their struggle against Barbarossa, he is also able to wage an attack on the Byzantine Empire now in decline. He is hailed a champion of the Third Crusade against Saladin: in fact, Norman troops were committed to rescuing Tripoli. He designates his aunt Constanza as his heir; she is betrothed to Henry, the eldest son of Barbarossa; thus the Swabian dynasty is permitted to claim legitimate rights to the throne of Sicily.

The Swabians and the Angevins

1186	The marriage of Henry IV (Barbarossa's son) to Constanza d'Altavilla is celebrated in Milan.
1190-97	Henry VI of Swabia is made Emperor and King of Sicily.
1198	Innocent III is elected pope. At his insistence, Constanza has young Frederick, who is growing up in the safety of the Palazzo dei Normanni, crowned in Palermo Cathedral.
1209	Frederick marries Costanza, the sister of Peter, King of Aragon.
1214	Innocent III excommunicates Emperor Otto of Brunswick and, in his place, nominates his rival Frederick II, already King of Sicily. Frederick arrives in Germany; he does not return to Sicily until 1220.
1228	Exhorted by Pope Gregory IX, Frederick leaves for the Holy Land, where he reaches a peaceful agreement with the Sultan. In 1229, he is crowned in Jerusalem.
1231	Frederick II issues the *Constitutions of Melfi*, a code of law designed for a centralised state, that is operational outside the jurisdiction of the feudal lords.
1250	Death of Frederick II.
1250-54	Conradin IV succeeds his father and is crowned Emperor despite the rivalry with Manfred, Frederick's natural son and heir.
1265	Pope Clement IV summons the Christian princes to rally against Manfred; the French, led by the Guelph sympathiser Charles of Anjou, rise to the call.
1266	Battle of Benevento: Manfred is defeated and killed.
1268	Final defeat of the Ghibellines (supporters of the Empire) at Tagliacozzo; Conradin, the 15-year-old heir to the Hohenstaufen throne, is beheaded in a piazza in Naples. The Guelphs of Anjou secure the power to rule southern Italy.

Sicilian Vespers and the Aragonese

| 1282 | Rebellion, provoked by an insult before Vespers, breaks out in Palermo and soon spreads across Sicily.

In 1282, a revolt by the so-called **Sicilian Vespers** *(see also p 256)* breaks out in Palermo. Corleone and Messina, the seat of the Angevin viceroy at that time, also rise to join the cause. Help in quelling the troubles is required: in the summer of 1282, an delegation of barons and town representatives request assistance from Peter II of Aragon who, being married to Costanza, |

Frederick II

It is difficult to draw a fair portrait of the Swabian emperor even if most of the great acclaim with which he is honoured by a large proportion of ancient and modern historians is ignored. The recent study by D Abulafia, together with other material published to mark the eight-hundredth anniversary of his birth (1994), provide a credible picture of the man rather than the great sovereign *"stupor mundi et novator mirabilis"*, by resisting the temptation to consider him as the powerful precursor of so many aspects of modern life.

Dante affirms Frederick's fame as a man of culture, describing the emperor as "a great logician and scholar". The learned Arab thinker **Ibn Sabin**, and the emperor's correspondent, laments Frederick's lack of familiarity with philosophical terminology. The *Cronica* written by the scholar **Salimbene de Adam** provides a lively description of the emperor's insatiable quest for knowledge. His intolerance of Aristotle is so disconcerting as to be considered the work of the devil himself. Credited as a lover of wisdom, patron of the arts as well as being a writer of courtly poetry himself, he showed considerable open-mindedness in his political dealings: a veritable "cavalier of intellect", in the words of the contemporary philosopher Manlio Sgarambro, a conscientious scholar of the Swabian thinker. What should not be forgotten is Frederick's wish to be regarded as the "Emperor of recent times" (ie, the modern emperor concerted with the science of the four last things: death, judgement, heaven and hell), summoned with a mission to restore the golden age of justice on earth. This legendary vision of his own personality and role, promoted by other tales of affectation (he pronounced Iesi, where he was born, as Iesus; the octagon of Castel del Monte was to reflect the ancient symbol of eternity; he wanted to be crowned in the sacred city of Jerusalem), conflicts violently with the vicious accusations made by the papal curia, which tended to regard Frederick as the Antichrist mentioned in the Bible.

Archivio Municipale. Asti/SCALA

Frederick II

the Swabian daughter of Manfred, believed he had a rightful claim to the crown of Sicily. Furthermore, the powerful Catalan fleet had been patrolling the Mediterranean for some time already, ready to conquer bases in Africa and Italy once the differences between Pisa and Genoa were settled. Peter II was offered the crown of Sicily. At first, there was little resistance, Charles of Anjou withdrew from Messina on 29 September. However, when war broke out in earnest, the Sicilian-Aragonese discovered an able military leader in Roger di Lauria, a great admiral, who won a decisive victory over the Angevin forces off Naples in June 1283.

1285	Charles dies in 1285, before he is able to return to Sicily.
1296	Frederick of Aragon concedes to the right for the parliament of the barons to be called at least once a year. During the 14C, Sicily is frequented by foreign merchants: traders from Genoa and England settle in Messina and Trapani. Groups of Greek and Albanian immigrants move

Sicilian Vespers by Erulo Eruli

to seven townships in Sicily. These communities preserve some aspects of their culture and religion until the 20C. There is also a considerable influx of "Lombards" – people from northern Italy – who settle in Palermo and Corleone.

1302 The war is concluded in 1302 with the Peace of Caltabellotta: Frederick of Aragon, Peter's son, is declared King of Trinacria on the condition that, at his death, his kingdom is returned to Robert of Anjou. The pact was broken and the Norman kingdom, once so prosperous and powerful, was divided into two parts. And so Charles of Anjou's attempt to make the Sicilian kingdom the hub of a potentate, in order to extend his influence throughout the peninsula, met with dismal failure.

1425-42 Alfonso V of Aragon intervenes against the Angevins in Naples. The island and the mainland are again united under one king.

Modern Sicily

1492 The Jews are forced to leave Spain; in Sicily also, prosperous communities are expelled from Salemi and Palermo.

1513 The *Tribunale di Sant'Uffizio*, otherwise known as the Spanish Inquisition, is introduced to Sicily.

1535 Emperor Charles V visits Palermo; he is celebrated following his hard-won victories in the Mediterranean over the Barbary pirates of Algeria.

1556 There are 72 barons on the island (by 1810 that number will have increased to 277) who hold the right to a seat in parliament; this institution is considered ancient and is therefore revered by the Sicilians as a symbol of the island's autonomy. It has three *Brazos* or Chambers with one each reserved for the clergy, the barons and military leaders, and for the representatives of towns directly answerable to the king; it only has the power to advise.

1570 The great Christian fleet (comprising galleys from Venice, Spain, the Papal States, the Duchy of Tuscany etc) that will sail into battle at Lepanto in October 1571 and secure its famous victory over the Turks is rallied at Messina. Large numbers of reserve galley crew and oarsmen are recruited from Calabria and Sicily.

1624 Plague ravages Palermo. The miraculous discovery of Santa Rosalia's bones helps, according to popular belief, to assuage the epidemic. Henceforth, the saint is acclaimed a patron of the city.

1647 Revolt in Palermo, coinciding with the insurrection in Naples led by Tommaso di Aniello. The anti-Spanish uprising is spearheaded by two commoners, Nino de la Pelosa and Giuseppe d'Alessi, but the rebellion is quickly suppressed.

	In 1674, Messina also rises up against the Spanish, with assistance from the king of France. The town is brutally recaptured by the Spanish in 1678.
1693	A terrible earthquake shakes south-eastern Sicily.
1713	The Treaty of Utrecht assigns Sicily to Savoy; Victor Amadeus, the new king, visits the island.
1714	The population of Sicily reaches 1 123 000; in 1570, it stood at 1 070 000.
1718-20	Spain recaptures Sardinia and threatens Naples and Palermo. The Spanish fleet is sunk, however, at Capo Passero, by the British fleet. Sicily is conferred upon the Habsburg emperor who, in return, cedes Sardinia to Savoy.
1733	The Scottish writer Patrick Brydone publishes his *Tour through Sicily and Malta*, an account of his travels in Sicily.
1735	The coronation of Charles Bourbon in Palermo heralds the dominion of the Bourbon dynasty in Sicily.
1781-86	Caracciolo is viceroy of the island: a number of reforms are avowed with the aim of increasing his powerbase. The Inquisition is abolished.
1794	Leblanc's discovery as to how to isolate sodium carbonate revolutionises several industrial processes: the price of sulphur becomes competitive. From 1790, Sicilian citrus fruits are exported on a large-scale across Europe. In 1814, English-owned distilleries in Marsala begin producing a sherry-like wine.
1806	British troops are stationed in Sicily to provide protection from the armies of Napoleon Bonaparte. These contribute to the economic prosperity.
1812	With help from Britain's representative in Sicily, Lord Bentinck, reforms are implemented for a more liberal constitution that abolishes feudal rights. Modelled on the British parliamentary system, the constitution comprises two chambers.
1816	Creation of the Kingdom of Two Sicilies: the kingdoms of Naples and Palermo are unified and the Sicilian flag is abolished. At the same time the 1812 constitution is abrogated.
1840	The issue of water and its illegally-controlled distribution comes to a head, most especially in the Palermo area, prompted by acute drought conditions. Smuggling and contraband also get out of hand.
1847	An investigation reveals that half of the island's woodland has been destroyed over the past 100 years, resulting in the climate becoming drier. Francesco Ferrara's *Letter from Malta* is published proposing Sicilian autonomy within a federation of Italian states.
1848-49	Insurrections in Palermo and across Sicily.
1860	In April, there is rioting in Palermo, provoked by agents from the north. The Thousand are sent to Sicily, headed by Garibaldi *(see MARSALA)*. On 21 October, a plebiscite sanctions (432 000 for and 600 against) the island's union with the Kingdom of Italy.

The landing of Garibaldi's Thousand at Marsala

Museo del Risorgimento, Roma/SCALA

1908: Messina after the earthquake

1866	Revolt in Palermo as a result of the acute economic situation (15 000 unemployed). In the end, the Italian fleet bombards the city while 4 000 soldiers quash the riots.
1886	The Jacini report on the state of Italian agriculture reveals that the island is heading towards a food shortage, aggravated by a rise in population. Between 1880 and 1914, about 1.5 million Sicilians leave the island, the majority heading for the United States. This phenomenon favours the repatriation of considerable funds by the émigrés (about 100 million Lire in 1907).
1893	The Notarbartolo scandal surrounding the director of the Banca d'Italia breaks out; he is assassinated after denouncing political and financial malpractice.
1894	A poor harvest, coupled with the inequalities in the distribution of ecclesiastical land, provoke disorder and insurrection rallied by the supporters of the so-called *Fasci di Lavoratori*, an organisation uniting less prosperous farmers (founded in 1889). When the Giolitti government falls, having been reluctant to use force, a government is formed by the Sicilian Francesco Crispi; he posts 50 000 soldiers on the island and imposes martial law.
1908	Serious earthquake in Messina causing over 60 000 fatalities.
1911	Population census: 58 % of Sicilians are found to be illiterate.
1925	The Fascist government extends the so-called "battle of wheat" to Sicily, with the intention of making Italy self-sufficient in the production of cereals.

Contemporary Sicily

1940	The government announces agricultural reforms which are impeded by the outbreak of war.
1943	On 16 July, the first units of the British Eighth Army and the American Seventh Army seize land at Licata and Augusta. The large-scale deployment of men and equipment under Eisenhower's command soon gains control over the four Italian and two German divisions drawn up to defend the island. On 22 July, first Palermo falls, then Messina, from where, to the detriment of their Italian counterparts, the German units succeed in reaching the mainland. On 3 September, at Cassibile, near Siracusa, emissaries of the Badoglio government sign the armistice with the Allied delegations.

The Sicilian Statute

On 15 May 1946, a royal decree promulgated a law on Sicilian autonomy. On 26 February 1948, the Constituent Assembly turns the Statute of Sicily into law, in accordance with provisions under Article 116 of the Italian Constitution listing the specifications and conditions for autonomous rule as granted to five Italian regions. The regional statute provides for a regional council, known as the Parliament, composed of 90 members. The Parliament elects a regional committee *(Giunta Regionale)* and a president from among its members by a majority consensus. The president has the right to sit in with the Council of Ministers in Rome during debates on issues affecting Sicily. The Parliament can approve legislation for the island, its powers, sanctioned by Article 117 of the Italian Constitution, being fairly extensive. Special delegations from the Council of State and the State Audit Court sit permanently in Palermo so as to ensure a certain degree of administrative decentralisation.

1947	In the elections, the separatists receive less than 10% of the vote. The aim of the movement is for the secession of the island from the rest of Italy. Many Sicilians dream of the island being annexed to the United States. The separatists seek to take up arms. Salvatore Giuliano, in hiding since 1943, is nominated colonel of EVIS (the Voluntary Army for Sicilian Independence). On 1 May 1947 Giuliano's men open fire on a group of demonstrating farmers at Portella delle Ginestre. There are 12 victims and national indignation is high. Giuliano is found dead on 5 July 1950 at Castelvetrano, in mysterious circumstances. The separatists disappear from the political scene with the elections of 1951.
1950	Agricultural reforms are implemented: estates of over 300ha/741 acres are expropriated and divided into numerous land-holdings (of 4-5ha/10-12 acres) for distribution among small-scale peasant-farmers: a total of some 115 000ha/284 165 acres are reallocated to over 18 000 farmers.
1951-75	A million Sicilians emigrate to northern Italy and Northern Europe.
1953	Crude oil is discovered at Ragusa and Gela; in 1966, 8 million barrels are extracted.
1958	A terrorist bomb shatters the headquarters of the Palermo daily newspaper *L'Ora* following its allusion to the power of the Mafia.
1968	A disastrous earthquake affects the Belice Valley.
1973-76	The Parliamentary Anti-Mafia Commission gets down to work.
1974	Bureaucratic problems come to the fore: more than 200 public authorities operate on the island at a cost of over 1 500 billion Lire in contemporary money and still there is no effective administration of goods and services.
1982	3 September: the Palermo Chief of Police, General Carlo Alberto Dalla Chiesa, his wife and a member of his police escort are killed in a terrorist attack.
1986	During the American-Libyan crisis across the Mediterranean basin, the Libyans launch missiles targeted at Lampedusa.
1987	End of the major court case held in Palermo against the Mafia, with 19 people sentenced to life imprisonment.
1992	12 March: the politician Salvo Lima is murdered in Palermo. 23 May: Giovanni Falcone, Director of Penal Affairs at the Ministry of Justice, is killed by an explosive device placed at a motorway crossing near Capaci. His wife and three members of his police escort also die in the blast. 19 July: in Via D'Amelio in Palermo, a car-bomb kills Judge Paolo Borsellino; three policemen and a policewoman also lose their lives. 6 September: the Mafia boss Giovanni Madonìa is arrested.
1996	13 March: the dome and a large section of the nave of the cathedral of Noto collapse.

The Ancient Greeks in Sicily

Contacts between Sicily and the Hellenistic world go back to the dawn of Greek civilisation: not only are references interwoven into the very fabric of Homer's epic poem, numerous archaeological artefacts testify to thriving maritime centres along the eastern and southern Sicilian coast trading with Crete and Mycenae from the middle of the 2nd millennium BC. However, this "pre-colonial" presence was strictly limited to the ports of call, for there are no traces of any permanent occupation between the 13C BC and the 8C BC. In fact colonisation only began when living conditions within Ancient Greece became untenable: famine followed civil war and a growing sense of social unrest was prompted by the emergence of a new "social class" drawn from restless second sons. They were rallying themselves in an attempt to contradict the established conventions, enforced by law, honouring the right of primogeniture that excluded the second-born from inheriting any agricultural land-holding. In the end, this was to prove reason enough for many to leave Greece in search of new lands where they could build a future for themselves. Sicily, and southern Italy in general, provided the broadest frontiers, despite their great hunger for land, and the ideal conditions for building a bigger and greater Greece of their own.

HISTORY AND SOCIAL PHENOMENA

Foundations – Just before the last quarter of the 8C BC, various small groups of Hellenes took part in colonising Sicily. The example was provided by the Ionians: in 735 BC the first major expedition involving a band of Chalcidians from Euboea led by Theocles, arrived in Sicily; they settled near Capo Schisò and founded Naxos. Settlements were instituted at Leontinoi, Catane and Zancle (later known as Messina). Almost simultaneously, a group of Dorians arrived from Corinth headed by Archias, they founded Syracuse, present-day Siracusa; meanwhile, colonists from Megara, led by Lamis, settled at Megara Hyblea. At the beginning of the 7C BC, Rhodians and Cretans arrived and founded Gela on the south coast of the island. This first phase of expansion did not result from any logical system of claiming the successive sites on a geographical basis, but rather on finding places with abundant supplies of fresh water that were easily accessible from the sea and remote enough from any other settlement to allow, in time, for secondary settlements to be developed further inland.

Founders – Each expedition, comprised predominantly but not exclusively of men, was led by an *oikistes* (founder) who, generally, belonged to one of the most renowned families in the city of origin. It is highly probable that, before setting out to found a colony, the *oikistes* would undertake several exploratory voyages during which he would find and choose the most suitable site for settlement. These voyages, however, were always preceded by a journey to Delphi, where the oracle of Apollo Archaghètas *(he who guides)* was consulted as to where the gods wanted the new colony to be founded. The founder-leaders disposed of great power and prestige: charged with transferring the holy flame and the lifeblood of the religious cult from the metropolis to their satellite colonies, their decisions were considered sacred and, when they died, they were honoured almost as if they had been gods. Accompanied by surveyors, engineers and soothsayers that had been recruited before departure, they presided over the construction of the citadel and the public buildings, and the administration of justice. They were also responsible for ensuring fair practice when the draw for plots of land took place, so that nobody should be unjustly privileged. Not all the land available was distributed immediately, however; a proportion was reserved for future colonists.

Colony – The founder would establish the new city's institutions, which were not necessarily identical to those implemented at home. Each colony (*apoikìa* in Greek meaning "new family") was, by right and in effect, completely independent. Despite Corinth's vain attempts to maintain control over its colonies, they forcefully embraced their autonomy by acting as independent political entities. In this way, Akragas (Agrigento) was able to develop excellent trading relations with Carthage, which officially was hostile to Greece, while Zancle and Reggio blockaded the Straits of Messina and demanded that Greek ships pay harbour taxes. The colonists lost their rights of citizenship in their city of origin and acquired the equivalent status in their new home. Restrictions on religious and sentimental practices were kept in place, as were rights of *isopolitia*, by which it was possible to "exchange" citizenship of one city with the resident of another by mutual consent. The colonies were not only independent from their motherland, but also from each other, with each individual city conducting its own political affairs in all but matters arising from an alliance with another, and then under special circumstances. The cities prospered and grew quickly, thanks to flourishing trade links and fertile territories: a sharp increase in population, partly as a result of the rise in birth-rate and partly resulting from the continuous influx of new immigrants, forced the authorities to establish secondary colonies further inland. Between the 7C BC and the 6C BC, a second wave of colonisation swept through Sicily, bringing with it a tendency towards territorial aggregation. The Chalcidians of

Zancle occupied Milazzo, affirming their supremacy over the Tyrrhenian coast of Sicily and the plain of the Mela; they also founded Himera to the west. Catane and Leontinoi claimed influence over territory inland towards Etna, to the valleys of the Simeto and its tributaries. Syracuse founded Acrae and then Kasmenai (Κασμεναι; Casmene), before assuming control over the plateau beyond and monopolising the means of communication with the central states and the plain of the Dirillo, where Camarina was subsequently founded. Megara Hyblaea, hemmed in by Syracuse and Leontinoi, hit upon a safety valve when they founded Selinus (Selinunte), the most westerly of the Greek colonies in Sicily. Towards the mid-6C BC, this precipitated the founding of Heraclea Minoa, a third-generation colony of Megara. In 580 BC, colonists from Cnidus settled in the Aeolian Islands. In the west of Sicily, specific areas of considerable significance – including Lilybaeum (Marsala), Motya, and Panormus – were subjugated first by the Phoenicians, later by the Carthaginians.

The Greeks and indigenous populations – Relations with the indigenous peoples were extremely varied. In some cases, the rapport was so serene as to inspire commercial and religious exchanges: although, in effect, the prime Hellenic settlements along the coast barely disturbed the pre-existing communities which, for the most part, were concentrated inland. It was only when the Greeks began to colonise the hinterland that resentment began to grow. Eventually, open conflict led to the systematic extermination of villages as happened during the great revolt by the indigenous population that gripped the eastern part of the island sometime in the mid 5C. With defeat came obligations to pay tributes and, in some cases, enforced conditions of slavery: it is known that in Syracuse, the descendants of the indigenous people (the Cilliri) were constrained to cultivating the land of their overlords (Gamòroi), who were descended from the ancient colonists. The Greek settlers were known as the **Siceliots**; these people, armed with weapons and endowed with sophisticated know-how drawn from the superior culture they had brought with them, were rapidly able to impose their civilisation upon Sicily like no other populating colony before them: between the 6C BC and the 5C BC, they managed to completely hellenise the territories they held.

Economy – Prosperity depended not only on the natural fertility of the Sicilian land but on good farming practices: yields from wild plants were improved by grafting, common wheat was allowed to adapt to being grown intensively, almond-trees and pomegranates were planted, and animals were bred selectively from fertile stock for best results. The most sophisticated cities set about reclaiming land where possible, most notably at Camarina and Selinus with direction from Empedocles. Besides their success at arable farming and careful husbandry, the Western Greeks amassed for tunes through commerce with intensive trade links established not only with the motherland, but also with Spain, southern Italy and North Africa. They imported fine ceramics, perfumes and metals against timber, wheat and wool. The upsurge in trade soon made it necessary for the Siceliot cities to introduce their own currencies. The earliest coins are of silver and feature an embossed head whereas the "tails" were impressed. At the beginning of the 5C BC, both heads and tails were moulded in relief, and two new materials were introduced, namely gold and bronze.

Political evolution – To qualify for citizenship, and thereby participate in the political life of the community, individuals were required to own a piece of land and to claim to have a fixed abode. In reality, most of the Greeks would have earned their living as skilled craftsmen, fishermen, traders and collectors of customs duties. In addition to these, a large number were involved in public works: it has been calculated that at least one-third of the population must have been engaged in building large-scale projects, be it a wood-cutter supplying timber or a painter employed on the decoration. Many more lived from one day to the next without a roof over their heads, without permanent employment. In the space of a few years, therefore, the very inequalities that the colonists thought they had escaped by leaving Greece had become issues of contention. The aristocracy, together with the owners of the best land, conferred all the power upon themselves; they repressed the new moneyed classes of businessmen and those who, for one reason or another, owned no land. The Siceliot cities had two ways of dealing with the continual crises provoked by fierce economic rivalry and the internal pressures caused by social inequality: some tried to correct the balance by overriding the written constitution with an oral legal system of oaths and undertakings that re-established the principle of equality, others resorted to straightforward tyranny. The first solution aimed at removing the administration of justice from the jurisdiction of the privileged few: the first codex, transcribed by **Charondas of Catane** (6C BC), was copied by many other cities, even outside Sicily – including Athens. It established duties and rights within the family; prescribed punishments for violence and perjury, and the death penalty for anyone entering a political meeting armed, and instituted a sort of citizens' jury, decreeing that a fine – proportional to earnings – be paid by anyone who refused to participate.

Tyrannic rule – The other way of averting economic and social crises was tyranny: this alternative consisted of compromise between patriarchal monarchy as practised effectively in the early Archaic period, and the demagogy of the Classical era of Antiquity. By preserving the external forms of state, the **tyrant**, who was generally a member of the new moneyed class or the army, invested himself with the maximum amount of power and delegated the rest to his most loyal supporters. It was precisely during the period of tyranny that Syracuse, first under **Gelon** and then under **Hieron** (Deinomenid dynasty), achieved its greatest splendour and managed to impose its authority throughout the island. The Siceliot cities, in a desperate attempt to resist the aggressor and salvage their independence, were driven to seek assistance from Carthage (Himera) or Athens, but this was to no avail. Meanwhile, the civil strife continued to split the Greek communities and the Carthaginian threat was growing. Syracuse found in **Dionysius** a means of averting the problem posed by its internal instability and the foreign threat. The new "tyrant" reinforced his authority over Syracuse by surrounding the entire Epipolae plateau with defensive walls culminating in the fortress of Euryalus; he set about transforming the island of Ortygia into a kind of stronghold for his soldiers. In 397 BC, he put himself in a position for attacking not only Carthage itself but the Punic colonies in Sicily as well, conquering Motya. The following year, the situation was reversed and Carthage turned on Syracuse. There followed a period of semi-anarchy after the demise of the Deinomenid dynasty in the latter half of the 4C BC. At last, **Timoleon**, who had arrived from Corinth to assist the colonies, succeeded in restoring democracy and peace to Sicily. Upon his death, the Greeks began to quarrel once more among themselves and with the Carthaginians: finally, in the second half of the 3C BC the citizens of Messina (Zancle) turned to Rome for help, opening their gates to the Imperial city and so precipitating her conquest of Sicily.

GREEK CULTURE IN SICILY

Legend relates how **Alpheus**, wandering across the Greek region of Arcadia, came across the water nymph **Arethusa** and fell in love with her; but as he tried to seize her, she was changed into a stream by Artemis, slipping from him into the Ionian Sea only to re-emerge as a spring in Sicily. Such was Alpheus' love for the nymph that he pursued her there, transformed as she had been *(see SIRACUSA)*. This myth, diffused among the Greek population of Sicily, was taken to symbolise the transference of the Greek civilisation from the motherland to Sicily. Far from being a marginal colony of Greece, the island in its own right attracted to its shores some of the most illustrious figures in Greek culture. It also succoured others born there who were to become famous throughout the Hellenic world. Furthermore, according to some scholars, Greek culture should be indebted to Sicily for one of its fundamental masterpieces, the *Odyssey*. Many of Ulysses' adventures were unequivocally set in the Island of the Sun, the name used by **Homer** to describe Sicily, so obviously that Apollodorus defined the *Odyssey* as a kind of "journey around Sicily". Many of the places are recognisable: Stromboli with its plume of smoke is the island of Aeolus; the Aeolian Islands are the kingdom of god; Scilla and Charibdis personify the impetuous currents in the Straits of Messina; the port at which Ulysses' companions steal Hyperion's flocks is based on Messina; even the famous episode involving Polyphemus was recognised by the ancients to have taken place in Sicily. The three little islands that lie north of Catania still bear the name of the Cyclops.

Tyrannical patrons – According to Aristotle, comedy in its Classical form was in part conceived by the Siceliot people; in fact, he goes further in conceding that it was invented by the Megareans of Greece and Sicily. Undoubtedly both **Epicharmus** and **Phormis**, the two earliest identifiable authors of comedies engaged at the court of Gelon, were Sicilian. Interestingly, the tyrants were noted for being generous patrons, summoning to their courts the best poets of the time, who celebrated their hosts in verse in exchange for the hospitality shown to them. Among the illustrious guests of the tyrants of Syracuse, we find the poet **Simonides**, famous as a writer of epigrams and funeral laments, who dedicated many of his verses to Sicily that tell of how the god of fire and Demeter disputed possession of the island. The simultaneous presence of poets of a certain renown also generated bitter rivalries: for years, **Bacchylides** and **Pindar** contested Hieron's favours, as they competed to compose songs of victory *(epinici)* exalting his successes with the quadriga at the games. At the height of his achievement, the great tragedian **Aeschylus** was based at the court of Hieron: so, to celebrate the conquest and re-naming of the city of Aetna (formerly Catane – later Catania) he arranged performances of *The Women of Etna* (now lost) and *The Persians*. Pindar marked the occasion by composing his Pythian Odes. **Theocritus** (c 300-260 BC), meanwhile, was a native of Syracuse; he is attributed with inventing pastoral poetry.

Philosophy – Two of the most interesting pre-Socratic thinkers were born in Sicily: **Empedocles** came from Agrigento and **Gorgias** from Leontinoi. **Empedocles** (c 500-c 430 BC) is a complex figure, being at the same time a mystic, miracle worker, doctor and student of natural philosophy: the founder, in fact, of a school of medicine which regarded the heart as the seat of life, an idea taken up by Aristotle. He also taught that all matter was composed of four elements (earth, water, air and fire) and that these, regulated by the two universal forces harmony and discord (love and hate), had given rise to the whole cosmos. According to legend, he hurled himself to his death by jumping into one of the fiery craters of Mount Etna in the hope of persuading his fellow citizens that he had been summoned by the gods. Gorgias

The theatre at Segesta

responded to a different cultural climate, one of sophism (false argument), that aimed to satisfy the requirements of the emerging democracy, with particular emphasis on moral and political issues. Gorgias became an orator of considerable renown, especially in Athens where he was acclaimed a "master of wisdom".

The first great philosopher of mathematical harmony was Pythagoras, and he advocated clarity and harmony of dependent parts. The doctrines of Pythagoras were widespread in Sicily, particularly in Agrigento and Catania. The **School of Pythagoras** was established at Croton in the 6C-5C BC as a sort of religious confraternity; in addition to sustaining theories on the arithmeogeometric structure of the universe, the Pythagoreans exercised considerable influence in political circles by putting forward ideas for an aristocracy drawn from the new classes involved in commerce and trade. Sicily was also the setting envisaged by **Plato** for his Utopian state, ruled by philosophers, as contemplated in his *Republic*. Plato came to Syracuse in 388-387 BC as the guest and friend of Dion, the brother-in-law and son-in-law of Dionysius I; so when the tyrant became suspicious of the Athenian, he had him incarcerated and ransomed as a slave on the island of Aegina. He later returned to Sicily after Dionysius II had succeeded his father; to begin with, Plato appears to have found Dionysius II the better disciple, that is, until Dion was sent into exile and Plato was detained as a prisoner.

Science and history – Archimedes (first half of the 3C BC) was the one person in the Greek world capable of consolidating the theoretical and practical aspects of scientific knowledge at that time. Besides his important discoveries in the fields of mathematics, geometry and naval engineering, his name is associated with the invention of war machines such as were used against the Romans; these weapons of mass-destruction managed to deceive the Romans into thinking they were at war with the gods.

Diodorus Siculus, born at Agyrion in the 1C BC, was the author of a universal history of 40 volumes entitled *Biblioteca*. In it he deals with Greek history from the mythical times that lead up to the Trojan War to contemporary times; this still constitutes a valuable source for scholars.

Plato

RELIGION

Religion touched upon everything in the life of a Greek man: being but a mere mortal, he saw every event, be it of major or minor importance, as a possible manifestation of the divine. In no way, however, was his religion in the least dogmatic. Indeed, on coming into contact with another people, the Greeks were always willing to admit their gods to the Olympic pantheon, or to assimilate them with their own deities. The Greek gods, who personified the forces of nature or some moral quality, were

57

endowed with the physical and psychological attributes of human personality; the main characteristic that defined them as different from humans was their immortality. Individuals as well as entire communities might turn to a deity for protection and favour. The cult depended upon prayer, sacrifice and purification. Prayers were usually accompanied by an offering (libations of milk or wine, sweets, *focacce* or fresh produce). In the event of more demanding requests, an animal might be sacrificed; parts were then burnt on the altar while the rest was divided between the priest and the faithful. However, the most important public ceremonies were those held in cele-bration of a particular festival, when they would be accompanied with activities that, to the modern mind, had nothing to do with religion: literary and poetry competitions, competitive sporting events or games like the pan-Hellenic games held annually at Olympia and Delphi, in which the Sicilian tyrants also participated on several occasions. Each part of Greece was especially devoted to a particular deity so when the colonists transferred themselves to new settlements, they took with them the same traditional cults, and their affiliated festivals, espoused by their native land. Of course, these cele-brations were in addition to those designated by the new state, which included the annual commemoration of the founding of the city with a great ritual banquet attended when possible by the original founders.

Three important figures – Among all the different gods and heroes to be venerated in Sicily, the most significant are **Demeter**, who was regarded as the protector of Sicily, and **Heracles**. Sometimes the Greeks embraced local cults and rites: a case in point are the nymphs who are supposed to have emerged from the hot springs at Termini Imerese; another is that of the **Palici** brothers.

Demeter, the goddess who embodies the earth's fertility, was the object of a cult preva-lent especially in Ionian Greece and naturally therefore in Sicily; here, when she assumed the role of mother-protector, she became a more complex deity modelled on a pre-existent indigenous allegory. Not only did the Greek colonists assimilate the maternal attributes of the earth figure, they adapted her mythological story so as to make it pertinent to the Sicilian soil, rooting it to the place with specific allusions to its topography. It tells of how Kore (Greek for maiden; Proserpina to the Romans), daughter of Demeter, was gathering flowers near the Lake of Pergusa (the Homeric *Hymn to Demeter* situates its version 19km/12mi from Athens at Eleusis) when Hades (Pluto), the king of the Underworld, saw her, fell in love with her, and carried her off. For nine days, Demeter wandered over Sicily in search of her lost daughter. Near Trapani, she dropped her sickle: this is supposed to be the origin of the sickle-shaped headland which lies before the town. One night, as she scoured the slopes of Etna by the light of flaming pine trees, she interpreted the sounds made as she passed through the lupins as the ring of their mocking laughter and spurning tongues: from that day forth, it is said, lupins lost their sweetness and became bitter. Frustrated at not having found her daughter, Demeter prevented the earth from bringing forth fruit by inflicting a terrible drought: men and animals began to die by the hundreds. This prompted her brother Zeus (also father of Kore) to intervene by agreeing to demand that Hades release Kore on condition that she had not eaten anything during her stay in the under-world. But before she departed from the kingdom of the dead, Hades forced her to eat a few pomegranate seeds as a symbol of fidelity. Thus betrothed to Hades, Kore – now called **Persephone** – was destined to spend a third of the year with him in the Underworld and the remaining months with her mother on earth. In the language of myth, Persephone thus came to stand as an allegory for the seed that must be planted in the earth for it to grow in spring and summer, before yielding up its own ripened seed before winter comes; the story also explains the cycle of seasons and provides hope for times of despair.

The second deity to enjoy a special following in Sicily was **Heracles**. This probably stems from another myth, established before the Greeks arrived on the island, involving a Phoenician deity that shared many elements with the story of the Greek hero. The legend tells of a Heracles that was born out of a union between Zeus and a mortal woman, Alcmena; he too had to undertake 12 labours in order to assuage a dreadful deed and become a god. According to tradition, the first people to attribute divine honours to the hero would seem to be the inhabitants of Sicily. Heracles came to the island in the course of his tenth labour, when he was forced to cross the Straits of Messina in pursuit of a bull belonging to Geryon. Almost every little place on the island claims to have been visited by the hero: Erice was where he wrestled and killed the son of Aphrodite and Butes, the king who shared his name with the town; at Syracuse he is said to have instituted a sacred festival near the Gorge of Cyane; Agiro was the place to honour him as a god; in recognition of this, the hero created a lake outside the city walls and raised two sanctuaries there.

The **Palici** rank among Sicily's own ancient divinities, which the Greeks later appropri-ated by adopting them as the twin sons of Zeus and the muse Thalia. The centre of their cult was Naftia, a small lake with bubbling sulphurous waters in the Plain of Catania, near Palagonia. The myth relates how Thalia, fearing the wrath of Hera, hid underground where she gave birth. The subterranean birth of the divine twins henceforth caused the waters of the lake to bubble and steam. Beside the sanctuary dedicated to the Palici, the Greeks pronounced solemn oaths and enacted a kind of ritualistic ordeal in the waters of the lake: if, when they submerged tablets bearing written agreements, the tablets sank, this was interpreted as a sign of perjury, which the Palici punished with blinding.

In general, the Siceliots were hugely sensitive to the indigenous cults and were deeply respectful of the cult of the dead and of the gods of the Underworld (referred to as chthonic deities). In fact, some gods which in Greece were completely extraneous to such things, assumed connotations with death and burial in Sicily: Aphrodite (Venus) and Artemis (Diana), for example, in addition to their traditional personalities, were regarded as companions and protectors of the souls of the dead.

Mysteries – Mystery rites were also particularly widespread in Sicily. These special religious spirits were developed to provide answers to the inexplicable, and to allay worries in the mind of individuals facing death. The Mysteries, to which individuals were admitted by special initiation rites, promised to purify the soul of the initiated and by doing so ensured other-worldly happiness after death. One of the most famous Mystery cults, the so-called Eleusinian Mysteries, revolve around Demeter and Kore: celebrations in the form of a spring festival was held at the time when seeds should be sown. It is therefore natural that they should quickly have been diffused throughout Sicily.

Homeric-Greek name	Virgilian-Latin name	Identity	Attribute
Hades	Pluto	Brother of Zeus; lord of the kingdom of the dead.	throne, beard
Aphrodite	Venus	Emerged from the sea. Goddess of love and beauty, wife of Hephaestus and mother of Eros.	dove, shell
Apollo	Phoebus-Apollo	Son of Zeus and Latona; the god of light, music and prophecy.	lyre, laurel, sun, dart
Ares	Mars	God of war; out of his union with Aphrodite Eros was born.	helmet, weapons
Artemis	Diana	Sister of Apollo, goddess of vegetation, hunting, of the moon; virgin and protector of chastity.	moon, bow, quiver
Asklepius	Aesculapius	Son of Apollo, god of medicine.	stick, snake
Athena	Minerva	Goddess of the arts, of justice, and wisdom; born from the brain of Zeus.	helmet, owl, olive, aegis (mythical shield)
Demeter	Ceres	Mother of the earth, fertility and agriculture.	sickle, ear of wheat, cornucopia of fruit
Dionysus	Bacchus	God of nature, wine and drunkenness.	wine, thyrsus
Hephaestus	Vulcan	Husband of Aphrodite and god of fire, he is depicted as a blacksmith.	anvil, hammer
Helios/Hyperion	Phoebus	God of the sun.	rays of sun, chariot
Hera	Juno	Sister and wife of Zeus, goddess of matrimony and fidelity.	crown, peacock
Heracles	Hercules	Son of Zeus and Alcmena; a hero during his earthly life and a god of Olympus after death. Eurystheus imposed the 12 labours on Heracles.	club, shield, lion's skin
Hermes	Mercury	Messenger of the gods and companion of souls beyond the grave. God of commerce and eloquence.	caduceus (stick with snakes entwined around it), sandals and winged bonnet
Hestia	Vesta	Goddess of the domestic hearth.	fire
Persephone/Kore	Proserpine	Daughter of Demeter, allegory for the seasonal cycles of nature.	plants, cock, pomegranate
Poseidon	Neptune	Brother of Zeus, god of the sea.	chariot, trident
Zeus	Jupiter	Lord over all the gods and mankind, guarantor of order and justice in the universe.	eagle, sceptre, thunderbolt

GREEK ART

Architecture: civil and military

Archaeological findings seems to suggest that the first military fortifications and examples of civil building in Sicily date from the late Archaic period, that is the end of the 6C BC. There are few traces of anything before that time, although it is presumed that military emplacements existed here as from the 8C when the various cities began to rival one another before the rise of tyrants.

Fortresses and fortifications – During the domination of the tyrants, the region was reinforced with fortified buildings that were constructed with materials that varied according to the local geology: in the east of the island, lava was commonly used, as at **Naxos** and **Lipari**. In the absence of suitable stone, walls were built using sun-dried brick with, at the bottom, a water-resistant foundation layer of broken stones, or a mixture of pebbles and clay.

Although archaeological surveys in Sicily have not yielded many emplacements of major significance, a few forts have survived. These guardian citadels ensured the defence of a city, its roads and other means of access. Maximum protection was provided by their strategic positions beside the city precincts or in their immediate vicinity, sited in as inaccessible a place as possible.

Urban planning – Almost on arrival, the Greek settlers organised the area into a rational system: different sections were designated as places of worship, for public buildings and residential quarters. Generally Sicilian cities conformed to the precepts for urban planning outlined by **Hippodamus of Miletus**, the 5C BC Greek philosopher and surveyor. The Hippodamian principles consisted of planning a city on a rectangular street-plan centred around two axes: the *cardo* (or *stenopos*, in Greek) which ran from north to south, and the *decumanus maximus* (*plateia* in Greek) which bisected it from east to west. The street network was then completed by other smaller streets running parallel to the two axes, forming an orthogonal network. A very precise set of buildings and various areas for particular purposes were then inserted into this plan, such as the *agorà*, the main square and the centre of public life, the *pritaneo*, which stood beside the *agorà* and was the setting for a range of civic activities, the *ekklesiasterion*, a secular public building reserved for the people's assembly (*ekklesia*), the most famous example of which can be seen at Agrigento, and the *bouleutérion*, where the citizen's council (*boulé*) met. The temples, sometimes built outside the city limits, were often surrounded by other sacred buildings, which in the most monumental structures could include porticoes, votive monuments, gymnasia and theatres. The urban area was usually fortified with walls; beyond lay the agricultural land, subdivided into family plots, and a specific area destined for use as a burial ground. All the Greek cities and, sometimes even the villages, were supplied with reservoirs for water and aqueducts: the most famous being that built by the architect Phaeax at Akragas (Agrigento), and the extremely complex one at Syracuse.

Architecture: sacred and religious

There are two forms of sacred building: the **temple** and the **theatre**. Located outside the city itself, these buildings were designed to be visible from a distance, hence the reason for their situation in the landscape, orientated so as to enjoy a splendid view.

Temples – From the 8C BC, Greek colonists came to Sicily bringing with them their own cults and gods, transforming the island into what is now regarded as one of the most extraordinary open-air museums of Doric temples, of the so-called "severe style".

Plan and structure – The heart of the building comprised the **naos** (*cella*), an oblong chamber which housed a statue of the god; temples normally faced east, so that the statue could be illuminated by the rising sun, the source of all life. Before the *naos* was the **pronaos** (a kind of ante-chamber), while behind stood the **opisthodomos** which served as a treasury. A **peristyle** or colonnade surrounded the building.

The Siceliot house

The Archaic houses were fairly simple affairs: walls marking the confines of the plot were built around the open space in which stood the rectangular sun-dried brick building, erected on a base of dry pebbles. The sloping gable roof was covered with flat tiles. In the courtyard were stored tools and those great terracotta jars in which provisions were kept; it also served as a communal area in which the family gathered, ate and received visitors. The terrace was used for drying fruit, as a place to sit and talk, pray and sleep. Among the foundations, a talisman was hidden, sometimes a bone or a votive object, to ensure the house remained sturdy and solid. Often it was sprinkled with the blood of a young animal, as were the threshold, the architrave and the door-jambs.

In time, the houses became more sophisticated: a raised floor was added complete with a stairway supported by a portico. The largest of the rooms facing onto the portico and connected to the kitchen was the one used for gatherings, for it was here that the men met for their *symposia*.

The temple was founded on a stepped base; onto the last step **(stylobate)** were erected the **columns** which rose to support the **architrave**. The building was covered by a sloping roof.

Style – The most splendid expressions of the **Doric style** are to be found in Sicily. First conceived in the Peloponnese, this style spread to mainland Greece and consequently to its colonies, including Sicily, where it exerted its powerful presence. The Doric order, which combines majesty with sobriety, comprises a base-less column shaft indented with 20 vertical grooves or flutes (as from the 5C) that sits directly on the stylobate. On the top of the shaft rests a simple capital, devoid of any sculptural decoration, that consists instead of a simple circular moulding *(echinus)* and an *abacus* (a square flat slab that supports the architrave). The Doric entablature consists of a plain architrave, the upper section of which comprises a frieze articulated by **metopes** (generally panels sculpted with shallow relief) and **triglyphs** (rectangular projections ornamented with two deep vertical grooves in the centre flanked by a narrower one at each edge).

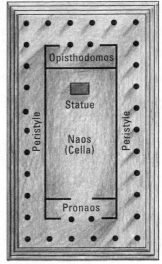

Temple

In the 6C BC, almost all the temples built in Sicily were peripteral (that is, surrounded by a line of columns) and hexastyle (6-columned front elevation); although some examples have more than six front columns, such as Temple G at Sellunte.

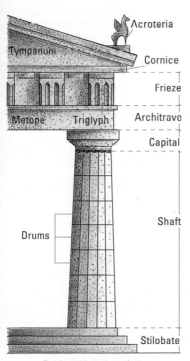

Doric order elevation

Proportion – As a result of its simplicity of structure and perfect harmony of proportion the temple was long considered to be the architectural prototype of ideal beauty. When building designers became aware of the tendency of the human eye to perceive emphatic architectural accents as distorted, they decided to correct the optical illusion. the central section of the architrave, which otherwise appeared to sag slightly, was fractionally raised, making it in effect imperceptibly concave; to restore an impression of perfect balance, the outer columns of the façades were slightly inclined inwards, thereby countering the natural tendency to appear lopsided. Finally, in particularly large buildings (such as the Temple of Concord at Agrigento and the temples at Selinunte and Segesta), as the rows of columns would otherwise appear exaggeratedly narrow at the top, to compensate for this optical illusion the columns were cut with a very slight central swelling (entasis) about two-thirds of the way up the shaft.

Decoration – When compared with the architecture of mainland Greece, the temples of Magna Graecia and Sicily are more monumental, pay more attention to spacial effect and show a particular taste for abundant decoration. Sculptures, often empowered with a didactic purpose, crown the prominent features, sometimes those elements with no structural function – on the **tympanum** of a pediment, for example, or above the **metopes** of the architrave and on the edges of roofs.

The temples were often decorated with groups of sculptures and low reliefs and were usually painted in red, blue and white in order to provide the sculptures and columns with maximum relief. Similarly, a "golden bronze" colour was used to throw other decorative features into relief, like the shields and **acroteri** (decorative elements set at the corners or apex of a pediment) or the sculptured ornaments called **antefixes** that functioned as gargoyles aligned along the gable cornices (along the edge of the roof).

Theatres – Beside most of the Greek sanctuaries there was a theatre where Dionysian celebrations were held (in honour of Dionysus, the god of wine) with hymns called "dithyrambs" from which, later, Greek tragedy was derived.

Built first of wood and then, from the 4C BC, in stone, a theatre would comprise:
– the *koilon* or *cavea*, a series of tiered ledges arranged in a semi-circle, the first row being reserved for priests and dignitaries. Access was from the base by means of side-entrances *(parodos)*; one passage *(diazoma)* led through to the central section, another up to the top rows of seating;
– the *orchestra* consisted of a circular area where the chorus and actors, wearing masks corresponding to their roles, took their places around the altar of Dionysus;
– the *proscenium (proskénion)* at the back, a kind of portico construction, served as backdrop scenery; behind it extended the *skéné* which at once fulfilled three functions:

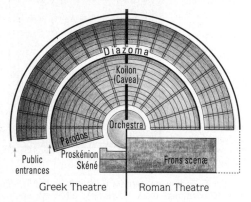

Greek Theatre   Roman Theatre

stage scenery, backstage and storage area. During the Hellenistic period, the *skéné* came to be reserved for actors. Given that these complexes are generally set in the most splendid landscape, on the slope of a hill or a mountain, the natural scenery provided the perfect background for productions (particularly spectacular at Taormina and Segesta). The *skéné*, almost always raised onto a platform, dominated the circular orchestra, where sacrifices were also sometimes made.

Sculpture

According to such Greek authors as Diodorus Siculus (1C BC historian) and Pausanias (Greek traveller of the 2C AD), Sicily had established an artistic heritage even before she was colonised. Either way, it is difficult to formulate a Sicilian style before the arrival of the Greek settlers (8C BC) given the full extent of artistic exchange between Sicily and Greece, particularly in the south of the island which at that time was occupied by the Sicani. During colonisation, indigenous artistic taste and aesthetics were naturally affected by Greek influences, leading to the gradual erosion and eventual extinction of a purely "Sicilian" style.
In such a way, the island succumbed to the three chronological phases used to define the evolution of Greek art: the Archaic, Classic and Hellenistic eras.

Actors and theatrical productions

In Antiquity, theatrical performances were held on public holidays. As such they were not regular occurrences or everyday events like they are today; instead, they were one of the salient highlights of a civic festival and, in most cases, lasted for up to three or four days. Performances took place by daylight and in the open air. The actors, exclusively male but adept at playing female roles, wore **high shoes** *(coturni)* and **wigs** that combined to make them more clearly visible (stature being synonymous with high standing, this provided an indication of a character's social importance). The wearing of **masks** helped to amplify the voice and allowed the actor to assume different roles as required (the handful of actors usually played several parts); these, however, prevented action from being emphasised with the appropriate facial expressions. To counteract this, expressive gesture was of vital importance. **Costumes** were brightly coloured, with shades appearing to have assumed different connotations: with black, for example, signifying mourning and misfortune. Indications of a character's age, social status, state of mind and origin were provided by the mask and by a range of obvious props: a crown denoted a king, a stick an old man, different hats for foreign characters, and so on. Besides the actors, the **chorus** was also reserved its place on stage, its primary function being to comment on the events as they unfolded.
Proper stage machinery was used to emphasise a particularly dramatic moment in the action or to mark the entrance on stage of an important character. Perhaps the most notable included the **thunderbolt machine**: a black board, painted with a thunderbolt in pure gold, which could be suddenly brandished so that it caught the sun (remembering, of course, that performances were held during the day); the **thunder machine** produced loud rumbles when stones were made to roll inside a brass container; the **mechané** was a hook and pulley used when deities were suddenly required to enter on the scene and intervene so as to resolve the situation. The expression "deus ex machina" (used to refer to a sudden and unexpected resolution) derives from these early theatrical effects.

The scarcity of marble and the particular Sicilian taste for pictorial and chiaroscuro effects resulted in the predominant use of limestone and sandstone as raw materials. Clay was widely used in the pediments and acroter of the temples, as well as for votive statues.

Archaic (8C-5C BC) – This phase coincides with the production of the first large, rather wooden, hieratic figures which, in the 6C BC, gave rise to two distinctive forms: the *kouros* – the young male nude, and the *koré* – the young female equivalent, though modestly dressed in a tunic.

The statue of the **Ephebus of Agrigento** is one excellent example of late Archaic sculpture: it suggests the sculptor was striving to conform to a predetermined aesthetic type, although its basic sense of balance has yet to be perfected (the right leg appears extremely rigid while the outstretched arms seem set too far away from the body). As far as Archaic sculptural ornament used to adorn temples is concerned, two examples are to be found in Sicily: the polychrome winged **Gorgon** that once ornamented the pediment of the Athenaion in Syracuse, and the **metopes of Selinunte**, now displayed in the archaeological museum at Palermo. Following the discovery of six metopes from 575 BC in the fortified wall of the acropolis at Selinunte (Selinus), the only ones bearing a distinctive type of decoration to have been found to date, it is assumed that the city must have had its very own local school of sculpture. Several of the metopes allude to gods worshipped at Selinus, like the Apollonian triad (Apollo, Artemis and their mother, Leto/Latona), Demeter and Persephone. The metopes from Temple C (bearing the *Chariot of Apollo, Perseus and the Gorgon* and *Heracles and the Cercopi*), carved from the local limestone, would have been brought to life by colour applied to details such as clothing and torsos. Thought to date from the mid-6C BC, these works demonstrate the perfected mastery of composition. The metopes from Temple E *(Hera and Zeus, Heracles Wrestling with an Amazon)* are veritable masterpieces in their own right, often compared to the decoration of the Temple of Zeus at Olympia.

Classic (5C-3C BC) – The Ionic style of sculpture, which appeared in Sicily from the 6C BC onwards, is characterised by a better portrayal of individual features, and a greater sense of realism and sensitivity, now free of the severe rigidity of the earlier phase.

The white marble **Ephebus of Motya** that was recovered without arms or feet, now on display in the Joseph Whitaker Museum near where it was found *(see MOZIA)*, provides a clear appreciation of this evolution: the graceful curves with which this youth, 1.81m/5.93ft tall, is modelled typify the style of the 5C BC; dressed in a long tunic of soft, figure-hugging linen, it flatters the muscular body of the athlete. It would seem that this marble, unique to Sicily, was imported in its raw state from Anatolia and then worked *in situ*. The identification of this Ephebus has generated various hypotheses, none conclusive.

The **Atlas figures** (or *telamons*) from the Temple of Zeus at Agrigento which once stood between columns against walls, are hugely impressive on account of their sheer size. The Regional Archaeological Museum in Agrigento has only one example (7.75m/25ft tall).

A variety of temple ornaments, like the lion's head antefixes (Palermo Archaeological Museum), confirm the huge improvement in artistry and skill of sculptors working in the Classical style.

B. Kaufmann

The Ephebus of Motya

Hellenistic (3C-1C BC) – During this phase sculpture becomes yet more expressive and Eastern: deities are portrayed with more realism, with human rather than ideal features and in a less formal state of dress (Aphrodite, the goddess of beauty and love, for example, is shown in a pleated, flowing shift nonchalantly revealing her glorious nudity). Sculpture from this period is expressive of both emotion and movement, sometimes powerfully so, be it demonstrations of muscular strength or of gracefully poised dance.

The discovery of the **bronze ram** at Castello Maniace betrays the major impact of Greek aesthetics, notably their canons of beauty, on a city such as Syracuse. Originally, this masterpiece from the 3C BC, would have been one of a pair of decorative ornaments intended for the local tyrant's palace (built in Antiquity on the island of Ortygia). This fabulous animal, the likes of whose exquisitely modelled features and superb craftsmanship has never been equalled, is now one of the most highly prized exhibits of the Palermo Archaeological Museum.

The terracotta **theatrical masks** in the Archaeological Museum on Lipari (over 250 examples) are fascinating in the great range and subtlety of expression they portray, influenced in the main by Greek tragedy which became widespread in Sicily from the 3C BC.

Bronze ram

Painting and pottery

Painting was considered by the Greeks to be the most noble and eloquent form of artistic expression, described by the poet Simonides (5C BC) as "mute poetry". Unfortunately, examples of this art form are rare because of the fragile nature of the pigments used to make the paints and their vulnerability to weather conditions. Large easel paintings, extolled by original sources, can be partially reconstructed from vase paintings, which often took the former as their model.

Shape and form – The *pithos* was used for storing grain, while the *amphora* had the dual purpose of storing and transporting oil and wine. The *pelike*, *crater* and *hydria* were jars used for oil, wine and water respectively. The *oinochoe*, which was also very common, was a jug for holding water or wine before it was dispensed into a *kantharos* or *kylix* (drinking-cups), or even a *rhyton* – a cup shaped like a horn or an animal's head. The *lekythos*, on the other hand, was a funerary vase.

Styles – Vases with black figures on a red or pale yellow background date from the Archaic and the beginning of the Classic phase. The detailing of the figures was obtained by simply scratching away the black paint with a steel-tipped instrument. The most common subject-matter were scenes drawn from mythology or from everyday life; sometimes purely geometric or abstract motifs were used as decorations, most especially on the early vases.

Red-figure vases appear in southern Italy towards the latter half of the 5C BC, earlier than in Greece where this style became prevalent from 480 BC. In this case, the black paint used hitherto for delineating the figures, is used exclusively as a background to the decoration, with the figures drawn in a brick red colour with touches of black and white. This inverted technique, allowing greater freedom of artistic expression, was a revolutionary discovery for artists; their designs acquired softer lines and contours than those obtained with a sharp steel point. The choice of subjects, however, does not change a great deal. Among the most beautiful examples of imported Attic vases are the magnificent two-handled craters from Agrigento (5C BC).

Pelike Amphora Hydria Krater Pithos

Rhython Lekythos Kylix Kantharos Krater Oinochoë

Architecture

Thermal baths

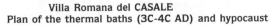

Villa Romana del CASALE
Plan of the thermal baths (3C-4C AD) and hypocaust

Pavement or floor

Hypocaust ducting permitting air to circulate

Suspensurae: small flat brick columns supporting the floor

Aqueduct supplying water to the complex

Tepidarium: warm bathing pool

Palaestra or gymnasium: bath complexes were often equipped with additional facilities for entertainment and physical exercise beneficial to mind and body

Calidarium: hot bathing pool and sauna

Laconicum: a room heated to high temperatures inducing greater perspiration after exercise

Apodyterium: changing room

Piscina or *natatio*: swimming pool

Frigidarium: cold bathing pool

Praefurnia or wood-burning stoves used to heat the water in the **fistulae** (lead piping) leading to the *caldaria*. These furnaces also heated the air that was then circulated throughout the complex

Vestibule: entrance to the baths

Bath kept at body temperature

Sala delle Unzioni: anointing room where oil and unguents were applied before exercise and where dead skin and perspiration were scraped away (using a **strigil**) before immersion in a bath

Tibuli: ducting through which hot air was circulated by convection up the walls

R. Corbel/MICHELIN

Religious architecture

RAGUSA IBLA – Duomo di San Giorgio (18C)

Latin cross floor plan with transepts

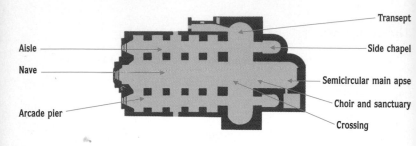

Aisle

Nave

Arcade pier

Transept

Side chapel

Semicircular main apse

Choir and sanctuary

Crossing

Cross-section of a church

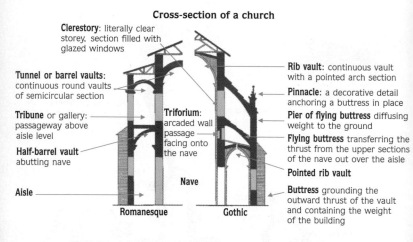

Clerestory: literally clear storey, section filled with glazed windows

Tunnel or barrel vaults: continuous round vaults of semicircular section

Tribune or gallery: passageway above aisle level

Half-barrel vault abutting nave

Aisle

Triforium: arcaded wall passage facing onto the nave

Nave

Romanesque

Gothic

Rib vault: continuous vault with a pointed arch section

Pinnacle: a decorative detail anchoring a buttress in place

Pier of flying buttress diffusing weight to the ground

Flying buttress transferring the thrust from the upper sections of the nave out over the aisle

Pointed rib vault

Buttress grounding the outward thrust of the vault and containing the weight of the building

NICOSIA – Cattedrale di San Nicolò: main doorway (14C)

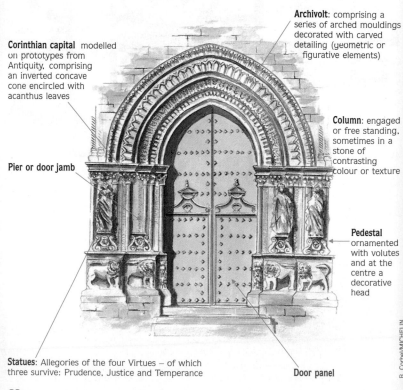

Archivolt: comprising a series of arched mouldings decorated with carved detailing (geometric or figurative elements)

Corinthian capital modelled on prototypes from Antiquity, comprising an inverted concave cone encircled with acanthus leaves

Pier or door jamb

Column: engaged or free standing, sometimes in a stone of contrasting colour or texture

Pedestal ornamented with volutes and at the centre a decorative head

Statues: Allegories of the four Virtues – of which three survive: Prudence, Justice and Temperance

Door panel

R. Corbel/MICHELIN

PALERMO – Cappella Palatina: ceiling detail (12C)

Muqarnas ceiling: complicated geometric plasterwork of interconnected stars and crosses elongated into stalactites

Schematic drawing illustrating the basis of Moorish decorative elements using the eight-pointed star

Stalactite decoration: a gay profusion of stucco pendants

Honeycombed plasterwork decorated with narrative scenes

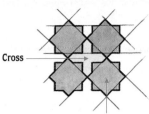

Cross

Eight-pointed star obtained by overlaying one square with another

MONREALE – Cathedral apse exterior detail (12C)

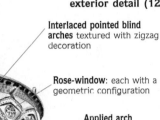

Interlaced pointed blind arches textured with zigzag decoration

Rose-window: each with a different geometric configuration

Applied arch

Column

CEFALÙ – Front elevation of cathedral (12C-13C)

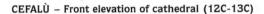

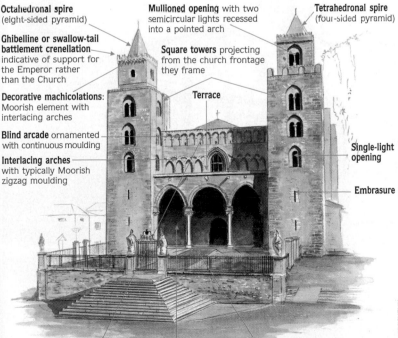

Octahedronal spire (eight-sided pyramid)

Ghibelline or swallow-tail battlement crenellation indicative of support for the Emperor rather than the Church

Decorative machicolations: Moorish element with interlacing arches

Blind arcade ornamented with continuous moulding

Interlacing arches with typically Moorish zigzag moulding

Mullioned opening with two semicircular lights recessed into a pointed arch

Square towers projecting from the church frontage they frame

Terrace

Tetrahedronal spire (four-sided pyramid)

Single-light opening

Embrasure

Gallery of blind arches   **Portico**

Spacious square terrace before the church known as the *Turriale*

RAGUSA IBLA – Palazzo Cosentini: balcony (18C)

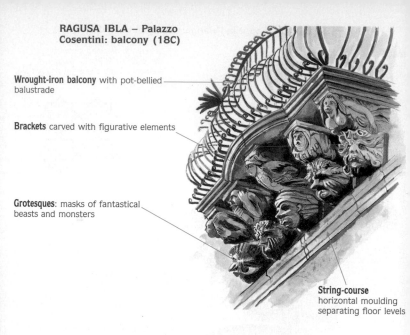

Wrought-iron balcony with pot-bellied balustrade

Brackets carved with figurative elements

Grotesques: masks of fantastical beasts and monsters

String-course horizontal moulding separating floor levels

RAGUSA – Baroque cathedral of San Giovanni (18C)

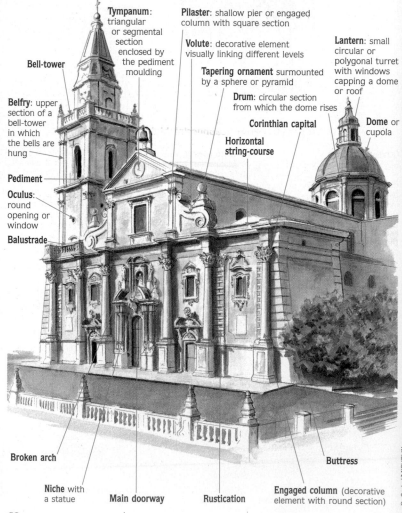

Tympanum: triangular or segmental section enclosed by the pediment moulding

Pilaster: shallow pier or engaged column with square section

Volute: decorative element visually linking different levels

Bell-tower

Tapering ornament surmounted by a sphere or pyramid

Lantern: small circular or polygonal turret with windows capping a dome or roof

Belfry: upper section of a bell-tower in which the bells are hung

Drum: circular section from which the dome rises

Corinthian capital

Dome or cupola

Horizontal string-course

Pediment

Oculus: round opening or window

Balustrade

Broken arch

Niche with a statue

Main doorway

Rustication

Buttress

Engaged column (decorative element with round section)

CASTELBUONO – Cappella di Sant'Anna (Castello dei Ventimiglia)(1683)

Putto: the angelic spirit represented as a Cupid-like infant, from the Latin *putus* – little man; sometimes an allegory of opulence and ease

Stucco: ornamental plasterwork, carved or moulded in low or high relief comprising figurative, geometric, architectural elements. A highly popular form of applied decoration during the late Mannerist to Baroque periods

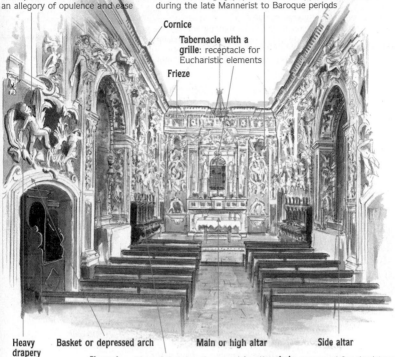

Cornice

Tabernacle with a grille: receptacle for Eucharistic elements

Frieze

Heavy drapery

Basket or depressed arch

Main or high altar

Side altar

Chancel: section of the church comprising the **choir** – reserved for choristers and furnished with wooden stalls, very often ornamented with carving and intarsia work, and the **sanctuary** – the area around the high altar

COMISO – Chiesa dei Cappuccini: high altar (17C-18C)

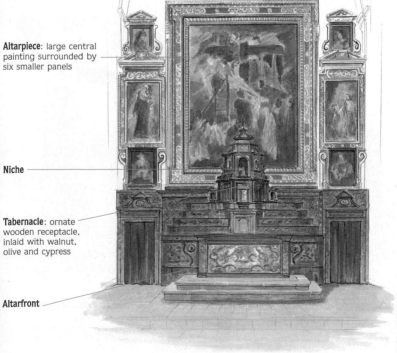

Altarpiece: large central painting surrounded by six smaller panels

Niche

Tabernacle: ornate wooden receptacle, inlaid with walnut, olive and cypress

Altarfront

Civil and military buildings

Sicilian stronghold or *baglio*

Complex of buildings arranged around a central courtyard, including living quarters and workshops. In some cases the complex includes a small private chapel. Fortifications are integrated for defensive purposes. Examples located in rural positions were often used as grain depositories and for storing farm equipment; those located by the sea were inhabited by fishing communities (especially tuna fishermen) and included areas reserved for processing the fish and for repairing boats. At Marsala these *bagli* served as wineries (hence by implication, an actual cellar). Today, most of these complexes have been transformed into museums or hotels.

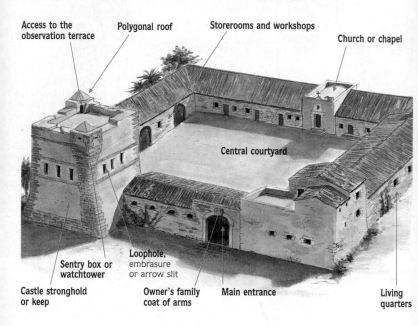

Access to the observation terrace

Polygonal roof

Storerooms and workshops

Church or chapel

Central courtyard

Sentry box or watchtower

Castle stronghold or keep

Loophole, embrasure or arrow slit

Owner's family coat of arms

Main entrance

Living quarters

CATANIA – Castello Ursino (1239-50)

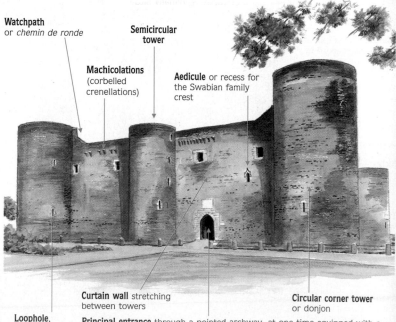

Watchpath or *chemin de ronde*

Semicircular tower

Machicolations (corbelled crenellations)

Aedicule or recess for the Swabian family crest

Curtain wall stretching between towers

Circular corner tower or donjon

Loophole, embrasure or arrow slit

Principal entrance through a pointed archway, at one time equipped with a drawbridge. The moat that surrounded the castle was largely infilled by a lava flow in 1669.

70

GLOSSARY OF TERMS

For terms relating specifically to **Greek Art**, see also p 60. The list below includes less common terms or those not explained in the illustrations on the previous pages.

Altarpiece (or *ancona*) – Painted or sculptured tableau on the front of or above an altar. The most common form of Gothic altarpiece is the **triptych**: a three-panelled painting or carving comprising a centrepiece and two wings, usually hinged so that the lateral panels can close over the central panel during Lent or periods of mourning. Variants include the diptych (two panels) and polyptych (many panels); the horizontal panel below the main centrepiece is called a *predella*.

Apsidiole – Small chapel opening onto the ambulatory of a Romanesque or Gothic church.

Arch – Curved architectural structure supported by columns or pilasters. The Romanesque arch has a semicircular profile; the Gothic arch is pointed, having two centres and equal radii; the ogee arch is pointed and has a combination of convex and concave profiles, having four arcs – often found in Catalan Gothic; the horse-shoe or Moorish arch is round-headed and tapers inwards towards the base, to form a horse-shoe shape; a trefoil arch has a cusped intrados with three round or pointed foils.
The Durazzo arch comprises a compressed pointed arch commonly found through central and southern Italy in the 15C, named after the princes of Durazzo, often out-lined with a round hood-moulding.

Atlas figure or **telamon** – A sculptured figure of a man used as a column (the female equivalent is called a caryatid). In Sicily, the most famous are the telamons of the Temple of Olympian Zeus at Agrigento.

Bay – Any of a number of principal divisions or spatial units of a building (or part of a building like an aisle of a church) contained within two or four vertical supports (piers, columns, pilasters).

Capital – The upper end of a column, pillar or pier crowning the shaft and taking the weight of the entablature or architrave. There are three Classical orders: **Doric** *(see illustration in the section on Greek Art)*; **Ionic**, with a scroll-like ornament – the Composite has the Ionic scrolls and acanthus leaf ornament; and the **Corinthian**, ringed with bur-geoning acanthus leaves, especially popular in the 16C and 17C for Baroque buildings.

Cardo – One of the main axes of the town plan as recommended by the Classical sur-veyor Hippodamus of Miletus, normally orientated north-south; the Greek equivalent is the **stenopos**.

Decumanus – A major thoroughfare bisecting a Classical town plan, running on a com-plementary axis to the **cardo**, orientated east-west; the Greek equivalent is the **plateia**.

Dosseret – Supplementary capital in the shape of the base of an upturned pyramid, often decorated, set above a column capital to receive the thrust of the arch.

Fresco – Wall painting applied to wet plaster.

Hypocaust – Underground heating system used in Antiquity, whereby floors were raised on a series of small brick columns, enabling hot air to circulate underneath.

Keep – The stronghold of a castle or fortress, usually situated in the centre of a well-protected area. It was the residence of the overlord, and used as an armoury, a treasury and a storage-place for provisions.

Ogive – Pointed arch.

Opus signinum – Floor covering obtained by mixing fragments of terracotta and other small pieces of rubble with lime. It is sometimes decorated with marble or stone cobbles.

Ovolo moulding – Egg-shaped ornament incorporated into the entablature.

Palazzo – Italian for town house or square building (housing commercial offices, for example) subtly different in connotation to the word "palace". In the Renaissance, the ground floor was usually reserved for storage or commercial activities, the first floor or *piano nobile* comprised the main apartments and the second floor *(alto piano)* was allocated to children and domestic staff.

Pendentive – The spherical triangular panel that provides the transition from a square or polygonal base (at a crossing) to a circular dome. In Sicily, these spandrels are often filled with figurative mosaics.

Peristyle – The range of columns surrounding a Classical building or courtyard.

Raceme – Ornamental vine motif with tendrils, leaves and stylised fruits.

Relief – High relief *(altorilievo)* is a sculptural term describing the modelled forms that project from the background by at least half their depth (half way between shallow relief and sculpture in the round). Low relief *(bassorilievo)* projects only very slightly from the background (also known as *bas relief*).

Rustication – Facing of a building that exaggeratedly replicates dressed stonework, raised or otherwise from the mortar joints. Rustication was used in the Renaissance to consolidate the impression of impregnability on the ground floor of a *palazzo*.

Squinch – Alternative to a pendentive comprising a compound number of miniature strainer arches, often intricately decorated with Moorish plasterwork.

Vault – An arched structure of stone or brick forming a ceiling or roof over a hall, room, bay or other wholly or partly enclosed space. **Barrel vault** – A vault having a semicircular cross-section. **Groin vault** (or **cross vault**) – Formed by the perpendicular intersection of two vaults. **Bowl-shaped vault** – A spherical vault enclosing a semicircular apse.

Art

DAWN OF SICILIAN ART

The numerous discoveries of prehistoric remains make it possible to affirm that Sicily, including the small independent islands offshore, was inhabited at that time. During the ensuing centuries, as the Greeks arrived *en masse*, the Phoenicians were forced to join their allies, the Elymi and the Carthaginians, on the west of the island, where they founded several cities, notably Palermo, Solunto, Selinunte and Motya. Little evidence of their culture survives from this period (Grotta del Genovese on Levanzo and Grotte dell'Addaura near Palermo are rare examples). Indeed, it would appear that art in Sicily only truly flourished after being subjected to the Greek influence.

From the Roman era to the present day, Sicilian creativity has never been idle. The complex history of this island, fashioned and formed by any number of foreign peoples and cultures, isolated by the sea, in part explains why and how the Sicilian temperament has found expression in such an eclectic and yet characteristic way through the centuries.

ROMAN (3C BC-5C AD)

Vestiges from Roman times are fewer and less impressive than those from the Greek period, largely because the Romans showed comparatively little interest in Sicily by comparison with their other colonies. Once the threat of a potential Carthaginian invasion had receded, the island lost its strategic importance and became prized exclusively as a resource for growing wheat to feed their campaigning troops. For many years, this "Roman granary" was regarded as one of the many provinces that had little appeal for its administrators, thereby enabling the enriched native land-owners to build splendid villas by the sea – as the ruins of such patrician villas as the one at Patti, near Tyndaris, testify. Not until the end of the 3C AD, during the reign of Diocletian, was this Roman province elected to the rank of *regio suburbicaria*; this propelled it to becoming one of the regions most sought after by the Roman aristocracy who set about acquiring large tracts of land on the island. During seven centuries of Roman occupation, Rome did not endow Sicily with any prestigious monuments other than the odd functional public building (amphitheatres, public baths), although they did lay the foundations for a comprehensive road system initially for use by the military, but which later served to underpin economic expansion. Several urban public areas (the *fora*, for example) have yet to be excavated.

Roman building – Unlike the Greeks, the Romans knew about cement and how to use it effectively. They erected walls, vaults and columns using casements filled with small bricks, and then poured concrete into them. Finishing touches were added in the form of marble facings (or high-quality stone), or for the interiors, ably applied stucco so as to suggest splendid stone walls.

Roman monuments – During this period, Greek **theatres**, like the ones at **Taormina** and **Catania**, underwent considerable transformation: the circular orchestra (reserved by the Greeks for the chorus) was reduced to a semicircle, while a stage wall was added for the machinery required to create special effects. The theatre provided a venue both for circus entertainment and combat with wild animals, and to protect the spectators, a wall was constructed along the bottom of the *cavea* (part of which can still be seen at Taormina). Those Roman monuments that may be of special interest include the **amphitheatre at Siracusa** built for extravagant gladiatorial combats and fights pitched against wild animals; that at Catania; the odeons at Taormina and Catania, and, finally, the **Naumachie of Taormina** (now badly damaged) which consists of a large-scale brick-built gymnasium (122m/400ft long) ornamented with niches. Besides these complexes dedicated to sport and entertainment, the Romans left nothing of value in terms of civic architecture: the fine **basilica** at Tyndaris suggest that the Romans introduced the art of vaulting to Sicily (for it was unknown to the Greek civil engineers), and more significantly, to towns removed from the major urban centres. Vestiges of public bath complexes *(terme)*, largely dating from the Imperial period, are preserved at Catania, Taormina, Comiso, Solunto and Tindari; traces of *fora* have been found at Taormina, Catania, Siracusa and Tindari.

Domestic architecture – The Romano-Sicilian house closely resembles its Hellenistic counterpart. The **town house** graced with a peristyle is introduced towards the close of the 3C-2C BC (Morgantina); only at Marsala and Agrigento have houses with an atrium and a peristyle courtyard (a model first conceived in Campania) been revealed. The most elegant homes, however, are to be found among the country villas, the most typical example being the magnificent **Villa del Casale** near Piazza Armerina. Here, the existence of its private bath facilities would indicate that this was indeed a highly sophisticated and luxurious house, decorated internally with notoriously sumptuous mosaics.

The Basilica at Tyndaris

PALEO-CHRISTIAN

Archaeological excavation undertaken in Palermo and Siracusa has uncovered complete cemeteries on the outskirts of the urban area dating from late Antiquity, when the Romans imposed Christianity on Sicily. The **catacombs** that preserve traces of painted decoration, most particularly those at Siracusa (4C-5C AD), provide the earliest examples of Christian art in Sicily. As was widespread in all the paleo-Christian world, Sicily was gradually coerced into erecting **churches**, modelled on the Roman prototype **basilica**: this consisted of a simple rectangular building, articulated by columns into three aisles, with a central nave terminated by a single apse. The other, more striking solution, was to incorporate a church around a pagan **Antique temple** – as with the Temple of Concord at Agrigento and the Temple of Athena at Siracusa: to achieve this, the walls of the *cella* were cut away to make arcades and the outer colonnade was in-filled with masonry.

In AD 535, as a result of the Byzantine conquest, links between the Church of Sicily and the Exarchate of Ravenna were reinforced: in 751 when Ravenna fell to the Lombards, this allegiance was transferred to Constantinople. Interestingly enough, the rift dividing the Roman and Byzantine Churches as a result of Pope Gregory II's opposition to Emperor Leo III's Iconoclast movement in 725-26 had serious repercussions in Sicily. The ban on the cult of holy icons imposed by the Byzantine Emperor prompted crowds of refugees to seek asylum in Sicily where the icon continued to be venerated. Whole monastic communities and numerous groups of skilled craftsmen found sanctuary in Sicily and set about applying their trades, notably in the art of mosaic.

This prosperous period gave rise to the building of numerous shrines (including the ones at Cava d'Ispica and Pantalica) and the institution of troglodyte settlements hewn into the bedrock (almost all now destroyed). It also resulted in the building of small centrally-planned square (typically Byzantine) churches, consisting of three curved walls or exedras enclosing a spatial cube contained by a dome, and fronted by a flat façade with an entrance (west facing). A few examples survive in the eastern part of the island, north and east of Etna (**Castiglione di Sicilia** – *see p 115*), in the vicinity of Noto and around Siracusa.

Other monuments erected in Byzantine times were completely transformed, dismembered or converted to another use through the ensuing centuries. What is certain is that the Byzantines introduced the art of mosaic to the island, although the skill of Sicilian artists in this field can only really be evaluated from the works commissioned by the Normans.

ARABO-NORMAN

After three centuries of Byzantine occupation and two of Arab domination, the Norman kings arrived and settled in Sicily in the latter half of the 11C. The composite term "Arabo-Norman" is used to describe an eclectic combination of elements: Moorish (Fatimid, Abbassid and Magreb in origin), Romanesque (introduced by various visitors to the royal courts, including a number of Franco-Norman Benedictine fathers), Roman (brought by Italian monks following the Normans as they travelled down to the south of Italy) and Byzantine (instigated by members of the monastic orders and the Greek Byzantine Patriarchate).

Arab occupation – The Arab conquest began in 827 in the area of Trapani. During their two and a half centuries of sovereignty, these people transformed the appearance of Sicily, transposing their power-base from Siracusa to Palermo, altering the countryside by instigating the use of irrigation and a range of new crops from the east, and, most particularly, by introducing architectural forms that, hitherto, had been unknown on the island. They were prolific builders and sensitive planners, ever conscious of a building's relationship with its natural setting: palaces, mosques and minarets were placed among gardens and fountains. In terms of design, their acute sense of line and elegance was applied to sophisticated decorative schemes: human figures gave way to geometric and arabesque forms, house interiors were transformed with coloured ceramic tiles, while ceilings were encrusted with rich honeycomb stalactite plaster decoration *(muqarnas)*.

Alas, no important monument survives intact from the Arab occupation. Indeed, most of their splendid buildings disappeared with the arrival of the Normans, who appropriated them for their own use, rebuilding and redecorating them, and in so doing, stripping them of their original integrity. A few examples of Arab craftsmanship survive, as do a number of intricate networks of irregular streets tucked away in the urban fabric of such cities as Palermo.

Norman eclecticism – Much of the wealth of Arabo-Norman art is rooted in the ardent wish harboured by the Norman sovereigns of emulating the splendour of Byzantium, a city they yearned to conquer. The new Sicilian master-builders set about channelling all their creative power to erect monuments of incomparable beauty. As from the end of the 11C and throughout the whole of the following century, large churches were conceived by architect-monks mainly from the Benedictine and Augustine orders, be they Greek, French or Latin (from mainland Italy). Designs were modelled on Classical prototypes: a transept was incorporated in a basilica giving it a Latin or Greek cross plan, towers were erected to house bells, a doorway was inserted in the front elevation, the choir was often crowned with a dome. At the same time, these edifices were given the latest contemporary decoration: Byzantine mosaics laid by Orthodox (Greek) artists and Moorish features (horse-shoe arches, arabesque and honeycomb ornament).

The result made for a curious mixture of buildings, all 12C, in which these three styles were blended to make something quite unique.

Byzantine influence – The Eastern elements incorporated into religious **architecture** include the square centralised plan, adapted in turn to the Greek cross, roofed with intersecting barrel vaults (Church of the Martorana, San Nicolò at Mazara del Vallo, or Santissima Trinità di Delia at Castelvetrano). Elsewhere, the intersection is vaulted with the typical Sicilian Byzantine dome rising from a polygonal drum. Even the capitals reflect an Arabo-Norman style adapted from the Byzantine, by incorporating a dosseret between the capital and the impost of the arch (Monreale Cathedral).

The reason for the lack of any Byzantine figurative representations of the human form in sculpture is threefold: firstly, the Christians' harboured antipathy for pagan statuary; secondly, the Iconoclastic movement forbade the veneration of anything that might be construed as an idol and, lastly, because of the Islamic – and hence Arab – influence. Similarly, the techniques used were also adapted; stone was no longer worked superficially but in the round, using small drills to make tiny holes and intricate fretwork effects that resembled stone lace.

The richest and most effective medium used by the Byzantine artists is the mosaic. This they applied to immense areas, animating them with figures and various decorative motifs, upgrading the art form to monumental proportions. Apart from the Martorana which fully conforms to Byzantine canons, the iconography and presentation of subject-matter were adapted in Sicilian churches to optimise its view from the royal throne. At Cefalù, Monreale and the Cappella Palatina in Palermo Christ Pantocrator fills the top of the vault above the apse; in Greek Byzantine churches meanwhile, He would always have been placed in the dome. Finally, the Norman kings had themselves depicted in sections traditionally reserved for saints, with the symbols of the *basilei* (Byzantine emperors), as a way of asserting their power.

Islamic influence – The Arabs brought with them new building methods and decoration know-how that enabled them to create veritable masterpieces. In architecture, they introduced the pointed arch and stilted arch (an arch resting on imposts treated as downward continuations of the archivolt), as well as what may perhaps be the most evocative import, the **horse-shoe** (or Moorish) **arch**: the upper part of this arch is semicircular, although it can be pointed at its apex, but tapers at the base to form a horse-shoe shape. The underside of such structures together with domes, pendentives, capitals and brackets, was often encrusted with stalactite plasterwork decoration called *muqarnas*; this in turn was painted, carved and textured into overhanging honeycombs. The interior decoration of Monreale Cathedral, the Palatine Chapel, the Zisa and Cuba *palazzi* are splendid testimonies to the influence of Islam. The characteristically Arab predilection for elaborate decoration can also be discerned in other forms of decoration: the serrated edge to the merloned cornice of San Cataldo in Palermo provides an elegant base from which spring the three pink domes. The Arabs also brought an alternative view of proportion and volume as indicated by the squat domes of San Giovanni degli Eremiti.

The Palatine Chapel

Romanesque influence – The most typical elements provided by the Romanesque style is the Latin-cross plan and the façade framed between massive towers, features that were devised by the Benedictine monks, most notably at Cluny, for the buildings they planned on a massive and monumental scale. According to scholars, the front elevation (two identical square towers) of the Duomo at Cefalù is modelled on the Church of St-Étienne at Caen; the interior meanwhile is graced with cornices and archivolts (also the underside of the arches) that are presumed to have been modelled on those in the churches of Caen. On the whole, the religious buildings did not allocate much space to Norman sculpture, which manifests itself exclusively in terms of geometric motifs on small arches and other decorative details – like strips of small leaves and ovolo moulding – applied to the dosserets of capitals. Their inclination towards stylisation touched representations of animals and plants which are reduced to simple palmettes or rather thin, flat, rigid-looking flower-less species (reeds and rushes). A handful of monuments, including the cloisters at Monreale, preserve some most splendid figurative capitals relating historical and biblical scenes founded in the Romanesque tradition.

Arabo-Norman creativity – Although many buildings from this period conform to a clearly defined influence, some combinations of styles end up becoming models and prototypes for other art forms promoted during the rule of the Altavilla (de Hautville) dynasty.

Religious buildings – The undisputed masterpiece of this Sicilian Norman School is the **Palatine Chapel** (Cappella Palatina). Here elements of Romanesque art – an extended plan comprising nave and side aisles and narrow windows through which suffused light is allowed to permeate – are married with the Moorish love for sumptuous decoration (notable in

The story of Samson, Monreale Cathedral cloisters

the ceiling), calligraphy (various Arabic inscriptions) and structural design (pointed arches), and merged with the monumental splendour of Byzantine art (dome pendentives, gold-background mosaics, marble wall-facing and inlaid floors). The chapel demonstrates how the centrally-planned Byzantine choir is superimposed onto the wooden-vaulted Latin basilica nave (set at a lower level). This came to be used as a new prototype and used subsequently at Monreale.

Palazzo Zisa

Like the earlier apse of Monreale, Palermo Cathedral is ornamented externally with a scheme of interlacing decorative arches detailed with geometric designs in lava. The effective outcome may in part have derived from the Lombard banded decoration applied to the exterior of Romanesque churches in the rest of Italy, and in part from the Eastern taste for geometric designs in contrasting colours (rosettes, chequer-board patterning).

Secular buildings – Besides the odd large castle built in strategic positions as at Palermo, Castellammare and Messina, the Norman kings built themselves various summer or pleasure palaces for rest and recreation purposes. At the end of the Altavilla (de Hauteville) rule, there were nine such residences in Sicily; today only the **Zisa** and **Cuba** *palazzi* in Palermo survive. These splendid houses are surrounded by large gardens ornamented with expanses of water. The interior space was divided into two main areas: the *iwan* (a room with three exedras) and an open courtyard containing one or more fountains and surrounded by porticoes. The first of these two distinctive areas originated in Abbassid Persia, the second in Fatimid Egypt. Together, they appear in Sicily sometime in the 12C, imported via the Maghreb (North Africa), which at that time extended as far as the coasts of modern Tunisia, and was under Sicilian rule. The decoration is also largely drawn from Islamic art: the floors are laid with marble or brick in a herringbone pattern, the walls are faced with mosaic (more a result of Byzantine craftsmen, but incorporating Moorish motifs) and finally, the ceilings and arches are encrusted with carved and painted *muqarnas*.

GOTHIC

For two centuries between the 13C and the 15C, Sicily suffered a long period of political instability under a succession of sovereigns: the Hohenstaufen of Swabia (1189-1266), the Angevins (1266-82), the House of Aragon (until 1416) and the Spaniards (from 1409). Common to them all was the way in which they came to appreciate the Gothic style on a grand scale – which was not the case in the mainland peninsula.

Hohenstaufen military constructions – Henry IV, and more particularly **Frederick II** who enjoyed a longer reign (1208-50), preserved the numerous religious and civil buildings erected by the Normans. They impressed their mark on the landscape by building fortresses designed by northern master-masons. The Gothic style was introduced to Sicily in the 13C in the form of fortified architecture. From this era date the castles at Siracusa (Castello Maniace), Catania (Castello Ursino) and Augusta, as do the fortifications of the castle at Enna (strategic centre of the island occupied since Byzantine times) from which there survive eight imposing towers. These buildings conform to a highly geometric ground-plan (square centrepiece defended with angle, and sometimes lateral, towers), doorways and windows set into pointed arches, austerely bare walls pierced with embrasures, that rise to battlements and, finally, quadripartite vaulted casemates.

14C: Chiaramonte style – If the 13C sovereigns of Sicily played a decisive role in encouraging the emergence of the Northern Gothic style on the island, the great feudal dynasties in power over the subsequent years, most especially the Chiaramonte, developed it by applying it with imagination to the construction of town houses and churches. The Palermo residence **Palazzo Chiaramonte** is a typical example of this Sicilian Gothic: the façade is extremely refined, the windows set into decorative pointed arches are unique and quite wonderful, the roof-line is crested with merlons.

Thereafter, all town houses conformed to this type. The windows were freely adapted with two or three lights surmounted by arches with tracery or polychrome geometric decoration. The Chiaramonte, who maintained their supremacy throughout the 14C as the royal power-base declined, sponsored many new buildings and restored others: from Mussomeli to Racalmuto, Montechiaro to Favara, they are responsible for at least 10 castles and *palazzi*.

15C: Catalan Gothic – The reason why the Catalan Gothic flourished so easily in Sicily rests in the importance wielded by the Spanish viceroys from the late 14C, under the rule of the House of Aragon. There were delays in the Gothic style being introduced to Sicily, especially if compared with the rest of Europe where the Gothic Flamboyant was reaching its peak. When it did travel care of the Catalan-Aragonese federation (which since the 13C had become one of the most powerful forces in the Mediterranean), it was a more sober form of Gothic characterised by elongated forms, a stumpy sense of proportion, a marked tendency towards breadth of space over height (particularly in the religious context), and ample windows alternating with bare flat wall surfaces. Typical examples include the Palazzo Santo Stefano and Palazzo Corvaja at Taormina and the main doorway of Palermo Cathedral.

Towards the end of the 15C, **Matteo Carnelivari** probably best epitomises the new influence, incorporating Catalan features in and among the Byzantine, Arab and Norman elements that were prevalent in the established vernacular style. Carnelivari is responsible for designing Palazzo Abatellis and Palazzo Ajutamicristo, and probably the Church of Santa Maria della Catena in Palermo.

Sculpture and painting – Only artists that were foreign to Sicily achieved any renown in these two fields at this time: sculptors were summoned from Tuscany, more particularly from Pisa, having already earned recognition for their work elsewhere. **Nino Pisano** completed a graceful and gentle-faced *Annunziata* that was true to his style for the cathedral in Trapani, a place that attracted a large number of sculptors to its marble quarries as from the 14C. **Bonaiuto Pisano** carved the eagle which stands above the gateway of Palazzo Sclafani in Palermo.

In painting, **Antonio Veneziano** (trained in Venice, worked in Florence), **Gera da Pisa**, and various Spanish artists such as **Guerau Janer**, also worked in Sicily for a time. Towards the end of the 15C, some of these painters became so successful that they decided to settle permanently in Sicily, among them **Nicolò di Maggio** (from Siena) who worked particularly in Palermo.

RENAISSANCE AND MANNERISM

As a result of the strong influence of the Spanish Gothic style favoured by the Aragonese court, the Renaissance and Mannerism which spread from Italy to the rest of Europe did not have a great impact on Sicily. It fell to artists trained by the great Tuscan masters to introduce the principles of the Renaissance to Sicily.

Painting – In the 15C, Sicily started to show an interest in the new Renaissance movement, prompted by the work of **Antonello da Messina**. Although his life and career have long been something of a mystery, there is no doubt that this artist is the most famous Sicilian painter. He was born in Messina in 1430; in 1450, he was in Naples, possibly engaged as a pupil to the workshop of the legendary Colantonio. There he would most certainly have come into contact with Flemish panting. In 1475-76 Antonello was in Venice where he must have encountered Giovanni Bellini and Piero della Francesca. Antonello's supreme reputation, however, is founded on the fact that he mastered and largely diffused the exacting practice of oil-painting techniques used by the Van Eycks. His mature style combines the detail so typical of Flemish art with the breadth of

Museo Mandralisca, Cefalù/SCALA

Portrait of an Unknown Man, by Antonello da Messina

form upheld by the Italian Schools. Indeed, his works all conform to being static in composition, exploring texture, and demonstrating an almost perfect tonal unity in terms of colour: his works found in Sicily include an *Annunciation* in Palazzo Bellomo (Siracusa), a *Polyptych of St Gregory* in the Museo Regionale in Messina and the *Portrait of an Unknown Man* in the Museo Mandralisca in Cefalù. These are among the most notable works of the Renaissance to be preserved in Sicily.

During the first half of the 16C, the painters **Cesare da Sesto**, **Polidoro da Caravaggio** and Vincenzo da Pavia played their part in spreading the Mannerist style prevalent in Tuscany and Rome. **Simone de Wobreck** meanwhile, who lived in Sicily until 1557, introduced the basic elements of Flemish Mannerism.

Sculpture – In the second half of the 15C, sculpture was completely revitalised by a range of Italian artists, notably Francesco Laurana and Domenico Gagini.

The sculptor and engraver **Francesco Laurana** spent five years in Sicily (1466-71) during which time he worked at the Cappella Mastrantonio in the Church of San Francesco and produced the bust of Eleonora of Aragon in Palazzo Abatellis in Palermo. Other paintings include a *Madonna and Child* in the Church of the Crocifisso in Noto, another in the Church of the Immacolata in Palazzolo Acreide and a third in the museum at Messina.

Domenico Gagini, who was born into a family of Italian sculptors and architects from Lake Lugano, moved south and settled in Sicily. There he practised his art in association with his son **Antonello** who was born in Palermo in 1478. Their workshop flourished in the capital, producing works that satisfied the contemporary predilection for elegant, refined forms in Carrara marble rather than travertine. Domenico's style and technique were later continued by his descendants, sculptors and goldsmiths who achieved fame up to the mid-17C. Numerous Sicilian churches preserve splendid statues executed by the Gagini, although their very proliferation has aroused accusations of their work being repetitive and therefore considered of a lesser value.

Mannerism exercised its influence on sculpture in the 16C largely thanks to such artists as the Florentine **Angelo Montorsoli** (1505-63) who was working in Messina around 1547-57. The fact that he had collaborated with Michelangelo in Florence and Rome gave Montorsoli a certain notoriety and his work demonstrates a shift from the Renaissance style to a Michelangelesque Mannerism. The works that survive include the Fontana di Orione (1547-50) in Messina which is regarded as one of the greatest masterpieces of the 16C. The Florentine **Camillo Camilliani** completed the fountain that was begun by his brother Francesco for the Florentine villa of Don Pedro di Toledo, and which was subsequently sold to the city of Palermo in 1573.

BAROQUE

During the 16C the Spanish authorities asserted their influence in the arts. They imposed the values promoted by the Counter Reformation (resulting from the Council of Trent 1545), before choosing to sponsor an elaborate, exuberant form of the Baroque that was more typically Spanish than Italian.

Counter Reformation – Sicily soon succumbed to the power and influence of the Society of Jesus (later known as the Jesuits), founded in 1540 by the Spaniard St Ignatius Loyola (1491-1556). Modelled on the Chiesa del Gesù in Rome, the **Jesuit churches in Sicily** were designed with the same features. The one broad nave is devoid of any element that might restrict the congregation's view of the main altar and obstruct or deflect the words of the preacher from reaching each and every one of the faithful. The solemnity, authority, opulence and luminosity of the internal space is in keeping with the exterior: the main body of the church, so tall and wide, is screened by a central bay; the lateral chapels which open directly off the nave are screened by a lower bay. The bare surfaces that lent a dignity to the Renaissance buildings is here textured with features that vary in weight and depth: engaged columns at ground level give way to superficial pilasters above as sharp contrasts effectively dissolve into lightness (the Church of Sant'Ignazio all'Olivella in Palermo is a good example of this style). The **painting of the Counter Reformation** revives a predilection for those images that had been rejected by Protestantism, subjects such as the Virgin Mary, the dogma of the Eucharist and the veneration of saints. Painting follows the example of Michelangelo and Raphael, although in Sicily the practitioners of this style active in Palermo like Vincenzo degli Azani are few and lesser known.

Politics and style – The Baroque which in Spain reached its apogee in the second half of the 17C, was quickly assimilated by the Sicilians, for they had enjoyed and appreciated the opulent use of marble and gilding since Arab and Byzantine tastes had prevailed in previous centuries. This movement placed great importance on detail, producing finely worked wrought-iron railings and gates, balcony brackets carved with the most original grotesques and imaginative designs interpreted in polychrome panels of *pietra dura*.

At the beginning of the 17C, the Spanish viceroy administration launched an ambitious building programme involving the founding of some 100 new towns in an attempt to underpin their plans for reorganising and then developing their extensive territories. The earthquake of 1669, followed by a more devastating one in 1693, destroyed almost all the south-eastern part of the island: the rebuilding of the towns was immediately initiated under the combined direction of the local authorities, the aristocracy, town planners (Fra' Michele la Ferla, Fra' Angelo Italia) and architects (Vaccarini, Ittar, Vermexio, Palma and Gagliardi). The earthquake laid bare a great expanse of land stretching from Catania to Siracusa, damaging Avola, Noto, Scicli, Modica, Ragusa, Vittoria, Lentini and Grammichele. As a result, Sicilian Baroque is concentrated in this part of the island and around Palermo (Bagheria, Trapani), being the seat of power.

Architecture – The majority of the Baroque architects had trained in Rome. They therefore modelled their ideas on Roman interpretations of the Baroque, sometimes exaggerating their iconographic forms, volumes and subject matter for sculptural effect. The delicate relationship between the fragility of life and the forces of nature was translated into an art-form that by now was far removed from any quest for beauty. Derision, excess, death, suffering and even ugliness (decrepitude of old age, poverty and physical deformity) underlie the expressions of exuberance that ornament every surface at this time. Contorted form, so easily applied to architectural elements, proved an ideal vehicle for expressing movement through façades or an internal decorative scheme. This same sense of movement and exaggeration pervades the towns that were rebuilt, not only with regard to the individual buildings but in their relationship one to another within their urban context.

So **Catania** was rebuilt and re-orientated by **Giovanni Battista Vaccarini** (born Palermo 1702, died Milazzo 1769). Vaccarini served his apprenticeship in Rome under Carlo Fontana, through whom he came to understand the ingenious creativity of the tormented architect Borromini; on his return to Sicily around 1730, Vaccarini settled in Catania and devoted the next 30 years of his life to rebuilding the city. The Elephant Fountain (in lava) harps back to the ones designed by Bernini in Rome (1735); his undoubted masterpiece, however, is the Church of St Agatha which is elliptical in shape and has a restless and undulating façade inspired by Borromini's oval Church of San Carlo alle Quattro Fontane in Rome.

Even **Palermo** bristles with buildings modelled on Roman prototypes. Most of these were built by one of the city's most highly regarded architects **Giacomo Amato** (1643-1732), who came from Palermo and was trained in Rome. He uses decorative elements borrowed from 16C Roman architecture: characteristic examples include the Church of Santa Teresa alla Kalsa (1686), the Church of the Pietà which rises through two imposing storeys articulated with columns (1689), the Church of the Santissimo Salvatore with its oval dome, as well as numerous private *palazzi*. The monument that best epitomises the urban Baroque style in Palermo is the Quattro Canti junction faced with four interacting building façades and fountains.

Noto, which had to be completely rebuilt following the 1693 earthquake, exemplifies the harmonious homogeneity of the Baroque style in the urban context in Sicily, largely as a result of being conceived as a vast theatre. Bold perspectives are defined by seemingly continuous cornices running in a straight axis along the narrow streets sloping uphill, brazen ornamentation incorporated into the frontages lends texture and relief at street level, while above, elaborately embellished window frames and bulging balconies allow stonemasons and master blacksmiths free reign to exalt their art. The author of this exceptional ensemble is presumed to be the enigmatic **Rosario Gagliardi**, about whom little is known other than his date of birth (Siracusa 1680) and death (Noto 1726). This man, the greatest Baroque architect of Sicily, exerted his considerable impact on this small area around Noto and its two neighbouring towns: Ragusa and Modica. In **Ragusa**, he is responsible for two churches – San Giuseppe and San Giorgio. The latter is preceded by a monumental flight of steps leading up from a long piazza, thereby heightening the dramatic effect of the front elevation which bristles with animated and gesticulating statues. Gagliardi, possibly with the assistance of other Noto architects, also designed the magnificent Church of San Giorgio with its distinctive slender bell-tower in **Modica** – Ragusa's nearby rival.

The most evocative Sicilian Baroque *palazzi* are to be found at **Bagheria**, a few kilometres from Palermo. One of the most remarkable of these refined residential buildings, endowed with luxuriously furnished halls and gardens populated with statuary, is the **Villa Palagonia** which is famous for its wildly extravagant interior decoration. The villa became a symbol of the absurd, renowned throughout Europe during the Age of Enlightenment, long before Goethe's famous visit in 1787 *(see BAGHERIA)*.

Sculpture and applied decoration – Baroque sculpture and decoration is characterised by rich ornamentation. Altarpieces are provided with carved marble panels and contained among twisted columns; cornices and pediments are crested with figures of angels. Ranking high among his many fellow artist-craftsmen, **Giacomo Serpotta** (1652-1732) excelled at using marble, stucco and polychrome decoration. After training in Rome, Serpotta returned to his home-town **Palermo** to work on an equestrian statue of Charles II before embarking on a long career as a decorator specialising in stucco. The Oratory of San Lorenzo (1686-96), the Oratory of Santa Cita (1686-88) and the Oratory of the Rosary at San Domenico (c 1714-17) are encrusted throughout with figures and swirling curlicues in bold relief, executed with an exquisite attention to detail. The other church interiors on which Serpotta worked include La Gancia, and Il Carmine; later in life, he was engaged on the decoration of the Church of San Francesco d'Assisi (1723) and that of Sant'Agostino (1726-28, with pupils) which contains a number of narrative panels in shallow relief that illustrate a rare degree of virtuosity. While Serpotta is regarded as the greatest exponent of Sicilian Baroque sculpture, he is also considered to be a precursor of the characteristic forms of Rococo.

Baroque painting – Baroque painters were predominantly engaged in experimenting with perspective and *trompe-l'œil*, constructing complex compositions on diagonal axes around swirling gestures. Their most common forms of subject matter were narrative scenes from the Bible or from among mythological allegories. The most representative adherent of this movement was **Caravaggio**: Michelangelo Merisi (1573-1610), known as Caravaggio after the town where he was born near Bergamo, began his career in Rome alongside Cavaliere d'Arpino in 1588. Implicated in various incidents provoked by his tempestuous temperament, Caravaggio was forced to flee the city in 1605, making for Naples, Malta and then Sicily. Venturing to the extremes of every artistic convention, Caravaggio perfected a highly personal style using low-life figures to animate his pictures and heightening the dramatic element of the narrative with bold contrasts of light and shadow labelled as "chiaroscuro". In the course of his visit to Sicily, he executed a number of important works, notably the *Burial of St Lucy* (1609, in Palazzo Bellomo in Siracusa), *The Adoration of the Shepherds* and *The Resurrection of Lazarus* (in the museum in Messina). These paintings fired the imagination of many subsequent artists, namely **Alfonso Rodriguez** (1578-1648) and **Pietro Novelli** (1603-47). Novelli was also influenced by the Dutch painter **Van Dyck** who, during a sojourn in Palermo in 1624, painted *The Madonna of the Rosary* for the oratory in the Church of San Domenico.

18C TO THE PRESENT DAY

Neo-Classicism – The Classical revival started in the mid-18C and was succoured by the reigning passion for Ancient Greek and Roman architecture following the discovery and archaeological excavation of Herculaneum, Pompeii and Paestum. In the graphic arts, this movement was translated into depictions of Romantic ruins and topographical views that met with great success. One of the most successful of the neo-Classical sculptors was **Ignazio Marabitti** (Palermo 1719-97) who trained in Rome under Filippo della Valle. Works by this artist include the altarpiece of St Ignatius commissioned for the Church of Sant'Agata al Collegio in Caltanissetta. In Palermo, the native-born **Venanzio Marvuglia** (1729-1814) met with measured success: a pupil of Vanvitelli in Rome, he was responsible for enlarging the Church of San Martino delle Scale, the Oratory of Sant'Ignazio dell'Olivella (Palermo) and the villa for the Prince of Belmonte. Marvuglia's predominantly Classical style is sometimes touched with the exotic, as the Chinese pavilion in the park of La Favorita in Palermo testifies.

Naturalism – Although sharing with many other contemporary Italian artists a keenness to portray reality, the sculptor **Domenico Trentacoste** (born Palermo 1859, died Florence 1933) still cannot be regarded a true exponent of Naturalism. The objective of this artistic movement, born out of the literary movement expertly represented in Sicily by Giovanni Verga, was to delve into the depth of being that belies every superficial appearance. Fascinated first by 15C exponents, Trentacoste then turned to the Naturalism of Rodin, whom he encountered in Paris in around 1880, before gradually directing his interest to popular painting, mythological subjects, portraiture and nude painting (*Little Faun* in the Galleria E Restivo in Palermo).

Ettore Ximenes (born Palermo 1855, died Rome 1926) trained first in Palermo then in Naples under Domenico Morelli. The Naturalism that pervades his works is sometimes compromised by his use of the serpentine lines that defined the contemporary fashion for the prevalent *Stile Liberty*.

Stile Liberty – The Art Nouveau style appeared in Italy on the back of the 19C by which time it was well established in the rest of Europe. Its main impact was impressed on the decorative arts; its most distinctive feature, the serpentine line insinuated itself into figurative depictions, wrought-iron work, and furniture. Its best exponent in Sicily is the architect **Ernesto Basile** (born Palermo, 1857-1932), son of the famous **Giovanni Basile** (designer of the Teatro Massimo in Palermo), who concentrated his studies on the forms of Arabo-Norman and Renaissance design before shifting to Art Nouveau. Examples of his work from this period include the decoration of Villa Igeia, notably the wonderful floral decoration of the dining-room, Caffè Ferraglia in Rome, and various villas in Palermo such as Villino Florio *(see p 283)*. He also worked on designing soft furnishings, fabrics and furniture.

The **Villa Malfitano in Palermo**, once owned by the Whitaker family, epitomises the success and effectiveness of the *Stile Liberty* in Sicily.

Contemporary art – Although Sicily has not given rise to an international movement, it can claim to have nurtured several interesting personalities.

The painter **Fausto Pirandello** (1889-1975), the son of the famous writer, was mainly interested in Cubist painting (Braque in particular) before later finding a balance between the abstract and figurative.

S. Chirol

B. Kaufmann

B. Kaufmann

The neo-Realist painter **Renato Guttuso** (1912-87) studied classics in Palermo before moving to Rome and then Milan. There he affirmed his political position as clearly anti-Fascist. During these years he turned to realist art. His paintings are characterised by a perspective which has been flattened and by form that has been refracted into geometric shapes in a way that is reminiscent of Picasso, yet his choice of subject always reflects his social predicament. Since 1958, Guttuso has been influenced by Expressionism. The result is a new painting style: the realism that pervaded his subject matter is now imbued with emotion, movement is suggested by the use of strong colour and boldly decisive line. One of his later works, the *Vucciria (see p 263)*, perfectly exemplifies this synthesis of styles, with its crude and realistic portrayal of the quarter of beef hanging in the foreground compared with the stacked pile of fruit crates and fish boxes that serve to suggest depth of field, and the central line of the characters – most especially the woman with her back to the viewer in the foreground, who animates and breathes life into the composition.

Among the contemporary Sicilian artists mention should be made of various sculptors. **Pietro Consagra**, who comes from Mazara del Vallo (b 1920), studied in Palermo before going to Rome where he came into contact with abstract art. His works show how he experiments with different materials, how he hones down the thickness of material to produce the finest end-result, a most fragile lamination. In Sicily, his name is directly associated with Gibellina *(see GIBELLINA)* where his imposing Star is situated at the entrance to the town, and with Fiumara d'Arte *(see La FIUMARA D'ARTE)*.

The sculptor **Emilio Greco** was born in Catania in 1913. He centres his work on Classical form, ever in quest of that elusive harmony and equilibrium, drawing his inspiration from Greek, Etruscan, Roman and Renaissance art. One of his favourite subjects is the female body; other concepts and ideas explored are associated with religion (the bronze doors of Orvieto Cathedral and the monument to Pope John XXIII for St Peter's in Rome).

Finally, **Salvatore Fiume** (1915-97), also known as Giocondo, was active in various media including sculpture, film and painting, that facilitated his early success. His paintings, which reflect a diverse source of inspiration, range from being ideal depictions of nature to flat portrayals of real and everyday life (depictions of women in a market). Pertinent influences evident in his work include the various cultures and civilisations that have been impressed through history on Sicily: an oriental inflection touches his interpretation of Moorish themes. In later life, Fiume also devoted himself to religious art, undertaking to illustrate various Biblical texts for the Catholic publisher Edizioni Paoline.

Letters

Sicilian literature has evolved in a curious way: nowhere has dialect been used as a literary language for such a long time and in such an uncompromising way as on this island. This is so much so that it has given rise to two linguistically different parallel streams, often present in the same author: one form being written in Italian, the other in the Sicilian dialect.

Sicilian school of poetry – **Frederick II** (1194-1250) was an exceptional patron of culture and art. At his court, the *Magna Curia*, he promoted the study of law, philosophy, medicine and languages: Arabic, Greek, Latin and Hebrew which at that time were the tongues used for philosophical and scientific knowledge. Literature developed there as a pursuit for aristocrats and was practised by princes and high officials of the court who regarded poetry as an elegant pastime and the finishing touch to their worldliness and sophistication. For their poetry, the Sicilian poets modelled their subject matter and style on the Provençal Troubadour poetry of courtly love: the sort of loving service that man, as a servant, dedicates to a Madonna. The language used is a refined Sicilian stripped of any base vernacular colloquialisms, enriched instead with Latin and Provençal phraseology: an illustrious, strictly literary language that excludes any form of realism, which in turn came to influence Italian lyric poetry as a whole. Another fundamentally important element of Sicilian poetry was meter: from this time the seven-syllable line and the hendecasyllable, favoured by the Sicilians, came to predominate Italian poetry. Among the Sicilian School poets ranked several sovereigns: **Frederick II** is attributed with four songs and a treatise on hunting; his sons **Henry**, **Frederick**, **Manfred** and **Enzo** King of Sardinia, wrote poetry. Other notable exponents of the genre include the court notary **Giacomo da Lentini**, who is regarded as the inventor of the sonnet, **Giacomo Pugliese**, **Rinaldo d'Aquino**, **Guido** and **Odo delle Colonne**, **Pier della Vigna** (who also found fame through an episode in Dante's *Inferno*: Canto XIII v 25) and **Cielo d'Alcamo**, author of the famous dialogue-poem *Rosa Fresca Aulentissima*. With the decline of the *Magna Curia*, so the Sicilian School's golden age dwindled: during the 14C-15C, the art of Sicilian poetry was modelled on Dante, Petrarch and Boccaccio; then it gradually faded, overshadowed by a more popular genre in local dialect.

Humanism and the Renaissance – The discovery of Classical texts, most particularly the understanding of Ancient Greek which underpinned the emergence of Humanism, resounded strongly in Sicily. As journeys were increasingly undertaken by scholars and detailed research was intensified by the specialised Academy factions (namely *gli Accesi* or the Enlightened, *i Solitari* or Solitaries, *gli Sregolati* or Immoderates, *gli Irresoluti* or Irresolutes), cultural exchanges between Sicily and the mainland peninsula became more comprehensive. Noto, Palermo, Siracusa, Catania, and Messina became leading cultural centres. Messina instituted at the monastery of San Salvatore a school for Greek which achieved international acclaim largely thanks to the teachings of **Costantino Lascaris** (1434-1501). Other illustrious Classical scholars and researchers included **Antonio Beccadelli** (1394-1471) and **Giovanni Aurispa** (1375-1459).

The 16C saw the recovery of Sicilian over the predominance of Tuscan, which by now had become the language of public officialdom. This period also saw the consolidation of local patriotism and pride, marked by the publication of the first Sicilian-Latin dictionaries and grammar primer for the regional dialect. As far as poetry is concerned, the preponderance of the Petrarchan style prevalent at that time found expression both in dialect through the works of **Antonio Veneziano** (1580-93) – the author of two volumes of poems entitled *Celia* – and in a language similar to Tuscan in the works of **Argisto Giuffredi** (1535-93).

17C-18C – The 17C witnessed, in keeping with the general mood of the Baroque, a upsurge of interest and development in the theatre, largely generated by **Ortensio Scammacca** (1562-1648) a tragedian both of religious and secular subjects. Comedy flourished both in Italian and in dialect using satire and humour to highlight the weaknesses of a decadent society.

In the course of the 18C, the Age of Enlightenment made its presence felt in Sicily, most especially by replacing historical preconceptions and superstition with scientific thought and reason. Expressions of this new culture include the History of Sicily written by the abbot **G Battista Caruso** (1673-1724) and the History of Sicilian Literature edited by **Antonio Mongitore** (1663-1743). Philosophical reflection inspired various other literary genres: Cartesian thought was voiced by **Tommaso Campailla** (1668-1740), who wrote a philosophical poem entitled *Adamo, ovvero il mondo é creato* (Adam, or How the World was Created); Leibniz meanwhile was exalted by **Tommaso Natale** in his work *La filosofia Leibniziana (The Philosophy of Leibniz)*. The precepts of Rousseau on the Noble Savage and the relationship between morality and the environment were promoted in poetry by the greatest poet of the century, **Giovanni Meli** (1740-1815), in his bucolic contemplations *La bucolica* and philosophical satires clearly influenced by the Enlightenment *L'origini du lu munnu, Don Chisciotti e Sanciu Panza*.

19C – The 19C opened with the debate between Classicism and Romanticism, often woven into the political arguments behind the Risorgimento. **Ellodoro Lombardi** (1843-94), one of the poets who encapsulate the spirit of the Risorgimento, expressed his commitment to Garibaldi's cause in verse. Romanticism encouraged the writing of lengthy histories and research into the origins of regional culture and tradition: **Michele Amari** (1806-89) initiated a new period of history criticism with his *La guerra del Vespro siciliano (War of the Sicilian Vespers)* and *Storia dei Musulmani di Sicilia (History of the Muslims in Sicily)*, while **Giuseppe Pitré** (1841-1916) can claim the merit for having begun to study folklore, and in so doing, raising the life and traditions of the Sicilian people to a level worthy of historical consideration *(see p 285)*.

Literature and reality: Realism – Realism was formulated as a reaction to Romanticism. It advocated that inspiration for art should come from the concrete reality of the natural world, and became widespread in Sicily towards the close of the 19C. Early foundations were laid by the positivist poetry of **Mario Rapisardi** (1844-1912); reinforcements came from the accomplished theorist **Luigi Capuana** (1839-1915), according to whom a work of art should embrace a sense of real life, examine the contemporary world and the laws of nature so as to document human life. His masterpieces – *Giacinta* and *Il Marchese di Roccaverdina* – reflect these values; furthermore they portray reality in an impersonal way. Even **Giovanni Verga** (1830-1922), after the late-Romantic inflections in his earliest work, show his move towards realist poetry as from his short story entitled *Nedda*. His masterpiece – *I Malavoglia* – intended as the first part of a cycle of novels entitled *I vinti (The Conquered)*, was followed by just one sequel *(Mastro Don Gesualdo)*. The main theme of the work by Verga concentrates on the description of the real Sicily, with the destiny of the humble portrayed objectively yet compassionately. He uses a sombre writing style and a language which, when compared to the Italian mainstream, succeeds in mimicking the cadences and rhythms of the spoken vernacular. Other adherents of the Realist School include **Federico de Roberto** (1861-1927) – author of *I Viceré (The Viceroys)* and *L'Illusione (The illusion)* and the poets **Giuseppe Aurelio Costanzo** (1843-1913) and **Giovanni Alfredo Cesareo** (1861-1937).

20C – Modern Italian literature is indebted to Sicily for one of its greatest protagonists: the 1934 Nobel Prize winner **Luigi Pirandello** (1867-1946). His early work as a poet and novelist lies in the Realist vein. Later works explore the theme of isolation, painting the individual at sea in a society that is foreign to him *(Il fu Mattia Pascal, Novelle per un anno)*. Pirandello's portrait of this human condition relative to his environment found its most poignant expression on the stage: there he experimented with form and

Luigi Pirandello

content. Pirandello's masterpieces include *Liolà*, *Pensaci Giacomino! (Think about it, Giacomino)*, *Così é (se vi pare) – That's How It Is (If You Like)* and *Sei personaggi in cerca di autore (Six Characters in Search of an Author)*.

Another figure that is central to the history of Italian culture is **Giovanni Gentile** (1875-1944): he championed a return to the idealism of Hegel, having worked for 20 years with B Croce on his "Critica" which revitalised Italian culture (Croce also founded *Il Giornale Critico della filosofia italiana*). Gentile joined the Fascist party and, as Minister for Education, promoted the reform of the Italian education system. On the opposing political front, the anti-Fascist and Member of Parliament for the Italian Communist Party (PCI) **Concetto Marchesi** (1878-1957) published studies on the history of Latin literature which are still regarded as classics today.

The decadence of the Sicilian aristocracy during the Risorgimento is poignantly, if bitterly, portrayed in *Il Gattopardo (The Leopard)*, the novel by **Giuseppe Tomasi di Lampedusa** (1896-1957), published posthumously. The satirical and grotesque narrator, **Vitaliano Brancati**, attacked the myths of eroticism and sexual conceit in his novels *(Don Giovanni in Sicilia, Il bell'Antonio and Paolo il Caldo)*. **Elio Vittorini** (1908-66) played a fundamental role in spreading awareness of contemporary American literature and in revitalising the Italian narrative tradition in the neo-Realist convention *(Conversazione in Sicilia, Uomini e no)*. The courageous, rough-and-ready style more often associated with police enquiries denouncing the curse of Italian and Sicilian society, animate the novels of **Leonardo Sciascia** (1921-89), which include *Il giorno della civetta (The Day of the Owl)*, *Todo modo*, and *Candido ovvero un sogno fatto in Sicilia (Candido, or a Sicilian Dream)*. **Gesualdo Bufalino** (1920-96) is a literary personality in his own right: having emerged at the age of 60 with *Diceria dell'untore*, he was immediately acclaimed by critics and the public alike following the publication of his many books of prose, poetry, memoirs and criticism *(Argo il cieco, Il Guerrin Meschino)*. The baroque prose of **Vincenzo Consolo** (b 1933) is full of precise reflections on history. The detective novels of **Andrea Camilleri** (1925), based on the fictitious character of police superintendant Montalbano, have enjoyed great success both in Italy and abroad; Camilleri's novels are infused with a strong Sicilian atmosphere and characterised by the use of extremely original language which uses Sicilian expressions and vocabulary and is very musical in tone. As far as poetry is concerned, **Salvatore Quasimodo** (1901-68), awarded the Nobel Prize for Literature in 1959, occupies a position of prime importance: his work revitalised the expressive modules of Hermeticism in an original way *(Ed é subito sera, La terra impareggiabile, Dare e avere)*. Less well-known, but nevertheless of interest, is the metaphorical poetry *(Canti barocchi, Plumelia)* of **Lucio Piccolo** (1903-69), as is the great sense of social commitment voiced by **Ignazio Buttitta** (1899-1997), who discovered, yet again, that dialect was the best vehicle for the Sicilian popular soul to sing *(Lu pani si chiama pani, La peddi nova)*.

The Grand Tour

Without Sicily, Italy leaves no image in the soul: it is the key to everything.

Italian Journey, JW Goethe

It was during the reign of the English Queen Elizabeth I (1533-1603) that the concept of a "Grand Tour" of the Continent first became popular. The medieval-style pilgrimages that used to be undertaken by superstitious gentry had been decried by the likes of Erasmus. Now, excursions were to be undertaken for education and pleasure *(utilitas et verits)*: Venice, Milan, Verona, Florence and Rome, of course, were the compulsory ports of call; but after Elizabeth I's excommunication and aggressive actions against Spain, (Protestant) travellers would have been wary of journeying south to Naples and Sicily, then under the dominion of the Spaniards and their Catholic Inquisition. Slowly the Papacy endeavoured to woo the English. Aristocrats sojourned at leisure in Italy (the Earl of Leicester's son, Sir Robert Dudley, was in Florence; Earl Arundel spent time in Padua); Inigo Jones (1573-1652) reported the delights of Classical and Palladian architecture. Finally, after the Restoration (1660) of Charles II, the frontiers were opened once more.

The **Age of Sensibility** exalted Italy as the cradle of civilisation. Instructive journeys were therefore undertaken by young intellectuals to complete their education. This involved travelling to the Continent, visiting places and cities endowed with a rich artistic heritage and cultural fervour, and coming into contact with everything that might enrich a man's spirit and intellect. Richard Boyle, then Lord Burlington (1684-1753), and Robert Adam (1728-92) followed in the wake of Jones to study the original Antique monuments.

As the **Age of Reason** dawned, still Rome and its academic institutions attracted the ambitions young artists to study, muse and acquaint themselves with life without responsibility. After the Seven Years War (1756-63) the Grand Tour became institutionalised: now not only the British **(Sir William Hamilton, Gavin Hamilton, Benjamin West)** came, but also the French, the Germans (notably **Winckelmann, Goethe**) and the Dutch. Visitors extended their tours to Naples and the south following the exciting discovery and excavation of Pompeii (1740s) and the neighbouring Herculaneum (1750s). This provided a genuine and "scientific" view of Roman life buried intact beneath layers of volcanic debris since the eruption of Vesuvius in AD 79, as had been described by Pliny the Younger. Scholars and tourists alike extended their travels to take in Paestum (documented by two other Englishmen, **John Berkenhout** and **Thomas Major**, in 1767-68). Before long, Sicily was also included in the itinerary. But these discoveries did not only encourage interest in things Roman relevant to neo-Classicism and the Greek Revival, they also precipitated an ever greater fascination for the latent power of volcanoes. This is encapsulated by Sir William Hamilton (Plenipotentiary at the Court of Naples 1764-1800) in his book *Observations on Mount Vesuvius, Mount Etna and other Volcanos* (1773).

Napoleon's invasion of Italy (1796) interrupted all forms of travel across the Continent, and when peace was restored the grandness of the scheme evaporated. After 1815, Thomas Cook began operating his package tours; foreign visitors urged the Italians to rise up against their Austrian occupiers; yet all the while, Italy provided a safe haven for those fleeing trouble at home, most especially those young and of a Romantic disposition (Byron, Shelley, Browning).

View of the interior of the Temple of Segesta, J Houel

G. Blot/RMN

Englishmen abroad – The first English traveller to compile a journal of his travels abroad is **Sir Thomas Hoby** (1530-66) who set out from England in June 1549 and travelled to Padua, Florence, Rome, Naples, Calabria and Sicily; in 1561 he published his very own translation of Castiglione's book of manners, *Il Cortegiano*.

In 1700, **John Dryden junior** was travelling in the Mediterranean (*A Voyage to Sicily and Malta* was published in 1776). In 1771, the Scotsman **Patrick Brydone** visited the island his impressions are contained in the entertaining letters that form his *Journey to Sicily and Malta* (pub 1773 – which library records prove to be the most popular book of the late 18C): the first thing that strikes him is the port of Messina, a harbour enclosed by a sickle-shaped tongue of land protecting it from all the winds. Here reality combines immediately with myth, with the terrible monsters of Scilla and Charibdis lurking in the underground caves on either side of the Straits of Messina. Then it is the luxuriant vegetation that catches the traveller's eye, and the humbler, sun-kissed cultivations of vines, olives and wheat, which alternate with flowers, bushes and prickly pears. Ever present in the background, stands the menacing form of Etna, smouldering benignly – the ultimate "curiousity" in this southern region. Then Taormina and the first leap into the Classical past, its magnificent theatre, and Etna looms up again, a sleeping giant, but ever vigilant and ready to prove its great power: *"in the centre...we could just see the summit of the mountain raising its proud head, vomiting clouds of smoke"*. The ascent was difficult, but the view from the top was worth all the effort: *"no imagination in the world has had the courage to depict such a marvellous sight. There is nowhere on the surface of the globe that can combine so many striking, sublimely beautiful details...The summit...is situated on the edge of a bottomless chasm, as old as the world itself, and it often erupts cascades of fire, thrusting up incandescent stones with a roar that shakes the whole island."*

For travellers, Etna acts as a powerful magnet: the very antithesis of the peace and serenity of the past inspired by the Greek ruins of Girgenti (Agrigento). It symbolised life in the form of fire and heat, an uncontrollable, unpredictable phenomenon. The fact that it is visible from a long way off seems almost to endow it with the inevitability of something that man cannot control, like life and death. The traveller journeys on towards the larger towns on the island: Catania, Siracusa, Agrigento and the *"beautiful, elegant"* Palermo, to which pages and pages of description are devoted. Not long afterwards, other travellers alight in Sicily. Often, the journey is restricted to a tour of the coastline: a diversion inland would have been risky for anyone attempting it given the poor state of the roads.

In his footsteps there followed **Henry Swinburne**, urged on by Brydone's "lies" and "nonsensical froth"; he published his travels in four volumes entitled *Travels in the Two Sicilies in the Years 1777, 1778, 1779 and 1780*. These, along with the Brydone account, were soon translated into French and German. **Johann Wolfgang Goethe** (1749-1832) used Brydone and JH Von Riedesel's *Reise* (1771) when he undertook his Italian journey, writing his own *Italienisch Reise* (1786-88).

As descriptions were penned, draughtsmen and painters flocked to the island eager to depict the natural landscape, the topography of the cities and views, the ruins and the people. A case in point were the artists sent by the **Abbot of Saint-Non** (Hubert Robert and Fragonard) for material to illustrate his *Voyage pittoresque de Naples et de Sicile* much like William Beckford sent JR Cozens to paint watercolours to illustrate his *Dreams, Waking, Thoughts and Incidents* (censored on publication in 1783).

Towards the end of the century, Sicily became the key destination for anyone undertaking the Grand Tour: it was the gateway of things Classical, but also a natural treasure trove of rare features that could not be found elsewhere.

Travelling diary – The diary was the traveller's faithful companion. In it he would transcribe his impressions, musings, pleasures and discomforts (Goethe's descriptions of sea sickness, for example) in an informal letter to himself or close friend. What is remarkable is how perceptive these observations are, touching upon technical and scientific details, curious facts, encounters, and images of a Sicily that has changed profoundly since. Yet the portraits of the Sicilians, their kindness and hospitality are true for all time. Goethe's *Italian Journey* aptly describes the members of the Cagliostro family and the furnishings of Villa Palagonia at Bagheria with the same consistently interested eye; the Prince of Palagonia, whom Goethe met strolling through the streets of Palermo, is portrayed as: *"A long, thin gentleman dressed in a coat fit for grand ceremonies, who proceeded with great calm and dignity along the middle of the street, through the rubbish. Smartly dressed and powdered, with clothes of silk, his hat under one arm, sword at his side, and elegant shoes with buckles decorated with precious stones: thus he walked along, calm and serious, and everyone's gaze was fixed upon him."*

Henry Swinburne observes: *"The next morning, being as the night had been, cold and stormy, the peasants went to church in short dark surtouts with capuchin hoods which, added to their swarthy complexions, sour looks, and greasy hair, composed the blackest congregation I ever beheld."* (Travels in the Two Sicilies).

Cinema

The silver screen in Sicily, or rather, Sicily on the silver screen, has challenged many an important film director to try and to recreate on celluloid a portrait of this complex island, populated by a simple people living amongst the most magnificent scenery, in a land of contradictions and veritable oxymorons in the broadest meaning of the word. For this is a bright and hospitable world, yet its people are haunted by the past: they are reserved, but also ever happy to extend warmth and generosity in equal measure to an extent rarely encountered elsewhere; this is a land of tacit complicity fired by the ardent will to fight it. Transcribing all these things into art is no simple task. The first great masterpieces were based on the classics: **Luchino Visconti** turned to Verga to make such films as **La Terra Trema** *(The Ground Trembles)* in 1948 based on his book *I Malavoglia*, and to Tomasi di Lampedusa for **Il Gattopardo** *(The Leopard)* in 1963 from the book of the same name. His determination to capture reality in all its different guises while peppering it with the local colour and poetry that such a major artistic undertaking demands prompted Visconti firstly to select his main cast from among amateur actors living in a typical community such as Aci Trezza who spoke in dialect. Secondly, he chose an historical epic that was respected and established in its own right, set in the magnificent, yet already decadent Palermo of the late 19C, illuminated by the sparkling star-performances of Claudia Cardinale, Burt Lancaster, and Alain Delon.

In the same vein, may be added the sad and agonising story related in **Stromboli terra di Dio** directed by **Roberto Rossellini** and interpreted by Ingrid Bergmann.

Films about the Mafia are a case apart. Since the making of the film-cum-denunciations – **In nome della legge** *(In the Name of the Law)* directed by Pietro Germi (1949) and **Salvatore Giuliano** directed by Francesco Rosi (1961) – the subject matter and circumstances were quickly exploited and transformed into a *genre* of its own, which for Italian viewers compares well with the popular Spaghetti Western elsewhere. This in turn generated a veritable industry of Mafia-family epics with the inevitable shoot-outs, clashes, and expressions in broad Sicilian dialect. These films were distributed all over the world, giving a somewhat negative impression of Sicily. However, also belonging to this *genre* are skillfully made films of social importance, such as **I cento passi** *(One hundred steps)* directed by Tullio Giordana (2000), which received the award for the best screenplay in the Venice Film Festival.

A very different portrait of Sicily is also portrayed on the cinema screen: a Sicily that is mournful but veined with humour as in the magnificent tales retold in **Kaos** *(Chaos)*, made in 1984 by the **Taviani brothers**, based on novels by Pirandello (brilliant performances by Franco Franchi and Ciccio Ingrassia in *La Giara (The Jar)*; a poetic view of Sicily is portrayed in Massimo Troisi's **Il Postino** *(The Postman)* made in 1994, and Giuseppe Tornatore's **Nuovo Cinema Paradiso** (1989). An ironic Sicily "in search of its lost tranquillity" is shown in the *Isole* episode (about the Aeolian Islands) of **Caro Diario** (1993) by Nanni Moretti and in the funny new **Tano da Morire** (1997), a musical about the Mafia, by Roberta Torre. *(For a list of films set in Sicily see p 26.)*

Scene from *Il Postino (The Postman)*

Popular festivals and traditions

By combining pagan rites, holy days allowed by the Christian Church and local festivals, the Sicilians ensure that the occasions they do celebrate are veritable high-points in their social calendars. These celebrations are intended to amaze, arouse emotion and inspire a heightened sense of occasion. Anyone who has participated in one of the great Sicilian festivals is bound to agree that it does just that. Everyone, but literally everyone from the local community, participates in the decoration of the floats, competes to be selected as one of the bearers of platforms and litters supporting the saints' effigies in the processions, jostles to organise the preparations and costumes and turns up on the day to join the crowd along the streets and cheer the procession on. The most important festivals are Easter, Carnival and the celebrations marking the local patron saint's feast day. Then there are the secular festivals like the **Palio dei Normanni** which commemorates **Roger II**'s delivery of Piazza Armerina and the **Festa della Castellana** at Caccamo. Others are derived from pagan rites: the **Sagra della Spiga** at Gangi largely revolves around the procession dedicated to the ancient goddess of Sicily, Demeter (Ceres) – the goddess of fertility; whereas the **Sagra del Mandorlo in fiore** (celebrating the blossoming of the almond trees) at Agrigento and the **Sagra della Ricotta** at Vizzini have their origins in feting the advent of Spring.

Some towns hold a **Carnival** with processions of brightly-coloured floats populated with *papier maché* figures through the streets, as at Sciacca and Acireale – which arguably claims to have the finest carnival celebration in Sicily with traditional allegorical floats painted in fabulous colours accompanied by others bedecked with flowers.

Every community, be it a large town or a remote hamlet, celebrates the *festa* of its **patron saint** in the most meaningful and spectacular way with processions, competitive events, sweet-vending street-stalls, firework displays, dancing and entertainment. As usual, all the activities associated with such a festival involve the entire local population. The most spectacular festivals are probably those held in the large towns where the patron saints are revered by the largest number of people. In **Palermo** *U fistinu*, dedicated to Santa Rosalia, lasts for six whole days: that is six action-packed days of wild celebration arranged around the slow yet triumphant procession of a float bearing the statue of the saint through the crowds. In **Catania** the citizens direct their hopes and aspirations to St Agatha so that she might protect them from any threat of devastation from some sudden fury sent by Mount Etna: for three days, her relics, contained in a precious silver bust of the saint, set with enamels and jewels, is processed by the *nudi*, dressed in simple jute sacks as the people were on that fateful night in 1126 when the relics were brought back to the city from Constantinople and the citizens poured into the streets, eagerly jumping out of bed without taking the time to get dressed. **Siracusa** meanwhile fetes its patron saint's day with a majestic procession led by people carrying votive candles; as the litter of St Lucy passes, eyes of wax, silver and bronze are fixed to it in grateful acknowledgement of grace received from the saint, the protector of eyes and eyesight. In **Messina** the most spectacular festival is held on 15 August (its patron, the Madonna of the Letter, is actually feted in June): an enormous statue of the Assumption is pulled by thousands of willing hands to the cathedral, where it remains for two days guarded by 14 young girls dressed in white. For the 15 August is the *Festa della Vergine* as well as the anniversary of the arrival of Count Roger. The sacred mixes with the profane in an inseparable cocktail of religious devotion, high spirits, social occasion and entertainment.

Popular Sicilian music

At the very mention of this island's name, anyone with a keen ear for music will call to mind an ancient popular shepherds' dance, the *siciliana*: this was transcribed in the 17C and 18C in a handful of pieces for instrument and voice. The traditional instruments of accompaniment for country dances are the straight reed pipe known in the vernacular as the *fiscalettu* or *friscaleddu*, and the *marranzanu* which in fact is the Sicilian name for the **Jew's harp**. The small tongue of this tiny instrument made entirely of metal produces a vibrating sound with different rhythms: as with any instrument, the sound produced varies according to the skill of the player. Unless the player succeeds in making the Jew's harp play properly with teeth, lips, cheeks, vocal chords and breath, the end-result will simply consist of some ugly noise.

The songs that brighten the passing of days are the songs called alla carrittera – literally "of the cart-driver", and those sung by the cantastorie – modern equivalents of minstrels who travel from town to town with a guitar and a large checked board depicting the scenes of the passionate story that is the subject of their song. The most famous is Ciccio Busacca (born Paternò 1926), the singer of the Lament for the Death of Turiddu Carnivali and Train of the Sun, written by Ignazio Buttitta with the collaboration of Dario Fo.

Easter – This is certainly the most eagerly-awaited festival in Sicily. In almost every town and small village, enormous amounts of effort are invested in preparing for the processions and the celebrations of a rite that have changed little through the centuries. The Crucifixion and Resurrection of Christ are re-enacted as acknowledgements of death and rebirth, not merely in the religious sense but in a more universal way. Each place chooses its own pace and timing: time is taken to prepare the mystery and time is given to actually performing it: processions move the sacred element – a representation of a holy figure – through the streets of the town, stopping here and there to re-enact the Madonna's desperate search for her son, what happened along the road to Calvary and the events of the Passion.

The most poignant elements of the ritual are re-enacted between the Thursday before Easter and Easter Sunday (the discovery of the empty tomb as evidence of the Resurrection), although these can be more protracted, as is the case for the celebrations held at **Trapani**. There, the evenings leading up to the Good Friday grand procession are devoted to the *discese delle Vergini*: at sunset, representatives of each and every *ceto* of the town (associations roughly comparable to the medieval trade guilds) bear on their shoulders the image of their patron Madonna (Madre dei Massari, Madre Pietà del Popolo) and carry her down to the old part of town by candlelight. The men (and many youngsters) compete to be chosen as bearers. The icon sways along its way progressing slowly and gently, stopping often opposite wayside crosses, shrines and churches, but also outside the houses and workplaces of people who have offered up a donation. In so doing, it is almost as though the Madonna is paying homage to the people who worship her. At the windows, people lean out to welcome benediction by the sacred image that will protect their houses through the coming year in exchange for a small offering. The elegant *palazzi* open their doors and gracious inner courtyards to visitors, to the crowd, and to the band, who at intervals interrupt the silence with a burst of music (silence being a relative term when the whole town is out thronging the streets). But this is still nothing compared with Good Friday when 20 figurative groups are continuously borne aloft round the town over a period of 20 hours: in a meaningful and symbolic succession of day, night and day (from early afternoon on the Friday through the night to Saturday morning) the faithful are reminded of, and learn to share in, the emotional endurance and physical pain suffered by the Madonna (it is no coincidence that the Madonna heads the procession) and by Christ in His Passion. An equally evocative occasion is the procession through **Caltanissetta** of 16 groups of statues. In **Marsala** the re-enactment of the Passion is assigned to real live men and women who take on individual roles in the different instalments. At **Enna**, the celebrations reach their climax on Good Friday, when hooded members (numbering some 2 000) of the confraternities that were instituted originally as trade corporations but which now act as religious organisations, process through the streets to the town centre carrying the two heavy statues of the dead Christ and the Addolorata (Our Lady of Sorrows) in complete, respectful, silence. The processions make their way independently to the cathedral where they meet and proceed together in an exhausting journey that lasts throughout the night. The whole thing is then repeated on the Sunday, but with one fundamental difference. This time, the meeting between the Madonna and the Resurrected Christ takes place in a happy, festive atmosphere. A rather unusual rite takes place in **Prizzi** on the Sunday morning. It is called the *Uballu di diavula*: devils, dressed in red, with goatskins slung across their shoulders, their faces covered by horrible tin masks, run through the streets of the town rattling iron chains accompanied by another masked figure this time dressed in yellow and armed with a wooden cross-bow, representing Death. Anyone who gets hit is carried off to the bar (identified as hell) where he pays for a complete round of drinks. These

At the height of the festival of St Agatha in Catania

LARA PESSINA

weird-looking figures lurching madly around as if engaged in a hellish dance, jump about uttering threats, trying to avert the Madonna from meeting the Resurrected Christ. The scene repeats itself several times until at last the two angels accompanying the Madonna strike them down, and the devils fall to the ground. Only Death itself cannot be touched, spared partly as a result of human resignation (man already has to live with the knowledge that he must die) and also because Christ has already overcome it. At **Terrasini**, the rite is tinged with the profane for the festival of *li schietti* – the eligible bachelors – involves them having to prove their virility by lifting orange trees *(see CARINI)*. Besides these, some places bedeck the actual streets with spectacular decorations: at San Biagio Platani, for example, the inhabitants build monumental triumphal arches and ornament them with sculptures made of bread.

A fast-disappearing art: the traditional Sicilian carts

Sadly it is increasingly rare to encounter the brightly-coloured Sicilian carts being pulled along the streets, for once these veritable works of art provided the family with the standard means of transport for the habitual Sunday outing. During the 19C, the *carretto* was simply a functional contraption. It was of basic construction, devoid of any decoration, used to transport fruit and vegetables, tools and farming implements. Then someone hatched the idea of decorating it: before long carts were being painted with brightly-coloured panels showing historical scenes (yellow, pale blue and red reigned supreme); the iron parts were contrived and painted into figurative forms, flowers and tendrils. The final impact was a fabulous show of exuberance, but the intricate detail of which deserves minute and painstaking analysis at close quarters. The taste for decoration assumed new dimensions: it came to signify the status of the owner of the cart and ward off the evil eye or *malocchio*, it might even be used to advertise a service or a product. Several different craftsmen were involved in putting the carts together: the *carradore* was in charge of cutting and carving the wood, the *fabbroferraio* contrived the metal fixtures as fabulous elements of decoration, finally the painter added his contribution to the side and rear panels. The choice of subject-matter was varied. Normally, the inside panels were ornamented with geometric motifs, often within a set framework. The narrative pictures were reserved for the outside, often presented as a series relating some chivalrous deed, a profane or religious story or legend.

In such a way, the Sicilian cart, that most humble vehicle in common use until the 1950s, should be regarded as an endangered species and respected as one of the richest expressions of popular art.

Sicilian puppets

The happy fate of puppets and marionettes in Italy took an upward turn in the 16C, when the aristocracy began showing an interest in the puppet shows put on using the wire-controlled marionettes. The spread to a wider, paying audience came about in the 18C. But it was not until the mid-19C that the puppet show as we know it today became a genre in itself, complete with shiny armour, swords and agile movements which pay off when it comes to a fight.

Sicilian puppet masters weave their stories around bandits, saints, Shakespearean heroes, not forgetting the vignettes that are strictly of local interest (often inserted at the end of a performance, or episode). The favourite source of subject matter are the popular **picaresque stories of chivalry**, from the **Carolingian cycle** in particular. The puppeteers prepare a text that follows the basic lines of the plot, and then set about exaggerating the clashes between the Paladins of France and the infidels because the fight is always the culmination of the show. In the Sicily of former times (as well as in the rest of southern Italy), the puppeteers' arrival was always awaited with great anticipation, most especially by the less fortunate classes, and no-one would dream of missing a single performance. Hence the reason why the puppeteers would break up the story into episodes and present them in series that might last several months. Each performance had to include at least one fight (such as the explanation for having to adapt the historical facts). The puppet master also prepared various boards with panels summarising the salient elements of the story. The main events that were relevant for that particular evening were illustrated on the board, and these were changed with each performance. The board, displayed outside the theatre, would act as an advertisement for the evening and also summarise for the public the story so far.

Principal characters – As mentioned above, the most famous protagonists were the Paladins of France who, under the leadership of Charlemagne, spent their lives fighting the infidels. The show hinged on predetermined precise values and sentiments: there were "goodies" (the Paladins), "baddies" (the infidels) and traitors, such as **Gano di Magonza** (who is always depicted with squinting eyes, because a traitor cannot look someone straight in the eye). Even the "goodies" have specific personalities. The two prime antagonists were Orlando and Rinaldo, companions at arms but divided by their love for a woman, the beautiful **Angelica**, the daughter of the king of Catai. **Orlando** is serious, reliable, a scrupulous person, dutiful but unlucky in love. **Rinaldo** is from a poor background, he has learned the art of survival from an early age; he is a cunning, jolly, rebellious womaniser who never misses an opportunity to sneak away if circumstances

Angelica (3)

Carlo Magno (1)

Gano di Magonza (2)

Rinaldo

Ferraù (4)

Orlando (5)

R. Corbel/MICHELIN 1, 2, 3.: da una foto di un pupo di Turi Grasso e figli – Acireale; 4, 5: da una foto tratta da *Album di Famiglia* di Mimmo Cuticchio – Palermo

LARA PESSINA

permit. The audience participates in the show and takes the side of one character or another: the heroes are challenged, encouraged and applauded; the "baddies" are derided and there is a great roar from the audience every time one of them is killed. The characters can easily be recognised by their clothes and by their shields, which bear the family coat of arms. The Saracens wear breeches and their shields are emblazoned with half-moons. Conversely, the Paladins wear skirts; Orlando has a crossed shield and Rinaldo and his sister **Bradamante**, who is also a warrior (but can be distinguished from her brother because of her long hair), have a lion on their shields.

Performance – The show has three main characters: the puppet who acts on stage; the puppet master who remains off-stage responsible for handling the puppet and providing the voice-overs of several characters at a time, and the music which emphasises the most dramatic moments, particularly when there is a duel – the sound of clashing swords must be accompanied by the frenzied strains of a mechanical pianola or wind instruments. As stated, the performance must include at least one fight, which is the moment the audience is waiting for. Special additional puppets are used for pulling off special effects: a puppet might lose its head or be torn asunder, only to be magically restored to one piece in the next show, or a witch might need to take on a disguise, turning from a pretty, angelic face to a death mask.

Two traditions – All puppets are made of wood and are jointed with metal hinges (the warriors, at least); their manipulation is controlled by lengths of wire connected to the head and right hand. The embossed armour is usually made of bronze or copper; sometimes it has additional applied metal decoration. However, not all puppets are the same. In fact, there are two main schools: one from Palermo and one from Catania (associated with the school of Acireale) which build puppets according to different criteria. The **Palermo puppet** is around 80cm-1m/2.62-3.28ft in height, weighs 8kg/17.6lb, has flexible knees and can draw and sheathe its sword. Its relative lightness makes it easily to manoeuvre: the puppet moves with extreme agility, reacting quickly and suddenly to provocation, and seemingly jumping about on stage to drive home or avoid blows during a duel. The **Catania puppet**, on the other hand, measures 1.40m/4.6ft in height and weighs between 16-20kg/35-44lb. Its knees are rigid (partly because supporting such a weight for any length of time would be a mean feat) and its sword is always drawn, ready to parry blows. Its movements are more ponderous and emphatic, its steps and its thrusts slower and more realistic. The **Acireale puppet** has the same features as the Catania puppet, but the height (1.20m/3.93ft) and the weight (15-18kg/33-39.6lb) are different. Such differences have resulted in the theatrical presentations and the way the puppet master animates his puppets being different: Palermo puppets are moved from the side, and the puppet master has to stretch out his arm to reach the centre of the stage. The puppets from Catania and Acireale, on the other hand, being much heavier, have longer pieces of wire and are controlled from above: the puppet master stands behind the stage on a platform, or on a manoeuvring bench (in the case of the Acireale puppets), 1.90m/6.23ft high

Arts and crafts

Ceramics – One of the most typical Sicilian crafts is ceramic work. The most important centres include Caltagirone and Santo Stefano di Camastra, followed by Sciacca. The shops of these small towns display a fine array of vases, statuettes, crockery, ornaments and knick-knacks, as well as traditional containers for mustard and quince jam.

The art of clay-working – The techniques used for creating articles from clay have remained unchanged for centuries. The ductile clay mixture is worked wet, by hand, using a potter's wheel, or is turned into a liquid and cast in a mould. The object is then left to dry and placed in an oven at a very high temperature. Once the object is baked it is ready for use.

There are a number of different techniques for decorating ceramics. These may include a final working of the clay (carvings, graffito designs or mouldings made with stones, shells or other objects on the unbaked article) or the use of colour which, depending on the type of technique and paint used, can be applied at different stages of manufacture (before or after baking, following a second baking, or cold).

Clay-working techniques allow a range of different articles to be produced, depending on the mixture, techniques and type of baking used. The most simple product is the porous reddish **terracotta**, typical of objects made in Antiquity. The first **maiolica** (terracotta decorated with enamel) appeared in the 16C.

Porcelain is produced from a different type of clay, a white paste known as kaolin, and usually has a glazed finish. Opaque porcelain is known as biscuit porcelain.

It is interesting to note that the name ceramic comes from the Greek word for clay, κεραμοσ (keramos).

Other traditional crafts – Apart from ceramics, there are plenty of other natural products and handicrafts which are typical of the island. Some of these are listed below:

Coral: especially in Trapani, where coral-working is a real art;

Sicilian puppets and traditional carts: these can generally be found at antique dealers and in second-hand shops, or, in Palermo, directly from the few remaining craftsmen who still make them;

Carpets: from the area around Erice;

Sponges: the best place to buy natural sponges is Lampedusa;

Papyrus: papyrus products (paper and cloth) are a speciality of Siracusa.

Sicilian ceramics

Regional specialities

FOOD AND WINE

Talk of food in Sicily is like talking about the weather in England – it is fundamental to life itself. Each region will boast about its own dishes being better and tastier than the next, each community will sing the praises of the way the sunshine has nurtured the home-grown vegetables and blessed the herbs which impart the flavour, texture and colour required where necessary.

Sicilian cuisine relies on an abundance of strongly-flavoured base products (fennel, for example) which are blended and fused with the ruddiest sun-blushed tomatoes, the most gleaming rich aubergine, delicate courgettes and freshest tuna. The food is a natural extension of the local landscape. It forms an integral part of the gastronomic culture of the Mediterranean, halfway between Greece and North Africa, Spain and Ancient Phoenicia (the Middle East).

Just as the landscape of the coast and the hinterland are radically different, so their cuisine is quite distinctive. Imagine, therefore, the gastronomy of Sicily as a palette of paints, with strong colours and subtle hints, a blend of flavours and suggestive memories, highly evocative and yet elusive.

As with all simple culinary traditions, the most popular **single-course meal** is often the tastiest. Pasta, prepared with seasonal vegetables and locally-made olive oil, is the main staple. *Pasta con le sarde*, originally a Palermo dish using freshly caught sardines, is now common across the whole island; pasta cooked predominantly with vegetables is more typical of the inland areas; more elaborate preparations include types of *pasta al forno* (baked pasta) such as *pasta 'ncaciata* from Messina, and Catania's *pasta alla Norma* (cooked with tomatoes, aubergines and salty ricotta cheese).

However, before pasta was invented, bread used to be the mainstay of the diet. The many varieties of bread available in Sicily have always been accompanied by what the local area had to offer: oil, origano and tomatoes resulted in the widespread and very simple *pane cunzato*: this is eaten hot straight out of the oven. The more unusual *pane ca' meusa* is toasted bread spread with a meat paste, often sold on little stalls dotted around the streets of Palermo.

It is easy to see analogies with the cuisine typical of the central part of the island, which is dominated by farming habits and uses a great deal of fresh vegetables. The aubergine is an important ingredient and forms the base of a whole range of delicious dishes, culminating in the glorious *parmigiana* (baked aubergine with ricotta and a touch of tomato sauce, maybe a sprig of basil). The by-products generated by sheep farming play an important role in the hills (providing the fresh and salted cheese known as *ricotta fresca* and *ricotta salata*); meat is usually reserved for special occasions, when *castrato* (literally castrated ram) is roasted (the ram is castrated to prevent it from developing a strong mutton flavour and to encourage deposits of fat which will help to baste the meat as it is being cooked over the open fire and keep it moist). The most common method of cooking meat is on the grill. Pork is also popular.

The eastern flank of the island preserves Greek cooking methods. The west meanwhile is marked by an Arab influence and by courtly practices. The cuisine is more elaborate, refined and full of unexpected contrasts. In an analogy with the landscape, the simple austerity of the Greek temples is replaced here with a sophistication imparted by a *Thousand and One Nights* prevalent in Moorish Palermo and its opulent Baroque architecture.

PRIMA PRESS

Pasta alla Norma

94

The *caponata di melanzane* is an example of the different approach to vegetables (cooked aubergine, tomato, onion, olives, celery and capers, served cold in a sweet-sour sauce); *falsomagro* (a large roll of meat stuffed with ham, cheese and eggs) or *involtini alla primavera* (rissoles made with breadcrumbs, sultanas, pine-nuts, cheese and flavoured with bay leaves and onion) demonstrate the different approach to meat, while *sarde a beccafico* (sardines fried with breadcrumbs, lemon juice and pine-nuts) do likewise for fish. The complexity of these dishes had the primary function of displaying wealth. However, even in the larger towns, a cuisine of popular inspiration is never far away: road-side shops sell food that has just been fried or cooked in the oven, and stalls sell all kinds of dishes around the clock

Pesce spada alla ghiotta

(*sfinciuni* and *panelle* to name but two, *see p 260*).

Returning to the historical influences on Sicilian cooking, the Arabs introduced citrus fruits, sugar, cinnamon and saffron, as well as rice to Sicily. Rice is cooked here in various ways that differ, in the main, with its usage in making risottos in northern Italy: take *arancine* for instance (delicious deep-fried rice balls filled with meat ragout and peas, or ham and cheese), a sort of symbol of the island's traditional cuisine, and often the first gastronomic encounter on a trip to Sicily.

As you would expect, there is an abundance of fish and hundreds of different ways of cooking it. Tuna fish has always occupied a prime position, possibly because of the ritual associated with its catch and killing; sardines and anchovies are common everywhere, while *pesce spada* (swordfish) is more common around Messina. Fish prepared with onions, olives, capers and tomatoes *(alla ghiotta)* is an unusual speciality and, around Trapani, the *cuscusu* is the island's version of the Moroccan dish from coastal regions where fish replaces meat.

Sicily's cake- and pastry-making tradition deserves special attention because it is part of daily life; its fragrance lingers as do the pungent smells of crushed herbs (rosemary, wild fennel, origano, basil, thyme) which grow in abundance throughout the countryside around the island.

Convent sweetmeats, like the brightly-coloured *frutta martorana*, named after the convent in Palermo where they originated, have gently asserted themselves throughout the island. *Cannoli, cassate, pignoccata, biancomangiare* and the traditional *gelo di mellone* (water-melon jelly) are the most common, but each province has its own particular varieties and surprises.

Then, we cannot forget the exquisite home-made ice cream and *granite* made by real experts, which are not merely products of great craftsmanship and culinary pride, but smack of habits and rites of another era. In summer, it is considered virtually compulsory to offer guests a coffee-, lemon- or almond-flavoured *granita* when they arrive. Literature even mentions such sophisticated delights as a jasmine *granita*, consumed by the Piccolo brothers in their refuge at Cala Novella.

Frutta martorana

95

Sicily's wines used to be regarded as *vini da taglio*, that is, they were used to boost the alcohol content of wines of other areas, but, today, although not all have acquired the fame of the fortified wine of **Marsala** *(see MARSALA)*, Sicilian table wines and proprietary wines such as Alcamo, Etna Rosso, il Corvo and Regaleali are delights in store for anyone who has not had the opportunity to taste them.

In addition to Marsala, dessert wines made here include **Moscato di Noto, Passito d Pantelleria** and **Malvasia di Lipari**.

Gelo di mellone

World Heritage List

In 1972, the United Nations Educational, Scientific and Cultural Organization (UNESCO) adopted a Convention for the preservation of cultural and natural sites. To date, more than 150 States Parties have signed this international agreement, which has listed over 500 sites "of outstanding universal value" on the World Heritage List. Each year, a committee of representatives from 21 countries, assisted by technical organizations (ICOMOS – International Council on Monuments and Sites; IUCN – International Union for Conservation of Nature and Natural Resources; ICCROM – International Centre for the Study of the Preservation and Restoration of Cultural Property, the Rome Centre), evaluates the proposals for new sites to be included on the list, which grows longer as new nominations are accepted and more countries sign the Convention. To be considered, a site must be nominated by the country in which it is located.

The protected cultural heritage may be monuments (buildings, sculptures, archaeological structures etc) with unique historical, artistic or scientific features; groups of buildings (such as religious communities, ancient cities); or sites (human settlements, examples of exceptional landscapes, cultural landscapes) which are the combined works of man and nature of exceptional beauty. Natural sites may be a testimony to the stages of the earth's geological history or to the development of human cultures and creative genius or represent significant ongoing ecological processes, contain superlative natural phenomena or provide a habitat for threatened species.

Signatories of the Convention pledge to cooperate to preserve and protect these sites around the world as a common heritage to be shared by all humanity.

Some of the most well-known places which the World Heritage Committee has inscribed include: Australia's Great Barrier Reef (1981), the Canadian Rocky Mountain Parks (1984), The Great Wall of China (1987), the Statue of Liberty (1984), the Kremlin (1990), Mont-Saint-Michel and its Bay (France, 1979), Durham Castle and Cathedral (1986).

In Sicily, UNESCO World Heritage sites are:

1997 Archaeological site of Agrigento

1997 Villa Romana del Casale

2000 Aeolian Islands

Caccamo

Sights

The town preserves a number of Baroque *palazzi* that were built following a major earthquake in 1693 which destroyed many towns in eastern Sicily and which prompted a great deal of reconstruction (Noto and Ragusa Ibla being among the most famous examples).

Acis and Galatea

The sea nymph Galatea, daughter of Nereus, fell in love with the shepherd Acis, son of the god Pan. Unfortunately, she also caught the eye of Polyphemus, the terrible cyclops and arch enemy of Odysseus (Ulysses). As the nymph continued to reject him, so his jealousy and hatred were aroused, until finally the monstrous creature from the caves of Mount Etna set out to kill the young shepherd boy. Zeus, moved to pity by the pain suffered by the young Nereid, transformed her lover into a river (the modern Akis) which, by flowing towards the sea, the realm from where Galatea had come, enabled the two lovers to meet together for ever more.

A popular legend tells of how the dismembered body of Acis became separated into nine parts and was scattered in areas which later became known as the nine *Aci*: Aci Bonaccorsi, Aci Castello *(see below)*, Aci Catena *(see below)*, Aci Platani, Acireale *(see ACIREALE)*, Aci San Filippo *(see below)*, Aci Sant'Antonio *(see p 185)*, Aci Santa Lucia and Aci Trezza *(see below)*.

This particular stretch of coastline is also known as the **Riviera dei Ciclopi** (Cyclops' Coast).

The main hub of the town is piazza del Duomo, from which emanates the principal artery – corso Umberto I to the north and corso Vittorio Emanuele to the south – lined by fine buildings, shops and **gelaterie** which do honour to the fame of the local ice cream. Acireale's renown as a spa town goes back a long way: the springs gushing sulphurous waters to the south of the town, where the Terme di Santa Venera are located, are documented since Antiquity.

It is also famous for its **carnival**, when processions of allegorical floats, many bedecked with flowers, stream through the main streets followed by masked revellers who might linger for a dance in the piazza. Another of Acireale's attractions is the Puppet Theatre which puts on vivid, animated interpretations of the most poignant and bellicose scenes taken from the French *chansons de geste*, especially from the *Chanson de Roland*. Shows are still performed in the Museo dei Pupi dell'Opra di Turi Grasso, just outside Acireale *(see below)*.

TOWN CENTRE

★**Piazza del Duomo** – At one time the piazza was called piazza del Cinque d'Oro (Square of the Golden Five), a reference to playing cards reflecting the arrangement of a platform surrounded by four small flower-beds that occupied the square. It was here that musical and theatrical events were performed at one time. The finely proportioned open space is enclosed by Baroque buildings: the **Duomo**, the **Basilica dei Santi Pietro e Paolo** with its fine façade marked by a single campanile, and the **Palazzo Comunale** (1659) graced with elegant wrought-iron **balconies**★ supported on richly decorated brackets bearing masks and gargoyles. Slightly set back, at the beginning of via Davì, sits the 17C **Palazzo Modò** which has two splendid balconies with brackets again decorated with grotesques; the façade still bears the name of the theatre the Eldorado that occupied the premises in the early 20C, crowned with a large mask.

Ice cream

The invention of sherbet, a mixture of fruit pulp, honey and snow, is often attributed to the Chinese; the recipe was introduced to the West by the Arabs and so to Sicily, an important Arab stronghold in the Mediterranean, where it has been known since Antiquity.

Indeed, the name sherbet or sorbet is derived from the Arabic **sharba** or **sciarbat** (a cold drink concocted from snow flavoured with essences). Furthermore, a 11C-tract on Arab cuisine has a section devoted to ice cream. Nowadays, Sicily is particularly associated with a number of ice-cream varieties: notably home-made *tartufo*, which consists of a chocolate ball nestling a cream core; **brioches** (the classic round type) filled with ice cream; **cassata** (the kind made during the summer with **ricotta** cheese, a typical Sicilian sweet) and the two-flavoured **mattonella** (ice brick).

Basilica dei Santi Pietro e Paolo

Duomo ⊘ – The cathedral is dedicated to the Annunciation and Santa Venera. Its two-tone neo-Gothic façade was designed by Giovan Battista Filippo Basile (1825-91), the architect of the Teatro Massimo in Palermo and father of the more famous Ernesto Basile, master of the Liberty style. Standing between two campanili with majolica spires, the front is ornamented by a fine 17C portal. Inside, the most interesting feature is between the transept and the chancel, frescoed by P Vasta. The right transept, its floor dominated by a 19C sundial by Wolfgang Sertorius and F Peters, harbours the Baroque chapel of Santa Venera.

Basilica di San Sebastiano ⊘ – *Corso Vittorio Emanuele, beyond piazza Duomo, on the left-hand side.* A statue-topped balustrade crowns the **Baroque façade★**, which consists of a harmonious combination of columns, pilasters, niches and volutes, drawn together within a frieze of angels bearing a continuous garland at the first cornice level. Inside, the transept and chancel contain frescoes by P Vasta depicting episodes from the life of St Sebastian, the patron saint of the town to whom the church is dedicated.

Piazza San Domenico – *At the end of via Cavour.* The fine Baroque façade of **San Domenico** dominates one side of the tiny piazza which is also overlooked by **Palazzo Musmeci** (17C) with its elegant wrought-iron balconies and Rococo windows.
A little further on, along the road on the right when facing San Domenico, is the **Biblioteca Zelantea**, the town library, annexed with an **art gallery** ⊘. Here reside the plaster modello for the statue of Acis and Galatea (now in the gardens of the Villa Comunale) by Rosario Anastasi, and the bust of **Julius Caesar** known as the *Busto di Acireale* (1C BC).

Villa Belvedere – *To the north of the town, at the far end of corso Umberto I.* The lovely, peaceful gardens, complete with a panoramic terrace, provide a magnificent **view★** of Mount Etna and the sea. It is here that the statue of **Acis** and **Galatea** is to be found. The platform at the entrance, on the left, is a reproduction of the one that used to ornament piazza del Duomo.

Terme di Santa Venera – *To the south of the town, entrance off the SS 114.* The neo-Classical baths complex dates back to 1873, built at the request of Baron Agostino Pennisi di Floristella (whose castle can still be seen behind the baths, near the old railway station).

The baths are fed with sulphurous water which is channelled from a spring about 3km/2mi inland, south of Acireale, in the district of Reitana. There, the remains of the **Roman Baths of Santa Venera al Pozzo** ⊘ have been discovered: including two barrel-vaulted rooms which are presumed to have served as **tepidarium** and **caldarium**.

ENVIRONS

Off the SS 114 to Catania, a left turning leads to the village of Santa Maria la Scala. Along this road the church of Santa Maria della Neve is signposted.

Grotta del Presepe di Santa Maria della Neve ⊘ – The Grotto of the Crib, adjacent to the church, is a winding lava ravine which, until the 18C, was used as a refuge by bandits and fishermen, before being transformed to represent the cave at Bethlehem. In 1752, a crib was arranged here comprising 32 life-sized figures with wax faces, dressed in sumptuous clothes (most especially the Magi).

Santa Maria della Scala – This picturesque village overlooking the sea, which grew up around the 17C parish church, has an attractive little harbour.

Return to the SS 114 and continue towards Catania, take the left fork for Capo Mulinit. About 100m/328ft along this road lies the Museo dei Pupi dell'Opra (via Nazionale per Catania, 193-195).

Museo dei Pupi dell'Opra ⊘ – The Turi Grasso Puppet Theatre displays a collection of traditional puppets (some dating from the last century) typical of the Aci area. These illustrate the high skill and craftsmanship involved in the making of the figures, the intricacy of their costumes and the individuality of the different painted faces. There is also a small functioning theatre *(for details of performances, ask at the museum).*

OTHER ACI IN THE AREA

The towns of Aci Catena and Aci San Filippo are almost natural extensions of Acireale.

Aci Catena – The little town, which owes its name to the cult of the *Madonna della Catena* (Madonna of the Chain), centres around the charming square, piano Umberto, onto which give the attractive late-19C and early-20C town hall and a number of other noble residences. Similar *palazzi* grace the neighbouring via IV Novembre and via Matrice where the 18C church and Palazzo Riggio (adjacent), sadly now in ruins, are to be found.

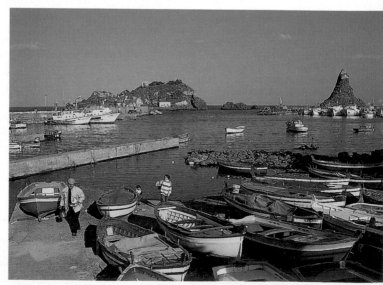

The harbour, Aci Trezza

Aci San Filippo – At the heart of the little town stands the church, ornamented with a fine 18C façade and, to one side, a campanile with a stone lava base.

From Aci San Filippo return to the SS 114 and continue towards Catania.

Aci Trezza – This small fishing town is dominated, on the seaward side, by the **Rocks of the Cyclops★** (Faraglioni dei Ciclopi), a treacherous pointed mass of black lava rising up from the crystal-clear waters. The *Odyssey* relates that these were the rocks hurled by Polyphemus against Ulysses, who had blinded him by thrusting a flaming stake into his only eye; the hero then escaped with his companions by clinging to the bellies of rams belonging to the Cyclops.

Next to these rocks sits the **island of Lachea**, now a biology research station run by the University of Catania.

The little harbour, bathed in sunshine and dotted with multi-coloured boats hauled up onto the beach, seems inhabited by the ghosts of fictitious characters created by the Italian author **Verga**: how easy to imagine Maruzzi and the other members of the **Malavoglia** family waiting here anxiously on the shore, ceaselessly searching the horizon, alas in vain, for the *Provvidenza* with its cargo of lupins.

How appropriate, therefore, that Aci Trezza should have been used by **Luchino Visconti** to shoot his film *La Terra Trema* (The Ground Trembles), based as it was on Verga's novel *I Malavoglia*.

After midnight, the wind began to raise merry hell, as if all the cats in the village were on the roof, shaking the shutters. You could hear the sea lowing around the high rocks so that it seemed as if the cattle from Sant'Alfio market were gathered there, and day broke as black as a traitor's soul... The village boats were drawn up on the beach, and well-moored to the boulders below the wash-place...

The only people on the beach were Padron 'Ntoni, because of that load of lupins he had at sea, along with the Provvidenza, and his son Bastianazzo to boot...

I Malavoglia (The House by the Medlar Tree) by Giovanni Verga.

Aci Castello – *2km/1.2mi S of Aci Trezza on the SS 114*. This small seaside town is situated on a stretch of coastline dotted with lemon trees (hence the name **Riviera dei Limoni**), agaves and palm trees.

★**Castle** – The Norman fortress, built of black lava, stands tall on a rocky spur surrounded by sea around it, a striking landmark even from the road. This place has been fortified since Roman times when it accommodated the Rocca Saturnia (Saturnia Fortress). On several occasions in 1189 it was destroyed and re-built by King Tancredi. Under the Bourbons (1787), the castle was used as a prison.

From the top there is a marvellous **view★** of the **Faraglioni dei Ciclopi★** and the island of **Lachea** *(see above)*. The castle houses a small **museum** ⊘ with an educational slant, containing mineral specimens and archaeological artefacts.

Population 55 665
Michelin map 432 fold 13 P 22

As the road picks its way to Agrigento, the almond trees gradually become more numerous. When in flower (January and February), their blossom appears like little clouds of white against the green fields and the bare earth of the hillsides. It is precisely at this time of year that the town comes to life and puts on its Sunday best for the Sagra del Mandorlo in Fiore (Almond Blossom Festival – see Practical Information: Calendar of events).

Visitors approaching Agrigento from the coast will be treated to a glorious sight, particularly if arriving at sunset when the houses along the crest of the hill are coloured with pastel hues and the Temple of Heracles dominates the foreground from on high, illuminated by the last rays of sunlight (enter the town from the Valley of the Temples). Having reached the town by way of the Porta Aurea, two high tufa walls mark and protect the entrance to the old town. The Church of St Nicholas appears on the left, built of the same rich gold tufa which characterises the vestiges from Antiquity and the old town.

Story of Akragas – The site★★ upon which Agrigento was constructed has been inhabited since prehistoric times, but it was not until about 580 BC that a group of people from Gela, originally from Rhodes and Crete, decided to found Akragas, taking its name from one of the two rivers which confine the city. Under the tyrant **Phalaris** (570-554 BC), the city was fortified and organised politically. It is to him that the ancients attribute the idea of using a hollow bronze bull (commissioned from the sculptor Perillus) as an instrument of torture for his enemies. These unfortunate victims were imprisoned in the belly of the animal and roasted alive; the screams of the condemned emanating from the animal were likened to the lowing of a cow. Hated by his people, Phalaris was publicly stoned to death.

The city reached its golden age under the tyrant **Theron** (488-472 BC): military might, having defeated the Carthaginians several times, enforced a rule which, among other things, forbade them from making human sacrifices. Economic stability, coupled with political strength, favoured a flowering of the arts: the Temple of Zeus was built, literature and the performing arts flourished. The philosopher Empedocles (c 492-c 432 BC) advocated a moderate form of democracy which lasted for some time. In 406 BC, Akragas suffered a crushing defeat at the hands of the Carthaginians, who all but destroyed it. It was rebuilt in the second half of the 4C BC by Timoleon, a mercenary general from Corinth engaged in the fight against the Carthaginians in Sicily. It was at this time that the Greco-Roman quarter was built, the remains of which give some idea of the town's reformed urban planning. In 210 BC, Akragas was besieged by the Romans, who conquered the city and changed its name to Agrigentum.

B. Kaufmann

Temple of the Dioscuri

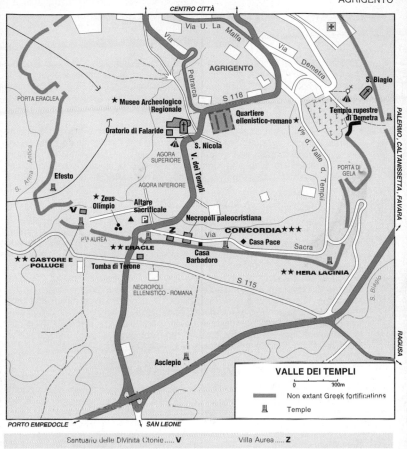

Via U. La Malta

Via

AGRIGENTO

Via Demetra

S. Biagio

PORTA ERACLEA

★ Museo Archeologico Regionale

S 118

Tempio rupestre di Demetra

Oratorio di Falaride

Quartiere ellenistico-romano ★

S. Nicola

AGORA SUPERIORE

V. dei Templi

Vie d' Valle d. Templi

PORTA DI GELA

Efesto

AGORA INFERIORE

★ Zeus Olimpio

Altare sacrificale

Necropoli paleocristiana

P.TA AUREA

Via

CONCORDIA★★★

Sacra

★★ ERACLE

Casa Pace

★★ CASTORE E POLLUCE

Casa Barbadoro

Tomba di Terone

★★ HERA LACINIA

S. Biagio

NECROPOLI ELLENISTICO · ROMANA

S 115

Asclepio

VALLE DEI TEMPLI

0   300m

Non extant Greek fortifications

Temple

PORTO EMPEDOCLE   SAN LEONE

Santuario delle Divinità Ctonie..... **V**   Villa Aurea .....**Z**

PALERMO, CALTANISSETTA, FAVARA

RAGUSA

Vicissitudes of Girgenti – With the fall of the Roman Empire, the city passed first to the Byzantines, then into Arab hands (9C). They built a new town centre higher up (at the heart of the modern town), calling it **Girgenti** — a name which lasted until 1927, when its Latin name was restored – which became the capital of the Berber kingdom. In 1087, the town was conquered by the Normans, prompting a new phase of prosperity and power which also enabled it to repel the frequent attacks of the Saracens. It was during the reign of Roger the Norman that the churches of San Nicola, Santa Maria dei Greci and San Biagio were built.

After a turbulent period which resulted in a gradual decline in the population of the town, Girgenti enjoyed a change in fortune, most notably in the 18C when the town centre was shifted from via Duomo to via Atenea. In 1860, the inhabitants, dissatisfied like the rest of the island with Bourbon misrule, enthusiastically supported Garibaldi's mission. During the Second World War, Agrigento suffered a number of air raids.

Two famous sons – Agrigento has nurtured famous personalities both in Antiquity and in more recent times. Among the most renowned are the philosopher **Empedocles** (5C BC), who died, according to legend, by leaping into the crater of Etna attempting to prove his divine powers (and, as if in confirmation of this, Etna is supposed to have thrown back his shoes, which had turned to bronze). In the 20C, the greatest figure with which it is associated is **Pirandello**, the famous playwright and novelist born in the small village of Caos *(see Il Caos, p 113)* below the town, where his ashes are interred. Pirandello enthusiasts should visit the **Biblioteca Luigi Pirandello** at 120 via Regione Sicilia, which also contains a vast selection of works by other Sicilian authors.

★★★LA VALLE DEI TEMPLI (VALLEY OF THE TEMPLES) ◷ *Tour 3hr*

Stretched out along the ridge, inappropriately called the "valley", and nestling in the area to the south of it, are a series of temples which were all erected in the course of a century (5C BC), as a testimony to the prosperity of the city at that time. Having been set ablaze by the Carthaginians in 406 BC, the buildings were restored by the Romans (1C BC) respecting their original Doric style. Their subsequent state of disrepair has been put down either to seismic activity or the

🎫 Via Cesare Battisti 15, ☎ 0922 20 454; Fax 0922 20 246.

GETTING TO AGRIGENTO

Visitors arriving in Sicily by **air** will land at either Punta-Raisi airport in Palermo (approximately 150km/93mi from Agrigento) or at Fontanarossa airport in Catania (approximately 160km/100mi). Cuffaro (☎ 0922 91 63 49) and Camilleri & Argento (☎ 0922 47 27 98) **bus companies** operate services from Agrigento to Palermo, while SAIS (☎ 0922 59 59 33) links the city with Catania. The bus terminal is situated in piazza Rosselli.

For **train** enthusiasts, the only enjoyable option is the Palermo-Agrigento Centrale service (make sure you don't leave the train at Agrigento Bassa!); the journey takes two hours and a number of services run daily. Train connections to other towns are long and tiring and the bus is usually a better option. Agrigento Centrale train station is located in piazza Marconi (☎ 0922 25 531).

CULTURAL EVENTS

Stoai – The atmosphere of the age-old covered market where shop-stalls once stood opposite each other among the arcades, survives just outside Agrigento (via Cavalleri Magazzeni, 1 ☎ 0922 60 66 23; fax 0922 60 83 53) in a multimedia environment used for craft shows and other events. A **show** staged in the evening (reservation only, 25 000L) presents the history of the city. Spectators, who are welcomed by the wealthy Greek Gellia (5C BC), will witness one of the most lavish weddings of Antiquity, between Timareta, the daughter of Antisthenes, and Menander. The show is a lively and colourful pageant which enacts the most important events to take place during the island's dramatic history, including scenes in an Arab market, a puppet show portraying the battles between the Normans and Saracens and the feast of the black San Calogero. The last scenes are dedicated to the great Pirandello, who was born near Agrigento.

WHERE TO STAY

Hotels are subdivided into three categories, each based on the price of a double room *(for further information see p 22)*, and are listed in alphabetical order. Visitors are advised to check prices and to book well in advance.

CAMP SITE

Torre Salsa has a camp site situated in an attractive, peaceful site by the beach, just 30min from the Valley of the Temples. Perfect for a picnic or a refreshing dip. Take the Torre Salsa exit from SS 115. ☎ 0922 84 70 74.

destructive fury of the Christians backed by an edict of the Emperor of the Eastern Empire, Theodosius (4C). The only one to survive intact is the Temple of Concord which, in the 6C, was converted into a Christian church. During the Middle Ages, masonry was removed to help construct other buildings. In particular, the Temple of Zeus, known locally as the Giant's Quarry, provided material for the church of San Nicola and the 18C part of the jetty at Porto Empedocle.

All the buildings face east, respecting the Classical criterion (both Greek and Roman) that the entrance to the *cella* (Holy of Holies) where the statue of the god was housed should be illuminated by the rays of the rising sun, the source and blood of life. On the whole, the temples are Doric and conform to the hexastyle format (that is, with six columns at the front), the exception being the Tèmple of Zeus, which had seven engaged columns articulating the wall that encloses the building. Built of limestone tufa, the temples provide a particularly impressive sight at dawn, and even more so at sunset when they are turned a warm shade of gold.

(The Greek form of the names of the divinities has been used to describe the temples, with the Latin equivalents given in brackets.) It is advisable to start a visit with the archaeological site around the Temple of Zeus as this is open at restricted times.

Sacrificial altar – Just beyond the entrance, on the right, slightly set back, are the remains of an enormous altar, used for large-scale sacrifices. As many as 100 oxen could be sacrificed at one time. The Italian word *ecatombe*, used today to mean a disaster, actually comes from the Greek words meaning to kill 100 – *Hecatòn* – oxen – *bôus*.

★**Tempio di Zeus Olimpico (Giove)** – Having been razed to the ground, the Temple of Zeus (Jupiter) was re-erected following the victory of the people of Agrigentum (allied with the Syracusans) over the Carthaginians at Himera (in about 480 BC) as a gesture of thanks to Zeus. It was one of the largest temples built in ancient times, being 113m/371ft long by 36m/118ft wide, and is thought never to have been completed. The entablature was supported by half-columns 20m/66ft high,

BUDGET

Camping Internazionale San Leone, via Lacco Ameno, San Leone *(S of Agrigento, see map of the Valley of the Temples)*, ☎ 0922 41 61 21 (pitches and bungalows), and **Camping Nettuno** Contr. Dune, San Leone, ☎ 0922 41 62 68 (pitches only).

MODERATE

Villa Eos – Contr. Cumbo, Villaggio Pirandello, SS 115. ☎ 0922 59 71 70; Fax 0922 59 71 88. Situated not far from Pirandello's birthplace, in a beautiful location near the sea, this hotel has 23 pleasant, well-appointed rooms (with air conditioning), a tennis court and garden with a swimming pool. An ideal place for resting up after a hard day's sightseeing.

EXPENSIVE

Villa Athena – Via dei Templi 33, ☎ 0922 59 62 88; Fax 0922 40 21 80. This restored 18C villa is situated in a delightful location, surrounded by citrus trees opposite the Temple of Concord. Not all the 40 rooms justify the price, but some, such as room 205, are truly splendid.

EATING OUT

RESTAURANTS

Kokalo'S – Via Cavaleri Magazzeni 3 (Valle dei Templi), ☎ 0922 60 64 27. This restaurant-cum-*pizzeria* offers traditional cuisine in a rustic setting. It also has a well-stocked wine bar. Approximately 35 000L per person.

Leon d'oro – Via Emporium 102, San Leone, ☎ 0922 41 44 00. Closed Mon. Situated in the seaside district of San Leone *(S of Agrigento, see map of the Valley of the Temples)*, this pleasant restaurant is renowned for its excellent fish dishes and extensive wine list. Approximately 60 000L per person.

LOCAL SPECIALITIES

The Benedictine nuns of the **Abbazia di Santo Spirito**, in via S. Spirito *(description below)*, make exquisite almond sweetmeats *(ricce, conchiglie, amaretti* and *paste nuove)* and the famous **cuscusu** (even its name recalls the more typical semolina dish using coarsely ground wheat, which is steamed and served with fish to make the Trapani variety of couscous) – a semolina pudding served in small bowls, sweetened with chocolate and pistachio nuts, and decorated with candied fruit.

which probably alternated with giant male caryatids (atlantes or **telamons**), an example of which can be seen in the local archaeological museum *(see below)*. A reproduction of an atlantes is displayed in the middle of the temple, giving some idea of scale proportional to the vast building. Instead of the more usual open colonnade, this temple is surrounded by a continuous screen wall sealing off the spaces between the columns which, inside, become square pilasters.

Some blocks still bear the marks made for lifting them into place: these are deep U-shaped incisions through which a rope was threaded and then, attached to a kind of crane, could be used to lift or haul the blocks one upon another.

★★**Tempio di Castore e Polluce o dei Dioscuri** – The Temple of Castor and Pollux or of the Dioscuri is the veritable symbol of Agrigento. Built during the last decades of the 5C BC, it is dedicated to the twins born from the union of Leda and Zeus while transformed into a swan.

Four columns and part of the entablature are all that remain of the temple, which was reconstructed in the 19C. Under one edge of the cornice is a rosette, one of the typical decorative motifs used.

On the right are the remains of what was probably a sanctuary dedicated to the Chthonic Deities (the gods of the underworld): Persephone (Proserpina), queen of the underworld, and her mother, Demeter (Ceres), the goddess of corn and fertility and patroness of agriculture. On the site are a **square altar**, probably used for sacrificing piglets, and another **round one** with a sacred well in the centre. This is probably where the rite of the Thesmophoria, a festival held in honour of Demeter, was celebrated by married women.

In the distance, last on the imaginary line linking all the temples of the valley, is the **Temple of Hephaistus** (Vulcan), of which little remains. According to legend, the god of fire and the arts had a forge under Etna where he fashioned thunderbolts for Zeus, assisted by the Cyclops.

Retrace your steps, leave the fenced area and follow Via dei Templi, on the other side of the road, on the right.

★★Tempio di Eracle (Ercole) – Conforming to the Archaic Doric style, the Temple of Heracles (Hercules) is the earliest of the group. The remains enable us to imagine how elegant this temple must have been. Today, a line of eight tapering columns stands erect, re-erected during the first half of this century.

From the temple, looking south, can be seen the erroneously called Tomb of Theron *(see end of this section)*.

Continuing along the path, deep ruts in the paving can be made out on the left: these are generally interpreted as having been caused by cartwheels. The reason for them being so deep has been put down to water erosion.

On the right is Villa Aurea, formerly the residence of Sir Alexander Hardcastle, a passionate patron of archaeology, who financed the re-erection of the columns of the Temple of Heracles.

Necropoli paleocristiana – The paleo-Christian necropolis is situated beneath the road, dug into the base rock, not far from the ancient walls of the city. There are various types of ancient tomb: *loculi* (cells or chambers for corpse or urn) and *arcosolia* (arched cavities like a niche), as often found in catacombs.

Before the Temple of Concord there is another group of tombs on the right.

★★★Tempio della Concordia – The Temple of Concord is one of the best-preserved temples surviving from Antiquity, thereby providing an insight into the elegance and majestic symmetry of other such buildings. The reason it has survived intact is due to its transformation into a church in the 6C AD. Inside the colonnade, the original arches through the *cella* walls of the Classical temple can still be made out. It is thought to have been built in about 430 BC, but it is not known to which god it was dedicated. The name Concord comes from a Latin inscription found in the vicinity. The temple is a typical example of the architectural refinement in temple building known as "optical correction": the columns are tapered (becoming narrower at the top so as to appear taller) and have a very slight convex curve at about two-thirds of the height of the column in order to counteract the illusion of concavity; those columns at the ends of the façade are also slightly inclined towards the central axis, avoiding the effect of divergence. This allows the observer standing at a certain distance from the temple to see a perfectly straight image. The frieze consists of standard Classical features: alternating triglyphs and metopes, without further low-relief ornamentation. The pediment is also devoid of decoration.

Antiquarium di Agrigento Paleocristiana (Casa Pace) ⊘ – Turn back through a section of the town, stopping perhaps to consult the various information boards set among the ruins that may be of interest: one in particular explains how the Temple of Concord was transformed into a basilica.

Antiquarium Iconografico della Collina dei Templi (Casa Barbadoro) ⊘ – In the modern but sympathetically designed building are collected together a series of drawings, engravings and prints of the Valley of the Temples as seen in the past by travellers undertaking the Grand Tour.

★★Tempio di Hera Lacinia (Giunone) – The Temple of Hera Lacinia (Juno) is situated at the top of the hill and is traditionally dedicated to the protector of matrimony and childbirth. The name *Lacinia* derives from an erroneous association with the sanctuary of the same name situated on the Lacinian promontory near Crotone.

The temple preserves its colonnade (albeit not in perfect condition), which was partially re-erected in the early 1900s. Inside, the columns of the *pronaos* and *opisthodomos* and the wall of the *cella* can still be seen. Built in about the mid-5C BC, it was set ablaze by the Carthaginians in 406 BC (evidence of burning is still visible on the walls of the *cella*).

To the east is the altar of the temple while, at the back of the building *(beside the steps)*, there is a cistern.

Tempio della Concordia

On the outskirts of the town are the so-called Tomb of Theron and the Temple of Asklepios (Aesculapius).

Tomba di Terone – *Also visible from the Caltagirone road.* The monument, erroneously believed to have been the tomb of the tyrant Theron, in fact dates from Roman times and was erected in honour of soldiers killed during the Second Punic War. Made of tufa, it is slighly pyramidal in shape and probably once had a pointed roof. The high base supports a second order with false doors and Ionic columns at the corners.

Tempio di Asclepio (Esculapio) – *Just beyond the Tomb of Theron, on the road to Caltanissetta. Look out for a sign (although obscured) on the right.* The ruins of this 5C BC temple are to be found in the middle of the countryside. It was dedicated to Aesculapius (Asklepios), the Greek god of medicine and son of Apollo – who it was believed had the power to heal the sick through dreams. The interior, it is thought, harboured a beautiful statue of the god by the Greek sculptor Myron.

ARCHAEOLOGICAL MUSEUM AND EXCURSIONS

★**Museo Archeologico Regionale** ⊙ – *Entrance from the cloisters of San Nicola.* Partially housed in the old monastery of San Nicola, the museum contains finds from the province of Agrigento.

Pre-Greek conquest – Among the prize exhibits is a fine two-handled cup with a very tall base, decorated with geometric patterns; its shape may stem from the custom of eating seated on the ground with the cup at chest level. Others of note include a small, elegant Mycenaean amphora, the mould of a **patera** with six animals (oxen) in relief, and two signet rings, again bearing animals. The most interesting, meanwhile, is a **dinos** (sacrificial vase) depicting the *triskelos* (literally "three legs"), the symbol of Sicily (in the guise of Trinacria, meaning "three-pointed").

Colonisation – The superb collection of **Attic vases**★ *(Room 3)* consists mainly of black-figure and red-figure ware, including the *cratere di Dionisio* (or cup of Bacchus) painted with Pan: the god of wine, dressed in flowing robes, holds a sprig of ivy in his hand, and has a leopard-skin draped over his arm. Among the other vessels, look for a *krater* with a white background, depicting the proud figure of Perseus on the point of liberating Andromeda from her chains.

B. Kaufmann

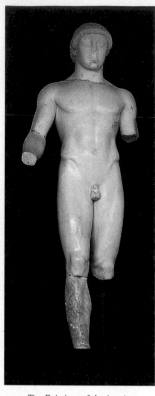

Museo/B. Kaufmann

The Ephebus of Agrigento

Room 4 contains a large number of votive statues, theatrical masks, moulds and other terracotta figures found during the excavations of the temples. The central well is filled by the massive figure of **Atlas★** from the Temple of Zeus, the only one to survive of the original 38 male caryatids which once adorned the building. On the left, in a case, are the heads of another three such powerful figures, one of which has well-preserved facial features.

The *Ephebus of Agrigento*★★ *(Room 10)* consists of a marble statue of a young man (5C BC), found in a cistern near the Temple of Demeter, which was transferred during the Norman period to the Church of San Biagio *(see below)*. It is thought to represent a young man from Agrigento who won various events at the Olympic games, and thus destined to be subjected to heroic status.

Other archaeological finds – Artefacts retrieved from various other sites in the province include sarcophagi, prehistoric remains and the magnificent *krater* from **Gela★★** *(Room 15)*, attributed to the painter of the Niobids. The upper half depicts a centauromachia (battle between centaurs and Lapiths) while the lower section shows scenes from battles between the Greeks and the Amazons.

Chiesa di San Nicola ⓥ – Built of tufa, the Church of St Nicholas was erected in the 13C by Cistercian monks in a transitional Romanesque to Gothic style. The stone blocks used were taken from the Giant's Quarry, as the ruined Temple of Zeus was known providing, as it did, an almost inexhaustible easy source of building material. The façade is dominated by two imposing reinforcing buttresses (added in the 16C), which flank a beautiful pointed-arched doorway.

The interior is enclosed within a single barrel-vaulted nave. Four chapels open off the south side. The second contains a fine **Roman sarcophagus★** (3C AD), known as the *Sarcophagus of Hippolytus and Phaedra*, with which Goethe was particularly smitten. Inspired by Greek prototypes, all four sides are sculpted in high relief, the compositions are animated by clean flowing lines and the figures are endowed with delicate features set in gentle expressions. The subject treated is the tragic story of Phaedra's unrequited love for her stepson Hippolytus, who is banished from the kingdom and killed by crazed horses under the shameful (and unfounded) accusation that he had tried to seduce her. On the sarcophagus *(going anti-clockwise, starting from the first long side)*, the hero is shown making preparations for a hunting expedition, at the moment when he rejects the message brought by Phaedra's nurse; Phaedra's resulting anguish and delirium, as she is waited upon by nine handmaidens; Hippolytus hunting wild boar on horseback and, finally, the death of the hero.

Beside the altar, on the left, is a fine 15C wooden crucifix, nicknamed *il Signore della Nave* (Lord of the Ship), which inspired Pirandello's short story of the same name included in his anthology entitled *Novelle per un Anno*. From the terrace before the church, there is a beautiful **view★** over the Valley of the Temples.

Oratorio di Falaride ⓥ – According to legend, the oratory occupies the site of the palace built by the tyrant Phalaris *(see Introduction)*, hence its name. The present monument was probably a small Greco-Roman temple, converted in Norman times.

Telamons and Atlantes (or Atlas figures)

These imposing giants from Agrigento, more often referred to as atlantes, are sometimes called Telamons (*Telamone* in Italian) after the Latin word derived by the Romans from the Greek, *Telamo(n)* which indicated their function, that is to carry or bear the structure. Their supporting role is accentuated by their position, with arms bent back to balance the weight upon their shoulders. The more common term alludes to the mythological figure Atlas, the giant and leader of the Titans who struggled against the gods of Olympus and was condemned by Zeus to support the weight of the sky on his head. When the earth was discovered to be spherical, he was often shown bearing the terrestrial globe on his shoulders.

Next to the oratory are the remains of an Ekklesiasterion, a small amphitheatre used for political meetings (from the Greek *ekklesia* – meeting), identified as an ancient agora (market place or place of assembly).

★**Greco-Roman quarter** ⊘ – This extensive urban complex contains the vestiges of houses in which survive fragments of ancient pavements laid with stone tesserae *(protected by roofing and plexiglass)* with geometric or figurative motifs. The network of streets follows the standard rules advocated by the Greek town planner Hippodamus of Miletus of having broad parallel avenues *(decumani)* bisected at right angles by secondary roads *(cardini)*.

Chiesa di San Biagio – *There is space to park in front of the cemetery. The church is on the left, and can be reached by a path.* The Norman church, erected in the 13C, stands on the remains of a **Greek temple** dedicated to Demeter. Just below the church, there is another more rudimentary **temple** to her (Tempio rupestre di Demetra) although inaccessible, which bears witness to the popularity of the cult of the goddess in ancient Sicily.

OLD TOWN CENTRE

The broad **viale della Vittoria**, shaded by trees, provides beautiful views of the Valley of the Temples and leads to a square before the station. On the right stands the 16C **Church of San Calogero**, dedicated to a saint who is particularly venerated in this area. The façade has a fine doorway with a pointed arch.

A little further on is piazza Aldo Moro, where the lovely **via Atenea** begins. Along this thoroughfare are to be found: on the right **Palazzo Celauro** (best admired from the street of the same name) where Goethe sojourned when on his Grand Tour and, on the left, the Franciscan Church of the Immacolata (Blessed Virgin), altered in the 18C. To the right of the church, beyond the gate, can be seen the façade of the 14C **Conventino Chiaramontano**, so called because of the style of the portal between the two-light windows.

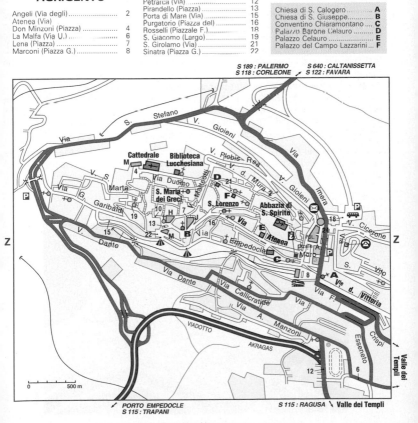

Traffic restricted in town centre

Return to via Atenea and continue to piazza del Purgatorio, which is overlooked by the splendid façade of **San Lorenzo★** ⊘ (18C), its golden ochre tufa contrasting dramatically with the whiteness of the doorway, ornamented with twisted columns. The **interior** contains stuccoes by Serpotta and a painting by Guido Reni. Nearby, level with via Bac Bac, stands San Giuseppe, a **church** dedicated to St Joseph.

In piazza Pirandello is the Town Hall, formerly a Dominican monastery (17C) and an adjacent church with a fine Baroque façade overlooking an elegant flight of steps. Set back, on the left side of the church, is the bell-tower.

★Abbazia di Santo Spirito ⊘ – *From via Atenea, take via Porcello, follow the steps up salita di Santo Spirito.* The church and its dependent convent date from the 13C. Sadly, the state of the buildings is gradually deteriorating. The front of the church has a fine Gothic doorway with a rose-window above. The Baroque interior consists of a single nave. On the walls are four high **reliefs★** attributed to Giacomo Serpotta: *The Nativity and The Adoration of the Magi* on the right, *The Flight into Egypt* and the *Presentation of Jesus at the Temple* on the left. To the right of the façade is a doorway into the cloisters, leading under two of the great buttresses supporting the church. At the far end is the beautiful **entrance★** to the chapter-house, consisting of an elegant doorway through a pointed arch, flanked by highly decorative Arabo-Norman two-light windows.

Via San Girolamo – This street is lined with elegant *palazzi*: of note in passing is the front of the 19C **Palazzo del Campo-Lazzarini** at no 14 (opposite Santa Maria del Soccorso) and that of the 18C **Palazzo Barone Celauro** at no 86, which has two rows of small balconies gracing the windows which are articulated with semicircular and triangular pediments.

Biblioteca Lucchesiana ⊘ – The library founded in 1765 by Bishop Lucchesi Palli contains more than 45 000 ancient books and manuscripts. The central hall, dominated by a statue of the bishop, is lined with beautiful wooden shelving. Books on profane subjects are kept to the left of the statue, while religious texts are on the right. This division is echoed by the two sculpted wooden figures behind the statue: on the left is a woman meditating, on the right, a woman holding a mirror, symbolising the search for truth in the inner self.

Cathedral ⊘ – The side of the cathedral facing onto via del Duomo still bears traces of the Noman original (notably the 11C windows). The main church was rebuilt in the 13C-14C, and remodelled in the 17C; it was then restored after the landslide of 1966. A broad double stairway leads up to the main door, marked by a tympanum, flanked by pairs of pilasters. On the right stands the unfinished bell-tower (1470), which on the south side is articulated with four blind arches in the shape of an inverted ship's keel, and a series of pointed arches above.

Inside★, the nave has a beautiful **wooden ceiling★** with tie-beams decorated with figures of the saints, painted in the 16C. The section beyond the triumphal arch is coffered (18C); the great two-headed eagle in the centre is the symbol of the Royal House of Aragon. The Baroque exuberance of the choir, with its angels and golden garlands, contrasts dramatically with the sobriety of the nave.

Santa Maria dei Greci – The 14C church dedicated to St Mary of the Greeks was built upon the foundations of a temple dedicated to Athena; it celebrated mass according to the Greek-Orthodox liturgy.

The chapter-house doorway, Abbazio di Santo Spirito

Ritorno

*A solitary house set amid my native
countryside: up here, on this plateau
of blue clay, to which the submissive
bitter African sea sends a fervour of
foam,
I see you always, from afar,
if I think of that moment in which my
life
opened up minutely to the immense,
vain world:
this, this, I say, was where I set out
along the path of life.*

Luigi Pirandello
in *Zampogna*, Rome 1901

Pirandello's Pine

EXCURSIONS

Il Caos – *In the Villaseta district, 6km/4mi W on the Porto Empedocle road (S 115). Turn left after Morandi viaduct.* This village, on the outskirts of Agrigento, was the birthplace of **Luigi Pirandello**, whose **house** ⊘ stands alone and silent in the middle of the countryside. The first floor of the writer's house is open to the public. A short film documents the most salient moments of his life and career, including the Nobel Prize award ceremony and his funeral. Pirandello last visited the house in 1934, but by then the house had been sold and he saw it only from a distance. The rooms contain written and illustrative material pertaining to the writer and Marta Abba, the actress to whom he became very close in the latter period of his life, pictures of stage performances, hand-written documents, editions of his plays and novels.

A small path to the right of the house leads to the **pine-tree** at the foot of which is buried the urn containing Pirandello's ashes. Beyond, lies the sea.

The Biblioteca Luigi Pirandello, located in Agrigento at 120 via Regione Sicilia, contains not only many works about the writer but also a vast selection of works by other Sicilian authors.

★**Scala dei Turchi** – *Access from Realmonte or Porto Empedocle. In both cases, follow signs to Madison Hotel. From Realmonte, the rock is visible once you have passed the road down to the hotel. A little further on, a small path (easy to find in summer because of the number of cars parked nearby) leads down to the beach.* This impressive smooth, white rock is shaped into a number of steps which slope gently towards the sea and is a popular place for sunbathing in summer. The other side of the "steps" *(scala)* has been more obviously shaped by the wind and the sea, forming a series of narrow, winding, wave-like formations.

EXCURSION INLAND

Favara – *12km/7mi NE of Agrigento (SS 640, then take a turn-off to the right).* A town of Arab origin, Favara reached its apogee under the powerful Chiaramonte family (13C-14C) who oversaw the building of the massive castle. Piazza dei Vespri is dominated by the imposing façade of the 18C Chiesa Madre, its tall dome resting gently on a ring of arches.

Racalmuto – *17km/10.5mi NE of Favara (head back to the SS 640, then take the turn-off for Racalmuto).* Fame for this little town comes from its status as the birthplace of **Leonardo Sciascia**, the 20C Sicilian writer and astute commentator who spent much of his life here. He is buried in the small cemetery.

In the centre of the town are the remains of the Chiaramonte castle, marked by two large towers.

Sant'Angelo Muxaro – *30km/19mi NW. From Racalmuto take the Aragona/Santa Elisabetta road and then the turn-off for Sant'Angelo.* Sant'Angelo clings to its craggy mountainside overlooking the surrounding countryside. It has been alleged that this was the capital of the ancient kingdom of Cocalus, that mythical king who is meant to have received Daedalus on his flight from Minos *(see HERACLEA MINOA)*. The 18C front elevation of the Chiesa Matrice is divided into three sections by strongly accented pilaster strips framing the three doorways, and rectangular windows above.

Grotta del Principe – *By the side of the road, just outside town. Leave the car on the verge so that it does not obstruct the traffic. Although the distance is short, the going is rough.* The Prince's Cavern is a proto-historic tomb (9C BC) consisting of two circular chambers. The first, the larger of the two with a domed ceiling, comprised the atrium for the actual burial chamber.

Bivona – *30km/19mi NW. There is a magnificent panorama from the road at Alessandria della Rocca.* At the centre of Bivona stands a lovely **Arabo-Norman archway**, all that remains of the former Chiesa Matrice. A little further on, **Palazzo Marchese Greco** preserves its fine, albeit damaged, façade ornamented with wrought-iron balconies and elegant Baroque stonework. The cornices of the French windows are decorated with bunches of grapes and other varieties of fruit.

Castronuovo di Sicilia – *30km/19mi NE. The road to Santo Stefano Quisquina offers some lovely views.* The picturesque little hamlet comprises a number of houses neatly built with carefully dressed stone. The little piazza is overlooked by the Chiesa Madre della Santissima Trinità (1404) and its fine bell-tower.

Mussomeli – *32km/20mi SE.* Mussomeli crams itself onto the bare hillside, in a place high enough to enjoy a scenic position. The houses jostle one with another, separated only by very narrow streets, apparently cowering below the watchful gaze of the **Castello Manfredonico** which perches on its lonely rock outcrop. Fort and rock are completely fused with man-made sections merely complementing those provided by nature.

The centre of the town is marked by the tall front elevation of the Chiesa Matrice (altered in the 17C) which peeps over the rooftops. Some way below stands the 16C white limestone Santuario della Madonna dei Miracoli with its attractively arranged doorway set between two spiral columns and broken pediment.

Gole dell'ALCANTARA★

Catania and Messina

Michelin map 432 N 27

Lost in the sands of time, a small volcano north of Mount Etna woke and poured forth enormous quantities of lava which flowed down to the sea and beyond, to form Capo Schisò. The tortuous route taken by the river of lava was followed by a torrent of water which ploughed a channel through it, smoothing the lava and clearing away the aggregate. Towards the end of its journey, the water encountered more friable ground and, sweeping onwards, exposed two sheer cliffs of very hard basalt that had cooled and hardened into fascinating prism-like shapes. This is the gorge, only part of which is now accessible.

The name of the river, and of its valley, *Al Qantarah*, dates back to the period of Arab occupation and refers to the arched bridge built by the Romans that was capable of withstanding the force of the river in full spate, still an impressive sight even today.

WHEN TO GO

The gorge is accessible when the water-level is low, for a stretch of 50m/164ft to 200m/656ft. At the entrance to the gorge, waders can be hired to keep out the perennially freezing cold waters of the river. Under normal conditions, it is possible to walk up river from May until September. During the rest of the year, only the entrance to the gorge is accessible. There is a lift to take visitors back up to the top of the gorge. Special camping facilities are available nearby.

The gorge ⊘ – The descent on foot affords a spectacular **view★** of the whole at the entrance to the gorge.

Once level with the river-bed, the stone cliffs tower some 50m/164ft above the narrow tongue of water awkwardly stretching their cumbersome monumentality upwards: geometric black forms seem to confront each other ominously as they surge skywards. Their axes intersect, forming pentagonal and hexagonal prisms, irregular shapes which interplay with the light, creating forms both graceful and monstrous. Their massive bulk, exaggerated by shadow, seems accentuated further up the gorge, where the world suddenly seems to be composed of three elements: rock, water and sky. All the while, the sun defines contour and profile by casting its bright light deep into the darkness; occasionally this is refracted into a thousand tiny mirrors by miniscule droplets of water that have been ejected by the waterfalls, which then collect together into rivulets that stream down the sheer rock face.

THE ALCANTARA VALLEY

Allow approximately 1 day (including the visit to the gorges and the walk along the river bed).

Etna looms over the Alcantara Valley, alternately featuring among, then disappearing behind the hills as the road winds its way, providing an ever changing kaleidoscope of marvellous **views★**.

Giardini Naxos – *See NAXOS.*

Continuing along the road, on the left, appear some disconcerting olive-wood sculptures by Francesco Lo Giudice, known as *il mago* (the magician).

★Alcantara Gorge – *See above.*

Motta Camastra – A road off to the right leads to the small town which stands at an altitude of 453m/1 486ft.

Francavilla di Sicilia – It was here that a violent battle took place between some Spaniards and Austrians, an event that is

Walking in the Alcantara Gorge

M. Magni/MICHELIN

recorded for posterity by a series of prints preserved in the Capuchin monastery which stands on top of the hill nearby. Founded in the 16C, the monastery still has a few original cells and houses a small museum about life in this offshoot of the Franciscan Order. In the church there are several works of art, including an 18C wooden aumbry for the tools of the Eucharist bearing a pelican plucking the flesh from its breast to feed its young, a symbol of the sacrifice of Christ.

Castiglione di Sicilia – Castel Leone (now reduced to a ruin) dominates the town from on high, set as it is on its amazing rocky spur of tufa as if fused to the earth. The **site★** of the castle has been a look-out point since ancient times. From here stretch magnificent **views★★** over the town and Etna. To the east lie the ruins of a fortress dating from 750 BC.

The main monuments are clustered around the highest part of the town.

The 18C church, **San Antonio** ⟨·⟩, has a concave façade and a campanile built of lava with an onion-shaped dome. The interior, decked with polychrome marble, has a magnificent triumphal arch (1796). There is a fine wooden organ in the chancel. **San Pietro** preserves in its campanile some of the primitive Norman original relieved by blind arcading. **Santa Maria della Catena**, preceded by a flight of steps, has a fine doorway with spiral columns.

At one time...

the Alcantara River flowed calmly along its course without crags, rapids or sheer drops, making the valley fertile. The people there, however, were evil: they hurt each other and had no respect for nature.

Two brothers lived in the valley and cultivated a field of wheat. One was blind. When the time came to divide up the harvest, the sighted farmer took the grain measure and began to share out the wheat. One measure for himself and one for his brother. Then, overtaken by greed, he decided to keep most of the harvest for himself. An eagle, happening to fly overhead, witnessed what was happening and reported the incident to God, who hurled a thunderbolt at the cheat, killing him outright. The thunderbolt also struck the heap of grain that had unjustly been set aside, turning it into a mountain of red earth from which poured a river of lava which flowed down to the sea.

Legend from the book entitled *Al Qantarah* by L Danzuso and E Zinna.

Off the road to Mojo Alcantara, a right fork leads to the remains of a **Byzantine chapel** (or *cuba*) dating from the 7C-9C.

Mojo Alcantara – The name of this little town comes from a small volcano which, when it erupted, gave rise to the creation of the gorge. Today, it is a green innocuous-looking cone.

Randazzo – *See RANDAZZO.*

From Randazzo it is possible to join the Circumtenea *(see ETNA)* or continue on towards the Nebrodi Mountains *(see SANTO STEFANO DI CAMASTRA).*

BAGHERIA

Palermo – Population 54 165
Michelin map 432 M 22

Bagheria is renowned for its Baroque villas, built from the 17C onwards by wealthy aristocrats from Palermo as summer residences. Alas, not all of them are visible and only a few, including the famous Villa Palagonìa, are open to the public.

Villa Butera – *This stands at the southern end of corso Butera.* The villa was built in the second half of the 17C by Prince Branciforti di Raccuia. Although now in a sad state of repair, the villa preserves on its eastern side (which can be seen by going around the left side of the building) an imposing tufa doorway to the *piano nobile* betraying Spanish influence: a drape held in place by ribbons and festoons of fruit and flowers bears an inscription in Spanish.

★**Villa Palagonìa** ◷ – The entrance is at the rear of the villa which faces onto the small piazza Garibaldi, at the end of the main street of the town, the fine corso Umberto I. This most celebrated of Bagheria villas, built in 1715, is an elegant building of unusual shape: the façade is concave, almost as if to welcome the visitor, while the rear is convex. The house was constructed by Prince Gravina's father, but it was the prince's idea to add the exuberant **sculptural decoration**★ along the top of the wall in front of the façade. This arrangement, consisting of about 60 crude and often monstrous tufa statues, has provoked various esoteric interpretations. They include mythological figures, ladies, gentlemen, musicians, soldiers, dragons and grotesque beasts with threatening expressions, creating a surreal atmosphere. What is especially peculiar is that the statues are placed facing in towards the villa and not, as was usual, the outside world with the idea of keeping evil spirits at bay. The outcome provides an insight into the mind and spirit of the prince, who aimed to surprise, if not frighten, his guests. This eccentricity runs through the villa's reception rooms. The great oval entrance hall, painted with *trompe l'œil* frescoes illustrating four of the twelve Labours of Heracles, leads into the Hall of Mirrors, an appropriate name given its ceiling encrusted with mirrors set at different angles, so as to distort the reflection of anyone entering the room, projecting it through a kaleidoscope of images multiplied a hundredfold to infinity or reduced to nothing with each step taken (today, sadly, this magical effect is barely discernible). The upper part of the hall is ornamented with a *trompe l'œil*,

A few of the fantastical figures

a balustrade enclosing a series of inquisitive animals and birds; these caught occasionally by a mirror in the ceiling, are reflected as though they existed under an open sky. The illusion is reinforced further by other decorative effects as panels of real marble are set alongside others of painted paper under glass: the real may be differentiated from the unreal from a few feet away.

Villa Cattolica – *Via Consolare 9 (SS 113). From the motorway, cross Bagheria following the signs to Aspra.* This massive, square building, built in 1736 by Giuseppe Bonanni Filangeri, Prince of Cattolica, houses the **Civica Galleria d'Arte Moderna e Contemporanea Renato Guttuso** ⊘, a modern art gallery which exhibits works by the painter and other artists close to him. Most of the works were donated by Guttoso to his native town in 1973. The villa gardens harbour a Camera dello Scirocco *(see p 272)* and the **tomb** of the painter, designed by his friend, Giacomo Manzù.

CACCAMO

Palermo – Population 8 650
Michelin map 432 N 23

Clinging to a rocky precipice among the lower spurs of Monte San Calogero, this pretty little town was probably founded by the Phoenicians. The earliest factual records, however, relate to Norman times when Camarina served as the crucible for the Sicilian barons' revolt against the Emperor William I (the Bad). During the Aragonese occupation, it fell subject to Spanish feudal lords; in the 14C it was assimilated into the dominion of the Chiaramonte, passing subsequently into the hands of various dynasties, notably the Prades-Cabrera, the Amato and the De Spuches families.

SIGHTS

★**Castle** ⊘ – *Entrance from via Termitana.* This is one of the best preserved castles in Sicily. It stands on a rocky spur and is arranged on several different levels, the result of spiralling extensions being added through the 14C, 15C and 17C. The main unit, complete with all the features of a small fortress, probably dates from the 11C. The defensive elements were reinforced by the Chiaramonte, while in the 17C, under Amato ownership, these were relaxed as the castle was transformed into a noble residence with terraces, and when single and two-arched windows were inserted.

Tour – Beyond the first gate, a 17C ramp leads up to a second gate. The broad, paved courtyard provides access to the Torre Mastra, from the top of which magnificent **views**★ open out in a full circle to include Termini Imerese, Mongerbina, Capo Zafferano, Rocca Busambra and the Vicari Castle. A fine 18C doorway leads through to the Sala delle Armi or Salone della Congiura where the rebellious barons gathered before confronting William the Bad. The interior of the castle has recently undergone radical renovation. The apartments to the left of the Weapons Hall give access to the Torre Gibellina; the rooms to the right include the Salotto dei Nobili with its lovely five-bay window, before leading out onto a terrace with a panoramic view.

Return to corso Umberto I and turn right to piazza Duomo.

★**Piazza Duomo** – The square provides an attractive open space split between two levels. The elevated northern side is fronted by a harmonious group of buildings, namely the **Palazzo del Monte di Pietà** (17C) flanked on the left by the **Oratorio del Santissimo Sacramento** and the **Chiesa delle Anime Sante del Purgatorio** on the right. This very special arrangement constitutes a sort of theatrical stage from which to survey the lower part of the square: the balustrade, which serves both to separate and to link the two levels, is surmounted by four statues representing the Blessed Giovanni Liccio, Santa Rosalia, San Nicasio and San Teotista.

Chiesa Madre ⊘ – The main church, dedicated to St George, stands on the western side of the piazza. On one side it clings to the rocky spur which rises to the castle, while on the other, it is supported by sturdy arcades and bastions. **Inside** hangs the dramatic, strongly highlighted painting of *The Miracle of Sant'Isidoro Agricola* (1641) by Mattia Stomer, while in the chapel of the Holy Sacrament, above the inlaid marble altar sits an unusual ciborium ornamented with marble reliefs by the Gagini School (15C). Also worth noting in passing, are the white marble font beside the high altar (1466) and the entablature over the sacristy entrance *(right transept)* with its delicate low reliefs by **Francesco Laurana**.
Down corso Umberto I, and off to the right, is piazza San Marco which is lined with the buildings of a former Franciscan monastery, the Church of the Annunciation with its twin bell-towers, the Chiesa della Badia and what was the 14C church of **San Marco** (the doorway with its pointed arch is still visible).

San Benedetto alla Badia ⊘ – The single-nave church has a superb majolica **floor** attributed to Nicolò Sarzana from Palermo (18C), although this is badly damaged in places and mostly covered by carpets. When possible, it is worth climbing up to the women's gallery, once the preserve of nuns of a closed order from the convent which once stood adjacent to the church. From the gallery there is an excellent view of the whole church, and, in particular, of the very fine wrought-iron railings (18C) at the far end. It is worth admiring the **stuccoes** in the apse by Bartolomeo Sanseverino (18C): the lunette, above, depicts *The Dinner at Emmaus*; the statues on either side of the altar are allegories of *Chastity* and *Obedience*.

Return to corso Umberto I. Just before piazza Torina turn left uphill.

Santa Maria degli Angeli ⊘ **(or San Domenico)** – The two-aisled church has a fine trussed **wooden ceiling** ornamented with paintings of Dominican saints (severely damaged by humidity). In the chapel dedicated to Santa Maria degli Angeli *(on the right)* is a lovely *Madonna and Child* by Antonello Gagini (1516), and, on the under-side of the main arch, a series of small paintings by Vincenzo La Barbera depicting The Mysteries of the Rosary (17C).

Before leaving Caccamo, it is well worth walking to the far side of town and turning right (signposted "Centro Storico"): at a certain point somewhere along this almost circular route, there is a wonderful **view**★ over the whole town with, down below the **Torre Pizzarone** – at one time part of the town's external defences – the Torre delle Campane (now the cathedral bell-tower), and the purpose-built bell-tower standing on the left of the Chiesa dell'Annunziata.

CALTAGIRONE★

Catania – Population 39 128
Michelin map 432 P 25

Visitors arriving in Caltagirone cannot fail to notice the outward signs of a thriving industry now synonymous with the name of the place: brightly painted ceramics not only fill shop windows with a profusion of vases, plates and other household goods, they decorate the bridges, balustrades, frontages and balconies. This bears witness to an art which, in this area, is as old as the origins of the town itself.

City of earthenware potteries – The reason behind it all rests in the inexhaustible deposits of clay in the area. The ease with which this raw material can be extracted has underpinned the success of the terracotta potteries, in manufacturing tableware especially, for distribution throughout the region. This soon became one of the town's main activities. Local shapes gave way to Greek influences (as trade increased), pro-duction improved, becoming more efficient and more precise with the introduction of the wheel (by the Cretans in about 1000 BC). The critical turning point, however, was the arrival of the Arabs (9C), for with them, practices were changed irrevocably. They introduced Eastern designs and, more importantly, introduced glazing tech-niques: a useful and innovative development which even rendered objects impermeable to water. The art became more sophisticated as exquisite geometric patterning and stylised decoration were modelled on plants and animals. The dominant colours were blue, green and yellow. The significance of the Arab contribution is honoured in the town's name which, according to the most intriguing hypothesis, might be derived from the Moorish for *castle* or *fortress of vases*.

With the advent of Spanish domination, tastes and demands changed. The painted decoration was predominantly monochrome (blue or brown) and comprised organic designs or the coats of arms of some noble family or religious order. The town enjoyed a period of notable prosperity thanks also to the area's other industries: honey pro-duction, which generated particularly high yields here, meant that apiculturists soon ranked among the potters' most assiduous customers. The *cannatari* (from the word *cannate* meaning jug) were supplemented by *quartari* (amphorae with a capacity of 1.25l equal to a *quartare*, a quarter of a barrel). The artisans organised themselves into confraternities which, in turn, helped build workshops in quite a large area south of the town but still within the town walls. In addition to ceramic table- and kitchen-wares, Caltagirone established its reputation for making tiles and ornamental plaques for domes and floors, church and palazzo façades. Among the great artists to work here during the 16C and 17C, the Gagini brothers and Natale Bonajuti are perhaps the most renowned. The main decorative elements are the same as those featured on domestic wares: geometric, floral and stylised motifs, such as the small Persian palm leaf transcribed from Tuscan designs (Montelupo). In the 17C, decorative medallions filled with figurative vignettes or effigies of saints (typical in products from all over Sicily) became popular; a century later, moulded relief was applied to vases with elab-orate volutes and polychrome decoration.

With the 19C there began a period of decline, arrested in part by the production of fig-urines, often used in Nativity cribs. In the second half of the century, this art-form reached new heights of excellence in the hands of such experts as Bongiovanni and Vaccaro.

🏛 Palazzo Libertini, ☎ 0933 53 809; Fax 0933 54 610.

WHERE TO STAY

La Scala 2 – Piazza Umberto 1, ☎ 0933 51 552. The owners of La Scala restaurant in the main square have 6 simple, but well-kept rooms without private bathrooms (2 shared bathrooms; 60 000L for a double room).

EATING OUT

La Scala – Scala S Maria del Monte 8, ☎ 0933 57 781. This restaurant is housed in a fine 18C building to the right of the steps leading up to Santa Maria del Monte. Spring water, the equivalent of running water at the time when the *palazzo* was built, still flows in some of the rooms on the ground floor. Meals are approximately 70 000L.

SHOPPING

Glazed earthenware is offered for sale by endless numbers of shops in the town centre and on either side of the Scala di Santa Maria del Monte. For an overview of what is produced locally, seek out the Mostra Mercato in via Vittorio Emanuele: this provides a venue for displaying representative examples of work by all the town's craftsmen.

THE TOWN

Via Roma, Caltagirone's main street, bisects the town, cutting its way to the famous steps up to Santa Maria del Monte, and continuing on up to the church entrance. Its way is lined with some of the town's most interesting buildings, many with maiolica decoration. Near its start, on the left, begins the elegant balustraded enclosure of the Villa Comunale (a public garden) and the Teatrino (housing the Ceramics Museum).

Bandstand

★**Villa Comunale** – This rather wonderful garden was designed in the late 19C by GB Basile, modelled on English gardens. The edge with via Roma is marked by an ornamental balustrade topped with vases with disturbingly devilish faces; these alternate with bright green pinecones and maiolica light stands. The garden is threaded by a series of shaded pathways which open out into secluded spaces ornamented by ceramic sculptures, figures and fountains. The most impressive open area is graced with a delightful bandstand decorated with Moorish-looking elements and glazed panels of maiolica.

Museo della Ceramica ⊙ – The **Teatrino**, an unusual 18C building decorated with maiolica tiles, houses this interesting museum which relates the history of the local ceramic industry from prehistoric times to the beginning of the 20C. The diffusion and importance of moulded clay is exemplified by an elegant 5C BC **krater**★ bearing a potter working at his wheel being watched by a young apprentice.

The 17C is particularly well represented, with albarello drug jars painted in shades of yellow, blue and green, and amphorae and vases with medallions depicting religious or profane subjects.

Further along via Roma, on the right, is the splendid 18C balcony-cum-terrace of **Casa Ventimiglia**, which is named after the local artist responsible for its maiolica decoration. Beyond the **Tondo Vecchio**, the curved stone and brick building, sits the remarkable façade *(on the right)* of **San Francesco d'Assisi**; this overlooks the maiolica bridge, also named after St Francis, which carries the road into the very heart of the town. Beyond the little Church of **Sant'Agata**, the seat of the ceramicists' confraternity, stands an austere prison block built under Bourbon rule.

Carcere Borbonico – The prison, a imposing square sandstone building, has been greatly improved by recent restoration. It was designed in the late 18C by the Sicilian architect Natale Bonajuto and used as a prison for about a century. It now houses the town's small municipal museum, thereby allowing access to its ponderous interior.

Museo Civico ⊙ – The displays on the second floor of this museum comprise a permanent exhibition of contemporary work in maiolica. One room harbours the gilt wood and silver litter of San Giacomo (late 16C), which continued to be used in processions on 25 July until 1966: note the caryatids' delicate facial features. The third room is devoted to the Vaccaro family: two generations of painters active during the 19C; Mario's *Little Girl Praying* is especially evocative.

The first floor accommodates the municipal art gallery containing works by Sicilian painters.

Piazza Umberto I – The most prominent building to face onto the square is the **Duomo di San Giuliano**, a great Baroque edifice that has been subjected to much remodelling, the most drastic involving the replacement of the whole front in the early 1900s. It comes into view from the steps below Santa Maria del Monte, at the foot of which, on the left, stands **Palazzo Senatorio** with the courtyard **Corte Capitaniale** behind, a fine example of early civic architecture (1601) by one of the Gaginis.

To the right, a stairway leads up to the **Chiesa del Gesù** ⊙, which harbours a *Deposition* by Filippo Paladini *(third chapel on the left)*. Behind it nestles the **Chiesa di Santa Chiara** with its elegant façade attributed to **Rosario Gagliardi** (18C) and, beyond again, the early 20C Officina Elettrica, the front of which was designed by **Ernesto Basile**.

Return to piazza Umberto I.

★**Scala di Santa Maria del Monte** – This long flight of steps acts as a conjunction between the old town (at the top), which in the 17C accommodated the seat of religious authority, and the new town, where the municipal administrative offices were in fact located. On either side of this axis lie the old quarters of San Giorgio and San Giacomo; among their narrow streets, both conceal some fine buildings *(see below)*. The 142 lava stair treads are complemented by highly decorative multi-coloured maiolica tile uprights bearing various combinations of geometric and organic designs inspired by the animal kingdom, echoing Moorish, Norman, Spanish, Baroque or some other more contemporary influence. Once a year, the stairway is brought to life by a multitude of flickering little coloured candles which pick out a kaleidoscope of ever changing patterns: swirls, volutes, plant tendrils, female figures and the recurring emblem of the town, an eagle emblazoned with a crossed shield. This fabulous spectacle, when thousands of little candles wrapped in red, yellow or green paper are placed on the steps and lit, takes place on the nights of San Giacomo, 24 and 25 July.

Presiding from the top of the steps, sits **Santa Maria del Monte** ⊙, formerly the town's main church and headquarters of the religious authorities. The high altar is graced with the Conadomini Madonna, a 13C painting on panel.

San Giorgio and San Giacomo quarters – Via L Sturzo, leading off to the right from the foot of the steps, has a number of fine buildings including **Palazzo della Magnolia** (no 74), which is ornamented by exuberant and elaborate terracotta decoration by Enrico Vella. Just beyond the *palazzo* are two 19C churches: San Domenico and **Santissimo Salvatore** ⊙. The latter contains the mausoleum of the politician Don Luigi Sturzo, and a *Madonna and Child* by **Antonello Gagini**. At the far end of via Sturzo stands the **Chiesa di San Giorgio** (11C-13C); this harbours the panel painting of the **Mystery of the Trinity**★, attributed to the Flemish artist Roger van der Weyden.

The logical extension of via Sturzo, on the opposite side of the steps, is via Vittorio Emanuele. This leads to the **Basilica di San Giacomo**, dedicated to the town's patron saint, in which a Gagini silver casket containing the relics of the saint is preserved.

ON THE EDGE OF TOWN

A stroll through the typical back streets of the old quarters on the periphery of town will reveal various unexpected surprises, like the neo-Gothic façade of the Chiesa di San Pietro (in the district of the same name, to the south-east), complete with maiolica decoration.

Chiesa dei Cappuccini ⊙ – The Capuchin church on the eastern edge of the town contains a lovely altarpiece by Filippo Paladini which depicts the Hodegetria Madonna (an icon representing the Virgin as a Guide or Instructress pointing to the Way of Redemption, said to be painted by St Luke) being carried on the shoulders of Basilian monks from the East (Jerusalem) to the West (Constantinople). On the left side of the nave, is a *Deposition* by Fra' Semplice da Verona which has an interesting play of perspective.

Additional paintings are displayed in the local art gallery next to the church, with art works drawn from the 16C to the present day. From here, there is access to the crypt where an unusual arrangement of figures re-enact different scenes from the life of Christ; one after the other, the different tableaux are illuminated and provided with a short commentary. The figures, all made by different local artisans, date from the 1990s.

CALTANISSETTA

Population 62 708
Michelin map 432 O 24

Situated at the very heart of Sicily, Caltanissetta extends itself across a plateau 568m/1 863ft above sea level. It started out as a small Greek town, before succumbing to the same fate endured by the rest of Sicily, passing from one domination to another. It enjoyed its greatest prosperity in the early 1900s when the extraction of local sulphur deposits was at its height, an activity which soon became the prime industry. Caltanissetta established itself as the leading exporter of sulphur, responsible for as much as four-fifths of world production. Fierce competition from America, however, soon threatened Caltanissetta's pre-eminence, forcing all the sulphur mines in the area to close.

The town is notorious for its extravagant celebrations of Holy Week: when, on the Thursday evening, groups of 19C statues arranged in tableaux representing scenes from the Mysteries of the Passion (the Deposition composition is particularly powerful), made by Neapolitan craftsmen, are processed through the streets; on Good Friday, the statue of a Black Christ is carried in procession across town. Outside Holy Week, these figures are kept in the **Chiesa di Pio X** in via Colajanni.

🛈 Viale Conte Testasecca 21, ☎ 0934 21 089; Fax 0934 21 239.

WHERE TO STAY

Hotel Plaza — Via Gaetani 5, ☎/fax 0934 58 38 77. This hotel, situated in the heart of the old town, offers 21 comfortable and spacious rooms (with air conditioning) at approximately 150 000L, including breakfast.

EATING OUT

Duomo — Vicolo Duomo 7, ☎ 0934 58 23 31. Closed Sun, Mon lunchtimes and Aug. Situated in a narrow street beside the Duomo in piazza Garibaldi, this restaurant serves traditional Caltanissetta dishes. Approximately 40 000L per person.

Legumerie Le Fontanelle — Via Pietro Leone 45, Contr. Fontanelle, ☎ 0934 59 24 37. Closed Mon. This farm, 2km/1.2mi north-west of the city, has a riding centre and a restaurant serving typical regional dishes. The outside tables, where guests eat in the summer months, offer beautiful views of the surrounding hills. Approximately 40 000L per person.

IN TOWN

The historic town centre clusters around **piazza Garibaldi** at the junction of the town's two main thoroughfares. Grouped around the square are the town hall (in the former Carmelite convent), the cathedral, the **Chiesa di San Sebastiano** with its Baroque frontage which, like Sant'Agata (at the end of corso Umberto) and Santa Croce (at the end of corso Vittorio Emanuele), is painted dark red, in marked contrast with the natural stone colour of the other architecture. In the centre sits the **Fontana del Tritone** (1956) by the local sculptor Michele Tripisciano, based on a 19C model. The bronze sculpture consists of a sea-horse being held back by a triton while under threat from two winged monsters.

Beyond the Town Hall in salita Matteotti, stands the 17C **Palazzo Moncada**, which although never completed, has a façade with intriguing carved corbels in the form of human and animal figures.

Cathedral ⊙ — The cathedral was erected in the late 16C. Its interior frescoes are by the Flemish painter Guglielmo Borremans (1720). The alternation of painted panels and stucco decoration combine to produce a dramatic impact. The 17C wooden figure of St Michael (1615) is by the Sicilian sculptor Stefano Li Volsi *(chapel to the right of the choir)*. The wonderful gilded wooden organ in the choir was built in 1601.

Sant'Agata al Collegio ⊘ – *Corso Umberto*. The 17C church has a composite front elevation fashioned in natural stone, red plasterwork and marble (doorway); inside, it contains elaborate inlaid polychrome marble decoration, and a beautiful marble altarpiece by **Ignazio Marabitti**.

Before the church stands a statue of Umberto I.

To the east of piazza Garibaldi stretches the Quartiere degli Angeli which preserves its medieval layout. At its centre stands **San Domenico** ⊘, a church with a fine Baroque façade with undulating panels. The painting inside of the *Madonna of the Rosary* is by Filippo Paladini. Further along via degli Angeli, the remains of the Saracen castle of Pietrarossa, perched on a rock, comes into view. Below, at the foot of the rock, stand the derelict ruins of Santa Maria degli Angeli (13C) and its lovely doorway (although propped up, this is difficult to see).

Museo Archeologico ⊘ – *Via Napoleone Colajanni, 1 (near the railway station)*. The museum gathers together artefacts recovered from around Caltanissetta and highlights the indigenous pre-Hellenistic civilisation and the impact made by Greek influences. The first two rooms are devoted to the Greek necropoli at **Gibil-Gabib** (where an unusual small clay cask from the 4C BC, later used as a funerary urn, was found) and **Vassallaggi** (where finds included a *strigil*, the tool used by athletes to scrape away oil, sweat and dead skin as illustrated in a mosaic at Villa del Casale, *see p 128*). The third room displays objects found in the Greek settlement of Sabucina: a small-scale terracotta model of a **temple★**, a votive object dating from the 6C BC, two large basins (one on a high pedestal) for holding drink or oil *(in the case on the left)* and a *krater* bearing a painting of the god Hephaestus, seated in his forge, hammering out hot iron (6C-5C BC). From the site at **Dessueri** there is a fine set of "tea-pots" used for boiling opium (indigenous culture, 13C BC) and an Attic *kylix* showing Heracles armed with a club, evidence of the hero's enduring popularity in Sicily. The last room contains a series of particularly sophisticated early artefacts from the local pre-Hellenistic cultures: note the refined geometric decoration and the stylised relief of the bull's head that appear on many of the clay pieces, and the two bronze statuettes with their arms outstretched (7C-6C BC) in the centre of the room. At the back, a bronze **shin-guard** and **helmet** dating from the Corinthian period (6C BC) are displayed.

ENVIRONS

Abbazia di Santo Spirito ⊘ – The abbey founded by Roger I (11C) and consecrated in 1153, is Romanesque in style. It has three typically Norman apses ornamented by decorative blind arcading. Inside, it has a wonderful 15C wooden crucifix and a deep early Romanesque baptismal font for the total immersion of infants, decorated with stylised palmettes.

EXCURSIONS

Archaeological sites – The archaeological excavations undertaken (and still in progress) in the Province of Caltanissetta are open to the public, even if they are difficult to find and rarely visited by tourists. Indeed, they remain the preserve of impassioned enthusiasts.

Sabucina – *Signposted off the main Enna road, 12km/7mi E of Caltanissetta*. Here, traces of an early hut settlement (12C BC) have been brought to light, together with elements from the subsequent phase (7C BC) in the local civilisation. A section of wall dating from the 5C or 4C BC has also been found.

Vassallaggi – *From Caltanissetta, take SS 640 towards San Cataldo. Follow to the junction with Serradifalco signed to the left and San Cataldo to the right: the sign (pointing right) for the excavations is wrong; the correct direction is straight on. After a few metres, a small tarred road branches right, passing through a gate which is usually open (information panel); follow the road until it degenerates into a dirt track (farm on the left). A green fence on the left delineates the excavated site.* The dig has so far uncovered an ancient settlement. The area includes a sacred precinct dedicated to gods of the underworld, surrounded by some 50 or so dependent buildings for use by officiators of the cult.

Gibil-Gabel – *6km/4mi S of Caltanissetta*. This site preserves the ruins of an ancient Sicani town and its necropolis.

CAPO D'ORLANDO ⚓

Messina – Population 1 669
Michelin map 432 M 26

A charming little seaside resort, Capo d'Orlando sits on a promontory of the same name surrounded by sea. Its history is intertwined with the legend of its foundation at the time of the Trojan War by Agathyrsus, the son of Aeolus. The legend also relates how the ancient settlement of Agathyrnis came to be renamed Capo d'Orlando by Charlemagne, who passing through these lands on a pilgrimage to the Holy Land, decided to call the place after his heroic paladin.

In 1299, the town watched the naval battle between James and Frederick of Aragon over the throne of Sicily.

Since 1955, the town has hosted a summer competition backed by the Messina painter Giuseppe Migneco, on the theme of life and countryside of Capo d'Orlando *(Vita e paesaggio di Capo d'Orlando)* whereby successful artists from Italy and abroad are commissioned to come and paint; some of the works, once the prize has been awarded, are acquired by the municipal art gallery.

The centre of the town falls between via Piave which is lined by smart shops, and the promenade which runs parallel, along the beautiful beach.

At the very tip of the promontory, up a flight of steps, is a purpose-built **viewpoint★** overlooking the ruins of the castle of Orlando and the 17C **Santuario di Maria Santissima di Capo d'Orlando**, to which pilgrims flock each year (22 October).

IN THE IMMEDIATE VICINITY

The coastal road continues beyond the cape, following the contours of the land and providing beautiful **views★** of the beach and the deep blue sea, its surface broken here and there by rocks.

Terme di Bagnoli ⊘ – On the outskirts of Capo d'Orlando at San Gregorio, in the district of Bagnoli, the remains of a bathing complex attached to a Roman villa dating from the Imperial period have been found. They include the **frigidarium** (marked 1-2-3), the **tepidarium** (marked 4) and the **caldarium** (marked 5 and 6). Clearly visible are the **suspensurae** which would have served to heat the various rooms. In rooms 4, 5 and 6 are fragments of mosaics with geometric decorations.

Villa Piccolo di Calanovella ⊘ – *4.5km/3mi W, marked by the 109km/68mi distance marker on the SS 113 between Messina and Palermo.* In keeping with the wishes of the last members of the Piccolo family, a museum-foundation was set up in the late 19C villa where they had lived since the 1930s. The Piccolos were an artistic family: in particular there was Lucio (who died in 1969), an acclaimed poet, and Casimiro, an enthusiastic painter and photographer, and a scholar of the occult. They were often visited by their cousin **Giuseppe di Lampedusa**, attracted as he was by the peace and quiet of the villa where he wrote a large part of his masterpiece *(The Leopard)*; in the room he once used is one of his letters to the Piccolo family, as is the bed in which he slept, ornamented with a beautiful ivory and mother-of-pearl bedhead depicting the Baptism of John (made by Trapani craftsmen in the 17C). Elsewhere in the villa are displayed porcelain from China, ceramics from Faenza and Capodimonte (notably a 10C Hispano-Moresque vase), dinner services, antique weapons, some Caltagirone 17C-18C ceramic water-bottles, and a fascinating series of fantastical **watercolours★** by Casimiro Piccolo, who enjoyed painting imaginary scenes from a fairy-tale world suffused with light and populated with amiable gnomes, elves, fairies and butterflies.

Before leaving, it is well worth taking a stroll under the pergolas in the villa gardens and seeking out the canine graveyard for the family pets.

EXCURSION INLAND *74km/46mi round trip*

This itinerary snakes its way inland from Capo d'Orlando on the eastern slopes of the Nebrodi Mountains *(for other excursions in the Nebrodi Mountains, see MADONIE e NEBRODI, La FIUMARA D'ARTE and SANTO STEFANO DI CAMASTRA).*

Leave Capo d'Orlando by the coastal road south towards Sant'Agata Militello. At Capri Leone, turn left towards Frazzanò.

Frazzanò – *22km/14mi S.* According to tradition, the town was founded in the 9C AD by people fleeing the Arab invasions. The **Chiesa Madre della Santissima Annunziata** (18C) has a fine Baroque façade ornamented with giant pilasters and an elegant portal with spiralling columns, flanked by niches containing statues.

The **Chiesa di San Lorenzo** ⊘ has a plainer façade relieved by a fine portal with spiralling columns and a flurry of sculptural motifs including plant fronds, cherubs and volutes. Inside, there is a fine wooden statue of the church's patron, St Lawrence (1620).

Proceed to the next right turning, signposted for the Convento di San Filippo di Fragalà.

Convento di San Filippo di Fragalà ⊙ – *3km/2mi from Frazzanò towards Longi.* The Basilian church, which has recently been restored, was built by Roger I of Altavilla in the 11C, very probably among the ruins of an earlier monastery dating from the 5C. It is worth pausing to view the exterior of the abbey complex from below: note the three apses in the Arabo-Norman style, articulated by brick pilasters, and the octagonal drum over the intersection of the transepts. The church is T-shaped in plan and inside, particularly in the central apse, there are traces of Byzantine-style frescoes.

The adjoining monastic buildings are also open.

The road continues to Portella Calcatirizzo. Beyond the town, turn left at the fork towards San Salvatore di Fitalia.

Eating out

The **Antica Filanda** trattoria (☎ 0941 43 47 15; closed 15 Jan to 15 Feb) in the Parrazzi district of **Galati Mamertino** serves excellent regional cuisine. Approximately 50 000L per person.

San Salvatore di Fitalia – Perched high among the Nebrodi Mountains, this small town has a fine church (1515) dedicated to **San Salvatore** ⊙. The exterior is somewhat severe, but the interior comes as a surprise; recent restoration has uncovered the 16C structure of the building with its nave separated from the aisles by sandstone columns supporting pointed arches. The fine **capitals** are sculpted with the plant and anthropomorphic motifs so typical of medieval decorative schemes. The capital of the first column on the right, bearing the name of the stone-mason who carved it, features a highly unusual mermaid with a forked tail. In the right aisle hangs Antonello Gagini's gentle *Madonna of the Snow* (1521) and, on the high altar, a highly prized **wooden statue of Salvator Mundi**★ (1603) at the moment of the Transfiguration.

Museo Siciliano delle Tradizioni Religiose ⊙ – The fascinating **museum of religious practices** documents the spirit of local popular cults with displays of simple objects, such as amulets against the evil eye, votive objects including a series of anatomical replicas made of wax originally from the Santuario of San Calogero (18C-19C); the *pillole* (meaning pills) consist of tiny squares of paper that were designed to be swallowed by the faithful while they recited prayers requesting divine intervention in the cure of disease or other malady; sheet music used by ballad-singers and terracotta whistles bearing figurative images sold on saints' days. An unusual 17C "priest toy" comprises a doll dressed as a priest complete with all the necessary holy vestments (sadly the liturgical objects have been stolen), reminiscent of the one described in Manzoni's 19C novel *Promessi Sposi (The Betrothed)* belonging to the nun from Monza since childhood. The collection also includes a series of engravings and lithographs of sacred images (17C-20C), special dress worn by the confraternities in sacred processions, various examples of devotional statuary in wood, plaster and terracotta, and small figures for cribs (19C).

Follow the road back to the coast and turn right towards Capo d'Orlando.

CAPO D'ORLANDO TO CAPO CALAVÀ *Approximately 16km/10mi*

The coast between the two headlands is dotted with beautiful beaches and small seaside resorts.

Eating out

At **Fiumara**, inland from Capo d'Orlando, try the **Ristorante Bontempo** (☎ 0941 96 11 89; closed Mon) which specialises in preparing food over a charcoal grill in the old-fashioned way, a practice which is unfortunately dying out. To find it, follow the restaurant signs, taking a right-hand turn off the coast road from Capo d'Orlando to Brolo (the restaurant is about 10km/6mi south-east from Capo d'Orlando). Approximately 70 000L per person.

Brolo – A flourishing port until the late 17C and now a seaside resort, the town has a fine medieval castle *(private)* built by the Lancia family in the 15C. Above the main archway is the family coat of arms, with the three pears of the Barony of Piràino.

Beyond Brolo, turn right at the next junction for Piràino.

Piràino – Stretched out along the spine of a hill enjoying a strategic position, Piràino retains much of its medieval form, scattered with religious buildings. Its legendary origins (supposed, as it is, to have been founded by the cyclops Piracmon – Arges in Homer – one of the three ministers of Vulcan) are probably rooted in the discovery of large bones in several caves nearby, erroneously believed to have belonged to the cyclops.

All the churches are strung along the main street of the town. The **Chiesa del Rosario** ⊙, the easternmost, dedicated to the Madonna of the Rosary, while retaining its 16C campanile, was re-built in 1635. Inside, it has a fine coffered wooden **ceiling** set with Byzantine-Norman rosettes, and an unusual wooden **high altar** painted with floral motifs (first half of the 17C) decorated with wooden medallions representing the Mysteries of the Rosary. The wooden figures in the centre of the altar represent the Madonna with saints.

Further along is the **Chiesa della Catena** ⊙, erected in the latter half of the 17C, where the first elections were held after the Unification of Italy. It contains some fine Byzantine-type **frescoes** from another church, the Chiesa della Badia.

Beyond is Piazza del Baglio, named after the complex of low-level workers' houses and workshops arranged around the **Palazzo Ducale**, built by the Lancia family (15C-16C).

Proceeding westwards, the way leads up to the highest part of the town which is marked by the beautifully preserved **Torre Saracena** or Torrazza (10C), from the terrace of which extends a magnificent **view**★ across the rooftops nestling below and beyond to Capo d'Orlando. The tower was part of a defensive system which would have transmitted signals from the 16C **Torre delle Ciavole** on the coast, via the **Guardiola** situated to the north of the town, to the Torrazza.

On the western edge of town is **Santa Caterina d'Alessandria** ⊙, the church dedicated to St Catherine of Alexandria, built in the 16C but altered in the 17C. Inside, the wooden altar is decorated with floral motifs. A low relief to the right of the altar depicts the patron St Catherine of Alexandria overcoming the infidel.

Turn back towards the coast; on the left stands the **Torre delle Ciavole** *(see above)*. Continue to the small seaside resort of **Gioiosa Marea** and follow the signs for San Filippo Armo and San Leonardo *(about 9km/5.5mi)* to Gioiosa Guardia.

Rovine di Gioiosa Guardia – The ruins of this medieval town, abandoned by its inhabitants in the 18C for Gioiosa Marea, are situated at 800m/2625ft above sea-level surrounded by romantic landscape. The idyllic serenity of the place is enhanced by the splendid **view**★ over the surrounding countryside.

Return to the coast.

A little further on is **Capo Calavà**, a spectacular rocky spur.

CARINI

Palermo – Population 24 907
Michelin map 432 M 21

Set on a hill overlooking its very own bay, Carini claims to have legendary origins. Allegedly, it was founded by Daedalus *(see ERACLEA MINOA)* who called it Hyccara in memory of his son Icarus; history then records how the town came to be destroyed by the Athenians in 415 BC, rebuilt by the Phoenicians and, after the Roman conquest, became a stipendiary town of the Empire. With time came changes in fortune: the town was assimilated into the feudal holdings of the most powerful Chiaramonte dynasty, before passing to the Moncada (14C) and, finally in the 15C to the La Grua-Talamanca, in whose hands it remains today.

A road snakes its way through broad bends up to a belvedere presenting sweeping views over the coast; here begins corso Umberto I, Carini's main street. A horse-shoe shaped flight of shallow steps makes its way up past the town's medieval water fountain, to a 12C archway and beyond to the old part of the town, threaded by narrow streets, and the castle.

SIGHTS

Castle ⊙ – The ancient Norman fortress-cum-castle, the famous setting for the tragic episode involving **Baronessa di Carini**, has been radically remodelled over the centuries, most especially since it has been owned by the La Grua-Talamanca family.

On the ground floor is the **Salone delle Derrate** (Victuals Hall), later transformed into a library, with its two elegant 15C stone arches springing from a single solid pier. On the floor above, the **Salone delle Feste** has a wonderful 15C coffered wooden **ceiling**, heavy with typical Catalan Gothic decorative pendentives. The square tower beyond is lit by a two-light window; above, the roof beams rest on a series of corbels, decorated with a profusion of organic elements, that alternate with machicolations.

Return to corso Umberto I.

Opposite the fountain stands the **Chiesa di San Vincenzo**. The space within is bisected by a wrought-iron grille (segregating the area reserved for the nuns from the adjacent convent) and decorated with white and gold neo-Classical stucco festoons, cherubs and grotesques.

Corso Umberto I opens out into **piazza del Duomo**, overlooked by two churches: San Vito on the right and the Chiesa Madre on the left.

A tale of love and tragedy

1563: Laura Lanza, the beautiful young daughter of the Count of Mussomeli, although betrothed to Don Vincenzo La Grua, falls in love with Ludovico Vernagallo, who reciprocates her love. Despite every effort by the girl's father to put an end to the affair, nothing will quell the passion of the two young lovers. Finding an accomplice in her nurse, the girl devises a plan with her partner, enabling them to marry in secret and run away together. The appointed day arrives: 4 December. The two youths pronounce their vows of reciprocal fidelity before a chaplain, when Laura's enraged father bursts in on the scene. The two surreptitious lovers are put to death, thereby salvaging the family's honour. The story is hushed up, no-one is punished, yet with time, the incident was assimilated into the colourful anthology of romance popularly celebrated in ballad and song.

Chiesa Madre ⊘ – Although subjected to considerable alteration in the 18C, the church preserves on its right side a loggia and a series of interesting maiolica panels depicting the *Crucifixion, Assumption, St Rosalia and St Vitus* (1715). **Inside**, the church houses a prized *Adoration of the Magi* by Alessandro Allori (1578), an eminent Tuscan painter who came to prominence at the Medici court; in the chapel dedicated to the Crucifixion sits an exquisite 17C wooden Crucified Christ with a crown of silver on cross of agate, set above an grandiose altar flanked by expressive stucco statues by Procopio Serpotta.

Oratorio del Santissimo Sacramento ⊘ – The oratory beside the Chiesa Madre dates from the mid-16C. Its interior is a glorious profusion of **stucco decoration★★** (18C) by the Trapani artist Vincenzo Messina, populated by life-size allegories (Faith, Charity, Strength and Penitence on the left; Hope, Justice, Divine Grace and the Roman Catholic Church on the right) and a crowd of smaller figures leaning on parapets below the windows, or engaged in scenes from the Mysteries of the Eucharist. Elsewhere, surfaces are encrusted with other Serpotta-like elements: cherubs, garlands of flowers and fruit, heraldic coats of arms and grotesques. The ceiling is frescoed with the Triumph of Faith.

Chiesa di Santa Maria degli Angeli ⊘ – *Behind the Chiesa Madre, in via Curreri.* This church once belonged to the Capuchin monastery; a ring of side chapels radiate from the nave, each one embellished with intricate intarsia. Pride of place in the elaborate Rococo chapel of the Crucifixion, among the various small reliquaries, is a lovely wooden **Crucifix** by the Capuchin Fra' Benedetto Valenza (1737), who also worked on the overall decor.

Chiesa degli Agonizzanti ⊘ – *Via Roma.* This church, completed in 1643, is richly decorated inside with white and gold **stucco★**: playful cherubs, eagles, garlands of flowers and fruit encircle frescoed panels depicting the scenes from the life of the Virgin, culminating in the ceiling *(Apotheosis of the Virgin)*. Half-way along the side-walls, two small stucco scenes below the frescoes represent the Death of Joseph and the Madonna.

EXCURSION

Terrasini – *15km/9mi W.* The seaside resort overlooks the sea, closed in behind by a lofty red **cliff★** which intermittently shelters little beaches and sweet little rocky creeks.

La festa di li schietti

The Saturday before Easter, all the eligible young men *(schietti)* of the town go out and cut a bitter-orange tree *(melangolo)*. They trim and tidy the top into a round shape and decorate it with coloured ribbons and bells of all shapes and sizes *(ciancianieddi)*. The dressed result, which must weigh at least 50kg, is then carried into the town ready for the Sunday morning, when each tree is blessed in the piazza before the main church. After the service and urged on by the local populace, each young man bears his tree to the house of his chosen love; there he must demonstrate his strength by balancing the tree on the palm of his hand for as long as possible.

This local festival has lost much of its importance today, for once it constituted a veritable test of virility: if the young man should fail to lift his heavy offering or, indeed, should fail to hold it up long enough, the engagement might, literally, be broken off.

Museo Civico ⊙ – Terrasini harbours an interesting local **museum**, although its presentation does not do justice to the quality of its collections. These comprise three departments: the most significant being the **natural history** section *(via Cala Rossa, 8)*. This comprises, among other things, the well-endowed Orlando collection of birds with species ranging from crows, nocturnal birds, storks, raptors, species approaching extinction or considered rare like the Griffon Vulture, Golden Eagle and Capercaillie.

The **archaeological** department *(next to the town hall in piazza Falcone e Borsellino)* displays marine artefacts retrieved from wrecks found off Terrasini – mainly fragments of amphorae from the 3C BC and objects from a 1C AD Roman ship.

The **ethnological** section *(via CA Dalla Chiesa, 42)* provides a small but excellent display of **Sicilian carts★**, among which are some truly remarkable examples from Palermo and Trapani.

M. Magni/MICHELIN

The coast at Terrasini

Villa Romana del CASALE★★★

Enna

Michelin map 432 ○ 25

This imposing Roman villa was probably built between the end of the 3C and the beginning of the 4C AD, undoubtedly by someone of importance, possibly a member of the Imperial family: one of the most likely candidates seems to be Maximian, one of the tetrarchs who jointly ruled the Empire from AD 286 to 305.

The country villa, surrounded by large estates, was only occupied occasionally until the 12C. It was destroyed by a fire, then buried in mud following floods and a subsequent landslide in about 1161; it was only partially re-discovered at the end of the 19C.

The large complex (c 3 500m²) was built on different levels. The main entrance (**A**) led into a polygonal courtyard, which provided access to the large peristyle overlooked by guest rooms (to the north – note: the map given has north pointing downwards) and the owner's private apartments (to the east). Beyond the guest rooms were the servants' quarters (**B**), complete with kitchen. The private apartments used by the members of the household were divided into two by a large basilica for meetings and official receptions. At the rear of these buildings stands a small separate octagonal latrine reserved for members of the family (**C**). The living area was situated to the south of the complex and consisted of a large elliptical atrium which gave onto a large apsed triclinium (dining-room), six small rooms and service amenities.

The western part of the complex housed the baths. The water was supplied by two aqueducts connected to a third which, in turn, was fed by the River Gela which flows only a few metres away.

Mosaics – What makes the villa unique is its floors, which consist almost entirely of mosaics that fortunately survive in excellent condition. The majority of panels are polychrome and feature a wide range of subjects: mythological scenes, incidents from daily life, special occasions – a great hunt, circus games, feast days honouring the gods and a grape harvest – alternate with geometric decoration incorporating medallions, stars and key patterns in a wonderful array of colours. What is particularly remarkable is the evocative way in which movement and action is portrayed thereby animating the various scenes with realism. The rare skill with which the wild and exotic animals have been portrayed has been interpreted as the work of North African craftsmen. In order that the various scenes might be seen from the best angle, the panels are laid facing the entrance to each room: the full impact, therefore, is delivered to the visitor as he or she enters the room.

GETTING TO THE VILLA ROMANA

The villa is situated 6km/3.5mi from Piazza Armerina and can be reached by bus from piazza Marescalchi. Bus services operate between Piazza Armerina and Caltagirone (1hr), Enna (40min) and Palermo (3hr). The closest railway station is in Enna.

TOUR ⊙

Some rooms contain geometric mosaics with a wide range of motifs: circles, stars, swastikas, hexagons and interlacing. The other, more figurative panels, are described below.

Terme – Just inside the entrance to the steam baths, on the left, is a section of the **aqueduct** that supplied the villa with water. Immediately beyond are the suite of rooms which make up the thermal complex. In the first are installed the great furnaces *(praefurnia)* (1) which heated the water in order to generate steam that was then circulated through cavities below the floors and in the walls, thereby heating the rooms. Sections of pipes which once ran along the length of the room can still be seen in the walls. The under-floor heating is visible in the **Tepidarium** (3): small brick columns support the actual floor, leaving a large cavity between the floor and the ground through which hot air could circulate freely. This room was maintained at a moderate temperature for use immediately after the **Caldaria** (2) where saunas and the hot baths were taken.

Sala delle Unzioni (4) – The function of the small square anointing room is reflected in the mosaic decoration. Slaves are shown preparing oil and unguents for application and massaging the bodies of the bathers *(the figures at the top left)*, with some of the tools of their trade: the *strigile*, a sort of curved spatula with a handle used for scraping and cleaning the skin, and a jar of oil *(the figure at the top right)*. Below, Tite and Cassi (from the names of the two slaves on the cloth draped around their hips) hold a bucket and a brush. The latter wears a pointed hat, of a kind typical in Syria.

Frigidarium (5) – The octagonal room set aside for cold baths has a fine central mosaic with a marine theme: cherub fishermen surrounded by tritons, nereids (sea nymphs) and dolphins.

One recess is filled with a man sitting on a leopard skin, attended by two servants. From the *frigidarium*, the **piscina** and the end of the aqueduct can just be seen. Beyond the **shrine of Venus** (6), thus called because fragments of a statue of the goddess were found there, is the **polygonal courtyard** articulated by a colonnade. In the centre are the remains of the *impluvium* – a basin or cistern in which rainwater is collected from the surrounding roofs. From here the water was channelled towards the great **latrina** (7).

The main entrance to the villa was from the courtyard: on the south side can be seen the remains of the entrance (**A**) comprising a central door flanked by two side-doors.

Peristilium – Pass through the **vestibule** (8). The mosaic features figures bearing a candlestick, a branch of laurel and, below, a figure with a diptych (a small book consisting of two panels) from which he might read a welcome addressed to the master of the house and any guests. Directly opposite is the **lararium** (9), where statues of the household gods, the *lari*, were kept.

The imposing rectangular portico (8 columns on the short sides, 10 on the longer sides) is dominated by a great fountain with a small statue as its centrepiece.

★★ **Peristilium mosaic** – Running along all four sides of the portico is a beautiful mosaic ornamented with round medallions set among squares with, at the corners, birds and leaves. The medallions feature the heads both of wild and domestic animals (bears, tigers, wild boars and panthers; horses and cows).

Piccola latrina (10) – The floor mosaic depicts animals, including a wild ass, a cheetah, a hare and a partridge.

★★ **Sala del Circo** – The long room, apsed at both ends, represents a circus, identified as the Circus Maximus in Rome. The decoration illustrates a chariot race, the final event in the festival honouring Ceres, the goddess of plenty and the harvest, whose cult was particularly popular in nearby Enna *(see introduction to chapter on ENNA)*. The scene is shown in great detail. Above the *spina*, the central line around which the horses are racing, the winner receives his prize, the victory palm, handed to him by a magistrate dressed in a toga, while another character blows a horn to signal the end of the race. On the left, around the bend in the track, are the spectators, among whom a boy picks his way distributing bread. The right-hand bend is dominated by a view of three temples dedicated to Jupiter, Rome and Heracles, before which a charioteer is being dressed: one child holds out his helmet, while a second gives him the whip.

The charioteers, dressed in green, white, blue or red tunics, indicate to which of the four competing factions they belong.

Along the south side of the peristyle are a series of rooms reserved for guests. Access to these was via a second **vestibule** (11), which is decorated with mosaics showing the lady of the house with her children and her servants holding lengths of cloth and a box containing oils. Other rooms (**B**) comprised the servants' quarters, complete with kitchen in which the oven can still be seen.

Sala della Danza (12) – The mosaic, incomplete alas, nevertheless gives an impression of women and men dancing. One girl in particular, at the top left, moves sinuously with a veil over her head.

Sala delle Quattro Stagioni (13) – The four seasons, after which this room is named, are represented in medallions, personified by two women (spring and autumn), differentiated by their clothing, and two men (summer and winter), with a bare shoulder.

★★ **Sala degli Amorini Pescatori** (14) – A few cupid-like cherubs concentrate on fishing with lines, tridents and nets while others play in the water with dolphins. In the upper section may be seen the shore, where a large building stands, fronted by a columned portico, among palm-trees and umbrella pines.

The walls bear traces of frescoes depicting a further number of cherubs.

★★★ **Sala della Piccola Caccia** – Here, in the **Room of the Small Hunt**, five panels depict the most important moments in the heat of the hunt. In the top left corner, a hunter walks with his dogs on a lead, before releasing them and encouraging them to chase after a fox *(on the right)*.

In order to give thanks for favourable conditions and a successful day, a sacrifice is offered to Diana, the goddess of hunting, a figure of whom is shown set on a column, in the middle ground. Two high-ranking officials burn incense on the altar while, behind them, a wild boar is brought forth in a net *(on the left)* and another hunter *(on the right)* holds up a hare that he has caught. The whole of the central part of the mosaic is dominated by a banqueting scene. Shaded by a red awning slung between the trees, game is being cooked over a fire. There is a pause in the day's activity: the horses are tethered, the nets are hung on branches, the

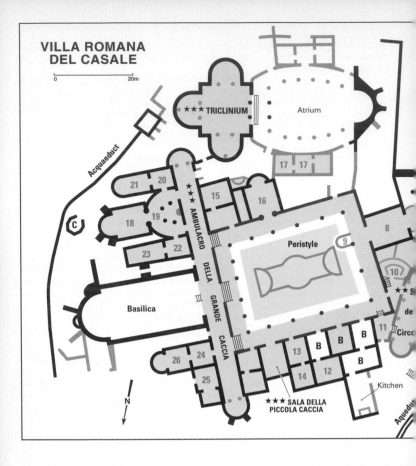

★★★ TRICLINIUM

Atrium

Acquaeduct

17 17

21 20 ★★★ 15 16

18 19 **AMBULACRO**

C

8

Peristyle 9

23 22 **DELLA**

10

Basilica **GRANDE** ★★ S

de

11 Circo

CACCIA

13 B B B

26 24 B

25 14 12

Kitchen

N

★★★ SALA DELLA PICCOLA CACCIA

Aqueduct

huntsmen, arranged in a semicircle, relax around the fire taking refreshment. All around are hunting scenes: at the top left, two falconers seek out birds hidden among the branches of a tree; on the right, in the bushes, a man encourages his dogs to follow a hare and, below, a huntsman on horseback tries to coax out another hare from under a bush. The last panel depicts the netting of deer and the hunt for a boar which, having injured the leg of a man (shown resting on the ground, on the left), is being hemmed in by fellow hunters as they plunge a spear into its chest.

Corridor of the Great Hunt

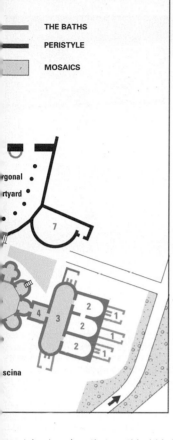

THE BATHS

PERISTYLE

MOSAICS

gonal
rtyard

7

scina

★★★Ambulacro della Grande Caccia

– The fabulous Corridor of the Great Hunt, 60m/197ft long with a recess at each end, is the most engaging and monumental part of the whole villa. The floor mosaic depicts an incredibly elaborate hunting scene. Panthers, lions, antelopes, wild boar, ostrich, dromedaries, elephants, hippopotamuses and rhinoceroses are captured and put into cages or bound prior to being loaded onto ships destined for Rome, where they will be shown to acclaim in the great amphitheatres. What makes this composition so extraordinary is the variety of its scenes, the realism with which men are shown vying with wild beasts, the strong sense of action and movement, the wealth of and articulate attention to detail. Note, for example, how the limbs of animals shown underwater are portrayed in a different colour to the parts above the surface.

Just beyond the mid-way point is a group of three figures: the central one is presumed to be the Emperor Maxentius, protected by the shields of two soldiers. Further on, another scene betrays the same tremendous sophistication of detail: a tiger pounces on a crystal ball in which an image of the animal is reflected. Nearby, a curious scene provoking considerable controversy illustrates a winged griffin holding a wooden box in its talons from which the head of a boy peeps out. Some maintain that the boy acts as human bait to attract the animal, while others interpret the scene as a warning against the cruelty of hunting, and that the protagonists have swapped roles.

In the right recess, Africa is depicted as a female figure with an ivory tusk, flanked by an elephant, a tiger and, above left, an Arab-style phoenix – that mythical bird symbolising immortality which took its own life by throwing itself into the flames, only to be re-born from its ashes.

Along the eastern side of this long corridor opened rooms used by the owners of the villa, including in the middle, the basilica destined for audiences and receptions *(for a description of these rooms, see below)*.

★★Sala delle Dieci Ragazze in Bikini (15)

– In the Room of the Ten Girls, the mosaic shows two rows of girls dressed in outfits that bear an uncanny resemblance to the modern two-piece bikini. In fact, they are pictured in their underwear, which was also commonly used when doing gymnastic exercises. The upper part was called the *fascia pectoralis* and the lower part *subligatur*. The young women concentrate on performing their various exercises: weight-lifting, discus throwing, running and playing ball-games. In the bottom row, the girl wearing a toga is about to crown another girl (also awarding her the palm of victory) who has been performing exercises with a hoop, trundling it with the aid of a stick.

★Diaeta di Orfeo (16)

– The Chamber of Orpheus is so called because it was reserved for playing music. At the centre is Orpheus (scarcely visible), seated on a rock, playing the lyre and enchanting all the animals which surround him. In the apse behind is a statue of the god Apollo.

The south wing of the villa accommodated the principal reception rooms: a spacious central atrium is flanked by six small units (three on each side) and a large apsed *triclinium* where meals were served. Two of the three rooms on the north side (17) contain mosaics of cherubs harvesting grapes from the vines.

★★Triclinium

– The large central square space extends into three broad apses.

Central area – The main mosaic is dedicated to the **Twelve Labours of Heracles** (Hercules to the Romans). Only some of them are recognisable. On the left is the Cretan Bull (or Bull of Minos), the famous and powerful animal sent from the waters by Poseidon to Minos, which having been captured by Heracles was eventually sacrificed to Athene by Theseus at Marathon *(see ERACLEA MINOA)*. Beside it is the Hydra of Lerna, whose many heads, one of which was immortal, were chopped off by the hero. In this case, the monster is represented with the body of a water-snake and a single immortal head. The Hydra, the younger sister of Cerberus, acted, with her brother, as guardians of the Underworld, reigning in the sweet, deep waters near Lerna, on the border with Argos. In this Labour, Heracles is

Girls in bikinis

assisted by his nephew and friend Iolaus, the figure, it is assumed, depicted next to the hero in the left apse. At the top, in the centre, is the great Nemean Lion, which terrorised a mountainous area. Having killed the monster, Heracles wore its pelt as a cloak and its head as a helmet. In honour of this great deed, Zeus, the divine father of Heracles, brought the lion to the heavens, making it into one of the constellations of the zodiac.

On the right is the hind of Artemis, which Heracles captured among the hills of Ceryneia in Arcadia. To the left of the animal is Cerberus, the many-headed huge and savage dog which was brought by Heracles from the gates of the Underworld.

Left apse – This mosaic represents the **glorification of Heracles**, who is depicted in the centre, holding the hand of his friend, Iolaus *(on the left)*, while Zeus bestows a laurel wreath on his head.

The panel below illustrates the metamorphoses of **Daphne** into a laurel *(on the left)* and of **Cyparissus** into a cypress *(on the right)*. This serves as a reminder as to why laurel is twisted into crowns honouring the heads of brave warriors, emperors and poets: Daphne was the nymph loved and pursued by Apollo; to escape his clutches she prayed to her father, a river god, and her mother, Earth, to be turned into a laurel tree. In consolation Apollo made himself a laurel wreath which, from then on, was awarded as a prize at the Pythian Games held in Apollo's honour.

Central apse – The scene represents a **battle of the giants**: five huge creatures have been struck by Heracles' poisoned arrows. Except for the central figure, the others have snakes' tails for legs. One of the labours consisted of Heracles stealing the oxen of Geryon and carrying them back to Greece. The return journey is particularly animated with exploits *(see Introduction: The Ancient Greeks in Sicily)*; it was as he crossed Italy that he encountered the giants, one of whom was called Alcyoneus, and fought them by the Flegraean Fields (near Naples).

In the mosaic below, **Hesione**, the daughter of Laomedon, king of Troy, is threatened by a sea monster sent by Poseidon: an incident resulting from Laomedon's failure to honour his agreement in paying Poseidon and Apollo for their assistance in building the walls of Troy; the only way to safeguard the city from the sea monster is to sacrifice Hesione. Heracles undertook to slay the monster on condition Laomedon give him his famous horses; when the king again reneges on his promise, Heracles raises an army against Troy and gives Hesione to Telamon. On the right is Endymion, who was thrown into perpetual sleep, awaiting Selene, the moon, his lover.

Right apse – This mosaic depicts the story of **Ambrosia and Lycurgus**. On the left, three maenads (literally *mad women*) attack Lycurgus, a legendary king of Thrace who, having surprised Dionysus (engaged in a bacchanal) on his land, chased him off, killing many maenads and satyrs. Among them, he even tries to kill Ambrosia who, in the scene depicted, is changing into a vine. Behind the maenads are the figures of Pan, Dionysus and Silenus.

Continue along the wall of the aqueduct. Just before a small hexagonal latrine (**C**), some steps on the left lead into room 18.

Diaeta di Arione (18) – The chamber of Arion was probably dedicated to making music and reading poetry, judging by the mosaic decoration which depicts the poet and musician Arion sitting on the back of a dolphin in the middle of the sea, holding a lyre and surrounded by nereids, tritons and cherubs astride wild beasts and sea monsters. Here is another example of the precise and minute detail demonstrated elsewhere by the mosaicists: one nereid on the right holds a mirror in which her face is reflected.

★★Atrio degli amorini pescatori (19) – The mosaic illustrates a delightful variety of fishing scenes which run right around the semicircular portico.

★★Vestibolo del Piccolo Circo (20) – The Vestibule of the Small Circus takes its name from another circus scene, this time with children as the protagonists. Racing around the turning-posts are the chariots drawn *(starting from the top right and working anti-clockwise)* by flamingos, white geese, waders and wood pigeons. Each pair of birds also seems to symbolise a season, as a motif on their collars would suggest: roses (spring), ears of wheat (summer), bunches of grapes (autumn) and leaves (winter).

Cubicolo dei musici e degli attori (21) – This particular *cubiculum* probably served as a bedroom for the owner's daughter. In the apse, two girls sit at the foot of a tree making crowns of flowers. The decoration of the rectangular room is divided into three areas populated by musicians and actors. The letters inscribed in the medallions in the second and third sections allude to musical notes.

Vestibolo di Eros e Pan (22) – Dominating the ante-chamber is the central horned and cloven-hoofed figure of Pan, the god of the woodlands, flocks and shepherds, fighting Eros, the god of love. Next to Pan is the judge, wearing a laurel wreath. Behind the two contestants is the audience made up of satyrs and maenads (carrying a thyrsus – the rod entwined with vine and ivy more often attributed to Dionysus) supporting the god of the woodlands, and the family of the owners of the house supporting Eros. The fight symbolises the difficulty for anyone who is ugly (Pan) to vanquish love. In the background, on a table, are aligned four hats set with diadems and palm leaves and, below, two bags full of money, as the writing indicates.

★Cubicolo dei fanciulli cacciatori (23) – This *cubiculum* was probably the bedroom of the son of the house-owner. The mosaic divides into two parts, which in turn are sub-divided into three sections. At the top, girls collect flowers and make garlands; a boy carries two rose-filled baskets on his shoulders. Lower down, hunting scenes show children killing a hare, capturing a duck and killing a small antelope. Walk around the large **basilica**, noting the fragments of the floor tiled with marble.

★Vestibolo di Ulisse e Polifemo (24) – These mosaics illustrate the famous story of Odysseus (Ulysses to the Romans) outwitting the Cyclops Polyphemus (shown here with three eyes) with a cup of wine intended to intoxicate him and send him to sleep. Behind him, the hero's companions are filling another cup.

★Cubicolo della scena erotica (25) – Surrounded by images of the four seasons (in the hexagonal medallions), a polygonal medallion enclosed within a laurel wreath shows a young man embracing a loosely clad girl. This is one of the few rooms that still bears traces of wall paintings depicting dancing figures.

In the room behind the vestibule (26) is a **mosaic★** with **fruit**, realistically represented with exquisite delicacy, set within medallions and among complex geometrical shapes, while the apse is ornamented with a delicate flower composition against a pale background.

CASTELBUONO

Population 9 797
Michelin map 432 N 24

This charming town grew up in the 14C around the **castle** built by the **Ventimiglia** family, a massive square construction with square towers, which has undergone many alterations over the years.

At the very heart of the town is piazza Margherita, which is overlooked by the Church of Madrice Vecchia and the old **Banca di Corte**. This currently accommodates the local **Museo Civico** ⊙, pending its relocation to the castle as soon as restoration work is completed, whose collections include treasures and furnishings from the Cappella Palatina *(see below)* and a fine selection of contemporary paintings, mainly by Italian artists.

Madrice Vecchia ⊙ – Built in the 14C on the ruins of a pagan temple, the church has a Renaissance portico, added in the 16C, and a splendid central portal in the Catalan style. On the left side rises a campanile with a fine Romanesque two arch bell-opening, culminating in an octagonal spire covered with maiolica tiles. The

🖪 Corso Umberto I 69, ☎ 0921 67 34 67.

WHERE TO STAY

Milocca – Contr. Piano Castagna, ☎ 0921 67 19 44, Fax 0921 67 14 37. This hotel is situated 7km/4mi south of the centre of Castelbuono and boasts a magnificent **panoramic view★★★** over Castelbuono, the Madonie mountains and the Tyrrhenian Sea dotted with the Aeolian Islands. On a clear day, it is even possible to make out individual houses on the islands with the naked eye. The hotel has 52 comfortable rooms and an outdoor swimming pool (at an altitude of 1 000m/3 280ft). Double rooms approximately 120 000L, including breakfast.

EATING OUT

Al vecchio palmento – Via Failla 2, ☎ 0921 67 20 99. Closed Mon. A family-run restaurant which offers a selection of dishes prepared with local produce. Approximately 50 000L per person.

Romitaggio – Loc San Guglielmo, ☎ 0921 67 13 23. Closed Mon and from 15 June to 15 July. Situated 5km/3mi south of Castelbuono, this restaurant, specialising in simple local cuisine, is accommodated by the medieval monastic buildings of San Guglielmo. In summer dinner is served in the arcades of the cloisters. Approximately 50 000L per person.

Pasticceria dei Fratelli Fiasconaro – Piazza Margherita. The Fiasconaro brothers' *pasticceria* makes the most delicious *panettone* (traditional Christmas cake), *colomba* (dove-shaped Easter cake) and, in the summer, *ciambelle* (almond doughnuts). On the opposite side of the piazza, excellent home-made ice cream is sold at **Extrabar** (owned by the same family).

Manna

Small whitish, slightly sweet stalactites hanging from ash trees; manna is the lymph of these trees which, when dried, is collected and used as a sweetener and a laxative. Although once one of the town's sources of income, it is now more of a curiosity sought by tourists, who can find it at the tobacconist's at the end of corso Umberto I (virtually in piazza Margherita).

---

interior, originally built as a nave with flanking aisles, was enlarged in the late 15C to its present plan with four aisles. It preserves several rare works of art, most remarkably, above the high altar, a splendid **polyptych★** depicting *The Coronation of the Virgin*, attributed to Pietro Ruzzolone (or possibly Antonello del Saliba). Note, in the bottom right, the unusual figure of a saint wearing spectacles. To the right is a statue of the *Madonna delle Grazie* by **Antonello Gagini**. Below the north aisle, the fresco of the *Sposalizio delle Vergini* (Betrothal of the Virgins) shows a strong Sienese influence in the elegant features and the symmetry of the composition.

A few of the columns separating the aisles are painted with frescoes; among these is the figure of St Catherine of Alexandria, characterised by her poise and delicate features. The crypt is entirely decorated with 17C frescoes depicting episodes from the Passion, Death and Resurrection of Christ.

Via Sant'Anna leads up to the castle. Through the Gothic arch appears the massive form of the castle with its square towers at each of its four corners.

Cappella Palatina ⊘ – The Palatine Chapel is located on the second floor of the **castle** and is decorated with some enchanting **stuccowork★** picked out from a gold-leaf background, attributed to Giuseppe Serpotta (1683), the brother of the more famous Giacomo.

Via Roma leads off from piazza Margherita.

Museo Francesco Minà-Palumbo ⊘ – Currently housed in the precincts of a former Benedictine convent, the **museum** evolved from the passion of **Francesco Minà-Palumbo**, a doctor living in the 19C, with a fascination for botany. The result is a lifetime's assemblage of conscientious and systematic collection, classification and representation on paper of the botanical species, reptiles and insects of the nearby Madonie mountains, some of which are now extinct.

A little further on is the church of **San Francesco** ⊘ together with its extension, the **Mausoleo dei Ventimiglia**, a late-medieval octagonal known as **la Madrice Nuova** ⊘, which contains a fine *Deposition from the Cross* by Giuseppe Velasco, and Baroque altars with spiral columns by Vincenzo Messina. In corso Umberto I is the **Fontana di Venere Ciprea** (reconstructed in 1614), with Andromeda *(at the top)*, Venus and Cupid in the central niche and four bas-reliefs depicting the myth of Artemis (Diana) and Actaeon.

WALKS

Il Sentiero degli Agrifogli giganti – To find the beginning of this path (the **Giant Holly Trail**), leave Castelbuono and follow signs for San Guglielmo and Rifugio Sempria, where the car can be left. The route is some 3.5km/2mi (allow 2hr 30min). For those seeking a ramble away from it all, the path leads from **Piano Sempria** along a beautiful path through woods of holm and young oak to **Piano Pomo** where a congregation of giant holly trees are to be found; these are not bushes but huge trees 15m/49ft tall, some estimated to be more than 300 years old.

Il Pollina and the Gole di Tiberio – An alternative walk leads to the **Pollina River** and the evocative **Tiberius' Gorge**. From Castelbuono, take the road down towards Cefalù, approximately 1km/0.6mi after the bridge over the Fiumara, follow the asphalted road on the right. At Contrada **Marcatagliastro** *(where the asphalt peters out)*, leave the car and proceed on foot to the river *(about 4km/2.5mi)*. The gorge is on the right.

Golfo di CASTELLAMMARE★★

Trapani – Population 13 972
Michelin map 432 N 20

This magnificent bay stretches from Capo San Vito to Capo Rama. It is characterised by gentle hills punctuated by harsh mountain ranges and is dominated to the west by the impressive bulk of Monte Cofano, which overlooks the promotory of Capo San Vito *(see SAN VITO LO CAPO)*. In addition to the stunning coastal scenery and well-known resorts dotted along the coast, this region is also of cultural interest with its many castles, tuna fisheries, fortified buildings and archaeological sites, all set against a landscape which is both agricultural and popular with tourists.

Castellammare del Golfo – Set in the beautiful bay of the same name, this town, now a popular seaside resort, was once the main port and principal trading post for the ancient cities of Segesta and Erice. In the centre of the town stands the **medieval castle** which gave it its name.

> ### Where to stay
>
> **Agriturismo Arabesque** – Loc Manostalla, Partinico (PA) ☎ 091 87 87 755; Fax 091 89 87 663. This beautiful guest-house is situated among vineyards and olive trees, only 2km/1.2mi from the coast. Swimming pool. Approximately 170 000L for a double room (including breakfast).

After Castellammare del Golfo, the road winds its way up a bare mountainside providing glorious **views**★ *(car park)* of the town and its harbour.

Scopello – The road leads onwards to Scopello, a small hamlet on the sea dominated by its 18C *baglio* (a large, fortified building – *see Introduction*) which faces onto the central piazza. After a bend in the road, a dirt road on the right leads down to the old tuna fishery (can be reached on foot).

Old tuna fishery

La Tonnara – The tuna fishery, now disused, testifies to an activity that once flourished in the fish-rich waters off this coast. Out of season, the place takes on an atmosphere all of its own. Silence reigns among the abandoned buildings; the only sound is the irregular rhythm of the waves. Time seems to stand still like the main buildings where the cruel rituals of killing tuna *(la metanza)* were enacted. The net weights sit impassively aside.

In the summer, on the other hand, the place bustles with sun-seekers and bathers. From here there is a wonderful view of the large monolithic rocks *(i faraglioni)*, that recall their more famous cousins off the island of Capri.

★**Riserva Naturale dello Zingaro** ⊙ – *The nature reserve between Scopello and San Vito lo Capo can be accessed from either of these two places.*

This, the first nature reserve to be designated in Sicily, measures some 7km/4mi in length and covers approximately 1 650ha/4 076 acres. The main track follows the coastline high above the sea offering spectacular **views**★ down over the successive creeks, bays, beaches (many of which are accessible), sheer cliffs and rocky headlands: these, seen together, provide a gloriously unspoilt area of Sicily. The wonderful, lush, Mediterranean vegetation (some 700 species) occasionally allows patches of red base rock to show through. This provides a provocative contrast of warm colour, offset by the deep green fronds of dwarf palms and the softer shades of green added by the shiny laurel bushes, matt agave spikes, tender asphodels and succulent prickly-pears; a further accent is provided by the garishly yellow flowering oxalis (also known as wood sorrel, Bermuda buttercup or Cape sorrel). Other equally attractive paths meander their way inland: as the scenery alters, so the vegetation changes until, at last, tumbling capers and flowering ash predominate.

The reserve maintains a number of nooks and crannies that provide sheltered burrows and nesting sites for a variety of animals (including small predators) and, more particularly, birds (with 39 different species documented including Peregrine falcons, Bonelli's eagles and kestrels).

The Zingaro Nature Reserve also preserves ancient vestiges of early man's presence in the area through the centuries: evidence of Neolithic and Mesolithic settlements have been uncovered near the Grotta dell'Uzzo, while vestiges of rural settlements, consisting of some 20 well-preserved houses, have been found at Baglio Cusenza; others have been found at la Tonnarella dell'Uzzo.

EXCURSION INLAND

Alcamo – *About 11km/6.5mi S of Castellammare del Golfo.* The name of the town is suggestive of the 13C poet **Cielo d'Alcamo**, author of a well-known work entitled *Rosa Fresca Aulentissima (The Fresh Fragrant Rose)*, one of the earliest texts to be written in Italian. One glance at the landscape, populated with vineyards, is likely to prompt more basic – though no less pleasant – associations with the local dry white wine which bears the town's name.

The town's churches contain works by members of the **Gagini** family (16C) and by Serpotta, one of the Sicilian masters of the Baroque. The main works are to be found in Santa Oliva, San Francesco d'Assisi, San Salvatore and the imposing **Chiesa Madre** ⊙ the principal church, which has a fine 15C chapel. Overlooking piazza Repubblica which has been laid out with gardens, is the **Castello dei Conti di Modica**. The castle built for the Counts of Modica in the 14C, is rhomboid in shape and has two rectangular and two round towers. Gothic two-light windows pierce the northern side.

CASTELVETRANO

Trapani – Population 30 160
Michelin map 432 N 20

Castelvetrano is a small farming town primarily concerned with the cultivation of vines and olive trees, and woodworking (for furniture). The first impression of the town is tainted by the large square glass building, the new hospital. Behind this extends the old town. The focal centre of Castelvetrano hinges on two adjacent squares, **piazza Umberto I** and **piazza Garibaldi**, and it is in this part of the town that the main monuments are to be found. In the nearby piazza Regina Margherita, overlooking a pleasant municipal garden, is the stark façade of **San Domenico** (15C) which, at one time, was attached to a convent (now a secondary school) from which it preserves the cloisters *(entrance to the right of the church)*; on the opposite side sits the 16C Church of **San Giovanni** complete with its massive bell-tower.

SIGHTS

Piazza Garibaldi – The square is lined with fine buildings such as the town's main church and the **Chiesa del Purgatorio** (now an auditorium), the latter an elegant conglomeration of elaborate detail (Classical friezes, false balcony, statues nestling in niches, volutes) drawn from a transitional late Mannerist-Baroque style. Next in line sits the 19C **Teatro Selinus**, which preserves its original stage.

Santa Trinità di Delia

Chiesa Madre ⊘ – The town's principal church dates, in its present form, from the 16C. The front elevation rises through two storeys: a pair of pilasters ornamented with garlands flank the entrance at ground level, the upper section is pierced by a rose-window. Swallow-tailed merlons run the length of the side walls. The internal space is arranged according to a composite Latin-cross/basilica plan typical of Norman churches: the nave is flanked by aisles with two transepts, the second terminating in apses (a square-ended one between two round ones). The glorious **stucco decoration**★ adorning the triumphal arch is attributed to **Gaspare Serpotta** (17C, father of the more famous Giacomo): a host of angels bearing festoons and garlands interplay with others brandishing musical instruments. The same elements are applied to the transept arch, although here the decoration is more restrained. The central ridge of the vaulted ceiling is painted with allegorical figures, inscribed with two dates: 1564 and 1570.

Piazza Umberto I – This delightful little piazza lies to the left of the church, providing a clear view of the bell-tower, which is hidden from the front. Gracing the square is a fine little fountain, the **Fontana della Ninfa**, named after the nymph nestling in a niche near the top, erected in the 17C in celebration of the restitution of an aqueduct.

Museo Selinuntino ⊘ – *Via Garibaldi.* The 16C *palazzo*, once home to the Majo family, now accommodates a museum for artefacts recovered from Selinunte. The well-presented displays are deservedly arranged around the prize exhibit: an elegant bronze statue of a young man (c 460 BC) which is famously known as *Ephebus of Selinunte*★. In a side niche nestles a lovely *Madonna and Child* by **Francesco Laurana** and his workshop from the Church of the Annunziata. The museum continues on the first floor with displays of religious objects and three shallow reliefs by the contemporary artist Giuseppe Lo Sciuto.

EXCURSION INLAND

Santa Trinità di Delia ⊘ – *4km/2.4mi W: follow directions from piazza Umberto I. The church is part of the Baglio Trinità farm complex.* This enchanting Arabo-Norman church (12C) conforms to a Greek-cross plan with three apses projecting on one side; it is capped by a pink dome. The exterior walls are pierced by single light windows screened with perforated stone panels, inset into articulated surrounds. Inside, the dome hovers above pendentives – a typically Moorish element – supported by four marble columns with Corinthian capitals. The apses are ornamented with delicate little columns. Resting here and in the crypt are various Saporito family tombs (19C), a powerful local dynasty.

A few metres from the church, on the opposite side of the road, extends the **Trinità forestry estate**, a lush area of eucalyptus, palm-trees and pines. This ideal spot for a picnic looks out onto an attractive **man-made lake**.

CASTROREALE

Messina – Population 2 972
Michelin map 432 M 27

The ancient town of Cristina, perched upon a series of spurs among the Monti Peloritani, became a dominion of considerable importance with jurisdiction over an extensive area following Frederick II of Aragon's concession of sovereignty in exchange for loyalty during the war against the Angevins. Re-christened Castroreale, it retains many medieval features, interconnecting little streets and alleys that open onto delightful little piazzas, and many churches, several containing a wealth of artworks that testify to the town's glorious past.

OLD TOWN

Chiesa Madre ⊙ – An elegant Baroque portal graces the front of the main church in stark contrast with the massive 16C campanile, which was probably used as a watchtower. **Inside** are hung a charming *St Catherine of Alexandria* (1534) and *Mother and Child* (1501) by Antonello Gagini and, in the north aisle, Andrea Calamech's *St James the Great (St James the Apostle)*. From the terrace, on the east side of the church, there is a magnificent **view**★ over the plain of Milazzo; an inscription records further privileges granted to the "royal town" by King Philip IV of Spain in 1639.

Continue along corso Umberto I, and then turn left towards the 15C **Chiesa della Candelora** – a church dedicated to Candlemas, the feast commemorating the purification of the Blessed Virgin Mary and the presentation of Christ in the Temple – with its simple brick façade and Durazzo portal.

Proceed along salita Federico II to a round **tower**, all that survives of the castle built by Frederick II of Aragon in 1324. From the top there is a fine **view**★ over Castroreale, the little Moorish dome of the Church of the Candelora, and the surrounding countryside beyond.

Back down to piazza Peculio; this owes its name to the former Peculio Frumentario (Wheat Reserve) which has since been replaced by the town hall. This was very probably the Jewish quarter: the arch on the viewing terrace behind Monte di Pietà is supposed to have been that of a synagogue transferred from hereabouts. The piazza is flanked by the 15C Church of the Holy Saviour **(San Salvatore)**, severely damaged, alas, in the earthquake of 1978, and its semi-collapsed bell-tower (1560) which once formed part of a chain of watchtowers with those of the cathedral and the castle.

Further along via Guglielmo Siracusa (formerly via della Moschita), there is a small art gallery on the right.

Pinacoteca di Santa Maria degli Angeli ⊙ – The art gallery houses various rare paintings and sculptures, including a panel of St Agatha (c 1420) in the Byzantine style, an unusually delicate Flemish triptych depicting *The Adoration of the Magi* with St Marina and St Barbara, a fine polyptych of *The Nativity* from the Neapolitan studio of GF Criscuolo, a marble statue of St John the Baptist by Calamech (1568) and a silver altar-frontal by Filippo Juvara (18C).

Museo Civico ⊙ – The municipal museum, housed in a former oratory dedicated to St Philip Neri, contains sculptures in wood and marble, including the splendid **funeral monument**★ of Geronimo Rosso (1506-08), an extremely fine work by **Antonello Gagini**, as well as a number of other notable paintings. Among the best are: a 14C Cross with scenes from the life of Christ, a lovely *Madonna and Child* by Antonello de Saliba (1503-05) – with the infant portrayed with the face of an adult – a Salvator Mundi (Saviour of the World) panel by Polidoro da Caravaggio betraying the clear influence of Raphael, and an altarpiece depicting St Lawrence by Fra' Simpliciano da Palermo.

Further along the same street is **Sant'Agata** ⊙, which was remodelled in the 19C and which contains an *Annunciation* by Antonello Gagini (1519), a statue of St Agatha (1554) by the Florentine sculptor Montorsoli, and an expressive 17C plaster and *papier-maché* image known as the **"Cristo Lungo"**, which is carried in procession on a 12-metre pole so as to be visible from every corner of the town. Nearby is the 16C **Santa Marina**, a church incorporating masonry from the Norman period and vestiges of fortifications typical of Spanish defences.

CATANIA ★

Population 339 271
Michelin map 432 O 27

Catania is overshadowed by Mount Etna, the volcano which has often betrayed the trust of the local people, sending forth great flows of lava, on one occasion down into the town itself. Reminders of the mountain, besides the physical presence of its towering profile on the horizon, appear in every sombre-looking monument, house and doorway detail which, when it is not made of lava stone, is of plaster painted to look like lava. The colours of the city are predominantly black and white, and these are used in combination to maximum effect. The saddest century in the city's history must surely be the 17C when lava flowed into the streets (1669) and, a mere 24 years later, a terrible earthquake destroyed most of the buildings (1693). This also marked the rebirth of a new city laid out according to a more modern urban plan with wide streets, piazzas and monuments. The main force behind the change was the architect **Giovanni Battista Vaccarini** (1702-68). For obvious reasons, therefore, Catania was predominantly rebuilt in a homogeneous style, so much so that the last vestiges of its more ancient past disappeared from view beneath an all-enveloping Baroque cloak: the theatre, odeon and amphitheatre from Antiquity are all hidden behind or beneath 18C *palazzi*. In the following century, Catania became home to the great composer, **Vincenzo Bellini** (1801-35), and the writer, **Giovanni Verga** (1840-1922).

A busy port and Sicily's second-largest city after Palermo, Catania is also one of the hottest places in Italy: in summer, temperatures can exceed 40°C.

For two days in early February, celebrations gain momentum for the feast day of St Agatha (5 February), the patron of the city who died a martyr there, and who is invoked against fire and eruptions of Mount Etna. At this time, the streets of the city are invaded by a cacophony of sound and colour as proof of a thriving cult following.

B via Cimarosa 10, ☎ 095 73 06 211; Fax 095 34 71 21.

GETTING TO CATANIA

For visitors arriving by **air**, Fontanarossa airport is situated 7km/4.5mi to the south of Catania (☎ 095 72 39 111). The airport is served by a number of airlines (Alitalia, Meridiana, Air Sicilia, Air Europe, Alpi Eagles) which operate services to all the major Italian cities. The Alibus links the airport with the city centre and the railway station (departures every 20 min from 5pm-midnight); the ticket is the same price as on the city buses.

The bus terminal is located in piazza Giovanni XXIII (by the railway station). The SAIS (via d'Amico 181, ☎ 095 53 61 68) and Etna trasporti (via d'Amico 181, ☎ 095 53 27 16) **bus companies** operate services between Catania and other major cities and tourist sites in Sicily; AST (via Sturzo 220, ☎ 095 74 61 096) links the city with other towns in the provinces of Catania and Siracusa.

Catania has good **train** connections with Messina (approximately 2hr) and Siracusa (1hr 30min); the service to and from Palermo is less frequent (just over 3hr). The main railway station is in piazza Giovanni XXIII (☎ 095 53 27 10).

GETTING AROUND

City buses – These are operated by AMT (Azienda Municipale Trasporti), via Plebiscito 747, ☎ 095 73 60 247, www.amt.ct.it A ticket costs 1 300L and is valid for 90min; a day pass costs 3 500L.

Sightseeing – The circular bus route no 410 provides tourists with a round tour of the main sights and points of interest. Services run by appointment only. For further information, contact ☎ 095 736 60 226; Fax 095 71 50 141.

WHERE TO STAY

CAMP SITES AND HOSTELS

Jonio – Loc. Ognina *(take via Messina from corso Italia)*, Via Villini a Mare 2, ☎ 095 49 11 39; Fax 095 49 22 77 (with bungalows).

Villaggio Turistico Europe – Viale Kennedy 91 *(the extension of via Cristoforo Colombo)*, ☎ 095 59 10 26 (with bungalows).

Ostello Agorà – Piazza Currò 6, ☎ 095 49 70 15. This hostel, housed in a 19C building, has rooms with bunk beds and a number of communal areas. Situated in an old square close to the fish market.

HOTELS

La Vecchia Palma – Via Etnea 668, ☎/fax 095 43 20 25. This family-run hotel is situated in a Liberty-style building and has 7 comfortable rooms, some of which have retained their original decor. Double rooms approximately 140 000L (including breakfast).

EATING OUT

For a quick bite at midday, select any one of the many bars in the centre selling sandwiches or one-course lunches, or make for one of the little *trattorie* near the fish market (behind piazza Duomo). Below are a few suggestions for dinner:

Cantine del Cugno Mezzano – Via Museo Biscari 8, ☎ 095 71 58 710. Closed at midday, Mon and during Aug. The former stables of Palazzo Biscari house this restaurant-cum-wine bar, which serves cuisine inspired by local traditions. Around 60 000L per person.

La Lampara – Via Pasubio 49 *(one of the roads crossing corso Italia)*, ☎ 095 38 32 37. Closed Weds and two weeks during Aug. A simple, family-run restaurant serving fish and seafood specialities. Around 50 000L per person.

★PIAZZA DEL DUOMO

The heart of the town, designed by Vaccarini, collects together its principal monuments which, in turn, impart to the square an endearing Baroque elegance. In the middle stands the **Fontana dell'Elefante**, the symbol of Catania. On the south side of the square, offset by the Chierici and Pardo *palazzi* behind, sits the more delicate **Fontana dell'Amenano**.

The most prominent ensemble is provided by the Duomo façade, flanked to the right by the Bishop's Palace and Porta Uzeda and, to the left, by the attractive front of the Badia di Sant'Agata, slightly set back. The north side of the square is almost completely taken up by the elegant front elevation of the **Palazzo Senatorio** or **Palazzo degli Elefanti** (now the town hall), designed by GB Vaccarini. In the courtyard stand two senatorial carriages.

Fontana dell'Elefante – This fountain, recalling Bellini's famous obelisk-bearing monument in piazza Minerva in Rome, was conceived in 1735. The black lava elephant standing on a high stone platform is possibly of Byzantine origin (documents confirm it to have graced the square in the 1500s) and bears on its back an Ancient Egyptian obelisk covered with hieroglyphics celebrating the cult of Isis. Isis is the Mother goddess, sister, wife and saviour of Osiris, who became the centre of a popular Greco-Roman mystery cult.

★**Duomo** ⊙ – The cathedral is dedicated to St Agatha, the patron saint of the city; it was erected in the late 11C by the Norman king Roger I, and rebuilt after the earthquake of 1693. The **façade★** is considered to be one of Vaccarini's masterpieces. Further along via Vittorio Emanuele II, the tall Norman lava apses can be admired from the courtyard of the Bishop's Palace. Its solid outward appearance relieved in part by the tall, single, narrow, slit-like openings underline the fact that the Duomo was conceived as a fortified church.

The north side is graced with a fine 16C portal ornamented with an entablature with cherubs.

Interior – *From the north entrance.* Restoration of the floor has revealed several column bases from the original Norman church.

Against the second pilaster on the right, in the nave, stands the funerary stele of Bellini who died at his home in Puteaux, near Paris, where he was originally buried. The transepts both harbour chapels, segregated from the crossing by a glorious Renaissance archway. The chapel to the right, dedicated to the Madonna, contains the sarcophagus of Constanza, wife of Frederick III of Aragon, who died in 1363. The southern chapel is dedicated to St Agatha: this although Renaissance in spirit, is encrusted with gilded stucco decoration that verges on the exaggerated. The especially elaborate Spanish doorway leads through to the reliquary and treasury *(on the left)*. The fine funerary monument straight ahead belongs to Ferdinandez de Acuña (1495), the figure depicted on his knees. The 16C carved choir stalls illustrate scenes from the life of St Agatha.

The sacristy has a large fresco (badly damaged, alas) showing a fairly accurate topographical view of Catania before 1669, with Etna on the skyline spewing lava which, lower down, is shown on the point of invading the city.

Below the church reside the vestiges of Roman baths, the **Terme Achilliane** *(normally accessible through a trapdoor in front of the building, but temporarily closed).*

★**Badia di Sant'Agata** – The church beside the Duomo contributes to the overall splendour of the piazza. The serpentine lines of the **façade★** are contained by a cornice that emphasises the ground level with, at the centre, a triangular pediment. This is another example of Vaccarini's mastery in design.

Fontana dell'Amenano – The fountain is named after the river that supplies it on its way past a few of the principal monuments from the Roman period (the theatre and baths or Terme della Rotonda). Locally, the fountain is called "Acqua a

The market

lenzuolo" by the people of Catania because of the way the water cascades down from the top basin, resembling a continuous fine veil. The open area behind is piazza Alonzo di Benedetto, where a bustling and picturesque **fish market** takes place each morning. The covered section, in times past, housed the military guard for the **Porta Carlo V**, which in the 16C used to be part of the city's fortifications. Its main frontage can still be seen from piazza Pardo.

Back in piazza Benedetto, down by the side of Palazzo Chierici, stands the Fontana dei Sette Canali.

The surrounding quarter

In the stretch of via Vittorio Emanuele II behind the Duomo nestle a number of important sights. A small square on the right harbours the lovely church of **San Placido** with its gently undulating façade by **Stefano Ittar** (1769). Opposite the right side of the church (via Museo Biscari) sits the former convent on which it depended, although little of the original remains besides the elements of a doorway and a few windows. The courtyard (access from via Landolina) preserves remains of the **Palazzo Platamone** (15C), namely a decorative balcony in coloured stone.

★ **Palazzo Biscari** ⊙ – This is the finest civic building in the city. It was erected after the earthquake of 1693, but reached its greatest splendour about 60 years later thanks to Ignazio Biscari, a man of eclectic interests, and an impassioned lover of art, literature and archaeology. It was he who promoted many of the excavations in the area and pushed for a museum of archaeology to be set up in this building. The south wing, in particular, is lavishly **decorated★★**: figures and volutes, cherubs and racemes fill the window frames along the long terrace, relieving the sombreness of the dark façade. The entrance to the palazzo (via Museo Biscari) is through an elaborate portal that leads into a courtyard with a fine stairway. The first floor accommodates the main reception rooms. At the far end, there is a splendid room with frescoes by Sebastiano Lo Monaco, complemented with stucco work, gilded mouldings and mirrors. The centre of the ceiling opens out into an oval dome, complete with gallery, behind which musicians once played: this was conceived as such so as to suggest the music descended from the heavens. The fresco depicts the triumph of the family being celebrated by a council of the gods. A pretty spiral staircase situated in the gallery next to the hall provides access to the little platform. From the gallery, an admirable view extends over the terrace on the south side of the building.

CATANIA

WESTERN DISTRICT

Continue along via Vittorio Emanuele II which, together with the more commercial via Etnea, constitutes the very heart of Catania and the most fashionable part of town. Begin at piazza San Francesco with its monumental church dedicated to St Francis, and turn down the lovely via Crociferi.

★**Via Crociferi** – This is regarded as Catania's Baroque street *par excellence*. The magnificent buildings ranged elegantly along either side, particularly in the first section, impart a graciousness that is quite unique. Through the gateway, **Arco di San Benedetto**, reside the Badia Grande and its diminutive Badia Piccola. On the left are aligned two churches dedicated to **San Benedetto** and **San Francesco Borgia**; between the two runs a narrow street with **Palazzo Asmundo** at the far end.

Further along via Crociferi on the left, stands a former Jesuit residence that now accommodates the Istituto d'Arte. The first courtyard, attributed to Vaccarini, is graced with a fine two-tiered portico: the same bay elevation has also been used in the University courtyard in piazza dell'Università. It also has a striking black and white cobbled pavement.

Palazzo Biscari (detail)

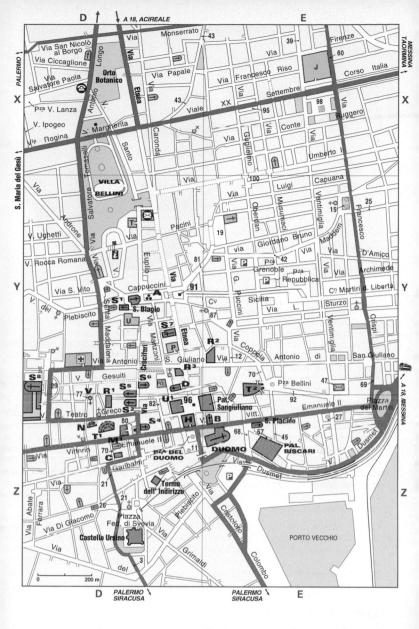

The elegant, curvilinear **façade★** of **San Giuliano** on the right was probably designed by Vaccarini. The internal space is arranged to a Greek-cross-cum-octagonal plan. Above the elaborate altar of agate and other semi-precious stones sits a 14C painted wooden Crucifix.

The street terminates at the gates of Villa Cerami, now the seat of the Faculty of Jurisprudence.

Museo Belliniano ⊙ – The house where **Vincenzo Bellini** (1801-35) was born now comprises a museum for displaying relevant documents, mementoes and portraits of the composer, together with a harpsichord and a spinette that once belonged to his grandfather. The last room contains various autographed original scores.

Museo Emilio Greco ⊙ – This archive-cum-museum houses the complete **graphic output★** of the native-born artist Emilio Greco (1913-95), who achieved particular fame as a sculptor. The subjects, for the most part female heads and nudes, illustrate his perceptive predilection for Hellenistic art, notably for its graceful lines and elegant forms.

Teatro Antico ⊙ – *Access via 266 corso Vittorio Emanuele II.* The present layout of the theatre dates from the Roman era. It is quite possible, however, that it occupies the site of an older Greek structure of which no traces remain other than in contemporary documents (notably a speech by Alcibiade addressing the people of

A composer of genius

The creator of *La sonnam-bula*, *Norma* and *I puritani* was a Romantic composer, who dedicated himself to his works with "the passion that is so characteristic of genius, convinced that a large part of success depends on the choice of an interesting theme, warm expressive tones and a contrast of passions".

LARA PESSINA

Catania during the Peloponnese War). It is built of lava stone, and would have had tiers of seats made of white limestone or marble (for the more important citizens) for a capacity audience of 7000 spectators. The *cavea* is supported on three vaulted inter-connected passageways; these also provide access to the auditorium by means of *vomitoria*, flights of steps that enabled large numbers of people to come and go quickly.

As far back as Norman times, the theatre was despoiled of its marble slabs for re-use in building the cathedral.

Beside the theatre stands an **odeon**, although this is later in date. It served as a more intimate context for musical shows, poetry readings and orations. At the back of the auditorium run a series of galleries: their exact purpose is not known.

Anyone particularly interested in Roman remains can request to be taken by a theatre custodian to visit the **Terme della Rotonda** *(via della Rotonda)*; little survives of these baths, however, other than a single circular domed chamber that was converted into a church in Byzantine times (6C). Access may also be arranged for the **Terme dell'Indirizzo** *(piazza Currò)*, a more extensive bath complex comprising at least 10 domed rooms. Here the wood-stoked burner that provided heating is clearly visible as are sections of rectangular hot-air ducting.

Casa di Verga ⊙ – *Via Sant'Anna 8*. The little house where the writer **Giovanni Verga** (1840-1922) spent many years of his life is preserved much as he left it; some items of furniture from his home in Milan have been added (especially to the last rooms). His study provides the opportunity of browsing through the author's "literary passions" and identifying his favourite writers such as Capuana, D'Annunzio and Deledda.

★VIA ETNEA

This straight, 3km/1.8mi long thoroughfare runs on a north-south axis making its way past Catania's best shops and boutiques, and running through piazza del Duomo *(see above)*, piazza dell'Università, piazza Stesicoro, before arriving at last before Villa Bellini, Catania's lovely public gardens.

Piazza dell'Università – The square piazza is surrounded on all sides by elegant *palazzi*. On the right stands Vaccarini's **Palazzo Sangiuliano**; on the left, the **University** arranged around an attractive courtyard surrounded by a portico with a loggia above. In the evening, the piazza is illuminated by four splendid lamps (1957) produced by a sculptor from Catania.

Further down the street rises the lovely concave frontage of the **Collegiata** (Santa Maria della Consolazione) designed by **Stefano Ittar** (18C). A short distance beyond, on the left, comes the gracious **Palazzo San Demetrio** (17C-18C) with its elaborate doorway and corbels. Just inside the entrance to the next church, the 18C **San Michele Arcangelo**, a double marble staircase climbs up to two Baroque stoups with angels drawing aside a marble drape to reveal the basin while the rest conceals the supporting ledge.

Piazza Stesicoro – The ruin in the middle of the square is all that survives of an enormous **Roman amphitheatre** (105m/344ft x 105m/344ft) that might have accommodated 15000 spectators. Most of the area it once occupied lies hidden below the piazza and the surrounding Baroque buildings.

San Biagio (Sant'Agata alla Fornace) ⓥ – The actual 18C building stands upon the foundations of a chapel dedicated to the patron saint of Catania, who was martyred here. In Roman times, the town's lime kilns were concentrated in this area. A chapel within the church *(at the far end on the right)* preserves the *carcara* (kiln or furnace) in which Agatha is meant to have met her death (other sources say she died in prison).

According to popular tradition, the Church of **Sant'Agata in Carcere**, behind the plazza, was built on the site of a Roman jail where the saint was imprisoned in 251. It has a fine Romanesque doorway. The wild olive tree growing next to the church was planted on the spot where another had sprouted after Agatha had stopped there on her way into the prison.

★**Villa Bellini** – The large, luxuriant park is thick with exotic plants. From the top of the hill (where a kiosk stands), there is a beautiful view over the city and out towards Mount Etna.

Orto Botanico ⓥ – *Entrance in via Longo.* The botanical gardens were laid out in the 1950s with various indigenous as well as exotic varieties, notably examples of Dracena Drago and Euforbia Brachiata.

ADDITIONAL SIGHTS

San Nicolò l'Arena ⓥ – The Benedictine Order, one of the richest and most powerful in the city, built a grandiose monastery (16C-17C) and an imposing **church** alongside, although the façade was never completed. Inside the huge and bare church, there is a lovely 18C organ case behind the altar. The meridian line was laid into the transept floor in 1841; this catches the sunlight precisely at 13 minutes past midday (at one time, this occurred dead on noon).

★**Monastery** – The present building dates from the 18C. The eye-catching doorway on the left of the church provides access to the courtyard, from where the east and south sides of the building, designed by Antonino Amato, may be admired. The opulent **decoration** recalls that of the contemporary Palazzo Biscari *(see above).* The first cloisters harbour a small neo-Gothic arcaded inner courtyard decorated with maiolica. The monastery now accommodates the University's Faculty of Arts; from the original have been preserved the fine oval refectory, now transformed into the main lecture-hall, and library along with the magnificent **Sala Vaccarini** that has wondrously large oval windows and an attractive 18C Neopolitan maiolica floor.

Santa Maria del Gesù ⓥ – Although built in 1465, this church has undergone considerable alterations. From the original there survives the Cappella Paternò complete with Renaissance archway surmounted by a lunette, inset with a Pietà, by **Antonello Gagini**. He is also the author of the Madonna and Child *(second altar on the right).*

Castello Ursino ⓥ – Frederick II of Swabia erected this austere, solid-looking castle on the seafront in the 13C; the reason why today the sea lies so far away is explained by the great river of lava that flowed down here in 1669, pushing the water offshore. The castle is supposedly named after a Roman consul (Arsinius), or possibly after the Orsini, an offshoot of the famous Roman family that fled to these parts in the Middle Ages seeking refuge after siding with the Ghibelline sympathisers (supporting the Emperor rather than the Church).

The castle is square in plan; it has a large round tower at each corner and two additional towers halfway along two sides.

Pinacoteca – The local art gallery assembles a collection of paintings, principally by southern Italian artists, that range from the 15C to the 19C.

Notable works include a polyptych with the *Virgin Enthroned with St Anthony and St Francis* by **Antonello de Saliba** (15C), a pupil of Antonello da Messina: see how delicately the features of the Madonna are rendered. Among the pictures influenced by Caravaggio's strong use of chiaroscuro and theatrical gesture for dramatic effect, look out for the expressive *St Christopher* by **Pietro Novelli**. There are two beautiful studies by **Michele Rapisardi**, an artist from Catania who came to prominence in the 19C: one pre-empted his depiction of the Sicilian Vespers, the other work is a sketched *Head of the Mad Ophelia* – a haunting image of a woman's hypnotic stare addressed accusingly towards the spectator. Examples by another Catanese artist, Giuseppe Sciuti, include a *Widow* – an expression of infinite sadness. Before leaving, cast an eye over the *Pastorello Malato (The Ailing Shepherd-boy)*, a delicate watercolour by Guzzone, and the vivid paintings by Lorenzo Loiacono.

Teatro Bellini – Catania's opera house commemorates its most illustrious musician. It was inaugurated with a production of his *Norma* in 1890. The acoustics of its beautiful auditorium are among the best in the world.

Palazzo Manganelli – This elaborately decorated *palazzo* provided the setting for a number of interior scenes in Luchino Visconti's film of *The Leopard*, based on the famous novel by Tomasi di Lampedusa.

CEFALÀ DIANA

Palermo – Population 987
Michelin map 432 N 22

The town, founded relatively recently (it has been inhabited since 1755, when Duke Diana received the *jus populandi*), deserves a visit even if it is solely on account of its 10C **Turkish baths**, the only example of its kind in Sicily. In the town, it is worth making a detour to see the ruins of a 13C **castle** of which a single square tower and fragments of the defensive outer walls remain.

The place once served as a defensive outpost between Palermo and Agrigento, or what is now a major road. During the ensuing centuries it was used as a grain depot until, in the 18C, it became a noble residence.

Other attractions include, in the main piazza, a series of expressive bronze sculptures by a contemporary artist from Corleone, Biagio Governali; the panels of the Door of Miracles of San Francesco di Paola; and the War Memorial and Monument to the Emigrants, which is so highly dramatic.

> **The baths** ⊘ – These are located just over 1km/0.6mi outside the town, beside the Cefalà River, within their tastefully restored complex. The original date for the baths is difficult to ascertain accurately although it is certainly pre-1570. It is thought that the outer buildings were probably used to accommodate those afflicted by aches and pains who came to bathe in the hot sulphurous springs to relieve their rheumatism.
>
> The rectangular brick building consists of a large room enclosed by a fine barrel vault, in the floor of which there are three pools – although at one time there was but one much larger one. This first section is separated from the elevated rear portion of the room by an elegant screen consisting of an arcade of three raised or Moorish-style arches supported on slender marble columns, terracotta capitals and dosserets (high block, inserted above the *abacus*). Beyond the screen is another, smaller pool, where the hot water bubbling out from the ground was collected before being channelled into the large pool. The vault is punctuated with ventilation holes, while the walls have niches which might have been used by bathers for their discarded clothes.

CEFALÙ ★★

Palermo – Population 14 007
Michelin map 432 M 24

Enjoying an exceptional **position★★**, and clearly visible from the road running north from Palermo, Cefalù started as a simple fishing village perched between the sea and a craggy limestone promontory. Now a small town, it is justly proud of the glorious Romanesque cathedral which towers over the network of narrow streets and ascending terraces of houses. Of Greek origin – hence its name corrupted from the Greek *Kephaloidon*, meaning head or chief – Cefalù was endowed with greatest splendour under the Normans and, in particular, by **Roger II** who, in 1131, decided to initiate work on the cathedral.

🚉 via Amendola 2, ☎ 0921 42 10 50; Fax 0921 42 23 88.

GETTING TO CEFALÙ

For visitors arriving by **car**, Cefalù is 70km/44mi from Palermo and 170km/106mi from Messina. Via Roma, easily accessible from the motorway, has a car park (fee payable) situated just a few minutes from the historical centre of the city. Cefalù can also be reached from Palermo by **bus**, operated by SAIS or by **train** which takes just over 1hr. Train connections are less frequent from Messina and the journey takes approximately 3hr. The railway station is about 10min walk from Corso Ruggero.

Boats leave Cefalù for the Aeolian islands (approx. 90min). Service operated by Aliscafi SNAV, corso Ruggero 82, ☎ 0921 42 15 95.

EATING OUT

La Brace – Via XXV Novembre 10, ☎ 0921 42 35 70. Closed Mon and from 15 Dec to 15 Jan. A welcoming bistro which serves Sicilian cuisine with imaginative Oriental touches. A meal is around 60 000L.

Porticciolo – Via CO Di Bordonaro 66, ☎ 0921 92 19 81. Closed Wed. Excellent pizza served in a small restaurant with a seafaring theme. Around 50 000L for a meal.

Pietro Serio, in via Giuseppe Giglio, is regarded as the best *pasticceria* in Cefalù. Ice cream addicts should try the renowned **Bar Duomo** in piazza del Duomo.

Corso Ruggero – Cefalù's main street overlies the ancient Roman *decumanus* which bisects the town on a north-south axis. The two resulting halves are quite different with their own particular character: to the west lies the medieval quarter, a labyrinth of narrow streets dotted with steps, arches and narrow passageways; to the east, a network of perpendicular, regular streets. The difference can probably be attributed to the two different social classes that lived in the two quarters: the western half was occupied by the common people, the eastern half by the clergy and the nobility.

The Corso starts at piazza Garibaldi, site of one of the four gateways of the town. Facing the piazza is the Baroque Church of Santa Maria alla Catena (Saint Mary of the Chain), the bell-tower of which incorporates remains from the ancient megalithic town walls.

★**Osterio Magno** – The legendary residence of King Roger, later the property of the Ventimiglia family, comprises two parts dating from different periods. The older, two-coloured part of lava and gold-coloured stone faces onto Via Amendola and has two elegant **two-light windows**; it dates from the 13C. The adjoining square tower, on the corner of Corso Ruggero, built in the 14C, has a fine three-light window set into an elaborate Chiaramonte-style arch. The palace, now completely restored, is used for temporary exhibitions.

Further along on the right, stands the **Chiesa del Purgatorio** ⊘ (formerly Santo Stefano Protomartire), its front graced by an elegant double staircase leading up to a Baroque doorway. Just inside is the sarcophagus of Baron Mandralisca *(see museum of the same name)*.

Towards the end, the street broadens out into **piazza del Duomo** which stretches out below the cathedral, enclosed with ranges of splendid *palazzi*: Palazzo Piraino (on the corner of corso Ruggero) with its late 16C portal, the medieval Palazzo Maria with a Gothic portal, possibly once a royal residence and, to the left of the cathedral, the 17C Palazzo Vescovile or Bishop's Palace.

★★**Duomo** ⊘ – The gold-coloured cathedral, a Romanesque jewel set back behind a series of palm trees, appears to merge with the limestone hillside called La Rocca behind. It was built by the Norman **King Roger II** between 1131 and 1240 following a vow he made when on the point of being shipwrecked when returning from Naples. It is also more evidently Norman than its counterpart in Palermo, notably in the Moorish style of façade framed by towers and, at the east end, its tall central apse flanked by two smaller ones. The façade, completed in 1204, is divided into two storeys by the portico which was rebuilt in the 15C by the Lombard architect Ambrogio da Como. The upper section is beautifully ornamented with blind arcading. The twin towers, built on a square plan, rise through levels with single and two-light openings to culminate in crenellations. The central doorway, known as the **King's Gate** (Porta dei Re), served at one time as the main entrance.

Interior – *Entrance from the right side of the church.* The church, with a Latin-cross floorplan, consists of a single nave flanked by aisles, subdivided by columns with fine **capitals★** carved in the Sicilian Arabo-Norman style.

The fabulous **mosaics★★** (1148), executed in a spectacular array of colours (emerald green in particular) on a gold background, adorn the chancel. The eye is immediately attracted to the huge majestic image of the **Christ Pantocrator** gazing down

Christ Pantocrator

from the apse, his right hand raised in benediction, his left holding a sacred scroll inscribed with text from St John's Gospel (Chapter 8, verse 12) in Greek on the left and in Latin on the right: "I am the light of the world: he who followeth me shall not walk in darkness, but shall have the light of life."

Below, on three different levels, the Virgin, attended by four Archangels and the twelve Apostles, are imbued with sensitivity and gentleness of a kind far removed from the more typical wooden face-on portrayals normally associated with Byzantine art. The side-walls of the choir are covered with more mosaics dating from the late 13C, depicting prophets, saints and patriarchs; the angels in the vault date from the same period.

To the right of the choir, note the old bishop's throne and, on the left, the royal marble and mosaic throne *(under restoration)*.

The stained glass windows designed by Michele Canzoneri depict biblical themes and date from the 1990s; they bathe the interior of the church in evocative coloured light.

In the cloisters, which have been closed for years, there are columns and capitals in the same style as the ones at Monreale.

At the bottom of corso Ruggero, turn left and along to piazza Crispi where the **Chiesa della Idria** (Church of the Hydria) stands, flanked by the Bastion of Cape Marchiafava from where the view encompasses a large stretch of the coastline. Not far away, along via Porpora and behind via Giudecca, there is a **tower** with a postern (an opening which allowed only one person to pass at a time) and the ancient remains of massive fortifications.

Climb back up and along via Ortolano di Bordonaro to piazza Marina. From here, via Vittorio Emanuele leads past Porta Pescara, which stands immediately off to the right.

This is the only surviving medieval gateway of the original four that once provided access to the town: it is currently used to display a collection of fishing equipment. A little further on is the picturesque via Mandralisca, leading to the museum of the same name. Set into the paving (towards the end of the street before piazza del Duomo) is the Cefalù coat of arms: three fishes with a loaf of bread, all symbols of Christianity (the fish being an acronym of the word Christ), while also referring to the town's economic resources.

Museo Mandralisca ⊘ – The museum was founded at the request of one of Cefalù's most generous benefactors, Baron Enrico Piraino di Mandralisca, a 19C art collector who bequeathed his art treasures and extensive library (more than

B. Kaufmann

6 000 books, including many from the 16C) to the town. The museum houses a collection of coins and medals; a series of paintings including **Antonello da Messina**'s wonderful *Portralt of an Unknown Man*★ from c 1470; archaeological artefacts, notably some from Lipari including an unusual bell-shaped *krater* (Antique vessel used to mix wine with water) depicting a tuna seller (4C BC); a changing selection of molluscs taken from an extensive collection of some 2 000, and a variety of *objects d'art*, including a Chinese puzzle in ivory.

Return to via Vittorio Emanuele.

A little further along on the right is the medieval **wash-house**, known by the locals as *u ciumi* – meaning the river – which was used by the town's womenfolk until comparatively recently.

La Rocca – *20min to the so-called Temple of Diana; another 40min to the top*. A path leads uphill from corso Ruggero and via dei Saraceni to the top of the outcrop. The first part of the route leads past ancient crenellated walls before rising steeply: particularly tiring in the midday heat of summer, it is best tackled in the early morning or at dusk.

From such height, the magnificent **view**★★ pans across from Capo d'Orlando to Palermo; below, to the east, the town is protected by the promontory marked by a look-out tower, the Torre Caldura, only the remains of which survive. On a good day the Aeolian Islands are quite clearly visible. Finds on this rocky outcrop confirm it to have accommodated the earliest settlements in the area, with evidence from different periods in history including the ruins of an Ancient Greek megalithic building, popularly called the **Temple of Diana**. On the top are the remains of a 12C-13C castle, recently restored.

EXCURSION INLAND *59km/37mi round trip*

This short circuit includes a climb up to the Sanctuary of Gibilmanna perched high on the Pizzo San Angelo, and the circuitous mountain road with panoramic views over the undulating countryside. From Cefalù follow the signs for the Santuario di Gibilmanna.

Santuario di Gibilmanna ⊙ – The **sanctuary**, dedicated to the Madonna, stands 800m/2 624ft above sea level surrounded by oak and chestnut woods: its name refers to its position (from the Arabic *Jebel*, a mountain) and the old tradition, now obsolete, of making manna *(see p 134)*. Of ancient origins – the monastery is supposed to have been one of the six earliest Benedictine communities or coenobites founded at the behest of Gregory the Great in the 6C – it passed into the hands of the Capuchin Friars Minor in 1535. The present building is the result of numerous remodelling, most especially in the Baroque period. The façade was rebuilt in 1907. The shrine is the object of a devout pilgrimage on 8 September, the festival of the Madonna.

Inside the chapel of the Madonna (1625) is an 11C Byzantine fresco of a Madonna and Child, from an earlier Benedictine building, and a statue of the Virgin, probably the work of Antonello Gagini, set into an ornate Baroque altar.

The building adjacent to the monastery, once used as a stable and guestrooms, have been converted into an interesting **museum** dedicated to the life and culture of the Capuchin Friars of the Demone Valley. On display are sacred vestments (17C-18C), paintings, tools (the community was completely self-sufficient), and objects worked from base materials such as wood, tin and wax, as was the custom for this order. Of particular interest are a polyptych by Fra' Feliciano (at the time he was Domenico Guargena), a 16C alabaster rosary belonging to Fra' Giuliano da Placia and a small 18C reed organ.

Down in the catacombs there are rare reliquaries in painted tin or wood made by the friars.

Isnello – This little holiday resort, the starting-point for many walks into the surrounding area, stands in a spectacular **position★** clinging to the rock in the middle of a gorge surrounded by high limestone walls. Its narrow streets have a typical medieval layout.

Take the road back towards the sanctuary; at the junction (signposted to Piano delle Fate), turn left to continue along the panoramic road. This leads through two small villages, **Gratteri**, the centre of which preserves a medieval feel, and **Lascari**, before continuing on down to the coast and Cefalù.

COMISO

Ragusa – Population 29 080
Michelin map 432 Q 25

This little town, which was thrown into the limelight in the 1980s with front-page reports of a controversial American missile base being built there (and subsequently dismantled in the 1990s), boasts several notable 18C buildings.

Piazza Fonte di Diana – The central square of the town is graced with a Neo-Classical **fountain** dedicated to the goddess Diana; this flows with water which would have supplied the public baths in Roman times. Archaeological excavations carried out in the little street directly opposite the fountain, connecting the square to piazza delle Erbe, have revealed parts of the **ancient baths**: an octagonal *caldarium*, and a nymphaeum with a black and white mosaic featuring Neptune surrounded by Nereids (2C AD).

Piazza delle Erbe – The main building overlooking the square is the town's main church, dedicated to **Santa Maria delle Stelle**. Its front elevation rises through three tiers of Doric, Ionic and Corinthian pilasters. The square also harbours the neo-Classical **covered market** (1871): this houses the **Museo Civico di Storia Naturale** ⊙ with its collection of cetaceans (whales and other such mammals) and sea turtles, and the **Biblioteca di Bufalino** ⊙, a library endowed by the author (who died in 1966) for his native town and refuge.

Chiesa dell'Annunziata ⊙ – The elegant neo-Classical front elevation of this church, raised high above an unusual flight of steps, comprises two levels linked by a single element: the palm leaf. The airy light interior, ornamented with white, blue and gold stucco decoration, harbours two paintings by Salvatore Fiume *(in the chancel)*.

Chiesa di San Francesco (dell'Immacolata) ⊙ – This Renaissance church contains the great **Naselli Chapel**; this rises from a square ground-plan, through pendentives, to an octagon from which springs a ribbed dome. Against the wall stands the funerary monument of Baldassare Naselli, surmounted by a small shrine, both by the Gagini. At the back of the church, there is a lovely 17C gallery, painted with baskets of fruit and flowers.

Piazza San Biagio – The square is graced with the **Chiesa di San Biagio**, a Byzantine church (buttresses) that was re-built in the 18C, and the **Castello Aragonese** which was converted into a baronial residence by the Naselli family.

Chiesa dei Cappuccini ⊙ – *In the southern part of the town.* The building dates from 1616. Inside, there is a fine intarsia (inlaid wood) **altar★** and a little statue of the Madonna full of delicacy (18C). The mortuary chapel preserves the mummified remains of various religious and illustrious men, like a miniature of the Capuchin Catacombs in Palermo *(see Index)*.

EXCURSIONS

Vittoria – *6km/3.6mi W*. The town which was founded in the 17C at the wishes of Countess Vittoria Colonna, after whom it is named, was partly spared by the 1693 earthquake. The town appears neat and orderly, organised into straight, perpendicular streets, through which are scattered elegant Liberty style *palazzi*. The heart of the town centres around piazza del Popolo, where **Santa Maria delle Grazie** with its harmoniously curvilinear façade and the neo-Classical municipal theatre are situated. In via Cancellieri, leading off the piazza, are a number of fine buildings: note the Liberty-style **Palazzo Carfi-Manfré** (no 71) and the Venetian Gothic **Palazzo Traina** (nos 108-116).

Via Cavour provides access to the town's main church and the museum. **San Giovanni Battista** (1695) has a distinctively linear front with three entrances and two small lateral domes. The interior is richly decorated with Classical stucco friezes picked out in white, pale and dark blue and gold; the chapel to the left of the altar has Serpotta-style stucco ornament. The **Museo Civico** ⊘ is accommodated in the countess's castle which was completed in 1785 on much earlier foundations. The well-restored rooms continue to reflect the fact that they were used as a prison until 1950. The small museum collects together old machinery for producing special theatrical effects (wind and hail-producing apparatus), a selection of traditional farming tools, and various ornithological specimens. The First World War **concentration camp** located just outside the town centre in Via Garibaldi was used primarily by Hungarian soldiers (who lived there on excellent terms with the local people); one of the dormitory blocks now contains a museum **(Museo Storico Italo-Ungherese)** ⊘ for documents, artefacts and photographs. Further information is provided on display panels which also provide an insight into the current relations between Italy (and, in particular, this little town) and Hungary.

> ### A commendable initiative
>
> **Guided tours of the historic centre** take place every Saturday morning. These are organised by the town council and take in the town's main monuments, including the picturesque local market. Tours leave at 9am from piazza del Popolo, in front of the tourist bus stop. For further information, contact ☎ 0932 86 40 38 (Signor Lo Piano).

Acate – *Approx 15km/9mi W*. In the past the little town was called Biscari; its modern name probably comes from the word for agate, a semi-precious stone commonly found locally. For generations, it formed part of the feudal holdings of the princes of Paterno-Castello (who also built a famous palace in Catania, *see CATANIA*), hence the presence of such a massive residence in the town centre. It is also worth seeking out the town's main church (Chiesa Madre) and San Vincenzo which claims to preserve the martyred saint's relics.

Cave di CUSA★

Trapani

Michelin map 432 ○ 20

Not far from **Selinunte**, the Cusa quarries were the main source of building stone for the town's temples and, more specifically, given the size of the blocks of stone extracted, for Temple G. The stone, a fine-grained and resistant kind of tufa particularly suitable for building, was quarried for more than 150 years, since the first half of the 6C BC. Work at the quarry ground to a brief halt following the outbreak of war when Selinunte was forced to confront the Carthaginian onslaught (resulting in the destruction of the town). The quarries were abandoned shortly after, as were the houses of the people who worked there. This is what is so unusual about the place: enormous blocks of rock destined for the temples still lie here half-quarried. The considerable number of such blocks makes it possible to calculate that there must have been about 150 stone-cutters engaged there. The quarrying technique was long and complex. Once the dimensions and profile of the piece to be extracted had been marked out, a double groove about half a metre deep was dug around it to enable the stonemasons to work more easily (the so-called chipping channel). The block was worked *in situ* and cut straight from the base rock. The tools used included picks, bronze saws and wedges. To split the harder layers, wooden wedges were inserted into cracks and then dampened with water so that, as they swelled, the stone would crack open. Once this was done, the block was severed at the base. The lighter blocks were removed by means of winches while the bulkier ones were slid down ramps (in this case, the material in front of the block was removed). The deep U-shaped grooves visible in some of the square blocks were made so that a rope could be fed through them for lifting (some can be seen at Agrigento in the Temple of Jupiter). Many blocks have a square hole at either end. Into these sockets were fitted special shafts that enabled the blocks to be moved and set in place. The blocks were transported on wooden frames with wheels, and pulled by oxen and slaves. A wide rocky track 12km/7mi long led from the quarries to Selinunte.

The modern name of the quarries comes from the owner of the land on which they were discovered.

QUARRY ⊙

3km/1.8mi S of Campobello di Mazara. Signposted.

The great cylindrical blocks which lie scattered on the ground or await to be quarried (some 60 in number) are a characteristic feature of the quarry, which is 1.8km/1mi long and extends along a ridge from east to west.

In the first section of the quarry, some blocks sit cut and ready for transporting; others barely sketched out, are ready for the stone-cutter. At the far end of the quarry is a capital in the making. Its cylindrical mass tapers from a square base into the 12 wedges intended as the echinus or ovolo moulding below the abacus. The cracks still show the marks made by picks. At Selinunte *(see SELINUNTE)*, among the ruins of Temple A, are examples of finished capitals with square bases, complete with the top of the column shaft and a section of the ovolo moulding intended as part of the entablature.

Stone quarries

Castello di DONNAFUGATA★

Ragusa
Michelin map 432 Q 25

The name, which is Arabic in origin, is misleading. It does not, in fact, refer, as first appearances might suggest, to a woman fleeing some tyrannical husband or father, nor to one of the legends lingering in some popular memory, but is a free interpretation and transcription of *Ayn as Jafât* (meaning Fountain of Health), which in Sicilian dialect became Ronnafuata and so was corrupted to its modern form.

The origins of the building, furthermore, are more recent than the name. The oldest part (which includes the square tower) dates back to the mid-17C when the Donnafugata fiefdom was acquired by Vincenzo Arezzo La Rocca. The building was continuously altered until the early 20C, when Corrado Arezzo transformed the façade into what can be seen today.

What is striking about the exterior of the castle is the elegant Venetian Gothic loggia which dominates the central section of the main facade. The trefoil arches become a recurrent motif repeated in the two-light windows throughout the building.

GARDENS ⊙

The large garden, shaded first by large banyan trees (*Ficus magnolioides)*, then by other Mediterranean and exotic species (succulents and cluster pines), conceals various follies intended to charm and bemuse its visitors, like the round temple and a Coffee House (where refreshments could be taken), the stone maze and several artificial caves encrusted with fake stalactites (below the temple).

VILLA ⊙

The first floor is open to the public. At the top of the black stone (*pietra pece* in Italian) staircase, ornamented with neo-Classical statues, is the **Salone degli Stemmi**, named after the armorial crests of great Sicilian noble families painted on the walls. Among the suites of rooms are some with delicately painted *trompe l'oeil* ceilings. These include the stucco-decorated **Salone degli Specchi** (the Hall of Mirrors), the **Billiard Room** and **Music Room**, each with painted landscapes projecting out beyond the walls, and the bedroom of the Princess of Navarre, paved in black *pietra pece* (a bituminous limestone mined locally, from which pitch is made) and white limestone where, it is said, Princess Bianca was kept segregated from Count Cabrera (an anachronistic legend, given that the princess lived in the 14C). The **Stanza del Signore** and the **Fumoir** are beautifully furnished; the decoration of the latter, a smoking room, is perfectly appropriate to its function. It is papered with pipe motifs and the ceiling is painted with medallions filled with cards and beautiful peacocks at the corners.

The castle has been featured in the making of many famous films including the *La Giara* scene in the film *Chaos* by the Taviani brothers.

Isole EGADI★

Trapani – Population 4 621
Michelin map 432 M-N 18-19

The three islands that form a mini-archipelago off Trapani are called **Favignana, Levanzo** and **Marettimo**. All three are blessed with lovely coastlines immersed in glorious crystal-clear water. The islands which are known to have been inhabited since prehistoric times (indeed, it is thought that Levanzo and Favignana formed part of the main island of Sicily in Paleolithic times), witnessed a very important event in Antiquity: for it was in these waters that the treaty sealing an end to the First Punic War (241 BC) was signed, whereby Carthage assigned Sicily to the Roman Empire.

Tourist Information – Two offices provide information: **Consorzio Turistico Egadi**, Largo Marina 14, Favignana ☎ 0923 92 21 21 and the **Pro Loco**, piazza Madrice 8, ☎ 0923 92 16 47.
The Pro Loco arranges guided tours of the tuna fishery and other excursions that change annually. The offices also act as points of reference for the other two islands in the archipelago, Levanzo and Marettimo.

GETTING TO THE ISLANDS

Several hydrofoil and ferry services (especially during the summer) operate every day out of Trapani (20-60min by hydrofoil and 1hr-2hr 45min by ferry). For information contact: **Siremar** ☎ 0923 54 54 55; Fax 0923 20 663.
In the summer, **Ustica Lines** (Naples ☎ 081 55 17 164, Trapani ☎ 0923 22 200) operates a return hydrofoil service between Trapani-Favignana-Ustica-Naples. The Favignana-Naples crossing takes approximately 6hr.

WHERE TO STAY AND EATING OUT

BUDGET

In addition to several traditional hotels, a number of **rooms** are available for rent (apply to the Pro Loco for names and addresses); there is also a delightful camp site surrounded by vegetation on Favignana called the **Camping Villaggio Egadi** (Contrada Arena, Favignana, ☎ 0923 92 15 55). The camp site also has small apartments equipped with kitchen and bathroom.

Egadi – Via Colombo 17, Favignana, ☎/fax 0923 92 12 32. Closed Oct to Mar. This hotel-restaurant is run with care and enthusiasm by the Guccione sisters. The hotel has 12 simple but well-kept rooms. Advance booking is highly recommended.

MODERATE

Aegusa – Via Garibaldi 11, Favignana, ☎ 0923 92 24 30; Fax 0923 92 24 40. Closed Oct to May. This building, dating from the beginning of the 20C, has 28 comfortable and well-furnished rooms (with air-conditioning). The hotel is situated in the village centre and has a restaurant.

EXPLORING FAVIGNANA

Mopeds and bicycles – The two most convenient ways of exploring the island are by bike or moped: cycling is especially popular because the island is so flat, thus requiring no great effort (so there is no excuse either!). To hire one, make your way into town; any of the shops will be happy to assist.

A. Safina/LARA PESSINA

Diving and snorkelling – Those who like to explore the underwater scene will find a profusion of flora and fauna. The best places are probably **Punta Marsala**, **Secca del Toro**, the submerged cave between Cala Rotonda and Scoglio Corrente, and the rocks off **Punta Fanfalo** and **Punta Ferro**.

Souvenirs – The most popular local specialities available on Favignana are of the edible kind: *bottarga* (dried tuna-fish roe) and *bresaola* (cured or smoked) tuna and swordfish. These local specialities will remind you of the delicious fish sampled during your stay on the islands.

★FAVIGNANA

The island is often referred to as *La Farfalla* on account of its shape, which has been likened to a butterfly a-flutter over the blue sea. Its proper name is, in fact, derived from *favonio*, the prevalent local wind, although in Antiquity, it was known as Aegusa. In more recent times, the fortunes of the island have been inextricably linked with the Florio family *(see MARSALA)* after they invested in a tuna fishery here, down by the harbour, where a prominent tower still marks the skyline. In times past, tuna fishing, and the **mattanza** (the traditional, but cruel ritual of killing the tuna trapped in the nets known as the *camera della morte*) comprised the principal means of earning a livelihood on the island.

Favignana covers an area of about 20km2/8sq mi. The west "wing" is dominated by **Montagna Grossa** which, despite its name, rises to a mere 302m/991ft. The eastern part of the island, on the other hand, is flatter and harbours the island's main town. The jagged coastline is interrupted, here and there, with short stretches of sandy beach.

Cave di tufo – Beside tuna fishing, tufa quarrying at one time provided the island with a second principal source of employment and income. Once cut, the blocks were transported elsewhere in Sicily and exported to North Africa. These quarries, a characteristic feature of the island's eastern flank, give the landscape an disturbing quality, as if great chunks had been bitten out of the hillside by some large square-jawed monster, leaving great, gaping, rectangular, stepped cavities. These are often overgrown with bushes, sometimes – alas – used as rubbish tips, or otherwise – luckily – transformed into secret small gardens, sheltered from the marauding winds. Near the sea, along the east coast, some of the old quarries have been partly flooded by waves let in by a landslip. Where it penetrates, the sea leaves small geometric pools of water. The most spectacular quarries are those grouped around Scalo Cavallo, Cala Rossa and Bue Marino *(see below: Bathing and beaches)*.

Favignana città – The main town of the island, indeed of the archipelago, is built around a small port that nestles in a large bay. On the skyline, perched up on its very own hill, sits the **Fort of Santa Caterina** *(now under military control)* which began life as an ancient Saracen warning station; this was rebuilt by the Norman King Roger II, and subsequently enlarged before serving as a prison under Bourbon rule (1794-1860).

Down by the seafront, Favigna boasts two buildings endowed by the **Florio** family, a wealthy dynasty involved in the production and export of Marsala wine before it developed any financial interests in tuna fishing. These comprise the **Palazzo Florio**, built in 1876, which is set back from the harbour and, at the opposite end of the bay on the right, the great **tonnara** or tuna fishery, now abandoned (plans are afoot to completely redevelop the old buildings to provide a multipurpose complex with a variety of facilities).

La mattanza

The complex and ritual method of catching tuna fish follows – or rather used to follow – very precise rules, timings and strictly disciplined practices established by the **Rais**, the head of the tuna fishermen and, at one time also the head of the village: a sort of shaman who specified when it should begin and what procedure should be followed. The methods by which the tuna used to be hunted and killed date back to ancient times, indeed possibly even to the Phoenicians, although it was not until the islands came under Arab domination that the most fundamental elements of the "rite" that underpin the fishing practices of today were firmly established. For the *mattanza* is a ritual in its own right, complete with propitiatory and superstitious songs (the *scialome*), concluding in a cruel struggle with these powerful creatures at very close quarters. The outcome, however, is always a foregone conclusion and rarely, if ever, in the tuna's favour.

In late spring, the tuna collect in great shoals off the west coast of Sicily where the conditions are conducive to breeding. The fishing boats put out to sea to lay the nets in a long corridor which the tuna are forced to follow. The last nets are dropped like barriers to form antechambers that will prevent too many fish from being gathered in a single unit, thus averting the risk of the nets being torn and the fish escaping. Beyond these antechambers is laid the *camera della morte*, an enclosure provided by tougher netting and often closed along the bottom. When an appropriate number of fish are deemed to be trapped in the chamber, the Rais orders the *mattanza* to begin. And so the killing of the fish is initiated: what is cruel is that, by now, the fish are exhausted after trying vainly to find a means of escape and panicked after being injured by inevitably knocking into others of their own kind crowded together. One by one they are speared or hooked and heaved aboard.

The term *mattanza* comes from the Spanish word *matar*, to kill, which derives from the Latin *mactare*, meaning to glorify, or immolate.

The little town centres around two piazzas: piazza Europa and piazza Madrice which are linked by the main street, where the evening "constitution" or *passeggiata* (stroll) is enacted each evening. On the north-eastern edge of town nestles the district of San Nicola (behind the cemetery) which preserves vestiges of the past: there is no access to this area, however, as long as it remains private property.

★**Bathing and beaches** – There are two main beaches: a small sandy bay south of the town in **Cala Azzurra** and, still in the southern part but a little west of Cala Azzurra, lies the broad beach called the **Lido Burrone**. For those without their own means of transport, there is an hourly bus service. The rocky bays are more exciting and thrilling, notably **Cala Rossa★** and **Cala del Bue Marino** nearby. What makes these spots especially unusual is the fact that they were once tufa quarries; deep in the grottoes where the roof has not fallen in, tunnel a network of long, dark and mysterious passages that can be explored by torchlight.

The other half of the island harbours such lovely bays as the **Cala Rotonda**, **Cala Grande** and Punta Ferro, which doubles as a popular area for diving.

The caves – The west side of the mountain slopes down into the sea, forming a number of evocative caves and grottoes. Each summer morning, when the sea is becalmed, the local harbour fishermen vie with each other to whisk visitors off to see the most picturesque: Grotta Azzurra (so called because of the colour of the water), Grotta dei Sospiri (The Grotto of Sighs which sounds its laments in winter), and Grotta degli Innamorati (Lovers' Grotto), so named because of two identical rocks standing side by side deep against the back wall.

★LEVANZO

Tiny Levanzo (pronounced with an emphasis on the first syllable) has a surface area of 6km²/2sq mi, and bristles with hills. The tallest, Pizzo del Monaco (278m/912ft), tumbles its jaggedly rocky skirts down into the sea: the most beautiful part being a section of the south-west coast.

Levanzo

Only one road bisects the island from south to north, making it a veritable haven of peace and serenity, beloved by nature-lovers and those who seek solitude and rhythms set by the breaking waves or by the sound of one's own feet on the stones. The northern part of the island consists of a succession of sheer drops, rocky outcrops and secluded little creeks. Between Levanzo and the coast of Sicily lie two minute islets: **Maraone** and **Formica** (on which there are the remains of an old tuna fishery).

Cala Dogana – The only hamlet on Levanzo overlooks a bay of the clearest water on the south side of the island. From here, a well-kept path snakes its way to the bays that open out along the south-western coast, each tightly embracing its very own miniature pebbled beach, as far as the Faraglione (a large rock).

★**Grotta del Genovese** ⊘ – *Accessible on foot (approx 2hr there and back), by jeep and then on foot along a steep slope, or by sea.* Discovered in 1949, this excavated hollow in the side of a tall cliff bears traces of prehistoric man. Vestiges of wall-painting have been identified as dating from the Upper Paleolithic era, while the incised drawings may be from the Neolithic period. The *graffiti* drawings, completed at a time when the island was still attached to the island of Sicily, represent bison and a **deer**★★ of the most pleasing proportions, elegance and foreshortening. The charcoal and animal fat paintings represent early attempts at fishing (both tuna and dolphins are discernible), animal husbandry (a woman leads a cow with a halter) and ritual images of men dancing and women with wide hips. These paintings are compatible with the Franco-Cantabrian cave paintings of Lascaux in south-west France *(see The Green Guide Dordogne Berry Limousin)* and Altamira in Spain *(see The Green Guide Spain)*.

★MARETTIMO

A steep rocky mountain with great limestone cliffs plunging down into the sea define this, the most remote island of the Egadi group. Its doors open only for the more curious visitors arriving at its tiny harbour knowing that there are no hotels there. The only accommodation available is that offered by local fishermen and that consists of rented rooms *(for addresses, contact the Pro Loco in Favignana)*. At the foot of the mountain, nestles the hamlet of Marettimo, a compact collection of square white houses and terraces collected together around the miniature harbour. Behind the Scalo Nuovo (the main landing-stage) stands the Scalo Vecchio reserved for the local fishermen. To one side, extends **Punta Troia**, topped with ruins from a Spanish castle (17C) that served as a prison until 1844. A series of rugged paths (manageable even astride a donkey) lead inland uphill to higher ground where Mother Nature, remote and wild, can provide companionship in contemplating the glorious views out over the sea.

★★**Boat trip around the island** – Down in the harbour, many a local fisherman will volunteer himself and his boat to provide excursions to the numerous caves that nestle among the precipitous cliffs along the coast. The most striking include the **Grotta del Cammello**, in which shelters a small pebble beach, **Grotta del Tuono** (Cave of Thunder), Grotta Perciata and, most notable of all, the **Grotta del Presepio**, likened to a Nativity scene because of the rocks it contains fashioned and crafted by the wind and the waves.

ENNA★

Population 28 475
Michelin map 432 O 24

Occupying a magnificent **position**★★ on a plateau 948m/3 109ft above sea-level, Enna is known as the belvedere of Sicily; it is also the highest provincial capital in Italy.
As the road winds gradually upwards to the town, beautiful views pan out across the valley to **Calascibetta**, the town perched on the concave slopes of the hill opposite.
In ancient times, the cult of **Demeter** (Ceres to the Romans), Earth mother and goddess of fertility, was especially important here, possibly because of the extensive cultivation of wheat that continues to characterise this area. Furthermore, according to the Greek myths, it was on the shores of Lake Pergusa, *(see section entitled From Enna to Piazza Armerina below)* which is not far from here, that Demeter's daughter Persephone (Proserpina) was abducted by Hades, the god of the Underworld; built at the highest point above Enna, in the place known as the belvedere, there used to be a temple dedicated to Demeter.

Historical notes – The origins of Enna date back to prehistoric times. Its elevated position, so easily defensible, made it especially desirable. It was probably inhabited by the Sicani, who exploited the strategic potential of the site to defend themselves from the threat of Siculi advances. There subsequently developed a Greek, and then later, a Roman town; in 135 BC it was here that the First Slave War erupted, prompted by the Syrian slave Euno, before spreading across the island and lasting for seven long years.
After being re-conquered by the Romans, it fell in the 6C, only to be absorbed into the Byzantine dominion (as did all the rest of Sicily), when it was quick to re-assume its defensive role pending the threat of siege by the Arabs. It capitulated only in the 9C. The name Henna, probably of Greek origin (from *en naien*: to live inside) was retained by the Romans who prefixed it with the Latin word for fortress, making it *Castrum Hennae*; with the advent of the Arabs, the name was transformed into *Kasrlànna (Qasr Yânnah* or *Qasr Yani)*, which was eventually vulgarised to Castrogiovanni. Enter the Normans, who made it the political and cultural stronghold of their kingdom, who were followed by the Swabians, the Angevins and the Aragonese. It was here that Frederick II took the title of King of Trinacria (the ancient name for Sicily) in 1314, and convocated parliament in 1324. Subsequently, the town followed the vicissitudes of the rest of the island, rebelling against the Bourbons and supporting Garibaldi. In 1927, the ancient name of Enna was restored under Mussolini.

🏛 via Roma 413, ☎ 0935 52 82 28; Fax 0935 52 82 29.

GETTING TO ENNA

SAIS **buses** (corso Sicilia 20, ☎ 0935 52 41 11) run between Enna and other towns in Sicily, including Caltagirone, Catania, Messina, Palermo, Piazza Armerina, Siracusa, as well as Rome.
By **train**, Enna can be reached from Caltanissetta (30min), Catania (approx 90min) and Palermo (approx 2hr). The railway station is situated outside the town, some 5km/3mi from the centre, between Enna and Calascibetta.

EATING OUT

If you are looking for a genuine taste of regional cooking, look no further than the **Ristorante Centrale** (piazza VI Dicembre 9, ☎ 0935 50 09 63; closed Sat except from June to Sept). Especially recommended are the meat and vegetable dishes. Approximately 50 000L for a meal.

TOWN CENTRE

With its plethora of churches, Enna has a great deal to offer the visitor. The axis of the town is charted by the **via Roma** which starts near the Castello di Lombardia and, after a sharp turn, leads down the hill to the Torre di Federico *(both of which are described below)*. It is along this principal thoroughfare that most of the monuments and points of interest are to be found.
One peculiarity of the residents of Enna is the fact that they are divided into confraternities, each having its "spiritual contrada or quarter". Every confraternity has its own hierarchy of officers, church and traditional costume, all of which are fiercely and proudly defended by its adherents. The most important popular event is the **Processione della Settimana Santa**, a week-long festival beginning on Palm Sunday when the Collegio dei Rettori (a council of governors) processes to the Duomo to begin celebrations in adoration of the Holy Eucharist. In turn, delegations from each confraternity leave their own churches and converge on the cathedral, followed by bands playing funeral marches. At noon on the Wednesday

ENNA

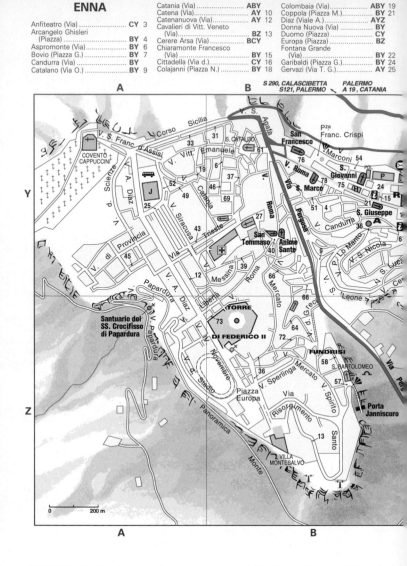

of Holy Week, the church bells are removed and the *troccola*, a special mechanical instrument made of wood, is sounded. The real and proper procession takes place on the evening of Good Friday: hundreds of representatives from the various confraternities, hooded and cloaked in mantles of different colour, process through the streets bearing first the Dead Christ, followed by Our Lady of Sorrows, on their shoulders. On Easter Sunday, the two statues are carried back to their respective churches.

Duomo ⊘ – Although largely rebuilt in the Baroque style in the 16C and 17C, the cathedral has retained its Gothic apses (best admired inside, especially in the left apse).

The cathedral front, preceded by a dramatic staircase, rises above a portico to a bell-tower through the three Classical orders: Doric (the portico has an entablature with metopes and triglyphs, as found in the temples of Antiquity), Ionic and Corinthian. The 16C south door, named after San Martino, has a marble relief panel depicting St Martin and the Pauper; this balances the Porta Santa, adjacent, which is Gothic. The **interior★** is divided into nave and aisles by columns of black basalt, each with finely sculpted bases and capitals (note, in particular, the reliefs incorporating allegorical creatures, *putti*, serpents and two-headed gargoyles on the second column on the right and the corresponding column on the left, which are considered to be by **Giandomenico Gagini**). The 16C woodwork is especially fine. The coffered **ceiling★** is finely inlaid, and graced at the end of each beam by unusual winged figures. At the end of the aisles, the organ loft and choir gallery, although in far from pristine condition, have elegant inlaid and painted wooden balustrading, and niches containing statues of Christ and the twelve Apostles. Behind the high altar, the wooden choirstalls are further decorated with scenes from the Old and New Testaments redolent with didacticism; this is echoed in the door-panels of the sacristy cupboard or *casciarizzo* which illustrate scenes from the life of Christ. Above the altar hangs a fine 15C Christ on the Cross with, on the reverse, a painting of the Resurrection: this is called the Christ of the Three Faces because Christ's expression appears to alter depending on the angle from which the painting is contemplated.

Museo Alessi ⊘ – *Entrance at the back of the Duomo.* In 1862, the museum was created to house the collections of Canon Alessi that include 17C and 18C sacred vestments embroidered with gold thread and coral *(in the basement)*, and a selection of **paintings** *(on the upper floor)*, notably a gentle *Madonna and Child* by an unknown 15C Flemish painter, a 16C *Pietà* with the symbols of the Passion, and two panels with John the Baptist and St John the Evangelist from a 16C polyptych attributed to Il Panormita. Displayed on the first floor are a canvas by Giuseppe Salerno (known locally as the Lame Man of Gangi) depicting a Madonna delle Grazie, together with the glorious **treasures** from the Chiesa Madre: sacred relics, a fabulous Madonna's **crown★** exquisitely enamelled and engraved with narrative scenes relating the life of Christ (17C), a magnificent 17C **pelican jewel★** – symbol of the Sacrifice of the Resurrection for Eternal Life, and the monumental **processional monstrance★** engraved with the graceful spires of a Gothic cathedral, a work of supreme quality attributed to Paolo Gili (1536-38).

On the second floor is exhibited a collection of Greek, Roman and Byzantine **coins**; an assortment of archaeological finds ranging from prehistoric times to the Late Middle Ages; not forgetting a series of interesting **Egyptian funerary figurines**, found

Embroidery detail

among grave goods recovered in Sicily, having been placed in tombs, it is thought, much in the way they were by the Ancient Egyptians: these so-called *ushebti* figurines (literally translated as "those who answer the call") were so interred so as to execute the earthly labours of the deceased.

Museo Archeologico Varisano ⊙ – On display are the archaeological finds, mainly in terracotta, recovered from the necropoli at Calascibetta, Capodarso, Pergusa, Cozzo Matrice and Rossomanno.

San Michele Arcangelo ⊙ – Erected in 1658, probably on the site of an old mosque, the church of the Archangel Michael has a square façade and is built on an elliptical plan with radiating side chapels. Follow via Polizzi out of the square and turn right into via del Salvatore to the church dedicated to the Holy Saviour **(San Salvatore)**, an old Basilian church remodelled in the 16C, and recently restored.

Santa Chiara ⊙ – *Piazza Colajanni*. The Church of St Clare, now a memorial to fallen soldiers, has a single nave. The tiled floor is set with two panels: *The Triumph of Christianity over Islam* and *The Advent of Steam Navigation*.
The church overlooks piazza Colajanni, which is bordered by fine buildings, including the **Palazzo Pollicarini**.

Campanile di San Giovanni Battista – *In a side-street off piazza Coppola*. The elegant bell-tower of John the Baptist, articulated by large ogive arches at ground level, a decorative three-light Gothic window above and round-headed arches in the upper storey, is all that remains of the church of the same name.
Further along via Roma is **San Giuseppe**, with its lovely (though rather dilapidated) Baroque façade, complete with bell-tower.

San Giovanni ⊙ – Originally built in the Romanesque style, the Church of St John has been remodelled, decorated with stucco and completely restored in 1967. Inside there is an unusual font: the base is Roman, the central section is a Byzantine capital made of red marble, the carved basin is medieval (14C).

San Marco ⊙ – This church, dating from the 17C, was erected on the site of an old synagogue, in what was Enna's Jewish quarter. **Inside**, the spacious hall church is decorated with fine stuccoes of cherubs, garlands of flowers, fruit and shells by Gabriele de Blanco da Licodia (1705). It is also worth noting the inlaid wooden women's gallery, reserved for nuns attending functions.
Almost directly opposite the belvedere in piazza Francesco Crispi, extends a fabulous **view★** of Calascibetta, Lake Nicoletti and the Lombardy Castle on the right. The fountain ornamenting the garden is graced with a bronze copy of Bernini's *Rape of Persephone*.
Further along is a monumental church dedicated to San Francis **(San Francesco)**. Right on the bend of the road is another, San Cataldo, with a square façade. Via Roma continues to piazza Neglia, onto which faces the **Chiesa delle Anime Sante** (All Souls) – with a fine Baroque limestone doorway – and the 15C **San Tomaso**, with its a fine gallery and campanile pierced by single openings, intended and used (around the 10C) as a watchtower.

Quartiere Fundrisi – *About half way along via Mercato*. The Fundrisi Quarter was established on the south-western end of the Enna plateau when, in 1396, King Martin of Aragon quelled the revolt on the island and razed several of the small towns in the vicinity of Castrogiovanni, as it was then, to the ground. The inhabitants of the town called Fundrò were transferred here and, over the centuries, constituted an separate community independent of the main town. A walk through the narrow streets of this part of the town, all up and down, among the typical single-storey houses with their distinctive galleries (especially along via San Bartolomeo) is particularly recommended. From here or piazzetta San Bartolomeo, which takes its name from the church that presides over the scene, extend various **prospects★** across the north-eastern part of the town. A short way below the piazza, sits **Porta Janniscuru**, the only gate to survive of the five that once served the city.

and, adjacent to this, the Grotta della Guardiola (literally translated as the Cave of the Guardroom) which is thought to have been the site of a cult long before the foundation of the town. Continuing on an axis with via Mercato, via Spirito Santo leads to the church which gives it its name, enjoying a splendid position, perched on a rocky spur over a vertical drop.

FORTIFICATIONS

★**Castello di Lombardia** ⊙ – *At the top of via Roma*. Situated uppermost on the plateau, the **castle** looks out over the town and the valley, including the Rocca di Cerere (Fortress of Ceres) where, it is thought, a temple dedicated to the fertility goddess was built.

This site has been fortified since earliest times because of its strategic position. Under Norman dominion, the castle was reinforced. It was made habitable by Frederick II of Aragon, who added a number of rooms that rendered it suitable for court life. Indeed, he intended it as his summer residence: it was here that he was crowned King of Trinacria and, in 1324, convocated the Sicilian parliament. The name of the castle dates from this same period, linked to the presence of a garrison of Lombard soldiers posted there to defend it. The ground-plan of the castle, which is roughly pentagonal, hugs the tortuous lie of the land. Of the original 20 towers, only six survive (some only in part). The most interesting and complete is the one called *La Pisana* or *Torre delle Aquile* (The Pisan Tower or Tower of the Eagles), topped by Guelph crenellations. From the top, a breathtaking **view**★★★ stretches over the best part of the Sicilian mountain ranges, Mount Etna and Calascibetta.

Enclosed within the walls are three courtyards: the one named after St Nicholas is used as an open-air theatre; the one named after Mary Magdalen was where the supplies were kept during times of siege; the Courtyard of St Martin, at the heart of the royal apartments, gives access to the Pisan Tower.

Just outside the castle precincts, in the direction of the Fortress of Ceres, stands the statue of **Euno**, a memorial to the slave who began the Slave War *(see also introduction to the chapter)*.

Rocca di Cerere – From the top of the hill, where the Fortress of Ceres – a temple dedicated to the fertility goddess – once stood, extends an all-encompassing **view**★★ including Calascibetta opposite, and Enna itself.

★**Torre di Federico** – *At the opposite end of via Roma from the castle*. At one time, Enna might have been called the city of towers. Their proliferation is explained by the defensive and strategic role of the town. Many have disappeared, many have been incorporated into churches as bell-towers; only a few survive as free-standing towers today. A case in point is the octagonal tower named after Frederick II of Swabia, which occupies pride of place in a small public park.

Frederick's towers

Frederick II, the Swabian King of Sicily, gave a considerable boost to civic building in the south of Italy. This architecture is characterised by rigorous geometry: buildings rise from a square base, imitating the form of the Roman *castrum*, also employed in the Islamic world, with cylindrical or square towers at the corners and one cylindrical or polygonal tower in the centre *(see the castle at Augusta or Maniace Castle at Siracusa)*. Through time, the *octagonal* ground-plan was evolved and applied to the one here, at Enna. The determination of such a choice lies in the mind of medieval man, fascinated as he was by precise geometry and the symbolic significance of such forms. The square – symbolising the Earth and humankind – contrasts with the circle, which symbolised the divine and the heavens. At that time, the octagon represented mediation, the fusion of the two opposing "rudiments".

ADDITIONAL SIGHTS

Santuario del SS Crocifisso di Papardura ⊙ – *Take via Libertà after the crossroads with viale Diaz; turn right down a minor road marked with the Stations of the Cross*. The Sanctuary of the Holy Crucifix of Papardura incorporates the cave where, in 1659, an image of the Crucifix was found painted on a stone slab. This has been attributed as the work of Basilian monks and can now be seen on the high altar. Inside, the fine **stuccoes** initiated in 1696 by Giuseppe and Giacomo Serpotta, were completed in 1699 by another artist, who also executed the statues of the Apostles. Note also the high altar silver **frontage**★ made by a craftsman from Messina (17C); the wooden coffered ceiling dates from the end of the last century; the side altar frontages are of tooled, painted leather.

AMONG THE HILLS NORTH OF ENNA *123km/77mi round trip*

Leave Enna as indicated on the plan and follow directions for Calascibetta.

Calascibetta – Benefiting from a glorious **setting★** which consists of a natural amphitheatre nestling in a rocky hollow on the side of a hill, this little town was probably founded during the Arab occupation. The **Chiesa Madre**, founded in the 14C, was completely rebuilt in the 17C following an earthquake; remains of the former building belie the present church, and can be seen below the north aisle. Inside, the nave is divided from its aisles by stone columns which rise from bases bearing carvings of monstrous figures to support the arcades of pointed arches. To the left of the entrance is a fine 16C font.

The **Norman tower** (11C), standing beside the ruined church of San Pietro, is ornamented with a shallow relief in stone. From the piazza on the left extends a marvellous **view★★**, with Enna on the right (where the castle and belvedere can be seen quite clearly) and the Lago di Pergusa below.

Leaving the town in the direction of Villapriolo, the road passes the rock-cut tombs of the **necropolis of Realmese** (4C BC).

Calascibetta

Return to the crossroads and take the left turning (SS 121) for Leonforte. The road winds its way inland across the hills around Enna beyond Regalbuto, offering **wonderful views★** over the countryside, particularly on the section between Nissoria and the turning for Centùripe, in the valley of the River Salso and Lago di Pozzillo.

Leonforte – The town perches on a hump enjoying a superb **position★**. The monumental silhouette of Palazzo Branciforte is discernible from a distance, a powerful reminder of the fact that the town was founded in the 17C by Nicola Placido Branciforte. The *palazzo*, dating from 1611, runs the whole length of one side of the enormous piazza of the same name. Of particular interest is the lovely fountain or **Granfonte** (1651) built by the Branciforte family: of gold-coloured stone it comprises 24 spouts, a series of small pointed arches crowned with a pediment bearing the family coat of arms.

Turn back down the same road, and at the fork, turn left for Assoro.

Assoro – At a height of 850m/2 788ft, the town is grouped around the little piazza Umberto I, which is attractively paved, has a fountain in the centre and a lovely **belvedere-terrace★**. Beyond the elegant archway linking Palazzo Valguarnera to the town's main church, is another little square with viewing terrace, which opens out before the Chiesa Madre, or **Basilica di San Leone** ⊙ *(closed for restoration: to visit the church, apply to the priest in the sacristy)*. The church, founded in 1186, has been subjected to major alterations: first in the late 14C and again in the 18C. It consists of a nave and aisles and has a doorway on the south side. The north porch was adapted in 1693 so as to accommodate the Capella dell'Oratorio del Purgatorio and given an elegant Baroque doorway. The **interior★**, enclosed by a fine ribbed-vault, is particularly attractive on account of its compactness and profuse gilded Baroque **stucco decoration**. The spiral columns were in fact embellished with their climbing plant ornament in the 18C, at the same time as the pelican *(right)* and the phoenix *(left)* were added above the apses. These emblems allude to the Sacrifice of the Crucifixion and the Resurrection of Christ: the first represents the bird which, according to myth, plucked flesh from its own breast to feed its young, while the second fabulous creature having burnt itself to ashes on an altar fire, re-emerged rejuvenated.

The main body of the church has a fine **wooden tie-beam ceiling**, painted and orna-mented with arabesques (1490); the attractive wrought-iron chapel **gates** (15C) are also worthy of note.

Beyond the town, follow the road past San Giorgio which intersects the SS 121 again at Nissoria. Turn right towards Agira.

Agira – Spread over the slopes of Monte Teja, at a height of 650m, the town is over-shadowed by the silhouette of the **castle**, which towers above it. Built under Swabian rule, this defensive outpost appears to have played an active role in various struggles between the Angevins and the Aragonese and, later, between the Aragonese and the Chiaramonte. From the ruins, there is a beautiful **view★** over Lago di Pozzillo.

Town and monastery – The story of Agira, home of the ancient historian Diodorus Siculus (90-20 BC), echoes the pattern in fortune of the Basilian monastery of San Filippo, which was founded by a Syrian monk some time between the 5C and 6C AD, and which quickly rose to become an important centre of culture and religion. It came to particular prominence when, during the Norman occupation, the resident com-munity was joined by a group of monks from Jerusalem who were forced into exile by the wrath of Saladin. The monastery also prospered on account of the enormous income generated by its immense holdings throughout Europe. In 1537, Charles V conceded the title of *città demaniale* upon Agira, providing it with a special "royal" status complete with privileges that included the right to administrate its own civil and penal justice system. The town's decline began in 1625 when King Philip IV of Spain, in a desperate effort to boost the dwindling finances of the monarchy, decided to sell the town to Genoese merchants: faced with the threat of losing their freedom, the citizens of Agira offered to raise the enormous sum required themselves.

Abbazia San Filippo ⊙   This abbey is the town's most important religious building. It dates in its present form from the late 18C and early 19C (the front was com-pletely rebuilt in 1928). **Inside**, it is decorated with gilded stuccowork: among the works of art is a dramatic wooden Crucifix by Fra' Umile da Petralia *(over the high altar)*, wooden choir stalls depicting scenes from the life of St Philip by Nicola Bagnasco (1818-22), three 15C polyptych panels representing the Madonna in Majesty with Saints, as well as paintings by Olivio Sozzi and Giuseppe Velasquez.

Regalbuto – Coming from Agira, the visitor is welcomed by the fine Baroque pink stone façade of **Santa Maria La Croce** (1744), graced with columns crowned by an elegant pediment. Turning left into Via Ingrassia, immediately on the left-hand side is the Jesuit school and, just beyond it, the Liberty-style **Palazzo Compagnini**. A little further, the town's main square provides a broad open space before the **Chiesa Madre** (1760), from which to survey the monumental Baroque frontage of the church dedi-cated to St Basil assembled from a miscellany of features, articulated by pilasters.

From the SS 121, a narrow road winds its twisted way to Centùripe.

Centùripe – This little town, which today seems rather off the beaten track, was at one time in the dark and distant past a strategic outpost on the main link-line between the plain of Catania and the mountains inland. This explains why, particu-larly in Roman times, Centùripe enjoyed considerable economic prosperity (in 70 BC, Cicero described it as one of the most prosperous towns in Sicily). And it is from the Roman era that Centùripe retains its most monumental vestiges. The **Tempio degli Augustali** (1C-2C AD) is a rectangular building raised above a colonnaded street onto which it faced (alongside the new archaeological museum). The two monumental tombs with towers are known as *la Dogana* (with only the upper floor visible) and the "castle of Conradin". Down a stone-cobbled side street on the far north-western side of the town, in the contrada of Bagni, sit the ruins of what must once have been a spectacular **nymphaeum** hanging above the ravine of the river, with fountains designed to delight visitors approaching the town. A brick wall containing five niches, the remains of a cistern in which water was collected and parts of the aqueduct are also visible.

Finally, the vast majority of artefacts recovered from the 8C BC to the Middle Ages are displayed in the **Museo Archeologico** ⊙ (via SS Crocifisso), including the statues from the Tempio degli Augustali representing various emperors and members of their families; a fine head of the Emperor Hadrian which, given its size, must have belonged to a statue of at least 4m; two splendid **funerary urns★** belonging to the Scribonii family (almost certainly imported from Rome); locally produced pottery (3C-1C BC) and an impressive collection of theatrical masks.

To return to Enna from Centùripe, continue in the direction of Catenanuova and take the motorway.

NATURAL HISTORY, ARCHAEOLOGY
AND SULPHUROUS DEPOSITS *127km/79mi round trip*

Leave Enna as indicated on the plan and follow directions for Pergusa.

Lago di Pergusa – The lake lies at the foot of Enna. Its shores, alas now encircled by a motor-racing track, provided the backdrop for a mythical story: the
abduction of **Persephone** by Hades. Legend describes how the daughter of Demeter
and Zeus was once playing here with her companions the ocean nymphs, when
her eye was caught by a particularly beautiful narcissus. As she reached out to
pick it, the earth gave way, forming a great abyss from which, with due majesty,
Hades and his immortal horses emerged. The god forced her to mount his golden
chariot before disappearing with her, near Syracuse, by the Cyane Fountain *(see
SIRACUSA)*, down into the Underworld. Her distraught mother, hearing her
daughter's piercing cries, set about searching for her. After wandering relentlessly,
she finally succeeded in discovering where the girl had been taken and arranged
to see her. Before allowing his bride to see Demeter, Hades (or Pluto, as he is also
known) made her eat some pomegranate seeds, thus binding her to him for the
winter months.

At the next junction, turn left, signposted for Valguarnera.

Parco minerario Floristella-Grottacalda – *Flagged along the roadside.* The park
consists of some 400ha/988 acres, including 200ha/494 acres that are privately
owned (comprising the Grottacalda Mineral Park, and its own *agriturismo* accommodation centre) and 200ha/494 acres belonging to the state (Floristella). The
sulphur mines at Floristella were operational until 1984. The park's main attraction, which may not immediately be evident, lies in the way it documents an
important area of activity that affected the lives and destinies of large numbers of
Sicilians, particularly of those living in the provinces of Enna and Caltanissetta.
A dirt track leads to a large open area and the *palazzina* Pennisi, a small building
erected by the barons of Floristella, who were the long-standing owners of the
mine since workings began around 1750. Behind the building, all the aspects of
the site and industrial archaeology can be seen. On the left stands Hoisting Shaft
No 1 (bricks and mortar) and a ventilation shaft (metal), which were in use until
1972. The small white hillocks are the so-called *calcheroni*, round pits lined with
inert material in which, using spontaneous combustion, the sulphur was separated
from its slag of impurities. Post-1860, the *calcheroni* were replaced by domed Gill
furnaces in groups of two, three or four, connected by small channels. This made
it possible to use the heat generated from the sulphur dioxide fumes produced by
the combustion in the furnaces, as a catalyst in breaking down the sulphur material in the next furnace. Opposite the *calcheroni* is a sort of gallery with arcades
and narrow slits, from which the molten sulphur would flow down to the collection point. There it was allowed to solidify in wooden trapezoidal moulds so as to
produce 50-60kg blocks. On the far right is the oldest section of the mine, where
the shaft-steps used by miners and *carusi* – the young boys employed to carry the
ore up to the surface in wooden structures on their backs – can still be seen.

Valguarnera – This small town, associated until only a few years ago with sulphur
mining, has a 17C church with an overbearing Baroque front made of limestone.

Return in the direction of Piazza Armerina. The road winds through a beautiful
valley★ with gently sloping hills, covered, in springtime, with a veil of emerald green.

Piazza Armerina – *See PIAZZA ARMERINA.*

★★★**Roman Villa of Casale** – *See Villa Romana del CASALE.*

*Proceed along SS 191 towards Caltanissetta to the fork signposted on the left for
Barrafranca.*

Barrafranca – At one time called Convicino (its current name dates from the 16C),
this simply consists of a collection of ochre-coloured houses clustered on the gentle
slopes of a hill. The entrance into the town is along via Vittorio Emanuele which
is flanked on either side by elegant town houses, including Palazzo Satariano and
Palazzo Mattina. The **Chiesa Madre** (18C) has a bare brick façade and a bell-tower
crowned with a small dome covered with polychrome tiles. The **Benedictine Monastery**
in piazza Messina is now virtually in ruins; just beyond it stand a large, eye-catching
18C building which once accommodated small shops (**i Putieddi**) and the **Chiesa della
Maria Santissima della Stella**, marked by its tall campanile topped with a maiolica spire.
Return to the town's main street, corso Garibaldi, which leads into piazza dell'Itria;
taking pride of place here is the 16C church of the same name with its front and
bell-tower of brick.

*From here it is possible to continue on towards Pietraperzia or undertake a detour
(13km/8mi) via Mazzarino.*

Mazzarino – This medieval hamlet largely developed as a result of the Branciforte family. The main features are collected along the main street corso Vittorio Emanuele. Alongside the Chiesa Madre sits Palazzo Branciforti (17C) and the contemporary Carmelite church. Just outside the little town, perched up on top of a small hill lie the ruins of the **castle** with its rather solid impenetrable round keep. No doubt the castle was built on the site of a Norman-Byzantine fortress, was enlarged and reinforced with fortifications during the Norman occupation in the course of the 14C before being converted into a major residence for its aristocratic owners towards the close of the 15C.

Pietraperzia – Here, too, the dominant colour of the stone is a yellow-ochre. The ruins of the Norman castle overlook the valley of the River Salso. On entering the town, in piazza Matteotti, is the 16C Chiesa del Rosario and, opposite, the fine neo-Gothic Palazzo Tortorici. The **Chiesa Madre** ⊘ (19C) has a square façade crowned with a squat pediment. Inside, hanging above the main altar, is the lovely *Madonna and Child* painted by Filippo Paladini.

Also of interest in passing is the **Pallazzo del Governatore** (17C) with its elegant square balcony ornamented with brackets provided by grotesque figures.

Caltanissetta – *See CALTANISSETTA.*

From Caltanissetta, return to Enna via the SS 117bis, a road providing fine views over the countryside.

Isole EOLIE★★★

Messina – Population 12 945
Michelin map 432 K-L 25-27

The blue of the sea off the north-eastern coast of Sicily is dotted with a gaggle of seven islands. They vary in character from being rough and untamed places (like the two most remote islands, **Filicudi** and **Alicudi**), to being tempered by residents and visitors (like **Lipari** and **Panarea**); they might be introverted and solitary (like **Salina**), or extrovert, like **Vulcano** and **Stromboli**, which, with timely precision one might say, puff out smoke before relishing the attention paid to them as they toss small incandescent lumps of stone high into the air.

The Greek myths ascribe the islands to **Aeolus**, the son of Poseidon, who Zeus made guardian of the winds; they suggest that it was here that the god ruled over an island encircled by walls of bronze (Lipari?), and that the hero **Odysseus** (Ulysses) sheltered temporarily during his travels and met the monster Polyphemus with his companions, the legendary forgers employed by the god of fire after whom the island of Vulcano is named.

The history of these islands is lost in the mists of time, when tectonic plates moved to create a great chasm in the Tyrrhenian Sea, thereby releasing a mass of molten magma that hardened into a great volcanic outcrop, some 1 000m-3 000m (3 280ft-9 840ft) from the ocean floor, of which only a minute proportion emerges above the water. According to the most recent theories, this happened during the Pleistocene Era, just under a million years ago. The first islands to be formed were Panarea, Filicudi

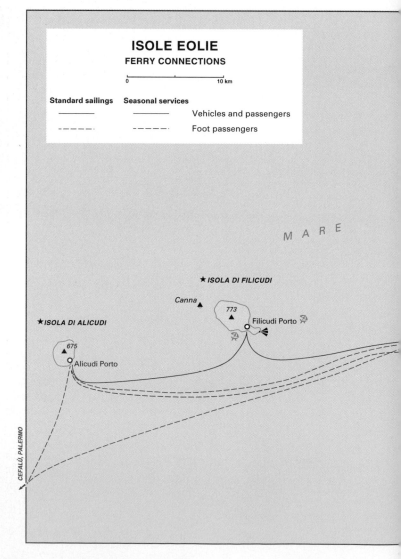

and Alicudi. The youngest are those which continue to be active today: Vulcano and Stromboli. Each successive eruption over the millennia has resulted in a variety of different phenomena: this ranges from the formation of pumice, a material so light that it will float on water, to the great streams of black obsidian, a glassy and friable material with edges so sharp as to be used by ancient peoples to make razor-like cutting tools.

The islands' resident population, which in places is sparse and liable to be cut off from the rest of the world for several months at a time, subsists on fishing, farming (especially vines and harvesting of capers for salting), quarrying pumice (as on Lipari, although this is a dying trade), and most particularly, albeit for a short season, from tourism.

The sea is clear and warm; the water's cobalt blue transparency gives way to ever greater limpidity the shallower it gets; the rocky shoreline nurtures a rich variety of aquatic flora and fauna: sea anemones, sponges, shell-fish, seaweed, crustaceans and molluscs as well as countless species of fish, making it a paradise for bathers, snorkellers, divers and spear-gun fishing enthusiasts alike.

Those who seek peace and quiet, far removed from the trappings of worldly life, may choose to go to Alicudi and Filicudi, or Salina which, although more populated and crowded by visitors, is still unspoilt. Even if Lipari, Panarea and Vulcano attract an ever-increasing number of tourists, catered for by a multitude of small shops, restaurants, stalls and the odd venues for whiling away the evening, they nevertheless provide an ideal context for a perfect holiday.

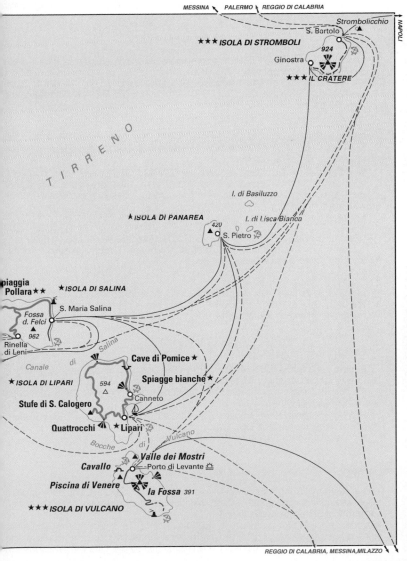

167

🛈 Corso Vittorio Emanuele 202, Lipari, 🛈 090 98 80 095.
🛈 Via Levante 4, Vulcano (July-Sept), 🛈 090 98 52 028.

GETTING TO THE ISLANDS

The Aeolian islands are linked to the mainland by hydrofoil *(aliscafo)* and ferry *(traghetto)*, which incur inversely proportional costs and times. On average, the hydrofoil (foot-passengers only) costs twice as much as the ferry and takes half the time. The closest port on the main island of Sicily, which logically runs the most frequent sailings, is Milazzo; buses run directly from the port to the main towns in Sicily.

Ferries run regularly from **Milazzo** (1hr 30min-4hr) and are operated by Siremar, via dei Mille, ☎ 090 92 83 242; Fax 090 92 83 243. The same agency also runs a hydrofoil service (40min-2hr 45min), as does Aliscafi SNAV, via Rizzo 9/10, ☎ 090 92 87 728; Fax 090 92 81 798.

Aliscafi SNAV operates a daily service from **Messina**, via San Raineri 22, ☎ 090 36 21 14; Fax 090 71 73 58, **Reggio Calabria**, Stazione Marittima, ☎ 0965 29 568, **Palermo** (June to Sept), piazza Principe di Belmonte 51/55, ☎ 091 58 65 33; Fax 091 58 48 30, and **Cefalù** (June to Sept only; not daily), corso Ruggero 76, ☎ 0921 42 15 95.

Ferries (14hr) and hydrofoils (4hr, June to Sept) also leave from **Naples**. The former are operated by Siremar, via Depetris 78, ☎ 081 55 12 112; Fax 081 55 12 114, and the latter by Aliscafi SNAV, via Caracciolo 10, ☎ 081 76 12 348; Fax 081 76 12 141.

For further information, contact **N.G.I.** (☎ 090 98 11 955) and **Co.Ve.Mar** (☎ 090 98 13 181).

WHERE TO STAY

In addition to traditional hotels, more moderately priced accommodation is available in **rented rooms and flats** (contact the tourist office for a detailed list). There are also camp sites on Lipari (**Baia Unci**, via Marina Garibaldi, Loc Canneto, Lipari, ☎ 090 98 11 909; Fax 090 98 11 540) and Salina (**Tre Pini**, via Rotabile 1, loc Leni, Salina, ☎ 090 98 09 155).

LIPARI

Oriente – Via Marconi 35, ☎ 090 98 11 493; Fax 090 98 80 198. This hotel (32 rooms with air conditioning) has a pleasant flower garden and a collection of traditional Aeolian articles.

Villa Augustus – Vico Ausonia 16, ☎ 090 98 11 232; Fax 090 98 12 233. Arranged around an attractive internal courtyard, this hotel looks over one of the traditional alleyways of the historical centre. It has 34 comfortable rooms with air-conditioning.

VULCANO

Conti – Loc Porto Ponente, ☎ 090 98 52 012; Fax 090 98 80 150. A hotel providing accommodation in a number of bungalows (67 rooms in total). Not far from the famous black sand beaches.

STROMBOLI

La locanda del Barbablù – Via Vittorio Emanuele 17, ☎ 090 98 61 18; 0335 31 73 14 (mobile); Fax 090 98 63 23. Closed Nov to Feb. A charming inn with 6 simple rooms, all of which are attractively furnished with period items and furniture.

EATING OUT

LIPARI

E Pulera – Via Diana, Lipari ☎ 090 98 11 158. Open for dinner only June to Oct. Guests dine *al fresco* in a beautiful garden setting. In July and August, typical Aeolian dishes are accompanied by traditional music and folk dancing. Around 70 000L per person.

Filippino – Piazza Municipio, Lipari, ☎ 090 98 11 002. Closed mid-Nov to mid-Dec. This restaurant is a local institution which has been serving regional dishes for almost a century. Around 70 000L per person.

★LIPARI

This is the largest and most densely populated of the Aeolian Islands. Its physical relief, with its areas of gentle lowland, has prompted a number of towns to spring up both along the coast and inland.

Inhabited since Antiquity, when it was famous for its obsidian, the island has enjoyed several periods of great prosperity, interrupted by frequent incursions and attacks: among the most famous is the one launched by the Turk **Kaireddin Barbarossa**

La Ginestra – Via Stradale 10, loc Pianoconte (5km/3mi north-west), Lipari, ☎ 090 98 22 285. This restaurant is situated inland on Pianoconte hill and serves typical regional dishes at reasonable prices. Pizza is also available in the evening. Around 50 000L per person.

Since 1930, the **Pasticceria Subba** in corso Vittorio Emanuele (no 92) in Lipari town has been making fabulous cakes and pastries: *cannoli* (filled with ricotta cheese), *cassate* (brimming with candied fruit), *pasta paradiso* (melting moments) and ice cream.

VULCANO AND ISLANDS

Cantine Stevenson – Via Porto Levante, **Vulcano**, ☎ 090 98 53 247. A colonial-style pub popular with the island's night-owls.

Da Franco – Via Belvedere 8, loc Santa Maria Salina, **Salina**, ☎ 090 98 43 287. Closed 1 to 20 Dec. A simple restaurant which serves excellent regional specialities. Superb views of the sea and the Aeolian islands. Around 60 000L per person.

Punta Lena – Via Marina, loc Ficogrande, **Stromboli**, ☎ 090 98 62 04. Open 3 June to 15 Oct. Delicious seafood specialities served under an arbour with magnificent sea views. Around 80 000L per person.

Remigio's *pasticceria* in Porto Levante, **Vulcano** offers an enticing selection of typical specialities such as *cannoli*, *cassate* and *granite*, as well as chocolate and cream Lulùs and delicious profiteroles.

EXPLORING THE ISLANDS

Boat trips – The most congenial and easiest way to explore the islands by far is by rubber dinghy. However, given the exorbitant cost of hiring one (140 000L-160 000L per day), there is always the option of joining an organised excursion by boat from Lipari or Vulcano (from the other islands, the boats are smaller and the services less frequent) which go to Stromboli (even at night, when the so-called Strombolian explosions can be watched from the sea); Filicudi and Alicudi (in the same day); Panarea, Salina, or circumnavigate them (Lipari and Vulcano). The trips usually take in all the islands, making the most interesting approaches from the sea to include a view of caves, rock formations, bays and beaches; they sometimes include stops for swimming and for brief visits to the main towns. Excursions take place two or three times a week; they can last a whole day (departing around 9am and returning between 5pm and 7pm) or half a day (departing early afternoon and returning late in the evening as for the Stromboli evening trip). The following companies operate services from Lipari: VIKING, vico Himera 3, ☎ 090 98 12 584; Compagnia di Navigazione G LA CAVA, via Vittorio Emanuele 124, ☎ 090 98 11 242; PIGNATARO SHIPPING, via Prof Carnevale 29, ☎ 090 98 11 417 or 0368 67 59 75; REGINA DEI MARI, Marina Corta, ☎ 090 98 22 237 or 0339 74 86 560; MOTOVELIERO SIGISMONDO, via San Vincenzo-Canneto, ☎ 0338 21 10 229; and ROBERTO FOTI, Marina Corta, ☎ 090 98 12 352 or 0368 30 61 503.

Recreation – As long as the sea continues to provide endless hours of fascination, the main sport has to be sub-aqua diving. For beginners and those without equipment of their own, contact the **Diving Center La Gorgonia** (☎ 090 98 12 060; mobile 0360 86 34 55) on Lipari.

The best way to explore the islands is to rent a bicycle or moped. Contact the tourist office for further information.

USEFUL INFORMATION

Banking facilities – Banks are available on Lipari, Vulcano (in Porto di Levante) and Salina (in Malfa). Visitors should note that the only cashpoint facilities in the Aeolian Islands are on Lipari, in corso Vittorio Emanuele, and that credit cards are NOT universally accepted.

Post offices – Corso Vittorio Emanuele 207, Lipari; via Risorgimento 130, Santa Maria di Salina; via Roma, Stromboli.

who, in 1544, landed at **Porto delle Genti** (a small hamlet near Lipari) before razing the town, killing or deporting the population as slaves to Africa.

The main moorings on the island are in the town of Lipari, which is served by two ports: Marina Corta is used by the hydrofoils and by smaller craft, whereas the ferries moo r at Marina Lunga.

From here it is easy to get to the island's other towns: Canneto, Acquacalda, Quattropiani and Pianoconte. The best way to explore the island is by private vehicle or with a hired moped.

★Città di Lipari

Lipari is also the main town on the island. Approaching it by sea, the top of the town may be glimpsed from away, with its fortified citadel and, behind, the former Franciscan monastery which now accommodates the town hall (visible when moored at Marina Lunga). Far below at its feet sit two bays. **Marina Corta** is watched over by a little church dedicated to the souls in Hell – **'Anime del Purgatorio'** (once isolated on a rock, but now linked to the mainland), and by the 17C **Chiesa di San Giuseppe** (which stands on the south side of the bay); **Marina Lunga** is the larger of the two inlets. On the last night of the festival of St Bartholomew (24 August), Marina Corta is illuminated by a magnificent display of fireworks, set off from the sea. The lower part of town or *città bassa*, with its very own corso Vittorio Emanuele lined with small shops and restaurants, provides the perfect context for the traditional *passeggiata* or early evening stroll.

★**Castle** – The citadel was constructed on a Greek acropolis before being surrounded by walls (13C); it was reinforced by Charles V (16C) after the town was sacked by Barbarossa *(see Introduction)*.

It is best approached from piazza Mazzini, by the most ancient route: beyond the Spanish fortifications and the Greek tower (4C BC) with its great medieval portcullis (12C-13C) lies the heart of the citadel. On the right is a church, Santa Caterina, with beyond it, an **archaeological area** which has been excavated to reveal superimposed layers of dwellings (huts), buildings and roads from various periods spanning the Bronze Age (Capo Graziano culture) through to Hellenistic and Ancient Roman times. Behind sits the **Chiesetta dell'Addolorata** and the 18C **Chiesa dell'Immacolata**. To the left of these, in the centre, stands the cathedral dedicated to the patron saint of the Aeolian Islands, **San Bartolomeo**: medieval in plan, it was rebuilt under Spanish rule; the façade is 19C. The adjacent cloisters are Norman. The flight of steps opposite the cathedral was inserted at the beginning of this century; in order to build it, some of the ancient walls had to be demolished.

★★**Museo Archeologico Eoliano** ⊘ – The collections are housed in several different buildings; these are displayed in sections relating the history of the islands from prehistoric to Classic times. There are also special displays devoted to marine archaeology and vulcanology. Most of the artefacts have been recovered from excavations since 1949.

At the entrance to each room are two different types of information panel: the more detailed one is intended for use by those wishing to complete a thorough tour of the museum; the other (red) one provides the basic facts pertaining to the successive development of cultures.

The **prehistory of Lipari** is outlined in a room dedicated entirely to obsidian, the glass-like volcanic stone which has been so prized for its strength and razor-sharp cutting edge; although fragile, it was widely used and exported in Antiquity for making tools. The Capo Graziano culture (1800-1400 BC), which takes its name from a site on Filicudi, and the ensuing Capo Milazzese culture from Panarea mark a particularly prosperous period for the islands *(Rooms V and VI)* when the population increased and goods began to be exchanged on a commercial basis. Evidence of this is provided by the presence of large Mycenean vases that were probably traded here for raw materials. The following period (13C-9C BC), known as the Ausonian period after the people who (according to the ancient historian Diodorus Siculus) arrived from the Italian mainland, is classified according to various criteria: there are many one-handled bowls with horn-shaped appendages (probably to ward off evil spirits) which, later on, evolve into stylised forms of animal heads *(Rooms VII-IX)*.

Room X onwards deals with the **Greek and Roman period**. Having been abandoned for a time, the acropolis at Lipari was then colonised by people from Knidos and Rhodes (6C BC). Note the interesting lid of the *bothros* (votive pit) of Aeolus, with its stone lion-cum-handle *(Room X)*. The cult of Aeolus seems to have been shared by both established residents and colonisers. The other glass cases contain the "offerings" found in the pit.

The buildings opposite contain rooms devoted to the prehistory of the smaller islands and to **vulcanology** *(building on the left)*; here the geological evolution of the islands is explained by means of boards, diagrams and scale models.

The chronological displays continue in the building north of the cathedral *(the numbering of the rooms has been inverted in the first three rooms: Room XVIII leads through to Room XVII and then Room XVI before continuing with Room XIX etc)*. The **reconstruction of the Bronze Age necropolis★** (12C BC) is particularly interesting: this compares burial after cremation (12C BC) – when urns containing the ashes were covered with bowls and placed inside small pits dug in the ground *(Room XVII)*, with inhumation burials (14C BC) – when large *pithoi* or jars (containing the curled-up body of the dead person) were simply interred in the ground.

Trading vessels encountering storms at sea often came in to shore to find shelter; on their route were two notable black spots renowned as being highly dangerous: Capo Graziano (on Filicudi) and the area known as Le Formiche (the Ants, which consists of treacherous rocks hidden just below the surface just off Panarea). From these two places have been retrieved the shipwrecked cargo of some 20 trading vessels that comprised large numbers of amphorae of various types, of which the museum has a vast **collection**★ *(see Marine Archaeology section)*.

The grave goods dating from the 6C-4C BC from Lipari include an unusual array of rather coarsely modelled clay figurines *(Room XXI)* but which are of particular interest in that they re-enact different domestic tasks: a mother washes a child, a woman is intent on making soup in a bowl and another grinds grain with a mortar, on the edge of which perches a cat. Among the fine examples of **red-figure ware**★, made in Sicily or mainland Italy, there is one depicting a highly unusual scene (360 BC): a naked acrobat balances in a hand-stand before Dionysus and two comic actors with exaggerated features. Behind the group, in two panels, are painted the portraits of two additional actors. The same case contains three vases by the so-called **painter of Adrastus** (King of Argos): the third one bears a very dramatic scene in which, under the portico of the palace of Argos, Tydeus confronts Polynices, the son of Oedipus, who was exiled from Thebes.

The cult of Dionysus, god not only of wine but also of the theatre and celestial bliss (for those who were initiated into its mysteries), explains the inclusion among the grave goods recovered from votive pits of **statuettes of actors** and **theatrical masks**; the museum has an extremely rich, varied and **ancient collection**★★ of such objects *(Room XXIII)* which is quite unique.

The last section of the museum is essentially devoted to Lipari's history in the Hellenistic and Roman periods (from which there are a considerable quantity of moulded oil lamps stamped with different kinds of decoration). It also displays various artefacts (particularly ceramics) relating to the Norman, Spanish, Renaissance and Baroque periods.

Parco Archeologico – *On the far side of the citadel on the right.* In the archaeological gardens are aligned numerous ancient sarcophagi. From the terrace there is a lovely **view**★ over the little Church of the Lost Souls, jutting out into the sea opposite Marina Corta, and Vulcano on the horizon.

Tour of the island

27km/17mi round trip: set out from Lipari città in the direction of Canneto, to the north.

Canneto – This small town set back from the great sweep of coast is a favourite spot from where to set out for the **white beaches**★ ⊘, visible from Canneto, that are accessible by a footpath. The brilliance of the white sand, and, in particular, of the clear sea is due to the high content of pumice dust *(see below)*. From the harbour of Canneto, it is possible to visit the pumice quarries near Porticello. The simplest way, and also the most picturesque and the most traditional, is to go by boat with one of the many fishermen down at the harbour; the other is by bus.

★**Cave di Pomice a Porticello** – This lovely bay is lined by a mass of pumice quarries and workshops; all, save the last and most northern, are now abandoned. Waste resulting from the extraction and working of the stone accumulates naturally along the shore in mounds of very fine white sand, which hardens with time. On the beach lie small fragments of black obsidian. The **scene**★★ is strangely compelling: the sea is of the palest tinges of blue, as clear as glass (revealing the pumice-lined seabed), old wooden jetties once used for loading pumice onto boats are ghostly still. One of the bathers' favourite pastimes is to climb the white mounds and cover themselves with pumice dust to smooth their skin. The keenest kids can then emulate the children in the scene from *Chaos* (the film directed by the Taviani brothers), who hurled themselves down the mounds, roly-poly fashion, straight into the sea (however, the sea is now about 1m/1.1yd away).

Pumice

White and sponge-like, light enough to float on water, pumice stone is used in pharmaceutical processes, cosmetics (it has delicately abrasive properties), buildings (to make earthquake-proof breeze-blocks) and most recently for stone-washed jeans and denim. The pumice from Lipari is of particularly high quality.

At sunset, the **view**★ from the road is dramatic as the white pumice pyramids in **Campo Bianco** catch the last sunlight of the day: for a split second, the scene might evoke some alpine context among tall snow-covered slopes. A little further on is the **Fossa delle Rocche Rosse** where the island's most impressive flow of obsidian can be admired.

Beyond **Acquacalda** is Puntazze, from where a wonderful **view**★★ opens out over five of the islands: from left to right, Alicudi, Filicudi, Salina, Panarea and Stromboli.

Stufe di San Calogero – *Turn right immediately after Pianoconte.* The waters of these hot springs have been famous for their therapeutic properties since Antiquity. Among the ancient ruins (alongside a modern spa which, alas, is closed) is a **domed chamber**. Since recent studies have revealed it to be from the Mycenean period, it may be considered the oldest thermal complex, and indeed the only Hellenistic building still in use today, even if it only provides people with "DIY" therapy requiring them to splash themselves with water that springs from the ground at a temperature of 60°C.

Quattrocchi – This viewpoint offers the most spectacular **panoramas★★★** in the archipelago, with Punta di Jacopo and then Punta del Perciato in the foreground. Behind sit treacherous crags of rock known locally as *faraglioni*, while the profile of Vulcano interrupts the skyline.
As Lipari looms back into the picture, a fine **view★** opens out onto the town.

★★Boat trip around the island – *Departures from Marina Corta.* A boat trip around the island provides the opportunity to explore its jagged coastline, dotted with arches, boulders and craggy rocks.

★★★VULCANO

It was on this island, with a surface area of 21km²/8sq mi, that Ancient Greek mythology placed the forge of Hephaestus, the god of fire who worked as a black-smith with the assistance of the Cyclops. But it was the Roman name of the god (Vulcan) that became synonymous with the island and, indeed, with vulcanology: the scientific study of volcanoes.
The very existence of the island results from the fusion of four volcanoes: the largest and most dominant peak, **Vulcano della Fossa**, is a 391m/1 282ft mountain of reddish rock; it is also the most active. Beside it sits the diminutive Vulcanello (123m/403ft) which erupted on the north side in 183 BC, to form a round penin-sula. The peculiar way in which these volcanoes behave, spewing acid lava and setting off a series of explosions until the plug is catapulted skywards, thereby releasing large incandescent masses of molten rock, has been classified as **Vulcanian** *(see Introduction: Volcanic phenomenon).*
Although the last eruption occurred in 1890, Vulcano has never ceased to betray signs of its activity; even today, such phenomena as fumaroles, jets of steam above and below sea-level, and sulphurous mud highly prized for its therapeutic proper-ties continue to be very much in evidence. The shoreline, so jagged in places as to resemble tentacles plunging into the sea, the range in colour of the rock from red to yellow ochre, and the desolate, lonely scenery endow the island with a strangely unnerving yet outstanding beauty.

Porto di Levante e Porto di Ponente – The main town of the island nestles midway between these two ports, and borrows both their names. A small place full of little shops, it is furnished with contemporary sculptures made of lava (*Hephaestus and Pandora's box* at the harbour, *Aeolus at Rest* in the main square).

★★★ Ascent to the crater – *Allow 2hr. From end of main road leading out of Levante.* The way to the crater is to be found at the far end of the road from Porto di Levante. As the track gently climbs up the mountainside in a series of broad zig-zags, it provides fabulous **views★★★** of the archipelago: in the foreground is the

M. Andreini/LARA PESSINA

Fumarole

Vulcanello peninsula. Lipari lies opposite, on the left is Salina – recognisable by its two humps – while in the distance sits Filicudi (on a clear day Alicudi may also be visible); off to the right, surrounded by its flock of islets, sits Panarea, with Stromboli some way beyond. About half way up to the top is an area of compacted red earth, cut with deep regular furrows, suggestive of some Martian landscape. The higher the path climbs, the stronger the smell of sulphur, accompanied by the occasional cloud of steam. At the top, the **sight**★★★ is unforgettable: the Cratere della Fossa's huge bowl stretches out below, its southern rim blurred by clouds of boiling sulphurous vapours released from cracks in the crust with a whistle that seems to emanate from deep within the earth; the rock is stained yellow ochre and red by the fumes that condense into the most delicate crystals while still hot. These are the fumaroles.

A **tour of the crater**★★★ *(about 30min)* permits an exploration of the southern part of the island and, from the highest point, enjoyment of one of the most stunning views of the archipelago.

★**Beaches** – Two beaches nestle near the main town: black beaches **(spiagge nere)** – so called because of the dark lava sand – line the lovely bay of Porto di Ponente, although these tend to become very crowded; the other **(spiaggia delle Fumarole)** is unusual in that its waters, heated by bubbles of sulphurous steam, can reach very high temperatures *(beware of being scalded).*

On the opposite side of the island is the remote, and therefore less frequented, **spiaggia del Gelso** (Mulberry Beach) which is accessible by sea, by bus from Porto del Levante *(check timetables as services are highly restricted)*, or by car along the road from Porto Levante to Vulcano Piano which forks for Gelso and Capo Grillo.

Grotta del Cavallo e la piscina di Venere – *Departures by boat from the black beaches.* The boat skirts around Vulcanello, with its so-called Valley of Monsters *(see below)*, before circumnavigating the most jagged part of the coast on the way to this glorious grotto named after the sea horses that once lived there. On the left is Venus's Pool, a shallow pool of the clearest water, an idyllic place for an unforgettable swim. *(Those who wish to stay for a few hours can go with one of the early boat trips, which run fairly regularly throughout the day, and return on one of the later ones; check with the fisherman.)*

★**I fanghi** – Mud is one of Vulcano's specialities. Leaving the port on the right, behind a rock of incredible colours ranging through every shade of yellow to red, there is a natural pool containing sulphurous mud renowned for its therapeutic properties.

A note of advice about mud therapy.

This special mud treatment is recommended for people with rheumatic ailments and dermatological conditions (greasy skin, acne, psoriasis).

It is NOT recommended for expectant mothers or people suffering from tumour-related diseases or with fevers, heart conditions, osteoporosis, gastro-intestinal upsets, uncompensated diabetes and Flajani's disease.

Recommendations: short immersions (never more than 20min at a time), in the coolest hours of the day, followed by a hot shower. Do not apply to the eyes. In the event of mud getting into the eyes, rinse liberally with fresh water. For any ailments resulting from mud baths, consult a doctor.

La Valle dei Mostri – *On Vulcanello*. A trip at dawn or sunset is particularly recommended when the evocative shapes of the rocks, caught by the sun's rays, are at their most impressive. The Valley of Monsters consists of a downward slope of black sand dotted here and there with blocks of lava that have cooled into weird forms and provocative profiles suggestive of prehistoric animals, monsters and wild beasts (including a bear reared up on its hind legs and a crouching lion).

Capo Grillo – *Approx 10km/6mi from Porto Levante*. The local road to Vulcano Piano and beyond to the cape, offers a variety of prospects of Lipari and the great crater. From the promontory, there is a splendid **view**★ of the archipelago.

★★★STROMBOLI

The island-volcano possesses a sombre, disquieting beauty all of its own: its coastline of steep crags emerging from the sea make it far from endearing. The almost total lack of roads, the untamed scenery and, more particularly, the volcano which methodically makes its presence felt with outbursts of fire and brimstone, have both a strange and awesome power of attraction.

In Rossellini's film *Stromboli, terra di Dio* (Stromboli, land of God – 1950), which highlighted the difficulties of living in such a place, the volcano plays the main role while the island is portrayed as the most fascinating and atmospheric of all the Aeolian isles.

There are two villages on the island: on the north-eastern slopes, surrounded by a green mantle that stretches to the north as far as San Bartolo, nestle the small square white houses of **San Vincenzo** (where the landing-stage is located); on the south-western side is **Ginostra**, which consists of a huddle of about 30 houses clinging to the rock, in desperate isolation (there are no roads, just a mule-track which winds along the side of the hill), but accessible by sea (although not all year around) by means of the smallest port in the world. The arid, precipitous northern flank which separates the two villages is the most impressive, scarred as it is by the *sciara del fuoco* – down which the burning lava flows each time the volcano decides to erupt.

Opposite San Vincenzo is the tiny islet of **Strombolicchio**, a single spur of rock topped by a lighthouse, bestowed by nature with a strange profile in which a horse's head may be perceived.

★★★**The crater** – The hike up to the crater of Stromboli makes for a unique and fascinating experience, as it provides the opportunity to wonder at the phenomenal workings of Mother Nature. The route itself is provocatively beautiful, casting unforgettable **views**★★ in all directions, before emerging, gently, gently, at the top of one of the very few active volcanoes in the world. The crater comprises five vents. A certain feeling of restlessness pervades the place. This atmosphere is charged and heightened by what is going on some few hundred metres away, as with each successive explosion, incandescent stones are thrust skywards: a spectacle which more than compensates for the steep and somewhat arduous climb.

When to go and what to take

To watch the eruptions at night is particularly exciting: we therefore recommend hiking up the mountain in the late afternoon and returning in the evening (don't forget to take a torch) or the following morning. Allow three hours for the climb up and two hours for the descent; it is not particularly taxing, but is not recommended for those who suffer from heart problems, asthma or vertigo and should not be undertaken by the faint-hearted, especially in rare cases of bad weather. **Qualified guides** ⊘ are available on Stromboli; they offer guided walks of the island and afternoon or evening excursions to the crater.

For the ascent, the following hiking equipment is recommended: walking boots (or sturdy trainers), an electric torch, wind-cheater, water (according to the weather), a pair of long trousers, a spare T-shirt and, if opting to stay the night, a good slee ping-bag and a jumper to wear at the top where the temperature can drop quite dramatically.

This excursion can be completed all year round. The best time is late spring when the weather is mild and temperatures are not too high; however, a night excursion during the summer months is also highly recommended.

Fire and incandescent stones

Ascent – *5hr round trip.* From the ferry jetty at San Vincenzo, head for the centre of the village and follow the tarred road to San Bartolo. Before long, the typical white houses dwindle to none, a mule-track begins *(follow the signs)*, at first paved with slabs of lava and then, after a few bends, degenerating into a well-worn footpath. After 20min, it reaches an observation point called Punta Labronzo (refreshments available; good view of the craters); beyond this point, the real climb begins. From here, the path heads straight for the summit, picking its way through the lush vegetation; ascending at a moderate incline, swinging first right then left, to its end at a ledge *(be careful)*, which provides a magnificent **view**★★ of the Sciara del Fuoco – the great black slope down which chunks of lava make their way from the crater to the sea. The footpath is reduced to a steep track cut deeply into the side of the mountain. This veritable trench, excavated by water erosion, leads to a reddish lava section where care should be taken in the awkward scramble upwards. After the next easy bit, a fine view opens out to the left, taking in the town and Strombolicchio, now almost 700m/2 296ft below. At this point, the path climbs up onto a broad, steep and sandy ridge to the summit. Level with the craters, safely tucked away behind low semicircular walls, are the first viewing points from where the eruptions may be observed at leisure. At this altitude, the craters appear between intermittent clouds of vapour; a final stretch of ridge leads to the highest point and the observation point closest to the crater vents.

On a day blessed with a favourable light wind, the view from here can be truly exceptional, providing an unforgettable **experience**★★★: one after another, the startling explosions shoot matter high into the air, tingeing the night's blackness with red.

★★★**Evening boat trip** – The easiest way of encapsulating an overall picture of this island and all its different aspects is, possibly, by means of a nocturnal excursion. Under normal conditions the rocky Sciara del Fuoco *(see above)* makes for an impressive sight; at night the impact is exaggerated a hundredfold as the volcanic eruptions, with incredible regularity, thrust fountains of luminous stones up into the black night sky in nature's most magnificent firework display (in daylight, the emissions merely look grey).

★SALINA

Recognisable from its distinctive two-humped profile (hence Didyme, its name in Antiquity, meaning twins), this remote and lonely island offers visitors the perfect place for a quiet holiday at one with nature. At one time it comprised six volcanoes, since when four have disappeared. It derives its name from the salt-works (a small lake) – now abandoned – at Lingua, a small town situated on the south coast. Today, the island is renowned for two specialities: capers which are gathered locally and the famous wine Malvasia delle Lipari, made from the island's grapes.

There are two landing-stages: **Santa Maria Salina** and the smaller **Rinella di Leni** (where there is also a camp site which gets extremely crowded during the second and third week of August).

Possible trips inland – *By car or moped (available from small car-hire firms on the island). Ask the local inhabitants for information. There is also a local bus service: timetables are displayed at the port of Santa Maria Salina.*

A panoramic road offering many **views★** of the jagged coastline links the harbour with the island's other hamlets. From the main town **Santa Maria Salina**, the road heads northwards, past Capo Faro, on its way to **Malfa**. The coast road climbs above Punta del Perciato, a beautiful natural arc visible only from the sea or from the beach a little further on at **Pollara**, which is considered to be one of the most attractive and atmospheric stretches of coast on the island. Before going down to the beach, take a peep through the vegetation for a glimpse of the house *(private)* where parts of the film *Il Postino* (The Postman) were made: it was here that the meetings between Neruda (Philippe Noiret) and the postman (Massimo Troisi) took place.

★★**Spiaggia di Pollara** – There are two paths down to this beautiful bay: one leads to a small anchorage enclosed by its own miniature shoreline of rocks; the other provides access to a broad beach overshadowed by a striking white semicircular cliff-wall, a desolate remnant of a crater.

On the way back to Malfa, the road forks inland to **Valdichiesa**, where a popular pilgrimage site – the sanctuary dedicated to the Madonna del Terzito – is located, and **Rinella di Leni**.

> The famous Malvasia delle Lipari is a strong, sweet, golden wine made from grapes that have been left to wither on the vine before being picked. Its smooth, aromatic flavour makes it an excellent dessert wine. There are various types of Malvasia available. The DOC-endorsed variety, produced only on the islands, must bear the words "Malvasia delle Lipari" in full on the label.

★**Fossa delle Felci** – Nestling inside the dormant crater of the taller of Salina's two mountains is a beautiful fern wood (known as Fossa delle Felci). This protected nature reserve is accessible on foot *(about 2hr)* by a path from the Santuario della Madonna del Terzito in Valdichiesa. A second track runs from Santa Maria Salina.

★PANAREA

The smallest Aeolian Island rises to its highest point with **Punta del Corvo** (420m/1 378ft high), the western flank of which plunges almost vertically down into the sea. Conversely, the gentler slopes on the eastern side accommodate Panarea's small resident community before terminating in a tall black lava coastline, skirted by small pebbled beaches. In the south-east, around **Punta Milazzese**, lie the remains of a prehistoric village set high above the bay of Cala Junco.

All around the island are scattered a collection of small islets and rocks, including the dreaded Formiche which, lying hidden just below the surface, have been the cause of so many shipwrecks since Antiquity.

★FILICUDI

Steep slopes and a rocky coastline, for the most part of basalt, determine the nature of this small island, which consists of a group of craters: the highest being the **Fossa delle Felci** (773m/2 535ft). An estimated population of 250 souls reside, in the main, in three hamlets.

Panarea

From the island's landing-stage at **Filicudi Porto**, it is simple to reach the **prehistoric village** situated on the promontory of **Capo Graziano** *(about 40min there and back)*; this contains the remains of about 25 roughly oval huts. The settlement dates from the Bronze Age and was transferred from its original site closer to the shore, so that it could be better defended against potential attack *(see also the Archaeological Museum at Lipari, where the finds from this site are displayed)*. From here, there is a beautiful **view★** of the bay, the summit of Fossa delle Felci and Alicudi (in the distance on the left).

If approaching by sea, a stop to visit the huge cave called **Grotta del Bue Marino** is a must. The tall volcanic chimney-stack formation which lies not so far offshore is known as **la Canna** on account of its shape.

★ALICUDI

Alicudi is the most isolated of the Aeolian Islands: it consists of a round cone covered with heather (hence its ancient name, Ericusa), inhabited by no more than 140 people; to all intents and purposes, it has remained unchanged since the dawn of time. A single village groups together the handful of pastel-coloured houses scattered at the foot of the mountain; this rises up to the **Filo d'Arpa** (literally, Harp String) which provides a magnificent view *(the footpath snakes its way from Chiesa di San Bartolo up through the cultivated terraces. About 1hr 45min to the top and back, at a brisk pace)*.

ERACLEA MINOA

Agrigento

Michelin map 432 O 21

The remains of the Greek city Heraclea Minoa enjoy a magnificent **situation★★** on the edge of a lonely hill with a fine view of the sea, at the beginning of Capo Bianco. At its feet, the coast opens out into a broad bay, lined with a long **beach★★** of the whitest sand extended up to a handsome glade of pine trees behind. Before the excavations, note on the right, the white "dunes" of rock (called **marl**, a mixture of clay and limestone smoothed by erosion) sculpted by the wind, echoing the cliff on the east side of the promontory.

The white dunes at Eraclea

Minos and Daedalus' labyrinth

Minos, the son of Zeus and Europa, was married to Pasiphaë (who was the daughter of Helios, the sun-god who charged across the oceans in a chariot pulled by four horses often identified with Hyperion and Apollo). Minos reigned over Crete and the islands of the Aegean, instituting their constitution and founding their naval supremacy. The Cretan Bull was sent by the god of the sea Poseidon for sacrifice. It was so magnificent a creature that Minos decided to spare it by substituting another at the sacrifice. This so angered Poseidon that he inspired Pasiphaë with an unnatural passion for the bull. Pasiphaë requested that Daedelus construct her a hollow cow that would allow her to hide inside; from her coupling with the Cretan Bull, the Minotaur was born. The Labyrinth was built by Daedelus in order to conceal and contain the monstrous creature with a human body and a bull's head to whom Minos insisted on sacrificing seven Athenian youths and seven maidens every ninth year (this he did to avenge the death of his own son Androgeus, but that is another story). On discovering Daedelus' treachery, Minos imprisoned him and his son Icarus in the Labyrinth; they were released by Pasiphaë whereupon Daedelus set about making wings to help him escape to Sicily *(see Monte KRONIO)*. When the third tribute was due, Theseus volunteered himself; on his arrival in Crete, Minos' daughter Ariadne fell in love with the Athenian hero; she gave him a sword with which to kill the monster and a ball of silk to help him retrace his way out of the inviolable maze.

Ancient foundations – The ancient settlement was probably called Minoa, the older of its two names. Legend links it to Minos, the ruler of Crete who, according to more recent traditions, is reputed to have followed Daedelus to Sicily to punish him for revealing the secret of the labyrinth to Ariadne and her accomplice Theseus. It is here that Minos is supposed to have been killed by the daughter of Cocalus. In fact, the kingdom of Cocalus was situated on the banks of the River Platani, with a capital called Camico, now identified by some as being the modern Sant'Angelo Muxaro *(see AGRIGENTO)*, by others as Caltabellotta. The city was probably founded in the 6C BC by Greek colonists from Selinus (now Selinunte). The addition of Heraclea to the name was prompted, it is alleged, by a subsequent influx of Greeks. Sometime in the 3C BC, the town passed into the hands of the Romans; thereafter it embarked upon a series of wars and was gradually abandoned. By the 1C BC it was deserted.

Ruins ⊘ – A concerted effort to undertake a thorough excavation of the area began in 1950: this has uncovered the remains of dwellings made of rough bricks, some still containing fragments of mosaic and, most excitingly, a **theatre** built of a very friable stone. This, inevitably, is not well preserved *(the transparent plastic coverings protect rather than preserve the extant parts)*. The complete layout of the *cavea* in relation to the horseshoe-shaped orchestra pit is easy to determine. A small **antiquarium** collects together various objects found for the most part in the necropoli.

★★**Beach** – *From Eraclea, return to SP 115 (Sciacca-Agrigento road) and continue towards Agrigento. Take the first exit sign-posted Montallegro-Bove Marina and then follow the signs for Montallegro Marina. A road off to the right indicates access to the sea.* This fabulous long beach is marked at one end by the tall white cliffs of the promontory and, at the south-eastern end, by a large pine grove.

ERICE★★★

Trapani – Population 31 141
Michelin map 432 M 19

Erice occupies a memorably beautiful site★★★. Developed as a Phoenician and Hellenistic town, it sits at a height of 751m/2 463ft, perched on the mountain of the same name, covering a triangular plateau with a glorious view over the sea. Enclosed within defensible bastions and walls, the town is a veritable labyrinth of little cobbled streets and passages wide enough to accommodate only one person at a time. The houses, packed one upon another, each have their own charming, carefully tended, inner courtyard that can be guarded from the gaze of neighbours or passers-by, and so allows family life to take its daily course in absolute privacy.

In Antiquity, Erice was famous for its temple where, in succession, the Phoenicians worshipped Astarte, the Greeks venerated Aphrodite and the Romans celebrated Venus. Mount Eryx served as a point of reference for sailors who, in time, adopted Venus as their protector. At night, a large fire would be lit within the sacred precinct and used as a guiding beacon. Venus Erycina became so famous that a temple was dedicated to her in Rome; meanwhile, her cult spread throughout the Mediterranean. Erice, like Janus, is two faced: there is the bright, sunny face that smiles during the long hot summer days, when light floods its tiny streets and distant views extend over the valley and far out to sea; there is also the mask of winter when, shrouded in mist, the town seems to hark back to its mythical origins, leaving the visitor with a feeling of unease and the impression of a place removed from time and reality. Its enveloping medieval atmosphere, cool mountain air, beautiful pine woods and pervading silence, combined with its rich local craft traditions, make Erice a highly popular destination for tourists.

Between myth and legend – The history of Erice is lost among local folklore and superstition. The name is the one given by Eryx, the mythical hero and king of the Elimi, to the mountain upon which the temple to his mother, Venus Erycina (later associated with the cult of Aphrodite), was built. The origins of the town are also linked with **Aeneas**, who also had a claim on the Elimian king's mother. In Virgil's narrative, Aeneas came ashore at the foot of the mountain to perform the funeral of his father Anchises. Having lost several ships in a fire, he was forced to abandon there a number of his companions, who set about founding the town.

Another major mythological figure associated with Erice is **Heracles**. The hero is alleged to have landed in this part of Sicily on his way back to Greece, having stolen the cattle of Geryon (one of the legendary Twelve Labours); during his sojourn he was forced to kill the Elimian king after he tried to steal the cattle from him. Notwithstanding this, Heracles decided to leave the rule of the kingdom in the hands of the Elimi, with the warning that one of his descendants, Dorieus, would later take over as ruler.

🛈 viale Conte Pepoli 11, ☎ 0923 86 93 88; Fax 0923 86 95 44.

GETTING TO ERICE

Visitors arriving by **car** are advised to leave their vehicle in the car park by Porta Trapani.
A.S.T. **buses** (☎ 0923 23 222) run between Trapani (piazza Malta) and Erice. Journey time is approx 30-60min.

WHERE TO STAY

The only options for moderately priced accommodation in Erice are the **youth hostel** (Ostello per la Gioventù, viale delle Pinete, ☎ 0923 86 91 44; open July to Sept) and the hostels run by **religious orders** (addresses available from the tourist office).
Baglio Santacroce – 2km/1.2mi east of **Valderice** on the N 187, ☎ 0923 89 11 11, Fax 0923 89 11 92. A 17C farmhouse which has been transformed into a hotel, while retaining its original fabric. Peace and seclusion are guaranteed by the delightful terraced gardens. Simple rooms, but a charming atmosphere and magnificent views. Approximately 200 000L for a double room.
Moderno – Via Vittorio Emanuele 63, Erice ☎ 0923 86 93 00; Fax 0923 86 91 39. The name of this hotel is misleading, as the building dates from the 19C and is situated in the historical centre of the town. The 40 rooms, each furnished differently, are located in two separate buildings. Approximately 200 000L for a double room.

EATING OUT

Monte San Giuliano – Vicolo S Rocco 7, Erice ☎ 0923 86 95 95; closed Mon, 7-12 Jan and Nov. Excellent local cuisine served in attractive surroundings. It is advisable to book for the evening. Approximately 60 000L for a meal.
The *pasticcerie* at via Vittorio Emanuele 14 and via Guarnotti 1 are highly recommended for those with a sweet tooth.

ERICE

S 187 TRAPANI, PALERMO VALDERICE

Addolorata (Viale d.) .... **AZ** 3
Cordici (Via) .... **ABZ** 4
Giudaica (Via) .... **ABZ** 6
Guarnotti (Via G. F.) .... **BZ** 9
Guarrasi (Via) .... **ABZ** 10
Rabata (Via) .... **AZ** 12
S. Cataldo (Piazza) .... **BZ** 13
S. Cataldo (Via) .... **BZ** 15
S. Domenico (Piazza) .... **BZ** 16
S. Giuliano (Piazza) .... **BZ** 18
Salerno (Via Gen. G.) .... **ABZ** 19
Umberto I (Piazza) .... **AZ** 21
Vittorio Emanuele (Via) .... **AZ**

Museo Cordici .... **AZ M**
Torre Campanaria .... **AZ R**

★★Access – *Both the two roads that wind up to the town afford superb views across the plain and out to sea (the one on the north side, overlooking Monte Cofano, is easier).*

The little town takes the shape of a perfect equilateral triangle, whose symbolism has provoked mystery and endless argument: hemmed in by the Castello di Venere (south-eastern axis) and the Chiesa Madre (south-western side). Exactly in the centre of the triangle is the Church of St Peter with its adjacent monastery that now houses the E Majorana Centre for Culture and Science. An intricate maze of narrow streets, each cobbled with rectangular stones, provides unexpected glimpses of churches and monasteries, of which there are over 60, scattered through the town.

It is advisable to park at Porta Trapani.

★Chiesa Matrice ⊘ – The town's main church is situated near **Porta di Trapani**, one of the entrances to the town. Built in the 14C, principally using stone from the Temple of Venus, its massive form and merlon-topped walls suggest it was intended as a church-fortress. The façade is graced with a fine rose-window (replicating the original), that is now partly concealed by the Gothic porch that was added a century later. Inside, fashioned in Neo-Gothic, sits a fine marble altarpiece from the Renaissance.

Bell-tower – The lonely tower to the left of the church was originally intended as a watchtower. The first level has simple narrow slits, while the upper section is graced with fine two-light Chiaramonte-style windows. The top is crenellated with Ghibelline merlons.

Museo Cordici ⊘ – Accommodated inside the town hall is the local museum which collects together various archaeological finds, statuary and paintings. Notable exhibits include Antonello Gagini's sculpture of the *Annunciation* (1525) and, on the first floor, beyond the library containing manuscripts and early books, a small marble **head of a woman**, modelled on a Greek original.

A little further along, on the right of the piazza, is via Cordici which leads into the picturesque **piazza San Domenico**, lined on one side by a street of the same name and on the other by elegant *palazzi*.

Giardino del Balio – The lovely public gardens are arranged around the Castello di Venere and the Torri di Balio which were built by the Normans as a forward defence for the castle. The towers and gardens are named after the Norman governor (Baiulo) who once lived on this site.

The glorious **view★★★** embraces Monte Cofano, Trapani, the Egadi Islands and, on a particularly clear day, Pantelleria and, possibly, Cap Bon some 170km/106mi away in Tunisia.

Castello di Venere – The 12C Venus's Castle is appended to the very tip of the mountain, looking out over the sea and the plain below; although the present building is Norman, the site itself has a more ancient history. Indeed, it was once occupied by a temple dedicated to Venus Erycina, who became completely associated with Aphrodite especially after a temple was dedicated to her in Rome (217 BC) when she gained popularity. By the time the Normans were in occupation the temple was in ruins, and so it was decided that the area should be cleared to make way for a fortress surrounded by great walls: the complex was designed to exploit the strategic nature of the site and have the added protection of forward defences in the form of towers **(Torri del Balio)** that would once have been accessible from the castle by a drawbridge. Its defensibility was further emphasised by the machicolations above the entrance; note the coat of arms of Charles V of Spain and the rather attractive two-light window.

This provides a perfect **viewpoint★★★** from which to survey Trapani and the Egadi Islands to the south-west and, to the north, the towers, the Pepoli turret *(down below)*, San Giovanni, Monte Cofano, the coast around Bonagia and, if the weather is fine, the island of Ustica.

★**Elimo-Punic Walls** – A mighty wall was built by the Elimini (8C-6C BC) around the north-eastern flank of the town – the only section open to possible attack. Massive blocks characterise the lowest and most ancient stone courses which were built up through successive ages with smaller components. The skyline was punctuated with look-out towers, steep stairways provided access to the *chemin-de-ronde*, while small openings allowed residents to come and go freely and supplies to be imported. The best-preserved stretch of walls runs along via dell'Addolorata, from Porta Carmine to Porta Spada.

Santa Orsola ⊘ – This church, built in 1413, preserves its original Gothic rib-vaulting down the nave. It is here that the 18C Mystery figures are kept when not being processed around the town on Good Friday before the Easter celebrations.

Quartiere Spagnolo – From the top of the so-called Spanish Quarter building, initiated in the 17C but never completed, there is a marvellous view over the bay of Monte Cofano and the area beyond, and down towards the tuna fishery at Bonagìa.

Remains of the Norman defences

EXCURSION

Tonnara di Bonagìa – *Approx 13km/8mi N. Drive down to Valderice and continue towards Tonnara (from the main Valderice road, turn left at the supermarket). At Bonagìa, follow signs for the Tonnara (tuna fishery) while looking out for its distinctive tower.* The tuna fishery, set up in the 17C, was once a simple self-contained village: clustered around a large central courtyard were the fishermen's houses, facilities for cleaning and processing the tuna, the boat-house (now a conference centre, although two examples of fishing-boats remain) and a small chapel where the tuna fishermen used to assemble before going out to sea.

Today, the tuna fishery accommodates an attractive hotel complex with 45 comfortable and attractive rooms and a number of two to three-room apartments. ☎ 0923 43 11 11; Fax 0923 59 2177.

The Saracen tower, intended for use in defending the place, now houses the **Museo della Tonnara** ⊙, a small museum displaying the tools and equipment required in building and repairing boats, fishing and the initial stages of sorting and processing the fish. On the second floor, a scale model shows the long corridors of net that the tuna had to enter before reaching the last chamber made of very strong twine, known as the camera della morte (death chamber). It was here that the cruel *mattanza* (the kill or slaughter) took place *(see p 155)*.

ETNA★★★
Catania
Michelin map 432 N-O 26-27

Mount Etna is Sicily's tallest peak. Although capped with snow for much of the winter, it is one of Europe's most famous active volcanoes. Its actual height is regularly modified by each eruption; it currently (1998) stands at 3 350m/10 988ft above sea-level. Mount Etna's other name **Mongibello** derives from the erroneous interpretation of the Arab word *gebel* meaning mountain: so, prefixed by the Italian word, it became *Mount Mountain.*

THE VOLCANO AND ITS STORY

Etna evolved as a result of submarine eruptions during the Quaternary Period (c 500 000 years ago), at the same time that the plain of Catania was formed, originally as a broad bay. Etna is known to have erupted regularly during Antiquity, as documented at least 135 times. In the Middle Ages, eruptions were recorded in 1329 and 1381; they disseminated terror among the people of the region. It was in 1669, however, that the most cataclysmic disaster occurred and a great river of lava flowed down to the sea, devastating part of Catania on the way.

In the 20C, the most violent eruptions took place in 1910 leading to 23 additional craters being formed; in 1917 a fountain of lava spurted 800m/2 624ft into the air from its base; in 1923 outpourings of molten lava stayed hot for more than 18 months after the eruption. In 1928, a lava flow destroyed the village of Mascali, and other eruptions followed in 1954, 1964, 1971, 1974, 1978, 1979, 1981, 1983 and 1985

B. Kaufmann

until the eruption of 1991 that continued to grumble for a further three years. A plume of smoke always hangs above Etna and it could burst into activity at any moment. The black lava around the craters dates from recent eruptions as compared with the older grey lava on which lichens are beginning to grow. The presence of both and, sometimes, their distressing effects (blocked roads and ruined buildings) are evidence of the volcano's constant activity.

On the slope of the central crater at around the 3 000m mark, in the vicinity of Torre del Filosofo where a refuge was destroyed by lava in 1971, there are four craters: the south-eastern crater that began suppurating in 1978, the immense **central crater**, the north-eastern crater at the highest point that has been dormant since 1971, and the Bocca Nuova (literally the 'New Mouth') which, in recent times, has been the most active.

For more detailed information about volcanic activity on Etna, see Introduction: Volcanic phenomenon.

NATIONAL PARK

The protected area designated a National Park in 1987 covers some 59 000ha/145 730 acres. The mountain consists of an enormous black cone, visible from a distance of up to 250km/155mi away. The extremely fertile lower slopes are heavily cultivated with dense groves of oranges, mandarins, lemons, olives, agaves and prickly pears, as well as bananas, eucalyptus, palm trees, Maritime (Parasol) pines and vines from which the excellent *Etna* wine is produced. Probably the most common of the wild plants is *Euphorbia dendroides* (tree spurge). Above 500m/1 640ft, plantations of hazelnuts, almonds, pistachio and chestnuts give way to oaks, beeches, birches and pines, especially around Linguaglossa *(see below)*. The landscape at this altitude is also characterised by a local variety of broom.

At 2 100m/6 888ft, the desolate landscape sustains desert-like plants like *Astragalus aetnensis* (a local variety of milk-vetch), a small prickly bush often found alongside colourful endemic varieties of violet, groundsel and other flowers which populate the slopes of secondary craters. Higher up, snow and, for a long time after an eruption, hot lava prevent any type of macroscopic vegetation from growing: this comprises the so-called volcanic desert.

MAKING THE MOST OF ETNA

Opportunities abound when it comes to walking in the park, with facilities for both short and long excursions (the longest and most complex being the **Grande Traversata Etnea** which involves five days of trekking, with daily 12-15km (7-9mi) hikes). There are also nature trails and, for the less agile, the **circum-navigation of Etna** by car *(see below)* or train: this latter option uses the section of railway that starts at Catania, goes around the mountain, and stops at Riposto (approximately 5hr); onward services to Catania are by bus or train. For information, apply to the Ferrovia Circumetnea (☎ 095 54 12 50).

For detailed information about routes enquire at the following:

APT di Catania (☎ 095 73 06 211), **Azienda di Soggiorno e Turismo** at via Garibaldi 63, Nicolosi ☎ 095 91 15 05, **Pro Loco information centres**, including Linguaglossa (piazza Annunziata 7, ☎ 095 64 30 94) and **Zafferana Etnea** (piazza Luigi Sturzo 3, ☎ 095 708 28 825), and the **Gruppo Guide Alpine Etna Sud at Nicolosi** (☎ 095 79 14 755).

Ascent to the top – Unpredictable and ongoing eruptions of the volcano undermine any permanent tourist amenity infrastructure (roads, ski runs, ropeways, refuges); favourite haunts and recommended itineraries, therefore, should be considered as temporary and subject to being closed at short notice following any recent eruption. Excursions across the higher slopes of the volcano in particular may be cancelled due to forecasts of bad weather (rain or mist). It is as well to bear in mind that, especially on the north-east side of the mountain, the period during which it is possible to go hiking varies each year according to the snowfall. At the start of the season (normally in May), shorter walks that stop well below the top are organised. When there is no snow, or if there is, only after the snowcat has cleared the roads through the highest sections, is it possible to reach 3 000m/9 840ft. The best time of the year for hiking on Etna is normally high summer, especially in the early morning.

Equipment – Whether aiming for high *(see below)* or low altitudes, it is important to remember that temperatures can plummet here. It is therefore advisable to carry a thick sweater, a wind-cheater and appropriate footwear (preferably hiking boots suitable for walking through snow higher up). Those arriving without suitable attire can, however, hire jackets and boots locally.

It is also advisable to have sunglasses and sunscreen to hand for the sunlight can be dazzling when reflected off the snow and the ultra-violet can be deceptively powerful in the clear mountain air.

The protected areas of Etna also harbour a large variety of small mammals (porcupine, fox, wild cat, weasel, marten and dormouse), birds (kestrel, buzzard, chaffinch, woodpecker and hoopoe), a few reptiles, including the asp viper, and a large variety of butterflies, including the Eastern orange tip *(Anthocharis damone, which is more commonly known in Italy as the Aurora dell'Etna).*

ASCENT TO THE TOP

A climb up the volcano can be approached from the south or the north: both routes offer different views over the landscape and contrasting qualities. The route from Nicolosi to Rifugio Sapienza is through a barren, black and desert-like environment when compared to the lushly green section up via Piano Provenzana.

① From the coast to the southern slopes

45km/28mi drive starting from Acireale: allow half a day.

There are various ways of approaching the southern slopes of the volcano, the bleaker side, where concretions of black lava form a lunar-like **landscape★★**. All along the edge runs a ring of little towns which all have one feature in common: dark lava stone paves the streets, ornaments the doorways and windows of the houses, fashions awesome black masks with exaggerated menace and articulates the lines of the churches.

✝ **Acireale** – *See ACIREALE.*

Continue by following signs to Aci Sant'Antonio.

Aci Sant'Antonio – Several of the town's most important monuments are collected around piazza Maggiore, most notably the Duomo with its imposing front, rebuilt after the terrible earthquake of 1693. Opposite stands the 16C church of San Michele Arcangelo.

At the far end of the town's main street, via Vittorio Emanuele, which leads out from the piazza, stands what remains of the Riggio family *palazzo*.

> **Where to stay**
>
> A beautiful avenue of plane trees leads up to the *agriturismo* guesthouse **L'Annunziata** (Viagrande, ☎ 095 78 94 438), an 18C villa which is part of a farm situated at 400m/1 312ft above sea-level. This is a particularly appropriate address for those interested in science, as the guesthouse is run by the Majorana sisters, descendents of the famous physicist from Catania who disappeared mysteriously in 1938 at only 32 years of age.

Viagrande – The centre of the village is paved with huge slabs of lava. The front elevation of the 18C Chiesa Madre is of the same dark stone, used here to emphasise the strong verticals of the doorways and windows above.

GOOD COOKING AND FOLKLORE

The **Villa Taverna** restaurant in Trecastagni (corso Colombo 42, ☎ 095 78 06 458; open evenings on weekdays and at midday Sat-Sun and public holidays; closed Mon) is cluttered with an unusual assemblage of artefacts in an attempt to recreate something of the historic centre of Catania in times past.
The menu offers a range of typical Sicilian dishes at 45 000L.

Pedara – Piazza Don Diego is graced with the Duomo which has an unusual spire covered in brightly-coloured maiolica tiles.

Nicolosi – Nicolosi is often regarded as the gateway to Etna: it is here that the official guides *(Alpine Etna Sud, via Etnea 49, ☎ 095 79 14 755)* are centred and it is from here that the road winds its way up to **Rifugio Sapienza**, the starting-point for all expeditions to the crater.

WHERE TO STAY

Hotel Corsaro – Loc. Piazza Cantoniera Etna Sud, 18km/11mi NW of Nicolosi, ☎ 095 91 41 22, Fax 095 78 01 024. Closed 15 Nov to 24 Dec. This comfortable hotel, situated at an altitude of 2 000m/6 560ft, has 20 attractively furnished rooms. Only 200m/219yd from the cable car and chair-lift, this is an excellent address for walkers and skiers. Approximately 150 000L for a double room.

Trecastagni – Literally, the name of this little town translates as Three chestnuts: however, contrary to what it might suggest, the name actually derives from *tre casti agni* (short for *agnelli*) which refer to the three chaste lambs that are worshipped here: Alfio, Filadelfio and Cirino. A festival in their honour is annually celebrated on 9 and 10 May: the highlight coming with the **procession of the wax effigies**, some immensely heavy, borne by strong bare-chested *ignudi* through the streets to the **Santuario di Sant'Alfio** on the outskirts of town.

Via Vittorio Emanuele, lined by fine buildings, leads to the foot of **Chiesa Madre di San Nicola** with its great central campanile. The front towers above a steep flight of steps that is flanked on the right by a projecting recess which rises to become a series of asymmetrical ramps above. The terrace at the top provides marvellous views over the plain below.

** **Up to the summit of Etna** – The route lies through a strangely unnerving landscape that might appear to the visitor like some fantastical set furnished with black lava below and blue sky above, relieved occasionally by a white patch of snow or lonely cloud as if for dramatic effect. Just before the refuge, a sign points to the **Crateri Silvestri**, a collection of moonlike craters a short walk away, at a height of 1 886m/6 186ft.

*** **Ascent from the south side** ⊘ – The section up to 1 923m/6 307ft can be made by cable-car (from Rifugio Sapienza), then to 2 608m/8 554ft by four-wheel drive vehicle, leaving a short distance to cover on foot. It is no longer possible to get close to the central vent for safety reasons, although a short walk away, there is a "hot area" where steam is released from the ground.

An excursion by vehicle includes a stop near the **Valle del Bove**, a vast sunken area (hence the description as a valley) enclosed by 1 000m/3 280ft high walls of lava, split with great crevasses and chasms. This zone often gives rise to violent eruptions, some notoriously dangerous, precipitating flows of lava that have succeeded in reaching the towns below (1950, 1952, 1979 and 1991).

② **The north-east flank**

62km/38mi drive starting from Linguaglossa: allow a full day.

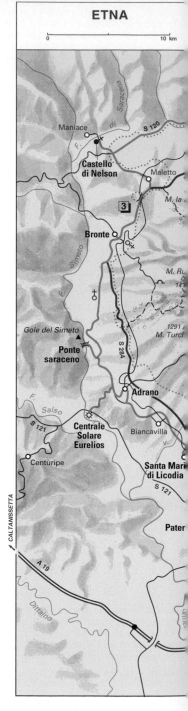

Linguaglossa – The name of this little town literally translates as "tongue" twice over (*lingua* in Latin, *glossa* in Greek), a reference perhaps to its vulnerable "red-hot" position on the slopes of Etna down which incandescent lava has flowed perilously on several occasions.

The **Chiesa Madre**, ⊘ built of sandstone and lava, is situated on the central piazza. Inside, it is furnished with lovely **wooden choir-stalls★** (1728) depicting scenes from the life of Christ.

The **Pro Loco** of Linguaglossa, located in the main street, serves as the main reference point for planning excursions up Etna. Information and explanatory boards provide details about the park and the volcano: these may be useful when organising walks in the area.

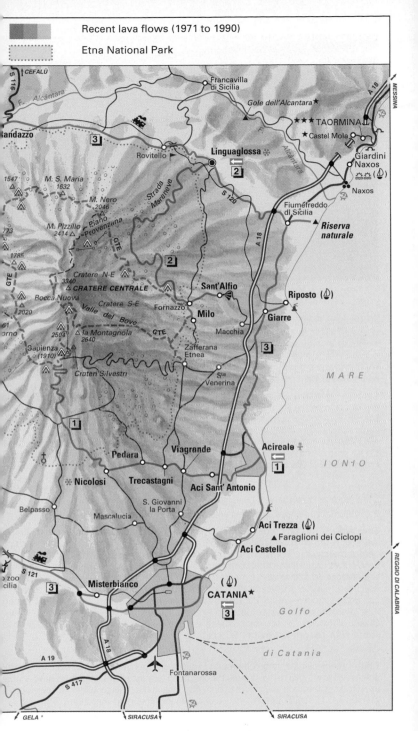

The **Mareneve** road leads through a wonderful larch and pine wood to the **Piano Provenzana** where cars may be left before undertaking the real climb up to the craters.

★★ Ascent up the north flank ⊘ – Four-wheel drive minibuses effortlessly make the ascent to 3 000m/9 840ft along a spectacular route. A new observatory has been built here, replacing the one destroyed by lava during the eruption of 1971 (lasting 69 days), which affected both the south slope (wiping out both the observatory and ropeway) and the eastern slope, where the lava flow threatened some of the towns below (Fornazzo and Milo – *see below*), before stopping about 7km/4mi short of the sea. From the observatory, at 2 750m/9 020ft, there is a magnificent **view★★**. The minibus can then transport the more intrepid to 3 000m/9 840ft before

187

The lunar landscape around Crateri Silvestri

abandoning them to the final leg and those awesome puffing vents, on foot. What is spine-chilling is that, at a whim, these craters can spare the surrounding area or cover it with spewing hot fire. The route may vary according to the latest outward signs given by the volcano.

On the downward return journey, there is an opportunity to stop at 2 400m/7 872ft and examine the craters that were the cause of the 1809 eruption.

★**Eastern approach** – From Piano Provenzana, the scenic Mareneve road skirts the eastern side of the summit before dropping back downhill. On the lower slopes of the east side of Etna, many farming villages have rallied to exploit the fertile volcanic soil by cultivating vines and citrus fruits.

Near **Fornazzo**, just before the road meets the more major Linguaglossa to Zafferana Etnea road, it passes the incredible lava flow which managed to spare the little **Cappella del Sacro Cuore** *(on the left)* in 1979, although lava did flow right up to one of the walls and even slightly penetrated the chapel. Regarded as having been preserved by sacred intervention, the chapel attracts people from far and wide who come here to give thanks, bearing *ex-voto* offerings.

From Fornazzo, a road down to the left leads to Sant'Alfio.

Sant'Alfio – This tiny little village has a monumental 17C **church**, remodelled in the 19C, with an unusual lava façade incorporating a campanile. From the terrace before the church, there is a splendid **view**★ of the Ionian Coast.

Sant'Alfio's main attraction, however, is a famous giant chestnut tree known as the **castagno dei 100 cavalli**★ ⊘ *(on the main road to Linguaglossa)*. This fabulous specimen, over 2 000 years old, comprises three distinct trunks with a combined circumference of 60m/196ft. Its name derives from a legend relating how Queen Joan (whether it refers to Joan of Aragon, Queen of Castile, or Joan of Anjou, Queen of Naples, is not clear) sheltered under its branches one night during a storm with her entourage of 100 knights.

Go back in the direction of Fornazzo and continue towards Milo.

Milo – This small farming community tenaciously survives, as it has over the years, against all odds given the unpredictable, blind advances of lava which have so far spared it: indeed, on many occasions, the lava has come to within a few metres (1950, 1971, 1979) before, at the last minute, changing direction.

Continue in the direction of Zafferana Etnea as far as Trecastagni and Nicolosi, then continue along the southern slope or towards Catania.

③ CIRCULAR TOUR OF ETNA

154km/95mi round trip: allow a full day.

The road runs around the circumference of Mount Etna providing a kaleidoscope of different views of the volcano, while passing through various picturesque little villages.

★**Catania** – See CATANIA.

Misterbianco – The imposing 18C church dedicated to **Santa Maria delle Grazie** ⊘ rises tall above the town roof tops, its elegant façade visible from miles away. In the south apse, nestles a *Madonna and Child* attributed to **Antonello Gagini**.

ETNA

Paternò – In 1072, **Roger II** built a castle here on top of a crag. Its square form is relieved on one side by a series of two-light windows: a line of four smaller ones with one larger opening above. The black lava stone provides a strong contrast for highlighting the white stone ornamental features. Clustered around the castle are the main religious buildings: the Chiesa Madre founded in Norman times and rebuilt in the 14C, and San Francesco. Below these developed the town's other buildings, predominantly in the 17C.

Santa Maria di Licodia – At the heart of this little town is piazza Umberto; this slightly raised square stretches before a former Benedictine monastery (now the Town Hall) and the Chiesa del Crocifisso. Down the left side of the church stands its attractive **bell-tower** (12C-14C) built in stone of two colours.

Adrano – This is one of the oldest settlements on the slopes of Mount Etna (the earliest traces found date from Neolithic times), founded, it is alleged, by the tyrant Dionysius I in the 5C BC under the name of Adranon. Evidence of the massive walls built of squared blocks of lava are still clearly visible *(follow via Catania and turn right at the yellow sign)*.
The **castle** ⊘ was built during the Norman occupation and still overlooks the centrally placed piazza Umberto. This unmistakable square edifice of dark lava stone owes its form to the Swabian era; inside, it contains three museums.
The **Museo Etnoantropologico** collects objects made by local craftsmen.
Over three floors, the **Museo Archeologico Regionale** displays artefacts relating to the history of the area (and from other parts of eastern Sicily) pertaining to Neolithic times until the Byzantine period. Of particular note *(on the second floor)*, there is the *banchettante* (which translates as the banqueting guest), an early bronze figurine of Samian workmanship (second half of the 6C BC) which probably adorned a bronze bowl or chest; the terracotta bust of a female Siculian deity found in the Primosole district (5C BC), a clay Locrian female bust (5C BC), a clay figurative group of Eros and Psyche, and a splendid **Attic vase★** with small columns (5C BC). The top floor is devoted to the **picture gallery** showing paintings on canvas (by the so-called Zoppo di Ganqi, Filippo Paladino and Vito D'Anna), glass and metal; sculptures in wood, alabaster and bronze dating from the early 17C to the early 20C, and a series of contemporary works by artists from Adrano and beyond.
The piazza extends eastwards into the delightful garden of the Villa Comunale, onto which face the imposing elevation of the **Church and Monastery of Santa Lucia**. The 18C church façade, in two colours of stone, is by Stefano Ittar.

Centrale Solare Eurellos – This experimental power plant lies a few kilometres from Adrano and was built within the framework of a European Community research project on solar energy sponsored by Italy, France and Germany. Following a brief period of trial and experimentation from 1981 to 1987, tests were halted (it succeeded in generating 1 mW). Currently, attempts are being made to generate electric power with solar energy using photovoltaic panels (composed of silicon cells) within the framework of Enel's plan to find ways of generating self-sufficient power for mountain refuges or similarly isolated buildings.

Ponte Saraceno – *The Saracen bridge is located outside the town, beside the River Simeto. Leave by the road south of Adrano and follow signs for Bronte. A sign at a crossroads indicates the way to the bridge: to the right and left, the road is tarred; straight on leads to a dirt track which continues on to the river and the bridge.*

Adrano: Saracen bridge

The so-called Saracen bridge was first erected by the Romans, rebuilt under Roger II and altered through the successive centuries. The pointed arches spanning the water are articulated with contrasting coloured stone.

A short walk north along the river bank leads to the amazing **Simeto Gorge** formed, like the gorges of Alcàntara *(see Gole dell'ALCÀNTARA)*, by a lava flow (this time from Etna) and then polished clean by water bearing away great blocks of basalt.

Bronte – Pride of place in the centre of town stands the Collegio Capizzi, a prestigious 18C boarding-school housed in a fine *palazzo*. A few kilometres away, near Maniace, although still falling within the Bronte district, is the lovely Benedictine Abbey of Maniace, later converted into "Nelson's Castle".

Castello di Nelson ⊘ – *Follow the signs from Bronte. The castle is situated by the entrance to the village of Maniace.* The Benedictine Abbey, founded in the 12C at the behest of Queen Margaret, wife of William the Bad, was situated on an important route of communication into the Sicilian hinterland. The adjacent **chapel** is graced with an elegant doorway ornamented with figurative capitals. Inside, it houses a 13C Byzantine icon, which is more popularly believed to be the original one carried by the Byzantine *condottiere* George Maniakes who inflicted a crushing defeat on the Saracens in this area in 1040. The prosperous monastery was subjected to various modifications before finally being given by Ferdinand III to the British naval hero Admiral Nelson in 1799. Nelson transformed the building into a private residence.

Randazzo – *See RANDAZZO.*

Linguaglossa – *See above, in the section devoted to the north-eastern slope of Etna.*

Pass through Fiumefreddo di Sicilia and head for the coast, taking the turning for Marina di Cottone.

Riserva naturale del fiume Fiumefreddo ⊘ – The River Fiumefreddo rushes down from the north-eastern slopes of Etna, swollen with snow melt which has permeated through the volcanic rock and reached the high water-table, an impermeable layer of clay, to be channelled across the plain. Essentially, the river rises from two springs, both 10-12m (33-39ft) deep, known as Testa dell'Acqua and Le Quadare (*paioli* in Sicilian dialect). It is well worth arranging a visit to the springs when the sun is at its height; this allows the depth and clarity of the water to be appreciated in full. The pH of the water in the river, which never exceeds temperatures of 10-15°C even in summer and flows remarkably slowly, provides the right conditions for an unusual range of water-loving plants more often associated with Central Europe (certain members of the Ranunculus family) or Africa as with papyrus. Other species include the white willow, aquatic iris, European aspen and horsetail. The springs also attract a variety of birds on migration: herons, oyster-catchers, golden orioles, and many species of duck.

Beside the nature reserve stands the 18C **Castello degli Schiavi** *(private, not open to the public)*, designed by the architects Vaccarini and Ittar.

Giarre – The little town was once part of the feudal estate belonging to the Mascali, having been bestowed upon the Bishop of Catania by **Roger II** in 1124. Its name, however, is taken from the jars in which the tithes on the harvest due to the bishop were collected. The **Duomo** is an imposing neo-Classical building with twin square-set bell-towers. The town's main axis is via Callipoli which is lined with elegant shops and noble town houses including the Liberty-style **Palazzo Bonaventura** (no 170); at no 154, **Palazzo Quattrocchi** is ornamented with Moorish designs.

From Giarre, head for the coast in the direction of Riposto.

Riposto – It was to Riposto that the tithes from the Mascali estates were brought pending their onward shipment by sea. The town itself developed around a colony of people from Messina (hence the popularity of the cult of the Madonna of the Letter) who established their warehouses here before it became an important depot for wine destined for the export market in the 19C. Indeed, the vestiges of a number of commercial buildings survive from the 1800s.

The charming **Santuario della Madonna della Lettera** ⊘ with its face turned towards the sea, was built in 1710, although a church probably existed on the site in Norman times. Four excavations undertaken beneath the sanctuary have revealed the existence of crypts containing funerary chambers dating from the paleo-Christian period, coins from the Arabo-Norman era and architectural remains from Aragonese times. The painting of the *Madonna and Child* on the 18C altar is of uncertain date. The choir has an interesting set of recently carved wooden stalls and an unusual Baroque lamp set with mother-of-pearl, probably made locally.

‡ **Acireale** – *See ACIREALE.*

Aci Trezza – *See p 103.*

Aci Castello – *See p 103.*

★ **Catania** – *See CATANIA.*

La FIUMARA D'ARTE★

Messina

Michelin map 432 M-N 24-25

Fiumara d'Arte literally translates as River of Art (*fiumara* means 'a broad river'). An appropriate name, given that it consists of an unusual attempt at exhibiting contemporary sculpture in a kind of open-air museum. Not only does the initiative take best advantage of the natural landscape to arrive at a symbiosis of art and nature, it provides interested visitors to the area an opportunity of exploring and appreciating in a highly original way a series of secluded and little-known places off the beaten track. The first short stretch of our recommended itinerary snakes its way along the coast before venturing for the most part inland through a naturally forested region between the Nebrodi and Madonie mountains. The scheme, which was initiated only a few years ago and continues to evolve, has already secured the cooperation of a number of contemporary artists from both Italy and abroad.

(For alternative itineraries in the Nebrodi and the Madonie, see CAPO D'ORLANDO, SANTO STEFANO DI CAMASTRA and MADONIE e NEBRODI).

Allow at least half a day.

An artistic trail – **Santo Stefano di Camastra** is as good a place as any to start out from. While driving westwards along the coast, the first gigantic sculpture looms into sight on the right, standing on the beach. Tano Festa's *Monument to a Dead Poet* is conceived as a type of window looking out to sea and to infinity; like the two elements (sea and sky) that surround it, it is blue. A little further on, a small bridge acknowledges the River Tusa: there, set in the middle of the almost permanently dry river bed, stands the second work: Pietro Consagra's *Matter could have not existed* – a linear conglomeration which breaks out onto two levels, one white, the other black. Turn left just before the bridge so as to follow the river upstream towards **Pettineo**. The **scenic road★** climbs up into the Nebrodi mountains providing **good views★** over the landscape. Before long, evidence of humankind dwindles and disappears, giving way in its stead to the overriding presence of nature. All along the sides of the road, the olive trees are contorted into forms resembling tortured, imprisoned souls; these make way for a sun-drenched landscape ablaze with startlingly yellow bushes of flowering broom. Pettineo crouches on the top of a small hill. Beyond it stands a work by Paolo Schiavocampo entitled *A Curve Thrown After the Wind*, shrouded in silence. At last **Castel di Lucio** comes into view; a sign on the left points to Italo Lanfredini's *Ariadne* standing lonely on a hill *(as the road turns in a hairpin bend to the left, keep straight on).* This windswept stone maze enclosed on all sides by a succession of towering mountains enjoys a fabulous **location★**.

Back down on the main road, follow the winding way to **Mistretta** *(see SANTO STEFANO DI CAMASTRA)* to view one of the last artistic creations: *The Ceramic Wall*, a work to which some 40 artists contributed. After Mistretta, a road forks left towards **Motta d'Affermo**; here Antonio Di Palma's blue wave entitled *Mediterranean Energy* dominates the landscape. Head back down towards the sea. At the *Hotel Atelier sul Mare* in **Castel di Tusa**, Antonio Presti, among the prime instigators and promoters of the Fiumara project, has made several rooms available to artists and allowed them to transform them into works of art in their own right.

LIVING ART IN CASTEL DI TUSA

The **Hotel Atelier sul Mare** (via Cesare Battisti 4 ☎ 0921 33 42 95) has succeeded in realising a truly original dream and exploring the concept of how to exploit art in a new form. Various rooms have been handed over to artists to be transformed into works of art. What is wholly original, however, is that these statements of interior decoration are not static: on the contrary, they are in a continuous state of flux. For each new "guest" is invited to leave his/her own individual imprint as he/she may feel inclined. The idea is to create an interaction between the existing work, which with time becomes inert and part of the everyday furnishing, and the artist who during his/her stay will contemplate and inwardly digest the decor before responding with his/her personal touch. The predominant theme is water – the sea, treated as a fundamental element and purifier of life, the return to man's basic origins and hence to humankind's very existence. Each artist interprets this idea in different ways. Every guest is given the choice of the passionate red of *Power* (by Maurizio Machetti), the white of the absorbing *Nest* (by Paolo Icaro), the minimalist *Mystery for the Moon* (by Hidetoshi Nagasawa), the deeply reflective *Denial of the Sea* (by Fabrizio Plessi), or the complicated and crooked *Room of the Prophet*, to name but a few.

The rooms are accessible only to those spending the night there; a double room costs approximately 250 000L.

One other work deserves a mention: *The Room of the Golden Boat* (by Hidetoshi Nagasawa) shelters within a cave on the bed of the River Romei *(near Mistretta)*. Inside, the rock is entirely faced with plates of polished steel – most disorientating. Somewhere within the enclosed space, a pink marble tree has been "planted" in the ground, on which the shell of an overturned boat has been built, and covered in gold leaf. This work, however, is not intended to be seen: the reason for its existence lies in the fact that it exists at all. As such, we are encouraged not to go and see it, but merely to imagine it.

The project is revitalised annually with a great event held in Pettineo when kilometres of canvas are laid out along the length of the main street and dozens of painters arrive to claim their stretch of allocated space. *(The event usually takes place in June. To confirm the dates, telephone the Hotel Atelier sul Mare.)*

GANGI

Palermo – Population 7 858
Michelin map 432 N 24

At one time, Gangi was identified with the ancient Engyum, a Greek town founded by colonists from **Minoa**; the town that survives today has largely evolved since the 14C. Gangi is scattered over the crest of Monte Marone, its picturesque narrow streets lined with stone-built houses which preserve its somewhat medieval character.

Guided tours – The Gangi Pro Loco organise guided tours of the town. Those interested should book at least a week in advance. For information, contact ☎ 0921 50 20 17 (9am-1pm and 3-7pm; closed Mon); www.comune.gangi.pa.it

WHERE TO STAY

At Gangi Vecchio, some 4km/2.5mi from Gangi itself, sits the former Benedictine monastery of **Santa Maria Annunziata** which was founded some time in the 13C. This was converted into a summer residence by the Barons of Bongiorno in the 18C, and now houses an informal guesthouse, the **Tenuta Agrituristica Gangivecchio** (90 000L for half-board), ☎ 0921 68 91 91.

The gracious 19C **Villa Rainò** (Contr. Rainò, Gangi, ☎ 0921 64 46 80, Fax 0921 64 49 00) has 15 tastefully decorated rooms and a restaurant which serves traditional regional cuisine using locally produced ingredients. Access to the villa is via a rather awkward descent on a narrow road. 120 000L for a double room (including breakfast).

CITTÀ ALTA

The tree-lined viale delle Rimembranze, commemorating every soldier killed in the Second World War, leads to the entrance to the higher town. The most obvious point of reference in **piazza San Paolo** is the simple stone front of the church (16C) dedicated to St Paul, with its fine entrance ornamented with shallow relief decoration. The later Chiesa della Badia (18C) has a similar, bare stone, front elevation. **Corso Umberto I** passes a number of harmonious pallazi, including the 19C **Palazzo Mocciaro**, on its way into the centre of town.

★**Palazzo Bongiorno** ⊙ – This rather imposing residence was built in the 18C for the ennobled Bongiorno family, one of the wealthiest in the area. Its most endearing feature is the elegant *trompe-l'œil* **frescoes**★ in the rooms on the piano nobile. These are by Gaspare Fumagalli, a painter from Rome who was active in Palermo around the mid-18C, and comprise a series of allegorical subjects, both sacred and profane *(Modesty, The Triumph of Christianity, Time)* set within an elaborate framework of architectural elements, ornamented with masks, volutes and medallions containing pastoral landscapes.

Piazza del Popolo – The town's main square is overshadowed by the Torre Ventimiglia. In one corner nestles a small grotto which harbours a fountain, the Fontana del Leone (1931).

★**Torre Ventimiglia** – The tower was erected in the 13C as a watchtower; in the 15C it came into the possession of the Knights of Malta; it was transformed into a belltower in the 17C when the Chiesa Madre was built. It is Norman Gothic in style and has a pointed arcade portico along the street side, with attractive three-light, double-arch windows above.

Chiesa Madrice ⊙ – The town's main church was erected in the 17C on the foundations of an older oratory; inside, it harbours several significant works of art. The eye is immediately drawn to the huge canvas occupying the left side of the chancel.

This depicts **The Last Judgement★** (1629) and is considered the main masterpiece of one of the two painters nicknamed The Lame Man of Gangi (Zoppo di Gangi), Giuseppe Salerno. The complex iconography underpinning this great theological statement is modelled on similar treatments of the subject by Michelangelo in the Sistine Chapel *(see The Green Guide Rome)*, among others: common elements include the standing figure of Christ, the skin of St Bartholomew whose head, some claim, is a self-portrait of the artist, and the figure of Charon, the devil's ferryman. The composition is arranged around the central upright figure of Christ; at his feet kneel the Virgin Mary and John the Baptist. They, in turn, are flanked by the Apostles in the foreground, and the rank and file of saints – male *(on the right)* and female *(on the left)* – behind. The tier below comprises 13 children representing the innocent martyrs; at their feet is the Book of Life. The level beneath is divided into two: to the left, the Archangel Michael *(in the centre)* drives away the dragon while presiding over the Elect who rise from the dead; to the right, are shown the Damned, with the jaws of Leviathan down in the corner. In the centre is Charon's boat. Each of the Damned embodies one of the capital sins, its name emblazoned upon a label, sometimes written in Sicilian. The Damned include various religious figures, but there is no priest, as it was a priest who commissioned the work.

The church also contains a number of fine wooden sculptures by Quattrocchi, among them a **San Gaetano★** *(at the far end of the south aisle)*.

From the church forecourt, there is a fine view of the lower part of Gangi including the so-called Torre Saracena on the left and the Capuchin Monastery.

The natural continuation of corso Umberto I, corso Fedele Vitale, is lined with "Roman shops" **(botteghe romane)** that date from the 16C – so called because they have next to the doorway a window and counter through which goods are sold. A little further up the street, Palazzo Sgadari houses the local **museum** ⊘ with displays of archaeological artefacts from Monte Alburchia. At the far end, sits the square mass of **Castello dei Ventimiglia**.

DOWN TO GANGI "BASSA"

Return to piazza del Popolo so as to turn down via Madrice (stepped) and find the **Chiesa del Santissimo Salvatore** ⊘. This contains a wooden Crucifix by Fra' Umile da Petralia and a painting by Giuseppe Salerno entitled *On the Road to Calvary*, which reflects the influence of Raphael's *Spasimo di Sicilia* commissioned for the Chiesa dello Spasimo in Palermo *(see p 275)*.

A little further down hill stands the **Chiesa di Santa Maria di Gesù** ⊘, which originally comprised a Benedictine Hospice (15C). The bell-tower, dating from the same period, is relieved by single and two-arch openings. The front façade of the church has an attractive doorway ornamented with shallow reliefs. Inside, there are several works by Quattrocchi, most notably a wooden group representing *The Annunciation*.

Santuario dello Spirito Santo ⊘ – A popular local story relates how, in the 16C, a deaf mute labourer was working in the fields when he came across an image of Christ painted on a rock, and miraculously began to speak. On the very spot the miracle occurred, a sanctuary was built; this continues to attract pilgrims from far and wide. Today, the image on the rock is masked by the painting behind the altar by Vazzano.

The popular epithet: Zoppo di Gangi

Interestingly enough, the last work of **Gaspare Vazzano** (or Bazzano), a cycle of frescoes in the Chiesa Madre at Collesano, is clearly signed "Zoppo di Gangi". Vazzano was born in Gangi in the latter part of the 16C and, despite being trained as a painter in Palermo, always gravitated towards the towns of the Madonie mountains in search of work. The other painter with whom he shares his nickname was a contemporary, also from Gangi, **Giuseppe Salerno**. It remains difficult to ascertain the relationship enjoyed by the two artists, despite a recent theory suggesting that Salerno collaborated with Bazzano, at least during his early career as a painter. The common pseudonym might possibly be explained as an act of homage by the pupil, who was a few years younger than Bazzano. The two painters fit into the same artistic movement, yet their styles are quite different. Bazzano's use of tonal colour, gentle facial expression and softer line endow his paintings with a certain sentimentality that contrasts sharply with Salerno's bolder style achieved by a strong use of line and precise draughtsmanship. His intention is to produce a cruder kind of work that dogmatically embodies a concept, a message or a doctrine. These different personalities and distinctive means of artistic expression are personified by two Sicilian painters who have each left an important legacy to their native land.

GELA

Caltanissetta – Population 77 702
Michelin map 432 P 24

The colony of Gela was founded by colonists from Rhodes and Crete towards the end of the 7C BC. The town prospered and expanded westwards, leading to the eventual foundation of Agrigentum, which soon surpassed it in importance. Gela reached its height during the rule of two tyrants: Hippocrates and Gelon, who in fact decided halfway through his reign to move to Syracuse. Over the ensuing period, the city gradually lost its political might but none of its cultural importance. Indeed, it was here in Gela that Aeschylus decided to spend the last years of his life.

Following each successive attack, the town was rebuilt; finally, in 1230, Gela was completely reconstructed by Frederick II.

A fatal case of mistaken identity

Aeschylus, the tragic poet who spent part of his life in Athens and part in Sicily, died at Gela. According to legend his death was caused by a tortoise which was dropped onto his bald head by an eagle that mistook it for a rock (eagles drop tortoises onto rocks so as to split the shell, thus enabling them to be eaten).

The surrounding plains, which hosted the landings by American troops in July 1943, are some of the most fertile areas of Sicily. Pockets of crude oil are being exploited to supply a refinery and a petrochemical plant, which in turn, are helping to improve the local economy of the area.

THE GREEK CITY

★**Museo Archeologico** ⊘ – *At the east end of the town in corso Vittorio Emanuele* The collections are beautifully presented in chronological order and by category, thereby displaying the locally found artefacts to best possible effect. Prefacing the exhibition is a *kylix* inscribed with the name of the city's founder, Antiphemus. The fine array of **antefixes** come from the acropolis area; some bear the features of gorgons, others the sneering traits of *sileni* or satyrs (6C-5C BC). Among the artefacts recovered from the wreck of a 5C BC ship with a valuable cargo, there is a delicate *askos* with a *silenus* and a *maenad*. The upper-floor displays relate to the sanctuaries outside Gela and to other sites in the area. The various iron agricultural implements, including a rake, were found in a votive pit near the temple precincts at Bitalemi. The last room *(on the ground floor)* gathers together a fine selection of **Archaic and Attic vases** from the necropoli at Navarra and Nocera and their collections.

Acropolis – *Alongside the museum*. The *plateia* (equivalent to the Roman *decumanus* or main street) divides the town neatly into two halves: to the south lie the sacred precincts with two temples (a single standing column survives from Temple C, built in the 5C BC to celebrate the victory at Himera); to the north lie the residential quarters, complete with shops.

★★**Fortifications** ⊘ – *West of the town, in the district of Capo Soprano*. Excavation has revealed some well-preserved fragments of the Greek fortifications. A stretch of wall, some 300m long, dates from the period between the 4C BC and 3C BC when Timoleon restored democracy and decided to rebuild the town after it had been razed to the ground by the Carthaginians (in 405 BC).

The wall consists of two courses: the lower, older section consists of well-appointed, regular, meticulously dressed, square blocks of sandstone.

The need to raise the wall came about following a major build-up of sand c 310 BC; extra height was achieved by using crudely made bricks of sun-dried clay to build a merloned *chemin-de-ronde* on the outermost side, parts of which are still visible. Although extremely fragile, this section was preserved by being covered by encroaching sand. Today, it is protected with plexiglass.

Complesso termale ⊘ – *A short distance from the fortifications, near an almshouse*. These two rooms date from Hellenistic times. The first is divided into two areas: one containing a series of small tubs arranged in a circle, the other set in a horse-shoe shape. The second room would have been the *hypocaust* (with under-floor heating), used at times as a sauna. The baths were largely destroyed by fire some time towards the end of the 3C BC.

EXCURSION

Licata – *31km/19mi E*. At the heart of the little town is piazza Progresso and from this radiate via Roma and corso Vittorio Emanuele, the two main streets along which the town's principal 18C monuments are aligned.

Via Roma harbours the church and cloisters of San Domenico and Chiesa del Carmine. Corso Vittorio Emanuele, meanwhile, claims Palazzo Frangipane with its fanciful brackets shaped like monsters and some other fantastic creatures, and the churches of San Francesco and the Chiesa Madre dedicated to Santa Maria la Nova.

GIBELLINA

Trapani – Population 4784
Michelin map 432 N 20

Gibellina was destroyed by the earthquake which struck the Valle del Belice in 1968. The ruins are still visible *(follow the signs for Ruderi di Gibellina, 18km/11mi west of Gibellina Nuova)*, although many have been petrified into a work of art called *Cretto (Crack)* by Burri. Indeed, much of what used to line the streets of the old town have been "veiled" in a gentle concrete blanket furrowed by cracks.

Consagra's *Star*

Gibellina Nuova has been rebuilt as an embodiment of a highly peculiar concept: to design the town as a kind of permanent museum with sculptures scattered through the streets and among the buildings which, in turn, could be seen as individual works of art. Contemporary artists such as Arnoldo Pomodoro, Consagra, Cascella and Isgrò (to name but a few) were commissioned to realise this unusual dream; this led to the installation of some 50 works of art, including the imposing **Star** at the entrance to the town by Pietro Consagra, Quaroni's piazza del Municipio with its **musical tower**, and his great white spherical **Chiesa Madre** that dominates the landscape from miles around.

EXCURSION

Partanna – *12km/7mi S*. This small town was also badly affected by the same earthquake of 1968. Its distinguishing feature, a battlemented castle, was rebuilt in the 17C by the princes of Graffeo (or Grifeo) on the foundations of an earlier, Norman, construction. The flat area behind the castle provides a splendid **view**★ of the valley. Unfortunately, the churches have been reduced to ghostly shells by the earthquake: all that remains of San Francesco along via Vittorio Emanuele is a lonely bell-tower (16C-17C) while, higher up, the church of the Madonna delle Grazie preserves its original tower.

Gli IBLEI

Catania and Siracusa
Michelin map 432 P-Q 25-26

The land and its people – The south-eastern corner of Sicily is dominated by the Iblei mountains, posted here almost as if to defend the area around Ragusa. The little mountain villages perched on the ridges or scattered among the woods and valleys have retained their rural aspect, in close harmony with the land that has sustained them for centuries. One of the most commonly recurring elements in the landscape is the **carob tree**, a large evergreen growing, often in isolation, in the middle of a field. The broad growth of characteristically shiny dark green leaves provides deep shade. Its beans, which can be used as a thickener or as an alternative to coffee when ground into powder, or as animal feed, once had a nobler use: the fact that their weight is ever consistent, meant that they came to be used as units of measurement for precious stones; the term "carat" derives from the Arabic name *Qirat*.

195

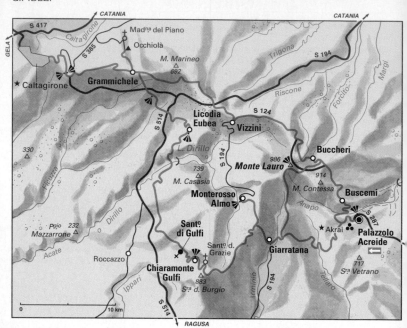

Dry-stone walling – An ever-present reminder of human impact on the rural landscape are the ribbons of dry-stone walling that extend in all directions: small, low-lying yet resistant courses of stone, no more than a metre high, enclose the cultivated fields. Interestingly, the very nature of these walls reflects the geological formation of the Iblei. For, just as with the base rock, the surface layer of limestone is impermeable: where this layer is damaged by erosion or fracture, water will penetrate through the underlying layers causing them to crumble, disintegrate into lumps: in the most dire cases, this can produce whole canyons. The broken lumps of rock litter the ground, requiring farmers to remove them before they can sow their fields: the walls are conceived as a way of re-using the stones so laboriously gathered which, instead of being heaped in a pile, are employed as building materials. However, this is no haphazard pastime but a skilled art learned from master-craftsmen known in the vernacular as *mastri ri mura a siccu*. The walls segregate different land holdings and enable flocks to graze unsupervised; they also support terraced land. The widespread implementation of the dry-stone walling was in part aided by the Counts of Henriquez-Cabrera, who decided to grant lands on a perpetual lease (the land was given to the farmers to manage on a long-term basis in exchange for a fixed annual rent).

A JOURNEY THROUGH THE MOUNTAINS

The round trip of approx 130km/81mi can be completed over two days, stopping for a night either in Palazzolo Acreide or, from the opposite direction, in Caltagirone. The latter has better accommodation options.

Palazzolo Acreide – See PALAZZOLO ACREIDE.

The road to Buscemi provides a succession of wonderful **views**★.

Buscemi – This particular little farming hamlet accommodates an unusual and provocatively interesting museum dedicated to rural craftsmanship: **I Luoghi del Lavoro Contadino**★ ⊙. The various venues, eight in all, however, are scattered throughout the town: each is dedicated to recapturing the life and work of the Iblei mountain people. These include the blacksmith's forge, the oil press (where some of the scenes of the film *La Lupa* by Gabriele Lavia were shot), a farmstead, the houses of a farm labourer *(lo Jurnataru)*, cobbler and carpenter, and a wine press to which the grapes were brought; a room attached to this last venue contains a small film library. Despite possible problems of language, the archive films showing the various activities in times past are most engaging. The eighth venue is the watermill (Mulino Santa Lucia) that was used to grind cereals at Palazzolo Acreide. There, a small display has been instituted (Museo della Maccina del Grano). A wander through the streets will also reveal a number of Baroque monuments, including the lovely façade of the Chiesa Madre, the curvilinear elevation of Sant'Antonio da Padova e San Sebastiano, as well as various other hidden corners of town, notably the farmers' quarter populated with low stone houses.

Immediately after rejoining the main road, a glance up at the rock face below the town will provide a view of the tombs excavated by the Siculi (12C-13C BC).

Buccheri – Perched at a height of 820m/2 689ft, this hamlet boasts a church dedicated to Mary Magdalen with a lovely façade (18C) articulated by two tiers of columns and pilasters, and another dedicated to St Anthony Abbot with a front elevation that rises in one sweep to a tall tower, exaggerated by a long, steep staircase up to the door.

Verga's Vizzini

The cry *"Hanno ammazzato compare Turiddu"* can be heard at the end of *Cavalleria Rusticana*, a Tuscan opera set in Sicily, very much inspired by the sunshine isle as seen and interpreted by Mascagni when placing Verga's novel in the opera house. For those familiar with these acclaimed works of Italian literature, an exploration of Vizzini might begin at the hostelry where Turiddo and Alfio challenge each other to a duel, or at the church of Santa Teresa where the friends go to pray (in the opera), or even the houses of Gnà Lola and Santuzza, and la Cunzirìa, the old tanners' district outside town, where the two friends fight. A careful search will also uncover the house and noble *palazzi* around which the story of *Mastro Don Gesualdo* unfurls.

Themed guided tours are organised by the Pro Loco at via Lombarda 8, ☎ 0933 96 59 05.

Vizzini – Vizzini was used by the novelist **Giovanni Verga** as a back drop for several of his books including *La Lupa – The She-Wolf* (the nearby district of la Cunziria was used for filming a number of scenes for G Lavia's film), *La Cavalleria Rusticana* (on which Mascagni based his famous opera), and *The Story of Mastro Don Gesualdo*.

Vizzini has grown up around piazza Umberto I, where the Palazzo Verga and the Palazzo Municipale are located. Alongside the town hall rises a flight of steps, the **Salita Marineo**, decorated with maiolica tiles featuring geometric and floral designs arranged around a central medallion painted

Eating out

The *agriturismo* **A Cunziria** (☎ 0933 96 55 07), near the district of the same name, has been installed in a series of naturally occurring caves used in the past as both troglodyte dwellings and shelter for animals. The caves now house a guesthouse with an atmospheric decor, which has been embellished by the addition of objects typical of the region. 50 000L per person (room only) or 80 000L (half-board).

with views of buildings in Vizzini. This scheme, completed in 1996, echoes a similar stairway by Santa Maria del Monte at Caltagirone *(see CALTAGIRONE)*.

The Chiesa Madre preserves a Norman-Gothic doorway *(right side)*, a lonely vestige of the original church that survived the earthquake of 1693 which destroyed much of the town and provided an incentive for major rebuilding. The town's Baroque constructions include the beautiful frontage of **San Sebastiano**.

Vizzini: Ricotta Festival

G. Iacono/LARA PESSINA

The church of **Santa Maria di Gesu** ⊘ contains a *Madonna and Child* by **Antonello Gagini**. From Vizzini, take the old road to Grammichele and Caltagirone (SS 124). The first stretch, which winds its way tortuously through the landscape, provides extensive views of the town on the left and untidy thickets of prickly pears on the right.

Grammichele – The development of Grammichele can be traced back to 1693 when a terrible earthquake shattered the south-eastern section of Sicily. The new town was laid out according to a highly singular and regular plan centred around a hexagonal piazza and six radial axes passing through the centre of each side. A series of orthogonal streets are then arranged in concentric hexagons around the central space.

The buildings overlooking the piazza include the Chiesa Madre and the town hall; this, in turn, houses the municipal **museum** ⊘ *(first floor)* which brings together various archaeological artefacts recovered from the nearby area of Terravecchia, where the ancient town of Occhiolà was situated before being destroyed by the earthquake and abandoned. The inhabitants of Occhiolà were eventually re-housed in the new town of Grammichele, named after the saint traditionally associated with protection from earthquakes.

The geometric town plan of Grammichele

Occhiolà is situated about 3km/1.8mi from Grammichele along the road to Catania, near a road-maintenance building before a tight bend. A stone on the left bearing an inscription marks the beginning of the road to the site where the old town stood, enjoying a **scenic position**.

A diversion – From here, it is possible to reach **Caltagirone**, located 15km/9mi away. The last section of the road, after a level crossing, some 4km/2.4mi before Caltagirone, provides wonderful **views**★★ over the vast plain that is intensely culti-vated with cereal crops. Beyond the hills which, according to Tomasi di Lampedusa, evoke *un mare bruscamente pietrificato* (a suddenly petrified sea), looms the dark majestic form of Mount Etna.

★**Caltagirone** – *See CALTAGIRONE.*

Following a visit to Caltagirone, return to Grammichele and continue towards Licodia Eubea.

The road up to Licodia Eubea provides a series of wonderful **views**★★ over the plain below.

Licodia Eubea – This hamlet, occupying a panoramic situation at the head of the valley of the River Dirillo, was probably built upon the ancient ruins of Euboia, which was founded by the colonists of Leontinoi in about the 7C BC. It comprises several 18C churches and **Palazzo Vassallo** *(Via Mugnos, at the end of via Umberto, on the right)*, a formal Baroque building with a doorway flanked by columns and a balcony with brackets bearing masks and volutes.

From the ruins of the medieval castle extends a sweeping **view**★ over the valley below and the artificial lake formed by the Dirillo.

Continue downhill from the centre of the town and, at the first junction, keep straight on (Grammichele is sign-posted to the right). The old road to Chiaramonte Gulfi winds its way through a lovely stretch of **mountain scenery**★. Follow this road until the **Lago Dirillo** dam comes into view on the left. A little further on, near a bend, just before a road-maintenance *casa cantoniera (on the right)*, turn left. The road leads to the Santuario di Gulfi.

Santuario di Gulfi ⊘ – Before the 1693 earthquake, a village occupied the broad site where the lonely sanctuary of Gulfi now stands, isolated. At that time it would have been an important landmark, built on the spot where, it is said, the yoked oxen transporting a statue of the Madonna "emerged from the sea" (found on the shore near Camarina) knelt down. The story is illustrated inside by four painted medallions, which also relate how the statue of the Salvatore (Saviour) came to be found and taken to the Church of the Saviour in Chiaramonte.

Chiaramonte Gulfi – The Greek town of Akrillai, renamed Gulfi by the Arabs, was razed to the ground in 1296 and immediately rebuilt by Manfred Chiaramonte, after whom it was renamed.

Although much of the fabric was destroyed by the 1693 earthquake, the hamlet preserves its medieval organisation. The Arco dell'Annunziata, an ancient gateway to the old town, is the only fragment to survive from the Chiaramonte era (14C). Among the principal Baroque buildings, look out for San Giovanni (at the top of the hill) and the **Chiesa Madre**. The main street, corso Umberto I, is lined with 18C and 19C *palazzi*; and at its western extremity, stands the Villa Comunale (Town Hall), from where a magnificent **view** opens out over the valley.

In the higher part of town, sits the Santuario delle Grazie surrounded by pine trees (picnic facilities) and an all-encompassing **view**★ over Chiaramonte and Etna. The legend that touches upon this little sanctuary relates how the local people offered up their prayers to the Madonna for salvation from the plague in 1576, whereupon a spring of clear water emerged from the ground on this very spot.

The road to Monterosso Almo snakes its way among gentle slopes covered with cultivated fields enclosed by **dry-stone walls**, an ever-present feature of the Iblei landscape. These transfer geometric figures onto the green fields, endowing the scenery with a sense of order and distorted perspective. At times, even the road is delineated by dry-stone walling.

> ### Eating out
>
> The **Majore** restaurant (via Martiri Ungheresi 12, ☎ 0932 92 80 19; closed Mon and during July) has been in business for over 100 years and specialises in pork dishes served with local products. The pork is produced in the adjacent workshops. Approximately 40 000L for a meal.

Monterosso Almo – The Church of **San Giovanni**★ ⊘ lends its name to the piazza onto which it faces: together they provide a focal point for the upper part of the little town that depends entirely upon agriculture. The front elevation of the church, attributed to **Vincenzo Sinatra**, rises through columns to culminate in a bell-tower. Inside, it is ornamented with friezes of stucco picked out against pastel backgrounds. The nave ceiling is punctuated with shallow relief medallions containing scenes from the life of St John.

In the lower part of the town (in the wake of the 1693 earthquake, Monterosso – like Ragusa and Modica – was divided into two rival parts), stands a church to rival San Giovanni, this time honouring **Sant'Antonio** (or Santuario di Maria Santissima Addolorata). The same square is graced with the neo-Gothic **Chiesa Madre**, and the elegant Palazzo Zacco.

Giarratana – Three monuments constitute the artistic heritage of this hamlet: the late-Renaissance Chiesa Madre, and two Baroque churches dedicated to San Bartolomeo and Sant'Antonio Abate.

An onion festival, the Sagra della Cipolla, is held annually in August in Giarratana.

From Giarratana it is possible to return to Palazzolo (see PALAZZOLO ACREIDE) or continue to the top of Monte Lauro.

Monte Lauro – The road that winds its way up the mountain through intense patches of colour provided by red Valerian *(Centranthus ruber)*, dark green carobs and pines, provides glorious **views**★ over the high plateau. It eventually links up with the road to Palazzolo.

Cava d'ISPICA★

Ragusa
Michelin map 432 Q 26

Situated between the *comuni* of Ispica and Modica, this great fissure some 13km/8mi long, is stacked with abandoned troglodyte dwellings, small sanctuaries and necropoli. The earliest signs of human occupation in the area date from Neolithic times. The hollows studding the walls of the gorge are a natural phenomena in karst rock; they came subsequently to be modified and adapted by humans according to their requirements.

THE GORGE

A tour of the gorge comprises two parts. The northern section between Ispica and Modica is open to the public via the Ufficio di Sovrintendenza *(follow signs for Cava d'Ispica)*; this first highly accessible part is fenced off. The second half of this site lies further north and encloses a more disseminated series of "monuments" which are difficult to find and less accessible. The best way of orientating a visit, therefore, is to follow a **guided tour** ⊘.
The second separate area, known as the Parco della Forza, is located outside Ispica; this automatically caters for organised tours.

Cava d'Ispica – The actual Cava d'Ispica harbours the **Larderia★** (from the word *ardeia* – with abundant water) which consists of a paleo-Christian catacomb (4C-5C) lined with an impressive number of burial chambers (464). The original entrance was at one time located at the opposite end of the corridor that is now used, off which branches the "main nave" that extends 35.6m/120ft. The two lateral passageways were added later.

La Larderia

The tour follows the contours of a rock wall. Beyond the Church of Santa Maria (high up in the cliff on the left) and the Camposanto or Holy ground, is located the **Grotte Cadute** which comprises a residential complex on several levels. Holes in the ceiling and steps cut in the walls below enabled the residents to move from one level to another with the aid of poles and ropes that could be pulled up in times of danger.
Opposite the entrance to the fenced area, on the far side of the main road, another road leads to the **rock-hewn Church of San Nicola** and the **Spezieria**, a little church perched on a sharp rocky outcrop. The name, corrupted from the local dialect, is linked to the mythical existence of a monk-cum-apothecary who prepared herbal remedies. The church interior is subdivided into two parts: a nave and a misaligned chancel with three apses.
Return to the car and drive up the main road to the first turning on the left.

Baravitalla – On the plateau, now scattered with dry-stone walls, stand the ruins of the Byzantine Church of **San Pancrati** *(on the left, fenced off)*. It was beside here that vestiges of a small settlement were recovered. A little further on, a path leads left to an area with other points of interest *(difficult to find without a guide)*: the **Tomb with decorative pilasters** has a double front entrance, and the **Grotta dei Santi** consists of a rectangular chamber containing fragments of fresco along the walls *(the haloes of the figures depicted can just be discerned)*.

Back on the main road, continue towards Cava d'Ispica, before looking and finding *(if accompanied by a guide)* the **Grotta della Signora** which shelters a spring considered sacred since ancient times. The walls bear traces of graffiti dating from the prehistoric or paleo-Christian Era (swastikas and crosses).

Meanwhile, in the opposite direction further towards Ispica, the central part of the gorge conceals the so-called **Castello**, an enchanting residential complex several storeys high that was abandoned only in the 1950s (very difficult to find: consult a local guide for detailed directions, *see above*).

Parco della Forza ⊙ – *Located at Ispica*. This, one of the earliest areas of settlement, has been occupied since Neolithic times and was abandoned in the 1950s *(very difficult to find: consult a local guide for directions)*. During the Middle Ages, the plateau above the gorge was fortified with a citadel. This was raised around the so-called **Palazzo Marchionale**, the basic layout of which may still be made out. Some rooms preserve fragments of the original floor covered with painted fired lime tiles. The small fortress also contained several churches including the **Annunziata** which has 26 graves inlaid into its floor.

The cave known as the **Scuderia**, so called because it accommodated stables in medieval times, bears traces of graffiti horses. An idea of just how considerable this settlement was may be gleaned from the known number of people residing there: before the earthquake in 1693, approximately 2 000 people lived within the precincts of the actual citadel, while an additional 5 500 people inhabited the nearby gorges. Perhaps the most striking feature is the **Centoscale**, an extremely long underground stairway (consisting of 240 steps cut into the rock) which descends 60m at an angle of 45° into the side of the hill to emerge on a level with the valley floor, below the riverbed. It is not known when exactly the passage was made; its function was to ensure a water supply even in times of drought. A total of 100 slaves (hence the name) were positioned along the length of the stairway to collect the water as it filtered down from the riverbed (at its deepest point, the passageway was 20m/65ft below water level); having been collected it was passed up in buckets to the surface.

Outside the actual park stands **Santa Maria della Cava**, a little rock-hewn church containing the fragments of fresco in successive layers *(for access, permission must be sought from the custodians)*.

LA CITTADINA DI ISPICA

The hub of the little town revolves around **piazza Regina Margherita**, where the Chiesa Madre, San Bartolomeo and Palazzo Bruno (1910) with its distinctive angular tower are situated. Corso Umberto I, running behind the church, passes between a series of fine buildings before leading to the Liberty-style jewel of the town: **Palazzo Bruno di Belmonte** (now the town hall) designed by **Ernesto Basile**. Almost opposite stands the lovely **covered market**, although now it is used to host events organised by the local council. Other additional buildings of quality lie beyond it, notably at no 76 and no 82.

Return to piazza Regina Margherita and turn down via XX Settembre to the church of **Santa Maria Maggiore** ⊙. The elegant semicircular arcade before the church was conceived by **Vincenzo Sinatra** as an effective **complement**★ to the church. Inside, the church contains a fine cycle of **frescoes**★ painted by the Catania artist Olivio Sozzi (1763) who was clearly influenced by the Rococo. The large central panel depicts scenes from the Old and New Testaments. Adam and Eve, Judith with the head of Holofernes, Moses *(below)*, the Apostles with St Peter *(centre)* and Christ holding the Eucharist *(above)*. The chapel in the left transept contains a canopy with an unusual carved wooden figure of Christ at the Column. This statue, His head bowed in an expression of defeat as if He were succumbing to the pain of His wounds, is processed annually during the Maundy Thursday (Thursday before Easter) celebrations.

In the opposite direction, corso Garibaldi leads to the elegant **Chiesa dell'Annunziata** ⊙ which is decorated internally by G Gianforma with 18C stuccoes depicting stories from the Bible.

Scavi del Monte JATO
Palermo
Michelin map 432 N 21

The first settlement is thought to have been founded by the Elimi (or possibly the Sicani) as early as the 1st millennium BC. The city of Jetae (later transformed into Iaitas during the Roman era and Giato in medieval times) was subjected to influences from the Ancient Greek world in the mid-6C BC. Certainly by 300 BC, it was enjoying its period of greatest splendour (various public buildings testify to this) before becoming, under the Romans, a stipendiary city of the Empire (that is, liable for tax). In the 13C, the Arabs who had rebelled against Frederick II barricaded themselves in the town, causing it to be subjected to a long siege that ended in 1246, with Giato being razed to the ground and its population being deported to Lucera in Puglia.

EXCAVATIONS ⊘

Turn off the Palermo-Sciacca road at San Cipirello and take the road signposted Corleone and Tagliavia. A turning on the left a short distance further on is marked with yellow signs for Scavi di Monte Jato. The road winds uphill for 5km/3mi (the asphalt gradually peters out into a dirt track that is fairly badly rutted in parts). A short, final section must be undertaken on foot.

The city extended over a large 40ha/99 acre site at an altitude of 852m/2 795ft above sea-level.

A striking feature of these archaeological remains is the contrasting solidity of the Greco-Roman walls, built with perfectly dressed, well-ordered stones, and the provisional aspect of the medieval walls, built in a very approximate, undisciplined manner at a time when Monte Jato was a temporary refuge rather than a permanent settlement. The houses erected during Swabian times occupy large sections of the Greco-Roman settlement (note in particular those in the area around the *cavea* of the theatre), contributing, in many cases, to their ultimate destruction, especially as building materials were systematically pillaged from those surviving constructions that, until then, had borne the test of time.

Agorà – The market place dates from 300 BC: on the west side stands its *stoà* (portico) with its a double row of columns. Off the west side sits the semicircular *bouleuterion*, a council chamber with a capacity of 200 people; between the two doorways, the orator would stand to address the assembly. Among the other buildings that flanked the western edge, all erected in Roman times, there was also a temple, possibly dedicated to Jupiter (only the ruins remain).

Traces of paving along the south-western side of the agorà are all that remains of what was once the town's "high street". On the south side of this axis stood a temple from the 4C BC: judging from its style of construction, this is thought to be of Punic origin.

Proceed westwards.

Teatro – The theatre dates from the late 4C-early 3C BC. It would have been lined with 35 tiers of seats, enough for a capacity audience of 4 400; the three lower rows of seats (including one with backrests) were reserved for dignitaries. The stage consisted of a long rectangular platform *(skene)* with two wings *(parascenia)* projecting forward.

Casa a peristilio – The house with the peristyle is one of the largest noble houses known to have survived from Hellenistic times. It was built over two storeys, around a porticoed courtyard, with Doric columns on the ground floor and Ionic columns above. The north range of the peristyle is distinctively arranged with three reception rooms. The position of the doorways, offset from the central axis (so as to accommodate the couches they used when eating), implies they were dining or banqueting rooms. One preserves its original *opus signinum* floor, complete with the inlaid inscription of thanks and farewell that a departing guest might give after a banquet. In the north-western corner of the peristyle is the bathroom, equipped with bath (note the drainage channel) and, in the servant's quarters behind it, traces of the fireplace that would have been used to heat the water. Next to the bathroom there is a service courtyard with a bread oven (now covered with earth). The south-western range of the peristyle is lined with rooms that suggest they were used as a *fullonica* (for dyeing cloth).

Tempio di Afrodite – *The temple stands opposite the south side of the house, on the far side of the paved street.* The Temple of Aphrodite was erected in about 550 BC, according to architectural standards that are characteristically Greek and, as such, is considered an expressive statement from the earliest cultural exchanges between the indigenous population and the Greek world.

The various Hellenistic buildings south of the temple would have accommodated shops.

Some 100m/110yd west of the first house, excavation has begun on a second, smaller one, also with a peristyle.

EXCURSION

San Cipirello – The **Museo Civico** ⊘ *(via Roma 320)* displays the artefacts recovered from the archaeological excavations at Monte Jato. The most significant pieces are undoubtedly the sculptures that adorned the theatre: two maenads and two satyrs, followers of Dionysus, god of the theatre, and a crouching lion. Furthermore, the history of the town may be traced through the pottery found there: indigenous pottery with incised decoration, Hellenistic black-figure ware, Roman red-gloss terra sigillata or Samian ware, and glazed ceramics from the Middle Ages. At one end of the room, the roof from the building erected on the stage of the theatre *(skene)* has been in part reconstructed with tiles bearing the inscription ϕΕΛΤΡΟΥ (meaning "of the theatre").

Monte KRONIO

The Kronion of Antiquity is an isolated peak 386m/1 266ft tall, set in a deserted landscape. The name of the mountain suggests an immediate association with Cronus (Greek Kronos; Roman Saturn), the god of time and one of the oldest figures of the pantheon, born out of a union between Mother Earth (Gaea) and her son, the god of heaven (Uranus). Banished to Tartarus along with his other siblings (the Titans) by his father, Cronus was assisted by his mother in rising up against Uranus and castrating him; there followed a Golden Age on earth that lasted until his youngest (oldest in Homer) son Zeus, assisted by the Cyclops and the Hundred-handed Giants, declared war on Mount Olympus and the other Titans: at this point the myths vary in detail. According to some, the gods were defeated by thunderbolts and falling stones before being imprisoned in Tartarus; other accounts prevalent in Sicily, relate how Zeus inveigled the gods by inebriating them with ambrosia and honeyed mead, chaining them up as they slept, and relegating them to a group of islands called the Isole dei Beati (Islands of the Blessed).

The other legendary hero associated with this place is Daedalus who, being an expert on labyrinths, as is well known, decided to redirect the boiling vapours that emanated from cracks in the rock in order to harness their power: and so the origins of the *stufe vaporose* – the steamy caves – are explained.

ASCENT TO THE TOP

The haul to the summit provides ample opportunity to survey the wonderfully spacious **panorama**★★ panning in an arc of 240° over the coast, the plain of Sciacca and the bare mountains inland. At the top sits the **Santuario di San Calogero**, built by the Franciscans. The natural occurrence of caves in which hot vapours are caught has been exploited to provide steam baths since Antiquity. The largest and most well known is the Stufe di San Calogero.

Stufe di San Calogero ⊘ – The caves were either inhabited or regularly used for cult-worship until the Bronze Age; they were finally abandoned some time around 2 000 BC when steam began to pour into them, possibly as a result of a landslide, making permanent occupation impossible. After a period of complete neglect, the caves began to be used again some time during the Greek occupation, possibly as a result of the steam being seen to emanate from the mountainside and interpreted as a mysterious (and hence divine) phenomenon. Indeed, numerous artefacts have been recovered from the caves, especially vases and votive figurines *(some of which are displayed in the archaeological museum at Agrigento)*. The various names by which the caves are now known are those bestowed upon them by a monk who came here in the 4C, having quickly realised the therapeutic potential of the vapours, he set about dividing the caves into rooms with stone benches on which to seat his patients. The largest caves include l'Antro di Dedalo and the Grotta degli Animali. The Grotta del Santo nearby, probably provided living quarters for St Calogero, who is depicted in the maiolica icon above the altar (15C).

Today, the caves are incorporated in the modern spa complex Grande Albergo delle Stufe.

How they work – The rational explanation for the phenomenon is that a vein of hot water runs deep within the mountain; when it comes into contact with direct heat the water evaporates and escapes upwards, mingling with the air as it rises through the fissures and cracks in the rock, to break through into the open at a temperature of 40°C.

The vapours are considered by the Italians as having great therapeutic powers, especially in cases of rheumatism, skin disease, gynaecological problems and allergic reactions.

Next to the Stufe, a small **antiquarium** ⊘ displays artefacts found in the immediate vicinity.

LAMPEDUSA★

The **Isole Pelagie**★, the islands of the "high sea", lie approximately 200km/125mi south of Agrigento, between the island of Malta and Tunisia. The archipelago comprises the large island of **Lampedusa** (surface area of 33km²/20sq mi) and the two small islands **Linosa** and **Lampione**. The latter, occupied only by a lighthouse, rises vertically from a depth of 60m/196ft or so as a series of sheer cliffs. The deep and therefore unpolluted sea provides ideal conditions for scuba divers to venture out for a glimpse of groupers, lobster, yellow and pink coral and the occasional grey shark.

LAMPEDUSA

The island of Lampedusa consists of a flat limestone platform which culminates, at the northern end, in a series of dramatic **cliffs★★**. The south coast, on the other hand, is jaggedly rugged as headlands alternate with small, precipitous creeks sheltering sandy beaches. Closer to Africa than Italy (forming a part, in fact, of the African continental shelf), Lampedusa is surrounded by a spectacular **sea★★** that ranges in colour from a transparent turquoise to emerald green and blue. The inhabitants of the island know nothing about farming: the interior of the island is white and yellow, stony and arid, like a miniature desert. Instead they depend on fishing for a livelihood, as the large fleet anchored offshore in the well-sheltered bays will testify.

A few finds confirm that the island was inhabited as early as the Bronze Age. In 1843, the island belonged to the illustrious Lampedusa family (of which Giuseppe, author of *The Leopard*, is the most famous member) when it was acquired by King Ferdinand II; he had a prison built there and sent a handful of people to reside there.

Marine underworld – Fabulously beautiful scenery awaits to be discovered by anyone prepared to don mask and fins for an expedition underwater to explore the island's rocky coastline: brightly-coloured rainbow wrasse, scorpion fish, bleney (lurking in small crevasses in the rock), starfish, salps, slender needle-fish, octopus, sea-cucumbers, sea-hares and sponges. The sea floor is a jigsaw of rocky and white sandy patches. At intervals these are suddenly monopolised by dark green underwater meadows of *Poseidonia oceanica*, the seaweed nicknamed "the lung of the Mediterranean" which efficiently oxygenates the water and sustains large colonies of fish.

GETTING TO THE ISLANDS

The simplest way to get to the islands is by **air**: flights operate out of Palermo (approx. 1hr), with additional services during the summer months operating out of the main Italian cities.

There is also a **hydrofoil** service during the summer months from Lampedusa to Linosa (1hr). For further information call ☎ 0922 97 00 03 (Agenzia Marittima Strazzera).

Ferries sail overnight from Agrigento (Porto Empedocle) to Linosa (6hr) and Lampedusa (8hr). For further information contact Siremar at Porto Empedocle, ☎ 0922 63 66 83 or ☎ 0922 63 66 85.

WHERE TO STAY

In addition to a number of traditional hotels, different types of **apartment** (book well in advance for the summer months) and *dammusi* (typical white-domed buildings with stone walls) in Borgo Cala Creta are available for rent. For further information contact the Pro Loco tourist office.

There are also two **camp sites** on the islands: *La Roccia*, via Madonna, Cala Greca, ☎ 0922 97 00 55 and *Lampedusa*, via Roma 171, Cala Francese, ☎ 0922 97 07 20.

Cavalluccio Marino – Contrada Cala Croce 3, ☎/fax 0922 97 00 53. This small, elegant family-run hotel, situated near an attractive bay, has 10 comfortable, well-maintained rooms with air-conditioning. Half-board only (c 180 000L per person per day). Signor Pietro, the owner, is a fisherman and so fresh fish is guaranteed.

EATING OUT

Lampedusa has a wide choice of small restaurants and *trattorie* all serving a wonderful variety of fresh fish. *Cuscus di pesce* (often made with grouper) is the one speciality based on a Tunisian dish that every visitor should at least try once. Good home cooking can be sampled at **Ristorante Lipadusa** (via Bonfiglio 6, Lampe-

dusa, ☎ 0922 97 16 91; approximately 60 000L for a meal) and the **Trattoria-Pizzeria da Nicola** near Isola dei Conigli.

SHOPPING

Natural sponges are collected from all around Lampedusa making them one of the most popular purchases available to visitors: a word of advice – the whiter sponges, although more attractive, have been treated with bleach making them less durable; the slightly brown sponges, on the other hand, last longer.

The locally grown produce available on Linosa includes lentils and miniature tomatoes; reed baskets are also on sale in the town centre.

M. Magni/MICHELIN

Divers ready and equipped for more prolonged ventures underwater will discover abundant groves of living coral, sponges and madrepores populated with colourful parrot fish and, off Capo Grecale (at a depth of 50m/164ft), lobster.

⌂ **Lampedusa** – The town shares its name with the island land-mass. Apart from the odd house scattered here and there, this is the only urban conurbation as such, and it hinges on via Roma. The main street comes to life in the morning at break-fast time, and again in the evening at sunset until late into the night. It hosts a cluster of small shops and *caffés* from which tables and chairs tumble out onto the pavement. In summer these bars proffer low-key entertainment (sessions of karaoke or live music).

★A BOAT TRIP ROUND THE ISLAND...

In summer, many a boat owner will tout for business down in the harbour, happy to take visitors out and round the island for a reasonable sum. Excursions usually take a whole day, departing at about 10am and returning at approximately 5pm, touring the island in a clockwise direction.

The low, jagged coastline is laced with little creeks and inlets including the one known as **la Tabaccara★★**: this lovely bay washed with the most stunningly turquoise sea is only accessible by boat. The next in line is the **Baia dell'Isola del Coniglio★★★** *(see below)* before the headland Capo Ponente, the most westerly point of the island. Here, the landscape suddenly changes: the **coastline★★** of the island's north flank consists of a single great tall cliff plunging straight down into the sea, indented here and there by a number of intriguing caves and grottoes. Eventually, the island contours open out into the huge **Baia della Madonnina★** (so called because of the shape of one of the rocks above it), and various impressive rocks. These are known as the **Scogli del Sacramento** and they guard the mouth of a deep cave with the same name and the one alongside it called **Grotta del Faraglione**.

The north-eastern tip of the island, Capo Grecale, is capped with a lighthouse that swings its beam across some 60 nautical miles offshore. Immediately after Cala Pisana, nestling in the Grotta del Teschio (Cave of the Skull) is a 10-15m long beach, accessible down a path on the right.

...AND FROM THE LANDWARD SIDE

The circular coast road is not asphalted all the way around the island; it is therefore recommended that mopeds or small four-wheel drive vehicles be hired for the day.

From the town of Lampedusa, head east towards the airport.

The dirt track that runs parallel to the runway skirts round many of the creeks and small rocky bays on the south coast. Beyond Cala Pisana the track continues out to the tip of Capo Grecale where the lighthouse is situated; from this lofty position, the fine **view★** pans in either direction along the coast and down to the sea stirring dizzily below. The road then links up with another that runs along the south side of the island. Turn right towards the telecommunications signalling station.

Albero del Sole – These steep cliffs are the highest point on Lampedusa (133m/436ft). The small round building contains a wooden Crucifix. From the other side of the stone wall *(be careful, as it conceals a horrendous drop)*, there is a dramatic **view★★** of the **Faraglione** – or Scoglio a Vela (shrouded rock) as it is also called – and the cliffs plunging steeply down into the sea. One way of enjoying the view without fear of falling is to lie flat on the ground, not too near the edge. Return back the same way and fork right along the partially asphalted road, that runs past a tree plantation on the right. At the far end of the enclosure wall, con-tinue along the vague dirt track leading to a small iron cross. The headland on the right provides a glorious **view★★** of the **Scoglio del Sacramento★** *(right)*. In the dis-tance on the left, can be seen the little island of Lampione. Return to the main road and head south towards the bay around Rabbit Island.

★★★ **Baia dell'Isola dei Conigli** – In this broad bay, petticoated with white cliffs and the most beautiful beach on the island, nestles a little islet. It could almost be a corner of the Caribbean: the whitest sand slopes gently down to the water's edge, delicate clear tints of turquoise and emerald green stretch out to sea. Annually, a colony of loggerhead turtles makes its way up the beach to lay its eggs. Today, this exciting event is threatened by the ever larger numbers of spectators who linger here until sunset (turtles lay their eggs at night, but their extreme shyness means that the slightest disturbance will frighten them away).

This is also the only place in Italy inhabited by an unusual species of stripy lizard of the Large Psammodromus *(Psammadromus algirus)* variety, more usually found in North Africa (Tunisia, Algeria and Morocco).

Madonna del Porto Salvo – This small, ancient shrine of uncertain date is sur-rounded by a pretty garden full of flowers.

The limpid waters around Baia dei Conigli

★LINOSA

The untamed beauty of Linosa resides in the blackness of its volcanic rock, and its three great lofty cones pitched dramatically against the blue sky. This island has evolved in different stages, and this is strikingly evident. The volcanoes, now extinct, leave the visitor with a lasting, if haunting, impression.

The only town, huddled around the little harbour, consists of a collection of houses attractively painted in pastel shades with strongly accented coloured corners, doors and windows. From here, there exist a variety of possible excursions on foot into the mountains, or by boat around the coast. The few resident inhabitants of this peaceful islet who once depended on rearing cattle, now eke out a living from tourism.

The tallest peak is Monte Vulcano (186m/610ft), a volcano, as its name suggests, though now extinct. The interior of the island, predominantly desert-like, still supports a few areas of cultivation (notably the so-called Fossa del Cappellano which is particularly well-sheltered from the wind).

Excellent fresh fish specialities can be sampled at **Ristorante Errera** (via Scalo Vecchio, ☎ 0922 97 20 41). Approximately 50 000L for a meal. Credit cards are not accepted.

Fringed with a jagged lava coastline, Linosa is considered to be a veritable paradise by scuba-divers and snorkelling enthusiasts *(underwater fauna and flora are described above under Lampedusa).*

The land-based fauna of Linosa includes large colonies of Maltese wall lizards and **Cory's shearwaters** – the seabirds that shatter the quiet summer nights with their plaintive cries. Loggerhead turtles still come up the black beach in Cala Pozzolana to lay their eggs.

A number of footpaths, popular among keen walkers, lead to the summits of the island's three main peaks: **Monte Rosso** – the crater of which shelters various garden allotments, **Monte Nero** and **Monte Vulcano**. From the top of Monte Vulcano, when the *libeccio* wind blows, it is possible to make out cars as they move along the roads of Lampedusa.

★★**Boat trip round the island** – *Excursions by boat can be arranged down at the harbour.* The boat sets out from the harbour leaving Monte Nero, Monte Bandiera and Monte Vulcano behind it. It skirts the **Fili**, a group of rocks surrounding a sort of natural swimming-pool, enclosed on the landward side by sheer walls of **rock**★

Loggerhead turtle (Caretta caretta)

This is the most common species of sea turtle in the Mediterranean. This wonderful sea creature is a docile, solitary being other than during the mating season; it lives in temperate waters all year round except for when it must haul itself up onto dry land to lay its eggs, every two or three years. The mother-to-be chooses a sandy beach undisturbed by lights or noise. With enormous effort, she heaves herself up from the water's edge (awkwardly deprived of all her natural dignity, agility and grace when in water) and, using her hind flippers, she digs a deep hole (40-75cm deep) in the sand. There she passively lays her eggs before covering them with sand. Her task now over, she turns round and shuffles back to the sea, abandoning the eggs to their fate. Hatching takes place six to eight weeks later. The baby turtles emerge from the sand and instinctively make their way down the beach towards the sea, a threatening and dangerous world at least until they grow to any size. Only a few will survive to adulthood. In fact, even before they hatch, the eggs easily fall prey to birds and man. As newly hatched turtles, their greatest threat come in the shape of fish, greedy for their tender meat. This is why it is important to protect and safeguard both the sites where the eggs are laid (thus eliminating or reducing the risks prior to hatching) and the seas they inhabit. Ordinary mortals should respect a few fundamental rules, notably disposing of their plastic bags with care: in the water, these take on the appearance of a tasty jellyfish for a turtle, and the mistake can cost it its life.

The Pelagie – notably **Lampedusa**'s bay of Isola dei Conigli with its long stretch of sand – have been chosen by the loggerhead turtles as suitable sites for laying their eggs. A special conservation-cum-education centre, **Centro Recupero, Marcaggio e Tutela delle Tartarughe Marine**, has been instigated on Lampedusa to monitor and protect the turtle population, with a programme involving local children under the supervision of Dr Daniela Freggi. The number to call should a turtle be found in distress, or for volunteers to participate in local monitoring is: ☎ 0338-219 85 33.

On **Linosa**, the black (and therefore warm) sands of Cala Pozzolana di Ponente seem to favour the birth of female turtles. For indeed, it has been established that the sex of a turtle is determined by the temperature of the sand: below 30°C males will predominate, temperatures in excess of 30°C favour females. By the beach the Associazione Hydrosphera runs its **Centro Studi sulle Tartarughe Marine** ⊙: this displays information concerning the life cycle of the turtles, complete with illustrations provided by enthusiastic volunteers who, during the summer months, flock to the island. The centre also has a small "Casualty department" for turtles found sick and exhausted or brought in by fishermen who have inadvertently caught them on a hook. The two centres (on Lampedusa and Linosa) are part of an Italian project run by the Department of Animal and Human Biology of La Sapienza University in Rome.

polished and moulded by the rain and wind into wave-like forms. The restless sea and a handful of clumps of caper plants complete the landscape. Beyond the Faraglioni rocks that stand guard outside the so-called natural pool or Piscina Naturale *(also accessible on foot)*, the lighthouse comes into view. This stretch of coastline is particularly jagged. Just before the circular trip draws to its conclusion, the boat steams across **Cala Pozzolana★★**; this shelters the only beach on the island backed by an amazing wall of incredible colour ranging from sulphur yellow through to rust red. The hydrofoils from Lampedusa moor here.

LEONTINOI

Siracusa

Michelin map 432 P 27

The ancient Greek colony lies south of **Lentini**, a small agricultural town dependent on growing citrus fruits, and greatly affected by the earthquake of 1693. The centre of town is marked by the **Chiesa Madre** ⊙ dedicated to Sant'Alfio (a hugely popular saint here and in the hamlets around Etna); preserved in its paleo-Christian underground vault are the relics, it is alleged, of St Alfio, St Filadelfio and St Cirino, as well as a 9C Byzantine image of the Hodegetria Madonna (Guide or Instructress pointing to the Way of Redemption based on an icon said to be painted by St Luke). A small **archaeological museum** ⊙ displays artefacts recovered from the excavations at Leontinoi.

ANCIENT TOWN ⊘

Access is easiest via Carlentini.

This area has been inhabited since protohistoric times (as the bases of huts on Collina di Metapiccola testify: these may be reached by a track that leads off to the right from the entrance to the archaeological zone). In 729 BC it was targeted by the Chalcidians of Naxos as a good place to found a colony. It was here that the philosopher **Gorgias** was born.

Excavation has brought to light the remains of various monumental pyramidal tombs and walling beyond. The Syracusan gate serves as the main entrance to the town. The way leads on towards what is assumed to be the site of an acropolis (on Colle San Mauro) where vestiges of a temple have been found. The track climbs up past the circular base of what was perhaps a defence tower. From the top, a wonderful view extends over Lentini and, in the distance, a man-made lake known as the **Biviere**. The mound to the left is Colle di Sant'Egidio where the town's necropolis was located, complete with tombs excavated from the base rock.

EXCURSION

★**Case del Biviere** ⊘ – *In the Contrada Biviere: from Lentini railway station, turn right and follow the sign for SP 67 to Valsavoia. By the fork in the road, on the right, stands a villa with a large green entrance.*

According to legend, when Heracles came to these parts intending to present the skin of the Nemean lion to Ceres, he fell in love with the area and created a lake which would bear his name; this was subsequently changed to Biviere (to mean drinking trough or fish-farm) during the Arab occupation. The house was built on the eastern edge of the lake which was infilled during the 1930s; when it came to be restored to its original state, it was made smaller and removed to some distance from the villa. The lovely gardens that now surround the house were initiated in 1967 at the behest of the Borghese princes. They comprise a broad variety of Mediterranean species including yuccas, palms, flowering trees (Jacaranda, originally from Brazil, and Judas trees), together with more exotic plants such as *Xanthorrea arborea* and *Encefaloartus horridus* – the silvery blue Prickly cycad which was thought to exist only in fossil form before it was discovered growing in Tanzania.

The stone jetties of the old port are home to a fine collection of succulent plants.

WHERE TO STAY

Agriturismo Casa dello Scirocco – Contr. Piscitello, Carlentini, ☎ 095 44 77 09, Fax 095 71 39 257. This interesting establishment is located in a complex of caves which date back to the pre-Greek era. It comprises a villa known as the "house of the scirocco", founded in ancient times. It is equipped with a ventilation system which keeps the house cool during hot weather; 10 one-room apartments are housed in prehistoric caves, fitted out with gas heating and bathrooms. Approximately 60 000L per person for bed and breakfast (minimum of 2 nights stay).

MADONIE e NEBRODI★

Messina and Palermo
Michelin map 432 M-N 23-25

Sicilian Apennines – The Sicilian Apennines form a natural extension in geological terms to the Calabrian Apennines. The range comprises the Monti Peloritani (above Messina) together with the **Nebrodi** and **Madonie** mountains: these are entirely consistent in terms of the landscape, flora and fauna. Recently, the two latter areas have been designated national parks so as to preserve the natural heritage. The scenery varies from gentle undulating slopes to a wilder escarpments where limestone predominates: this is especially the case around San Fratello and Rocche del Crasto in the Nebrodi and on the northern flank of the Madonie around Piano Battaglia and Battaglietta. Pizzo Carbonara – the highest peak in the Madonie – and the Serre di Quecella are often referred to as the "Sicilian Alps" on account of their resemblance to the Dolomites. The valleys accommodate rivers and mountain streams that nestle in gorges cut by erosion: one of the most spectacular is the **Gole di Tiberio**, near Borrello. The vegetation varies with altitude: the coastal strip, up to 600-800m (1 968ft-2 624ft), is covered with oaks (cork, holm) and scrubby shrubs typical of the Mediterranean maquis (tree spurge, myrtle, Pistacia lentiscus, wild olive, strawberry tree/arbutus, juniper); above, at 1 200-1 400m (3 936-4 592ft), grow various species of oak; over 1 400m/4 592ft, the slopes are covered with glorious beech woods. Between Vallone

THE TWO NATIONAL PARKS

Parco dei Nebrodi – The Nebrodi Park, designated a nature reserve in 1993, covers a large area, touching upon several local districts or *comuni*. Its 85 687ha/211 647 acres are divided into four categories consistent with the level of conservation implemented: special, general, protected and controlled. The park authority (Ente Parco) provides a number of information centres which dispense advice and guidance about footpaths and nature trails. These are to be found at **Caronia** (via Ruggero Orlando 126, ☎ 0921 33 32 11), **Alcara Li Fusi** (via Ugo Foscolo 1, ☎ 0941 79 39 04); **Cesarò** (in strada Nazionale ☎ 095 77 32 061); the latter organises free guided walks of different grades and duration, especially in summer: book first by phone.

Parco delle Madonie – The Madonie Park encompasses since 1989 some 39 679ha/98 007 acres. Its roughly rectangular perimeter also contains four categories of reserve designated special, general, protected and controlled according to different guidelines. For detailed information, illustrated material and advice on excursions (by car or on foot), contact the Ente Parco at **Petralia Sottana**, corso Paolo Alliata 16, ☎ 0921 68 08 40 and 0921 68 40 11, or their administrative headquarters at contr Farchio, **Isnello** ☎ 0921 66 27 95 37 or 0921 66 27 37.

Madonna degli Angeli and Manca li Pini (northern side of Monte Scalone), grow 25 Nebrodi spruce, the only examples of this endemic, and now rare, species (one other stands by the ruined castle at Polizzi). One of the most interesting places for plants is Piano Pomo where the giant holly grows: a few, considered to be over 300 years old, reach over 14m/46ft in height and have a circumference of 4m/13ft *(see CASTELBUONO)*. The area harbours a variety of indigenous birds and animals, although the increased presence of humans (and increased hunting or poaching) has virtually annihilated many of the larger species (red and fallow deer, wolf, lammergeier and griffon vulture). Those still found, however, include porcupines, wild cats, foxes, martens and some 150 or so species of bird such as hoopoes, buzzards, kestrels, red kites, Peregrine falcons, ravens, golden eagles and grey herons. Among the area's most interesting groups of residents are the many (70 or more) species of butterfly, many of which are brightly coloured.

The itineraries proposed below follow **scenic routes★★** which, depending on the direction in which they are followed, provide a completely different set of views.

For alternative itineraries in the Nebrodi area, consult the chapters headed SANTO STEFANO DI CAMASTRA, FIUMARA D'ARTE and CAPO D'ORLANDO.

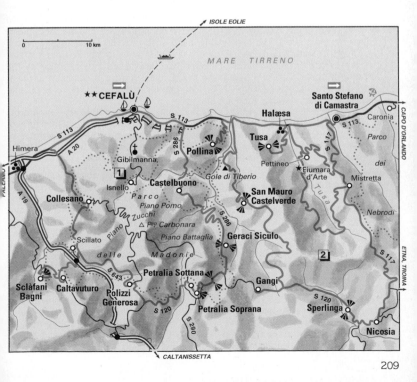

1 THE HEART OF THE MADONIE

162km/100mi round trip starting from Cefalù: allow a full day.

★★Cefalù – *See CEFALÙ.*

Take the road out of Cefalù along the coast eastwards, enjoying the views of the look-out tower on the promontory. A signpost a little further on indicates the road, right, for Castelbuono.

Castelbuono – *See CASTELBUONO.*

The road continues onwards towards Geraci Siculo.

Geraci Siculo – A medieval quality continues to prevail in this hamlet, notably in the upper part of town riddled with a maze of narrow cobbled streets. All that survives of the castle built for the Marchesi Ventimiglia *(accessible by road by turning right by the entrance to the town)* is a sad ruin and the little church of Sant'Anna, once the family chapel. From here, marvellous **views★** extend in every direction.

At the centre of the community stands the Gothic **Chiesa Madre** ⊘, its nave separated from its side aisles by a stone arcade. Nestling in the second chapel of the north aisle is a Madonna and Child by **Antonello Gagini**, commissioned by the Ventimiglias.

The road from Geraci to Petralia proceeds through a glorious, sweeping open landscape with lovely **views★** of the mountains, the high outcrop on which Enna is perched, and Mount Etna.

Petralia Soprana – Petralia "up town" stands at 1 147m/3 762ft, making it the highest town in the Madonie. From its situation, it appears to survey the outlying landscape and open space, enthralled by its unforgettable all-encompassing views. The origins of the town seem to go back to Petra, a town founded by the Sicani which they could defend from enemy attack. In feel, however, it remains rooted firmly in the Middle Ages, thanks to the local regulation dictating that all houses must be built in natural stone. The narrow streets weave between austere *palazzi* and churches, all built of local stone, occasionally opening out into picturesque little squares and onto breathtaking scenery. The **Belvedere** (by piazza del Popolo) probably provides the best vantage point from which to survey the **panorama★★** that takes in Enna *(on the far left)*, Resuttano, Monte Cammarata and Madonna dall'Alto *(on the right)*.

The focal point of the town is **piazza del Popolo** where the town hall is located, occupying the former premises of a Dominican convent that retains its Gothic appearance, complete with pointed arches. The street to the Chiesa Madre leads through the delightful piazza Quattro Cannoli past its stone fountain. The right flank of the **Chiesa Madre** ⊘, preceded by a lovely portico, is open for all to admire. The **view** from here extends over Piano Battaglia, Polizzi, Mount Etna and Enna. **Inside**, it shelters a fine wooden crucifix by **Frà Umile da Petralia** *(right of the altar)* and a lovely wooden altar carved by Bencivinni in the Cappella del Santissimo Sacramento *(left of the main altar)*. The rear wall is taken up by an 18C organ case.

The Church of **Santa Maria di Loreto** ⊘ stands on the site of a former Saracen fortress. Its convex front elevation, framed between two bell-towers, was designed by the Serpotta brothers. The large altarpiece inside, depicting the Madonna and Child, is attributed to Giacomo Mancini (15C). From behind the church extends a splendid **panorama★★★** with views of Mount Etna.

Another church, dedicated to the Great Redeemer **(Santissimo Salvatore)** ⊘ conforms to an elliptical plan and has an 18C decoration. It contains a wooden figure of St Joseph by Quattrocchi and, in the sacristy, two works by **Giuseppe Salerno** *(see p 193)*: *St Catherine of Alexandria* and the *Madonna with a Cat*; both pictures show an intimacy and gentleness that is unusual for this painter.

Petralia Sottana – Petralia "down town" is situated in a lovely position overlooking the valley of the River Imera. Despite this, Petralia Sottana is nonetheless perched on a rocky spur 1 000m/3 280ft above sea-level. Corso Paolo Agliata, where the headquarters of the Madonie Park Authority (Ente Parco delle Madonie) are located, leads past the church **Santa Maria della Fontana** with its lovely 15C doorway. Further along the same street stands **San Francesco** ⊘, with its fine bell-tower rising from a pointed arch; inside, it contains a number of paintings by Giuseppe Salerno. As the street curves round to the right, the eye is drawn to the bell-tower-cum-archway of the Chiesa della Misericordia inlaid with a meridian line. A little further on lies piazza Umberto I and the **Chiesa Madre** ⊘ (17C), an imposing building overlooking the valley. The internal space is articulated into nave and flanking aisles by a series of monolithic stone columns cut from Balza Sant'Eleuterio. There hang various paintings by **Giuseppe Salerno** *(see p 193)* including a *Triumph of the Eucharist (first altar on the left)* and *The Five Wounds of Our Lord* (once erroneously thought to be a *Deposition*). In the chapel to the right of the high altar is preserved a picture of the *Nativity*: the delicate rendering of the Christ Child is by **Antonello Gagini**.

Continue on through the bell-tower-cum-archway, uphill to the 16C **Chiesa della Trinità** ⊘ (sometimes called la Badia). A fine Gothic doorway leads through into the church which cedes pride of place to a large 23-panel **marble altarpiece★** by **Giandomenico Gagini**. The central section shows the Mystery of Easter; this is surrounded by the Trinity *(above)*, the Crucifixion, the Resurrection and the Ascension. The lateral panels *(top left to bottom right)* relate incidents from the life of Christ. At the end of the nave, on the right, stands a fine 18C organ.

Excursion on foot – *Allow 3hr 30min to the top.* On the northern edge of Petralia, a track worn by pilgrims leads up to the **Santuario della Madonna dell'Alto** (1 819m/5 966ft). This houses a painting of the Virgin and Child from 1471.

Proceed to Polizzi Generosa.

Polizzi Generosa – Like the other preceding hilltop towns, Polizzi enjoys its splendid **situation★**, sitting on a limestone spur dominating the northern and southern slopes of the Imera Valley. The most suggestively Romantic view may be glimpsed on crisp mornings when low cloud *(la marella)* collects around the foot of the mountains, shrouding the base in shadow while the tops, caught in the sunshine, appear to float on the mist.

Despite the town's elusive origins, it seems to have played an active role in ejecting the Arab invader: **Roger II** had a castle built and took up defences in preparation against an attack from the infidels. Later, Frederick II was so impressed by the warmth of hospitality extended to him on his visit that he bestowed the title of *Generosa* on the little town.

A good place from which to begin a tour of the town is the main piazza, marked by the ruins of the castle on the highest point (917m/3 008ft). Also located on the piazza is the Palazzo Notarbartolo (16C) which houses the **Museo Ambientalistico Madonlta** ⊘. This natural history collection is presented as a series of reconstructed natural habitats (note that the preserved animals died of natural causes or were retrieved from poachers): the flora and fauna are displayed in tableaux that range from the water that nestles in the bottom of the valley (the river as it was 30-40 years ago) to the highest peaks in the Madonie range; intermediate stages include woodland, beech forest (1 300m/4 264ft-1 800m/5 904ft) and the fauna that thrives at the lower and higher altitudes, including vultures (notably the griffon vulture which disappeared in the 1920s) and golden eagles.

Via Roma leads downhill past Palazzo Gagliardo (16C-17C) and, opposite, the **Chiesa Madre** ⊘, which although largely dating from the 19C, still preserves a number of earlier features from the 14C-15C (portico and pointed arch). Inside, it contains a number of works of art: a Flemish triptych *(presbytery)* and a lovely *Madonna of the Rosary* by **Giuseppe Salerno** – one of the two Zoppi di Gangi *(see GANGI)*.

Beyond lies piazza Umberto I. From here, via Garibaldi leads to San Girolamo with its fine Baroque doorway before finally terminating at piazza XXVII Maggio. This square offers a dramatic **view★★★** that pans across the highest peaks of the Madonie: in the centre there is the northern valley of the River Himera (along which the motorway runs today); to the left, sits Rocca di Caltavuturo, Monte Calogero (right in the middle, in the far distance) and Monte Cammarata; the far right is marked by the Dolomite-like profile of Quacella, followed by Monte Mufara and Pizzo Carbonara. Almost directly opposite extends the lower section of the Massicio dei Cervi, known as the *Padella* (meaning a frying pan). According to local hearsay, this is where a secret entrance leads into a cave full of treasure, the whereabouts of which may only be revealed during Easter Mass. Below lies the Valle dei Noccioleti.

Local delicacies

The **Pasticceria al Castello** in piazza Castello produces excellent pastries and cakes including the typical *sfoglio* (mille-feuille) made with unsalted *fromage frais*.

Continue on down to the coast; at the first fork, turn left towards Caltavuturo.

The road runs past the turning for **Scillato** *(2km/1.2mi NE)*, picking its **way★** through ever-changing scenery as bare tracts of mountain might alternate with gentle green slopes and steep limestone escarpments.

Caltavuturo – Clinging to the foot of the Rocca di Sciara, the "Fortress of the Vulture" – derived from the Arabic *(calaat, fortress)* and the Sicilian vernacular *(vuturo, vulture)* – preserves a few prized 16C works of art in the **Chiesa Madre** ⊘. These include an attractive *Madonna of the Rosary surrounded by the Mysteries,* executed by followers of Pietro Novelli and, at the back of the church, a fine Baroque organ by Raffaele della Valle.

Leave Caltavuturo by the SS 120 towards Cerda; at the fork, turn left for Sclàfani Bagni.

Sclàfani Bagni – Crouched on the edge of a rocky crag in a wonderful **position**★, the little hamlet retains a certain medieval quality. The entrance is boldly stated by the **Porta Soprana**, a gate comprising a pointed arch surmounted by the Sclàfani family coat of arms. On the left sits the *castelletto*, probably conceived as a defence tower. Just beyond stands the **Chiesa Madre** ⏱, graced with a decorative Gothic doorway (15C). Inside, it contains a painting by the Zoppo di Gangi **Giuseppe Salerno** entitled *L'Agonizzante*, and a sarcophagus carved with a bacchanal from Himera *(see TERMINI IMERESE)*. The organ *(under restoration)* at the back of the church is by Raffaele della Valle (1615).

Up to the right of the church may be seen a tower, the last vestige of the 14C fortifications. From here, a wonderful **view**★★ extends across to the Madonie mountains, over the sea below Himera and Caltavuturo.

Return to the SS 643, following it to Collesano.

Collesano – The heart of this small holiday resort preserves its original medieval fabric. Its most interesting building is the **Chiesa Madre**, theatrically placed up a great flight of steps. The façade betrays nothing of the marvellous works of art – paintings and sculptures – it conceals within. Above the nave hangs an enormous Crucifixion, painted in 1550. A protective case in the south aisle hosts a 17C sedan chair. Among the many paintings, look out for *St Catherine* (1596) in one of the first bays in the south aisle, completed by Giuseppe Alvino who was also known as *Il Sozzo* (which literally translates as the Soak!), and more particularly, for works by Zoppo di Gangi **Gaspare Vazzano** *(see p 193)*, such as the wonderful great canvas of **Santa Maria degli Angeli**★ *(north aisle)* and the **cycle of frescoes**★ in the chancel illustrating scenes from the lives of Christ *(ceiling)* and of St Peter and St Paul *(left and right walls respectively)*. The elegant tabernacle in the south aisle is the work of Donatello Gagini (1489).

The way up to piazza Gallo, in the oldest part of town, leads past the ruins of the castle, from where a splendid view opens out over the valley bottom and the coast beyond.

From Collesano, turn down towards the coast signposted for Cefalù.

② BETWEEN THE NEBRODI AND THE MADONIE

177km/110mi round trip starting from Santo Stefano di Camastra: allow one full day.

Santo Stefano di Camastra – *See SANTO STEFANO DI CAMASTRA.*

Follow the early stages of the itinerary given in that chapter, following the signs for Mistretta, to the junction with the Troina/Nicosia road: turn right to Nicosia.

Nicosia – *See NICOSIA.*

A few kilometres further on, the road reaches Sperlinga, a little town overlooked by its castle, backed up against a vertical cliff-face.

Sperlinga: the castle

Sperlinga – The compact hamlet stretches along the side of a spur of rock shaped like an upturned ship's keel. It seems to have started life as a troglodyte community contemporary with the Sicani; several such cave dwellings are open to view below the town. At the highest point, overlooking the other rooftops, stands the strategically placed **castle-fortress** ⊙ firmly rooted to the base rock to which it clings. On the way up to the castle entrance, there are two spacious caves that were once kitted out as stables; today they house a small ethno-anthropological museum. Through the first gateway stands a second archway, this time consisting of a pointed arch with an inscription above extolling the virtue of the town: *Quod Siculis placuit, sola Sperlinga negavit* ("That which pleased the Sicilians was only rejected by Sperlinga"). The significance of such a proclamation must be sought in history for, in 1282, at the height of the War of the Sicilian Vespers, a band of Frenchmen sought refuge in the castle: instead of being treated as hostages, they were shown kindness and understanding by the town residents. Elsewhere, the episode caused a great outcry. The castle is built on several levels. The caves excavated from the rock *(to the left of the entrance)* were used for stabling animals, as prison cells and forges and probably for making weapons. At the front is the prince's reception room. Opposite, on a single level, lies the chapel and the residential quarters: the undercrofts in this section of the castle served as granaries. Centrally placed between the two wings, a steep staircase cut into the bedrock climbs up to the look-out tower: from here the **view**★★ pans 360° over the Gangi plateau with the Madonie range behind, the Nebrodi to the north, Mount Etna and the Erei mountains.

To the right stretches the long undulating ridge that runs from Monte Grafagna to San Martino, and links up with the Nebrodi mountain chain. This good scenic road snakes its way towards Gangi, the largest town in the Madonie.

Gangi – *See GANGI.*

From Gangi, it is possible to link up with itinerary **1**, extending it with a drive to Petralia Sottana. Gangi reappears in the foreground on the left, before the looming shape of Mount Etna behind.

Alternatively, if proceeding with itinerary **2**, make your way back to the fork and turn left towards San Mauro Castelverde.

San Mauro Castelverde – On a clear day, this ideally situated little hamlet enjoys a range of bird's-eye **views**★★ from the top of its own hilltop across to the Aeolian Islands and the mountain ranges: the Nebrodi and Madonie (visible from Piano San Giorgio in the higher part of the town).

The centre is typically medieval in feel and layout. The church, **Santa Maria dei Franchi** ⊙ (13C), and its 18C bell-tower are surrounded by tortuous narrow streets like a beetle caught in a web. Inside, it contains a Madonna by **Domenico Gagini** and a font by **Antonello Gagini**.

From here, turn back down towards the coast: at the fork, turn left, following the coast road. Turn right up the road signposted for Pollina (about 7km/4mi).

Pollina – The hilltop town of Pollina is in a perfect **position**★ to enjoy picture-postcard **views**★ of the coast below. The **Chiesa Madre** ⊙ (16C) passively sitting at the heart of a complicated network of medieval streets, preserves within various prized works of art including an attractive and engaging **Nativity**★ by **Antonello Gagini**. In the Middle Ages, the top of the town was marked by a castle: today only a square tower remains. Alongside, a theatre has recently been built according to ancient Greek and Roman prototypes, complete with spectacular **panoramic views**★★ over the mountain landscape and the sea; linking the two is a winding road that leads from the theatre all the way to the coast.

Continue back down towards the coast and Cefalù. Signs on the right indicate the way to Tusa and thereby to the archaeological site of Halaesa which lies before the village itself.

Halaesa – The vestiges of Halaesa are to be found just beyond the chapel of Santa Maria di Palate. The little town was originally founded by the Siculi in the 5C BC; later it passed first into Greek then Roman hands, before being completely destroyed by the Arabs. **Excavations** ⊙ have revealed the precincts of a Roman forum complete with its associated sanctuaries, a patrician family house and sections of bastions along the enclosure walls from the Greek era; opposite, a temple is supposed to have stood, occupying a strategic position above the River Tusa. Another temple was located at the top of the hill *(closed to the public)*.

Tusa – *Approx 10km/6mi S.* This little town, enjoying its fabulous position high on the brow of a hill, was probably founded by the people who managed to escape Halaesa as it was being ransacked and razed by the Arabs. The upper part of the town preserves its medieval appearance. Access to it is through the main gateway. This is where the most interesting churches are to be found, including the **Chiesa Madre** with its entrance set in a decorative pointed arch. Inside, a delicate marble Annunciation from the Renaissance (1525) ornaments the altar; the wooden choir stalls carved with dragons, cherubs and masks are 17C; the *Madonna and Child* is by followers of Gagini. Alongside the church rises a free-standing bell-tower.

Nestling among the other narrow streets is the little stone Church of San Nicola with its distinctive tile-topped campanile.

Return to the coast road which continues on to Santo Stefano di Camastra. Alternatively, after crossing the River Tusa, turn away from the coast by taking a road that leads up to the right; this links up with the itinerary described under FIUMARA D'ARTE.

MARSALA

Trapani – Population 80 546
Michelin map 432 N 19

Marsala nestles on the headland which continues to bear the town's ancient name, Lilybaeum (from *Lily* meaning water and *beum* referring to the Eubei, its pre-Phoenician inhabitants). The settlement is presumed to be have been founded in 397 BC by the Phoenicians who fled from Motya following their defeat by the Syracusans. Its name in current use probably derives from the Arabic *Marsah el Ali*, meaning port of Ali, which would indicate that it has been a maritime town of considerable importance since its early history. Later, the harbour witnessed one of the most momentous events in the history of Sicily: the landing of Garibaldi's Thousand in Sicily.

The ethnic diversity (including a large Tunisian minority), the harbour and the city's web of narrow streets combine to suggest that the visitor has been inadvertently catapulted into some North African town.

Marsala becomes progressively more animated in the period leading up to Easter: celebrations begin with a **Maundy Thursday procession** (the eve of Good Friday) when the Stations of the Cross are re-enacted in the streets of the town centre by local men and women in the different roles involved in the Passion. In the evening, the Crucifixion and Resurrection are also re-enacted.

Grazie ... mille

Early May 1860: accompanied by 1 000 volunteers dressed in red shirts, **Garibaldi** set sail from Quarto (near Genoa) bound for Sicily. Their mission was to overthrow the Bourbon government and liberate the Kingdom of the Two Sicilies. On 11 May, the two ships – the *Lombardo* and the *Piemonte* – moored at Marsala. The *Mille* (one thousand) made their way inland, winning their first battle at Calatafimi: this opened up the way to Palermo. As the campaign progressed, the band was swollen by new volunteers so that by the time they reached the Straits of Messina, their number exceeded 20 000. In less than two months, Sicily had been liberated from Bourbon government. The expedition continued to sweep through the rest of the kingdom until, following a plebiscite, the island was admitted on 21 October to the nucleus of northern states (Piedmont, Lombardy, Liguria, Emilia Romagna, Tuscany and Sardinia) that later were to unify to form the Kingdom of Italy.

🗎 via XI Maggio 100, ☎ 0923 71 40 97.

GETTING TO MARSALA

The city can be reached by **train** from Trapani (approx 30min) and by **bus** from Palermo (piazza Pizzo), Agrigento (piazza Caprera) and Trapani (piazza del Popolo). For timetables and departure information contact the tourist office.
The railway station is approximately 15min walk from the town centre, in via Fazio.

FOOD AND WINE

In addition to the numerous Marsala wine producers *(see below)*, the **Cantina Sperimentale Istituto Regionale della Vite e del Vino** is open to the public, and allows visitors to sample a number of experimental wines. *Via Trapani 218, Istituto Tecnico Agrario A Damiani. Visits by appointment only,* ☎ *0337 89 93 53 or 091 62 78 111 (Palermo office); www.infcom.it/irvv*
The restaurant at **Tenuta Volpara** farm (contr Digerbato, ☎ 0923 98 46 67; closed Mon) is situated in a panoramic location in the district of the same name and serves typical local cuisine, including a special warm ricotta cheese, known as *zabbina*. Approximately 35 000L for a meal and 140 000L for a double room (including breakfast).

TOWN CENTRE

The centre of Marsala radiates from **piazza della Repubblica**, where the Chiesa Madre and Palazzo Senatorio, completed in the 18C and known as the Loggia, are located. The main thoroughfare leading from the piazza is the corso XI Maggio, the old *Decumanus Maximus* of the Roman town, lined as ever with splendid buildings. Perpendicular to the principal axis, **via Garibaldi** leads southwards to **Porta Garibaldi** on the edge of town, running past the town hall, a former Spanish military bar-racks, on the way. The area behind is brought noisily to life each morning by a bustling fish market. The 17C Chiesa del Collegio, nestling among a series of fine 18C buildings line via Rapisardi, the northern extension of via Garibaldi.

Chiesa Madre ⊘   The main church with its tufa front decked with statues was built during the Norman occupation, but extensively remodelled in the 18C. Inside, it contains a number of works by the Gagini: most notably a fine icon by **Antonello Gagini** and Berrettaro *(north apse)*, and a delicate Madonna by **Domenico Gagini** from 1490 *(south transept)*. Above this hangs a good Renaissance painting by Antonello Riggio depicting the Presentation of the Virgin at the temple.

Museo degli Arazzi ⊘ – *The entrance to this museum housed in rooms behind the Chiesa Madre is in via Garraffa.* The collection comprises eight large 16C Flemish **tapestries**★ relating scenes from the war waged by Titus against the Jews.

Porta Garibaldi

215

The sweet nectar of Marsala

History – 1770: a violent storm forced a British ship to take shelter in the harbour of Marsala. A certain merchant by the name of **John Woodhouse** disembarked and went into town to sample the Marsala wine in one of the humble taverns. Although more accustomed to the liqueur wines of Spain and Portugal, his palate immediately detected their similarity, prompting him to risk despatching a considerable consignment of wine (blended with alcohol so as to better withstand the journey) to his native land to sound out the market. The response being positive, the merchant set up his own company in Marsala. A little later, a second English merchant landed in town: **Ben Ingham**, a great connoisseur of fortified wines. With his intervention, the quality of the wine was gradually improved using carefully selected blends of different, improved, grape varieties. His business passed into the hands of his nephews, the **Whitakers** *(see p 283)*. In 1833, the entrepreneur **Vincenzo Florio**, a Calabrese by birth and Palermitano by adoption, bought up great swathes of land between the two largest established Marsala producers and set to making his own vintage with an even more exclusive range of grape. At the end of the 19C, several more wine growers joined the competition, including Pellegrino (1880). After the turn of the century, Florio bought out Ingham and Woodhouse, and retained the two labels. Florio in turn succumbed to a takeover by a conglomeration of other producers; again the famous, well-established, labels continued to be made and marketed.

Marsala wine – Marsala is registered as a DOC wine (a State-designated label of controlled quality); this means that production is restricted to an exclusive area around Trapani, and a collection of additional vineyards in the provinces of Agrigento and Palermo. Only grape varieties with a high natural sugar content are used to make Marsala: these, once pressed, are left to ferment, and/or caramelise, before being blended with ethyl alcohol to produce the different types and flavours of Marsala.

Relative to the sugar content, Marsala may be categorised as dry, semi-dry or sweet. Its main denomination, however, is relative to the length of time it is left to mature: Marsala Fine (1 year), Superiore (2 years), Superiore Riserva (4 years), Vergine (5 years) and Vergine Riserva (10 years). Dry Marsala is usually served as a refreshing aperitif (below 10°C) while the sweeter forms are drunk as a dessert wine (no more than 18°C).

CANTINE FLORIO

Florio ⊘ – A tour of this long-established winery provides the opportunity of comparing old techniques and installations with the new. The huge wine-cellars *(cantine)* themselves are somewhat close and stuffy: the environment is carefully maintained at a constant temperature of 18°C by means of tufa walls (insulation), a tiled roof (aeration) and sand on the floor (temperature control and humidity). Perhaps the most interesting part of the process, however, is the explanation relating to the **Soleras Method** to which the wine is conditioned by the pyramid arrangement of oak barrels. This practice, imported from Spain, is used to age the wine: the young wine is added at the top, this is then allowed to percolate gently down through the interconnected barrels as the older, matured vintage is drawn off from the bottom tier of casks. This ensures that the wine is perfectly blended and remains of a consistent high quality.

The winery also has a small museum where the requisite equipment and tools are displayed.

Pellegrino ⊘ – This is another of the large producers: besides Marsala they also make Passito and Moscato di Pantelleria. Five wonderful **Sicilian carts** decorated in the 19C with historical scenes are to be admired at the entrance. Another memento of times past is the grille which once segregated the bottles on which custom duties were to be levied, subject to inspection.

Marco De Bartoli ⊘ – *292 contrada Samperi.* This producer, situated in the Samperi district, is responsible for one of the best Marsalas, achieved by traditional methods.

Vivid colours and a strong sense of composition determine the central panel as well as the borders of flowers, fruit and allegorical figures. The sixth tapestry, illustrating a violent fight, manages to convey a great sense of movement and action.

Museo Archeologico di Baglio Anselmi ⓥ – This archaeological museum is accommodated inside a former wine warehouse designed by Basile. Pride of place is given to the remains of a **Punic ship★** (3C BC) recovered in 1969 near the island of Motya. This probably consisted of a *liburna*, a type of fast warship (35m long) used and lost at the end of the First Punic War, in the Battle of the Egadi (241 BC). The detailed analysis of these fragments has provided valuable information on the ship-building methods practised by the Phoenicians using prefabricated units marked with letters. Furthermore, the metal-alloy nails used for assembling the hold have proven to be quite remarkable: after more than 2 000 years under water, they show no sign whatsoever of deterioration.

The museum also displays important artefacts relating to the historic evolution of Marsala and its surrounding area from prehistoric times to the Middle Ages. Among the most interesting cases are those devoted to Motya and to various examples of finely crafted Hellenistic **jewellery** found off Capo Boeo.

Insula di Capo Boeo ⓥ – *At the end of viale Vittorio Emanuele.* Right on the tip of the headland are situated the remains of three Roman *insulae*. Almost the whole of one is taken up by a large **villa**, built in Imperial times (3C BC), complete with its own private set of baths. Fragments of the mosaic floors are still in evidence, as are a number of the small pillars *(suspensurae)* used to support the floor, thereby enabling hot air to circulate through the cavity. The access roads to the area were paved with white stone from Trapani.

A little further on stands the Church of **San Giovanni al Boeo** ⓥ, built around the Sibyl of Lilybaeum's legendary grotto.

MAZARA DEL VALLO
Trapani – Population 51 986
Michelin map 432 O 19

The settlement founded by the Phoenicians at the mouth of the River Mazaro became an important harbour in Antiquity on account of its protected position and its proximity to Africa. The trading post that so flourished under the Ancient Greeks, however, reached its apotheosis under Arab and then Norman dominion. The cosmopolitan range of different ancestries that have been attracted to this town through the ages, not least from nearby North Africa, are still much in evidence today, constituting a considerable proportion of the local population.

As in times past, Mazara continues to be regarded as one of the most important deep-sea fishing-towns in Italy, accounting for 20% of the national catch.

> **Eating out**
>
> Enjoy a range of fish specialities at **Il Pescatore**, via Castelvetrano 191, ☎ 0923 94 75 80. Closed Mon. Approximately 50 000L for a meal.

OLD TOWN

Harbour and shipping canal – The heart of the town is the harbour; this throbs with life early in the morning when the fishing fleet returns with its catch. The quays jostle with activity as refrigerated trucks manoeuvre into place; the harbour echoes with the sounds of fishermen, merchants, packers and drivers who see to the offloading, processing, packaging and despatching of the fish. Meanwhile, the fishermen go about preparing their boats, moored to the jetty, sorting and folding the nets, stacking up the lobster-pots and stowing the cages in readiness for the next expedition. Overlooking the scene with benign approval, set back from the actual harbour front, is the Norman church, San Nicolò Regale.

San Nicolò Regale ⓥ – This evocative building erected under William I, has a square plan with the three apses contained by a bulbous dome characteristic of Arabo-Norman architecture *(see PALERMO: San Giovanni degli Eremiti or San Cataldo)*. The skyline is edged with rounded battlements.

Below the floor inside, fragments of mosaic have been discovered: these, from paleo-Christian times, probably form part of a Roman floor.

Among the streets behind sits **piazza Plebiscito**, graced with the elegant façade of **Sant'Ignazio** (18C), and the former **Jesuit College** (17C) with its lovely doorway. This currently accommodates the municipal library and small local **museum** ⓥ containing artefacts from various periods, predominantly from Neolithic to the late Byzantine Eras. The separate **Sala Consagra** ⓥ is devoted to a contemporary artist born in Mazara: it contains etchings, acquatints and relief panels together with small-scale *modelli* of his best-known sculptures.

The museum also maintains a large reserve collection of paintings for which permanent exhibition space has yet to be found.

Cathedral ⊙ – The main building dates from the 11C although this was subjected to considerable remodelling in the 17C. The façade, completed in 1906, is ornamented with an decorative doorway and a 16C shallow relief panel depicting Roger I, on horseback, felling a Moor.

★**Interior** – The somewhat overall theatrical effect is achieved by interspersing a few genuine elements of gilded stucco decoration among frescoed *trompe-l'œil* stucco volutes, curlicues and little cherubs. The most complex group resides in the central apse where a large drape richly embroidered with gold "stitching" is suspended and drawn aside by angels, to reveal the **Transfiguration**★. The whole composition by Antonello Gagini sits upon a majestic Renaissance altar. In the first chapel on the right is an ancient *ciborium* which may have been used, according to the inscription, at the christening of Frederick II's son. The Chapel of the Crucifix, also right of centre, takes its name from the fine painted wooden crucifix (13C) contained in the adjoining room.
Set into the floor is a glass plate that provides a view of the ancient foundations. Elsewhere, the church contains a number Roman sarcophagi.

Piazza della Repubblica – This pleasing piazza laid out in the Baroque period acts as the focal point to the old town. The statue (1771) gracing the centre is by **Ignazio Marabitti** and represents San Vito, the patron saint of Mazara. On all sides rise a harmonious collection of *palazzi* from the 18C: at the far end sits the cathedral overshadowed by an elegant Baroque campanile, along the left side stands the Bishop's Palace and, to the right, extends the **Seminario dei Chierici** complete with its lovely neo-Classical portico and round-headed arched loggia. The former seminary now houses a small **Museo Diocesano** ⊙ *(entrance at 3 via dell'Orologio)*.

Lungomare Mazzini – *South of piazza della Repubblica*. The seafront is flanked by gardens shaded by magnolias and palm trees, making it a perfect place for the habitual Italian "constitutional". At its eastern end, piazza Makara contains all that remains of the Norman castle (11C), namely a pointed gateway.

MEGARA HYBLAEA
Siracusa
Michelin map 432 P 27

The archaeological site is situated in a strange landscape, stranded between the sea and the chimneys of the Augusta oil refinery.
The Greek colony of Megara Hyblaea, founded by the Megarians of Greece in 728 BC, was twice razed to the ground: once in 483 BC by Gelon, the tyrant of Gela, and again by the Romans in 213 BC.

Excavations ⊙ – The **necropolis** lies outside the town walls, alongside the older enclosure walls *(before crossing the railway bridge, by the bend, take the dirt track off to the right)*.
Beyond the entrance extends one of the *decumani* that once led to the **agorà** (marketplace). One of the particular characteristics of the site is the clear evidence of successive building phases as Archaic constructions give way to Hellenistic ones above. On the left of the piazza sits a sanctuary, recognisable by the semicircular north end wall. Follow D 1, a street on the left, which passes alongside a large **Hellenistic house** from the 4C-2C BC (entrance marked by iron steps): this comprises some 20 rooms arranged around two courtyards, a rectangular one with a well in the middle, and a second diamond-shaped one. Some rooms preserve remains of *opus signinum* floors (an amalgam of clay particles mixed with minute pieces of rubble, bound together with lime). In each case, the thresholds of the various internal doorways are clearly visible, together with the grooves into which fit the door jambs. To the left of the *agorà*, lie the **Hellenistic baths**. The boiler is discernible (below the metal walkway) as is a round room used for ablutions which once would have been ringed with basins. Further along C 1 (right of the baths) is a *Pritaneo* (where magistrates would meet) from the Archaic period (6C BC) built of characteristic square, regular-cut stones. The *decumanus* continues beyond the square, as far as the **West Gate** and fortifications from the Hellenistic period, built with regular blocks and reinforced with defence towers.

EXCURSIONS

Augusta – *Approx 15km/9mi N of Megara Hyblaea*. Augusta is an important Italian commercial port concerned primarily with oil refineries and the production of "green" (lead-free) petrol. This industrial conglomeration has incurred considerable damage be it as a result of the 1693 earthquake, the Allied bombing of 1943 or, indeed, following major seismic tremors as recently as 1990.

Industrial skyline

B. Kaufmann

The town was founded by Frederick II on account of its strategic position with regard to defending the Bay of Augusta: hence the overpowering defensive quality of the Swabian castle, despite its neglected state of repair. The entrance to the citadel is by the **Spanish Gate**, flanked by two imposing bastions.
The main axis of the old town is corso Principe Umberto, the commercial thoroughfare which runs north to south.

Brucoli – *23km/14mi N of Megara Hyblaea*. This charming fishing-village clusters around its picturesque little **harbour** which nestles in the mouth of the River Porcaria. The 15C **castle** *(closed to the public)* occupying the very tip of the headland where the village has grown up, enjoys a marvellous **view★** of the harbour on one side and the ample Golfo di Brucoli on the other.

MESSINA

Population 261 134
Michelin map 432 M 28

Five kilometres separate Messina from mainland Italy, making it the obvious landing stage for people arriving from the peninsula. The bulk of this traffic has helped boost the sickle-shaped commercial harbour that in ancient times was given the name of **Zancle** by the Greek colony in the 8C BC. The history of the town is therefore inextricably linked to the sea and to the straits that bear its name. According to tradition, sailors have long claimed that the straits are guarded by two monsters, Scylla and Charybdis. **Scylla** was the daughter of Phorcys and Hecate (Greek goddess associated with the lower world and with night; she later assumed the role of queen of the ghosts and magic, haunting crossroads attended by heel-hounds, protectress of enchanters and witches). In art she is represented in triple form looking down three roads). She was loved by Poseidon and this aroused the jealousy of his wife Amphitrite who, using magic herbs, turned Scylla into a monster that devoured mariners who sailed too close to her cave under a cliff on the Calabrian side of the strait. She is said to have had 12 feet and six heads. It was she who flung herself at Ulysses' ship, catching and devouring six of his sailors. On the Sicilian side of the strait, under another rock, lived **Charybdis**, who used to drink the sea water and regurgitate it three times every day; when trapped by this whirlpool, the sailors often fell prey to Scylla (*Odyssey*, Book XII, v 234-259).
Strategically situated as far as commerce was concerned, Messina acted as a trading post for the interchange of goods and people, and therefore artistic trends and ideas. From this dynamic and stimulating context emerged such figures as the 15C painter Antonello da Messina.
In more recent times, the town has suffered the effects of devastating earthquakes, most notably in 1783 and in 1908, when 90% of the town was destroyed, leaving more than 60 000 victims. During the Second World War, the town was subjected to several intensive bombing raids.

🛈 via Calabria isol 301 bis, ☎ 090 67 42 36, Fax 090 67 42 71.

GETTING TO MESSINA

From mainland Italy – Messina handles the principal ferry services from mainland Italy. **Ferries** run from Reggio Calabria (45min, Stazione Ferrovie Stato, ☎ 0965 86 35 25) and Villa San Giovanni (20min, Caronte Shipping, via Marina 30, ☎ 0965 75 14 13 and Ferrovie dello Stato, piazza Stazione, ☎ 0965 75 60 99). For **hydrofoil** services (20min), contact SNAV, Stazione Marittima, Reggio Calabria, ☎ 0965 29 568.

For visitors arriving by **air**, the nearest airports are in Reggio di Calabria (connections with the Cavalieri bus services, via I Settembre 137, ☎ 090 77 19 38) and Catania (connections with the SAIS bus services, piazza della Repubblica, ☎ 090 77 19 14).

From Sicily – Messina is linked by **train** with Palermo (3hr), Taormina (1hr), Catania (approx 2hr) and Siracusa (3hr).

The SAIS **bus company** *(see above)* operates services to Palermo, Taormina and Catania, while TAI (viale S Martino 20, ☎ 090 67 51 84) serves Capo d'Orlando, Patti and Tindari.

Connections with the Aeolian islands – Trains (approx 40min) and buses (Giuntabus, via Terranova 6, ☎ 090 67 37 82) run from Messina to Milazzo, from where ferries cross to the Aeolian islands. Alternatively, daily hydrofoil services are operated by Aliscafi SNAV from Messina (1hr 20min), via San Raineri 22, ☎ 090 36 21 14, Fax 090 71 73 58.

EATING OUT

Le Due Sorelle – Piazza Municipio 4, ☎ 090 44 720. Closed Aug, Mon and at lunchtime. A pleasant restaurant in the heart of the historical centre, serving innovative local specialities. Approximately 40 000L for a meal.

Savoja – Via XXVII Luglio 36, ☎ 090 29 34 865. Closed 15 to 31 Aug, Sun evening and Mon. A simple, family-run establishment offering regional cuisine. Approximately 60 000L for a meal.

PASTRY SHOPS

Pasticceria Irrera at 12 piazza Cairoli and **Pasticceria P Gordelli** at 86 via Ghibellina 86 are both well worth a visit for their cakes and pastries.

SIGHTS

★**Museo Regionale** ⊘ – The chronological arrangement of the displays begins with the history of the area and the artistic climate that prevailed through the Byzantine and Norman Eras. The first rooms are dedicated to paintings and sculpture: shallow reliefs and capitals. Among the most notable examples, there is a fine early-15C polychrome wooden Crucifix *(third room on the right)* and a glazed terracotta medallion from the Della Robbia workshops of a sweet-faced Madonna gazing down at her Child.

The works in the next room betray the strong influence exerted by the Flemish style: a strong sense of realism and an astute attention to detail characterises the edge of the mantle and cuffs of the garments in the **Madonna and Child** attributed to a follower of Petrus Christus (15C). The same exquisite technique is evident in Antonello da Messina's beautiful, though badly damaged **Polyptych of St Gregory** (1473). His style assimilates several Northern qualities, namely the international Gothic predilection for linearity (stance of the figures, the crisp folds of falling drapery), the Flemish fascination for conveying the quality of texture and detail – as the Madonna's clothes demonstrate. The overall balance of composition is achieved with the use of perspective tapering to a single vanishing point and extending out from the central panel through to the side-panels. Note how the dais on which the Madonna is seated broadens out into the platform on which the two saints are standing, so making the three figures united in a single space. The predella (central lower panel) defines the limit of the picture plain, as does the necklace hanging down from the step. This early example of a *Sacra Conversazione* may have been pioneered in collaboration with his contemporaries Piero dell Francesca and Giovanni Bellini, while Antonello was in Venice between 1475-76 (The *Sacra Conversazione* is a picture composition, usually with the Madonna at its centre, that includes figures of Apostles, saints and martyrs – sometimes donors – as if they existed within a single space and within a single time span).

Antonello da Messina

Antonello "of Messina" was born around 1430 at a time when Sicily was under Spanish rule, and while the town was particularly prosperous. He transferred to the Spanish domain on the mainland, settling in Naples so as to study, possibly in the renowned studio of Colantonio. This proved to be a highly dynamic and stimulating environment. Spain also ruled Flanders at that time and so the artistic currents of Flemish, Spanish and Provençal schools merged here in Naples; Antonello assimilated them all to formulate his own highly personal style of painting. From the Flemish masters, he learnt to paint with oils (becoming the first in the southern part of Italy to practise the new technique; Piero being among the first in northern Italy), aped their realism and copied the way they portrayed textures in exquisite detail. These stylistic elements, however, did not affect the formal – and distinctly Italian – way in which he constructed his compositions and unified his picture space with light. The unified harmony of his paintings is achieved by his use of a rich and warm palette, clear and rational perspective and soft lighting effects. In a different domain, Antonello painted several portraits showing a three-quarter view of his sitter as was common among Flemish artists of the time, rather than the more common Tuscan and Umbrian side profile or face on view. His ability to reproduce the different effects of light, in contrast with a plain dark background, concentrates the impact of the picture on the noble yet serene facial features of his sitters. Certainly, his style is further enriched by the influences exchanged with other contemporary artists. During his sojourn in Venice, Antonello met Giovanni Bellini: the encounter made a lasting impression on both artists. Antonello began to use colour tonally and more gently as in the *Annunciation* in Palermo, perhaps the most famous of his Annunciations.

Other pictures hanging in the same room include the striking Colijn de Coter's *Deposition*: in this the drama of the scene is heightened by the anguished expressions of the mourners bent in supporting the weight of the dead Christ, and in the predominant use of burnt, dull colours.

The adjacent room is devoted to the Messina painter Girolamo Alibrandi. The most striking include the huge *Presentation at the Temple* of 1519 (note the noble expression and gentle features of the woman in the foreground) and *St Paul*. The elegant statue of the *Madonna and Child* in the same room is by **A Gagini**.

The Roman painter Polidoro da Caravaggio and the Florentine sculptor and architect Montorsoli introduced Mannerism to Messina. Their work, together with that of their followers, is displayed in galleries 6 and 7. Michelangelo Merisi, better known as **Caravaggio**, spent a year in Messina between 1608 and 1609; during this time he painted the *Adoration of the Shepherds* and the *Resurrection of Lazarus (Room 10)*. The short time he spent here was sufficient to influence contemporary artists living in the city.

The splendid **Senator's Coach★** *(Room 12)*, dated 1742, incorporates a number of exquisitely made furnishings, including small gilded wooden carvings and painted panels.

The top floor of the museum is devoted to displaying decorative and applied arts.

Chiesa di San Giovanni di Malta – *Via San Giovanni di Malta*. The west front of this square late 16C building, overlooking via Placida, is articulated with white stone pilasters, niches and windows (some blind) and, in the upper tier, a gallery.

Chiesa di San Francesco o dell'Immacolata – *Viale Boccetta*. This monumental church was almost entirely rebuilt following the earthquake of 1908, retaining a few original features such as the three rather austere 13C stone **apses**, relieved in part by tall narrow arches that contain the windows; the two doorways are set into pointed archways that post-date the main building of the church; and the fine rose-window on the façade.

Monte di Pietà – *Corner of via XXIV Maggio and piazza Crisafulli*. The front elevation of this late-Mannerist building is ornamented with a massive rusticated doorway framed between rather solid columns and a broken pediment; above, the balcony rests on brackets carved with volutes. The upper storey, destroyed by the earthquake, has not been rebuilt, making it look unfinished. Today it is used for concerts and recitals. The left side of the building is interrupted by a gate which leads through to what used to be the consecrated ground leading up to a majestic symmetrical flights of steps and the Church of Santa Maria della Pietà. Of the church, only the façade survives.

Duomo ⊙ – After the 1908 earthquake, the **cathedral** was almost completely rebuilt in the style of the Norman original. The façade rises in tiers and is relieved with one-light windows and a small central rose-window. The **central doorway★**, one of the three, was re-erected using elements of the original fabric (15C). It is flanked by small column supported by lions, and surmounted by a lunette filled with a *Madonna and Child* from the 16C.

Projecting from the right flank is a small building lit with elegant two-light Catalan Gothic windows.

The fine-beamed and painted **ceiling** contained within replaces the older one, destroyed by bombing raids during the Second World War. The ornamental carved rosettes along the central beams betray the influence of Eastern design.

Treasury ⊙ – *Access from inside the Duomo*. On display are a number of religious objects and vestments. The most ancient exhibit (from the Middle Ages) is the Pigna, a lamp made of rock crystal. Much of the silver plate was made in Messina, including the arm-shaped reliquaries (the one of San Marziano is inscribed with Moorish and Byzantine patterns), candlesticks, chalices and a fine 17C **monstrance** (containing a host) with two angels and a pelican on top presiding over the rays.

★**Orologio astronomico** – The **astronomical clock** is the most interesting component of the 60m/197ft high bell-tower to the left of the cathedral. The mechanism dates from 1933 having been built in Strasbourg. It comprises several layers, each bearing a different display endowed with a separate movement. At the bottom, a two-horse chariot driven by a deity indicates the day of the week; above, the central figure of Death waves his scythe threateningly at the child, youth, soldier or old man – the four ages of man – that pass before him. At the third stage, the Sanctuary of Montalto *(turn left to compare it with the real one)* sets the scene for a group of figures which, according to the time of year, represent the Nativity, Epiphany, Resurrection and Pentecost. At the top, the tableau enacts a scene relating to a local legend whereby the Madonna delivers a letter to the ambassadors of Messina in which she thanks and agrees to protect the inhabitants of the town who were converted to Christianity by St Paul the Apostle: the same **Madonna della Lettera** (Madonna of the Letter), is patron saint of the city.

The two young female bell-strikers are the local heroines Dina and Clarenza, who were alive during the period of resistance against the Angevins (1282). The very top is capped with a lion.

A. Picone/LARA PESSINA

Astronomical clock

The south side of the bell-tower *(starting from the bottom)* shows a perpetual calendar, the astronomical cycle marked by the signs of the zodiac, and the various phases of the moon.
When the clock strikes midday, all the mechanical figures come to life in tune to a musical air: the lion, the symbol of the vitality of the town, roars three times while the cockerel crows from between the two girls.

Fontana di Orione – Gracing the centre of piazza del Duomo, is an attractively elegant **fountain**, designed by the Tuscan sculptor Montorsoli to commemorate the inauguration of an aqueduct. Sculpted in a pre-Baroque style (16C), it incorporates allegories of four rivers: the Tiber, Nile, Ebro and Camaro – the River Messina was diverted into the new aqueduct.

Santissima Annunziata dei Catalani – A short way from the cathedral, nestling among fine *palazzi* in via Garibaldi, sits the Catalan Church. This was built in the 12C when the Normans were in power, and named after the Catalan merchants who patronised it later. The **apse★** is a fine example of the Norman composite style, incorporating Romanesque elements (small blind arches on slender columns), Moorish influences (geometrical motifs in polychrome stone) and Byzantine features (dome on a drum).

Santa Maria Alemanna – The sad ruin (no roof or façade) still manages to convey something of the original Gothic style, so rare in Sicily, with its pointed arches supported on pilasters and clusters of columns topped by splendid capitals that once articulated the aisles.

TOUR ROUND THE CAPO PELORO

This excursion starts from Messina and follows a panoramic road around the edge of the headland, past the glorious beaches that skirt the tip, before continuing along the Tyrrhenian shore.

Ganzirri and Torre Faro – *15km/9mi N.* The houses that make up the lively little fishing village of Ganzirri are clustered around two wide saltwater lagoons used for farming shellfish. The road along the "lakeside" bristles with restaurants and *pizzerias*, and continues to hum with activity late into the summer evenings.
Continuing north beyond the Straits of Messina lies Torre Faro, a small fishing village overlooked by a lighthouse and great electricity pylons bearing cables across the strait. Drive through **Lidi di Mortelle** and on to Divieto, before turning inland towards Gesso. On past this little town, after some 6km/4mi, the road that forks right leads up to the top of Antennammare.

Monte Antennammare – The road winds up to the San Rizzo pass. There a second road forks right for the **Santuario di Maria Santissima di Dinnammare** which is situated right on the top of Mount Antennammare (1 130m/3 706ft). From here, a spectacular view spans the **panorama★★** of Messina with its port, Capo Peloro and Calabria to the east, the Ionian coastline with the sickle-shaped promontory of Milazzo, and Rometta perched on a hill to the west.
On the way back, continue down to the crossroads and then turn right. This road coasts its way down the wooded slopes of Colle San Rizzo.

Santa Maria della Valle o Badiazza – The **Benedictine abbey of Santa Maria della Valle**, known also as Santa Maria della Scala, was probably built in the 12C and restored in the 14C. The actual church is not open to the public and the precincts are enclosed behind a tall concrete wall that protects it when the river is in full spate. The exterior, however, has windows set into pointed arches finished in volcanic stone. Through these, the interior can be glimpsed with its two-coloured ribbed vault and sculpted truncated pyramid capitals.
Return to Messina.

IONIAN COAST: MESSINA TO TAORMINA

The 40km/25mi round trip taking in a number of outposts dotted along the coast or a brief excursion inland can be undertaken just as easily in reverse, starting out from Taormina.

Monastero di San Placido Calonerò ⊘ – *On the road to Pezzolo, a short distance before Galati Marina.* The **Benedictine monastery**, now the headquarters of a technical institute for agriculture, preserves two attractive 17C cloisters with columns with high dosserets and Ionic capitals. A fine little Durazzo Gothic portal to the right of the atrium leading into the first cloisters, provides access to a vaulted chapel articulated with clustered columns.

Scaletta Zanclea – Scaletta Superiore *(2km/1.2mi inland)* boasts a **castle** that was built originally to serve as a Swabian military outpost (13C); it was eventually acquired by the Ruffo family who used it as a hunting lodge until the 17C. The massive fortress, gentrified by elegant two-light windows on the first floor and one-light windows above, houses the **Museo Civico** ⊘ and its collections of weaponry and historic documents.

Itàla – *2.5km/1.5mi inland from Itàla Marina*. The little hamlet of Croce jostles around the Basilian Church of **San Pietro e San Paolo** ⊘ which was rebuilt in 1093 by Count Roger, apparently in celebration of a victory over the Arabs. It comprises a tall nave and two lower aisles. The crossing is marked with a dome rising from a square drum. The brick exterior is relieved on the façade with occasional insertions of volcanic stone and by low, in places interlacing, blind arcading inspired by Eastern influences.

Continuing back along the coast, the road passes **Capo Alì** which is topped by a small round watchtower probably from the Norman period. It then proceeds through the seaside resorts of **Alì Terme**, **Nizza di Sicilia** and **Roccalumera**.

Sàvoca – *Approx 3km/1.8mi inland*. This picturesque typically medieval town occupies a splendid position on the top of a hill. What is somewhat remarkable is the way this divides into two ridges and yet interconnects with three spurs on which the districts of San Rocco, San Giovanni and Pentefur are built; together they form the star-shaped town.

Beyond the Town Hall, but still outside the old town sits the **Convento dei Cappuccini** ⊘, a Capuchin monastery with a **crypt** that contains the mummified bodies of 32 former town dignitaries and friars from the 17C and 18C. Several of these, some having been daubed with green paint by vandals, are displayed in niches, others in wooden sarcophagi. From the sacred area before the church there is a wonderful view of the town, the ruined castle and il Calvario or hill of "Calvary" in the distance.

Go back the same way and turn up via Borgo and then immediately left on to via San Michele.

This leads to the gateway to the old town centre. Just beyond the pointed archway on the right stands the 15C Church of **San Michele** with its fine transitional Gothic-Renaissance porches. Alongside sit the ruins of the Archimandrite community precincts (accommodating the highest officers of an Eastern monastic order). As the same street continues, a number of wonderful **views**★ extend over the rooftops and the valley below or up to the ruins of the Norman **castle** and the church San Nicolò (or Santa Lucia) differentiated by its peculiar crenellations perched on a rocky spur above. At last, the **Chiesa Madre** comes into view with its fine 16C portal surmounted by a beautifully carved oculus and the coat of arms of Sàvoca, bearing the elderberry *(sambuco)* branch from which the name of the town is supposed to derive. A visit to the town might then conclude with a climb up Calvary hill to the ruins of the Church of Santa Maria delle Sette Piaghe (St Mary of the Seven Sorrows).

The road continues to meander its way (2km/1.2mi) inland to the town of Casalvecchio.

Casalvecchio – This little town, called Palakorìon (old hamlet) in Byzantine times, enjoys a fabulous position with a panoramic view: from the terrace before the **Chiesa Madre di Sant'Onofrio** ⊘ this **view**★ takes in the Ionian Sea lying off Capo Sant'Alessio and Forza d'Agrò and, to the south, Mount Etna. **Inside**, the church has a fine coffered wooden ceiling ornamented with anthropomorphic figures, and a stone floor inlaid with the local black and red Taormina marble; both date from the 17C.

In a neighbouring former vicarage is housed the rather eclectic **Museo Parrocchiale** ⊘ which displays local farming tools, a silver life-size statue of Sant'Onofrio (1745), a painting of San Nicolò by a follower of Antonelli (1497), liturgical furnishings and sacred vestments.

Follow directions for Antillo and, after about 500m/550yd, fork left along a minor road which twists and turns to its destination.

Chiesa di Santi Pietro e Paolo d'Agrò ⊘ – The **church**, founded by Basilian monks, was largely rebuilt in 1117 and then restored in 1172 by a master builder called Gherardo il Franco; or so the inscription above the architrave of the main doorway claims. It is striking not only on account of its unusual appearance achieved by the use of brick, volcanic stone, limestone and sandstone, but also as a homogeneous expression of Byzantine, Arab and Norman influences. The **exterior** is ornamented with decorative banding, interlaced arcading and herringbone patterns. The main façade is graced with a portico flanked by twin towers. The **interior** space is divided into nave and aisles by Corinthian columns with high dosserets that rise to pointed arches. A large ribbed dome contains the central area, hovering on its tall drum suspended by pendentives.

The choir is enclosed by a smaller dome springing from an octagonal drum.

Turn back down towards the coast to Capo Sant'Alessio.

★**Capo Sant'Alessio** – This lovely rocky headland, distinctively shaped, is crowned with a round fortress on the western side and a polygonal castle on the eastern tip *(neither are open to the public)*.

On the south side nestles the wonderful **beach** of **Sant'Alessio Siculo**⌂.

A road extends from the fortresses to Forza d'Agrò.

Forza d'Agrò – This attractive medieval hamlet caps the furthermost spurs of the Monti Peloritani, enjoying a splendid **prospect**★ of the coast broken into inlets and bays. The best viewpoint is probably the terrace of piazza del Municipio. Behind this climbs a flight of steps through a fine Durazzo Gothic archway up to the sacred area before the **Chiesa della Triade**. The **combination**★ of the steps, archway and church façade is especially effective. Tortuous lanes wind their way up the hill towards the castle past the 16C **Chiesa Madre** that has been remodelled in the Baroque style. The Norman **castle** is now but a ruin; sheltering among the walls is the cemetery: silence and serenity endow this **secluded corner**★, populated at random with tombstones, with particular atmosphere.

★★★**Taormina** – See TAORMINA.

MILAZZO

Messina – Population 32 317
Michelin map 432 M 27

Mylai, the ancient city of the sea, sits at the base of the neck of Capo Milazzo, the sickle-shaped promontory that juts into the Tyrrhenian Sea, pointing like a finger towards the Aeolian Islands *(for information about boat services to the islands, see MESSINA)* which lie only a few miles offshore. This part of Sicily is often featured in Classical mythology: the promontory, regarded as prime pasture, provided grazing for the flocks of the sun god while the islands were considered to be home to Aeolus, the keeper of the winds, as well as to pretty nymphs, dancing satyrs and sileni (spirits of wild nature later associated with Dionysus) drunk on wine; it was possibly here that Ulysses and his companions were shipwrecked and encountered Polyphemus.

Milazzo also has its own history: its strategic situation meant that it has been inhabited and fought over since time immemorial and has been the scene of many a bitter battle. A silent witness to this eventful past is the fortress, which has served many different masters.

A boat in the port

THE BORGO

The *borgo* is the oldest part of the town: this consists of a medieval quarter stretched along the slope of the hill, loftily presided over by the fortified citadel, where an antiques fair is held on the first weekend of each month.

The entrance to this district coincides with the beginning of via Impallomeni which is lined on both sides by the Spanish Military Barracks (1585-95). There are many religious buildings within the *borgo*: on the right, in the steep street with the same name, is the **Santuario di San Francesco di Paola** ⊙, a church founded by the saint during his stay in the town (1464), remodelled in the 18C. The attractive **façade**★ is graced with an effective interplay of curvilinear stairway, windows and gallery, crowned with an elegant pediment. **Inside**, in the Gesù e Maria chapel, there is an unusual carved wooden altar decorated with gilt and mirrors, set with a charming *Madonna and Child* central panel by Domenico Gagini (1465).

🏛 piazza Caio Duilio 20, ☎ 090 92 22 865.

GETTING TO MILAZZO

Milazzo is linked to **Messina** by train (40min) and by bus, operated by the Giuntabus company (via Terranova 6, Messina, ☎ 090 67 37 82). **Palermo**, approximately 200km/125mi away, can be reached by train (approx 2hr 30min). Milazzo's railway station is situated in piazza Marconi, approx 3km/1.8mi from the historical centre of the town.

EATING OUT

Al Castello – Via Federico di Svevia 20, ☎ 090 92 82 175. Closed Mon and from 15 June to 15 Sept, also Tues at lunchtime. A pleasant, attractive restaurant, at the foot of the castle, serving typical seafood dishes of the region. Outdoor dining on the pavement during the summer months. Approximately 60 000L for a meal.

L'ugghiularu – Via Acquaviole 101, ☎ 090 92 84 384. Closed Wed. This *trattoria* is housed in an old olive-oil storehouse. The cuisine is simple and based on seasonal ingredients. Approximately 40 000L for a meal.

Bar Washington – Via Marina Garibaldi 94. A selection of ice creams, pastries, cakes and snacks.

A little further on, up salita San Francesco, is the Viceroy's residence **(Palazzo dei Vicerè)**, built in the 16C and altered in the 18C when the balconies with Baroque brackets were added. Beyond, on the other side of the road, is the **Chiesa del Santissimo Salvatore**, whose 18C façade was designed by Giovan Battista Vaccarini. Continuing along via San Domenico, on the right, is the **Chiesa della Madonna del Rosario** ⊘ which, until 1782, served as the main seat of the Inquisition Tribunal. Erected in the 16C, it was radically altered during the 18C when the interior was given its stucco decoration and frescoed by the Messina painter Domenico Giordano. Salita Castello, on the left, leads up to the city walls built by the Spanish, the outermost and the most impressive of the town's three sets.

★**Citadel and castle** ⊘ – The main fortification of the town was initiated by the Arabs (10C) on what had been an ancient Greek acropolis, and which had been modified and extended over the centuries. Through the **Spanish walls**, there is a large open space with, on the left, the **Duomo Vecchio** (1608), an example of Sicilian Mannerism. At one time this area might have accommodated the houses of those Milazzo citizens charged with public functions; however, after the political and administrative offices were transferred to the lower part of the town, the importance of the cathedral gradually dwindled, until it became used first as a warehouse, then as a prison and finally as a stable or cowshed. The **Aragonese city walls** (15C) are punctuated by five truncated-cone towers: two, set closer together, flank a fine gateway set into a pointed arch bearing the coat of arms of the Spanish monarchs, Ferdinand and Isabella – a shield divided into four sections (representing the monarchs under which Spain was unified), supported by the eagle of St John. Within, stands Frederick II's **castle** with later additions. The fine Gothic doorway is surmounted, however, by the Aragon coat of arms, added in the 1400s. It was here in the great hall that representatives from the five *campate* (regions of Sicily) met to constitute the Sicilian Parliament of 1295. The top of the castle provides a breathtaking view of the Aeolian Islands (from the left: Vulcano, Lipari, Panarea and, on particularly clear days, Stromboli) and the Bay of Tono.

CITTA BASSA

The lower part of town is the more modern section of Milazzo, built in the 18C when the decision to abandon the old town centre was taken in favour of a flatter site, nearer the sea. At the heart of this part of town is the piazza Caio Duilio, beside which a fish market takes place every morning. Facing onto the west side of the piazza is Palazzo Marchese Proto (once Garibaldi's headquarters); the eastern side is graced with the **Chiesa del Carmine**'s elegant **façade★**, composed of a lovely doorway (1620), an architrave sculpted with garlands and volutes, and a niche containing the statue of the Madonna della Consolazione (1632). This is flanked by the graceful frontage of the Convento del Carmine, where municipal offices are now located.

Continue along the old strada Reale, now via Umberto I, past the occasional noble *palazzo*, now in a poor state of repair. On the parallel street, via Cumbo Borgia, is the **Duomo Nuovo** ⊘, built in the 1930s. Its interior is hung with a few prized paintings: on the high altar, figures of St Peter and St Paul (1531) frame the wooden effigy of St Stephen; these panels are from a dismantled polyptych by

Antonello de Saliba, who also painted the *Adoration of the Shepherds*, the luminous *Annunciation* painted with vibrant colours typical of the Venetian School and the *St Nicholas Enthroned with Scenes from his Life* are both attributed to Antonio Guffrè, a painter of the Antonelli School (end of the 15C).

Posted at the crossroads with via Cristoforo Colombo is the Liberty-style **Villino Greco**, with its fine friezes of stylised flowers and organic decoration.

SIGHTSEEING EXCURSION *About 8km/5mi by car*

Take the **Lungomare Garibaldi** along the seafront, overlooked by the elegant proportions of the 18C frontage of Palazzo dei Marchesi D'Amico, and cross the waterfront district of Vaccarella which begins with the piazza before the church Santa Maria Maggiore; follow the **panoramic road★** which runs along the eastern side of the Milazzo promontory to the end. Arriving at **Capo Milazzo★**, pause to take in the wonderful **view★★** of the surrounding landscape: intense greens merging with the burnt browns of the Mediterranean *maquis* extend over the rocky spur to blend with the dazzling blue of the sea beyond.

From the left side of piazza Sant'Antonio, a short flight of steps drops down to the **Santuario di Sant'Antonio di Padova** and the bay it overlooks, to which it has lent its name. The place is so called after, it is said, St Antony of Padua sought refuge in a cave here during a storm in 1221. Since then, it has been a place of pilgrimage; it was transformed into a sanctuary in 1575 under the patronage of a nobleman, Andrea Guerrera; in the 18C it was further endowed with altars and decoration of polychrome marble, and some new panels in shallow relief depicting scenes from the life of the saint.

To return a different route, take the road along the ridge of the little peninsula: cruise past several of the many elegant villas, and fork right along the road to **Monte Trino**, the highest point on this tongue of land, unfortunately spoilt by the erection of telecommunications transmitters. The name is all that remains of a temple, dedicated, it would seem in Greek and Roman times, to the pagan triad of Apollo, Diana and Isis (or Osiris). From the little piazza before the small **Chiesetta della Santissima Trinità**, there are wonderful **views★** over Milazzo, its citadel and the sickle-shaped promontory.

To the west, the coast opens out into a beautiful long strip of sand. This is followed by the coastal road to the **Grotta di Polifemo**, where Ulysses' mythical meeting with the Cyclops is supposed to have taken place.

In front of the cave stretches the broad beach that lines the glorious **Baia del Tono** (known locally as *Ngonia*, from the Greek word for bay). A little further on may be seen the remains of the former **tuna fishery**, although these are now incorporated into a tourist complex.

EXCURSIONS INLAND

Santa Lucia del Mela – *13km/8mi S*. The little town is overshadowed by the silhouette of the **castle** which was built in the 9C by the Arabs, and altered during the Swabian and Aragonese occupations. Little survives other than a massive round tower fortifying the main gateway, part of a triangular bastion, and sections of the defensive walls which shelter the **Santuario della Madonna della Neve** ⊘ (1673). Inside hangs a lovely *Madonna of the Snow* by **Antonello Gagini** (1529). The terrace to the left of the church affords good views of the surrounding countryside, of the stone-dressed church corner and window surrounds.

On the way down into the town, there is an elegant Renaissance **doorway★** gracing the front of the **Chiesa Madre di Santa Lucia** (17C): note the lunette containing a relief of the Madonna attended by St Agatha and St Lucy, with the royal eagle, symbol of regal patronage. To the left of the church is piazza del Duomo and the Bishop's Palace, marked by its heavily rusticated entrance.

Left of the **Chiesa dell'Annunziata** *(in via Garibaldi)* stands a wonderful 15C campanile with three tiers of single openings surrounded with volcanic stone. The doorway, which dates from 1587, is ornamented with panels of delicate relief illustrating the *Annunciation*, surrounded with a garland of organic decoration.

★ **Roccavaldina** – *Approx 15km/9mi SE*. The main attraction of this little town is the extraordinary apothecary's **pharmacy** ⊘ which in itself is quite unique. The shopfront consists of a fine 16C Tuscan-style doorway flanked by a stone counter from which members of the public used to be served. Inside, arranged on the fabulous old wooden shelves are a rare **collection of maiolica drug jars★★** (or *albarello*) datable from about 1580. Indeed, what is truly exceptional about this collection is that all the pieces come from the famous Patanazzi family workshop in Urbino, having been commissioned by the Messina herbalist Cesare Candia (whose coat of arms, a dove and three stars on a turquoise background, can be seen on each and every one of the 238 jars assembled). The collection, acquired by a priest from Rocca, has been in the town since 1628; it includes long-necked vases, small jugs with handle and spout, and *albarelli* (typical, tall, pharmacy jars) bearing scenes from the Bible, Classical mythology or the history of Ancient Rome. There are two magnificent display amphorae (note their wonderful handles) decorated, in relief, with characteristic grotesques and a narrative panel: Julius Caesar receiving Senior Captivi *(right)* and the contest of Apollo versus Marsyas who, on losing, was tied to a tree and flayed alive.

Overlooking the same piazza is the 16C **castle**, a transitional building between a fortress and an aristocratic residence; the massive walls along the right side are tempered by the elegant balconies and their voluted brackets.

On the edge of the town, set in the gardens of the former Capuchin monastery, stands a gracious **municipal villa**, enjoying a privileged situation with a panoramic **view**★ over the promontory of Milazzo and the fortress of Venetico Superiore with its four round towers.

Rometta – *20km/12mi SE*. Strategically positioned at a height of 600m/1 968ft, Rometta has earned its place in history by courageously resisting the Arab invaders: it was the last town to fall into their hands in 965. Little remains of the city walls other than the two pointed gateways, Porta Milazzo and Porta Messina.

The **Chiesa Madre** dedicated to the Madonna of the Assumption, has a fine doorway *(left side)* decorated with a frieze of organic and animal motifs. From the ruins of Frederick II's **castle**, there is a wonderful **view**★ of Capo Milazzo and the Aeolian Islands.

MILITELLO IN VAL DI CATANIA

Catania – Population 9 076
Michelin map 432 P 26

The Baroque town of Militello is largely indebted to Joan of Austria (1573-1630), Charles V's grand-daughter, for its prosperity: when she married Francesco Branciforte, she came to the place with her predilection for sophisticated culture and her taste for beautiful things. Militello was transformed into an aristocratic court and enjoyed living its period of glory to the full. As a result, the streets of the old town centre bristle with a multitude of fine Baroque buildings.

Monastero Benedettino ⊘ – *Piazza del Municipio*. The imposing Benedictine monastery (1614-41), now used as the town hall, has a highly decorative frontage. The main **façade** of the **church** next door is ornamented with rusticated window surrounds, a common feature peculiar to the Militello style of Baroque. Inside, it contains Sebastiano Conca's painting of *The Last Communion of St Benedict (third chapel on the left)* and a fine set of carved wooden choir stalls depicting the Mysteries and scenes from the life of St Benedict (1734).

Continue along via Umberto, past the 18C Palazzo Reforgiato, to piazza Vittorio Emanuele.

Museo di San Nicolò ⊘ – The museum is housed in the undercrofts of the Chiesa Madre, built in 1721. The objects displayed are **fabulously arranged**★ so as to enhance their beauty and heighten their impact. These include a fine collection of 17C and 18C religious vestments, prized treasures from the town's various other churches – notably the silver plate from Santa Maria alla Catena, as well as the jewellery, votive and liturgical objects from Sant'Agata. The last rooms are devoted to pictures: an altarpiece Annunciation by Francesco Franzetto (1552), a strongly lit Caravaggesque *Attack on San Carlo Borromeo* by the Tuscan painter Filippo Paladini (1612), and a gentle treatment of the *Immacolata* by Vaccaro.

Santa Maria alla Catena ⊘ – The oratory was rebuilt in 1652. Its fine **interior**★ is encrusted with lovely **stuccowork** by artists from Acireale; this represents in the upper tier, scenes from the Joyful Mysteries, while the lower tier harbours various Sicilian saints surrounded by cherubs, festoons and cornucopias. The overall effect is completed by an elegant coffered wooden ceiling from 1661.

Turn left onto via Umberto. Beyond the attractively concave façade of the Chiesa del Santissimo Sacramento al Circolo, lies piazza Maria Santissima della Stella.

Maria Santissima della Stella ⊘ – This church, with its fine doorway and spiral columns, was erected between 1722 and 1741. Inside, it preserves a magnificent glazed terracotta **Nativity altarpiece**★ (1487) by the early Renaissance Florentine master **Andrea della Robbia**. The **Treasury** contains a fine late-15C altarpiece with scenes from the life of St Peter by the Maestro della Croce di Piazza Armerina, and the *Portrait of Pietro Speciale*, a shallow relief by **Francesco Laurana**.

Palazzo Majorana, one of the few buildings dating from the 16C, extends along the same side of the square beside the church. Note its heavily rusticated corner stones bearing carved lions.

At the far end of the palazzo, turn left, then immediately right for Santa Maria la Vetere up ahead.

Chiesa di Santa Maria la Vetere – Most of church collapsed following the earthquake of 1693, leaving only the wall of the south aisle intact. Above the front entrance with its 16C porch, sits a lunette enclosing shallow reliefs. The overall **impact★** is heightened by the splendid orientation of the church, nestling in its green valley, right on the edge of town.

Return the way you have come and turn left so as to skirt around the ruins of the Branciforti castle (comprising a round tower and sections of wall), pass through the town gate – Porta della Terra – and reach the piazza beyond.

At the centre of what once constituted the castle courtyard sits a fountain: **Fontana della Ninfa Zizza**, built in 1607 to commemorate the opening of Militello's first aqueduct, sponsored by Branciforte.

Pass back through the town gate and turn immediately left for the Chiesa dei Santissimi Angeli Custodi.

The **Chiesa dei Santissimi Angeli Custodi** ⊙ contains a wonderful maiolica **floor★** laid with tiles from Caltagirone (1785).

AND IF, AFTER EXPLORING THE TOWN....

...hunger sets in – The oil-mill *trattoria*, U' Trappitu (via Principe Branciforte 125; ☎ 095 81 14 47; closed Mon) preserves its very own olive-press from 1927. Carefully converted, the building effectively retains its original character, although it is its unusual furnishings that lend atmosphere to the place: the assortment of tools and equipment includes mill-wheels, olive-presses and *coffe*, sisal recipients for containing the olive pulp from the first pressing. Approximately 35 000L for a meal.

... or your sweet tooth needs satisfying – The seasonal specialities in the sweets line associated with Militello range from the *cassatelline* – made with ground almonds, chocolate and cinnamon; the *mastrazzuoli* – Christmas titbits made with almonds, cinnamon and vermouth (cooked wine); to the *mostarda* – concocted from semolina or wine must, boiled with prickly-pear extract (available around the second or third Sunday in October, for the Sagra della Mostarda).

EXCURSIONS

Mineo – *17km/11mi W*. The place where the writer Luigi Capuana (1839-1915) was born has its origins in Antiquity, especially since it has been identified as the ancient town of Mene, founded by Ducetius, the king of the Siculi. The town's main gateway, Porta Adinolfo, is 18C; beside it sits the Jesuit College; while beyond lies the main square and the **Chiesa del Collegio**. Via Umberto I leads into piazza Agrippina, where a 15C church (apses) with the same name is to be found. At the top of the town, next to the Church of Santa Maria, lie the ruins of a castle. From here, a wonderful view extends over the whole valley.

Scordia – *10km/6mi E*. Scordia is built on a rectilinear town plan, arranged around the *palazzo* of the Branciforti family, the lords of the town during the 17C. The main square, piazza Umberto, is enclosed by noble *palazzi* and a church with a lofty front elevation, dedicated to San Rocco.

The 18C **Santa Maria Maggiore** has an interesting façade incorporating a bell-tower. From Scordia, it is possible to drive to Palagonia without a detour via Militello in Val Catania. The SS 385 picks its way through **rolling landscape★** past the lush groves of lemon and orange trees for which the area is famous, and the small rocky hills known as *Coste* to the south.

Palagonia – *15km/9mi NE*. For the Siculi, Palagonia was important in both political and religious terms: according to local legend, it was from the bubbling sulphurous waters of the **Laghetto di Naftia** that their gods, the **Palici**, were born and it is to them that they dedicated the temple built on the edge of the lake. Nowadays, the lake is masked from view by installations for collecting the natural gas for industrial purposes.

Eremo di Santa Febronia – *Follow the S 385 from Palagonia towards Catania; take the right fork signposted for Contrada Croce. 4.5km/3mi further on, as the road curves to the right, look out for a track on the left barricaded by a metal barrier. The hermitage is a 15min walk up the track.*

The evocative little hermitage is named after Santa Febronia, known locally as *a' Santuzza*, because her relics are brought here each year in a great procession from nearby Palagonia. The small retreat, carved out of the rock, is Byzantine in date (7C). Inside, the apse contains a fine, albeit damaged, fresco of Christ flanked by the Madonna and an angel.

MODICA★

Ragusa – Population 52 257
Michelin map 432 Q 26

Modica before the earthquake and after; Modica before the flood and after: twice the town has been devastated, turned upside-down, destroyed or badly damaged, and twice it has pulled itself together ready to face the future. Before the earthquake, a large proportion of the population lived in troglodyte dwellings cut into the steep lime-stone cliffs surrounding the modern town. In the centre, stood the castle enclosed on the north side by walls, isolated on its rocky spur. Nestling in the valley, there flowed two rivers which converged midway to form the River Scicli (or Motucano). Then, as the threat of attack slowly dwindled, the people moved down into the valley; it was not until the terrible earthquake of 1693, however, that the cave dwellings were finally abandoned. The town clustered naturally into a Y-shape around the confluence of the two rivers. Unity was ensured by a succession of 20 bridges between the different banks, transforming the place into a veritable city on water and earning it the epithet "Venice of the South". Then the second disaster struck: a series of freak storms in 1902 raised the water level to a terrifying height of 9m/29ft at the confluence. The town took it all in its stride: the waterways were sealed off and transformed into wide streets that became the main thoroughfares of modern-day Modica.

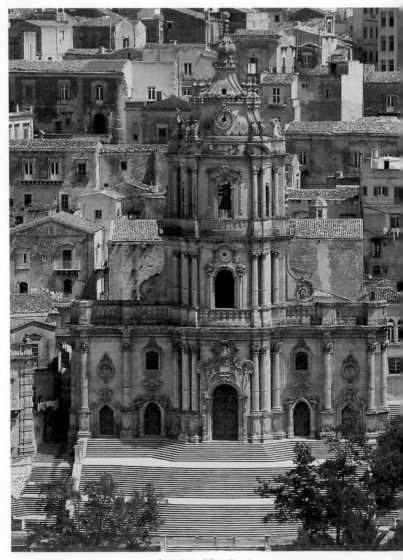

Cathedral of San Giorgio

🏠 corso Umberto I 246, ☎ 0932 75 27 47, Fax 0932 75 28 97.

GETTING TO MODICA

The most convenient way of reaching the town is by **car**, although **train** (20min from Ragusa and approx 2hr from Siracusa) and **bus** services are also available (for information contact the tourist office).

EATING OUT

Fattoria delle Torri – Vico Napolitano 14, ☎ 0932 75 12 86. Closed Mon. This attractive restaurant serves a range of interesting and creative dishes based on local specialities. Excellent wine list. Approximately 70 000L for a meal.

L'Arco – Piazza Corrado Rizzone 11 (at the end of corso Umberto I), ☎ 0932 94 27 27. Closed Mon. A trattoria serving home-made, regional cuisine. Approximately 35 000L for a meal.

The **Antica Dolcerìa Bonajuto**, corso Umberto I 195, offers delicacies such as *mpanatigghi*: sweet pastries with an unusual filling of minced meat and chocolate; *liccumie*: consisting of aubergine (egg-plant) and vanilla- and cinnamon-flavoured chocolate made according to the original Aztec recipe; and *riposti*: delicately decorated almond sweets, originally produced for weddings. Closed Mon.

Caffè delle Arti – Via Umberto I. Closed Wed. This café sells sweet Sicilian specialities such as *cannoli* and *cassate*.

A TWO-TOWN CITY

Modica divides naturally into two parts: the centre lies in the lower town, hemmed in by high ground; the upper town, dominated by the castle, occupies that same high ground. Modica Bassa (lower Modica) aligns itself with the two main streets **via Marchesa Tedeschi** and **corso Umberto** that converge to form a Y *(see above)*. Since the 19C, the two sections of the town have been dramatically linked by a fabulous stairway leading up from corso Umberto to San Giorgio, Modica's most beautiful church: this most magnificent among Baroque buildings must surely be the obvious point with which to begin a description of the city.

★★San Giorgio ⊘ – The flight of almost 300 steps pays homage to the elegant façade, merging with it to produce a most dramatic **composition★★**. Traditionally, its conception has been attributed to Rosario Gagliardi, although some claim the design to result from a collaboration of architects from Noto, notably Paolo Labisi; either way, it was completed in the 19C. The stairway was finished in 1818. The lofty front elevation rises through three levels to a single bell-tower; a sense of sweeping movement is imparted by the projecting convex central bay, flanked to each side by twin bays that accommodate the double aisles. A balustrade and a pair of compact volutes act to soften the strong horizontal transition between the ground and first levels.

Inside, St George's contains a highly prized chased silver altar front upon which sits a fine **polyptych** (1513) by Bernardino Niger. The three tiers show the Holy Family between St George and St Martin with, above, the Joyful Mysteries and the Glorious Mysteries. The transept floor is inlaid with a 19C meridian line by A Perini. The third chapel on the right contains an Assumption altarpiece by Francesco Paladini.

Beside the church stands **Palazzo Polara** which houses the **Pinacoteca Comunale** ⊘, and its collection of contemporary paintings.

Via Posteria harbours the **Casa Natale di Salvatore Quasimodo** ⊘, the house where the 20C poet was born, containing furniture and possessions from the writer's study in Milan.

Continue on down to corso Umberto I, the main thoroughfare of the Città Bassa (lower town), lined with elegant 18C *palazzi* and religious institutions. At the north end sits **Palazzo Manenti**, ornamented with carved stone portraits of various famous figures living in the 18C. As the street approaches the centre, it passes the lovely undulating façade of **Santa Maria del Soccorso** and, a little further on, the Church of San Pietro.

San Pietro – St Peter's was also rebuilt after the earthquake: a flight of steps lead up to the front **façade★**, ornamented with statues representing the twelve Apostles.

Chiesa Rupestre di San Nicola Inferiore ⊘ – Nestling in the apse of the rock-hewn church are a series of Byzantine-style frescoes dating from the Norman era. Pride of place is given to Christ Pantocrator (in the centre) surrounded by His almond-shaped aura; at His sides, stand the Madonna and Child and the Archange Michael, together with a host of saints in attendance. The church, probably consecrated to serve the Greek Orthodox community, consists of a simple hall church its nave terminated with an apse would originally have been segregated by a wal in accordance with Basilian prototypes.

At the intersection with the other branch of the Y (via Marchesa Tedeschi) stands **San Domenico** with, beyond, the town hall. This provides a good view of the round tower of the castle above, clinging to its rock, surmounted since the 18C with a clock tower. Almost opposite, the little via De Leva leads through to the *palazzo* which shares its name, and which is graced with a fine **Chiaramonte Gothic** entranceway. Before the end of the street stands the Baroque **Chiesa del Carmine** which only preserves a doorway with, above, a magnificent rose-window from the original Chiaramonte church. Continue as far as the junction with via Mercé and turn right: up ahead are located the Church of the Madonna delle Grazie and the **Convento dei Padre Mercedari** which now houses the **Museo Civico** ⊘. This displays artefacts from the local area and a collection of locally-made examples of rural handicraft.

★ **Museo delle Arti e Tradizioni Popolari** ⊘ – This museum, dedicated to the rural arts, crafts and practices, displays a vast collection of farming tools, furnishings and hand-made bits and pieces. What makes this museum especially unusual and effective is the way objects are presented in their "natural context" as part of an integral arrangement. The reconstituted workshop interiors are self-explanatory alongside the farmstead, the mainstay of any agricultural peasant community, there is the bee-keeper, blacksmith, cobbler, tailor, cartwright, pastry cook, not forgetting the barber's shop.

Behind the castle in via Crispi, sits **Palazzo Tomasi Rosso** with its decorative limestone doorway and balconies; note the stone-carved grimacing masks and acanthus leaves and finely wrought iron railings.

Via Marchesa Tedeschi, the other arm of the Y, climbs up to *Modica Alta* (upper Modica). At one time, these two towns were legally and administratively autonomous.

Santa Maria di Betlem ⊘ – This church preserves *(at the far end on the right)* through an elegant 15C doorway, the attractive **Capella Cabrera**.

An elaborate 19C Nativity scene in the north aisle comprises 60 or so terracotta figures modelled by G Papale.

The street continues uphill past the 19C Baroque-fronted Church of **San Giovann Evangelista**, elevated up a broad set of steps. At the top (Belvedere del Pizzo), a splendid **view**★ extends over the town encompassing, in particular, the Jewish quarter known as *il Cartellone (on the right, beyond corso Umberto I)*, and the Francavilla district *(the near side of corso Umberto I)*, the oldest part of town dominated by San Giorgio.

MONREALE★★★

Palermo – Population 29 128
Michelin map 432 M 21

Monreale perches high above the Conca d'Oro, enjoying a splendid view over the broad
bay with Palermo in the distance. In Norman times Monte Reale was a royal hunting
ground where, before long, the reigning monarch had a hunting-lodge built. It was not
until William II decided to build the famous cathedral, with a royal palace and monastery
attached, that a town developed in its own right in the area. Even today, the life and
soul of the place radiates very much from around these same buildings. On the north
side lies piazza Vittorio Emanuele with its Fontana del Tritone. The main front, however,
overlooks the smaller piazza Guglielmo which provides access to both the cloisters and
a small **public garden** *(last doorway on the right facing the cloisters entrance)*. The garden
extends beyond a large courtyard, offering a magnificent **view★★** over the Conca d'Oro.
In the warren of neighbouring streets nestle a variety of little souvenir shops, bars
and small restaurants.

🛈 piazza Duomo, ☎ 091 63 98 011, Fax 091 63 75 400.

GETTING TO MONREALE

If travelling to Monreale by **car** from Palermo on viale Regione Siciliana, take
the Calatafimi-Monreale exit and then follow the N 186. For visitors without
their own transport, bus nos 309 and 389 connect piazza dell'Indipendenza
with Monreale. For information contact AMAT, ☎ 091 35 01 11.

WHERE TO STAY

Baglio Conca d'Oro – Via Aquino 19c, ☎ 091 64 06 286, Fax 091 64 08 742. This
magnificently restored 18C paper mill is situated in Borgo Molara, just outside
Palermo *(from viale Regione Siciliana follow signs to Sciacca and the N 624)*,
3km/1.8mi from Monreale. The hotel has 27 elegant rooms, some of which
enjoy views of the Conca d'Oro, Monreale and the Gulf of Palermo. A double
room costs approx 300 000L.

EATING OUT

Taverna del Pavone – Vicolo Pensato 18 (☎ 091 64 06 209; closed Mon and from
26 Sept to 10 Oct). This restaurant specialises in creative, traditional cuisine.
Approximately 50 000L for a meal.

★★DUOMO

In addition to the cathedral, this splendid complex of buildings comprising a
Benedictine abbey and a royal palace (converted in the late 16C into the
Archbishop's Seminary), was initiated by the grandson of Roger II, **William II**, around
1172. Legend relates how the Madonna appeared to him in a dream to suggest
that he build a church with money concealed by his father in a hiding place that
she would reveal. The building should be so grandiose as to rival the splendour of
the greatest cathedrals of other European cities and should outshine the beauty of
the Palatine Chapel in Palermo built by his grandfather, Roger. And so the most
highly skilled craftsmen came to be employed to work on the project, with no
expense spared. To the north, the church was flanked by the royal palace and, to
the south, by the Benedictine monastery, of which the magnificent cloisters can
still be admired today.

Exterior

The church is the product of a blend of artistic styles implemented by a combination of craftsmen. The two great towers on either side of the main front are
quintessentially Norman in concept, as are the apses (one tall one flanked by two
smaller ones), the basilica plan and, therefore, the fundamental arrangement of
the cathedral. The superficial decoration applied to the **apses**, on the other hand,
is clearly Moorish in origin: this can best be **viewed★★** from via dell'Arcivescovado.
From the same street, it is possible to make out the vestiges of the original royal
palace now incorporated within the Archbishop's Palace.
The apses are articulated with three tiers of intersecting blind arcading: the pointed
arches, of varying heights, rise from tall bases through slender columns. The decorative effect is heightened by the use of two different kinds of stone (warm
gold-coloured limestone and black lava) as the ribs enclose rectangles filled with
miniature circular rose-windows traceried with kaleidoscopic star patterns. The
same elements are repeated on the façade, although the full impact is marred some-

233

what by the portico that was rebuilt in the 18C. This shelters the magnificent great bronze **doors**★★, designed in 1185 by **Bonanno Pisano** – the architect and sculptor responsible for the famous Leaning Tower of Pisa. It comprises 46 panels illustrating scenes from the Old and New Testaments. The surprisingly modern feel to this work is accomplished by an economical use of figures and a refined degree of stylisation. The two doors are hung within an elaborately moulded stone door frame in which panels of geometric motifs alternate with animals and human figures concealed among branching plant fronds in shallow relief and narrow strips of mosaic. The lateral entrance, beneath a 16C portico, also consists of bronze **doors**★ with several narrative panels, this time by Barisano da Trani. The three Biblical stories and scenes from the lives of various saints are incoporated among a range of decorative elements, only this time the style is more wooden, more firmly rooted in the Byzantine tradition, even though they were executed only four years later.

Interior ⊘ *Entrance from the west end. Visitors are advised to take several 500L coins for the coin-operated lighting of the mosaics.*

For a brief moment the elaborate, predominantly golden mantle of mosaics is spellbinding. Gradually the eye grows accustomed to the crowded mass of forms and gleaming designs, focusing on the internal space enclosed by the individual parts of the church. The wide nave is separated from the two much smaller side aisles by columns with splendid capitals, some Corinthian, others of a composite order with acanthus leaves below and portraits of Demeter and Persephone (Ceres and Proserpine) above. The capitals and the intrados (curved inner surface of the springer arches) sandwich dosserets decorated with Moorish mosaics. Just beyond the half-way mark, the nave is interrupted by a monumental triumphal arch preceding the spacious area contained by the transept and apses, that rise up and above the level of the nave and aisles. This section of the floor is of inlaid marble, as are the skirting and lower part of the walls, echoing Byzantine influences. The wooden ceiling above the choir is 19C.

The church contains the tombs of William I and William II *(south transept)*; the altar in the north transept encloses the heart of Louis IX (St Louis), King of France, who died in Tunis in 1270 while his brother Charles I ruled Sicily.

The Cappella del Crocifisso★ ⊘, situated in the north apse, is elaborately decked with marble Baroque decoration: with a profusion of inlay work, shallow- and high-relief carving, figurative statues and volutes. The wooden Crucifix dates from the 1400s. The **treasury**, set to one side, houses various reliquaries and other cult objects.

Below the arch across the far side of the transept sit two thrones with mosaic scenes above: the right one, above the archbishop's throne, shows William II's symbolic tribute to the church (the king offers up a model of the cathedral to the Madonna); on the left, the royal throne stands as confirmation of the Divine Protection conferred upon the king (Christ Himself crowns William). This latter panel depicts two lions facing each other (Eastern in derivation) in the tympanum: these symbols of Norman power also feature on the armrests of the royal throne.

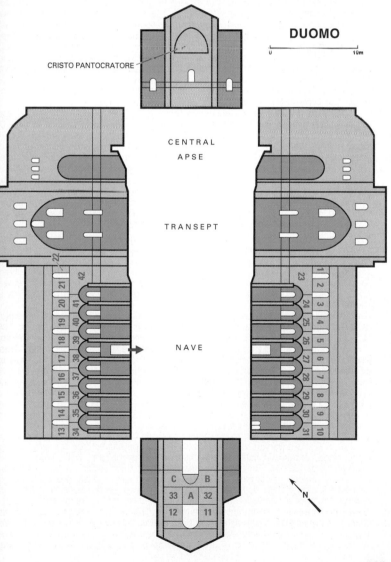

★★★ **Mosaics** – Against a gold background, the characters of the Bible re-enact their stories. The colours are not as bright as those of the contemporary mosaics in the Palatine Chapel, but the figures are represented with greater realism and are endowed with more expressive personality. These mosaics were completed during the late 12C and early 13C by craftsmen from Venice and Sicily. The compositions and their component elements, together with the symbols used, are often the same as those used in the Palatine Chapel. The sequential order of the scenes represented follows a precise programme in accordance with recommendations laid down under the papacy of Adrian I by the Seventh General Council at the Second Council of Nicaea, that was convened so as to end the Iconoclastic Controversy (787). This specified that art should be an instrument of religion and the liturgy, and serve to educate the faithful in the teachings of the Christian Church. The mosaics tell the story of Divine Redemption, beginning with the Creation of the Earth and Man, who by committing the act of Original Sin was forced thenceforth to toil and expiation, until God intervened by choosing the people that He will prepare for salvation *(nave)*. The sending of Christ His own Son represents the realisation of redemption through the sacrifice of His life *(transept)* and works *(aisles)*. Christ's mission is then continued with the foundation of the Church and the example given by those men that followed in His example *(smaller apses)*.

The individual scenes are full of realistically portrayed incidental detail: the ropes that bind the scaffolding erected around the Tower of Babel (**29**); the knives on the table of the Wedding at Cana *(high up on the left-hand side of the crossing)*; the coins falling from the table upset by Christ when He chased the moneylenders from the temple *(about half way along the north aisle)*; the astonishing variety of fish depicted in the Creation (**6**) and caught in the fishermen's nets illustrating the Miraculous draft of fishes *(north transept)*. Many iconographic symbols are used like the cloud *(used to denote transportation to another world)* that wraps itself around the figures that have fallen asleep as in the angel appearing to Joseph *(crossing, on the right)*, or the little dark figure that appears in several scenes representing the devil, being cast out of those possessed or simply haunting evil people. Note also how the soul of Abel is depicted as a small red figure of spilt blood (**20**). Christ Pantocrator majestically fills the **central apse**, with the Virgin and Child below pictured among angels and Apostles. The lowest tier is populated with saints. Below the arch, in the middle, is the Throne of Judgement.

The vaults of the **lateral apses** accommodate the figures of St Peter *(right)* and St Paul *(left)* with scenes from their lives below.

The life of Christ is depicted in the **chancel**, starting at the crossing where stories from His childhood are related. Christ's adult life is represented in the transept *(starting with south side)*, up until the descent of the Holy Spirit. The aisles illustrate a selection of Christ's miracles. In the **triumphal arch**, above the archbishop's throne *(right)*, King William II offers up a model of the cathedral to the Virgin; above the royal throne *(opposite)*, William II is crowned by Christ.

The **nave** is devoted entirely to the Old Testament: listed below are the chapters from this extraordinary picture book. Where appropriate, explanatory notes are given to help unravel some of the more complex stories.

Nave – *Starting from the beginning of the nave on the right-hand side (south wall)* (**1**) The spirit of God moving upon the face of the waters. (**2**) God dividing the light from the darkness in the presence of seven angels (for each day of the Creation). (**3**) The making of the firmament (Heaven) to divide the waters above the heavens from those below. (**4**) Separation of the waters into the seas from the land that was Earth. (**5**) Creation of the sun, the moon and the stars. (**6**) Creation of the birds of the air and the fish of the oceans. (**7**) Creation of Man. (**8**) God resting. (**9**) God leads Adam into the Garden of Eden. (**10**) Adam in the Garden of Eden. (**11**) Creation of Eve. (**12**) Eve is presented to Adam. (**13**) Eve is tempted by the Serpent. (**14**) Original Sin. (**15**) God discovers that Adam and Eve are ashamed of their nudity. (**16**) Adam and Eve are expelled from Earthly Paradise. (**17**) Adam working. Eve is seated with a spindle in her hand. (**18**) Sacrifice of Cain and Abel. *Only the sacrifice of Abel pleases God, symbolised by the ray of light shining straight from the Lord's hand.* (**19**) Cain slays Abel. (**20**) God discovers Cain's crime and curses him. (**21**) Cain is slain by Lamech *(a story from the Jewish tradition and not mentioned in Genesis)*. (**22**) God commands Noah to build an Ark. (**23**) Noah builds the Ark. (**24**) The animals board the Ark. (**25**) Noah welcomes the dove carrying the olive sprig, the sign that the waters have abated. (**26**) The animals come out of the Ark. (**27**) Noah's sacrifice as a sign of thanks to God. Behind him is the rainbow, the symbol of God's covenant with Man. (**28**) The grape-harvest *(on the left)*. On the right, Noah, drunk and half-naked, is discovered by his son, Ham, who calls his brothers to deride him. They are more respectful of their father's dignity and cover his nudity. *Hence the reason for Noah to curse Ham and his descendants, the Canaanites. This is why, henceforth, fathers often express the hope that their sons should not take a Canaanite wife.* (**29**) Noah's descendants unite and build the Tower of Babel in an attempt to reach heaven; this results in chaos. *God, fearing that the force of Man might overthrow Him, caused the people to quarrel with each other, to confound their language and scatter them abroad: this story is often taken to be a parable for upholding Church authority in the face of Man's litigiousness*

(**30**) Abraham, *having settled in the land of Sodom and Gomorrah*, encounters three angels sent by God and invites them to his house. *The angels represent the Trinity.* (**31**) The hospitality of Abraham. (**32**) *God sends two angels to destroy Sodom. Lot, Abraham's nephew, shows them hospitality.* Lot tries to prevent the inhabitants of Sodom from entering the house where the two angels are.

(**A**) *The following scene does not come from the Old Testament but relates to the story about St Cassius, St Castus and St Castrense (patron saint of Monreale) which continue in the tier below.* Cassius and Castus, condemned to being thrown to the lions because they refused to renounce their faith in Christ, are saved when the lions are suddenly tamed and lick their feet. (**B**) Cassius and Castus are taken to a pagan temple causing it to collapse onto the infidels. (**C**) St Castrense cures a man possessed of the Devil who throws himself into the sea and causes a storm. (**33**) Sodom in flames while Lot flees with his daughters; his wife, turning round to look back, is transformed into a pillar of salt. (**34**) God appears to Abraham and bids him to sacrifice his only son, Isaac. (**35**) The angel of the Lord stops Abraham from sacrificing his son. (**36**) *Abraham sends a servant to seek a wife for Isaac.* At the well, Rebecca offers up water to Abraham's servant and his camels to drink. (**37**) Rebecca sets out on the journey to her chosen bridegroom, Isaac. (**38**) Isaac with his favourite son Esau, and his second son Jacob. (**39**) Isaac blesses Jacob, believing mistakenly that he is Esau *(depicted on the right, as he returns from hunting). Isaac, who is almost blind in his old age, is deceived by the goatskins covering the arms of Jacob who, unlike his brother, is smooth-skinned.* (**40**) Jacob flees from the vengeful anger of his brother, from whom he has stolen his father Isaac's blessing. (**41**) On his journey, Jacob dreams of a ladder leading from earth up to heaven being ascended by angels. God, at the top, grants him the land on which he has fallen asleep; on awaking, Jacob takes the stones he had been using as pillows and lays them down as a foundation for his city. (**42**) Jacob wrestles with the angel. *On his journey back to his brother Esau's, fearing lest he should be angry, Jacob sent forth his sheep and goats as offerings to him. That night, having made his family ford the stream, an angel approached and wrestled with him until dawn, when the angel blessed Jacob and bestowed upon him a new name: Israel (meaning the one who has fought with God and with Man, and has prevailed).*

★★ **Ascent to the terraces** ⊙ – *Access from the far end of the south aisle; but beware, it involves a long and arduous climb.* The first outlook provides a marvellous view down over the cloisters. Further round, there is a wonderful view of the **apses**★★. The last, highest section provides wonderful **views**★★ of the Conca d'Oro.

★★ Cloisters ⊙

The huge cloisters, one of the finest examples of a building inspired by Islamic architecture, present a series of pointed arches supported by sets of splendid small paired columns, many decorated with polychrome mosaic that is Eastern in inspiration. Those columns marking each corner of the cloisters, together with those at the corner of the tiny square cloisters surrounding the fountain *(south-west corner)* are sculpted with animals and human figures interwoven among fronds of luxuriant vegetation. The true jewels in the crown, however, are the fabulous **Romanesque capitals**, each distinctively different and imaginatively carved. The subject matter is drawn both from medieval and Classical iconography. Without following any particular sequence – implying that the capitals were intended as merely decorative – scenes from the Gospels alternate with stories from the Old Testament, symbolic and purely

The cloisters

ornamental images, each possessing an originality all of its own. Even the Classical subjects betray a certain inventiveness: the acanthus leaves of the Corinthian capitals, for example, although surprisingly natural-looking, appear to be being ruffled by the wind (b). To these are added a variety of other subjects: birds stretching down to peck the plant volutes of the capital (h), Atlas figures reaching up to support the weight of the arch (m), cherubs feeding animals (u), exotic characters wearing turbans with snakes (t). Perhaps the most remarkable capital is the one (s) in which William II offers up the church to the Madonna: note the detail with which the south side of the church has been carved. One capital depicts a man killing a bull, the sacred symbol of the cult of Mithras (p). Another features an acrobat (o): his position, his weight supported by his arms, his back arched so that his feet rest on the back of his head *(his head in the centre)*, recalls the Trinacria, the ancient symbol of Sicily. The tiny cloisters nestling in the south-west corner, are graced with a lovely **fountain**. The column in the centre of the circular bowl is sculpted with banding and crested with a cluster of animals. The serenity and graciousness of this corner of the cloisters is peculiarly evocative of Persian splendour.

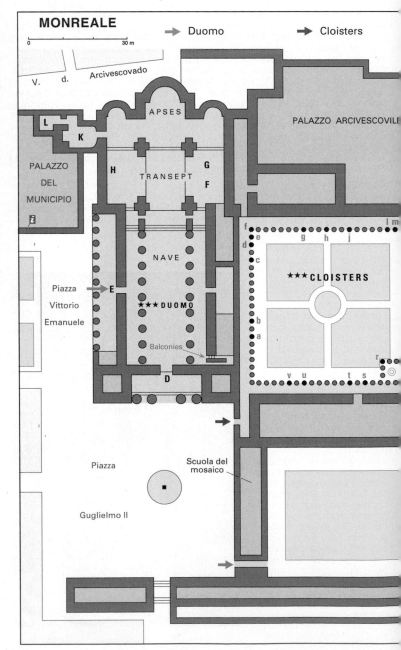

EXCURSIONS

San Martino delle Scale – *10km/6mi W of Monreale*. Pleasantly situated at a height of 548m/1 797ft, this retreat has long been prized for its cool climate during the burning summer months endured by the coast. The town has assumed the name of the Benedictine monastery that was founded in the 6C by St Gregory the Great, and which was rebuilt and enlarged in the 16C. The **church** ⊘ preserves a wonderful **wooden intarsia choir stall**★ dating from the 16C.

The road leading up to the town affords spectacular **views**★★ over the roofs of Monreale, the cathedral, the Conca d'Oro and Palermo.

Castellaccio – *3km/1.8mi W*. The ruins of the late-Norman castle perch on **Monte Caputo**, making for a popular excursion among the locals in the spring and summer as it offers an excellent place for a picnic *(some facilities available)*.

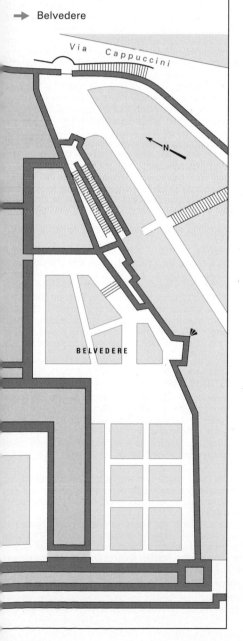

CLOISTERS

a The parable of Dives and Lazarus

b Corinthians capital with windswept leaves

c The story of Samson

d The Massacre of the Innocents

e The Four Evangelists dominated by a mermaid

f The Annunciation

g Owls, symbols of vigilance formerly placed above the monk's cells

h Birds pecking the volutes of the capital

j Joseph sold into slavery in Egypt

l The Resurrection

m Telamons

n Constantine and Helen present the cross of Christ rediscovered on Calvary, symbol of the Church's victory over the Synagogue

o Acrobat

p The cult of Mithras

q The Apostles' mission to evangelise the world: they are depicted in groups of three, in tabernacles protected by a flying angel

r The 12 months of the year

s William II offering Monreale cathedral to the Virgin

t Men of oriental appearance

u Cherubs feeding animals

v The story of Noah

MOZIA★
Trapani
Michelin map 432 N 19

This tiny island in the middle of a lagoon is so small as not to arouse the least suspicion that it might have played any role in the history of its larger neighbour Sicily. Yet, San Pantaleo – its modern name – was chosen by the Phoenicians as a suitable site for a vital and later prosperous colony. Its strategic position, surrounded by the shallow waters of the **Laguna dello Stagnone** *(see below)* and naturally protected by Isola Longa on the seaward side, meant that it was coveted as a strategic trade-post as much by the Carthaginian as by the Syracusan antagonists. In the end, this was to be its undoing: besieged by the Syracusan forces, the old town of Motya was completely destroyed and left abandoned until it was rediscovered at the end of the 19C.

A PHOENICIAN CORNER

The ancient Phoenician colony therefore, was founded in the 8C BC on one of the four islands of the Stagnone Lagoon now known as the **island of San Pantaleo** (the name it assumed in the high Middle Ages when a group of Basilian monks settled there). Motya, the Phoenician name by which it was known before, is alleged to translate loosely as "spinning centre", after wool carding and spinning cottage industries were instituted on the island. Like most other Phoenician colonies, the island became a commercial trade-centre-cum-staging-post for Phoenician ships plying the Mediterranean. The 8C BC also saw the beginning of the Greek colonisation of Sicily which, for the main, was concentrated on the east side of the island. It therefore seemed appropriate for the Phoenicians to consolidate their activities in the west, enabling Motya to grow in importance and to evolve into a small town. In the 6C BC, the struggle for Greek or Carthaginian supremacy over Sicily gained momentum, and Motya was forced into taking sides. Hefty defensive walls were erected around the settlement to provide better protection. In 397 BC, the tyrant of Syracuse, Dionysius the Elder, laid siege to the town until at last it capitulated, snuffing out every last will to continue. Its surviving inhabitants sought refuge on the mainland, and soon integrated themselves among the people of Lilybaeum, modern-day Marsala.

The rediscovery of *Motya* is associated with the name of **Joseph Whitaker**, an English nobleman living in the 1880s related to the family that owned a well-established and flourishing business producing and exporting Marsala wines. The house on the island built for Whitaker now accommodates a small museum.

Access ⊘ – *Leave the car at the landing-stage. Local fishermen assure a regular boat service to and from the island.*

As recently as 1971, it was still possible to ride in a horse-drawn cart across the old Phoenician causeway linking the island to the mainland. Given that the causeway lay just below the surface of the water, passengers had the strange impression that they were "walking on water" *(see Porta Nord below)*. This was also the usual means by which the Grillo grapes grown on the island since the 19C were transported for use in making Marsala. As the island is approached, a profusion of colour and smells seems to emanate from it like a warm welcome: in spring the typical Mediterranean vegetation is especially lush, a perfect excuse in itself for inspiring a visit. In the centre stands the lovely 19C house built by the Whitakers, now a museum.

Excavations – Footpaths run along the perimeter of the island and lead in and among the vestiges of the Phoenician town *(allow 90min; furthermore, you may be well advised to follow the path in an anti-clockwise direction)*.

Fortifications – The island lies in the lee of what was once a peninsula – modern day Isola Longa, naturally protected from attack, therefore, by the mainland and the shallow waters of the lagoon. In order to increase its natural defences, Motya was enveloped by an enclosure wall with watchtowers in the 6C BC. These fortifications were later modified and reinforced. The footpath skirts past the remains of several towers, notably the **east tower** (with a rectangular base) with its staircase up to the ramparts.

Porta Nord – The North Gate is the more important and better preserved of the town's two entrances. The remains of the towers flanking the gateway are still clearly in evidence. Inside, a section of the original main street shows signs of wear, its surface rutted by ancient cart-wheels.

On the seaward side, just below the surface of the water, extends a paved causeway linking Motya to Birgi on the mainland. It covered a distance of some 7km/4.5mi and was just wide enough to accommodate two carts abreast. Today, the way is "waymarked" above the surface allowing the keenest visitors to walk the causeway (although the wearing of rubber flip-flops or plastic sandals is highly recommended).

Enter through the gate and proceed along the main street.

Cappiddazzu – This alludes to the areas that lie just inside the North Gate: among the various buildings, the one divided into three aisles may have served a religious function.

Make your way back towards the shore.

Necropolis – A series of stelae and urns indicate the area used for Archaic cremations and burials. A second necropolis was located on the mainland at Birgi, at the far end of the submerged causeway directly opposite.

Tophet – The sacred area consists of an open-air sanctuary where urns containing the remains from human sacrifices to the goddess Tanit and the god Baal Hammon were deposited. At that time, the immolation of firstborn male children was widespread. A little further along the track, the little island of Schola comes into view: this is the smallest of the Stagnone Lagoon islands, and is distinctively recognisable by its three pink roofless houses.

Cothon – The small rectangular man-made harbour is linked to the sea by a narrow channel. Its exact purpose is not known. Some experts believe it to have been built as a harbour for the smaller, lighter craft that might have plied between the island and the ships moored in the lagoon, ferrying passengers as well as merchandise.

Porta Sud – The South Gate is situated beyond the harbour: like the North Gate, it too is framed by towers.

The small man-made harbour

Casermetta – As its name suggests, this building was reserved for the military: the vertical stone shafts are a typical feature of Phoenician constructions.

Casa dei Mosaici – The house with the mosaics is so called because it preserves two fine black and white pebble panels with a winged griffin chasing a deer, and a lion attacking a bull.

Museum ⊘ – The museum is devoted to displaying artefacts recovered from the island itself, from Lilybaeum (Marsala) and from the necropolis at Birgi, on the shore opposite Motya. In the front courtyard, are arranged a series of stelae from the Tophet. The Phoenician and Punic pottery is simple in shape and devoid of any decoration; the imported Corinthian, Attic and Italiot vases, meanwhile, are decorated with black or red figures. The sculpture collection includes allegorical statuettes of motherhood, like the figurine of the *Great Mother*; terracotta heads betraying a Greek influence; not forgetting the superb **Ephebus of Motya**★★, a noble, proud looking figure wearing a long, pleated garment, most evidently influenced by Hellenistic prototypes.

Casa delle Anfore – The House with the Amphorae is located behind the museum, beyond the houses. It owes its name to the simple fact that a considerable number of amphorae were found there.

LA LAGUNA DELLO STAGNONE

Since 1984, Sicily's largest lagoon (2 000ha/4 940 acres) has been designated a nature reserve of special interest – **Riserva Naturale Orientata**. This area extends into the sea, and includes the section of coastline between Punta Alga and Capo San Teodoro. The water here is shallow and very salty, the ideal conditions for salt-works to be set up all along the coast and on Isola Longa, where it soon became the main industry; many of these have since dwindled into disuse.

The lagoon harbours four islands: Isola Longa is the largest. Santa Maria is covered in vegetation. San Pantaleo is the most important and Schola is a tiny islet with a few roofless houses that give it an eerie air of decadence.

The most common plant species to thrive here include the Aleppo pine, dwarf palm, bamboo (Isola Grande), **sea marigold** *(Calendula maritima)* which, in Europe, grows only here and in Spain, glasswort or sea samphire (with fleshy branches), sea scilla with its star-like white flowers, the sea lily and the sea rush. The islands are also populated with a multitude of bird species, namely the lark, goldfinch, magpie, Kentish plover, tawny pipit and Sardinian warbler – to mention but a few.

The waters of the Stagnone (which literally means large pool) provide fertile habitats for a broad variety of underwater flora and fauna: sea anemones, murex – collected by the Phoenicians so as to extract a valuable purple dye used for colouring textiles – and over 40 different kinds of fish: sea bass, gilthead, white bream and sole. The seabed also supports colonies of the **Poseidonia Oceanica**, a ribbon-leafed seaweed which grows in clusters and produces flowers not unlike an ear of wheat from its centre. This plant is fast becoming a menace to others, spreading itself through the Mediterranean like wildfire: its contribution, however, is to thrive in polluted and slightly stagnant conditions; it stabilises the seabed, oxygenates the water and provides a source of nutrients for other species, thereby playing a role similar to that of the forests on land.

NARO

Agrigento – Population 9 517
Michelin map 432 P 23

Naro was probably founded by the Greeks; what is certain is that it was subjugated, like the surrounding area, to the successive rule of the Greeks, Romans, Arabs and Normans – during whose sovereignty the Duomo was built. Under Frederick II of Swabia it was granted a royal charter and, in the 17C, given the authority to administer justice. The town accumulated considerable wealth in the 17C and 18C, providing it with the means to construct many Baroque *palazzi* and churches; this style continues to be the predominant one of the town, even if, today, a large proportion of buildigs are now rather decrepit.

The town is dominated by the bulky silhouette of the **castle**. This is built in the Chiaramonte style out of irregularly shaped blocks of tuff (consolidated volcanic ash); the only relief is provided on one side of the square tower, by two blind arches and by a fine entrance way.

From here, down via Archeologica, and on the left, sits the **Norman Duomo**. All that now remains is a sad ruin, although fragments of the beautiful Chiaramonte doorway do still grace the main front.

Via Dante – The town's central axis, running from east to west, is lined with elegant Baroque buildings. The street begins at piazza Cavour, passing on the right, the **Chiesa del Santissimo Salvatore** with its elaborate façade; a little further on, in via Cannizzato *(off to the right)*, is another church, **Santa Caterina** ⊙, which was built in 1366, altered in the 18C, and subsequently has been restored to its original appearance. A bold linearity pervades the interior arrangement, relieved in part by a highly decorative Chiaramonte archway.

Santissimo Salvatore, doorway detail

Return to via Dante.

Chiesa Madre ⊙ – This church, built in the 17C by the Jesuits, became the town's main one when the Duomo began to crumble (1867). At the same time, many of the furnishings and works of art were transferred here from the abandoned cathedral, including the carved wooden sacristy furniture with spiral columns intertwined with vines and ornamental half busts (1725). To the left of the entrance is a lovely font from 1424.

A little further on stands the **Chiesa di San Nicolò di Bari** which also boasts a fine early Sicilian Baroque façade.

South of via Dante lies piazza Garibaldi, which is enclosed on all sides by gracious buildings, among the most notable the front of **San Francesco**. The adjacent former Franciscan monastery has attractive cloisters overlooked by municipal offices.

Santuario di San Calogero ⊙ – This is to be found at the far end of corso Umberto I, the eastern continuation of via Dante. The open space-cum-belvedere before the church enjoys lovely views over the Valle del Paradiso. The church, built in the 16C, was completely remodelled during the Baroque period. Inside, standing against the wall of the stairway down to the crypt, is a remarkable **Wounded Christ★** in pink marble, its dark veins suggestive of the blood being shed.

The crypt is built around the cave where San Calogero, the patron saint of Naro, is supposed to have lived. The black statue of the saint by the altar is the one carried in procession on 18 June, the saint's feast day.

Catacombe paleocristiane – *In the contrada Canale, just south of the town.* This rural catacomb comprises several passageways lined with niches and shallow hollows containing a sparse number of grave goods. The main underground chamber or hypogeum is the Grotta delle Meraviglie (Cave of Marvels), which extends some 20m/66ft.

EXCURSIONS

Reggia di Cocalo – The Palace of Cocalus is the popular epithet for a small ruined castle perched on an isolated rocky outcrop, about 2km/1.2mi from the centre of town. The foundations are provided by great blocks of stone cut from the base rock; according to local folklore, this is where Cocalus might have lived while ruling over his mythical kingdom *(see ERACLEA MINOA)*.

Palma di Montechiaro – *17km/10.5mi S of Naro on the S 410.* The town was founded in 1637 by Carlo Tomasi, Prince of Lampedusa – one of whose descendants, **Giuseppe Tomasi di Lampedusa** (1896-1957) wrote the famous novel *The Leopard* which was published in 1958. This book, on which Luchino Visconti based his magnificent film, retells the decline of an aristocratic family from Palermo between 1860, the year in which Garibaldi's Thousand landed in Sicily, and 1910.

Chiesa Madre – Standing at the top of a long flight of steps, the broad Baroque **façade★** of the town's main church, built in white limestone, is framed by two bell-towers with attractive onion domes.

Set to one side of the great stairway up to the church is the so-called "palace of the holy duke", **Palazzo Tomasi**.

Castello di Montechiaro – *8km/5mi SW along the road to Marina di Palma, then right towards Capraia.* Crouched high upon a rocky crag above the sea, the 14C castle has a rather bleak and proud quality about it. In 1863, the name of the castle was incorporated into the name of the nearby town of Palma.

NAXOS

Messina

Michelin map 432 N 27

Capo Schisò is a promontory formed originally as a consequence of a great lava flow. It was here that the first Chalcidian colonisers, led by Theocles, founded Naxos in 734 BC, making it the oldest Greek colony in Sicily, or so it is commonly claimed. The name is borrowed from the Cycladic island where, according to legend, Dionysus met and then married Ariadne after she was abandoned by Theseus. In 729 BC Theocles founded the two colonies Catane and Leontinoi that lie further south.

From the 5C BC, the domination of Naxos became a prime objective for aspiring empire-builders, notably Hippocrates of Gela and, later, Hieron of Syracuse who, in 476, evicted the inhabitants of Naxos and deported them to Leontinoi. Eventually, the support offered by Naxos to the Athenian expedition against Syracuse (415 BC) led to the demise of the city: in 403 BC, Dionysius the Great razed it to the ground, leaving the exiled survivors to found Tauromenion.

EXCAVATIONS ⊘

Access to the site is from via Stracina, the continuation of via Naxos, or, during opening hours, via the museum in via Schisò.

The Archaic settlement (7C-6C BC) was replaced in the 4C BC by a new urban scheme that was laid out on a rigidly geometrical grid system, possibly as a result of a redevelopment initiative prompted by Hieron of Syracuse. The new town followed the same boundaries as those of the ancient town: all but the old city walls and the **temenos** (or sacred precinct) were removed and replaced by a regular orthogonal (right-angled) street plan as advocated by the 5C BC architect-urban planner Hippodamus of Miletus, with three **plateiai** (principal avenues – **decumani** in Latin: A, B, and C, oriented on an east-west axis) intersected at right angles by an indeterminate number of **stenopoi** (minor roads or **cardini**).

On entering the site from via Stracina, follow the path along the boundary walls of the ancient city which, pierced by four gateways, are built with polygonal blocks of lava stone. On the south-west side, they incorporate the older walls of the **temenos** (late 7C-early 6C BC) which enclose what are now the ruin of a large temple (B) from the late 6C BC built over an older **sacellum** or sacred precinct from the late 7C BC. The site is scattered with various heaps of stones which date from the same period; among these

N. Reitano/LARA PESSINA

Aphrodite Hippias

remains are several small altars and one larger, quadrangular one with three steps on the west side. Nearby sit two kilns: the larger rectangular chamber would have been used for firing architectural elements in terracotta, while the smaller round one served in the production of vases and votive objects.

Skirt around the kilns and leave the sacred precinct by its northern entrance (or **propylaeum** – traces of which are still visible) to emerge onto plateia B. Follow this broad avenue some distance while surveying the way in which the separate units or blocks are disposed into the greater 5C BC urban scheme; the crossroads are marked with identical quadrangular stones which, possibly, once served as bases to altars. At stenopos 6, turn left towards the museum: on the left, level with stenopos 11, are the remains of a small temple from the 7C BC.

Archaeological museum ⊘ – *Via Schisò*. Situated alongside a small Bourbon keep, the museum houses artefacts from the excavations. The ground floor contains pottery which testifies to the existence of settlements on Capo Schisò from Neolithic times and throughout the Bronze Age, before the arrival of the Greeks. Of particular interest is a bowl inscribed with Stentinello-style decoration (4-3 millennium BC) and other ceramics bearing Cassibile designs (1 millennium BC). A fabulous range of broken **cymae** (decorative roof ornaments) painted with animated elements in different colours and drip-mouldings for channelling rain water, possibly from Temple B (early 6C BC), are displayed on the ground and first floors. Also on the upper level are arranged various examples of votive objects for hanging on the wall in the shape of a female breast or face, antefixes (decorative end-pieces) with silenus masks – testifying to the cult of Dionysus – and a fine altar reconstituted in 1990 (with one fragment retrieved from Heidelberg). Among the other exhibits to look out for are the lovely **figurine of a veiled goddess** (probably Hera) dated as 5C BC, a delicately contrived **statuette of Aphrodite Hippias** identified as 5C BC and a collection of objects from a **surgeon's tomb**, including small ointment jars, a strigil, a specillum – used by doctors to examine wounds – and a beautiful glass dish probably imported from Egypt or Mesopotamia. There is also a fine 4C BC Thracian bronze helmet and a miniature bust of Athena (5C-6C AD) used as a weight for scales.

Inside the keep are displayed various objects found at sea: anchor shafts, amphorae and grindstones.

☆☆GIARDINI NAXOS

This seaside resort lies on the landward side of the **lungomare**, the long road and promenade which echo the lie of the beach as it sweeps around the bay between Capo Schisò in the south, and Capo Taormina in the north-west. For a long time the "garden town" merely served as a sheltered anchorage for nearby Taormina; the epithet originated from the cotton and sugar-cane plantations which, through the ages, were replaced by citrus orchards. These for a long while provided the main source of income until, in the 1950s, the place developed into an important holiday resort, thanks partly to the attraction of nearby Taormina, which provides a splendid backdrop.

🖪 via Tysandros 54, ☎ 0942 51 010.

GETTING TO NAXOS

Giardini Naxos is just 5km/3mi from Taormina and is linked to the city by bus (departures every 30min).

WHERE TO STAY

For details of further accommodation options, see TAORMINA.

Agriturismo Villa Antonella – Via Fondaco d'Accorso, Trappitello (from the motorway, take the Giardini Naxos exit and follow the SS 185 in the direction of Francavilla for 2km/1.2mi), ☎ 0942 65 41 31. This beautiful *agriturismo* guesthouse has 10 simple, well-maintained rooms and is attractively situated among fruit and citrus trees. Half-board only for 75 000L a day per person.

Arathena Rocks Hotel – Via Calcide Eubea 55, ☎ 0942 51 349, Fax 0942 51 690. This elegant, quiet hotel enjoys an isolated location and has a beautiful garden and swimming pool overlooking the sea. It has 47 well-appointed, comfortable rooms (without air-conditioning or TV). Half-board only (approx 115 000L a day per person).

Hotel La Riva – Via Tysandros 52, ☎/fax 0942 51 329. A family-run *pensione* on the seafront, with 38 rooms furnished in original style and a dining room on the fourth floor with superb views. Approx 110 000L for a double room (not including breakfast).

NICOSIA

Enna – Population 15 051
Michelin map 432 N 25

Founded during the Byzantine era when it acquired its eastern sounding name (possibly a corruption of "Città di San Nicolò"), the little town clusters around the castle (now in ruins) that once dominated the highest crag. Nicosia shares the same fate as the rest of Sicily, having passed from Norman hands into Swabian, Aragonese, Castilian and then Bourbon control, but with a difference, as with each successive occupier it managed to resist subordination. This came about because of a strong rivalry between the upper and lower parts of the town, with each faction clinging fiercely to their respective church (San Nicolò and Santa Maria), so as to exclude all other preoccupations. This predicament also faced other towns in Sicily (Ragusa and Modica being two examples), but here it assumed an unusual level of determination and aggression. Scuffles would break out in the street during religious processions until, finally, a gate was set up to mark the official division of the town into two. Even as recently as 1957, two Crucifixes were borne through the town in separate processions celebrating Good Friday.

The historical centre is served by a network of cobbled streets which narrow and then widen, go up and down with the lie of the land in a typically medieval way, sometimes revealing dwellings that have been carved from the rock (now often converted into stores or garages) – now a mere reminder of the troglodyte cave habitations that were widespread in former times, particularly in south-eastern Sicily.

The town contains a number of interesting buildings and monuments, especially churches and *palazzi*, although most are closed due to staff shortages or for ongoing restoration work.

   Piazza Garibaldi – The piazza at the heart of the little town becomes especially atmospheric in the evening when it is suffused with artificial light. It is lined with distinguished-looking buildings, including San Nicolò and the 19C **Palazzo di Città**, which encloses an elegant internal courtyard ornamented with a fine wrought-iron lamp.

Nicosia

Cattedrale di San Nicolò ⊘ – The cathedral was originally built in the Gothic style (conceived in 1340 as an extension to a chapel), but has undergone several remodellings through the ages. Evidence of its original splendour, however, is to be found in the elegant main **doorway★** decorated with flowers, acanthus leaves and palmettes; the bell-tower which, although much altered, retains enough on the second level to suggest the impact of two and three arched openings enclosed within elaborate ogive arches. The left flank of the cathedral facing onto Piazza Garibaldi has an entrance ornamented with pointed arches, also from the Gothic period. Further up towards the apsed east end, carved into the external walls, are a set of sample weights and measures. The **interior** results from the many alterations undertaken: not least the ceiling completed in the 19C and crowned, in the dome, by an unusual statue of St Nicholas "suspended" from on high. This 17C figure is by Giovan Battista Li Volsi who, with his son Stefano, also built the **choir stalls★** out of walnut (1622), and finely decorated with flowers and *putti*. The first stalls harbour four scenes depicting *Christ entering Jerusalem (first on the left)* and, opposite, the *Coronation of the Virgin* (note, in the lower section, a representation of Nicosia before the landslide of 1757 which seriously affected the higher part of the town), while the *Martyrdom of St Bartholomew (second on the left)* has as its pennant the *Miracle of St Nicholas*.

The roof of the church, however, holds a secret: above the vault spans another earlier trussed and painted wooden ceiling from the 14C-15C (closed to the public). Attached to the inside wall of the main façade is an organ by Raffaele della Valle installed in a wooden loft by Stefano Li Volsi. The church preserves examples of Gagini workmanship (baptismal font and pulpit), a sculptural arrangement of *Christ in Glory between the Virgin and John the Baptist* attributed to Antonello Gagini *(second chapel on the left)*, and the **chapter-house** ⊘ is hung with three fine 17C

Legend of Santa Claus

St Nicholas, or Santa Claus to Anglo-Saxons, was a bishop at Myra in Lycia (southwest Turkey) in the 4C. According to legend, he is reputed to be the mysterious benefactor of three eligible young girls whose father, unable to provide dowries for them, proposed to send them out as prostitutes until the necessary funds were raised. One night, the saint slipped unseen into their house to leave three full bags of coin, thus preserving their moral integrity. And so was born the figure of Santa Claus (or Father Christmas) who bestows gifts on well-behaved children.

---

paintings: *Madonna and Child between John the Baptist and Santa Rosalia* by **Pietro Novelli**, a *St Bartholomew*★ by *Lo Spagnoletto* José de Ribera, in which the flayer and other onlookers are animated by intense realism, and a *Martyrdom of St Sebastian* by **Salvator Rosa**.

Turn up salita Salomone between buildings from a more splendid age; continue along via Ansaldi to **Chiesa di San Vincenzo Ferreri** ⊙ which is frescoed by Guglielmo Borremans, and then on to Santa Maria Maggiore, strategically situated with glorious views of the hills and the lower part of the town.

Santa Maria Maggiore ⊙ – In 1757, a landslide swept away the upper part of the town including Santa Maria Maggiore. Very soon after, work was initiated on a replacement church, slightly taller than its predecessor, while all the local residents set to business in order to meet the cost. The noble La Via family gave a lovely 17C doorway from their *palazzo*; this now adorns the main front. Inside, the eye is immediately caught by the **Cona**, a large marble composition in six tiers illustrating scenes from the life of the Virgin, crowned with a figure of St Michael: a work by **Antonello Gagini** and his pupils. At the end of the south aisle is the throne of Charles V, so called after use by the Emperor when he passed through the town in 1535.

Atop the steep rocks behind the church stood the castle, now reduced to a mere ruin. This is accessible by car along via San Simone, a road leading uphill from just outside the town centre, thus saving a long walk.

Castle – Little remains of the castle other than a pointed entrance archway, in a bastion, and the paltry vestiges of a tower. From here, a wonderful **view**★ extends over the town and the mountains all around.

Returning towards piazza Garibaldi, take via Fratelli Testa. On a rise off to the right sits the Chiesa del Santissimo Salvatore.

Santissimo Salvatore – The church, graced by a portico, stands on a rise enjoying a fine **view** over the town.

Continue along via Fratelli Testa, then via GB Li Volsi; at the intersection with via Umberto I, turn left uphill.

Chiesa dei Cappuccini ⊙ – Inside nestles a fine wooden 18C wooden tabernacle attributed to **Bencivinni** and a prized series of paintings by the "Zoppo di Gangi" (The Lame Man of Gangi), **Gaspare Bazzano**, depicting the *Madonna of the Angels*, *St Barbara* and *St Lucy*.

NOTO★★

Siracusa – Population 22 777
Michelin map 432 Q 27

In a region populated by olive and almond trees, Noto sits on a plateau dominating the valley of the Asinaro and its citrus plantations. This tiny Baroque jewel endowed with an opulent beauty that verges on the theatrical, is the result of a single tragic event: the earthquake of 1693. But despite bringing death and destruction to this part of Sicily, it also sparked a huge effort to rebuild. Previously, the town that stood some 9-10km/6mi away *(see below, Noto Antica)* had its origins way back in Antiquity. It witnessed the birth of **Ducetius** who, in the 5C, made the Greeks quake in their shoes for having incited the Siculi against his Sicilian nationalist movement.

The 1693 earthquake completely destroyed the old town. A broader and less vulnerable site was chosen for the new town, one that might accommodate a straightforward, linear town plan – with intersections at right angles and wide, parallel streets – in accordance with the new Baroque taste. Three of the main streets run on an east to west axis, so that they might always be bathed in sunshine. Three different social categories were catered for: the highest part was reserved for the nobility, the centre for the clergy (all except the "hundred-year-old" Palazzo Landolina), while the ordinary people were left to fill the rest of the town. Uniformly, the buildings are majestic: all are built of the soft, compacted limestone found locally that loses its glaring whiteness with time as a glorious patina develops imparting a magnificent golden or rosy hue to each facet, especially when these are caught in the last rays of the setting sun. Many Sicilian artists co-operated in the reconstruction of Noto conducted under the supervision of the Duke of Camastra, the acting representative of the Spanish viceroy; these included **Paolo Labisi**, **Vincenzo Sinatra** and **Rosario Gagliardi** who, being a close follower of Borromini, was perhaps one of the most inventive. The town was built like a stage set might be: its perspectives were configured and implemented in an entirely original way, flattered and enhanced with curvaceous forms and curvilinear accents in façades, decorated brackets and keystones, curlicues and volutes, masks, cherubs, and balconies with gracefully bulging wrought-iron railings. Although Noto was rebuilt entirely by local craftsmen, it fits into a much larger picture as Italian hands modelled, fashioned and realised expressions of the Baroque movement all over Europe and beyond, to the new Russian capital, St Petersburg.

🖪 piazza XVI Maggio, ☎ 0931 83 67 44.

GETTING TO NOTO

Noto is 55km/34mi from Ragusa and 30km/19mi from Siracusa, from where there are **train** (90min and 40min respectively) and **bus** (1hr to Ragusa and 40min to Siracusa) services. The bus station is situated in piazzale Marconi, behind the park *(giardino pubblico)*, while the railway station is in via Principe di Piemonte, a 10min walk from the historical centre of the town.
The AST (☎ 0931 46 49 06) and Interbus (☎ 0931 66 710) bus companies operate services between Noto and Fontanarossa airport in Catania (approx 80km/50mi).

WHERE TO STAY

Villa Al Canisello – Via Pavese 1, ☎ 0931 83 57 93, Fax 0931 83 77 00; www.villacanisello.it Not far from the historical centre, this elegant establishment has six rooms, some of which have a sink and refrigerator. Approximately 120 000L for a double room (including breakfast). Credit cards are not accepted.
Villa Mediterranea – Viale Lido, Lido di Noto (7.5km/4.5mi SE of Noto), ☎/fax 0931 81 23 30. This attractive Mediterranean-style villa is located along the seafront at Noto Marina. The hotel has seven comfortable and well-appointed rooms with air-conditioning, and is surrounded by a garden. A double room costs approx 160 000L.

EATING OUT

Trattoria del Carmine – Via Ducezio 1/A, ☎ 0931 83 87 05; closed Mon. Situated near the Carmine church, this restaurant serves good home cooking at reasonable prices (approximately 30 000L for a meal).

GUIDED TOURS

Through the streets – Throughout the 18C rectilinear town centre layout, popular districts have "sprung up" (Agliastrello, Mannarazze, Macchina Ghiaccio, Carmine) among the tightly knit, tortuous and often maze-like streets more usually associated with medieval towns. The Allakatalla association not only provides guided tours of the historic quarters, but also organises "alternative" routes coloured with local stories and popular legend. These veritable leaps into the past are even more captivating in the evening, when the subdued light casts an almost magical atmosphere. **Allakatalla**, corso Vittorio Emanuele 47, ☎ 0931 83 50 05, Fax 0931 83 60 21; www.allakatalla.it

BAROQUE CITY CENTRE

The main axis is provided by **corso Vittorio Emanuele** which runs through three piazzas, each with its own church. The street extends from **Porta Reale**, a monumental gateway modelled on a triumphal arch, erected in the 19C. Above the entrance is a pelican, the symbol of self-denial – a reference to King Ferdinand II, who visited the town in 1838 – flanked on one side by a tower (shorthand for a fortress and thereby a symbol for strength) and on the other by a *cirneco* (an old Sicilian breed of dog, a symbol of loyalty). Beyond stretches an avenue of trees and to one side the public gardens (Giardino Pubblico) dotted with patches of purple-flowering bougainvillaea and palm trees, and the occasional marble bust of a famous local figure.

This is a common meeting-point for the townspeople to congregate and a good spot from where to watch the daily *passeggiata*.

Piazza Immacolata – The square is overlooked by the fairly austere Baroque façade of **San Francesco all'Immacolata** ⊙ (designed by Sinatra). An important stairway leads up to a terrace with a statue of the Virgin in the centre, stretched out before its dependent monastery. The church contains several notable works of art removed from the Franciscan church abandoned in the old town of Noto: these include on the main altar a painted wooden *Virgin and Child* attributed to Antonio Monachello (1564) and, set into the floor of the nave on the right, the tombstone of a Franciscan priest (1575).

To the left of the church, by the entrance to via San Francesco d'Assisi, sits the lovely **Monastero del Santissimo Salvatore** marked by an elegant tower rising tall above the curved frontage, once a watchtower. The windows are graced with the most wonderful pot-bellied wrought-iron balconies, echoed across the street at the **Convento di Santa Chiara**, by Gagliardi.

*Piazza Municipio – This is the most majestic and the busiest of the three squares, overlooked on the left by the eye-catching elevation of the Palazzo Ducezio, and on the right by the broad flight of steps to the cathedral entrance, flanked by two beautiful horse-shoe-shaped hedges.

**Cathedral – The broad façade with its two tall bell-towers do not completely obscure the remains of the dome which tragically collapsed in 1996 destroying a large section of the nave.

The wide stairway appears to sweep up from the piazza with a great movement, accentuated no doubt by the two tall exedra side hedges, each with a paved area above echoing and thereby emphasising their serpentine line. Alongside the cathedral, on the same level, stand the 19C **Palazzo Vescovile** (Bishop's Palace) and **Palazzo Landolina di Sant'Alfano**, both sober in their countenance in contrast with the exuberant style of the other buildings in the square.

On the opposite side of the square sits the **Palazzo Ducezio**, a well-proportioned building with curvilinear elements, enclosed by a Classical type of portico designed by Sinatra. The upper section was added in the 1950s.

The main feature on the east side of the square is the façade of the **Basilica del Santissimo Salvatore**.

*Via Nicolaci – *Right off corso Vittorio Emanuele.* The eye is naturally drawn along the street as it gently rises up to the **Chiesa di Montevergine** with its fine concave frontage framed between bell-towers, designed by Sinatra. Both sides of the street

A view of the cathedral

M. Guillot/MICHELIN

are lined with fine Baroque buildings: on the left, note **Palazzo Nicolaci di Villadorata** with its fabulous **balconies★★★**. See how the richly carved brackets are ornamented with arrays of fantastical cherubs, horses, mermaids and lions, grotesque figures among which, in the centre, is a figure with distinctively Middle-Eastern features. It is intended that the interior will be opened to the public once restoration is completed.

Towards the middle of May, the citizens recreate brilliantly coloured tableaux of flowers inside the doorways of the *palazzi*: these panels, composed entirely of petals, are in celebration of the *Infiorata* festival. The cobbles of Via Nicolaci are transformed into some gigantic canvas onto which the artists apply their multi-coloured brushstrokes picked from palettes of petals; each year the designs are different.

Returning to corso Vittorio Emanuele, on the left stands the imposing complex of the **Jesuit Church and College** attributed to Gagliardi. The fine central doorway is enclosed between four columns and, at the top, grotesque masks.

Piazza XVI Maggio – The most striking feature on the square is Gagliardi's elegant convex façade for the **Chiesa di San Domenico★** ⊘, designed with an emphatic use of line and boldly contained by two tiers of columns separated by a high cornice. The interior, predominantly white and encrusted with stucco, is graced with polychrome marble altars.

In front of the church lies the delightful **Villetta d'Ercole**, a public garden with an 18C fountain in the centre named after Heracles. Opposite, stands the 19C Teatro Vittorio Emanuele III.

The second street on the left off corso Vittorio Emanuele, via Ruggero VII, leads to

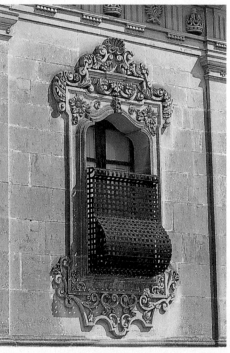

A typical window and its grille

the **Chiesa del Carmine**; a church with an elegant concave frontage and a Baroque doorway. Return to piazza XVI Maggio so as to turn up via Bovio, which passes, on the right, the former Carmine convent known as Casa dei Padri Crociferi.

Via Cavour – This noble street runs parallel to, but on a level above, corso Vittorio Emanuele, between a series of interesting buildings: **Palazzo Astuto** (no 54) has wonderful balconies with bulging wrought-iron railings; and **Palazzo Trigona Cannicarao** (no 93).

Beyond the *palazzo* turn left onto via Coffa, then left again at the end so as to pass before the late-Baroque **Palazzo Impellizzeri**; and turn right onto via Sallicano. This in turn leads right up to the **Chiesa del Santissimo Crocefisso**,⊘ designed by Gagliardi, and containing **Francesco Laurana**'s sensitive painting entitled the *Madonna della Neve*.

EXCURSIONS

Noto Antica – *9-10km/6mi NW*. Along the road to the site of the original Noto there is a sign for **Eremo di San Corrado fuori le Mura**: this 18C sanctuary set in among the green countryside was built beside the cave where St Corrado lived in the 14C. The main road then continues past the **Santuario di Santa Maria della Scala** which preserves a lovely Arabo-Norman arch behind the font. The road leads on to the site where the town of old Noto stood before the terrible earthquake of 1693: it was stretched along the ridge of Monte Alveria, squeezed in between two deep gorges, making it easily defensible. Beyond Porta Aurea, the gateway to the now deserted, picturesquely overgrown city, the street system remains intact: how strange, therefore, to think of it as bustling with people in the 17C. A few eerie ruins protrude from the rubble and weeds.

★★**Cava Grande** – *19km/12mi N.* An excursion to Cava Grande provides the opportunity of exploring a small and forgotten corner of the Iblei mountain landscape, that karst range dominating the south-east part of Sicily. This itinerary off the beaten track will be of particular interest to nature-lovers.

Turn off the road from Palazzolo Acreide to Noto for Avola; then take the secondary road signposted for Cava Grande. Leave the car at the viewpoint from where there is a magnificent **view**★ over the **Cava Grande Gorge**★ plunging down between impressively tall and sheer limestone cliffs. Along the valley bottom winds the river which opens out intermittently to make a succession of tiny lakes, accessible by a path leading down into the gorge. Slightly to the left, a cave may be seen excavated from the rock: this is the so-called **Grotta dei Briganti** (Bandits' Cave), just one of the many rock-hewn dwellings in this settlement, and another example of the type so commonly found throughout the rocky landscape of south-east Sicily. It is thought that this particular cave was used as a tannery.

Descent – It takes half an hour to walk down to the river, or *cava* as it is known locally – allow twice that time to climb back to the top. The track, which at times becomes quite difficult to follow, cuts its way along the river through luxuriant vegetation. After a few hundred metres, the bush gives way to an open clearing around a series of **natural rock pools**★★ created by the river, complete with flat rounded slabs of rock ideal for whiling away a moment or two in the sunshine. In summer, the cool water is very tempting. Furthermore the rock pools are surrounded on all sides by the most idyllic scenery, far removed from anything found elsewhere in Sicily, and so providing an unusual and highly recommended alternative to a swim in the sea off the Syracuse coast.

Eloro – *11km/7mi SE.* Ancient Helorus was probably founded by the Syracusans some time in the 7C BC. It enjoys a splendid **situation**★ on a hill overlooking the sea, not far from the mouth of the River Tellaro.

Excavations – On entering the site, to the east, the ruin of a great *stoà* (portico) stands which once would have marked the entrance to the sacred precinct where the **sanctuary** dedicated to Demeter and Kore was located, now buried below vestiges of various Byzantine buildings erected later.

Down towards the river lie the remains of a **theatre** cavea, badly scarred, alas, when a drainage channel was dug under Fascist rule. Westwards, sits the base of a **temple** thought to have been dedicated to Asclepius (Aesculapius), the son of Apollo and god of medicine and healing. Beyond, northern and western sections of the **enclosure walls** are still much in evidence, as is the **north gate** (complete with the foundations of flanking towers) which marks the beginning of the main street, running on a north to south axis, rutted by cart-wheels. In an area east of the principal thoroughfare, set among rectangular buildings, lies an open space that must surely have been the *agorà* (market place).

Villa Romana del Tellaro ⊘ – *7km/4mi W.* Beside the River Tellaro, west of the main Noto-Pachino road, the remains of a Roman villa dating from the second half of the 4C AD have been recovered. These fragments, found in the 1970s while excavations were conducted on a nearby rural complex, seem to suggest that its internal decoration must have been at least as sumptuous as the famous Roman Villa del Casale, near Piazza Armerina.

Tour – The residence is planned around a square peristyle: excavations of the north wing have revealed mosaic floors with geometric designs, notably diamonds and spirals. Three rooms in the northern range preserve mosaics with an intensity of colour far in excess of anything found at the Villa del Casale: these, composed of smaller tesserae, feature hunting scenes, erotic scenes and Apollo's deliverance of the body of Hector to Priam, after avenging the death of his friend Patroclus, a story taken from Homer's *Iliad (unfortunately these mosaics are preserved elsewhere for the time being).*

Before leaving, note on the right, the traces of additional buildings annexed to the main complex – possibly intended as the servants' quarters, and the remains of a wall from the Greek period.

PALAZZOLO ACREIDE

Population 9 261
Michelin map 432 P 26

The new town of Palazzolo, which derives from the ancient town of Akrai (founded in 664 BC), occupies a plateau dominating the gorges of the upper valley of the River Anapo, at the heart of the Iblei mountains.

★ANCIENT TOWN OF AKRAI ⊙ *Area lying SW of the town*

At the top of the hill where the acropolis used to lie, all that is visible of the small Greek theatre built of white stone is the floor of the orchestra, and this actually dates from Roman times. To the right lay the *bouleuterion*, a stepped meeting-area, connected to the theatre by a narrow passage leading straight into the cavea. Near to the gate that seals off the excavation area on this side, may be seen a section of the old *plateia* (main road running from east to west) paved with large slabs of lava stone.

Two former Greek quarries next to the theatre were converted by the Christians for use as catacombs and troglodyte dwellings. Near the entrance to the **Intagliatella**, the narrower of the two quarries, on the right, there is a low relief of a heroic figure participating in a banquet *(right)* and offering up a sacrifice *(left)*.

Excavation of the area along the fence has uncovered vestiges of a residential quarter and a circular building, probably a temple built in Roman times.

The track that skirts around the edge of the archaeological site provides a lovely **view★** over the surrounding valley, reinforcing the strategic positioning of the ancient city, founded as a defensive outpost of Syracuse.

I Santoni – *1km/0.6mi from the archaeological site*. Tucked away in a small valley nearby, 12 rock-hewn figures dating from the 3C BC testify to the existence in Sicily of a cult of Oriental origin. The main sculpture represents the **goddess Cybele** (Demeter), seated between two lions, or standing surrounded by smaller figures. No II, one of the best-preserved, personifies the Dioscuri - Castor and Pollux on horseback on either side. No VIII shows the goddess seated.

The theatre

MODERN CITY OF PALAZZOLO ACREIDE

Palazzolo was largely rebuilt in the 18C and so has many Baroque buildings lining its main thoroughfares: corso Vittorio Emanuele and via Carlo Alberto, which intersect at piazza del Popolo. The square is dominated by the majestic façade of **San Sebastiano** raised up a flight of steps.

At the western end of the *corso* stands the **Chiesa dell'Immacolata** ⊙ with its convex frontage, in which is preserved a most delicate Madonna and Child by **Francesco Laurana**. Via Carlo Alberto passes between a series of *palazzi* with wonderful Baroque details. One of the streets off to the right (via Machiavelli) leads to the **Casa-Museo dell'etologo Antonino Uccello** ⊙ – a *palazzo* once owned by Baron Ferla and later turned into a house-museum by another owner, the ethnologist Antonio Uccello. On the ground floor is displayed an oil-press *(third room)* and the Casa del Massaro: the house of the baron's most trusted man, furnished with everyday objects.

At the end of the street, turn right onto piazza Umberto I where the Church of **San Paolo** is situated. The striking frontage, possibly designed by **Vincenzo Sinatra** (an architect who worked mainly at Noto), rises through three tiers of rounded arches and columns capped with Corinthian capitals. The top storey comprises the bell-tower.

Follow via dell'Annunziata out of the piazza to the church of the same name: its façade, which remains incomplete, has an interesting **doorway★** flanked with spiral columns. Return back along via dell'Annunziata and turn left down via Garibaldi to take a look at **Palazzo Iudica** (at nos 123-131) and its amazingly long balcony supported by brackets carved with monsters, fantastical figures, masks and other such elements so typical of the Baroque period.

E. Baret

PALERMO ★★★

Population 686 551
Michelin map 432 M 22

Palermo, Sicily's main port, nestles in the middle of a wide bay, enclosed to the north by Monte Pellegrino and to the south by Capo Zafferano. It is built on the edge of a very fertile plain that was called, in the 15C, the **Conca d'Oro** (meaning the golden shell or the horn of plenty) on account of its lush citrus plantations, palm trees and olive-groves. Palermo, at one time, was the favoured haunt of writers, poets and artists, seduced by its inherent atmosphere of Eastern exoticism and by its esoteric beauty. The city, built over the course of centuries to provide for a range of diverse cultures and traditions, alas has suffered terrible damage, especially during bombing raids in the Second World War (1943) when much of the old fabric of the picturesque quarters was destroyed, and has never really been rebuilt. Certainly the construction of large modern crumbling buildings in the suburbs has done nothing to improve the city's image. Despite this, Palermo manages to hang on to its essential fascination, ever drawing its personality from the peoples who have populated its streets over the ages – be they Byzantine, Arab, Norman or other – and who have left their indelible mark not only in the form of a rich artistic heritage but in the very vital rhythm of life in the city.

Palermo becomes particularly lively in July for the festival of its patron saint, Santa Rosalia, which is celebrated with a programme of events lasting five whole days.

An endearing place – Many writers have dipped their pen into an inkwell with the intention of encapsulating the elusive spirit of Palermo or of using the city as the backdrop to their stories. Here is an excerpt from a Sicilian text by a writer who transforms Sicily into a dream, evoking images, smells and sounds through words that are sometimes lyrical, sometimes nostalgic and sometimes crude. "To Palermo the red, Palermo the child... Red, Palermo, which we might imagine the likes of Tyre or Sidon, perhaps Carthage, like the purple of the Phoenicians; of rich red earth, with springs of water where the palm grove rises tall and slender, creating sweet shade, bending with the wind, vibrant with the echo and nostalgia of an oasis, a green mosque, a carpet of comfort and prayer, image of the eternal garden of the Koran. A child because she is sleeping and still, content with her own beauty, having always had to be subservient to foreigners, obedient in particular to her mother, her own natural mother who locks her children in an eternal adolescence.

She settles down, relaxed and happy, in the gentle hollow of a shell ..."
From *La Sicilia Passeggiata* (Strolling through Sicily) by Vincenzo Consolo.

CUSTOMS, ART AND HISTORY

It was the Phoenicians who laid the foundations of the city in the 7C BC, calling it *Ziz*, meaning flower. This, in time, was conquered by the Romans who gave it the name Panormus (from the Greek words meaning "large port or rock") from which Palermo (corrupted by the introduction of the Arabic name *Balharm*) has been derived for us today. The city's golden age began under Arab domination (9C), when it was established as one of the main Islamic centres in the west. The town expanded as new quarters were developed beyond the confines of the old centre known as the Cassaro (from the Arabic *Qasr* meaning castle; also the old name of the main street of Palermo, now corso Vittorio Emanuele); the Kalsa (from *al Halisah* – the chosen one), in particular, flourished down by the seafront and, once fortified, provided a residence for the Emir. In 1072, the city fell into the hands of the Norman **Count Roger**, but the transfer was not a violent one as merchants, artisans and Muslims in general (but also people of other races and religions) were permitted to continue to live and practise their chosen professions as though nothing had changed. Indeed, it was precisely this magnanimity that made it possible for the so-called Arabo-Norman style, that glorious mix of structural and decorative elements, to develop in architecture. The city prospered while benefiting from the wealthy investment of different cultures. **Roger II**, son of the "count", harbouring a predilection for luxury, built gardens in the Oriental style to complement his sumptuous palaces (La Zisa and La Cuba); he surrounded himself with men of letters, mathematicians, astronomers and intellectuals from far and wide.

Sicilian Vespers

Charles of Anjou arrived in Palermo in 1266, supported by the Pope. The French were disdained by the people, to such an extent that, given their inability to pronounce Italian properly, they were nicknamed *tartaglioni* (stutterers). In 1282, on Easter Monday, before the Church of Santo Spirito *(see p 284)*, just as the bell was calling the faithful to Vespers, a French soldier directed an insult at a Sicilian woman, thereby sparking off a reaction of indignation in the crowd. The situation deteriorated and, with the help of the local aristocracy, the quarrel was transformed into a revolt which then spread throughout Sicily. Any Frenchmen unabl to pronounce the word *cicero* correctly was massacred, while the others we driven out. Eventually, Peter of Aragon, husband of Costanza d'Altavilla, t daughter of Manfred, was called upon to rule the island.

After a short period of disorder and decadence, Palermo and Sicily passed into the hands of Frederick II of Swabia (1212), under whom the city regained its importance and vigour. The Swabians were succeeded by the Angevins; they in turn were driven out at the end of the so-called War of the Vespers, by the Spaniards and, in the 18C, the Bourbons of Naples, who embellished the city with Baroque palaces.

The 19C heralded the opening of the city to trade and relations with Europe. The entrepreneurial bourgeoisie became the new economic driving force and the new "commissioners". The city outgrew its boundaries. The viale della Libertà, an extension of via Maqueda, was inaugurated; the surrounding district mushroomed, populated with elegant Liberty-style buildings. Sadly, this was to be the final flurry before a period of stagnation. The city succumbed to the bombing raids of the last war, and there followed an earthquake in 1968. Meanwhile the slow but sure decline of its medieval quarters continued. Today, this trend is being reversed as a new sense of determination prompts a systematic re-evaluation, restoration and improved use of the city's magnificent monuments in an attempt to stir this wonderful giant of the East from its protracted slumber.

OLD DISTRICTS

Palermo's urban plan is centred around the intersection of two main streets: corso Vittorio Emanuele and via Maqueda. Corso Vittorio Emanuele corresponds roughly to the historical **Cassaro** (from the Arabic al-Qasr), the city's main artery which once linked the Emirate's palace to the sea and was enclosed at either end by Porta Nuova and Porta Felice. In time the district around the street gradually assumed the same name. Via Maqueda was created at the end of the 16C, when the medieval quarters were demolished and the city was divided into four areas, known as *mandamenti*.

Mandamento Palazzo Reale or Albergheria to the south-west coincides with the oldest part of the city: here the Phoenicians settled, followed by the Romans, Arabs and Normans, who built their most important civic buildings in the western section of the district. The eastern part of the *mandamento*, towards via Maqueda, was originally an irregular and densely populated urban centre, which grew up around via Albergheria, and included the Jewish quarter.

Mandamento Monte di Pietà or Capo to the north-west was the area mostly inhabited by the Islamic population, where much of the city's artisanal and commercial activity took place. This is still the case today, as shown by the lively Capo market which takes place in this district.

Mandamento Castellammare or Loggia to the north-east, changed by the creation of via Roma at the end of the 19C and badly damaged by bombing raids in 1943, included the port area, which brought bustling mercantile activity to the district, and merchants from Amalfi, Pisa, Lucca, Genoa and Catalonia. The historical Vucciria market bears witness to this commercial past.

Mandamento Tribunali or Kalsa to the south-east, which takes its name from Palazzo Chiaramonte, the headquarters of the Court of the Inquisition, grew up around the Kalsa, the old fortified citadel, and via Alloro, along which a number of noble mansions were built in the 15C. From the 18C onwards, large aristocratic *palazzi* were built along the seafront, with terraces overlooking the Passeggiata della Marina (the present Foro Italico).

★★PRINCIPAL MONUMENTS

★★Palazzo dei Normanni

The **Norman Palace** is located at the heart of the original town, probably on a site occupied in Punic times by a fortress. The earliest documents, however, date from the Arab occupation; these confirm this to be where the Emir's palace was once situated, linked to the port by the Cassaro. The castle was abandoned in 938 for reasons of security and the Emir's residence transferred to the Kalsa *(see below)*. The area returned to favour when the Normans re-established a royal seat there, having extended and embellished the place. Life in the palace revolved around the green hall, an ample space in which regal ceremonies, assemblies and banquets were held. The building comprised various wings, each assigned to different people and functions, interconnected by a terrace or a lush garden ornamented with pools of water and fountains. Four towers punctuated the corners: the Greek, the Pisan, the Joaria (from the Arabic for airy) and the Kirimbi. Sadly, only the central part of the original complex survives today, together with the massive Pisan Tower, although the dome is a later addition dating from when an observatory was installed there in 1791. The palace then endured a period of abandonment and decline (all, that is, save the Palatine Chapel) that lasted well into the 17C when, under the Spanish viceroys, it was restored. It was then that the impressive south front and the beautiful internal courtyard with its three storeys of loggias were inserted.

ℹ Piazza Castelnuovo 34. ☎ 091 58 38 47; Fax 091 58 27 88; www.aapit.pa.it
The tourist office publishes a monthly magazine listing up-to-date information on events in Palermo, as well as opening hours for museums, churches and mansions.

GETTING TO PALERMO

By air – This is certainly the easiest and quickest way to get to Palermo. **Falcone-Borsellino** airport (once known as Punta-Raisi airport, ☎ 091 70 20 111) is situated 30km/19mi north of Palermo, on the A29 motorway. It is served by a number of airlines (Alitalia, Alpi Eagles, Air Sicilia, Med Airlines, Meridiana, Air Europe), which link Palermo with other major Italian cities.

Car hire at the airport:
Avis ☎ 091 59 16 84
Europcar ☎ 091 59 16 88
Hertz ☎ 091 21 31 12
Holiday Car ☎ 091 59 16 87
Maggiore ☎ 091 59 16 81
Sicily by Car ☎ 091 59 12 50

Connections with the city centre – A bus links the airport with the city centre every 30min from 5am until the arrival of the last flight of the day, stopping in viale Lazio, piazza Ruggero Settimo (in front of Politeama Hotel), and at the main railway station. The journey takes approx 1hr and costs 7 500L (one-way). For information, call ☎ 091 58 04 57.
The cost of a taxi from the airport to the city is approx 60/70 000L. Beware of individuals who offer transport at considerably lower prices.

Connections with other cities – Segesta buses (☎ 091 61 67 919) link Palermo airport with **Trapani** in just under 1hr (10 000L one-way). The Licata bus company (☎ 0922 40 13 60) operates services to **Agrigento** (approx 3hr, 15 000L), while Gallo (☎ 091 61 71 141) runs three daily services to **Sciacca** (approx 1hr 30min, 14 000L).

By car – Close to Palermo the motorway joins the ring-road around the city (the viale Regione Siciliana), from where various exits lead to the major sites of interest. The **corso Calatafimi** exit is the most convenient for the historical centre, as this road eventually continues into corso Vittorio Emanuele, one of the main streets through the old town.

Car parks – The difficulty of finding somewhere to park in Palermo discourages many visitors from driving in the city. Large car parks can be found on the outskirts of the city (marked by a P on the map); it is also sometimes possible to park in via Lincoln, next to the Botanical Gardens, which is a short walk from piazza della Kalsa.
The following guarded car parks are situated in the old town:
piazza Giulio Cesare 43 (railway station)
via Guardione 81 (running parallel with via Cavour to the north, in the port area)
via Archimede 88 (north of Politeama)
via Sammartino 24 (north-west of Teatro Massimo)
These car parks cost around 30 000L for 24hr, but often have special arrangements with hotels nearby.
Visitors are advised not to leave luggage or valuables in their car.

By boat – Ferries leave for Palermo from the following Italian ports:
Genova: Grandi Navi Veloci, via Fieschi 17 ☎ 010 58 93 31, Fax 010 55 92 25 (20hr) and Tirrenia navigazione, Stazione Marittima, via Milano 51, ☎ 010 26 981; Fax 010 24 98 255 (24hr).
Livorno: Grandi Navi Veloci, varco Galvani Darsena 1, ☎ 0586 40 98 04, Fax 0586 42 97 17, (only operates on certain days, 17hr).
Naples: Tirrenia Navigazione, Stazione Marittima, molo Angioino, ☎ 081 31 72 999, Fax 081 25 14 767 (11hr); Aliscafi SNAV, via Caracciolo 10, ☎ 081 76 12 348, Fax 081 76 12 141 (from Apr to Oct; 4hr 30min).
Cagliari: Tirrenia Navigazione, agenzia Agenave, via Campidano 1, ☎ 070 66 30 04, Fax 070 66 38 53 (once a week, 14hr 30min).

By bus – There is a direct daily service between Rome (Stazione Tiburtina and Castro Pretorio), Messina (piazza della Repubblica), Palermo (via P Balsamo 26 and via Turati 3) and Trapani (via Ammiraglio Stairi 13), operated by Segesta Internazionale. The service departs Rome at 9.30pm and Palermo at 6.30pm; journey time 12hr. 110 000L (round trip). ☎ 091 30 05 56 (weekdays) and 091 32 07 57 (Sat-Sun).
Palermo can also reached from all other major towns in Sicily. The main bus companies are **SAIS**, via Balsamo 16, ☎ 091 61 66 028 (Caltagirone, Caltanissetta, Castelbuono, Catania, Cefalà Diana, Cefalù, Enna, Messina, N Piazza Armerina, Siracusa), **Cuffaro**, via Balsamo 13, ☎ 091 61 61 (Agrigento), and **Segesta** (Messina and Trapani, *see above*).

By train – Travelling to Sicily by train from mainland Italy involves crossing the Straits of Messina; the train drives directly onto the ferry; the crossing is included in the price of the train ticket. For information, contact the Italian State Railways *(Ferrovie dello Stato)*. For visitors travelling from Sicily, Palermo has train connections with Messina (approx 3hr), Caltanissetta (approx 2hr) and Catania (just over 3hr, but the service is infrequent). Palermo's main railway station is situated in piazza Giulio Cesare.

WHERE TO STAY

Hotels are subdivided into three categories, each based on the price of a double room *(for further information, see p 22)*, and are listed in alphabetical order. Visitors are advised to check prices before booking and to book in advance.

BUDGET

Hotel Azzurro di Lampedusa – Via Roma 111, ☎ 091 61 66 881, Fax 091 61 00 105; azzurrolampedusa@tiscali.net This hotel is situated on the 5th floor of a *palazzo* in the old town (lift) and has 12 rooms with private bathroom, television and telephone. Some rooms have air-conditioning. Good value for money (approximately 90 000L for a double room, including breakfast).

Hotel Gardenia – Via Mariano Stabile 136, ☎ 091 32 27 61, Fax 091 33 37 32; www.gardeniahotel.com Small family-run hotel on the 7th floor of a building in the old town (lift available). Total of 16 rooms with private bathroom, television, telephone and air-conditioning, some of which have private balconies. Garage (25 000L/day). 140 000L for a double room (including breakfast).

Hotel Moderno – Via Roma 276, ☎ 091 58 82 60, Fax 091 58 86 83. This simple and well-kept hotel, on the 3rd and 4th floor of this building (lift available), has 38 rooms with air-conditioning.

Hotel Posta – Via Gagini 77 *(the road leads off piazza S Domenico and runs parallel with via Roma to the east)*, ☎ 091 58 73 38, Fax 091 58 73 47. A simple, family-run hotel. Total of 27 well-appointed rooms with air-conditioning.

MODERATE

Massimo Plaza Hotel – Via Maqueda 437, ☎ 091 32 56 57, Fax 091 32 57 11. On the first floor of a building situated opposite Teatro Massimo, this small, elegant hotel has 15 comfortable and spacious rooms with air-conditioning.

Hotel Principe di Villafranca – Via Turrisi Colonna 4, ☎ 091 612 18 523, Fax 091 58 87 05. This hotel is built on the site of a famous garden which once belonged to the Prince of Villafranca. Total of 34 well-appointed rooms, elegantly furnished with antique furniture. Beautiful public rooms.

EXPENSIVE

Centrale Palace Hotel – Corso Vittorio Emanuele 327, ☎ 091 33 66 66, Fax 091 33 48 81. The elegant, tasteful Centrale Palace is located in an 18C mansion and offers excellent hospitality. This hotel has pleasant public areas, including a panoramic restaurant on the top floor. Total of 63 attractively decorated and comfortable rooms.

PALERMO'S HISTORIC HOTELS

Grand Hotel et des Palmes – Via Roma 398, ☎ 091 58 39 33, Fax 091 33 15 45. This building came to prominence in the mid-1800s when used as a residence by Ben Ingham, the Englishman who played a key role in the history of Marsala *(see p 283)*. Soon converted into a hotel, it has provided hospitality to all the persons of note passing through the city: musicians (Wagner finished *Parsifal* here – his stool is still there), painters (sketches by Guttuso and Fiume furnish one of the salons), writers, politicians past and present (President Andreotti for one), great names from the theatre world and countless numbers of aristocrats have silently passed through its corridors over the years. It has provided an objective context for important political occasions, newsworthy events, inexplicable and mysterious incidents linked to the world of spies, *omertà* (tacit complicity demanded by the Mafia), and intrigues which might be more typical of a royal court rather than a hotel. It was here, in 1957, that a secret dinner was held for the top henchmen of the Italian and American Mafia; that a secret agent died in mysterious circumstances (and disappeared), having fallen from the seventh floor straight through the skylight of the great hall of mirrors (before being immediately rushed "to hospital" by two equally mysterious figures on stand-by); it was here that Vittorio Emanuele Orlando, a famous politician, gave a sumptuous 12-course dinner; here, too, that, in 1933, a French poet ended his dissolute and tragic life by committing suicide (or overdosing on hallucinogenics). Another strange story involves the Baron of Castelvetrano who lived hidden away in his suite on the first floor for more than half a century; allegedly, this enforced exile was levied upon him for having killed, so it is said, a boy guilty of petty theft; the sentence, pronounced by the father of the unfortunate victim, seems to epitomise the high respect for dignity and a word of honour so typical of a bygone age.

An atmosphere of times past still lingers in the hotel's great hall – designed by Basile – in the great hall of mirrors, the room with the fireplace, the restaurant where people still request to dine "at that table" or at the bar, where many a client has made his "confession" to the barman over a drink or two.

Villa Igiea – Salita Belmonte 43, ☎ 091 54 37 44, Fax 091 54 76 54. This very large building is scenically positioned on the slopes of Monte Pellegrino. It began life as a nursing home for Igiea Florio (who suffered from tuberculosis), adapted from a pre-existing neo-Gothic building to designs by Ernesto Basile for a exotically luxurious home. The dining-room in particular, now the **Sala Basile★** (accessible by request and subsequent permission from the hotel staff, who are always most kind), was completely renovated: lovely wooden panelling was installed, and the interior decoration with beautiful female figures surrounded by delicate, long-stalked flowers was commissioned from Ettore de Maria Bergler, a well-known Liberty-style painter. On the walls of the corridor are photographs depicting illustrious guests who stayed here in the past, including many European kings and queens.

EATING OUT

Capricci di Sicilia – Via Istituto Pignatelli on the corner of piazza Sturzo, ☎ 091 32 77 77. Simple surroundings offering excellent food, with the emphasis on regional specialities. Approximately 70 000L for a meal.

Trattoria Biondo – Via Carducci 15 *(N of piazza Castelnuovo)*, ☎ 091 58 36 62. Closed Wed and from 30 July to 15 Sept. A quiet, welcoming restaurant, famous for its mushroom-based dishes. Approximately 50 000L for a meal.

Santandrea – Piazza S Andrea 4 *(S of piazza S Domenico)*, ☎ 091 33 49 99. Closed Tues (also Sun in July and Aug) and in Jan. This pleasant restaurant in the heart of the Vucciria district serves traditional Sicilian cuisine. Approximately 80 000L for a meal.

Tonnara Florio *(off the map)* – Discesa Tonnara 4, quartiere Arenella, ☎ 091 63 75 611. Pizzeria closed Mon. This attractive Liberty-style building, unfortunately in need of restoration, has a beautiful garden and a number of rooms once used for processing tuna and repairing fishing boats. The building now houses a night club and a pizzeria. Old fishing tools and mementoes belonging to the Florio family can still be seen in the old tuna rooms where the pizzeria is now located.

SNACKS

Local specialties include *u sfinciuni* or *sfincione* (pizza topped with tomato, anchovies, onion and bread crumbs), *panino con la milza* (spleen-filled roll) and *panelle* (fried chickpea flour pancakes), which are often sold in the local markets. The **Antica Focacceria San Francesco**, situated in the heart of the old town opposite San Francesco church, serves *focaccia farcita* (flat pizza-dough baked with various fillings), *arancini di riso* (deliciously moist, deep-fried rice balls sometimes with tomatoes and peas stuffed with meat sauce; otherwise filled with melted mozzarella), torte salate (Sicilian savoury "cake"), fried ricotta cheese, and sfincione. Another famous address is **Focacceria Basile**, at via Bara all'Olivella (runs parallel with via Cavour to the south) and piazza Nascé 5. Visitors who find themselves in the viale della Libertà district should try the *panini* (sandwiches) at **Di Martino** (via Mazzini 54), while sitting at a table outside.

PASTRY SHOPS

Two of the many excellent pastry shops in Palermo are **Oscar** at 39 via Mariano Migliaccio (not shown on the map), whose best-known speciality is the Torta Devil (Devil's Cake), and **Bar Costa** at 15 via G D'Annunzio (not shown on the map), which specialises in all kinds of cakes and pastries (especially lemon and orange mousses). Also worth a visit are the **Pasticceria Scimone** at 18 via Miceli (not shown on the map) and the long-established **Pasticceria Mazzara** at 19 via Generale Magliocco (the second street on the right off via Pignatelli d'Aragona, immediately north of Teatro Massino), where Giuseppe Tomasi di Lampedusa, author of The Leopard, used to stop for breakfast.

EXPLORING THE CITY

Getting around – It is best to avoid driving in Palermo because of traffic congestion and the difficulty of finding somewhere to park *(see above)*. By far the best way to see the city is by public transport and taxi for longer distances and on foot once in the old town.

A slower, yet nonetheless enjoyable way of soaking up the atmosphere is to take one of the horse-drawn carriages available for hire outside the central station or elsewhere in the city. It is advisable, however, to agree a price before setting off.

Buses – There are two types of bus ticket: one valid for up to an hour (1 500L) or one for a full day (5 000L); the latter is worth purchasing if public transport is likely to be used several times in the course of the day.

Radio Taxis – Autoradio Taxi ☏ 091 51 27 27. Radio Taxi Trinacria ☏ 091 22 54 55.

Guided tours – The CST (Compania Siciliana Turismo) organises visits to several of the main sights in combination with a visit to the Duomo at Monreale every Saturday morning. On other days of the week, it also arranges accompanied day trips to Segesta, Erice and Trapani; Mount Etna and Taormina; Agrigento and Piazza Armerina; Il Capo market; Mondello and the Capuchin Catacombs in Palermo (half-day visits only). The CST office is located at via Emerico Amari 124, ☏ 091 74 39 611, Fax 091 58 22 18; www.web.tin.it/cst

The AMAT (Azienda Municipale dei Trasporti) organises various bus tours around the sights of the city and Monreale. Tours leave at 9am and last approx 3hr 45min. 20 000L. Via Stabile, on the corner of via Ruggero Settimo, ☏ 091 35 04 15.

The Cooperativa Solidarietà offers 4 themed tours entitled *"I percorsi della memoria"* (I Beati Paoli, Il Piano della Cattedrale, Le Logge delle Nazioni and La Boucherie), as well as the "Palermo underground" *("Palermo ...sotto sopra")* speological tour which explores the passageways under the city *(this tour is not suitable for children under 11 years of age)*. For reservations, contact ☏ 091 65 20 067.

100 open churches – The aim of this excellent initiative is to provide access to a number of buildings hitherto closed to the public. The idea is to appoint groups of volunteers to administrate and oversee opening times (ideally 9am to 5pm) and provide guided tours. Those buildings to have benefited from the scheme so far include a number of churches (Sant' Eulalia dei Catalani, Santa Maria dei Miracoli, Madonna della Mercè, Madonna dei Rimedi, San Carlo, Santa Caterina, dell'Itria or dei Cocchieri, Santa Ninfa dei Crociferi, Sant' Orsola, Santa Teresa alla Kalsa), the Convento di Santa Maria del Gesù and Stand Florio. For information and reservations, ☏ 091 740 60 35.

SHOPPING

Local markets – The most colourful and picturesque markets are, without doubt, those selling food, with their array of multi-coloured awnings, their brightly painted stalls decked with assortments of fruit, vegetables or fish, lit with bare light-bulbs.

La Vucciria – This historic market is certainly Palermo's most famous, always bustling with colour and noise, and is the most important food market in the city. It takes place set back from the waterfront in via Cassari-Argenteria and the surrounding area (stretching as far as piazza San Domenico). The origin of the name is controversial: some maintain that it comes from the French term *boucherie* (meat), others are of the opinion that it refers to the deafening clamour of the traders' voices drawing attention to their wares.

Ballarò – Ballarò market is held in the area stretching from piazza Casa Professa to corso Tukory. The food stalls cluster around piazza del Carmine, while clothing and second-hand items can be found near **Casa Professa**. A lively atmosphere, especially in the morning.

Il Capo – The first, more picturesque, food section is along via Carini and via Beati Paoli; the clothing and shoe stalls congregate in via Sant'Agostino and via Bandiera. In addition to the brightly coloured stalls, it is worth noting the interestingly named streets in this area, such as Sedie Volanti (flying chairs) and Gioia Mia (my love).

Mercato delle Pulci – A range of antique and modern bric-a-brac can be found in the flea market (located between piazza Peranni and corso Amedeo), where haggling over prices is mandatory!

I Lattarini – The name of this market derives from the Arabic *suk-el-attarin* (grocery market). Once a food market, its stalls now sell clothing, work tools and ironmongery.

Shopping – The most elegant shops are concentrated in the new development along via della Libertà and the main streets of the city (via Roma and via Maqueda). Via Principe di Belmonte has been pedestrianised and is also lined with elegant shops. The central section has been planted with trees to provide shade for tables spilling onto the pavement from bars such as the Antico Caffè, the *Gelateria Liberty*, Au Domino (*crêperie* and *bistro*) and the Café de Paris.

Opening hours – Most shops are closed Monday mornings (food shops close Wednesday afternoons). Shops generally open between 9am to 1pm and from 3.30pm to 7.30pm (4pm to 8pm Saturday afternoons).

ENTERTAINMENT

IL TEATRO DEI PUPI

The name synonymous with the ancient tradition of the puppet theatre in Palermo, is that of the Cuticchio family. For generations not only have these highly skilled puppeteers put on performances, they have themselves made the actual puppets. Alas, puppet shows no longer attract the same large crowds they used to, for at one time they were the talk of the day, followed by everyone and, as such, provided work not only for puppeteers (of which there were many companies in business), but also for many a skilled craftsman who specialised in giving form to their fabulous creations, ever attentive to every detail and so complex as to demand several days in the making. A simple suit of armour, for example, might comprise some 35 to 36 individual parts before being assembled by hand. The family continues to be quite numerous; some members devote themselves to inventing new shows while others concentrate on constructing the puppets.

Working puppets – Opposite the Teatro di Mimmo Cuticchio *(via Bara all'Olivella 52* ☎ *091 32 34 00)* is the workshop (visits welcome) where the puppets and stage machinery are kept (for producing wind and rain). The puppets are hung on the walls according to category: just inside on the left, are little Orlando and his companions (used for shows for children of nursery and primary school age); these are followed by two rows of Paladins (above) and Saracens (below). At one time, puppet shows were so popular that members of the audience immediately recognised the different characters on sight. For the less initiated, the simplest way to determine who is who is by looking at the shields: Orlando's bears a cross, those of Rinaldo and Bradamante (who has long hair) have a lion. A little further on is the workshop of the famous puppet-maker Nino Cuticchio. The workshop and theatre of Girolamo Cuticchio is in via dei Benedettini. The Ippogrifo, belonging to Anna Cuticchio, is situated in vicolo Ragusi ai Quattro Canti di Città, ☎ 091 32 91 94. The workshop is at via Orologio 14.

CONCERTS, OPERA AND THEATRE

Teatro Massimo – Piazza Verdi, ☎ 091 60 53 515 or 800 65 58 58 (toll-free number). This renowned theatre stages opera performances, concerts and ballets.

Teatro Biondo – Via Roma 258, ☎ 091 58 23 64. Classical drama from Nov to May.

Teatro al Massimo – Piazza Verdi 9, ☎ 091 58 95 75. Light drama and operettas from Nov to May.

Politeama Garibaldi – Piazza Ruggero Settimo, ☎ 091 60 53 315. Concerts and ballets from Nov to May.

Teatro Golden – Via Terrasanta 60, ☎ 091 30 52 17. Concerts.

Teatro Zappalà – Via Aut. Siciliana 125, ☎ 091 54 33 80. Plays in Sicilian dialect.

Today, the *palazzo* serves as the seat of the Sicilian Parliament (or ARS: Assemblea Regionale Siciliana). The entrance hall, graced by a monumental staircase (where a senator's beautiful carriage is displayed), dates from 1735.

***Cappella Palatina** ⊘ – *Up on the first floor (take the staircase on the left).* Before entering the Palatine Chapel, it is worth pausing a moment to admire the superb **courtyard** enclosed by three superimposed loggias. Set into the wall on the left is an inscription in Latin, Greek and Arabic: this would originally have come from the base of a bell-tower that once stood before the chapel on the right. The inscription sings the praises of a water-clock that was made during the reign of Roger II. The actual chapel was built by the king between 1130 – the year of his coronation – and 1140. In the beginning it would have stood alone, with the apse at the east end. Then, through the course of time, it became incorporated into a complex of other buildings which now conceal it completely. Currently, the entrance is via the narthex that precedes the chapel proper. What can still be seen is the exterior of the side wall (corresponding to the north aisle) with its two-tier decoration. The lower section echoes the decorative arrangement at the same level inside: slabs of white marble surrounded by *pietra dura* decoration (inlay of semi-precious stones). The upper tier comprises composite panels dating from the 19C, depicting scenes from the life of David. At the rear, next to the entrance, Roger II is represented handing a decree instituting the royal ecclesiastical body to the *ciantro* (literally a singer, but, in this case, the person in charge of the chapel). Once inside, attention is immediately drawn to the fabulous Arabo-Norman interior decoration of blazing gold set off by the marble.

Structure – The internal space, with a rectangular ground plan, is divided into two parts: the first section is articulated into three aisles by 10 granite columns; the second, up five steps, comprises the chancel, which is contained within a marbl

La Vucciria by Renato Guttuso

MICHELIN – © ADAGP PARIS 1998

EXHIBITION HALLS

Cantieri culturali alla Zisa – Via Gili 4, ☎ 091 65 24 942. The old Ducrot warehouses, near Castello della Zisa and once home to a well-known furniture factory, have been transformed into exhibition rooms which now host a range of exhibitions, concerts and plays.

Lo Spasimo – Via Spasimo (piazza Magione), ☎ 091 61 61 486. The complex of Santa Maria dello Spasimo provides an atmospheric environment for a range of cultural events *(see p 275)*.

balustrade. On the right, near the division of the two halves, is the double **ambo**, supported by four beautiful columns and two small pilasters, with integrated lecterns borne by the eagle of St John and the lion of St Mark. To one side is the fine Paschal **candlestick** (12C), a wonderful piece of sculpture, tall, slender and richly decorated: its square pedestal is formed by four lions intent on mauling two men and two animals; a braid of plant-like branches intertwines the figures of wild beasts and an armed man preparing to defend himself. Above, Christ sits in a mandorla supported by angels, holding the Gospels in his hand while, below, a figure in bishop's clothing kneels before him (possibly Roger II himself). Two tiers of birds (vultures pecking the tails of slender storks) support three figures representing the three ages of man. The acute sense of realism of these figures might suggest they are of a later date; perhaps the figures were added when the candlestick was moved, and required further refinement.

Set against the back wall of the chapel is the majestic **royal throne**, which also forms an integral part of the mosaic above depicting Christ seated, attended by the Archangels St Michael and St Gabriel (representing death and birth respectively) and by the Apostles St Peter and St Paul (a Jew and a Gentile, founders of the Christian Church). The actual throne is inlaid with mosaic and porphyry; the coat of arms in the centre is that of the House of Aragon. The porphyry octagon probably bore the image of the reigning monarch.

The pavement comprises a geometric arrangement of marble tiles and mosaic, that form large Oriental-style rectangles.

The remarkable **wooden muqarnas ceiling**★★ in the central nave, a masterpiece by North African artists, depicts a number of scenes from daily life: courtly and hunting scenes, drinking, dancing, games of chess, animals etc. This exceptional work of art comprises the most extensive cycle of Fatimid painting to have survived to the present day.

CAPPELLA PALATINA

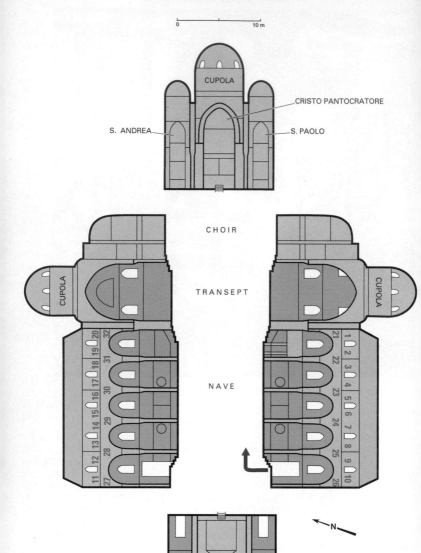

1 The creation of light and of the seas
2 The dry land separated from the waters
3 The creation of plants and trees
4 The creation of the sun, moon and stars
5 The creation of fish and birds
6 The creation of land animals
7 The creation of Adam
8 God resting from his labours
9 God pointing out the tree to Adam
10 The creation of Eve
11 Original sin
12 The shame of Adam and Eve
13 Paradise lost
14 Adam and Eve at work
15 The sacrifice of Cain and Abel
16 Cain kills Abel and lies to God
17 Lamech confesses to his two wives that he has killed two men
18 Enoch taken up to heaven on account of his deep faith

19 Noah with his wife and three sons
20 Building the Ark
21 Return of the dove
22 God tells Noah to leave the Ark
23 Noah planting a vineyard and getting drunk
24 Noah's descendants build the city of Babel
25 Abraham meets three angels and offers them hospitality
26 Lot on the threshold of his house tries to restrain the Sodomites
27 Destruction of Sodom, and Lot leaving the city
28 God tells Abraham to sacrifice Isaac, but an angel intervenes
29 Rebecca at the well and departure for Canaan
30 Isaac blessing Jacob
31 Jacob's dream
32 Jacob wrestling with the angel

Mosaics – The mosaics, exquisitely laid, comprise pieces of coloured paste (cement and pigment) and glass onto which gold leaf has been applied, thus imparting an inherent brilliance. They recount the story of the Old Testament *(nave)*, a selection of the most important episodes in the life of Christ *(chancel)*, and of St Peter and St Paul *(aisles)*. The silent witnesses include a host of prophets, angels and saints, either shown full-length or enclosed in medallions.

The mosaics were executed in two different phases: the oldest ones date from the 1140s, the ones in the nave, echoing the style of those at Monreale, date from the 1160s and 1170s.

The sequence of scenes in the nave serves a single function, and that is didactic: this is a prime example of teaching through pictures. Of particular note is the illustration of the earth being separated from the sea: the terrestrial globe is shown as a sphere of water in which there are three areas of land (America and Oceania had not yet been discovered). These are divided by sea which takes the form of a Y – the symbol of the Holy Trinity; the firmament, all around, is not yet illuminated by stars. Look out also for the **Creation of Adam**: note the striking resemblance in the face of Adam with that of God, thereby underlining the inscription in Latin: *"creavit ds ominem at imaginem sua"* (And God created Man in His own image). The scene recounting the story of **Original Sin** sounds an unusual note as both Adam and Eve are shown with the forbidden fruit in their mouths as they reach for a second one. The section that follows on from the second half of the panel illustrating the **Sacrifice of Cain and Abel**, when the latter lies to the Lord, up to the scene showing the family of Noah (including Noah himself) was substantially remodelled in the 19C: this is evident from the radical change in style.

In contrast, the iconography of the scenes in the chancel is modified for contemplation by the clergy and is therefore conducive to reflection rather than teaching by example. This explains why the scenes from the life of Christ are not arranged sequentially but in order of importance *(note especially above the right-hand apse)*. The **cupola** above the choir contains the figure of Christ Pantocrator, flanked by the three Archangels (St Gabriel, St Michael and St Raphael) and Tobit, and four angels. Biblical figures line the inside of the drum, and the Evangelists fill the pendentives (triangular corner sections).

The Annunciation is represented above the arch of the apse, placed there as a reminder of the word of God that foretold Christ in Benediction (in the vault) and the enthroned Madonna, the Queen of Heaven. On the underside of the arch, at its apex, is a medallion containing the throne of justice, the cross hung with the crown of thorns, and the dove.

In the **south transept**, pride of place is given to the figure of St Paul (apse vault) surrounded by scenes from the life of Christ; the barrel vault has a medallion filled with the symbol of Pentecost, a dove flying down among the Apostles (figures below). The story of the *Nativity* is particularly well related: the three kings are represented on their journey towards Bethlehem and the Christ Child (note that the Magi on the left wear Phrygian caps, a pointed hat with the top folded forward, to denote the fact that they come from the East. Historically, the Magi were astrologers of the Persian court, the priests of the cult of Mithras, which was widespread throughout the Roman Empire). St Joseph, on the left of the Virgin Mary, is seated on a typical type of Sicilian chair. The blue lunette below the scene symbolises the washing of the Christ Child.

Dominating the **north transept** is St Andrew (apse vault), but only since the 14C when he replaced the original mosaics of St Peter; beside him is the so-called Hodegetria Madonna and Child (Guide or Instructress pointing to the Way of Redemption based on an icon said to be painted by St Luke). To one side, St John the Baptist preaches in the desert.

Some of the mosaics in the apse were substantially reworked in the 18C.

The **aisles** are covered with scenes from the life of St Paul *(starting from the beginning of the south aisle)* and St Peter *(last section of the south aisle, along the length of the north aisle)*. A list of the scenes depicted in the nave is given below.

Nave: Old Testament – *Begin from the top of the right-hand side of the nave, follow the length of the top register, along the left-hand side of the nave; continue with the second register, starting again on the right-hand side of the nave. For an explanation of the less well-known biblical stories, see the description of the mosaics of Monreale, under the same heading.*

★★**Royal Apartments** ⊘ – The visit begins in the Salone d'Ercole (1560), now the chamber of the Sicilian Parliament, so called after the large frescoes by Giuseppe Velasquez (19C) depicting the *Twelve Labours of Heracles (see p 131)*. Today, only six panels are visible (the others being hidden behind the gallery), namely: *starting from the far end of the hall*: Heracles and the giants (not, in fact, related to the Labours), the slaying of the many-headed Hydra of Lerna, the capture of the Ceryneian hind, the taming of the three-headed dog Cerberus, the capture of the Erymanthean boar and the Cretan Bull. The frescoed ceiling illustrates the birth, triumph and death of the hero.

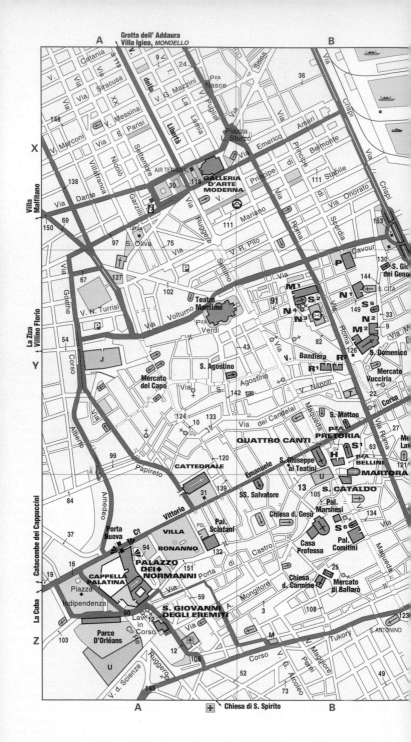

Street and monument in

Across the hall of the viceroys is a small entrance room which once constituted the heart of the **Joaria**, one of the Norman palace's original towers, now incorporated into other buildings. The wall apertures were designed to provide ventilation, allowing cool and warm air to circulate through the cavities between one wall and another. On the left is the most interesting room in the palace, **Sala di Ruggero II**, which is decorated in a way that is reminiscent of the Palatine Chapel. From the high marble panelling, framed within friezes of mosaic, springs the golden mantle that covers the upper sections of the wall and ceiling. Hunting scenes alternate with symbolic animals such as the peacock (for eternity, as it was alleged that its

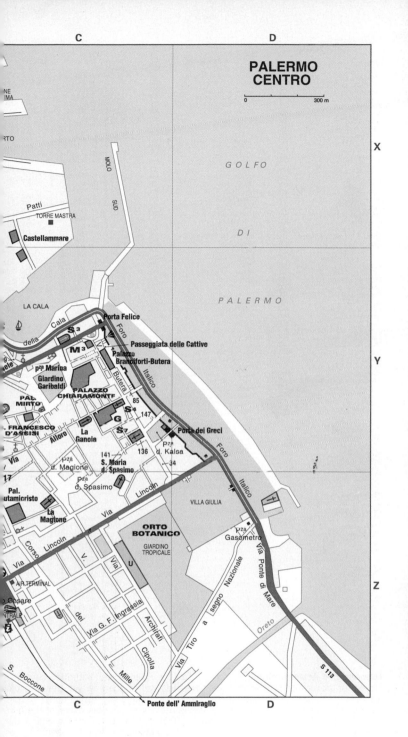

PALERMO CENTRO

0   300 m

GOLFO

DI

PALERMO

MOLO SUD

Patti
TORRE MASTRA
Castellammare

LA CALA

Porta Felice
Passeggiata delle Cattive
Palazzo Branciforti-Butera

della Cala
S³
M³
pⁿ Marina
Giardino Garibaldi
PAL. MIRTO
PALAZZO CHIARAMONTE
85
S⁴
147
G
Porta dei Greci
. FRANCESCO D'ASSISI
Alloro
La Ganoia
S⁷
Pⁿ d. Kalsa
136
34
Via
pⁿ d. Magione
141
S. Maria d. Spasimo
17
Pal. utamicristo
pⁿ d. Spasimo
La Magione
Lincoln
Via
Lincoln
Via
VILLA GIULIA
Corso
Lincoln
V.
Via
ORTO BOTANICO
GIARDINO TROPICALE
pⁿ Gasometro
U
Via Ponte di Mare
AIR TERMINAL
Cesare
Via G. F. Ingrassia
Via Tiro a segno Nazionale
Via del
Archiafi
Oreto
S 113
S. Boccone
Cipolla
Mille
Ponte dell' Ammiraglio

X

Y

Z

C   D

ne following page

flesh would never decompose) and the lion (for royalty and strength): all are portrayed in accordance with an Eastern iconography, which demanded that they be
shown in pairs, one facing the other. Representations are exquisitely detailed, as
the figures wander through a typically Sicilian landscape with palms and citrus
trees. At the centre of the ceiling is a medallion with the Imperial emblem: an eagle
holding a hare between its talons. There follows a number of other 18C and 19C
rooms, including the Yellow Hall or Hall of Mirrors, named after the beautiful gold
candlesticks it contains.

267

PALERMO

Osservatorio Astronomico ⊘ – *Top floor of the Pisan Tower*. Although currently closed for restoration, the **astronomical observatory** will re-open as a museum of old instruments used in astronomy, meteorology, seismology and topography; visitors will be able to relive a fundamental event in astronomy: the discovery of the first asteroid, on this very spot, on 1 January 1801, by Father Piazzi, to whom the observatory is dedicated. From the top, there is a fabulous bird's-eye **view★★★** over Palermo.

CASSARO QUARTER

Porta Nuova – Built under Charles V, the gateway is topped by a Renaissance-style loggia; note at the end of the pitched roof, the Imperial eagle. Beyond the gate stretches **corso Vittorio Emanuele**, a long, straight road which runs across town to **Porta Felice**.

Palazzo e Parco d'Orléans – This is the house and garden in which Louis Philippe d'Orléans, the future King of France, lived in exile from 1810-14. Today, it is used by the Sicilian regional authorities. The garden has magnificent banyan trees *(Ficus magnolioides)* with their spectacular array of roots, and various exotic animals.

San Giovanni degli Eremiti

★★ San Giovanni degli Eremiti ⊘ – The Church of **St John of the Hermits** and its garden are situated not far from Palazzo dei Normanni, providing a tiny haven of peace where even the noise of the Palermo traffic seems muffled.

Nestling in a luxuriant garden of palm trees, agaves, bougainvillaea, orange-trees, Chinese mandarin-trees and shrubs of various kinds, stands the church that was built around the middle of the 12C at the request of King **Roger II**. This is one of the most famous Arabo-Norman monuments in Palermo. Its simple, square forms which enclose perfect cubes of spaces rise to a red roof with five squat domes (echoing the profile of San Cataldo not far away), are clearly the work of Moorish craftsmen. The interior, simple and bare, is shaped into a Latin-cross plan: the central space is divided into two halves above which hover two domes. The transept is subdivided into three, each part contained by a dome; the south bay rising first to become a bell-tower that is then capped by a dome.

At one time, the church was flanked by its monastery, the abbot of which was employed as the king's private confessor. Today, only the delightful little 13C **cloisters★** with their paired columns remain.

★ Villa Bonanno – These lovely public gardens lie behind the Palazzo Reale (Norman Palace). The elaborate 17C monument is of Philip V of Bourbon. Excavations conducted in one part of the garden have revealed the **remains of Roman patrician houses** containing mosaics featuring the seasons and Orpheus, now housed in the Museo Archeologico Regionale *(see below)*.

Palazzo Sclafani – The front of the building (1330) overlooking piazzetta San Giovanni Decollato is ornamented with fine Gothic two-light windows within interlacing arches so typical of the Arabo-Norman style, and an elegant cusped doorway surmounted by the royal eagle. It is from this *palazzo* that the famous fresco *The Triumph of Death* was transferred to the Galleria Regionale di Sicilia.

★ Cathedral ⊘ – Palermo's cathedral is an imposing edifice. It was built in the late 12C in the Sicilian-Norman style, but has undergone considerable alteration over the centuries. A notable addition from the 15C is the Catalan Gothic south porch with, on the outermost wall, the symbols of the four Evangelists (St Mark's lion and St Matthew's angel on the right, St Luke's ox and St John's eagle on the left), its fine inner doorway and fine, carved wooden doors. The neo-Classical dome was added in the 18C, when the interior was also completely refurbished. The original fabric of the building, however, can still be seen in the **apses★** which retain their typical yet effective geometric decoration.

Inside, the first chapel on the right contains the tombs of members of the Swabian royal family: Frederick II, his wife Costanza of Aragon, Henry IV and, at the rear, Roger II and his daughter Costanza d'Altavilla.

Treasury ⊘ – *Access from the south transept.* The **treasury** contains a fine carved ivory staff made in Sicily in the 17C, and various jewels belonging to Queen Constanza of Aragon. Among these various rings and the magnificent **Imperial gold crown★** set with precious stones, pearls and enamels.

B. Kaufmann

Cathedral apses

Crypt – A number of tombs from different periods are preserved in the crypt, a large proportion belonging to former bishops. Note the Classical Roman sarcophagus decorated with the figures of nine muses, Apollo, and a seated man wearing a toga.

Chiesa del Santissimo Salvatore ⊘ – The present oval Church of the Holy Saviour, built on the foundations of a Norman predecessor, was designed in the late 17C by **Paolo Amato**. The interior is richly decorated in the Baroque style complete with polychrome marble and stucco. Within the dome may be discerned fragments of a large fresco of the **Triumph of St Basil** (1763). Today, the church is principally used as an auditorium.

Further along corso Vittorio Emanuele is **piazza Bologni**: among the alignment of fine 18C buildings sits **Palazzo Alliata di Villafranca** which displays proudly the elaborate coats of arms of two aristocratic families including that of the Bologna family. In the centre of the piazza is a statue of Charles V, the Spanish monarch.

★★QUATTRO CANTI AND ITS NEIGHBOURHOOD

★**I "Quattro Canti" (piazza Vigliena)** – The intersection of Palermo's two main thoroughfares, via Vittorio Emanuele and via Maqueda, is marked by a spacious octagon: the in-filled corners of the square are furnished by four elegant 18C Baroque *palazzo* fronts, their elevation subdivided into sections with Classical columns (Doric, Ionic and Corinthian); with, at the centre, an elaborate fountain dedicated to one of the four seasons. The niches of the middle storey harbour statues of the four Spanish kings of Sicily, those at the upper level contain effigies representing the patron saints of Palermo, who protected the districts lying behind them: St Christina, St Ninfa, St Oliva and St Agatha (who was subsequently replaced by St Rosalia) *(see p 286)*.

San Matteo ⊘ – The Church of St Matthew was built in the mid-17C. Its façade consists of three orders, the niches and projecting surfaces of which contrast to produce striking *chiaroscuro* effects. The richly decorated interior reflects the church's ties with the Unione dei Miseremini, founded with the aim of hearing masses for souls suffering in Purgatory. The valuable works of art housed here include two beautiful canvases by P Novelli (*The Presentation at the Temple* and *The Marriage of the Virgin*, fourth chapel in the side aisle), the 18C frescoes in the vault and dome by Vito d'Anna, and the statue of *Faith and Justice* to the side of the presbytery and the lunette portraying *Christ Freeing Souls from the Flames of Purgatory* opposite, by the great Serpotta. Serpotta himself is buried in the crypt of the church (access from the left aisle).

★★**Piazza Pretoria** – At the centre of this lovely piazza is a spectacular **fountain**★★ by the 16C Florentine sculptor Francesco Camilliani, originally intended as a garden ornament for some Tuscan villa. Comprising concentric circles of gods and goddesses, nymphs, monsters, animals' heads, allegories, ornamental staircases and balustrades, this fountain is a veritable Mount Olympus. Spouting water brings the whole to life, animating it with sparkling light, yet never upsetting the balance of the composition: a rare quality typically often found in Tuscan Renaissance works of art.

The top basin is divided into four sections; below each is a smaller bowl which, in turn, is overlooked by one of the four allegories of the rivers of Palermo: Gabriele, Maredolce, Papireto and Oreto. Among the statuettes guarding the ramps is Ceres, the Classical patroness of Sicily, who holds a sheaf of wheat and a horn of plenty. The wrought-iron railing surrounding the fountain is by Giovan Battista Basile.

B. Kaufmann

The fountain in piazza Pretoria

The piazza is confined by fine buildings: to one side rises the dome of **Santa Caterina**; on the south axis stands the **Palazzo Pretorio** (also known as Palazzo Senatorio or Palazzo delle Aquile), the City Hall. Across the road is the church of San Giuseppe ai Teatini.

Palazzo Pretorio ⊙ – Concealed by the present rather austere exterior, the result of 19C renovations, lie the vestiges of a succession of earlier façades in various styles, the oldest of which dates from the 1300s. Since then, it has been the seat of the City Council. The main entrance, especially on the inside, is ornamented with a profusion of Baroque elements (1691), including spiralling columns; beyond, lies an attractive courtyard with a monumental staircase up to the *piano nobile*. Here, on the first floor, there is a shallow relief *(on the left)* of a crowned Ceres, a homage to the patroness of Sicily. The rooms open to the public include the **Sala del Lapidi** lined with marble tablets bearing inscriptions and now used for Council meetings (note, in passing the magnificent central 17C chandelier carved from a single piece of wood), and **Sala Garibaldi**, so named after the Italian hero who addressed the assembled crowds from the balcony in 1860. A glass case on the right contains some fine weapons and scabbards inlaid with gold and mother-of-pearl belonging to Napoleon Bonaparte.

San Giuseppe ai Teatini ⊙ – The piazza Pretoria is bordered by the side of the striking Baroque church. The most eye-catching element is the original campanile which rises to an octagonal section with spiral columns at the top. The sides are ornamented with flaming vases. The **interior★**, in the form of a Latin cross, is theatrical, endowed as it is with a majestic ceiling, a stunning array of white and gold stucco decoration and frescoes on a grand scale. Each aisle bay is capped with a small round dome, itself encrusted with stucco. Set diagonally from the rear wall are two fine organ cases. Sitting to either side of the entrance are a pair of unusually impressive 18C **stoups★** each one consisting of an angel in flight with a basin in its arms.

★Piazza Bellini – This small square is contained by three churches: **Santa Caterina** (dating from the end of the 16C, with an 18C dome), la Martorana and San Cataldo which, with its three red domes, endows the place with an Eastern flavour.

★★La Martorana ⊙ – This church is named after Eloisa Martorana who, in 1194, founded the nearby Benedictine convent, to which the church served as a chapel. The church, in fact dedicated to **Santa Maria dell'Ammiraglio** (St Mary of the Admiral), had been founded in 1143 at the request of George of Antioch, an admiral in the fleet of Roger II.
The linearity of the Norman original is unfortunately concealed behind the Baroque façade (on the south side of the church) that faces onto the piazza. The main entrance is through a fine portico-cum-bell-tower, articulated by three orders of columns and double arch openings. At one time, this was free-standing; it was attached to the church in the 16C when the church was extended by two bays, at the same time as the apse was replaced by a square choir.
Mass is celebrated according to the Greek Orthodox dogma.

Interior – The building is divided into two parts. The first two bays, added in the 16C, were frescoed in the 17C; the older church shelters a wonderful array of glorious **mosaics★★** that strictly conform to Byzantine iconography, possibly, executed by the same craftsmen as those employed at the Capella Palatina. The wall which once constituted the main façade has two mosaic panels representing George of Antioch prostrate at the feet of the Virgin *(on the left)* and Roger II receiving the crown from Christ *(on the right)*. Filling the nave dome is Christ Pantocrator sur-

271

Frutta martorana

Frutta martorana, also known as *pasta reale* and one of the most typical kinds of Sicilian *pasticcerie*, is named after the church of the same name. According to tradition, the origins of this delicacy can be traced back to medieval times when every convent specialised In making a different kind of confectionery. The ones made by the Benedictine convent of la Martorana in early November for the feast-day of All Saints, were of marzipan, shaped and coloured into various fruits. The tradition continues today: during the Fiera dei Morti at the beginning of November the district between via Spicuzza and piazza Olivella is invaded by brightly-coloured stalls selling *frutta martorana*, dolls made from sugar and children's toys.

Marzipan is also of medieval origin: the term is derived from the Arabic *mauthaban* which originally denoted a coin, then a unit of measurement and, finally, the container used to store the paste, made of almonds, sugar and white of egg.

rounded by the three Archangels (St Michael, St Gabriel, St Raphael) and St Uriel. In the register below are eight prophets and, in the pendentives, the four Evangelists. In the nave vault may be seen the Nativity *(on the left)* and the Death (Dormition) of the Virgin.

The gratings of the nuns' gallery are a fine example of wrought-iron work.

★★San Cataldo ☉ – The church, the main seat of the Knights of the Holy Sepulchre, was built during the Norman period (12C). A distinctive Moorish quality is imparted by the combination of its rather severe square forms, crenellated walls, perforated window screens and characteristic bulbous red domes (likened, by the Italians, to a eunuch's hat).

The austere interior is articulated into three aisles by antique columns stolen from more ancient buildings. The nave is crowned with three domes, each supported on squinches. The polychrome marble paving is original.

Le Camere dello Scirocco

The custom of excavating artificial caves under the seigniorial mansions of Palermo can be traced as far back as the 15C. These caves provided refuge on days when the scorching south-east wind swept through the city, drying out both mind and body. Palermo's limestone soil was ideal for this purpose and the presence of numerous springs allowed for the construction of small pools in which to escape the heat. One of the oldest of these *scirocco rooms* is under the cloisters of the 15C **Palazzo Marchesi** ☉, at a depth of 8m/26ft. An enormous Arabic cistern, once used for the city's water supply, has been found next to this room. *From piazzetta SS Quaranta Martiri, go into passageway no 14 (to the left of the tower), and from the courtyard take the staircase on the left. Ring the bell if the door is closed.*

Sant'Orsola ☉ – This 17C church was once the headquarters of the Compagnia dell'Orazione della Morte, an organisation responsible for burying the deceased of the district. The façade is late-Renaissance in style and the interior 18C with unusual communicating chapels. In the last chapel to the right, decorated by Serpotta, the usual rejoicing *putti* are replaced by skeletons and dangling bones.

Palazzo Comitini ☉ – *Via Maqueda 100*. The *palazzo* (1768-71), built for the Prince of Gravina, incorporates two older ones belonging to the Roccafiorita-Bonanno and Gravina di Palagonia families. The front is graced with two large entrances and nine openings (now windows) on the ground floor, and a series of bulbous balconies (evocatively described in Italian as a *petto d'oca* which translates as goose breasted) on the first floor. The building was radically altered in 1931 with the addition of another floor for use as the administrative offices for the Province of Palermo. A wide staircase leads up from the internal courtyard to the loggia on the first floor and the Sala delle Armi (Armoury), now the Salone dei Commessi: the two masks flanking the doorway served as torch extinguishers. Off to the left is the Green Room, furnished with a fine 18C Murano glass lamp. **Sala Martorana★**, now the seat of the Provincial Council, is lined throughout with 18C wood panelling inlayed with mirrors: these add luminosity to the room and enhance the impact of the ceiling which is frescoed with *The Triumph of True Love*: the chariot of Wisdom has overcome Avarice, Falsehood and Perfidy; as it crushes Eros and Envy, it is celebrated by cherubs bearing garlands of flowers. The theme is picked up in the four corner medallions which depict the four Virtues: Fortitude, Temperance, Prudence and Justice. Sadly, the tiled floor is in poor condition.

Adjacent to the Sala del Presidente, at one time the prince's bedroom, are two small boudoirs; these are panelled in wood and furnished with shelves bearing early-20C maiolica plates.

Sicilian wine exhibition

The permanent exhibition of Sicilian wines **(Mostra permanente dei vini di Sicilia)** ⓥ is a must for wine lovers. It is housed in the beautiful Palazzo Ramacca (*via Maqueda 92, ☎ 091 61 62 288, open weekdays 9am-12.30pm*). The visit includes a wine tasting.

Chiesa del Gesù ⓥ – When the Jesuits arrived in Sicily in the mid-16C, the Spanish government gave them its generous support. It was here that they founded their first church, although this was considerably altered before arriving at its present form at the end of the same century. Sadly, the church suffered serious damage during the bombing of 1943 and has been partially re-built.
Its sober façade is in marked contrast to the Baroque exuberance of the interior which is encrusted with stucco and *pietra dura* decoration. The **chancel decor★** executed by the Serpotta brothers is especially fine, populated with a euphoric display of cherubs engaged in all manner of activities: gathering grapes, holding garlands of flowers, torches, musical instruments, rulers, set squares, and lances with which they pierce devils.
The second chapel on the right has two fine paintings by **Pietro Novelli**: *St Philip of Agira* and ***St Paul the Hermit★***, in which the last figure on the left is a self-portrait of the artist.
The **sacristy** is furnished with a splendidly carved cupboard (16C).
Next to the church stands **Casa Professa**; this houses the **municipal library** which contains a large number of incunabula and manuscripts. The first and second room (reading rooms) are hung with the portraits of 300 illustrious men.

Chiesa del Carmine ⓥ – Piazza del Carmine, before the Church of Our Lady of Mount Carmel, is brought to life each day by the picturesque **Ballarò food market**. Before entering the church, it is worth taking the time to admire from afar the splendid tile-covered **dome** supported by four giant Atlas figures.
Inside the church, the two most interesting features are the sumptuous **altars★** in the transepts, decorated with pairs of golden twisting columns on which spirals of stucco tell the story of the life of the Virgin Mary *(on the left)* and of Christ *(on the right)*. They are the work of Giacomo and Giuseppe Serpotta. Above the left-hand altar is a fine canvas of *La Madonna del Carmine* (Our Lady of Mount Carmel), dating from the 15C.

★★ LA KALSA

This quarter grew up during the period of Islamic domination around the fortified citadel where the emir and his ministers lived, preserving its original name (*al halisah*; the elect, the pure). Even today, an unusual Oriental atmosphere pervades the place, accentuated by the presence of monuments in the Arabo-Norman style. Centrally located and densely populated, the neighbourhood offers an intriguing insight into Palermo life. For example, on passing before the Church of St Teresa it is not unusual to encounter some local engaged in cooking and selling *babbaluci*: tiny snails marinated in oil, parsley, garlic and pepper and sold in paper cornets to passers-by.
The heart of the quarter is piazza della Kalsa, although the district itself stretches as far as corso Vittorio Emanuele, and contains many of the city's most interesting monuments.

Count of Cagliostro

Giuseppe Balsamo was born in Palermo in 1743. He became fascinated by occult science and founded a Masonic lodge; assuming the name Count of Cagliostro, he embarked upon his travels around Europe practising the "arts" of healing and magic with his miraculous "water of eternal youth". In France, he became involved in court intrigues which led to him being imprisoned in the Bastille. Following his return to Italy, fortune still refused to smile upon him and he was again arrested: this time, accused of belonging to the sect of the *Illuminati*, he was incarcerated in the fortress of San Leo, in the Montefeltro near Urbino. Here, he died in poverty, and his body was taken to the cemetery in Palermo. His house is located off piazza Ballarò, in via Cagliostro (in a bad state of repair).

The heart of the quarter

The main entrance to the quarter appears to be **Porta dei Greci** beyond which lies the piazza and the church of **Santa Teresa alla Kalsa**, a monumental Baroque church built between 1686 and 1706 by **Paolo Amato**, with an imposing façade with two orders of Corinthian columns.

Turning onto via Torremuzza, note the beautiful stone-framed Noviziato dei Crociferi at no 20 and, further along on the opposite side of the street, **Santa Maria della Pietà** designed by Giacomo Amata: inside, in the section reserved for the closed order of Dominican nuns which founded the church, is a choir screen emblazoned with a rising sun.

Via Alloro – Throughout the Middle Ages, this served as the quarter's main street. Today, most of the elegant *palazzi* that once lined the thoroughfare have, sadly, either been destroyed or have fallen into disrepair. The few surviving buildings include Palazzo Abatellis, which accommodates the Galleria Regionale di Sicilia, and, next to it, the lovely Chiesa della Gancia.

★★ **Galleria Regionale di Sicilia** ⊙ – The regional art gallery is housed in **Palazzo Abatellis★**, a magnificent Catalan Gothic building with some Renaissance features, designed by Matteo Carnelivari who was active in Palermo towards the end of the 15C. Its elegant front has a great square central doorway ornamented with fasces (literally faggots), and a series of two– and three-light windows. Within, the *palazzo* is arranged around an attractive square courtyard.

The gallery's internal layout is most interesting having been completed in the 1950s by Carlo Scarpa, one of Italy's foremost contemporary interior designers. For each important work of art, the designer has contrived a tailor-made solution in terms of support and background, using different materials and colours so as to display it in the best possible manner while exploiting natural daylight to the full.

The gallery collects together sculptures and paintings from the medieval period. The first exhibit to draw attention on the ground floor is the magnificent fresco of the *Triumph of Death*★★★ *(Room II)*, from the Palazzo Sclafani. The title probably refers to the thirteenth Tarot card as the cards, which were highly popular in the Middle Ages, were also known as *Trionfi* (Triumphs). The painting shows the cruel and realistic figure of Death, astride a skeletal horse and armed with a bow and arrows, in the act of striking down men and women in the full flush of youth. Note, in particular, how colder shades of colour have been used to portray Death, the horse, and the faces of those who have been struck by his arrows. On the left, among the group of beggars and the afflicted who have been "spared" by the terrible rider, is painted a figure *(top)* who gazes out from the picture at the observer; the brush in his right hand denotes this to be a self-portrait of the unknown author of the picture. The modernity with which some of the details – such as the stylised nose of the horse – have been rendered is quite extraordinary.

The admirable *bust of Eleonora of Aragon*★★ *(Room IV)*, with its gentle expression and delicate features, together with the bust of a young woman, are by the sculptor **Francesco Laurana** who worked in Sicily in the 15C. This was also when the Gagini family were active and works by them are to be found all over the island. Included in the gallery is a fine *Madonna and Child*★ by **Antonello da Messina**.

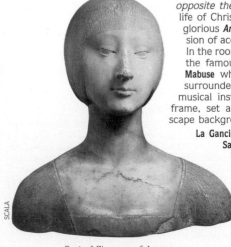

The first floor is entirely devoted to painting (with many works from the Sicilian School). Note the lovely portable Byzantine icon *(first room opposite the entrance)* with scenes from the life of Christ, and in Antonello da Messina's glorious *Annunciation*★★, the peaceful expression of acceptance in the face of the Virgin. In the room devoted to Flemish painting sits the famous *Malvagna Triptych*★★ (1510) by **Mabuse** which shows the Virgin and Child surrounded by angels singing and playing musical instruments in a lavishly decorated frame, set against an equally fabulous landscape background.

La Gancia ⊙ – The church dedicated to **Santa Maria degli Angeli** was originally built by the Franciscans in the late 15C; numerous alterations have since modified its appearance, particularly the interior. The exterior retains from the original its square profile and rustication. Before entering, look out for the *Buca della*

Bust of Eleonora of Aragon

SCALA

Salvezza on the left: this so-called Hole of Salvation was made by two patriots who had hidden in the crypt of the church during the anti-Bourbon rebellion so that they could be pulled to safety by a handful of local people.

The **interior**★ gives the impression of being Baroque although various elements date from several different periods. The fine wooden ceiling painted with stars on a blue background, the magnificent **organ**★★ by Raffaele della Valle (late 16C), the elegant marble **pulpit** and Antonello Gagini's relief tondoes of the *Annunciation (on either side of the altar)* all date from the 16C. Most of the superficial decoration, notably the stucco work in the nave and in some of the chapels by the Serpotta brothers, although in poor condition, dates from the 17C. Among the parts of the original fabric that survive are some very fine details including an original *novice monk*★ peeping out over the top of a cornice in the chapel to the left of the altar.

Complesso di Santa Maria dello Spasimo – *Via dello Spasimo*. The church and convent were built just inside the walls of the Kalsa in 1506. The patron of the project was Giacomo Basilicò who, to mark the occasion, commissioned **Raphael** to paint a picture of the anguish of the Madonna before the Cross (now in the Prado in Madrid). Building work on the church was slow and not yet completed when the Turkish threat made it necessary to build a new bastion just behind the church. In turn the complex was transformed into a fortress, a theatre, a hospice for plague victims (1624) then, later, for the poor (1835) and finally a hospital; the place was abandoned in 1986. The church and old hospital have been restored and transformed into unusual exhibition spaces and venues for cultural events. The section that is currently accessible to the public is the part arranged around the 16C cloisters: this is endowed with simple lines. Beyond sits the **church**★, the only example of Northern Gothic in Sicily. The tall, slender nave reaches up towards the open sky without a roof and ends with a lovely polygonal **apse**. The original entrance is given prominence by a *pronaos* in which were installed two side chapels. The one on the left is still visible, complete with its distinctive little bulbous dome. This, in turn, provides access to the old Spanish bastion, now laid out as a garden. The whole complex is most evocative, particularly when caught by the rays of the setting sun.

La Magione ⊘ – An attractive little avenue of palm trees leads up to the Romanesque church that was founded in the 12C by Matteo d'Ajello, a prominent official in the service of the Norman sovereigns. In 1197, it was conceded by Henry IV to the Order of Teutonic Knights, in whose hands it remained for more than 300 years. The **front elevation**★ rises through three tiers of pointed arches which at the lowest level are ornamented with decorative features and enclose the doorways. The interior, divided into three aisles, is simple and austere. The church also has a fine **cloisters** from the original Cistercian monastery, unfortunately severely damaged during the Second World War. Vestiges of pre-existing constructions, including a 10C Arab tower, are visible from the cloisters.

Via della Magione runs along the side of **Palazzo Ajutamicristo**, a large 15C building designed by **Matteo Carnelivari**.

Piazza della Rivoluzione – This delightful little square is so called because it was here that the anti-Bourbon rebellion of 1848 was sparked off. In the centre is a fountain graced by the so-called **Genio di Palermo**, who symbolises the city.

North of via Alloro

★**San Francesco d'Assisi** ⊘ – Very little of the original 13C church survives. As it succumbed to damage, repair and alteration on successive occasions, it owes its current appearance to the fact that, last time it was restored, great efforts were made to respect its original design. The simple front elevation is graced with a fine rose-window and magnificent Gothic **portal**★ from the original 13C structure. Inside, a strong sense of airiness and space, so typical of Franciscan churches, has been preserved despite subsequent structural remodelling. Of note, there are eight statues by Giovanni Serpotta, while the fine entrance **doorway** to the Mastrantonio Chapel is by **Francesco Laurana** and **Pietro di Bonitate** *(fourth chapel on the left)*.

Rose-window of San Francesco

B. Kaufmann

275

Next to the church stands the Oratorio dell'Immacolatella and, a little further on, the **Oratorio di San Lorenzo**.

***Oratorio di San Lorenzo** ⊙ – This masterpiece created by a mature **Giacomo Serpotta** has been described as a "cave of white coral". On the walls paintings alternating with statues of the Virtues illustrate scenes from the life of St Francis (to the right) and St Lawrence (to the left); the martyrdom of the latter is depicted opposite these works. Nude thinkers on the upper sections of the walls recall figures by Michelangelo. The lofty detachment of the Virtues and the veiled sadness of the nudes contrast sharply with the triumph of the delightful rejoicing *putti*, depicted in the most imaginative poses (note the figure making a soap bubble and the two characters kissing each other tenderly). However, the innocent vitality of these figures is in stark contrast to events that have taken place in the church, the most notorious of which was the theft in 1969 of Caravaggio's *Nativity*, painted to hang above the altar of the church.

***Palazzo Mirto** ⊙ – The *palazzo* that provides the princes of Lanzi Filangeri with a residence has been altered several times to meet the family's needs. Its current form dates from the late 18C. Just inside, on the left, are the fabulous **stables**★ (19C) complete with stalls and ornamental bronze horse-heads. A red marble staircase leads up to the first floor which is still furnished in the main with original pieces. Among the rooms open to the public there is the **Chinese sitting room** with its leather-covered floor, painted silk walls depicting scenes from everyday life, and fine *trompe-l'œil* ceiling: this was used as an intimate smoking-room or for playing cards. The next room, a small vestibule, contains a good set of 19C Neapolitan plates decorated with people in costume; it is said that the service was used for masked balls and that each guest was supposed to sit in front of the plate featuring their particular costume. Leading from the vestibule is another unusual **smoking room**★ this time panelled with painted and embossed leather, a material suited to such rooms because it does not become impregnated with smoke.

The most striking element of the **Pompadour sitting room**★ is the fabulous wall silks embroidered with flowers. The mosaic floor is the only original one.

The dining room contains a Meissen service (18C) exquisitely painted with flowers and birds.

Piazza Marina – The centre of the piazza, which in itself lies at the very heart of medieval Palermo, is graced with an attractive garden, the **Giardino Garibaldi**, which is planted with magnificent **banyan trees**★★ with their large, exposed, trunk-like roots.

The piazza is enclosed on all sides by fine buildings: Palazzo Galletti (no 46), Palazzo Notarbartolo (no 51) and the famous Palazzo Chiaramonte. Diametrically opposite this, on the far side, sits the lovely **Fontana del Garraffo** (from the Arabic *gharraf*, meaning abundant water) which was constructed at the close of the 17C by G Vitaliano, to designs by Paolo Amato.

The banyan trees in Giardino Garibaldi

M. Magni/MICHELIN

*★ **Palazzo Chiaramonte** – This splendid *palazzo* was built in 1307 for the Chiaramonte family, one of the wealthiest and most powerful dynasties of the Aragonese period. The building also came to be called **Lo Steri** from *Hosterium*, a fortified residence, an obvious function given its clean, square form. It passed into the hands of the Spanish viceroys, and thence, in the 17C, served as the headquarters of the Court of the Inquisition; this situation lasted until 1792 when the institution was abolished in Sicily.

The main front is ornamented by two tiers of elegant two– and three-light **windows**★★ (note the fabulous stone inlays on the underside of the arches on the first floor). The style, which in essence was distilled from the Gothic, is so distinctive as to be described simply as Chiaramonte; this may be discerned in many other Sicilian civic buildings of the same period.

★★Museo Internazionale delle Marionette ⊘ – The International Puppet Museum contains a fabulously rich collection of *pupi* (Sicilian puppets based on characters from the French *chansons de geste*), marionettes (articulated puppets operated with strings), shadow puppets, scenery and panels from all over the world. The first rooms are devoted to Sicilian puppets, many being presented "on stage". Notice, in particular, the delicate facial features of Gaspare Canino's theatre puppets (19C). The second section presents the European tradition, including such renowned figures as the English *Punch and Judy*, and the non-European, which comprises a vast Oriental collection: Chinese glove-puppets; string-puppets from India, Burma, Vietnam, Thailand and Africa; shadow puppets from Turkey, India and Malaysia (made of leather). All the caricatures are evocatively displayed in semi-darkness (for preservation purposes) as if to suggest the remoteness of their origins in the distant past and from far afield. In Room IV a *hsaing waing* has been arranged: this consists of a Burmese orchestra pit where, an hour before the performance, musicians used to sit and play pieces of music that constituted a symbolic rite. The final section is dedicated to special puppets destined for a violent, spectacular death. The museum also has an active theatre *(details of performances are available from the museum)*. The walls are hung with decorative puppeteers' posters, which were used by story-tellers to illustrate their stories.

Passeggiata alla Marina – Up until the 16C this promenade (the present Foro Italico), with its esplanade overlooking the sea, was a popular meeting-place and area for strolling for Palermo's elegant aristocracy, as well as the site of festivals and parades. A number of fine *palazzi* were built here, including the 18C **Palazzo Branciforti-Butera**, with terraces that enjoyed splendid and exclusive sea views. In 1847 the German writer Fanny Lewald was to write in *Diogena*: "Night never completely falls in Palermo, especially along the seafront, which is perhaps one of the most beautiful promenades in Europe...Under the row of terraces along the *corso*, starting at seven, the evening *passeggiata* takes place. At ten o'clock the orchestra strikes up and the music continues until midnight; it is only around ten that the marina really comes to life." The atmosphere of days gone by is evoked by the natural beauty of the setting and the neo-Classical bandstand *(immediately after the crossroads with via Alloro)*; however, the noise of the traffic and fairground rides makes it difficult to imagine the refined qualities of Palermo during the era of the Grand Tour.

Passeggiata delle Cattive – *Access by the steps in piazza S Spirito*. Built in 1823 along the wall which marked the end of the Passeggiata alla Marina, this promenade owes its unusual name to the popular expression "*mura di li cattivi*", which translates as the "wall of the wayward women". The walkway provided widows with a higher degree of privacy (as well as a better view) than the promenade below.

THE OLD HARBOUR DISTRICT

The *cala*, the city's ancient harbour, was once protected by the **Castellammare**, which was built by the Arabs, and later transformed for use as a fortress, prison and private residence. The massive construction was, however, badly damaged in 1922 when the new jetty was extended. A description of the Cala quarter which extends behind the old harbour must begin with the church, as this was where the chains that were used to close off the area were kept through the centuries, hence its dedication to Santa Maria della Catena.

★Santa Maria della Catena ⊘ – The design of the church is attributed to Matteo Carnelivari. Its elevation is dominated by the broad square portico with three arches; behind these are doorways set with low reliefs by Vincenzo Gagini. A decorative fretwork stone cornice runs along the top and sides of the portico (the flight of steps in front of the church was added at a later date). The overall style is transitional Gothic-Renaissance (1490). The lovely interior is articulated by blind arcading into square bays with pointed cross-arches, the stone ribs being offset by the white vault. The chancel is lit by traceried two-light windows. The second chapel on the right harbours fragments of a frescoed Madonna and, on the altar, symbolic chains. The church is especially evocative at sunset, when the façade is dramatically set alight by the colours of the setting sun.

Close by stands the monumental **Porta Felice** (1582), which marks the eastern end of via Vittorio Emanuele. This is designed in the late Renaissance style, its two massive upright elements softened by an interplay of volutes and openings surmounted by pediments.

Further along the broad curve of the harbour lies piazza Fonderia, beyond which (between via Cassari and piazza San Domenico) extends the picturesque and historic **Vucciria** market.

Market scene

San Domenico ⊘ – Before the church stretches an attractive **piazza** with, at its centre, a statue of the Madonna raised on a column.

The church was initiated in the 17C and completed only a century later. The Baroque front elevation rises in three ordered tiers of Doric and Corinthian columns and square pilasters framing a statue of St Dominic. The spacious interior is divided into nave and aisles, with a side chapel off each bay. A fine scheme of inlaid *pietra dura* decoration ornaments the fourth chapel on the right and the Chapel of the Rosary in the north transept. Adjacent to the church are lovely 14C **cloisters** with paired columns.

The neighbouring buildings accommodate the **Sicilian Historical Society** (Società Siciliana per la Storia Patria) which, in turn, has its own small **Museo del Risorgimento** containing mementoes of Garibaldi. From the windows of the museum, there is a splendid view of the cloisters of San Domenico.

★★★ **Oratorio del Rosario di San Domenico** ⊘ – The oratory is a veritable treasury of stucco decoration by **Giacomo Serpotta**, who succeeded, as always, in conferring a profound sense of movement to the antics of his cherubs. These are characterised by a spontaneous playfulness so often found in children; their unusually expressive faces, exuding happiness or thoughtfulness, highlight Serpotta's skill at working with stucco, a medium devoid of any inherent life of its own when compared to stone or marble.

The stucco or plasterwork provides frames for a series of paintings relating to the Joyful Mysteries of the Rosary *(left and rear walls)*, some of which are by **Pietro Novelli**, and the Sorrowful Mysteries of the Rosary *(right wall)*, which include a *Flagellation* by Mattias Stomer. In the niches which alternate with the paintings, nestle allegories of the Virtues, a series of extraordinary female figures remarkable for their poise and for the delicate way in which their drapery is rendered. In some instances they are attended by *putti*; the statue of Meekness, for example, holding a dove, is flanked by a *putto* dressed in a monk's attire stretching a podgy little hand towards her.

In the large ovals above the paintings, Serpotta has depicted scenes from the Apocalypse of St John: note how the figure of the Devil writhes as he falls, having been driven from heaven.

Above the dome of the altar, more winged cherubs hold up a great sheet. On the high altar itself, sits the splendid painting by Anthony Van Dyck of the *Madonna of the Rosary* (1628) with St Dominic and the patron saints of Palermo; this, in turn, is framed by two female allegories who look onto the scene as if witnessing a theatrical performance. The ceiling, frescoed by Pietro Novelli, illustrates the *Coronation of the Virgin*.

Santa Maria di Valverde ⊘ – An elegant marble portal by Pietro Amato (1691) leads into this small church. The **interior** is extravagantly decorated in the Baroque style using different types of marble, sculpted into soft drapery on the side altars. In the first chapel on the right, dedicated to Saint Lucy, note the delicate perspectives created by the different marbles.

Santa Cita ◷ – This church was badly damaged by the bombing raids in 1943, which destroyed its side aisles. Note the beautiful **marble chancel arch**★ by Antonello Gagini in the presbytery: the Nativity and Dormitio Virginis are represented inside the arch; Dominican saints can be seen in the pilaster panels on the arch, and portraits of St Thomas Aquinas and St Peter the Martyr grace the two medallion tondi, on the corners. In the eight coffers of the arch intrados are episodes of the life of St Zita. Also worthy of note is the beautiful **Cappella del Rosario** to the right of the presbytery, with its delicate stuccowork and polychrome marquetry. Access to the **crypt** ◷ (cripta della Cappella Lanza), decorated with different types of marble, is from the chapel to the left of the presbytery.

★★**Oratorio del Rosario di Santa Cita** ◷ – *Access from via Valverde or via da S Cita.* The oratory is a remarkable work by the leading Baroque decorator **Giacomo Serpotta**, who worked here between 1686 and 1718. A host of angels and cherubs are endowed with carefree expressions and realistic attitudes, completely intent on playing among themselves, climbing up onto the window frames, larking about with garlands of flowers, turning their backs irreverently, crying, sleeping, and hugging their knees deep in thought.

The eye is immediately drawn towards the wall at the back of the nave where a great drape hangs across the entire wall, supported by a struggling crowd of cherubs. A central panel depicts in relief the Battle of Lepanto; this is flanked by two emaciated youths, symbolising the horrors of War. All around the oratory, even below the side windows, are panels depicting the Mysteries of the Rosary. On the left wall begin the series relating to the Joyful Mysteries: the Annunciation, Visitation, Nativity and Presentation at the Temple. On the right are the Sorrowful Mysteries: Jesus in the Garden at Gethsemane, the Flagellation, Crowning of Thorns, and Calvary. At the far end are a second series of Joyful Mysteries *(starting bottom left)*: the Resurrection, Ascension, Descent of the Holy Spirit, and the Assumption of Mary. At the top, in the centre, the Crowning of Mary.

The high altar has a fine painting by Carlo Maratta of the Madonna of the Rosary (1690).

The eight windows along the side walls are "guarded" by allegorical figures.

A little further on, sits **San Giorgio dei Genovesi** ◷ overlooking its own piazza: this is one of the rare expressions of the late Renaisssance. It was built by a community of Genovese merchants to shelter those among them who died in Palermo; having been deconsecrated, the former church is now used to house temporary exhibitions.

In via Cavour, is the **Prefettura**: a Venetian Neo-Gothic building that was once known as the Villa Whitaker, having been erected by one of the 12 grandchildren of Ingham, the British Marsala magnate *(see p 283)*.

Stucco decoration: the Battle of Lepanto

FROM VIA ROMA TO THE CAPO QUARTER

★**Museo Archeologico Regionale** ⊘ – The Regional Archaeological Museum is installed in the 16C confines of the Olivella monastery which, with the adjoining Baroque church of **Sant'Ignazio all'Olivella** *(see below)* was founded in the 17C by the fathers of St Philip Neri. The museum contains a magnificent collection of arte-facts recovered from Sicilian sites, in particular those from Selinunte.

Ground floor – The visit begins in **small cloisters★** with a hexagonal fountain in the centre. At the back, high up in the wall, is a beautiful single-light window with a decorative surround. The portico shelters an assortment of Punic and Roman anchors (also on display in the large cloisters). One small room devoted to Phoenician art displays two sarcophagi from 6C BC with organic decoration; another is dedicated to Egyptian and Punic finds, including the hieroglyphic inscrip-tion known as the **Palermo Stone** (the other three parts are in Cairo and London) which narrates 700 years of Egyptian history, and a Punic one recovered near the harbour at Marsala bearing the figure of a priest before a perfume-burner, worshipping the god Tanit.

Beyond are the large cloisters, off which are arranged a series of rooms devoted to artefacts from **Selinunte**. The first displays the twin steles formed by pairs of busts representing the gods of the underworld, both in shallow relief and in the round. This leads into the Sala Gabrici *(interactive information terminals)* which contains a reconstruction of the front elevation of Temple C and a selection of the original triglyphs. Sala Marconi has various lion masks with water-spouts from the Temple of Victory at Himera. The exhibits in the following larger room are principally from

Perseus slaying Medusa

Selinunte, including the range of marvellous **metopes★★**. The oldest (smaller) artefacts, notably from a 6C BC Archaic tem-ple, are displayed below the window on the right: one fragment depicts the Rape of Europa by Zeus in the guise of a bull. On the left are three more marvellous metopes from Temple C (6C BC). The high relief, which in places verges on being in the round, shows Perseus severing the head of Medusa while from her breast springs Pegasus, the winged horse born from her spilt blood *(central scene)*; above is the figure of Athena with, to the left, the four-horse chariot of the sun god Apollo and, to the right, Heracles captur-ing the Cercopi (two thiev-ing brothers) and hanging them from a stick.

Against the back wall are four metopes from Temple E: these are considered to be the finest in terms of their expressiveness, their sense of movement and their realism which has been described as "modern" in concept. Starting from the left, these show Heracles fighting with an Amazon, Hera before Zeus (who, seated, lifts the veil from her face), Actaeon being transformed into a stag (the muzzle of the animal can just be seen behind the head of Actaeon as he is attacked by the dogs), and Athena fighting the giant Enceladus. The four rooms filled with Etruscan finds contain some fine cinerary urns and *bucchero* ware.

First floor – Among the various **bronzes** from the Greek, Roman and Punic periods, are a couple of truly superb ones: **Heracles catching the stag★**, perhaps the central dec-oration for a fountain and, more particularly, the fabulously lifelike bronze **Ram★★**, a Hellenistic work of extraordinary quality, from Syracuse.

The following room displays small marble statues include a fine **Satyr★**, a Roman copy of an original by Praxiteles.

Second floor – On this floor are arranged the museum's prehistoric collections, a se-lection of its finest Greek vases, Roman mosaics and frescoes. The room with the mosaics includes panels illustrating **Orpheus with the animals★** (3C AD), the seasons, and representations of allegories and myths closely associated with the cult of Dionysus found in Palermo.

Sant'Ignazio all'Olivella ⊘ – This fine Baroque church was initiated in the late 16C on the site where, according to tradition, the villa of the family of Santa Rosalia once stood. An interpretation of Olivella would confirm this: *Olim villa*, once a villa (was here). The front incorporates two bell-towers which add a certain freedom to the overall composition.

Inside, an eye-catching inscription in bright red proclaims *jahvé* in the centre of the Gloria behind the altar. The first chapel on the right contains a great wealth of decorative inlay in the form of polychrome *pietra dura*. *Access to the Oratorio di San Filippo Neri (or Sant'Ignazio) is from the south transept.*

Oratorio di San Filippo Neri ⊘ – *Access from the piazza or from Sant'Ignazio.* This was designed by the architect **Venanzio Marvuglia**. Inside, the stucco work relates the Gloria: the attractive composition with the angel surrounded by groups of cherubs in twos and threes, is the work of **Ignazio Marabitti**.

★**Oratorio di Santa Caterina d'Alessandria** ⊘ – *Via Monteleone 50; ring the bell.* Although more static and less vigorous than work by his father Giacomo, this stuccowork by **Procopio Serpotta** elegantly portrays various scenes from the life of St Catherine, the protector of scholars, alongside allegories of the sciences: Rhetoric, Ethics, Geography and Astrology to the right; Dialectics, Physics, Geometry and Theology to the left and, under the beautiful triple-arched tribune of the entrance wall, Knowledge and Science. The ceiling is decorated with delicate foliage patterns. *Continue along via Monteleone as far as the crossroads with via Roma.*

On the far side of piazza San Domenico, directly opposite the church, is the narrow **via Bandiera** which marks the outer fringe of the **Capo market**, and harbours a number of fine buildings, notably **Palazzo Termine** (no 14) built in 1573 with hints of the Spanish Style. Its most striking features are the lovely two-light stone traceried windows divided by slender columns; the window on the corner was added during restoration at the beginning of this century. Next door is **Palazzo Oneto di Sperlinga**, an elegant 18C residence of some other noble family.

Chiesa di Sant'Agostino ⊘ – The splendid 13C St Augustine's was built at the request of the Chiaramonte and Sclafani families. The **front★** is graced with a beautiful entrance decorated with duotone geometric and flower motifs, and a lovely rose-window. The Gaginiesque side entrance in Via Sant'Agostino is also worthy of note. The interior is largely dominated by Baroque alterations, which include stuccoes by followers of the Serpotta School, signed on the shelf under the second statue on the right with Serpotta's mark, a lizard (*serpe* in Sicilian).

The heart of the quarter which lies further along via Sant'Agostino, is brought to life every morning by a busy market, the **mercato di Capo**. It was in this part of the city that a large number of the *Beati Paoli* stories were set. This massively popular novel by Luigi Natoli was published in instalments between 1909 and 1910, capturing the imagination of large numbers of Palermitani who read it avidly and who spent hours speculating on the suspense maintained with each new edition. Its vivid style succeeds in painting a provocative yet faithful picture of Palermo in times past. Notice in via Cappuccinelle (no 6) the shop sign above the **Panifico Morello**: this consists of an elegant Liberty-style mosaic panel with a female figure enclosed within a "niche" of wheat sheaves, with a lotus-flower motif below and further wheat sheaves above.

Return to via Maqueda and head north, towards Teatro Massimo. **Via dell'Orologio**, to the right just before the theatre, provides an unexpected view of one of Sant'Ignazio's two bell-towers, the clock of which might even have lent its name to the street.

CITTÀ NUOVA

At the beginning of the 19C, the city underwent a period of considerable expansion. The wealthy merchant bourgeoisie chose the north-west side of the city to build fine residences in keeping with the new aesthetic taste, lavishly decorated with wrought-iron work, glass and floral panels. The hub of high society shifted from via Maqueda to its extension, which took the name of **via della Libertà**. Here they built the great temples of opera, two theatres – the Massimo and the Politeama – and a large number of modern *palazzi* scattered through the neighbouring streets. Even today, a walk along via XX Settembre, via Dante and via Siracusa, to name but three, will reveal a flavour of the splendour promoted by the wealthy upper-middle classes in the late 19C.

Teatro Massimo – This opera house, under the watchful eye of Giuseppe Verdi, is one of the largest in Europe. The front of this imposing neo-Classical structure is composed of six columns and a broad triangular pediment, modelled on the *pronaos* of an ancient temple. Set back, a great dome rises from its high drum. The initial design was completed by Giovan Battista Basile in 1875; building work was concluded by his son Ernesto, who took it upon himself to add the two small distinctive

A tour of the main Liberty-style buildings

Besides the ones described below, Palermo's best Liberty-style residences should include **Palazzo Dato** with its pink external detailing on the corner of via XX Settembre and Via XII Gennaio; Ernesto Basile's **Villa Favaloro Di Stefano** in piazza Virgilio and the Villino Ida at no 15 via Siracusa, with its fine wrought-iron balcony and tiled frieze.

Another must, albeit in a completely different part of the city, is the **Villa Igiea** with its truly amazing **Sala Basile★**.

Liberty-style kiosks in front of the theatre (the one on the right, built of wood and wrought iron, is known as the Vicari al Massimo Kiosk, while the one on the left, made of iron, is the Ribaudo Kiosk).

Teatro Politeama – The Politeama Theatre, as imposing and built in the same neo-Classical style as the Teatro Massimo, faces onto the vast piazza Castelnuovo. Its façade is dominated by a quadriga of bronze horses.

Inside, it accommodates the Galleria d'Arte Moderna Empedocle Restivo.

★ **Galleria d'Arte Moderna Empedocle Restivo** ⊘ – The Empedocle Restivo Gallery of Modern Art is contained within an elegant Liberty-style interior (note the large, wrought-iron lights). The collection comprises a highly prized selection of 19C and 20C paintings and sculptures by a number of Sicilian artists and a few foreign artists. The sculptures include a delightful *Faun* by **Trentacoste**, a marble figurine of Classical proportions, but gracefully coiled upon itself like a spiral ready to burst free.

Sicilian 19C art developed in different directions while simultaneously giving rise to a new generation of concepts. Artists specialised in using the medium they found most congenial. The great themes tackled often revolved around psychological introspection, interspersed with intervals of inactivity and neo-Classical composure, history and landscape. From this period stem the portraits by Patania, such as his *Study of a Sick Priest* in which the man's suffering is rendered with piercing realism, and those by Salvatore Lo Forte, who managed to impart to his subjects so much strength of character. This is also the age of patriotism, which Erulo Eruli encapsulated in his great composition *The Sicilian Vesper*: the incident, in fact, is set in the 19C, although here, the subject has been transposed into an example of heroic rebellion against all kinds of foreign domination.

Different trends may also be detected in the style and expression of the various landscape painters represented: Lo Jacono's realism *(Wind in the Mountains)* becomes loaded with feeling in the works of A Leto who paints "impressions" by dabbing strong, warm colours onto his canvas (three studies for *The Rope-makers*); Michele Catti absorbs all the tenets of Impressionism before painting his hazy landscapes with horizons lost in infinity *(Last Leaves)*. Onofrio Tomaselli *(The Carusi)* adds a note of compassion (in the sense of the Latin word, implying a sharing of pain) with his bold use of warm colours. A few works both from the Italian and other foreign schools exemplify the new trends that emerged at the close of the 19C and the beginning of the 20C: Expressionism in the *Nativity* by Lienz, Symbolism in the works of Von Stuck *(The Sin)*, and Pointillism in Terzi's *Summer Morning*.

The last few rooms collect together paintings from the 1930s and the years following the Second World War: *The Tram* by Sironi, with its cold colours; *The Schoolchildren* by F Casorati, with its geometric lines that seem to accentuate the sadness and immobility of the children (what is haunting is the blank, staring eyes

Onofior Tomaselli, *I Carusi*

of one child in the foreground); an expressive *Self-portrait* by Guttuso. These rooms also accommodate a number of sculptures, including the fine *Acrobat* by T Bertolino, with its curving, sinuous lines.

★★ Villa Malfitano ⊘ – The famous Liberty-style Villa Malfitano, contained within its glorious **garden★★**, was begun in 1886 by **Joseph Whitaker**, a grandson of the mighty **Ingham**, that English gentleman-cum wine-merchant who came to live in Sicily in 1806. Ingham was an entrepreneur who managed to build himself a veritable commercial empire out of producing Marsala wine, a business he founded and developed until it became one of the three leading producers, and a large steamship company. In stark contrast to his grandfather, Joseph was fascinated by ornithology and archaeology: to satisfy his interest he travelled to Tunisia where he studied the birds (later writing a treatise on the subject) and initiated a programme of excavation on the island of Mozia which he had purchased *(see MOZIA)*. Another of his passions was botany: he arranged to have trees sent from all over the world so that he could plant them around his villa; these gardens soon comprised a whole range of rare and exotic species: palm trees, Dragon's Blood trees, the only example in Europe of *Araucaria Rouler* and an enormous banyan tree. The villa soon became one of the main points of reference for high society at that time. Lavish parties were held there and important guests, such as the reigning monarchs of Great Britain and Italy, were received and entertained. The point came when the villa would epitomise the pre-eminence of the family. It was remodelled upon the Villa Favard in Florence, and endowed with elegant wrought-iron verandas which reflect a taste for the new Liberty-style (the one at the back is especially beautiful).

The internal furnishings are exquisitely chosen: a profusion of Oriental items (often purchased at the most famous English auction rooms) include, for example, a pair of *cloisonée* elephants from the Royal Palace in Beijing, and a pair of large waders riding on the back of a turtle symbolising the four elements (the birds represent the air, the turtles water, the snake wound around the neck and held in the beak of the bird represents the earth and the lantern which acts as a lamp symbolises fire). The best craftsmen from the area and the most famous local artists were employed to work on the villa (the dining-room furniture was all made in Palermo, except for the table, which is English). Worthy of particular note is the *Safari in Tunisia* by Lo Jacono (in the corridor) and the pastel portrait of Joseph's daughters by Ettore de Maria Bergler, which hangs above the lovely spiral staircase leading up to the first floor, decorated in the then fashionable Pompeian style, as is the ceiling of the corridor.

The real highlight of the Whitaker house, however, is the **decoration** conceived by the same artist for the **Sala d'Estate** (Summer Room): this consists of a *trompe l'œil* composition covering the entire room (walls and ceiling), transforming the enclosed space into a cool veranda surrounded by vegetation.

★Villino Florio – *Viale Regina Margherita 36*. This fantastic house was built for one of the most powerful families in Sicily in the 19C: the Florio. It is, without doubt, one of the finest examples of the Palermo Liberty style. Designed by Ernesto Basile, it was originally surrounded by a large garden.

Villa Trabia – *Via Salinas*. A wonderful garden surrounds the villa of the same name, built in the 18C and bought the following year by Giuseppe Lanza Branciforte, prince of Trabia and Butera. The current appearance of the villa is the result of the many alterations undertaken at the end of the last century. The building, now used as municipal offices, has a splendid entrance with a monumental staircase.

Albero di Falcone – This tree stands at the beginning of via Notarbartolo, on the right, outside the house of Giovanni Falcone, who was killed by a Mafia bomb in 1993. Since his death, the tree seems to have become a token shrine in its own right: messages, photographs, and small offerings bear witness to the people's esteem and affection for the judge.

Museo della Fondazione Mormino ⊘ – *Viale della Libertà 52*. The Mormino Foundation Museum is housed on the first floor of the Banco di Sicilia (Villa Zito). It was formed so as to display an accumulation of art work, original creations and recovered artefacts acquired over the years by the Banco di Sicilia. The first rooms are devoted to artefacts recovered during the excavations of Selinunte, Himera, Solunto and Terravecchia di Cuti, a small town further inland where a village from the 6C-5C BC was unearthed. A second section displays maiolica from Sicily and from the rest of Italy (with a few examples from Turkey and China). The third section is devoted to a large collection of 13C-19C coins and medals; this is complemented by a fine series of Sicilian engravings on the walls. No 936 in particular, dating from the 16C, provides a view of Palermo as it was, completely surrounded by defensive walls: Palazzo Reale can be pinpointed at the top and, to its left, San

> ### The green parks of Palermo
>
> The custody of Palermo's parks and gardens goes back to ancient times. The real and true garden culture was introduced to Sicily by the Arabs, and quickly taken on by the Normans, who created extensive areas of parkland for recreational purposes or as settings for their wonderful summer palaces. Palermo has managed to nurture these oases down the centuries and to create new ones throughout the centre of the city. These havens of peace, planted with a host of exotic plants and trees, are veritable corners of paradise, ideal for relaxing or rediscovering the pleasures of walking amid the greenery: the exotic garden of San Giovanni degli Eremiti, Villa Bonanno, Villa Giulia, the Botanical Gardens, Villa Malfitano, Villa Trabia, Giardino Garibaldi in piazza Marina, or the beautiful **English Garden**, extremely well kept, with an enormous number of palms, cactuses, Parasol (Maritime) pines and banyans, where walking is a sheer delight.

Giovanni degli Eremiti; at right angles to the *palazzo* runs the axis of modern-day via Vittorio Emanuele, which continues down to the harbour; this is guarded on the left by the Castellammare falling into ruin; in the centre is La Martorana.

On the ground floor is displayed the bank's philatelic collection with stamps dating from the era of the Kingdom of Two Sicilies.

BEYOND THE CITY GATES

★**Orto Botanico** ⊘ – The Botanical Gardens have occupied their present site since 1789. The French architect Dufourny designed not only the gardens but also a series of buildings for use as research laboratories and experimentation. The gardens contain a huge range of different species, including fine examples of Oriental and exotic plants, such as the majestic Dendrocalamus Giganteus – a giant kind of bamboo – or the incredible **banyan tree**★★ *(Ficus magnoloides)*, the tallest and most far-reaching tree in the garden. There are various South American plants such as *Chorisias* and *Bombacaceae* characterised by their strange, swollen, prickly trunks, brought to Palermo in the late 19C. From the large, deep pink flowers develop the fruits which, when mature, split open, dropping their seeds and their enveloping thick hairy padding, once used like horsehair. One greenhouse contains a fine variety of cactus; note, at the entrance, the enormous *barili d'oro* (literally "barrels of gold" – also ironically called "mother-in-law's chairs").

Ponte dell'Ammiraglio – *Corso dei Mille*. The picturesque medieval bridge once straddled the waters of the River Oreto, which was then diverted. It was built in 1113 by George of Antioch, an admiral serving under **Roger II**.

★**San Giovanni dei Lebbrosi** ⊘ – *Via Cappello*. St John of the Lepers may be the oldest Norman church in Sicily. Its most endearing feature is the red dome which caps the bell-tower-cum-entrance. The church is supposed to have been founded in 1070 (although some say it may have been a century later).

Chiesa di Santo Spirito o dei Vespri ⊘ – *Inside the cemetery of Santa Orsola*. The Church of the Holy Spirit or of the Vespers was built in 1178 during the reign of Roger II. It came to fame on 31 March 1282 when, during Evensong (Vespers), a French soldier cast some insult at a Sicilian woman, provoking the bystanders to jump to her defence and so providing a pretext for an outburst of growing resentment towards the invaders from beyond the Alps. The incident sparked off the War of the Sicilian Vespers which, in turn, led to the eviction of the French from the island.

The front of the church, although incomplete, points promisingly upwards, while a decorative system of duotone interlacing arches, typical of Norman art, extends down the sides to the apses.

The interior is austere and simple (largely thanks to the restoration work carried out in the late 19C, when it was restored to its original state by removing the elaborate decoration added during the Baroque era); the internal space is divided into a nave and flanking aisles by pointed arches that spring from round piers. The east end comprises three apses, in accordance with the Norman tradition. The painted *Christ on the Cross* above the altar is 16C.

Santuario di Santa Maria di Gesù ⊘ – Follow viale della Regione Siciliana to where it meets the narrow alleyway called via Oreto; turn right down via Santa Maria di Gesù (look out for the green sign above the shoe-shop at the corner). The 15C Sanctuary of St Mary of Jesus occupies a peacefully serene and cool spot on the slopes of Monte Grifone. The way to it leads through a cemetery where, traditionally, aristocratic families have kept their mausoleums. The area in front of the church is surrounded by fine patrician tombs mainly from the 19C or the beginning of this century, including the Liberty-style chapel belonging to the princes of Lanza di Scalea. The main entrance has a marble surround decorated with delicate shallow reliefs depicting Christ among angels and Apostles. The doorway on the left side is Gothic in style; it has attractive capitals carved with organic decoration. **Inside**, the chancel has two bays articulated by pointed arches; Antonio Alliata's marble sarcophagus is attributed to Antonello Gagini (in the chancel, high up on the right); there is a rare **wooden statue of the Virgin**★ (1470); and a fine coffered wooden **ceiling**, painted with flowers and angels (early 16C), spans the entrance to the church and the organ above it. It is also worth taking note of the brightly coloured wooden organ loft, painted with scenes from the life of St Francis (1932).

Albergo delle Povere – *Corso Calatafimi 217. Open to the public during exhibitions and conferences.* This complex was originally intended at the end of the 18C as a hospice for the poor of the city; in the 19C, it was reserved for spinsters who set up a weaving workshop there; it is now used for temporary exhibitions and conferences.

The **fountain** in front is 17C. The complex, which includes the buildings on the other side of the road, consists of two parts arranged round two large, beautiful cloisters; these, in turn, are connected by a central courtyard onto which faces the Church of Holy Trinity. The left wing still shelters Opera Pia, a charity providing assistance to the poor; the right wing serves as operational headquarters for the exclusive carabinieri hit-squad unit charged with protecting Sicily's artistic heritage – facilities include exhibition rooms and a lecture hall with a capacity for 350 people.

> ## And, if you get the chance...
>
> ... take up position at one end of the semicircular wall enclosing the fountain and get someone else to stand at the other end; a mere whisper will carry from one side to the other. Who needs a mobile phone?

★★**Catacombe dei Cappuccini** ⊘ – The Capuchin Catacombs hold a certain macabre fascination: in simple terms they consist of a maze of corridors containing thousands of mummified bodies, contorted in expression and posture, perfectly dressed, appended (as if they had been hanged, with a rope around the neck) to the walls, in niches or propped up against the wall. The overwhelming sense of tragedy, which never fails to touch visitors, is heightened by the fact that these figures are shut away behind railings. The catacombs contain the remains of almost 8 000 Capuchin friars (the oldest corpses date from the late 16C), as well as those of illustrious or wealthy Palermitani, children and virgins, each category having been allotted its own special area. What is particularly extraordinary is the condition of the corpses, preserved intact by the special environmental conditions causing gradual desiccation. The one exception is the little two-year old girl who died in 1920; she is so well preserved that she seems merely asleep; her body was injected with a concoction of chemicals (the doctor who administered them died without revealing his secret potion).

In the cemetery adjacent to the Capuchin monastery is the tomb of Giuseppe Tomasi di Lampedusa, author of *The Leopard*, who died in 1957 *(third avenue on the left)*.

Parco della Favorita – *3km/1.8mi N, along viale Diana.* The large park situated at the foot of Monte Pellegrino was created in 1799 by Ferdinand III of Bourbon, when the Napoleonic troops drove him out of Naples (where he had reigned as Ferdinand IV). The parkland became the king's private hunting estate; he had a house built there, the delightful **Chinese palace**, a curiously shaped building with an exotic decor, designed by Marvuglia. The servants quarters were accommodated in the building next door which was similar in style to the first, but arranged around a lovely courtyard onto which faced the kitchens (connected to the palace by an underground passageway); this now houses the G Pitré Museum.

Museo Etnografico Pitré ⊘ – The Pitré Ethnographic Museum houses a large quantity of artefacts associated with local folklore, in an attempt to explain their significance and use in the customary practices, especially in rural areas. Reconstructions of houses, tools, needlework and embroidery, fabrics, a wonderful 17C wrought-iron bed-head, everyday pottery, "Sunday-best" clothes for high days and holidays, splendid engraved horn goblets and gourd containers for water or wine provide an introduction to life in Sicily in days of yore. In the rooms around the courtyard are displayed various examples of Sicilian carts, all decorated with an incredible array of elaborate carving, painting and wrought-iron work *(pause to admire the intricate detail of these exhibits)*, two 17C council carriages and children's toys; amulets and trinkets linked with magic and popular superstitions, together with the fine collection of hand-made votive objects, bear witness to the strong faith of the country people. The museum also has a library *(open mornings only)* of books about popular traditions in Sicily and beyond.

MEMORIES FROM THE EAST

The parks around Palermo in the time of the Normans covered great areas of land: the one lying west of the city, known as the *Genoard* or the Paradise on Earth, was chosen by the sovereigns as an apt place for a summer residence or a pleasure palace in the Oriental sense of the word: providing a peaceful haven set among gardens of exotic plants, with pools containing fish, water courses and even wild animals from distant lands. Such were the dreams that inspired the building of **la Zisa**, **Scibene Castle** – still visible, although much restored, from viale Tasca Lanza – **Cuba Sottana** and **Cuba Soprana** – now part of the crumbling Villa Napoli complex (a few arches are just visible) – and **la Cubola** – a small, square pavilion surmounted by the characteristic bulbous red dome *(see San Cataldo and San Giovanni degli Eremiti)*, which is accessible from via Zancia, one of the roads crossing corso Calatafimi. The two best-preserved monuments are, without doubt, la Zisa and la Cuba Sottana.

★**La Zisa** ⊘ – *Piazza Guglielmo il Buono.* The name is derived from *El Aziz*, meaning the splendid or noble one. Today, sadly, only the shell of the palace remains, yet this retains an undeniable aura. It was initiated by Guglielmo d'Altavilla and completed by his son Guglielmo II between 1166 and 1175; work on the building was entrusted entirely to Moorish craftsmen. In the 14C, after a period of neglect, it was transformed into a fortress, then into a depository for objects contaminated by the plague (16C), before being converted (and then extensively altered) into a *palazzo* for some noble family; recent restoration has endeavoured to return it to its original state.

Tour – The main attraction on the ground floor is the room with the fountain: built on a cruciform plan, open at the front, the room has two square pools that collect water from the main channel in the centre of the room, fed from a waterspout. The upper section of the walls carries a mosaic frieze of peacocks and archers. From here are arranged a succession of rooms, each equipped with a special ventilation system whereby draughts of cool air could circulate through gaps in the walls. The niches and windows have *muqarnas*, a highly decorative honeycomb of miniature vaults and stalactite pendants, a characteristic feature in Islamic architecture. The *palazzo* houses a collection of objects, mainly from Egypt (from the Mameluke and Ottoman periods), that typify the art and style of furnishings that might once have adorned the original palace. The 15C *mushrabiyya*, a sort of perforated wooden screen placed in front of doors and windows as protection against excessive heat and light, are particularly fine.

★**La Cuba** ⊘ – *Corso Calatafimi 100.* The Cuba Sottana, now incorporated into military barracks, was probably surrounded by a vast artificial lake that was known as the Pescheria (fishpond). In the old stables, just inside the entrance on the right, is a model reconstruction of how the palace must have looked originally. On the wall, the engraved Kufic inscription celebrates the completion of the building, thereby confirming that it was erected in 1180 at the request of William II.

The decoration of the building is exquisitely simple: above a series of tall pointed arches of different widths are inserted various other smaller openings. La Cuba was built according to a rectangular plan, with four small projections at the centre of each side. The internal space was divided into three parts (the first, or last in the order of our visit, also accommodated two service rooms). In the central section there is an eight-sided star-shaped pool: from here the water would trickle gently into the Pescheria without breaking the surface so as not to disturb the reflections of the building and garden.

EXCURSIONS

Monte Pellegrino – *14km/9mi N.* The road up Monte Pellegrino offers magnificent **views★★★** over Palermo and the Conca d'Oro; in places it is crossed by a wide, much steeper, paved path dating from the 17C (used by those going up on foot). As the road climbs, it passes on the left, the **Castello Utveggio**, a massive pink construction that can also be seen from the city; it then continues on to the **Santuario di Santa Rosalia** (17C), a sanctuary built around the cave where, according to legend, St Rosalia lived. It is also said that this was where her bones were found in 1624 and that these, when carried in procession down through the city, liberated it from the plague. Following this event, St Rosalia became the patron saint of Palermo. The cave is covered with zinc guttering which helps collect the dripping water from the walls, as this is considered to have miraculous properties.

Further on up, the road comes to a look-out point which, though dominated by a statue of the saint, provides breathtaking **views★** out to sea.

★**Grotte dell'Addaura** ⊘ – *Between Mondello and Arenella, off the Lungomare Cristoforo Colombo, level with the road turning for Punta di Priola.* A series of caves among the lower slopes of Monte Pellegrino have revealed that they were inhabited during Palaeolithic times (5th millennium BC). In one of these caves have been found various extra-ordinary **rock engravings**, possibly associated with some initiation ceremony or a ritual. The inscriptions consist of animals and a group of **nine human figures**★ wearing strange head-dresses, standing in a circle around another two figures arching their bod-

ies and holding their arms stretched out in front of them, almost as if they are dancing.

⌂ **Mondello** – *11km/7mi N.* The road passes below the tall rugged slopes of Monte Pellegrino. This area, now an elegant holiday resort, was "discovered" at the beginning of the century by well-to-do Palermitani who decided that it provided the ideal conditions for a weekend away or for a short seaside holiday. As a result, large numbers of elegant villas (many of which still stand) sprang up along the sea front, the length of viale Principe Scalea (Villa Margherita at no 36), via Margherita di Savoia (especially at the beginning) or in the streets behind, like no 7 via Cà da Mosto (Villino Lentini).

The seafront promenade is graced with a picturesque bathing establishment dating from the beginning of this century, which continues to function as such (although part of it has been converted into a restaurant and accommodates a private club).

PANTALICA★

Siracusa

Michelin map 432 P 27

Pantalica, identified as the ancient Hybla (founded, it is alleged, as Megara Hyblaea in 728 BC by a group of colonists from Megara with the blessing of their last king Hyblon), has been inhabited since the Bronze Age. Towards the middle of the 13C BC, the Sicani moved inland from their original settlements in the coastal regions to a chosen site at Pantalica: for the coast at this time was subjected to attack and regular waves of settlers, and therefore no longer secure. The narrow valley through which the River Anapo ran, together with the Cavagrande (which becomes the Calcinara in its final section) were naturally defensible in that they comprised two deep gorges with one means of access (the saddle of Filiporto, to the west); furthermore, the area had two rivers that were considered of inestimable value. Today, little survives of the original town, which was probably destroyed by the Syracusans before the foundation of Akrai in 664 BC, save for an incredible number of tombs in the steep limestone cliffs (excavated at the cost of huge efforts, probably using bronze or stone axes, given that iron had not yet been discovered). New life was breathed into Pantalica by the Byzantines, who installed small communities in rock-hewn dwellings there. It is probable that the site continued to be occupied during the Arab and Norman periods before being completely abandoned until the beginning of the 20C, when the archaeologist Paolo Orsi began excavating.

★ARCHAEOLOGICAL SITE ⊘

Access – The archaeological site may be reached from two directions: from Ferla and from Sortino. The former is to be recommended as it provides better views of the necropolis and saves on the need to climb down to the riverbed, fording the river and climbing up the other side.

More than 5 000 burial chambers honeycomb the walls of this quarry to make five necropoli through successive periods. The earliest in the north and north-west necropoli (13C-11C BC) are elliptical in shape, whereas the most recent (850-730 BC) are rectangular. What is distinctive about these tombs is the way in which they are organised into compact family units, rather than into the more usual extended groups.

Follow the signs for Pantalica from Ferla; after 9km, stop and park at Sella di Filiporto *(yellow sign)*, the ancient gateway to the town, where the remains of the fortification trench can still be seen. From here, a path runs along the southern edge of the upland plateau from which, looking back, the **Filiporto necropolis** can be seen nestling within a broad amphitheatre of rock. Further along the way there are splendid **views**★★ over the Anapo gorge below; the path then continues down to a Byzantine settlement with rectangular rock-hewn dwellings, and to the Oratory of San Micidiario. Follow the path and, after about 1km/0.6mi, turn left for the **anaktoron** or Prince's Palace: this is also accessible by car, by continuing along the

The necropolis

main road some 1.5km/0.9mi (note in passing the **north-west necropolis** on the left) and then taking a short path *(yellow sign)*. The site accommodates the remains of a megalithic construction which, demonstrating clear Mycenean influences, is thought by Orsi to be built by Mycenean workmen in the service of the prince. *Return to the car.* 11km/7mi before Ferla the tarred road peters out (note the Byzantine village of Cavetta just before this). Leave the car and take the steep path down, enjoying, along the way, the marvellous **views★★** of the gorge of Calcinara and of the vast **northern necropolis** harboured by the wall on the opposite side *(20min on foot to the river).*

★PROTECTED NATURAL AREA ⊙

Access – *There are two entrances to the Anapo valley, via the Fusco gate (off the Floridia-Sortino road, turn left after about 12km/7mi at the fork marked with a yellow sign for Valle dell'Anapo; 700m/2 296ft further along, continue left – red road with wooden barrier), or via the Cassaro gate (from Ferla, follow the signs for Cassaro; at the first fork, turn left and continue to the bridge over the river, the Ponte Diga gate is located thereabouts – 4km/2.5mi from Ferla).*

An expedition through the protected area (soon to become a nature reserve) around the Anapo valley reveals an extraordinary **landscape** comprising a succession of gorges defined by vertical cliffs, along which ran the old Syracuse-Ragusa-Vizzini railway. For those who do not wish to walk the whole route (13km/8mi), there is an alternative, clearly marked track which combines both natural and archaeological points of interest, leading to the **Cavetta necropolis** *(on the right immediately after the first tunnel)*, the **southern necropolis** *(on both sides after the second tunnel)* and the **Filiporto necropolis** *(after 4km/2.5mi in the wall on the right)*. Furthermore, at the start of the alternative route, immediately on the right (level with a pier of the fallen bridge), can be seen a series of vents associated with the Galermi aqueduct, built by the tyrant Gelon to convey water from the river to Syracuse, which continues to be used for irrigation purposes.

Flora and fauna – The geological formation known as the **cave iblee** (or Hyblaean quarries), a series of deep canyons cutting through the landscape, harbours a broad range of plants in a concentrated area. The tree varieties that make up the thickly wooded section up the rocky slopes include white and black poplars, and willows; there is also a profusion of tamarisks, oleanders, wild orchids and the nettle *urtica rupestris*, a relic from the Ice Age. Clinging to the slopes elsewhere are patches of Mediterranean maquis: forest of holm and cork oaks interspersed with, in the more arid parts exposed to the sun, an aromatic scrub of sage, thyme, giant fennel, euphorbia and thorny broom. The Oriental plane-tree deserves a special mention as it only grows wild in a very few places in Italy; the threat of a spreading fungus, a pathogenic canker, seems to have been checked here for the time being, thanks to appropriate measures.

As regards fauna, the Anapo valley also accommodates a large number of different species: foxes, pine martens, porcupines, hares and hedgehogs; painted frogs and other amphibians; dippers, stone chats, kingfishers, partridges and a pair of Peregrine falcons.

EXCURSIONS

Ferla – Isolated on the limestone upland plateau crossed by the River Anapo, the town boasts several 18C religious buildings. **San Antonio** ⊙, built on a Greek-cross plan overlooking an attractive square-cum-forecourt cobbled with geometric designs, is graced with an elegant frontage comprising five convex panels, articulated with columns, and surmounted by two towers, one incomplete. Inside, the stucco and painted wall and ceiling decoration, panels and statues combine to make a charming Baroque whole.

The church of **San Sebastiano** has a highly decorative façade and bell-tower.

The road from Ferla to Sortino provides evocatively panoramic **views**★ over the surrounding plateau and the deep cleft hewn by water erosion.

Sortino – Completely rebuilt in the 18C on the top of a hill, the town is laid out on a rectilinear grid-like plan. The **Chiesa Madre** ⊙, fronted by a **forecourt cobbled** with lozenge-shaped stones, has a fine **façade** of warm golden stone. The elevation comprises a doorway flanked by spiral columns ornamented with organic decoration and garlands of fruit; a level articulated by statues; and, along the top, an open balustrade. The overall **composition**★ is strikingly effective, especially at sunset. The interior ceiling and apse is frescoed (1777-78) by Crestadoro.

The church belonging to the Montevergine monastery, enclosed within a secluded square, has a harmonious front and a bell-tower, contrived with concave and convex lines (18C).

The **Museo dell'Opra dei Pupi** ⊙ is housed in the former monastery of St Francis. This museum contains the puppet theatre and puppets which once belonged to the puppeteer Ignazio Puglisi (1904-86), a collection which is organised by theme, with rooms dedicated to monsters (devils, skeletons and giants), to Paladins and Saracens and to the so-called *cartoni*, large sections of cardboard portraying the puppets used as a background. One of the last rooms is dedicated to the characters of farce which spoke in Sicilian dialect and brought the show to an end.

PANTELLERIA★★

Trapani – Population 7 444
Michelin map 432 Q 17-18

Pantelleria is the largest of Sicily's satellite islands with a surface area of 83km2/32sqmi; it is also the most westerly, lying a mere 84km/52mi from the African continent, at the same latitude as Tunisia. Its warm climate, however, is constantly being tempered by ever-present strong winds blowing in from the sea, hence the justification for the island's Arabic name *Qawsarah or Bent el Rion*, meaning Daughter of the Wind. The current name is, in fact, late Greek or Byzantine in origin and may mean "rich land of offerings".

The island is endowed with a jagged coastline bathed by clear blue sea, that hides a wealth of varied marine life; its rocky slopes, fashioned by dry stone walling into terraces fit for cultivation, together with the local *dammusi* (typical kind of house), combine to confer upon the place an exceptional and unique beauty. The distinctive colours of the soil and base rock, which for the most part are basaltic, have earned the island a nickname, "the black pearl of the Mediterranean".

Volcanic land – The highest point on the island is Montagna Grande (836m/2 742ft), an ancient crater. The rocky black lava coastline is riddled with caves and small headlands projecting into the sea. The land mass, being volcanic, is extremely fertile and well drained, and therefore suited to the cultivation of the vine. *Solimano*, a sparkling wine with a delicate bouquet, together with the *Passito di Pantelleria*, made with *zibibbo* grapes, are the principal specialities of the island. Second to these are salted capers, which are harvested from plants that produce abundant numbers of exquisitely delicate flowers.

Various phenomena provoked by volcanic activity are still much in evidence on Pantelleria: hot springs emerge from the sea floor just off the coast, sulphuric vapour emanates from natural caves, and jets of steam (known locally as *favare*) are intermittently emitted from the volcanic rock, especially in the vicinity of the craters *(see below)*.

Evolution of a house style – The first residents of Pantelleria may have come from Africa in Neolithic times to extract its black gold, namely obsidian which, at that time, was highly sought after. Near to a village dating from this period with fortifications of a type found elsewhere only at Los Millares in Spain (near Almerìa), are a number of megalithic funerary structures of a kind that is distinctive to the island, known locally as **sesi** *(see below)*, yet reminiscent in shape of the *nuraghi* of Sardinia.

Next came the Phoenicians: they called the island Kossura and provided it with a large harbour on the exact spot occupied by the island's main port today. There followed waves of Carthaginians, Romans, Vandals, Byzantines and Arabs, who boosted the local agriculture by introducing cotton, olives and figs, and improving the cultivation of the vine. Many of the island's farming communities preserve their Arab names: Khamma, Gadir, Rakhali, Bukkuram, Bugeber and Mursia.

During the Second World War, Pantelleria's key strategic position right in the middle of the Canale di Sicilia separating North Africa from Italy, earned it the attentions of the Fascist government, which began to fortify the place. As a result, it was subjected to systematic bombing raids in 1943 by the Allies based on the Tunisian coast.

The traditional type of house found on Pantelleria is the **dammuso**; this is Arab in origin. The square constructions are built with square stones (now only used to face the exterior). The roof doubles as a terrace, but rather than being completely flat, the surface is gently undulated so as to permit rain water to be channelled away, and subsequently collected for domestic use. At one time, each individual house constituted a single residential unit, more often than not divided into two rooms: one for human habitation, the other for sheltering animals. Nowadays, however, many have been bought up and converted into summer homes, often grouped into a residential complex comprising several units.

Tourist information – Several tour operators, some private, are able to provide information on the types of accommodation and facilities available. Most can also arrange holiday packages, car and boat rentals. **Pro Loco** ☎ 0923 91 18 38; **Associazione Turistica Pantelleria** ☎ 0923 91 29 48; **Promozione Turistica di Pantelleria** ☎ 0923 91 22 57.

GETTING TO PANTELLERIA

The quickest and easiest way of getting to the island from mainland Italy is by **air**. Direct flights from Trapani and Palermo are operated by Alitalia and Air Sicilia; during the summer, both airlines offer services from both Rome and Milan. A shuttle bus links the airport, situated 5km/3mi south of the city, to piazza Cavour in Pantelleria.

Those already in Sicily, ideally in the area of Trapani, might like to consider the **ferry** travelling overnight on the outward journey (approx 6hr) and returning by day (approx. 5hr). For information contact **Siremar** ☎ 0923 54 05 15; Fax 0923 54 54 44 (Trapani office) or 0923 91 11 04 (Pantelleria office). Ustica Lines ☎ 0923 22 200, operates a **hydrofoil** service (2hr 30min) from June to Sept.

WHERE TO STAY

If you are planning to stay one or more nights on the island, it is well worth renting a *dammuso*, one of the typical local Arab-style houses *(see below)*. Tourist information providers will be happy to give information on terms and conditions.

Hotel Papuscia – Contrada Sopra Portella 28, Tracino, ☎/fax 0923 91 54 63; www.pantelleria.it/papuscia This small, friendly hotel has 11 comfortable rooms housed in 3 *dammusi*. 130 000L half-board a day per person.

EATING OUT

I Mulini – Via Kania 12, Tracino *(12km/7.5mi south-east of Pantelleria)*, ☎ 0923 91 53 98; open from Easter to Oct. A popular restaurant, housed in an old restored mill, serving cuisine which is both traditional and innovative. Around 70 000L per person.

GETTING AROUND

The best way of exploring the island is by **car**, enabling visitors to discover the island's many surprises at a leisurely pace. The road running around the island is asphalted but very narrow. **Bus** services from piazza Cavour link Pantelleria with other parts of the island.

To explore the coast from the sea, rubber dinghies may be hired; organised boat trips are also provided. Further details and costs are available from tourist information providers.

SHOPPING

Visitors should not really leave the island without buying some capers and a bottle of the excellent dessert wine, the Passito di Pantelleria, for which the island is renowned. These can be bought from shops in the built-up areas or from the land-holdings where they are produced.

The inhabitants of Pantelleria, who by trade tend traditionally to be farmers rather than sailors, have tried to resolve the problem posed by the strong winds that blow during the greater part of the year and prevent trees from growing tall (even the olive-trees have been adapted and helped by man to grow at ground level by pruning them into a circular fan of low-lying espaliers). The solution they have devised is the **Pantelleria garden**, a circular or square enclosure with high stone walls, in which one or more citrus trees might grow, protected from the wind. Sometimes these gardens are physically attached to a house, others might be situated in the centre of some field – an oasis of green, especially when seen from the air.

★★TOUR OF THE ISLAND BY CAR *Approx 40km/25mi round trip*

A scenic coast road provides glorious views of the landscape.

Pantelleria – The houses of the island's main built-up area are clustered around the harbour, having been reconstructed without any formal planning after the Second World War. The main landmark is the **Castello Barbacane**; this was probably founded in Roman times, since when it has been demolished and rebuilt on a number of occasions. It owes its present appearance to Frederick II of Swabia.

Follow the west coast, heading south.

Neolithic Village – The archaeological site is situated some 3km/1.8mi beyond Mursia and the **Kuddie Rosse**, ancient craters of a reddish colour. The only discernible feature among the low stone field boundary walls and scattered piles of rubble is the **Sese Grande★** (just beyond the quarry, at the end of a long wall, continue left some 50m/55yd. The *sese* lies behind a villa, on the left.) This structure rises from an elliptical base of large blocks of lava into a kind of tower. It is surrounded by an ornamental ledge which spirals its way up to the top. The base has 12 entrances serving as many low passages that interconnect the same number of domed funerary chambers. Here, the dead were entombed in the foetal position, with the head pointing towards the west, surrounded by their personal grave goods.
A little further on, the rocky black **Punta Fram** points out to the sea. Past the tip of the headland, a flight of steps leads down from the right side of the road, to the **Grotta di Sataria** which contains pools of water fed by hot springs.

★**Scauri** – High up on the cliff edge, enjoying its spectacular **position★**, Scauri overlooks its picturesque little harbour, fed by hot springs. Marvellous **views★** are to be had from the cemetery.

Specchio di Venere

After continuing some way along the coast, park the car and walk into Nikà.

Nikà – *30min on foot there and back.* The minuscule fishing village nestles in a lava gorge. Among the nearby rocks emerge a number of hot springs.

Back on the coastal road, turn left at the junction for **Rekhale**, one of the few villages that preserves various *dammusi* and Pantelleria gardens in their original state. Return to the coast, which at this point drops steeply down to the sea. After a bend in the road appears **Saltalavecchia** (which literally translates as the "old lady's leap"), a village perched on the cliff at one of the highest points; enjoy the incredible and very dramatic **view**★★ down a sheer face to the sea, over 150m/492ft below *(be very careful here as the ground can give way)*.

Balata dei Turchi – This was where the Saracens used to land on the island unseen. It is one of the few sheltered coves with access to the sea (a broad, flat rock), protected from the wind and therefore overgrown with tall vegetation, notably bushes of wild juniper and sweet-smelling pines.

Dietro Isola – The road provides splendid **views**★★ out over the coastline which here is dominated by this great headland.

★**Punto dell'Arco** – At the far end of the promontory sits the **Arco dell'Elefante**★, a rather spectacular naturally formed archway of grey lava which, in colour and shape, resembles the head and trunk of an elephant.

Gadir – The little harbour full of fishing smacks bubbles with water from thermal springs (in the harbour hollow).

A short way beyond, a path leads off to the right of the road to the lighthouse on **Punta Spadillo**. When the lighthouse comes into view, branch left along a second track towards a collection of abandoned houses; then climb up to the batteries. Behind the white one, follow the path downhill between low stone-lava walls which eventually opens out by the tiny **Lago delle Ondine**★ (lake of waves). Almost completely surrounded by glorious tall cliffs and wonderful lumps of volcanic rock, this small lava hollow collects water from the breaking waves to form a small emerald-green pool of stillness.

After the fine **Cala dei Cinque Denti**★ (the bay with five teeth), turn left at the fork.

★**Specchio di Venere** – This Venus' looking glass (besides being an attractive purple wild flower) is a delicious lake of green water fed by a sulphur-rich spring on its western flank. Its name is bestowed by the ancient myths for, according to the legend, Venus studied her reflection in this lake when comparing her beauty with that of her rival Psyche.

★★INLAND

Leave the town of Pantelleria by the airport road and continue to Sibà. Beyond the village is the Benikulà Cave or Bagno Asciutto (natural sauna).

Grotta Benikulà – *Coming from the direction of Sibà, there are no signs: access to the cave is down a road on the left (signposted from the other direction). Leave the car and proceed on foot. It takes 10min to walk there and back. Those intending to have a sauna should take a swimming costume and a towel.*

Looking down over the valley from above, two Pantelleria gardens may be seen. Inside the cave, the temperature of the steam rises the deeper in one goes. It is worth pausing at the cave entrance and to enter only once you are accustomed to the heat. It is advisable not to spend too long inside as the temperature can be overwhelming.

★★ **La Montagna Grande** – The road up to the Montagna Grande offers magnificent **views**★★ over the surrounding landscape. The mountain is covered with pine forest *(with prescribed picnic sites)*. By the building marking the end of the road, leave the car and continue on foot past two other buildings (a *dammuso* house and a chapel); a little further on the left, a series of stone steps lead up to the **Grotta dei Briganti**, a large cave in which the temperature is constantly warm, which is why in the past it served as a refuge for outlaws (hence its name).

Ghirlanda – Costa Ghirlanda, on the east side of the island, conceals a number of tombs of indeterminate age. Access to them is by an extremely bumpy dirt track for which a four-wheel drive vehicle (or a horse) is recommended. In an oak wood *(on the left)* is a collection of rock-hewn **tombs**, which local tradition claims to be Byzantine. The exceptional beauty of this mysterious place alone makes the excursion worthwhile.

★ **Monte Gibele** – This old volcano, now extinct, provides the perfect context for an agreeable walk: from Rakhali, head inland and, at the junction, fork right until a path appears on the left. Continue on foot. The path leads to the crater, now covered in vegetation. On the way, the track skirts past the **Favara Grande**, a powerful geyser which issues jets of boiling hot steam.

★★TOUR OF THE ISLAND BY BOAT

The perfect complement to an exploration of the island's land mass, is to go off and discover her other splendid attributes by sea. The opaque blackness of the lava rocks contrasts sharply with the deep blue sea which, in places, appears an emerald green. The coastline is interrupted by little, delightfully secluded creeks, ravines and intriguing caves. Starting out from Pantelleria, a clockwise tour of the island will first reveal the jagged and low-lying north coast; in the area of Cuddia Randazzo, the rocks assume strange black profiles which can be construed as figures of animals or other weird creatures. There follows a series of inlets and caves, perfect for swimming. Then comes the **Arco dell'Elefante**★ *(see above)* and a further succession of caves and hollows divided by pillars of lava. The most dramatic grottoes are situated between Punta Duca and Punta Polacca, however these can only be fully explored by the smallest craft: **Grotta del Duce**, **Grotta del Formaggio** and Grotta della Pila dell'Acqua. This is the most spectacular stretch of the island's coast, with its towering great cliffs reaching far into the sky and large monolithic rocks pointing sharply out of the sea until, at last, the drama culminates with a view of **Saltalavecchia**. Ever taller rocky outcrops follow (like sections of coastline around Scauri), before settling out among flatter and low-lying boulders as in the vicinity of Cala dell'Alga.

Golfo di PATTI ⚓

Messina
Michelin map 432 M 27

The bay stretches from Capo Calavà to Capo Milazzo which juts out into the sea like a sickle. The broad sweep of beach which stretches along the ample width of the bay – a favourite haunt of sun-seekers – is briefly interrupted halfway by Capo Tindari, crowned by its sanctuary.

Patti – This small town in the hinterland extends down to the sea at Marina di Patti, where the remains of a Roman villa were recently discovered *(see below)*. The old town centre still retains its medieval network of narrow streets, spanned by arches, clustered around the cathedral.
Elevated to a bishopric by King Roger in 1131, then nominated a royal town by Frederick III of Aragon in 1312, the title of *magnanima* (generous) was bestowed on Patti by Charles V for having made a generous tribute to the crown. Very little remains of this glorious period of the town's history, Patti having succumbed to repeated earthquakes (particularly the one in 1693).

Low tide below Capo Tindari

The present **cathedral** ⓥ building dates from the 18C, its beautiful 15C **portal** having been restored to the main façade. The small clusters of columns which flank the main entrance are graced with magnificent capitals, typical of the late Romanesque, carved with grotesques: two-headed, winged animals and fantastical human monsters. **Inside** stands the **sarcophagus of Queen Adelasia** *(in the right transept)* – wife of Roger I – a 16C restoration of the 1118 original.

On the northern side of the town, beside the River Montagnareale, is Porta San Michele, the only fragment of the Aragonese defensive town walls to survive. Beyond the gate sits the little church of **San Michele**, which contains a fine marble ciborium by Antonello Gagini (1538) and a triptych featuring a group of angels flanked by St Agatha and Mary Magdalene *(Sa Maddalena)*.

Villa Romana di Patti ⓥ – *In Patti Marina, near the underpass of the motorway on the right.*

The large Imperial Roman villa was discovered during construction work on the motorway. The complex is arranged around a peristyle with a columned portico from which lead various rooms, including one with three apses, paved with mosaic featuring geometric motifs and depictions of domestic and wild animals. There would also have been baths on the east side of the house.

★**Tindari** – *See TINDARI.*

Laghetti di Marinello – This is the name given to the pools of water left by the tide on the wide sandy strip below Capo Tindari *(see also TINDARI)*, some of which harbour a rich variety of aquatic plants. The area also attracts an interesting selection of birds: gulls and migratory species, including grebes, coots and little egrets. These pools can be reached on foot (about 30min) from Oliveri. The beach tails off into a glorious **bay**★★ of clear blue water. In summer this is a veritable paradise for bathers although the beach is rarely crowded *(swimmers are strongly recommended not to bathe in the actual pools, since the water is stagnant: it is preferable to swim in the bay)*.

★**Villa Romana di Terme Vigliatore** ⓥ *(in the district of San Biagio)* – The luxury suburban residence, dating from the 1C AD, has not been excavated fully. The villa comprises the actual residential quarters *(on the left)* and a small bath complex for the owners of the villa and their guests *(on the right)*.

To the left extends a square **peristyle** with eight columns down each side (of which only part has been excavated). Straight ahead is a large **tablinum** (archive room) with an *opus sectile* floor made up of black and white stone pieces laid in geometric patterns, surrounded with a marble tile border. The rooms on the left served as a kitchen (adjacent to the *tablinum*) or bedrooms.

The most interesting part of the complex, however, is the private baths *(to the right of the entrance to the site)*, which were extended in two different phases. First there is the semicircular bath, to the left of which is the **frigidarium** paved with a fine black and white mosaic depicting a boat with two oarsmen and a fisherman (with a line). Around the central panel are dolphins (at the four corners), with a swordfish above. The heating system of the various sections of the baths is clearly visible.

Hot air from a furnace located behind the complex circulated by convection through the cavities in the walls formed by rectangular pipes and between the ground and the floor, which was raised by little columns of bricks is known as *suspensurae*.

Milazzo – *See MILAZZO.*

EXCURSION INLAND

Montalbano Elicona – *42km/26mi SE of Patti and 27km/17mi SW of Terme Vigliatore.* Perched 900m/2 952ft high among the Nebrodi mountains, this town offers excellent opportunities for walking through woodland (bosco di Malabotta) and rambling among the rocky crags of Argimosco. On arrival, the most impressive feature is the great **castle** ⊘ which dominates the rest of the town. This was erected by Frederick II of Swabia on the site of an earlier small Arab fortress, and destroyed by him following the Guelph uprising in 1232. It was then rebuilt by Frederick II of Aragon in the early 14C, as an elegant fortified residence so typical of that time. Situated on the highest outcrop on the western edge of the town, it is surrounded by a network of narrow medieval streets, atmospheric in the extreme, running up and down. Inside the castle complex is a large courtyard in the middle of which stands a chapel complete with traces of frescoes.

It is well worth walking around the ramparts, although this may be awkward in parts *(special care required climbing up)*, so as to take full advantage of the views in every direction.

Novara di Sicilia – *40km/25mi from Montalbano Elicona, retracing your route back to the SS 185 (approximately 1hr).* This small mountain town, between the Peloritani and Nebrodi mountain ranges, lies some way inland along a wonderfully scenic drive: the road winds its way from the coast through a landscape of pine forests and lush Mediterranean vegetation. The town itself is laid out on medieval lines, complete with a towering Saracen castle, now in ruins. In the centre stands the **Duomo**, which shelters a remarkable carved wooden altar, candlesticks and lecterns, sculpted with unusual figures with primitive features.

The road continues inland on the SS 185 to a mountain pass, **Portella Mandrazzi** (1 125m/3 690ft), from where wonderful views stretch over the Alcàntara valley and beyond, Mount Etna. From here, it is easy to follow on to Francavilla di Sicilia and to explore its fascinating valley *(see Gole dell'ALCANTARA)*.

PIANA DEGLI ALBANESI

Palermo – Population 6 340
Michelin map 432 N 21

Towards the middle of the 15C, the area occupied by the Balkans was invaded by the Turks. Many inhabitants emigrated, some settled in Molise and Apulia. A century later, an Albanian condottiere was summoned by Alfonso of Aragon to contain a spate of revolts thereabouts: the soldiers then stayed in southern Italy, particularly in Calabria, before trickling through into Sicily over the ensuing years, and arriving at Piana degli Albanesi. Here they were welcomed with open arms and obtained permission to continue practising their faith in accordance with the Greek Orthodox Church. Small-time farmers became small-time merchants and set about securing their community's prosperity. The Church granted them ever-greater administrative and religious autonomy, enabling them to maintain their traditions, language and literature. One of their most important communities is centred around Piano degli Albanesi and, although completely integrated within the local population, the Albanians retain their own ancient traditions, especially during religious festivals. The main season comes with Epiphany (12 days after Christmas), then celebrations are completed with all the pomp and majesty of the Eastern Byzantine Church, complete with a re-enactment of the baptism of Christ; while at Easter, the locals don their most splendid costumes, typically embroidered with gold and silver, before pouring out onto the main street and rallying before the churches of Santa Maria Odigitria, San Giorgio (not far away but actually in via Barbato) and San Demetrio, the town's main church. Outward signs of their heritage are evident at all times in the local dialect they speak and in the Greek Orthodox masses they celebrate; even the road signs and street names are inscribed in two languages. The town itself has another name, *Hora*, meaning the town.

The "gelu i muluni"

Although there are no actual Albanian specialities as such to have gained popularity in Sicily, at least one typical Palermo sweetmeat is said to be of Albanian origin. It is the *gelu i muluni* which consists of watermelon sweetened with sugar and mixed with starch, pieces of chocolate, candied pumpkin, pistachio nuts, cinnamon and vanilla, and served with ice cream.

A short way south-west, a lovely artificial lake nestles silently in among the lushly green countryside: a view of this pastoral idyll may be espied from the Basilian monastery just above the town.

EXCURSION *21km/13mi*

From Piana degli Albanesi take the SP 5 to Ficuzza. The winding road leads upwards and offers splendid views of the town and artificial lake.

Palazzo Reale ⊘ – The small village of Ficuzza is arranged around the piazza in front of this **hunting lodge** built for Ferdinando III of Bourbon at the beginning of the 19C. The limestone walls of Rocca Busambra (1 613m/5 290ft) act as an impressive backdrop to the elegant neo-Classical lines of the building. The rather bare interior has a beautiful **dining room** decorated with stuccowork depicting hunting scenes. Attractive gardens *(parco reale)* lie behind the palace.
To the right of the palace, the **Centro di Recupero della Fauna selvatica di Ficuzza** (Ficuzza Wildlife Protection Centre) provides visitors with a wealth of information on local fauna.

The forest – *A road to the left of the palace leads into the woods and is the starting point for a number of excursions.* The **Bosco della Ficuzza**, once a royal hunting ground, is a plateau covering approximately 7 000ha/17 297 acres of land dominated by Rocca Busambra. The forest comprises mainly holm oak, maple, oak and cork oak, while its rich fauna includes porcupines, martens, hedgehogs, tortoises, golden eagles and peregrine falcons.

PIAZZA ARMERINA

Enna – Population 22 530
Michelin map 432 ○ 25

Piazza Armerina is rather overshadowed by the fabulous nearby Roman villa of Casale *(see Villa Romana del CASALE)*, yet its attractive historic centre clustered around a Baroque cathedral is worthy of interest in its own right. The town comes to life each 13 and 14 August, when the townsfolk don medieval garb in order to re-enact the arrival of the Gran Conte Ruggero d'Altavilla and his troops.

The palio and its legend – It all stems from the people's huge admiration for great Count Roger: in those days, the town was held by the Saracens, the infidels, so the Norman advance in Sicily was considered a kind of holy war. Very soon, the inhabitants of Piazza rose in revolt, acclaiming Roger Guiscard de Hauteville (known in Italy as Ruggero d'Altavilla) as their leader. On arrival, the paid mercenary/condottiere gave the town a banner which earned great admiration from the faithful. The banner was then furled and put away until the mid-1300s, when it was recovered and borne with great ceremony to the town church. As if by a miracle, the plague which was then decimating the town, suddenly died out and the banner became a cult object. According to tradition, the standard in question is the one bearing the Madonna delle Vittorie, now in the cathedral.

★MEDIEVAL QUARTER

The little town is visible from a good distance away with, at its centre, the Duomo dominating the highest point (721m/2 364ft). Around the great church grew up the old town, threaded by a jumble of narrow medieval streets, lined by fine Renaissance and Baroque town houses.

Duomo ⊘ – The monumental Baroque building, crowned with a great dome, towers over its own **piazza**, an open space enclosed by the likes of the Baroque **Palazzo Trigona**.
The current church stands upon the 15C foundations of another, from which a bell-tower survives down the right side, with Catalan Gothic windows on the two lower levels and Renaissance equivalents above. The front elevation comprises a broad façade ornamented with pilasters and engaged columns; a sandstone string-course articulates the horizontal planes balancing the important emphasis given to the elegant central doorway framed by spiral columns, surmounted by a single wide, square window, with the eagle above, the heraldic emblem of the Trigona family, who originally commissioned the church.
Inside, it preserves a number of notable works of art: immediately on the right, the baptismal font stands through a Gagini-style Renaissance archway. Above the main altar, at the far end of the nave, sits the **Madonna delle Vittorie★**, the Byzantine image which is popularly linked to the banner given by Pope Nicholas II to his legate Roger I "to go before him and inspire his army in its future campaigns" at the Council of Melfi, the capital of the Norman kingdom of Puglia, where several councils were held. In the little chapel to the left of the chancel is a fine **painted wooden cross★** from 1455, with the Resurrection depicted on the back. Overlooking

the nave there are two gilded wooden organ cases; one ornamented with a medallion enclosing the Trinacria, the ancient symbol of Sicily *(on the left)*, the other bearing Count Roger on horseback *(on the right)*.

A walk through the streets – In via Cavour, behind the Duomo, stands a 17C **Franciscan complex** (now a hospital); its sandstone and brick church is marked by a bell-tower with a conical spire covered in maiolica tiles. The south face of the convent buildings is graced with an elegant **balcony** supported by Baroque brackets, designed by GV Gagini.

Continue on down the street to slargo Santa Rosalia and **Palazzo Canicarao**, which now comprise commercial offices (Azienda di Promozione Turistica). The main buildings enclosing **piazza Garibaldi** include the **Chiesa di Fundrò**, dedicated to St Roch, and the 18C Palazzo di Città.

Turn down via Vittorio Emanuele which opens out before two church fronts face to face: **Chiesa di Sant'Ignazio di Loyola** is preceded by a staircase that divides into two above the first flight; **Chiesa di Sant'Anna** has a noticeably convex façade. Above, towers the solid, square profile of the **Aragonese castle** (1392-96). From here, return to piazza Duomo so as to take via Monte down to the **Chiesa di San Martino di Tours**, which was founded in 1163.

On the outskirts

On the western side of town, at the far end of via Sant'Andrea, stands a 12C hermitage, l'**Eremo di Sant'Andrea** and, a little further on, the precincts of **Santa Maria del Gesù** (17C), now sadly abandoned but which preserves nonetheless its fine portico with a loggia above.

EXCURSIONS

From Piazza Armerina take the SS 228 (7km/4mi).

Aidone – The small town, a few kilometres from the ruins of Morgantina, accommodates the **Museo Archeologico Regionale** ⊙: this small regional museum housed in a former Capuchin monastery displays prehistoric and protohistoric artefacts found in the immediate area. Access to the museum is through the Church of San Francesco, which still contains a lovely 17C wooden tabernacle. The exhibits include some fine antefixes from the mid-6C BC, bearing masks of Gorgons, lions and maenads.

Scavi di Morgantina – *From Aidone follow signs for Scavi di Morgantina (approx 5km/3mi).*

The area of **Serra Orlando** has been inhabited since the Bronze Age. During the Iron Age, one particular settlement on the hill became the focal point of the area, and it was this that grew to become Morgantina, probably named after the king of the Morgeti, an Italic tribe from central-southern Italy. In the 5C BC, the town re-founded a short distance beyond the original, at Serra Orlando. The archaeological site has been excavated since 1955: this has brought to light the remains of the Siculi centre that was colonised by the Greeks, grew to prominence in the 1C AD, and was then abandoned.

The **site** ⊙ extends from one hill, into a small valley and up the next rise. The **agorà**, a small **theatre** and, on the northern hill, fragments of mosaics under protective roofing are all in evidence.

B. Kaufmann

RAGUSA ★

Population 69 683

Michelin map 432 Q 26

Ragusa is a town with ancient origins and a troubled history, one of the places where life was thrown into disarray by the earthquake of 1693 and then determinedly rebuilt. As a result, there are, in fact, two towns: the lower, older town, arranged according to a medieval plan yet Baroque in appearance, and the higher, more modern town. After that most terrible earthquake in January 1693, the inhabitants all turned their efforts to re-erecting their town. However, a straightforward settlement of the way forward was prejudiced by conflicting opinions: rebuilding began in the newly cleared open spaces according to the Baroque ideal vision for a city planned with wide avenues bisected by perpendicular streets, piazzas and avenues providing calculated vistas of the great monuments, most notably the Cathedral of San Giovanni.

Then attention was turned to rebuilding Ibla: and so the nightmare began, largely as a result of the confines of the site itself. Here, too, plans were drawn up for a new town with fine Baroque buildings but instead of the intended clean lines and straight avenues opening out into broad open squares, the designers inherited a site riddled with a complicated network of interconnecting narrow medieval streets.

In more recent times, the ugly profiles of industrial processing plants have been put up, prompted by the discovery of two major natural resources: crude oil and pitch. The black pitch in question is mined locally: once used for building, it is now principally used for making tarmac for road surfacing.

★★RAGUSA IBLA

A visit to the old town will logically begin from the long stairway of Santa Maria delle Scale, which leads down from the new (higher) part of town to the heart of Ragusa Ibla. At certain points, it provides the most splendid **views**★★ of the town's rooftops, notably the dome of Santa Maria dell'Itria *(left)* and the neo-Classical dome of the cathedral.

RAGUSA

Aquila Sveva (Via)	**AZ**	
Bocchieri (Via C.)	**BZ**	3
Cabrera (Via)	**BZ**	
Camerina (Largo)	**BZ**	4
Camerina (Via)	**BZ**	5
Chiaramonte (Via)	**BZ**	
Convento (Via)	**BZ**	6
Duomo (Piazza)	**BZ**	
Ecce Homo (Via)	**AZ**	9
Giardino (Via)	**CZ**	
Guidi (Via)	**AZ**	
La Rocca (Via T.)	**BCZ**	
Margherita (Viale)	**CZ**	10
Marini (Piazza G.M.)	**CZ**	12
Mazzini (Corso)	**AZ**	
Mercato (Via d.)	**ABZ**	
Minzoni (Via)	**AZ**	13
Montereo (Via)	**CZ**	15
Odierna (Piazza G.B.)	**CZ**	16
Orfanotrofio (Via)	**BZ**	17
Ottaviano (Via)	**ABZ**	
Ottavio (Via T.)	**ABZ**	18
Paternò Arezzo (Via M.)	**ABZ**	
Peschiera (Via)	**CZ**	
Pezza (Via)	**AZ**	
Pola (Piazza)	**BZ**	19
Porta Modica (Via)	**BCZ**	
Portale (Via d.)	**CZ**	21
Repubblica (Piazza)	**AZ**	22
Risorgimento (Via)	**AZ**	
S. Agnese (Via)	**AZ**	24
S. Domenico (Via)	**CZ**	25
S. Lucia (Via)	**AZ**	27
Solarino (Piazza D.)	**BZ**	28
Solarino (Via D.)	**ABZ**	28
Stefano (Via T. d.)	**AZ**	
Toppulo (Via)	**AZ**	
Torre Nuova (Via)	**BZ**	
XI Febbraio (Via)	**AZ**	29
XXIV Maggio (Via)	**AZ**	30
XXV Aprile (Corso)	**BCZ**	

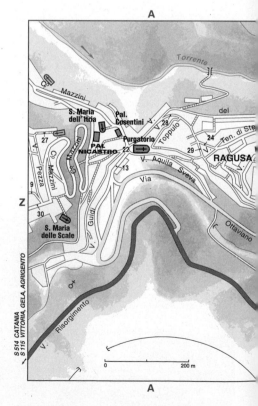

Cappuccini	**CZ**	Palazzo Cosentini	**AZ**	Palazzo La Rocca	**BZ**
Giardino Ibleo	**CZ**	Palazzo		Palazzo Nicastro	**AZ**
Palazzo Arezzi	**BZ A**	Donnafugata	**BZ**	Purgatorio	**AZ**

Santa Maria delle Scale 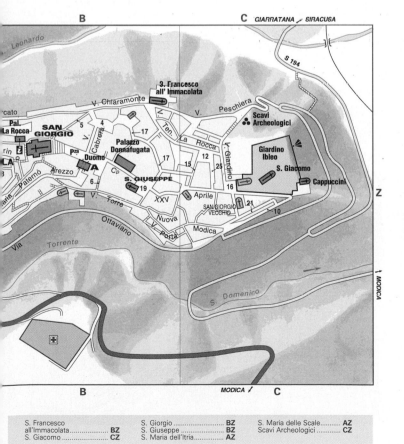 was largely rebuilt in the 18C; from the original fabric of the earlier church it preserves the Gothic south aisle, with its elegant **pointed arches★**. Nestling below the second archway sits a large Gagini School terracotta panel depicting the Dormition of the Virgin.

In Ibla itself, as if guarding the entrance to the salita Commendatore *(on the right)*, stands the statue of San Francesco di Paola set against a corner of **Palazzo Cosentini**, which has beautiful **balconies★★** and brackets carved with caricatured figures and masks. This comprises one of the most secluded corners of town, with a warren of intersecting stepped alleyways among which are hidden a number of interesting buildings.

The church **Santa Maria dell'Itria** ⊘ is marked, on the outside, by a campanile which at the top is ornamented with lovely floral panels of maiolica from Caltagirone; inside, the church contains various chapels articulated with lovely columns, all different (note the spiral columns of the chapels flanking the main altar).

Just beyond it sits **Palazzo Nicastro★★** or Vecchia Cancelleria (1760) – the old prison: note its marvellous doorway surmounted by an attractive balcony. The steep slope downhill on the left comes out before the flight of steps leading up to the elegantly convex front of the **Chiesa del Purgatorio**.

Palazzo La Rocca – *Via Bocchieri 33. Azienda Autonoma Provinciale del Turismo headquarters.* This Baroque *palazzo* still bears traces of the original medieval building that preceded it. An elegant double staircase shows the way up to the main entrance on the first floor where the tourist office is located. The six **balconies★★** along the main façade are ornamented with portrait heads of real people of the day; note the flute, lute and trumpet players, and a mother nursing a baby.

★★ Duomo di San Giorgio ⊘ – When seen from a distance, the most striking feature is the neo-Classical dome with its blue lantern articulated with Corinthian columns, added in the 19C. From the piazza, on the other hand, the eye is drawn up the steep and imposing flight of steps to the wonderful pink façade. The elegant and harmoniously proportioned front elevation comprises a central, slightly convex bay contained by three tiers of columns, flanked by a side bay surmounted by a volute. Delicately carved decoration ornaments the doorway and cornice. The figure of

S. Francesco all'Immacolata................. **BZ**	S. Giorgio .... **BZ**	S. Maria delle Scale........... **AZ**
S. Giacomo .... **CZ**	S. Giuseppe .... **BZ**	Scavi Archeologici .... **CZ**
	S. Maria dell'Itria............... **AZ**	

🛈 via Capitano Bocchieri 33, Ibla, ☎ 0932 62 14 21.

GETTING TO RAGUSA

There are daily **bus** services from Agrigento (2hr 30min), Catania airport (2hr), Palermo (4hr) and Siracusa (approx 2hr), as well as a **train** service from. Siracusa. Both trains and buses arrive in the modern town. For further information and timetables, contact the tourist office.

WHERE TO STAY

An old **monastery** a short way from Ragusa, in the district of Giubiliana (9km/5.5mi off the main road to Marina di Ragusa), has been restored and converted into the **Eremo della Giubiliana**. Guests sleep in the old monks' cells, all furnished with traditional Sicilian furniture. An ideal location for a relaxing break. Around 350 000L for a double room. ☎ 0932 66 91 19, Fax 0932 63 38 91.

EATING OUT

The most typical restaurant in Ragusa Ibla is **U' Saracinu** (via del Convento 9, ☎ 0932 24 69 76; closed Wed), which offers a choice of typical Sicilian dishes for approximately 40 000L.
La Pergola, an attractive restaurant in the new town (piazza Sturzo 6, ☎ 0932 25 56 59; closed Tues and from the beginning of Aug to 10 Sept), serves pizza and seafood specialities. Approximately 60 000L for a meal.

St George on horseback driving a spear into the dragon, is incorporated both into the façade (above the left volute), and as the centrepiece of the beautiful railings at the bottom of the steps. The building was erected in the 18C by **Rosario Gagliardi**. The **interior**, divided into nave and aisles, is graced with the same frieze along the nave as the one on the exterior, thereby linking the two into an ideal whole.

Piazza – The space before the duomo is, in fact, rectangular in shape and set at a slight angle to the church, on a slope. The other buildings enclosing it include **Palazzo Arezzi** which has a wonderful balcony projecting over an archway through to the street beyond; further on, on the opposite side of the square, sits **Palazzo Donnafugata** with its delightful little wooden balcony.

★**San Giuseppe** ⊙ – The elegant front elevation bears a remarkable resemblance to that of San Giorgio, and for this reason has been attributed to Gagliardi. It rises through three tiers of Corinthian columns and figurative statues. The **interior**, an

San Giorgio

oval space, is enclosed below an oval dome; the splendid floor is a striking combination of maiolica tiles and black pitch-stone. Note the gratings which enabled the enclosed nuns to follow mass out of sight of the congregation.

Giardino Ibleo – These public gardens containing several religious buildings are laid out at the far end of Ragusa Ibla. Just outside the entrance, on the right, stands the elaborate Catalan Gothic portal of **San Giorgio Vecchio** (15C).
The church just inside the gardens, on the left, is **San Giacomo** ⊘, better known as Chiesa del Crocefisso because of the wooden effigy contained within, left of the main altar. It dates in the main from the 14C (the 1693 earthquake caused the lateral aisles to collapse; these were never rebuilt), and encloses a ceiling painted with historical panels from 1754 – unfortunately several are missing. The *trompe l'oeil* dome is especially effective.
On the side of the garden stands the **Chiesa dei Cappuccini** ⊘. This hosts a lovely **triptych★** by **Pietro Novelli** showing the Virgin Mary flanked by St Agatha and St Lucy. The figure in the left-hand section of the central panel looking out of the picture is a self-portrait.
A wonderful **view** from the gardens extends over the Irminio valley.
Archaeological excavation conducted on a site just beyond the garden has unearthed a street and residential quarter dating from the Classical period underlying various medieval constructions.

Chiesa di San Francesco all'Immacolata – The church, largely rebuilt in the 17C, preserves a 13C Chiaramonte doorway *(west flank)*.

NEW TOWN

The "modern" town has been developed on a framework of straight, parallel streets intersecting at right angles to each other, to form a regular grid-like pattern up the side of the Patro hill. The elegant **via Roma** bisects the town on a parallel axis to the side of the hill; the perpendicular **corso Italia** runs down towards Ibla between wonderful buildings.
On the right opens out piazza San Giovanni, overlooked by the church with which it shares its name.

Cattedrale di San Giovanni ⊘ – The cathedral dates from the early 18C. Its imposing Baroque front elevation, flanked by its campanile, is graced with a broad, raised terrace.
Further along corso Italia, on the left, sits the 19C Chiesa del Collegio di Maria Addolorata, with **Palazzo Lupis** – note the fine brackets – beyond. There follows via San Vito *(right)*: no 156 is **Palazzo Zacco**, marked by a great coat of arms supported on decorative brackets on the corner. Note the balcony **brackets** projecting from the lateral façade carved with figures and grotesques. Still in corso Italia, but a short distance further on the left, rises **Palazzo Bertini** which was built towards the end of the 18C. Three large **masks★** peer down from the carved window keystones, as if watching the pedestrian traffic. According to tradition, these personify a pauper – ugly, hungry and toothless *(left)*, a nobleman – serene in the assurance of his social status, and a merchant – wearing a turban and a self-satisfied expression assured by the weight of money in his pocket.

Museo Archeologico Ibleo ⊘ – *Via Natalelli; under the Ponte Nuovo, on the first floor of a building, above a garage.*
The local archaeological museum displays artefacts recovered from the surrounding area. Among the most interesting exhibits is a reconstruction of the Classical necropoli at Camarina and Rito, and one of the kiln at Scornavacche.

C Cappello Sculpture Collection

Carmelo Cappello, a native of Ragusa (b 1912), began to work in the 1930s. His style, which evolved from being highly figurative in the early years to becoming pure abstraction in his latest creations, is well-represented in this small, but interesting collection. *Il freddoloso (Shivering with Cold* – 1938), one of his most famous works, is a realistic figure charged with great expression. In the later works, facial features become abstracted by being reduced to a minimum: compare the expressive faces of the two women with well-defined noses and eyes, no hair or mouth in *Le prime stelle (The First Stars)* to the faces of the two athletes in *Acrobati* (1953-54); for in this latter work, individual personality and detail has been distilled, abstracted and replaced by a concentration on rhythm and movement of line. Cappello's latest works are austere studies of pure line, clinically cold (an impression imparted by the polished steel) yet which twist and merge, attempting to encapsulate in form the fluid dynamics of the universe.

The collection is housed in the industrial estate (ASI) south of Ragusa. Open Mon to Fri, 8.30am-12.30pm. Three afternoon openings, from 3pm-5.30pm, are also scheduled.

SEASIDE

This part of the coast is blessed with wonderful beaches and an especially limpid sea. Resorts include **Marina di Ragusa Soleil** which is especially popular during the summer and **Sampieri** and **Marina di Modica**.

Some 2km/1.2mi out of Ragusa lies the **Riserva Naturale della Foce dell'Irpinio**.

Rovine di Camarina – *16km/10mi NW of Marina di Ragusa.* Camarina was founded as a Greek town at the behest of Syracuse; it suffered assaults from both the Carthaginians and the Romans who finally destroyed it in 598 BC. **Excavation** ⊙ has revealed the remains of a temple dedicated to Athena (incorporated in the masonry of the 19C building which now houses the museum), sections of plateia B, the market-place and stoà – the portico over the covered market – and a residential quarter dating from Hellenistic times *(marked by the fence on the other side of the road).*

Museo Archeologico Regionale di Camarina ⊙ – *In the first room the most recent finds*

Santa Maria dell'Itria, Ragusa

recovered as a result of ongoing work are displayed; these are gradually replaced and transferred to the permanent collection. The layout is therefore subject to reorganisation. The sea off Camarina has proved to conceal a wealth of treasures lost in numerous wrecks: a wonderful **Corinthian bronze helmet**★ (6C-5C BC), an Attic-Etruscan helmet (4C BC), an elegant bronze and enamel perfume container (2C AD), and a hoard of more than 1 000 bronze coins (AD 275). There is also an unusual set of **lead weights** recovered from the sea bed from the area below the market-place. The museum possesses a vast collection of Corinthian (older and therefore more crudely made) and Attic **amphorae**★. The Etruscan and Punic amphorae are different, being more elongated. The section devoted to the Archaic period contains a fine aryballos (a small bucket-like vessel used for drawing water from a well) decorated with two lions facing each other (T 2281), from the necropolis at Rifriscolaro.

Not far away, between Punta Secca and Casuzze, is the **Parco Archeologico di Kaucana** ⊙. There are two entrances to the archaeological site: one along the coastal road, the other on the way from Punta Secca to Marina di Ragusa. It encloses the ruins of a residential area and a small paleo-Christian church.

Pozzallo – *30km/19mi E of Marina di Ragusa.* This sleepy hamlet lies on the edge of a long beach. Its most characteristic landmark is the **Torre dei Conti Cabrera**, which was originally built by the local count as a watchtower at a time when pirates frequently assaulted the community. Although destroyed by the 1693 earthquake, it has been rebuilt as it was.

RANDAZZO

Catania – Population 11 626
Michelin map 432 N 26

This small town, situated on the slopes of Mount Etna, is so close to the volcano that only by a miracle has it never been threatened by a flow of molten lava. Randazzo began to prosper during the Middle Ages (12C). Its good fortune continued until the 16C, when heavy tax policies implemented by the Spanish sovereigns, coupled with a drastic plague epidemic, brought the town to its knees.

LARA PESSINA

★OLD TOWN CENTRE

Randazzo could be called the black town, black because of the lava used not only to pave its streets and highlight arches above doorways and windows (at corso Umberto 100, for example, is a building with lovely two-light windows divided by small spiral columns), but also as the main building material for the town's principal monuments like the Church of Santa Maria.

Chiesa di Santa Maria – Although the building dates from the 13C it has undergone considerable modifications through the centuries. What survives from the original is the plan, the characteristic tall Norman **apses**★ ornamented with blind arcading, and the south wall pierced by its two– and three-light windows. The neo-Gothic façade and bell-tower are 19C. The black lava building stone contrasts effectively with the white window and door surrounds. The sacristy, which stands proud of the main church, once accommodated an ecclesiastical tribunal.

Corso Umberto, the main thoroughfare, cuts through the historic centre. A short distance along it, via Roma leads off right; this, in turn, is bisected by a street which to the left leads to piazza San Nicolò. The church after which the square is named was erected in 1594, and has a front elevation articulated by dark lava stone; the campanile dates from 1783. The other buildings overlooking the square include Palazzo Clarentano (1508) graced with decorative two-light openings

WHERE TO STAY

L'antica vigna – Loc Montelaguardia, ☎ 095 92 40 03, Fax 095 92 33 24. This agriturismo guesthouse, beautifully situated at the foot of Etna 4km/2.5mi SE of Randazzo (SS 120) and easily accessible from the Circumetnea road, has 8 simple, but comfortable rooms. 100 000L for a double room, including breakfast.

EATING OUT

The **Trattoria Veneziano** via Romano 8, ☎ 095 79 91 353 (closed Sun evening and Mon) serves typical regional cuisine made from local products. Approximately 50 000L for a meal.

separated by slender columns, and the 14C Church of Santa Maria della Volta. To the right of it opens the delightful **via degli Archi** ornamented, as its name suggests, with a series of arches. Via Polizzi, on the right, leads from the piazza to **Casa Spitaleri**, with its fine lava doorway.

Turn down via Duca degli Abruzzi to its intersection from the right by via Agonia: this street is so called because, it is said, condemned prisoners were led along here from their castle-prison to the Timpa, before San Martino, to face their executioners. Look out for the one house that conforms to the 14C archetype, with a single large open space on the ground floor and two square rooms above on the first floor *(only visible from the outside)*. Via Duca degli Abruzzi leads back into corso Umberto. An archway on the right marks the old entrance to the **Palazzo Reale**. Only part of the façade, a lovely two-coloured string-course and a pair of two-light windows now remain from this elegant country town residence: before the *palazzo* was destroyed in the earthquake of 1693, it accommodated such famous guests as Joan of England, the wife of the Norman King William II, Constanza of Aragon (the town was chosen as the summer residence of the Spanish court) and, in 1535, Charles V.

Chiesa di San Martino ⊙ – This church was rebuilt in the 17C, although the fine **campanile★** beside it dates from the 13C-14C. Battlemented at roof level, a tall octagonal spire points skywards. Lower down, it is ornamented with elegant single openings, emphasised by deep polychrome strips, and decorative pointed three-light windows.

Inside, it preserves two Madonnas by followers of the Gagini and a polyptych attributed to Antonello de Saliba – a pupil of Antonello da Messina.

Across from the church lie the ruins of the castle-prison. This began life in the 13C as a fortified tower set into the city walls that extended around the medieval citadel. **Porta di San Martino**, just beyond, constitutes one of the entrances to it.

SALEMI

Trapani – Population 11 927
Michelin map 432 N 20

The small town of Salemi enjoys a lovely position surrounded by the vineyards that are so typical a feature of the Trapani region. The older parts of Salemi bear the indelible imprint of Arab influences; the narrow cobbled streets wind their way to the top of the hill crowned with the inevitable castle. Salemi was inadvertently blessed with a moment of unexpected glory when, after Garibaldi landed in Sicily, Salemi was declared the first capital of Italy.

In 1968, the town was badly damaged by the earthquake.

Castello Normanno – The Norman castle was erected at the wishes of Roger d'Altavilla on the foundations of a fortress: the castle has two square towers and one high round one.

On its right stand the remains of the **Chiesa Madre**, destroyed as a result of the earthquake of 1968. Turn down via D'Aguirre and along past the church.

Chiesa e Collegio dei Gesuiti – The rather elegant façade of the church is Baroque, complete with a portal flanked with spiral columns of tufa. The Collegio, meanwhile, accommodates the **Museo Civico** ⊙ which contains various religious works of art rescued from the churches destroyed in the earthquake in 1968: a particular highlight is the lovely *Madonna della Candelora* (Candlemas) by Domenico Gagini. Beyond the last room of the museum sits an 18C chapel that replicates the Casa Santa di Loreto.

Further downhill, lies the picturesque **Rabato** quarter complete with all its Moorish flavour. The outside streets provide wonderful **views★** of the valley. Here, on 3 February each year, the residents distribute tiny, very elaborate and strangely shaped loaves of bread for the feast day of San Biago.

Bread also plays its part in the celebrations of St Joseph's day (19 March), when special large votive loaves are baked in the shape of angels, garlands, flowers, animals and work-tools so as to represent every aspect of daily life.

EXCURSION

Calatafimi – *13km/8mi N.* This little town is well defended in spirit by its **Castello Eufemio**, a Byzantine fortress that was rebuilt in the 13C and now lies in ruins. From here, a fine **view★** stretches over the valley and town.

Every five years, during the first three days of May, the Festival of the Holy Crucifix **(Festa del Santissimo Crocefisso)** is held: an important procession takes place through the streets with representations from all the various town "corporations". The Massari delegation may be distinguished by its float decorated with bread.

On the hill opposite stands the **Pianto Romano**, a monument commemorating the followers of Garibaldi who died in action (Calatafimi was the scene of an important battle). From there, a marvellous **view★★** extends back over the Calatafimi, the surrounding hills, and the sea beyond.

The site of San Marco, 550m/1 804ft above sea-level and only 9km/6mi from the coast, was probably inhabited during the pre-Hellenistic period. Each phase in Sicilian history has left its mark here, with the site occupied by the Greeks and becoming *Municipium Aluntinorum* under the Romans. It was renamed San Marco dei Normanni in memory of the first town conquered by the Normans in Calabria. Robert Guiscard erected the **castle**, now ruined, that still dominates the town. In 1398, King Martin of Aragon conceded it to the Filangeri family as part of their feudal domain.

Before entering the heart of the town itself, isolated on the left of the road stands the Church of **San Marco**. This was built on the foundations of a **temple** dedicated to Heracles (4C BC), of which only a few blocks of tufa stone remain. The church, which is open to the sky, preserves its stone walls and a re-erected doorway.

Eating out

The restaurant **La Fornace**, via Cappuccini 115, ☎/fax 0941 79 72 97 (closed Mon in winter), is renowned for its *maccheroni al ragù*, cooked in a terracotta bowl, and for its chargrilled meat. Approximately 40 000L for a meal.

San Teodoro (or **Badia piccola**) ⊘ – San Teodoro was built in the 16C on the site of a Byzantine chapel. It is built on a Greek-cross plan with each square arm enclosed by a little dome. The interior is ornamented with magnificent Serpotta-style **stuccowork**★ depicting *Judith and Holofernes*, *Manna falling from Heaven in the Desert (at the sides of the altar)*, scenes from the parable of the prodigal son; saints and the four Theological Virtues grace the pilasters that rise up to the vault.

Monastero delle Monache Benedettine – The former Benedictine convent built in 1545 has recently been renovated so as to accommodate a **museum** ⊘ dedicated to Byzantine-Norman art. On the ground floor, two of the three apses that once formed part of the **Cappella dei Santissimi Quattro Dottori** (11C) have been uncovered, with splendid **Byzantine frescoes**★ largely intact. Those in the right-hand apse are very well-preserved: the Madonna in the vault has beautifully delicate hands (unfortunately her face is obscured); in the tier below (separated by a clear boundary symbolising the separation of heaven and earth), the four Doctors of the Orthodox Church – St John Chrysostom, St Gregory of Nazianzus, St Basil the Great and St Athanasius – are shown against a bright blue background.

San Giuseppe – Sheltering in the Church of St Joseph is the Parish Museum (**Museo Parrocchiale**) ⊘ whose collections comprise sacred furnishings, wooden reliquaries, a wooden polychrome Madonna Odigitria, a charming wooden figure representing Mary Magdalene (17C) and a painting of the Deposition (18C).

Centro storico – The main street, via Aluntina, runs through the centre of San Marco past the Chiesa Madre dedicated to **San Nicolò**, which has an austere façade relieved in part by three doorways in red Alunzio marble, also in profusion inside. In piazza Sant'Agostino some way ahead stands **Santa Maria delle Grazie** ⊘, which preserves the Filangeri funeral monument by Domenico Gagini (1481) with its fine reclining figure exuding gentle serenity.

It then continues to the 18C **Church of San Basilio** with its arcade of pointed arches, and on to the 17C **Church of Ara Coeli** ⊘, graced with a lovely doorway flanked by fluted columns and ornamented with volutes and floral elements. Inside, contained within the **Cappella del Santissimo Crocefisso**, encrusted with fine **stuccowork**★ by Serpotta depicting saints, lively cherubs, angels and festoons of fruit, is an expressive 17C Spanish wooden **Crucifix**★.

San Salvatore ⊘ – San Salvatore is also known as the **Badia Grande**, since the time it used to adjoin an important Benedictine convent; now alone, it stands in ruins not far from the football pitch. Its elegant **doorway**★ made of Alunzio marble is ornamented with columns, angels and cherubs. **Inside**, visitors are greeted by a band of serenading angels playing trumpets, various allegorical figures, playful cherubs bearing heavy drapes, scrolls and garlands of flowers; the exuberant **stucco decoration**★ culminates in sumptuous drapery hanging from the wooden canopy over the tabernacle.

SANTO STEFANO DI CAMASTRA

Messina – Population 5 105
Michelin map 432 M 25

Santo Stefano is famous for its hand-painted ceramics and so it comes as no surprise that its streets are lined with a myriad of small shops offering locally made pots, vases, plates and ceramic trinkets to suit every requirement, taste and more. Its most interesting buildings include **Palazzo Sergio**, which once belonged to the Duke of Camastra, and which now houses the **Museo della Ceramica** ⊘. Pride of place in the museum is given to S Lorenzini's *Andare (Departing)* on the right of the entrance. This comprises a group of five warriors gradually "sinking" into the ground. Several rooms in the *palazzo* preserve their original **tiled floors★**, frescoed ceilings and 18C furnishings.

Outside the town (beyond the Ceramics Institute), lies the **Cimitero Vecchio**: a cemetery that was used for two years only, between 1878 and 1880, and which contains a number of graves ornamented with maiolica.

A DAY IN THE NEBRODI MOUNTAINS

Approx 182km/113mi – Allow 1 day

The recommended itinerary follows a wonderfully scenic (although fairly long and windy) route inland, forming a roughly square circuit at the heart of the **Nebrodi mountains** which, with the Madonie, form part of the Sicilian Apennines *(Appennino Siculo, see p 208)*.

In order to ensure that the natural scenery and the indigenous species it harbours are effectively preserved intact, a large area has been designated a National Park (Parco dei Nebrodi); *for alternative excursions into the Nebrodi, consult the chapters MADONIE e NEBRODI, CAPO D'ORLANDO and FIUMARA D'ARTE.*

This circuit may also be undertaken from Sant'Agata Militello, although it is worth doing it in an anti-clockwise direction so as to enjoy the best views of Mount Etna, notably those savoured from Lago Ancipa.

The road from Santo Stefano to Mistretta provides wide prospects over the valley.

Mistretta – This small hamlet is located 950m/3 116ft above sea-level, and comprises a collection of simple stone houses grouped around the ruins of a feudal castle: the best vantage point from which to enjoy the view. A second glance will reveal a clutch of striking buildings including the Church of **San Giovanni** (1530) which is graced with an elegant double stairway and a bell-tower with a pair of openings at the top.

The front elevation of the 16C **Chiesa Madre** ⊘, dedicated to St Lucy (the popular saint martyred in Syracuse), lacks its second bell-tower (the left side being incomplete): one can but wonder whether it might have had two bell-openings like its right counterpart. Although partly rebuilt in the 17C, it preserves from the original a fine marble doorway *(right side)*. Inside, a chapel dedicated to the Madonna shelters a *Madonna of Miracles* attributed to Giorgio da Milano; a larger side chapel honouring St Lucy contains a fine altarpiece by **Antonello Gagini** with statues of St Lucy, St Peter and St Paul (1552). The elegant choir stalls behind the main altar are 17C, the organ is 18C.

At the top of the town nestles the Renaissance Church of **Santa Caterina**.

Annually, on 7 and 8 September, the town celebrates its festival for the *Madonna of Light (Madonna della Luce)* when a Madonna is borne aloft in solemn procession, escorted by two giant figures representing Mythia and Kronos (the legendary founders of Mistretta). At one time, an ugly, deformed dwarf – *i figghiu ri gesanti* – also took part, but this was discontinued because, it is said, he frightened the young women in early stages of pregnancy.

Some of the most taxing excursions on foot into the Nebrodi mountains set out from Mistretta.

From Mistretta follow the S 117 to the fork signposted right for Nicosia (see NICOSIA, MADONIE e NEBRODI) and left for the S 120 to Cerami; turn left and continue on to Cerami; the road goes straight on for Troina, or forks left for Lago Ancipa (see below).

Troina – A medieval citadel perched high above the town's rooftops shelters Troina's main church: sadly, only the bell-tower survives from the original Norman building (11C), built in blocks of sandstone spanning the road.

From Troina, return towards Cerami so as to turn right down to Lago Ancipa.

Lago Ancipa – This man-made lake, formed when the great San Teodoro dam (120m/394ft) was built, nestles in a glorious stretch of countryside. The road skirts the lake before leading on to Cesarò. Although narrow and badly rutted in places, it picks its way scenically through woods and along open valleys, providing unforgettable **views★★** of Mount Etna.

Cesarò – The town is overshadowed by the volcano. Just outside the hamlet, follow the signs for Cristo sul Monte from where a wonderful but haunting **view★★** extends across to Mount Etna.

The road twists and turns up to the narrow pass, Portella Femmina Morta e della Miraglia, through the mountain scenery and extensive beech woods. At the top of the pass, a dirt track leads up to the summit of **Monte Soro**, the highest peak in the Nebrodi mountains (1 847m/6 058ft). Continue along the scenic road to San Fratello.

San Fratello – This town, founded by a group of Lombard settlers, was partly destroyed by a landslide in the 18C. San Fratello is linked by name to the *san-fratellani*, a fine breed of horse, examples of which may be spotted roaming freely on the edge of town. The San Francesco monastery preserves 16C cloisters with fragments of fresco.

On the north side of the hamlet, by the cemetery, a track provides access to a Norman church, the **Chiesa Normanna dei Santi Alfio, Filadelfio e Cirino** ◷ (11C-12C). A marvellous **view★★** extends over the surrounding landscape from the area behind the church.

The S 289 leads out of San Fratello and tumbles its way downhill, over the motorway, to join the coastal road: turn right for Sant'Agata di Militello.

Sant'Agata di Militello – This comparatively recent resort has been developed along the seafront with access to a long stretch of beach. The main buildings, the Castello dei Principi Gallego and the adjacent 18C Chiesa dell'Addolorata, are both located on piazza Crispi. The town has a small natural history museum dedicated to the inland mountain region, the **Museo Etnoantrolpologico dei Nebrodi** ◷ *(via Cosenz)*. Sant'Agata is a good place to stay as it is conveniently situated close enough to the mountains for short excursions to escape the summer heat, and within easy range of other coastal sights like Capo d'Orlando to the east, Halæsa and Tusa to the west.

From here, the main road leads back along the coast to Santo Stefano di Camastra: after 16.5km/10mi, a road is signposted left for Caronia (4km/2.5mi inland); this little town has one of the tourist information centres for the Nebrodi National Park (Parco dei Nebrodi – see p 209).

SAN VITO LO CAPO ♒♒

Trapani – Population 3 913
Michelin map 432 M 20

San Vito is a well-known seaside resort, noted in particular for its beautiful coastline. This opens out into a bay lined with wonderful beaches lapped by limpid water that seems tinged with ranges of blues and greens, from aquamarine to navy. In the 18C, the small town comprised simply a collection of whitewashed houses clustered around the **Chiesa Madre**. The church continues steadfastly to act as the town's focal point, square and massive in profile, a constant reminder of its early beginnings as a Saracen fortress. Inside, it used to preserve a small church dedicated to San Vito (erected over the site where the saint is supposed to have lived) but this grew to be too small to accommodate the many pilgrims, and so it was enlarged until it actually incorporated the very building which once harboured it.

🮲 via Savoia 57, ☎ 0923 97 24 64.

WHERE TO STAY AND EATING OUT

Camp sites – El Bahira, in the Salinella district, Bahira, ☎ 0923 97 25 77, is an attractive camp site located 4km/2.5mi south of the town. **Camping La Pineta** is closer to San Vito, in via del Secco, ☎ 0923 97 28 18. Both camp sites also have chalets and apartments to rent.

Halimeda Hotel – Via Arimondi 100, ☎/fax 0923 97 23 99. The only drawback to this attractive and welcoming hotel is its location away from the seafront. The hotel has 9 comfortable, well-appointed rooms, all furnished in different styles, taking various parts of the world as their theme (England, the Far East, the Mediterranean, Northern Europe). Approximately 150 000L for a double room.

Da Alfredo – Contrada Valanga 3 (1km/0.6mi south), ☎ 0923 97 23 66. Typical regional cuisine served under a delightful shady arbour. Approximately 60 000L for a meal.

BOAT TRIPS TO THE RISERVA DELLO ZINGARO

Two boats offer trips from San Vito Lo Capo: the *Leonardo da Vinci* (☎ 0924 34 222) and the *Nautilus* (☎ 0347 57 66 391). The latter has a glass bottom, which allows visitors to admire the colourful underwater life *(for a description of the Riserva dello ZINGARO see Golfo di CASTELLAMMARE).*

Capo San Vito

HEADLAND

The road from **Custonaci** to the headland offers wonderful **views**★ out over the Golfo del Cofano. Before San Vito, it passes on the left one of the many 16C watch-towers that punctuate this area; it then continues past an attractive, characteristically cube-like, little chapel dedicated to **San Crescenzia** (16C).
Beyond San Vito, on the left of the road, stands an old and now abandoned tuna fishery **(Tonnara del Secco)**. Up ahead sits the solitary **Torre dell'Impio**, another watch-tower (hidden on the way there, but clearly visible on the return journey). At the end of the road extends the marvellous Riserva dello Zingaro *(see Golfo di CASTEL-LAMMARE)*.

Monte Cofano – The towering limestone peak and the bay that surrounds it, now a nature reserve, make for a magnificent **sight**★ as the steep pinky-red cliffs extending skywards are mirrored (hopefully) in the crystal calm sea. Turn up the road on the right before Custonaci that leads to the bottom of the hill before con-tinuing past a number of quarries gouged into the rocky flank. From these are extracted the marble known as *Perlato di Sicilia*, a startlingly white stone by com-parison with the other brownish natural rock of the area. Not far from the quarries *(follow the signs)* nestles the grotto known as the **Grotta Mangiapane** (in the vicinity of Scurati). Inside, it shelters a tiny rural hamlet, complete with chapel and cobbled street. The endearing charm of this abandoned village, with its vaguely Mexican air (especially because of the square, mud-coloured houses), is especially poignant at Christmas, when it provides a setting for a captivating human enactment of the Christmas story.

SCIACCA⚓

Agrigento – Population 40 276
Michelin map 432 O 21

The striking thing about Sciacca, with its collection of white buildings scattered over a flank of Monte Kronio *(see Monte KRONIO)*, right on the edge of the sea, is its Arab feel. Long-established local industries include the thermal spa and fishing, as a glance at the harbour will confirm: it is full of fishing smacks with attractively fronted colour-washed houses behind. Sciacca's main attraction, however, is its prodigious output of maiolica on sale in a host of pottery workshops dotted about town.
It was in the waters off Sciacca that the French airship *Dixmude* crashed in 1923.

The island that came and went

July 1831: at the time, anyone looking out to sea from Sciacca was unlikely to imagine what was about to happen. For, in a very short space of time, a great land mass emerged from the water. Rather than being some monstrous raptor from the underworld, this apparition comprised a volcanic outcrop that gently settled back into a truncated cone. This precipitated a huge stir and prompted a host of heatedly contested theories. The island was christened **Ferdinandea**, in honour of the reigning Spanish monarch. But it was short lived: after a mere five months, the island disappeared into oblivion.

SIGHTS

Piazza Scandaliato – The perfect kernel at the heart of Sciacca is this piazza with its broad terrace overlooking the multi-coloured harbour packed with boats, and the open sea beyond. Dominating the west side of the square is the 18C Church of **San Domenico**; the longer flank accommodates the former **Jesuit College** (complete with fine 17C cloisters), now used as the town hall. Behind lies piazza del Duomo.

Duomo ⊙ – The cathedral was founded by the Normans (from which time only the exterior wall of the three apses survives), and rebuilt in the 1600s. The Baroque façade remains unfinished. The **interior** nave and side aisles preserve various works of interest. The barrel-vaulted nave is frescoed (1829) by the local artist Tommaso Rossi with the Apocalypse and several episodes from the life of Mary Magdelene. The chapel to the right of the chancel contains a lovely Renaissance marble altarpiece (1581) by Antonio Gagini; its walls are hung with paintings of scenes from Christ's Passion.

*Palazzo Scaglione ⊙ – This 18C residence, now a museum, displays the *objets d'art* and other works of art collected in the 19C by Francesco Scaglione. All the rooms are crowded with pictures – the majority by Sicilian painters – engravings, coins, archaeological artefacts, bronze sculptures and ceramics in a clear demonstration of the eclecticism and encyclopedic collecting mania so typical of the period. The last room contains a fine 18C ivory and mother-of-pearl Crucifix. The *palazzo* has maiolica floors and frescoed ceilings throughout.

Surrounding streets – The central thoroughfare, **corso Vittorio Emanuele**, runs to the right of the Duomo, past the 15C-17C **Palazzo Arone Tagliavia** *(on the right)*, its fine castellated frontage accommodating three pointed entrances and, above the central arch, a lovely three-light Gothic window. A little further on the left sits the 19C Imperial-style **Palazzo San Giacomo** (or Tagliavia), with its south-facing façade graced with four sphinx-like herms. The Venetian neo-Gothic front of the building overlooks piazza Friscia.

Carnival colours

M. Magni/MICHELIN

Eating out

Hostaria del Vicolo – Vicolo Sammaritano 10, ☎ 0925 23 071; closed Mon and 14 Oct to 1 Nov. In the centre of the old town, this pleasant restaurant serves innovative regional dishes. Good wine list. Approximately 60 000L for a meal.

The **Bar delle Terme** stocks excellent homemade cakes, pastries and ice cream.

Down by the harbour, **Aurelio Licata** is famous for his *granite al limone* served, for those who wish it, with a bun – in traditional Sicilian style.

In **viale della Vittoria** which leads off the piazza, on the right, stands the **Convento di San Francesco** ⊘. This, after being completely restored, has been transformed into a conference-cum-exhibition centre. The fine monastery cloisters display sculptures by contemporary artists, including three large *Bathers* by Bergomi (1989).

At the far end of viale della Vittoria, **Santa Maria delle Giummare** (entrance in via Valverde) rises tall above the surrounding buildings. This was founded by the Normans and rebuilt in the 16C. The actual church is contained within the main body of the building (graced with a Baroque doorway); the two square "towers" provide residential quarters for the dependent monastery. The austerity of the battlemented façade is in part relieved by two decorative two-light windows.

A little further on the right lie the ruins of **Castello della Luna**. This was built in the late 14C, rebuilt in the 16C and almost completely destroyed in the 19C. Today, only the perimeter walls and an imposing cylindrical tower remain. The street passes before the castle before leading down to the lovely Norman church, San Nicolò la Latina.

San Nicolò la Latina ⊘ – This church was founded in the early part of the 12C by Giuletta, the daughter of Roger I. Its simple façade is graced with a doorway with a heavily moulded surround, and three similarly accented single openings above (the two side ones are blind). The interior comprises a Latin-cross plan, complete with nave, short transepts and three semicircular apses typical of transitional Arabo-Norman prototypes. The light filters through small, single openings set deep into the wall, reminiscent of arrow-slits.

Climb back up to the castle ruins and follow via Giglio to the town gate – **Porta di San Calogero** – where remains of the medieval walls may be seen. On piazza Noceto is situated **Santa Maria dell'Itria**, an annexe to the larger Chiesa Madre with a fine Baroque façade, **San Michele Arcangelo** ⊘ (17C-18C). Inside it shelters a lovely 18C gallery and a carved, painted wooden organ case set against the back wall; on the right note the fine Catalan Gothic cross and, in the south aisle, an altarpiece of St Jerome dating from 1454.

Continue down towards corso Vittorio Emanuele to the junction with via Licata which accommodates two fine 18C buildings: **Palazzo Inveges**, and further up on the right, **Palazzo Ragusa**. At the next intersection with via Gerardi, turn left: on the corner with corso Vittorio Emanuele is the building known as *Lo Steripinto*.

Palazzo Steripinto – The Catalan-style *palazzo* dates from the 15C. Its splendid façade is articulated with diamond-cut rustication and two-light openings; it is battlemented with Ghibelline merlons.

Via Gerardi opens out into piazza del Carmine, named after the Carmine church which stands there, laid out before the 16C town gateway, **Porta San Salvatore**, ornamented by two lions facing each other. The Norman-built **Chiesa del Carmine**, although remodelled several times, retains its original rose-window.

Santa Margherita ⊘ – The original church fabric dates from the 13C; the alterations were implemented in the late 16C. The main front has a lovely Catalan Gothic doorway, although the Renaissance-Gothic side door on the left side with *St Margaret and the Dragon* by Pietro da Bonitate and Francesco Laurana (apparently only the figure of Mary Magdalene on the left jamb is his) is more famous (unfortunately the stonework is shored up with scaffolding). Inside, the coffered ceiling is painted to suggest a star-spangled sky. A monumental 19C organ takes up most of the back wall, and a splendid marble altarpiece in the right chapel relates scenes from the life of St Margaret.

The other church nearby with a fine stone doorway is **Chiesa di San Gerlando**. A little further on the left stands the 15C **Palazzo Perollo**: its main façade has three late-Gothic three-light windows and its inner courtyard is furnished with a lovely, although dilapidated, Catalan staircase.

Thermal baths

The thermal treatments in the region surrounding Sciacca have been famous since Antiquity *(see Monte KRONIO)*, yet it was only some time in the mid-19C that a spa was opened outside the town centre in the so-called Valle dei Bagni *(this awaits to be restored and reopened)*. The most modern thermal facilities at the **Nuovo Stabilimento Termale** ⊘ date from 1938: this extensive, Liberty-style complex lies south-east of the town, right by the edge of the sea, in its own private landscaped gardens. Here, the naturally occurring sulphurous waters are used in mud-therapy (for relieving arthritis), balneotherapy (recommended for osteo-arthritis and skin conditions) and inhalation treatments. Other such degenerative conditions are treated with various therapies also available from the Stufe di San Calogero on Monte Kronio, and at the thermal pools at Molinelli. These baths are supplemented by mineral-rich waters that issue from the ground at a constant temperature of 34°C. Such treatments have proved effective for skin conditions as well.

OUTSIDE TOWN

Castello Incantato ⊘ – *2km/1.2mi W: take via Figuli out of Sciacca and follow signs for Agrigento (SS 115).* This incredible garden, peopled with sculpted stone heads, was conceived by Filippo Bentivegna. Over a period of half a century, *Filippu delli Testi* – as he is called here – sculpted these faces out of the rock in every corner of his extensive estate, with expressions that range from the worried to the serene.

INLAND

A circuit of approx 110km/68mi taking at least half a day. From Sciacca, head NE in the direction of Caltabellotta (19km/12mi).

Caltabellotta – The two roads up to the town offer wonderful **views**★★ over the surrounding valley; the route via **Sant'Anna** is especially scenic. Caltabellotta enjoys a fabulous **position**★★, 900m/2 952ft above sea-level. Its name (deriving from the Arabic *Kal'at al-ballut* meaning Fortress of the oaks) seems to conjure up a picture of the town precariously clinging to a bare spur of rock. Given its high position, which made it difficult to storm, Caltabellota came to be considered over the centuries as a place of safety, and as a consequence became transformed into a military outpost. It was here that the Angevins signed a peace treaty that sealed an end to the War of Vespers (1302).

The tallest point is claimed by the chapel and hermitage of San Pellegrino, and the ruins of the Norman castle that blend into the landscape. At the foot of the castle reside the extant Arabo-Norman **Chiesa Matrice** and **Chiesa del Salvatore** with its fine late-Gothic doorway.

Drive back along the same road (15km/9mi) to the junction and turn right; 10km/6mi further on, at the T-junction with the S 624, turn right; another 10km/6mi further on, fork right, following signs for Sambuca (9km/5.5mi).

Sambuca di Sicilia – The town reclines lazily on a gentle slope. Noble *palazzi* run the length of the central street corso Umberto I: at the far end, a stairway provides access to a viewing terrace; behind stands the hamlet's main church.

From Sambuca, follow signs for Scavi di Monte Adranone (7km/4mi).

Scavi di Monte Adranone ⊘ – *32km/20mi N of Sciacca.* The ancient Greek settlement (6C BC) overlies another earlier, indigenous, one. The site, perched high on a mountain top, overlooking the surrounding countryside, is naturally defended on one side and reinforced by strong defensive walls on the other two, making it into a vaguely triangular area. The town, loosely identified with Adranon, a place documented by the Classical historian Diodorus Siculus, was probably destroyed in 250 BC during the First Punic War.

Tour – Outside the walls, on the south-eastern side, lay the **necropolis** containing subterranean funeral chambers, including the so-called **Tomba della Regina** lined with square-cut blocks of tufa.

A short distance further on stands the **Porta Sud** (south gate) framed between turrets. The building nestling within has been identified as a farmstead. The way up to the **acropolis** passes on the right a large rectangular construction, probably intended for public use; ahead extends a complex of stores, shops and houses. At the top, the **acropolis** overlooks the entire valley: the **view**★★ up here pans round in a complete circle, taking in the rooftops of the living hamlet of Sambuca and **Lago Arancio** below.

The most significant building would have been the large **Punic Temple** with, on the right, its large cistern. The rectangular temple would have comprised an inner sanctum open to the sky, with a *cella* adjacent on the eastern side.

Make your way back down to Sambuca and return to Sciacca by means of the S 115.

SCICLI

Ragusa – Population 25 775
Michelin map 432 Q 26

Scicli is tucked away high up in the hinterland, slightly off the beaten track. Its other name, the town of the Siculi, suggests that it is ancient in origin. The first settlers, it would seem, established their colony strategically on the very top of the hill of San Matteo, overlooking the surrounding landscape. Yet even here, the people came to be pestered successively by the Greeks, Romans, Arabs and Normans who came to occupy and dominate them, as they did everywhere else in Sicily, leaving in their wake their indelible mark in terms of culture and art. Alas, here, as with the rest of the Val di Noto, the 1693 earthquake spared neither its inhabitants nor its monuments: the Scicli of today proffers its new and reformed guise, risen like a phoenix from the ashes.

A feast of festivals

Three festivals are honoured and celebrated by Scicli. The first, the **Cavalcata di San Giuseppe**, takes place on the 18 (evening preparations) and 19 March. This essentially commemorates the flight of Joseph and Mary into Egypt, although it also fetes the rite of spring after the passage of winter with all the affiliated pagan rituals required. Colour is the festival's dominant element as flowers are used to bedeck the horses' harnesses and great wood bonfires are lit along the route followed by the fugitives, lighting up the garish costumes of the onlookers who throng the streets. Meanwhile the air rings with jingling horse bells, with people's voices animated with merriment after the procession, gathering for great feasts partaken in each other's houses.

At Easter, the **Festa dell'Uomo Vivo** celebrates life itself with a lively procession of a statue representing the Resurrected Christ, raced along by young men, through the town's streets.

Before the advent of summer, on the last Sunday in May, the **Festa della Madonna delle Milizie** takes place: this consists of a statue of the Madonna on horseback being processed, defeating and trampling over Saracen soldiers (long ago, this festival took place on the Saturday before Easter).

Bird's-eye views – Two spots provide a good **overview** of the town's rooftops: one is Colle della Croce before the 16C-17C Church of Santa Maria della Croce; the other, offering the marginally better prospect, is Colle di San Matteo set before a church of the same name, now sadly abandoned. Behind it rise the ruins of a castle that was possibly constructed during the Arab occupation.

Piazza Italia – The **Chiesa Madre** ⊘, dedicated to St Ignatius, shelters the **wooden statue of the Madonna on horseback**: her other name, Madonna delle Milizie, is explained by popular legend. This tells of how she is supposed to have fought at Roger I's side, thus ensuring his victory over the Saracens. Originally, the carved figure was kept in her own sanctuary about 6km/4mi west of the town.

On the corner of the piazza, a narrow staircase to the right of the church leads up to Via Duca d'Aosta and **Palazzo Beneventano**. This building, an elegant example of secular late Baroque architecture (18C), is flamboyantly ornamented with corbels sculpted with fantastical figures, decorative pilasters and, over the windows, masks of Moors and Muslims, and aggressive wild tiger-like animals baring their teeth. The first corner of the house to come into view is ornamented with shields.

Go back down to piazza Italia. Opposite the church stands **Palazzo Fava**; its corbels are carved with emblems of chivalry. The balcony overlooking San Bartolomeo is especially fine.

Chiesa di San Bartolomeo ⊘ – *Located at the end of via San Bartolomeo which begins in piazza Italia.* The elegantly restrained façade, verging on the neo-Classical, rises through three tiers of columns to a bell-tower capped with a ribbed dome. Inside, it contains an 18C **Nativity scene★** fashioned by the Neapolitan craftsman Pietro Padula. All 29 carved wooden figures (originally there were 65) are most beautifully crafted, each endowed with a lovely face and exquisitely rendered costumes.

The church is shouldered by **Colle di San Matteo**. The caves that punctuate the side of the hill form part of the **Chiafura troglodyte settlement**, which continued to serve as dwellings until the 1960s (the majority of cave-dwellers moved down into the valley below after the earthquake of 1693).

Via Mormino Penna – This elegant street passes between the fine Baroque exteriors of several *palazzi* and three churches. The first in line is that of **San Giovanni Evangelista** ⊘, a church with a fine **façade★** fronting a convex central section reminiscent of the peculiar style of Rosario Gagliardi, to whom it is attributed. The elliptically planned building is decorated inside with neo-Classical stuccowork. A few paces up the street stands a second church, **San Michele**, that is laid out according to the same oval plan as San Giovanni.

The 19C building opposite, **Palazzo Spadaro**, preserves its original decoration inside and out (the interior may be viewed during office hours when the local council's cultural affairs department is at work). The street comes to an end before **Santa Teresa** ☉, a church with a late Baroque interior including columns encrusted with stucco.

Walk back along via Mormino Penna and turn down via Nazionale to piazza Busaccasu. The buildings facing onto the square include a Rococo church, **Chiesa del Carmine** and its adjacent convent, and **Palazzo Busacca** complete with clock. From the front of the church may be seen two additional churches: Santa Maria della Consolazione and, in the distance, **Santa Maria la Nova**.

SEGESTA★★★

Trapani

Michelin map 432 N 20

Segesta occupies a splendid **position**★★, among gently sloping hills of yellow-ochre and ruddy brown that, at times, are thrown into marked contrast by patches of variegated greens around the excavated areas. All the while, the timeless landscape is presided over by the majestic silhouette of the Doric temple.

Ancient Segesta was probably founded by the Elimi; under Greek sponsorship, it soon ranked, like Erice (Eryx), among the leading towns of the Mediterranean basin. In the 5C BC, it was pitched against its great rival Selinunte (Selinus): in an attempt to rally its defences against this threat, Segesta appealed for help from Athens in 415 BC, but these reinforcements were defeated by Syracuse whose forces were allied to Selinunte. In 409 BC, Segesta turned to Carthage for support; on landing in Sicily, these troops destroyed both Selinus and Himera. In turn, Segesta was destroyed by the Syracusan tyrant Agathocles in 307 BC, and rose again under the Romans. Subsequent developments are not documented, although it is thought that the city probably succumbed to further damage by the Vandals in the 5C AD. What is certain is that the area was inhabited in medieval times, as ruins of a Norman castle and a small three-apsed basilica (later abandoned and rebuilt as a hermitage in the 15C), situated in the northern part of the ancient acropolis, testify. This part of the site extended over two areas separated by a hollow. The south-eastern section was predominantly residential, whereas the north was populated by public buildings, including the theatre.

EXCAVATIONS (GLI SCAVI) ☉

★★★ **Tempio** – The Temple of Segesta, one of the most perfectly preserved monuments to survive from Antiquity, stands in majestic solitude on a hill surrounded by a deep valley, framed by Monte Bernardo and Monte Barbaro where the theatre is situated. Built in 430 BC (although scholars are divided about its exact date), the temple is a Doric building of extraordinarily harmonious proportions.

The 36 columns of the peristyle are almost completely intact, their gloriously mellow golden-tinged limestone flattered by their smooth finish. The fact that the shafts are unfluted, coupled with the absence of a *cella*, has prompted the suggestion that the temple was abandoned before completion. This theory is dismissed by some scholars who claim that the lack of a *cella* (which usually comprised the first part of the sanctuary to be undertaken) might indicate that the building was intended to consist merely of a peristyle, making it a pseudo-temple. Furthermore, the mystery surrounding the purpose such a construction would serve is exacerbated by the lack of any indication as to which deity it might have been dedicated. The road up to the theatre *(approx 2km/1.2mi: regular minibus service)* provides fabulous **views**★★ back over the temple. Before the theatre, on the right, are the remains of the Hermitage of San Leone, with a single apse, built over the foundation of an earlier three-apsed church and, behind it, the ruins of the Norman castle.

Temple of Segesta

★**Teatro** – The theatre was built in the 3C BC during the Hellenistic period, while the area was under Roman domination. It consists of a perfect semicircle with a diameter of 63m/207ft, apparently slotted into a rocky slope. The tiers of seats face west towards the hills, beyond which, to the right, may be glimpsed the broad Bay of Castellammare.

Every two years, during a summer festival, the theatre is revived by throngs of spectators eager to savour the great Classical tragedies and comedies so beloved to the ancients, in a timeless setting.

Antica città di SELINUNTE★★

Trapani
Michelin map 432 O 20

Selinus is derived from the Greek name for the sweet-smelling herb they called *Selinon*: wild celery *(Heleioselinon – Apium graveolens)*, as well as mountain parsley *(Oreoselinon – Petroselinum* from which the English term is corrupted). Funnily enough, this herb, that the ancients held in such high esteem, was dedicated to Persephone; it was widely used to crown victors at the Isthmian games and to make wreaths for adorning the tombs of the dead. It grew in profusion in this part of Sicily and appears on the first coins minted by the town.

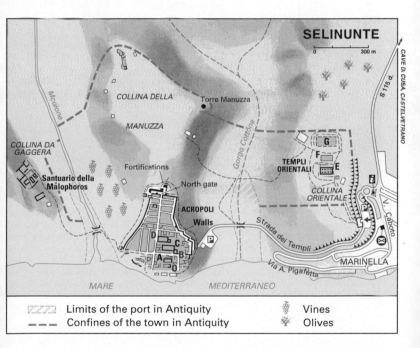

The colony was founded by settlers from Megara Hyblaea during the 7C BC. Thereafter, Selinus enjoyed a short but intensive period of prosperity (almost two centuries of splendour), perhaps thanks to prudent government practised by the continuous line of successive tyrants. Evidence of the town's flowering is to be found in the extensive area allocated to sacred ritual and public use, concentrated in three distinctive districts.

For a long time, Selinunte allied itself to Carthage, in the hope of securing support in the fight with its rival, Segesta, although, in the end, it was destroyed in 409 BC by the Carthaginian Hannibal, who used ferociously cruel methods in winning supremacy: this resulted in the death of 16 000 Selinuntini and the capture of a further 5 000 as prisoners (according to the account given by Diodorus Siculus). When the survivors begged him for their freedom and for the temples of the city to be spared in return for a substantial payment, Hannibal consented; once he had the cash in hand, he sacked the temples and pulled down the walls.

Selinus invested every last effort in repairing the damage and, against the odds, struggled to survive until the Second Punic War, when it was razed to the ground.

315

RUINS (LE ROVINE) ⊘

The ruins are scattered over an almost deserted area, having been completely abandoned since Silenus' downfall: the ruined temples continue to point their impressive great columns to the sky; other buildings, reduced to heaps of rubble, probably by an earthquake, inspire a tragic air of utter desolation. The fine metopes which once adorned several of the temple friezes are displayed in the archaeological museum in Palermo.

There are three main areas: the first, spread across the hill on the eastern side, contains three large temples, one having been re-erected in 1957. The second, on the hill to the west and surrounded by walls, comprises the acropolis, south of the actual town. The third, lying west of the acropolis, beyond the River Modione, also consisted of a sacred precinct complete with temples and sanctuaries. In the absence of any sure knowledge as to which gods the temples were dedicated, scholars have identified them with letters of the alphabet.

To complete the picture, it is well worth visiting the quarries from where the stone was brought *(see Cave di CUSA)*.

Temple C towers over the other ruins

Templi orientali – The first of the eastern temples to come into view is **Temple E**, which, re-erected in 1957, was dedicated to Hera. It dates from the 5C BC and has a complex ground plan. The entrance to the *pronaos* was from the east-facing side, up several steps and through the colonnade. Only the capitals remain, lying on the ground, from the two free-standing columns that marked the doorway. Beyond lay the *cella* off which opened a small secret chamber (the *adytum*) where the statue of the deity was kept. Behind this, opened the *opisthodomus* which was identical to the *pronaos*.

On the right, lie the ruins of **Temple F**, on a smaller scale than Temple E and probably dedicated to Athena.

Lastly, **Temple G** – the second largest Greek temple in Sicily, after the Temple of Olympian Zeus at Agrigento – would have been the most impressive. Conceived on simply gigantic proportions – 17 columns long and 8 wide, each with a diameter of almost 3.5m and a height of more than 16m/53ft – it was probably dedicated to Apollo. Today, it is reduced to a mass of fragments scattered over the ground. The cylindrical blocks with which the columns were built, each weighing several tons, retain distinctive grooves that suggest to scholars that the temple was never completed.

Acropoli – *Drive from the eastern temples car park to the next one.* The acropolis stretched across a hill on the far side of the dip called Gorgo di Cottone, through which the River Cottone flowed down to the sea where the town's **harbour** *(now overgrown)* was situated. The site was enclosed within defensive walls built in the 6C-5C BC. The streets were laid out according to the Classical town plan proposed by Hippodamus of Miletus, with three main arteries bisected at right angles by a grid of smaller streets. This area contained the town's public and religious buildings, together with a few houses for the highest ranking members of society.

The path skirts a section of the powerful graduated **walls** surrounding the eastern side of the acropolis.

Temples – The first to be made out as the track climbs uphill is the ruin of **Temple A**. Within the wall with the doorway into the *naos* are two spiral staircases, the most ancient examples known to date. This precinct, however, is dominated by 14 of the 17 columns of **Temple C**, which were re-erected in 1925. This, the earliest surviving temple at Selinus (initiated early 6C BC), was probably dedicated to Apollo or Heracles. It is hard to imagine the full impact of the pediment (ornamented with a clay Gorgon's head in shallow relief) as it lies broken on the ground. It is from this temple that the finest metopes, now in the archaeological museum in Palermo, come; there is also a reconstruction of the pediment there. It is interesting to follow the evolution in building techniques implemented during the temple's construction: the columns on the south side are monolithic, whereas the others are composed of cylindrical segments, being far easier to transport. Traces of three further temples have been configured in the acropolis.

Fortifications – At the far end of the *decumanus maximus*, rises the curtain wall which once surrounded the acropolis. What may now be seen consists, in fact, of the fortifications built using recycled building stone (the columns split lengthways come from an unidentified temple from an unknown site) after the site was destroyed in 409 BC. Beyond the north gate, the **Porta Nord**, stands an impressive three-storey structure comprising two superimposed galleries surmounted by a series of arches which allowed for soldiers and equipment to move quickly through them.

The residential part of the town was situated on the hill of Manuzza: from the 4C BC, this area was gradually abandoned and used as a necropolis for burials.

Santuario della Malòphoros – *The sanctuary may be reached by following the track that extends from the first cardo to the left of the decumanus maximus (from the acropolis); allow 20min there and back.* The sanctuary is in honour of Demeter Malophoros (she who bears the pomegranate), the goddess of plants and thereby the protector of farmers and growers. It was built inside a sacred precinct (temenos) on the opposite side of the River Modione, where a harbour and the town's trading emporium were located. Beyond the propylaeum (identifiable by the remains of columns) stands a large sacrificial altar. A channel bearing water from the Gaggera mountain spring separates it from the temple. The latter, without columns or foundations, comprised a *pronaos*, a *cella* and an *adytum* containing a statue of the deity.

... Syracuse,
Where settlers once from Corinth's isthmus built
Between two harbours their great battlements.

Ovid, *Metamorphoses*

Siracusa has for ever depended upon the sea, rallying herself around the Island of Ortygia, overlooking a wonderful bay on the east coast. Its name is synonymous with an ancient Greek past, a series of valiant tyrants, the rivalry between Athens and Carthage: a past which has left a number of vestiges for the modern-day visitor to see and enjoy. Alongside this dramatic historical background, there exists another less obvious past that can be explored among the streets of the island, where time seems to stand still somewhere between the medieval and Baroque eras. Just behind Ortygia stretches a flat area called Akradina – yet another name inherited from Antiquity. The district of Neapolis, literally meaning the "new town", is one of the most evocative quarters, claiming the theatre, the Ear of Dionysius and the *Latomia del Paradiso* within its boundaries. On the eastern side lies Tyche, so called because there was a temple there dedicated to the goddess of fortune (from the Greek *Tyche* – fortune or luck). Dominating the remainder of the city is the part called Epipolae, guarded and defended by the castle of Euryalus, strategically built in the most advantageous position.

HISTORY

Syracuse was colonised some time in the 8C BC by Greeks from Corinth, who settled on the island of **Ortygia**. Soon this power base was seized by a succession of mighty tyrants. Under their rule the city enjoyed success and great splendour (5C-4C BC); its population stabilised at the 300 000 mark, and it established its supremacy over the rest of Sicily. Between 416 BC and 413 BC, there developed a furious conflict between Syracuse and Athens. The Athenian warriors were captained by Alcibiades. So the people endured one of the most famous and cruel periods of ancient history. At last the city fell to the Romans, and so to subsequent invaders – Barbarians, Byzantines, Arabs and Normans.

Tyrants of Syracuse – The tyrant in Antiquity corresponds with the modern dictator, and several such figures populate the history of Sicily during the Hellenistic period, particularly in Syracuse.
Gelon, already tyrant of Gela, extended his dominion to Syracuse in 485 BC. His expansionist ambitions baited the hostile Carthaginians to such an extent as to provoke open conflict. Gelon, in alliance with **Theron**, the tyrant of Akragas (Agrigento), succeeded in defeating them at the famous battle of Himera in 480 BC. He was succeeded by his brother **Hieron I** (478-467 BC), and it was during his reign that Cumae was assisted in averting the Etruscan threat (474 BC): from this battle there exists a bronze helmet, found at Olympia and now displayed in the British Museum in London.
After a brief period of democracy, punctuated by battles against Athens, the famous **Dionysius the Elder** acceded to the throne (405-367 BC). He refused the discredited title of tyrant and adopted instead that of *strategòs autokrátor*, meaning absolute general. This shrewd strategist underpinned his government with popular consensus, which he secured with gifts and favours, and by his reputation as the defender against the Punic threat, which he did not, however, succeed in eliminating. During his tyrannical rule, Syracuse became an independent and mighty force in its own right. On a more personal level, Dionysius I appears to have been haunted with suspicions, ever fearful that someone might be plotting against him. His fears developed into manias of persecution and culminated in his decision to retreat with his court to the castle of Ortygia, which he made into an impregnable private fortress. The story of his life is dotted with strange happenings from which were hatched numerous malicious rumours, half fiction and half fact. Such writers as Valerius Maximus, Cicero and Plutarch describe how the tyrant was so distrustful of the Barbarians that he entrusted the task of shaving to his own daughters but, fearing that even they might be tempted to murder him, he insisted that sharpened walnut shells be used rather than razors or scissors; he had a small ditch dug around his marital bed with a small bridge that he could remove when he retired for the night and, to show that the life of a ruler was fraught with danger, he had a sharp sword suspended from a single horsehair above the head of an envious member of his court called Damocles (hence the expression "the sword of Damocles" to allude to a looming threat). His greed, it is said, led him to take possession of the golden mantle from the statue of Zeus, replacing it with a woollen one. Upon his death, he was succeeded to the throne by his young son **Dionysius (II) the Younger**, who lacked the political astuteness of his father; he was briefly toppled by his uncle **Dion** in 357 BC who, in turn, was assassinated four years later (Dion's life

🅱 via Maestranza 33, ☎ 0931 46 42 55, Fax 0931 60 204.

GETTING TO SIRACUSA

The nearest **airport** is Fontanarossa airport in Catania, which is linked to Siracusa by buses which run daily (1hr).

Buses leave from piazzale San Antonio to Catania (approx 1hr), Palermo (4hr), Ragusa (2hr) and a number of other destinations. For further information, contact the following two bus companies: AST, ☎ 0931 46 27 11, and SAIS, ☎ 0931 66 710.

A **train** service also operates from Siracusa to Catania (90min), Messina (3hr), Ragusa (approx 2hr) and Taormina (2hr 15min). The railway station is situated in piazza della Stazione, ☎ 0931 69 650.

Taxis are available from piazza della Repubblica (☎ 0931 64 323), piazza Pancali (☎ 0931 60 980) and piazza Stazione (☎ 0931 69 722).

EXPLORING THE CITY

Siracusa by sea ◷ – Boat trips around the **Porto Grande and Ortygia★** by motorlaunch are operated by **Selene**. Excursions along the coast provide a different perspective of the town. Outings last on average 35min, but can be extended on request; they can also include lunch or dinner by prior arrangement. Those timed around sunset and nightfall, when monuments are floodlit, are especially enjoyable.

This is also the only means of seeing Castello Maniace, since it is now a military barracks and out of bounds; otherwise, the only view from dry land is from the eastern shore *(see ORTYGIA)*.

WHERE TO STAY

The province of **Siracusa** offers visitors a number of alternatives to traditional hotels, including camp sites and *agriturismi*. A full list and details of accommodation options and addresses are available from the Siracusa Azienda Provinciale per l'Incremento del Turismo.

Azienda Agrituristica La Perciata – Via Spinagallo 77 *(11km/7mi W of Siracusa on the Miramonti road towards Canicattini)*, ☎ 0931 71 73 66; www.sistemia.it/ perciata This beautiful *agriturismo* in the middle of the countryside has 9 comfortable, tastefully decorated rooms. 140 000L for a double room (including breakfast).

Bed & breakfast Dolce casa – Via Lido Sacramento 4 *(take the SS 115 towards Noto, then the road on the left to Isola)*, ☎/Fax 0931 72 11 35; www.iblea2000.com/ dolcecasa. This elegant villa with a garden has 10 spacious, comfortable rooms. 130 000L for a double room (including breakfast).

Domus Mariae – Via Vittorio Veneto 76, ☎ 0931 24 854, Fax 0931 24 858. This small, elegant hotel is situated in the heart of Ortygia and is run by nuns. It has 12 spacious, comfortable rooms, some of which have magnificent views of the sea. 250 000L for a double room.

EATING OUT

Darsena – Riva Garibaldi 6 *(turn right as soon as you arrive in the Ortygia district)*, ☎ 0931 61 522; closed Wed. An attractive restaurant serving seafood specialities. Approximately 50 000L for a meal.

L'Orto di Epicuro – Largo della Gancia 5 (at the end of via Nizza), ☎ 0931 46 45 24; closed Wed. A pleasant *ristorante-pizzeria* known for its fish dishes.

is celebrated in a poem by William Wordsworth). Dionysius II was expelled a second time following a desperate plea from the Syracusans to the mother-city Corinth; in 344 BC Timoleon, an effective general, was sent to the rescue; as a wise and moderate statesman he restored peace to Sicily. There followed **Agathocles**, who in order to secure power harboured no qualms in murdering the aristocracy; his attempts to rout the Carthaginians from Sicily were also unsuccessful (culminating in his defeat at Himera in 310 BC).

The last tyrant to govern Syracuse was **Hieron II** (269-216 BC), a mild and just ruler celebrated by Theocritus *(Idyll xvi)*, who oversaw the last golden age of Syracuse and signed up to an alliance with Rome against the Carthaginians in the First Punic War. In 212 BC, despite the clever devices designed by Archimedes, the town fell to Roman rule and became the capital of the Roman Province of Sicily.

Ortygia

Archimedes – There exists no reliable source of information for details on the life of Archimedes, the famous mathematician, born in Syracuse in 287 BC. It is said that he was so absent-minded and absorbed by his research that he even forgot to eat and drink; his servants were forced to drag him by force to the public baths and, even there, he continued to draw geometric shapes in the ash. It was while he was soaking in his bath that he came upon the principle which was to ensure his fame endured thereafter: a body immersed in a liquid receives a force equal and opposite to the weight of the volume of the liquid that has been displaced. Thrilled with his discovery, he is supposed to have stood up suddenly and rushed out of the house shouting "Eureka!" (I've got it!).

Besides his contributions to the study of arithmetic, geometry, physics, astronomy and engineering, Archimedes is credited with several significant mechanical inventions, notably the Archimedes' Screw – a cylinder containing a spiral screw for moving liquid uphill, like a pump *(see VIA DEL SALE)*; the cog-wheel; celestial spheres; and burning glasses – a combination of lenses and mirrors with which he succeeded in setting fire to the Roman fleet. According to tradition, Archimedes was so deeply involved in his calculations when the Romans succeeded in penetrating the city, that he died from a sword wound inflicted by a Roman soldier, more or less oblivious of what was happening.

Poetic muses – Syracuse played its own part in developing its artistic prowess in Antiquity. Several of its rulers became so taken with the power of patronage and the benefits of promoting the arts that before long established foreign poets and writers were being welcomed to their court. Some, like Dionysius the Elder, tried to establish themselves as writers but without any great success. The first to take a truly effective interest was Hieron I who proclaimed himself protector of poets and invited to his court such illustrious figures as Bacchylides, Xenophon and Simonides, and highly competitive rivals **Pindar** and **Aeschylus**, one of the most eminent early Greek dramatists and author of *The Persians* (c 470 BC) and *The Women of Etna* (now lost): both plays are known to have been performed in the Greek theatre in Neapolis.

By contrast, **Plato** was to endure difficult relations with Syracuse, most particularly with its rulers. Dionysius the Elder welcomed him reluctantly, only to expel him shortly afterwards; after his demise, the philosopher returned (under the protection of the

R. Mazin/DIAF

regent Dion), only to be expelled a second time – by Dionysius II – after failing to persuade the tyrant to accept the principles of his Utopian state (outlined later in his *Dialogues* in the section entitled *Republic*).

Theocrates, the protagonist of a kind of bucolic poetry at which Virgil was later to excel, was probably a native of Syracuse.

In more recent times, **Salvatore Quasimodo** (1901-68) was born in Siracusa: a poet obsessed with the malaise of life, which he expressed in verses that became ever-more terse and concise; he wona Nobel Prize for literature in 1959.

★★ORTYGIA

"Sicanio praetenta sinu iacet insula contra

Plemyrium undosum; nomen dixere priores

Ortygiam. Alpheum fama est huc Elidis amnem

occultas egisse vias subter mare, qui nunc

ore, Arethusa, tuo Siculis confunditur undis."

"Stretched in front of a Sicanian bay lies an island, over against wave-beaten Plemyrium; men of old called it Ortygia. Hither, so runs the tale, Alpheus, river of Elis, forced a secret course beneath the sea, and now at thy fountain, Arethusa, mingles with the Sicilian waves."

Virgil, *The Aeneid*, Book III (lines 692-695).

There are so many wonderful buildings and interesting outlooks as to make it impossible to set an itinerary including all that might be worth seeing. The descriptions given below therefore mention only the most interesting streets, leaving a large section of the historical city without commentary for visitors to explore at will according to inclination.

A word of advice: remember to raise your gaze as often as possible so as not to miss any understated secret lurking in the narrow streets among their splendid buildings.

A look at the coast...

The island, the most ancient area of settlement, is linked to the mainland by the Ponte Nuovo, a natural extension of one of the main thoroughfares of Siracusa, corso Umberto I. A powerful awareness of the sea and all things associated with it pervades this area: the harbour, filled with colourful boats, moored or going about their business, stretches both to the right and to the left.

As the eye roams the seafront, its attention is caught by the lovely neo-Gothic palazzo on the corner: this red-plastered house with two-light windows was once the home of the poet and writer **Antonio Cardile** (b Messina 1883, d Siracusa 1951). Its distinctive appearance may perhaps arouse the curiosity of visitors to these parts, inspiring them to take a walk around the perimeter of the island, and explore the intriguing quality of the place, absorbing its atmosphere, quieter and more peaceful than elsewhere, and contemplating the attenuated sounds that signal life within its walls. To the right lies the sea; to the left, the old Spanish walls stand as a reminder of times when (until 1800) the old town was fortified.

The bold linearity of the **Porta Marina** is interrupted by a decorative Catalan aedicule framing the entrance to passeggio Adorno, a walkway created along the top of the walls in the 19C.

Finally, a glance will also take in the great Porto Grande, the scene of several major naval battles.

★**Fonte Aretusa** – The Fountain of Arethusa played a significant part in persuading the first group of colonists to settle here in Antiquity. Legend relates how Arethusa, one of Diana's nymphs, tormented by the demonstrations of love from a hunter

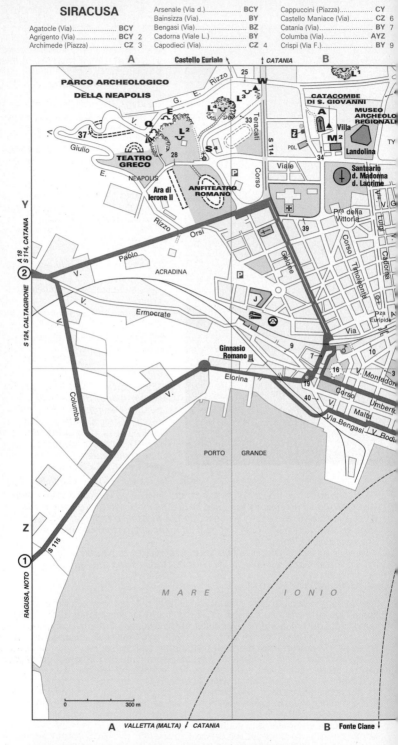

SIRACUSA

named Alpheus, turned to the goddess for help. Diana intervened by turning Arethusa into a stream so that she might escape underground and re-emerge on the island of Ortygia as a beautifully clear fresh-water spring or fountain. Alpheus, meanwhile, was not to be defeated: he, too, changed himself into an underground river, crossed the Ionian Sea and came up in Ortygia having mingled his waters with those of Arethusa.

Today, the fountain sustains palm trees and clumps of papyrus, ducks and drakes. The fronts of the houses painted in pastel shades make for an attractive picture, a harmonious three-dimensional visual entity that extends along the streets of the island.

C

Piazza Cappuccini

Latomia dei Cappuccini

Via Teocrito
Torino

Riviera Dionisio il Grande

S. Lucia extra Mœnia

Monte Grappa
Piazza Sta Lucia

Arsenale
12

Y

MARE IONIO

RTO PICCOLO

P

ISOLA DI ORTIGIA

ORTIGIA
V
S. Pietro

Via Veneto
Mastrarua S¹
21
22
R⁴
I. DEI CANI

Pta arina
C¹
R¹ R²
3
S²
18
Belvedere S. Giacomo

GGIO INO
13 D
S³
M¹
C²

Roma
Forte Vigliena
Z

PAL. BELLOMO

Fonte Arethusa
36
6
S. MARTINO
Spirito Santo
38

Castello Maniace

C

Looming on the horizon on the far side, sits the solid profile of the **Castello Maniace** *(closed to the public)*, a sandstone fortress built by Frederick II of Swabia in the first half of the 13C. Its name honours the Byzantine general, George Maniakes who, in 1038, tried to rescue Ortygia from the Arabs, and then fortified the island, especially the area where Frederick II would later rebuild the castle. The massive square structure is a typical example of Swabian building: the architectural features are both functional and cosmetic, suggesting that the castle was conceived to function as a defensive stronghold and also as a bold visual reminder of Swabian authority.

323

Cross the tip of the island to reach the eastern shore, from where a series of wonderful views extend over the castle (the best view, however, is from the sea); pass before the Church of **Santo Spirito**, with its fine three-tiered white façade unified by volutes and decorative pilasters. Leave **Forte Vigliena** behind and make for Belvedere San Giacomo, once a defensive bastion, which offers a magnificent **view★** back across to *Siracusa*.

...and a stroll through the narrow streets

★Piazza Duomo – The attractively presented irregular square precedes the cathedral, curving gently at one end to accommodate its majestic front elevation. The open space becomes especially effective when the cathedral façade is dramatically caught by the setting sun or floodlit after nightfall. The other fine Baroque buildings enclosing the square include the striking **Palazzo Beneventano del Bosco**, which conceals a lovely internal courtyard, and opposite, **Palazzo del Senato**, whose inner courtyard displays an 18C senator's carriage; at the far end stands the Church of **Santa Lucia**.

★Duomo ⊘ – The area now occupied by the cathedral has been a place of worship since early Antiquity. A temple erected in the 6C BC was replaced by a temple dedicated to Athena, honouring the goddess with some of the profits from the fateful and decisive defeat of the Carthaginians at Himera (480 BC). In the 7C AD, the temple was incorporated into a Christian church: walls were raised between the columns of the peristyle and a double arcade of eight arches was inserted in the cella to provide two lateral aisles. Still today, the majestic Doric columns may be seen along the left side of the church, both inside and outside the building. Possibly converted into a mosque during the Arab domination, it was restored for Christian use by the Normans. The 1693 earthquake caused the front façade to collapse; it was rebuilt in the Baroque style (18C) by the Palermo architect Andrea Palma. He used the column as the basic unit module for his design. The entrance is preceded by an atrium screening a fine doorway flanked by a pair of twisted columns, the spirals of which are decorated with vines and grapes (a symbol of the Passion).

Inside, the right side of the south aisle incorporates the columns of the temple; today these frame the entrance into the lateral chapels. The first bay on the right contains a lovely font made from a Greek marble krater, supported by seven small 13C wrought-iron lions.

The next **chapel**, dedicated to *St Lucy*, is furnished with an 18C silver altar-front. The silver figure of the saint nestling in the niche is by Pietro Rizzo (1599). Elsewhere, the cathedral is furnished with several statues by the various *Gagini*: the Virgin is by **Domenico**; St Lucy is by **Antonello** (north aisle); the Madonna della Neve in the north apse is by Antonello.

Via Landolina, north of the piazza, accommodates the powerfully fronted **Chiesa dei Gesuiti**.

Galleria Civica d'Arte Contemporanea ⊘ – The former convent and Church of Montevergini (entrance in via delle Vergini) presently houses the municipal collection of contemporary art. This consists mainly of paintings by Italian and foreign artists (Sergio Fermariello, Marco Cingolani, Aldo Damioli, Enrico De Paris).

★Galleria Regionale di Palazzo Bellomo ⊘ – *Via Capodieci*. Palazzo Bellomo, initiated under Swabian rule (13C), was extended and raised in the 15C. Such is the reason for the two markedly different styles: at ground level, the combination of the pointed archway and narrow arrow-slit openings give it the appearance of a fortress; the first floor is graced with elegant three-light windows separated with slender columns. The *palazzo* was built as a private residence before being acquired by the nuns from the adjoining convent of St Benedict in the 18C. Today it is all part of the same museum. The Church of **San Benedetto** ⊘ standing alongside contains a fine coffered ceiling.

Inside, the palazzo shelters a lovely internal porticoed courtyard with a staircase leading to the first floor. The top part of the parapet is ornamented with rosettes and trilobate tracery. At the top of the first flight of stairs, note the fine Flamboyant aedicule above the doorway.

Museum – The museum is dedicated in the main to Sicilian art. Byzantine influences clearly pervade a series of paintings *(Room IV)* by Venetian artists working in Crete (at a time when it formed part of the Venetian Empire). These show *The Creation* (six panels), *Original Sin* and *Earthly Paradise*. The upper floor is largely devoted to painting: perhaps the most striking, despite being damaged, is the **Annunciation★** by **Antonello da Messina**. As with other paintings by the same artist, there is an inherent Flemish quality to this picture especially in its minute attention to detail (the saint's mantle, crowded landscape through the window); the overall formality, spacious composition and precise definition of perspective is more typically Italian. The *Entombment of St Lucy★* by **Caravaggio** might even be modelled on the saint's actual

tomb in the catacombs nearby in *Siracusa* which bear her name. The characteristically dramatic and provocative style of this artist's work is here evident in the
arrangement of the crowd: the main figures jostling around the saint, who lies
dead upon the ground, are the gravediggers, including one in the foreground
turning his back to the onlooker. Atmosphere is imparted by the strong light which,
in turn, casts disturbing shadows.

The museum also displays an eclectic collection of objects: furnishings, holy vestments, Nativity figures, furniture and ceramics.

A short walk from here, tucked away in via San Martino, stands a church which
is dedicated to St Martin and has a Catalan Gothic doorway. The original church
was founded in the 6C.

★**Palazzo Mergulese-Montalto** – *Via Mergulensi*. This superb *palazzo*, although
rather dilapidated, dates from the 14C. The main elevation rises through two
storeys separated by an indented string-course. The upper section is ornamented
with wonderful highly elaborate **windows**★★, set into richly carved arched settings
subdivided by delicately slender twisted columns. The ground floor is graced with
a pointed arched entrance surmounted by a decorative aedicule.

Beyond the palazzo lies **piazza Archimede**. This square was constructed more recently.
Presiding over the central space, overlooked by fine buildings, is the 19C fountain
of Artemis. Via della Maestranza leads off the piazza.

★**Via della Maestranza** – Not only is via della Maestranza one of Ortygia's main
thoroughfares, it is one of the oldest. It threads its way between a succession of
aristocratic residences, predominantly Baroque in style. Among the most interesting, look out for: **Palazzo Interland Pizzuti** (no 10) and, a little further on, **Palazzo
Impellizzeri** (no 17) with its sinuously linear arrangement of curved windows and
balconies. **Palazzo Bonanno** (no 33), which now accommodates the headquarters of
the Tourist Office, is an austere medieval building sheltering a lovely inner courtyard and a loggia on the first floor. At no 72 stands the imposing **Palazzo Romeo
Bufardeci**, with its exuberant frontage and Rococo balconies.

The street opens out into a small square before the Church of **San Francesco
all'Immacolata** flanked by a 19C bell-tower. The light-coloured, curved and elegant
front elevation is gracefully articulated with columns and pilasters. At one time the
church used to host a ritual rooted in Antiquity: during the night of the 28
November the *Svelata* (literally, the unveiling) took place, during which an image
of the Madonna was unveiled. This event was timed to occur in the early hours of
the morning before dawn (so that people could go off to work, in an era when
the working day started very early) after a long vigil accompanied by local bands.
Almost at the end of the street may be discerned the curved façade of **Palazzo Rizza**
(no 110). **Palazzo Impellizzeri** (no 99) dominates the street, rising to its full height
through a sumptuous and highly original frieze ornamented with human faces and
grotesque masks, surmounted with organic decorations.

Behind this last section of the street extends the **Quartiere della Giudecca**, a quarter
that retains its medieval street plan, threaded by narrow perpendicular streets.
During the 16C a considerable community of Jews settled and thrived there until
expelled.

Mastrarua – Renamed via Vittorio Veneto, this street was once the main thoroughfare of Ortygia. This was the route followed by kings as they entered the
town, by official parades and royal processions. It is logical, therefore, that it should
be lined with fine *palazzi*. **Palazzo Blanco** (no 41) is graced outside with a niche in
which stands a statue of St Anthony; it has a lovely internal courtyard and staircase within. **Casa Mezia** (no 47) has a doorway surmounted by a projecting griffin.
Beyond the Church of **San Filippo Neri** there follows **Palazzo Interlandi** and **Palazzo
Monforte**, badly damaged alas. This last *palazzo* marks the corner with via Mirabella,
which is also contained by yet more fine buildings. Note, right opposite Palazzo
Monforte, the elegant **Palazzo Bongiovanni**: the doorway is surmounted by a mask
and, above, a lion holding a scroll bearing the date 1772 which, in turn, acts as
a central support for a balcony; its central window is ornamented with volutes.
Continue along via Mirabella. A small diversion to the right allows for a detour past
the neo-Gothic **Palazzo Gargallo** (Archivio Distrettuale Notarile – Records Office).
Another **Palazzo Gargallo** graces piazzetta del Carmine (no 34), built in the same
style. Via Mirabella also heralds the beginning of the Arab quarter, characterised
by extremely narrow streets known as *ronchi*. One of these streets conceals the
paleo-Christian Church of **San Pietro** distinguished by its fine doorway, which is now
used for concerts and presentations. A little further along via Mirabella stands the
Church of **San Tommaso** which was founded in Norman times (12C). Turn back along
the Mastrarua; no 111 has a lovely doorway decorated with monstrous creatures.
No 136, on the other hand, is the birthplace of the writer, **Elio Vittorini** (born
23 July 1908).

Tempio di Apollo – *Piazza Pancali*. This temple of Apollo, built in the 6C BC, is
the oldest peripteral Doric temple (that is, enclosed by columns) in Sicily. According
to one inscription it was dedicated to Apollo; according to Cicero it was dedicated

to Artemis – before being transformed into a Byzantine church, then a mosque, and back again into a church by the Normans. The remains of the peristyle columns and part of the wall of the sacred precinct are still in evidence.

Corso Matteotti, described as the drawing room of Ortygia, leads off the piazza, flanked on either side with elegant shops.

★★★PARCO ARCHEOLIGICO DELLA NEAPOLIS ⊙

There are two different entrances: one is in via Rizzo and the other in viale Paradiso. To follow the itinerary prescribed below, begin from the entrance in via Rizzo.

★★★**Teatro Greco** – This is one of the most impressive theatres to survive from Antiquity. The *cavea* was completely cut out from the bedrock, taking advantage of the natural slope of Colle Temenite. The date of construction has been established as the 5C BC, largely on the basis of factual reports documenting the first performance of Aeschylus's play *The Persians*. It is also known who the builder was, namely a certain Damocopus, known as Myrilla, because he used unguents *(miroi)* at the official opening of the theatre.

The theatre was modified by Hieron II in the 3C BC, when it was divided into nine wedge-shaped sections, and a passageway was inserted around the cavea about half way up. The wall in front of each section is inscribed with the name of a famous person or deity. Today, certain letters may still be distinguished, including those spelling out Olympian Zeus ΔΙΟΣ ΟΔΥΜΠΙΩΥ) in the central section; to the right, facing the stage, appear the letters naming Hieron II himself (ΒΑΣΙΔΕΟΣ ΙΗΡΩΝΩΣ – *of King Hieron*), his wife (ΒΑΣΙΔΙΣΣΑΣ ΘΙΔΙΣΤΙΔΟΣ – *of Queen Philistis*) and his daughter-in-law (ΒΑΣΙΔΕΟΣ ΝΗΡΙΔΟΣ – *of Queen Nereis*). It was altered in Roman times so as to host water sports (it is thought) and gladiatorial combats before the amphitheatre *(see below)* was completed. Later it was put to other uses. In fact, the Spaniards installed various water-driven millstones in it: the furrows left by two mill-wheels in the central part of the cavea may still be seen as can the drainage channel bearing the water away.

Nazionale del Dramma Antico, Siracusa

Behind the cavea is a large open area with, in the centre, the Grotta del Ninfeo (Nymph's Cave). The rectangular tank set before it was filled with water drawn from the aqueduct that was built by the Greeks to carry water over a distance of some 35km/22mi from the rio Bottigliera, a tributary of the River Anapo, near Pantalica *(see PANTALICA)*. Having fallen into disuse during the Middle Ages, the aqueduct was restored in the 16C by the Marchese di Sortinoto in order to power the watermills erected in the theatre.

To the left extends the **via dei Sepolcri** (Street of Tombs). Pock-marking the rock face on each side are a series of Byzantine tombs and votive niches in which offerings used to be placed. Today, the theatre is still the used during the summer for performances of Classical Greek and Latin plays *(in June of every even year)*.

★★★**Orecchio di Dionisio** – The haunting cave known as the Ear of Dionysius is situated in one of the most striking former limestone quarries *(latomie)* in *Siracusa*: the one that is aptly named **Latomia del Paradiso★★**, now a delightful garden shaded with orange trees, palm trees and magnolias. As its name suggests, the cave resembles an auricle (cavity inside the ear), both in the shape of the entrance and the winding internal space beyond. It was the artist Caravaggio who gave the cave its

Ear of Dionysius

name during his visit to Sicily in the early 1600s on hearing the intriguing explanation of how Dionysius the Elder was able to hear his enemies without seeing them, thanks to the cave's extraordinary echo.

The smoothness of the walls, so tall and even, together with the maze-like interior permanently swathed in shadow make it difficult to imagine that this was once a quarry. In fact, its peculiar shape is explained by the way the limestone was quarried. A small crack was made in the surface at the top; this was then broadened into a narrow channel that was gradually excavated downwards (possibly with the aid of water) until the good stone was reached. The cave has amazing acoustics which the occasional guide or visitor will put to the test by suddenly bursting into song.

Many stories concerning the cave once quarrying ceased are circulated by guides and guidebooks: the most likely hypothesis is that it was used as a prison (like all the other *latomie*); the most imaginative tells of how it came to be used as a hearing trumpet by Dionysius; others say it was used by choirs performing at the nearby theatre.

The neighbouring **Grotta dei Cordari** earned its name from its use until fairly recently by rope-makers for twisting long stretches of sisal and twine, as it provided them with a pleasantly cool area in which to work. Although only visible from the outside (for safety reasons), it clearly shows how it was quarried.

Ara di Ierone II – This enormous altar, some 200m/656ft long and partly carved out of the rock, was commissioned by the tyrant Hieron II in the 3C BC for public sacrifices. Originally, there may have been a large rectangular area stretched out before it, probably with a portico and a central pool.

★**Anfiteatro Romano** – The Roman amphitheatre was built during the Imperial Era. Its situation makes best use of the natural lie of the land and required only half of the *cavea* to be cut out of the bedrock. This is the best preserved section. The other half of the circle was built using large blocks of stone which have been pillaged through the successive centuries. Two entrances may be discerned: one on the north and one on the south side. The rectangular pit in the centre of the arena is connected to the southern entrance by a ditch. This "technical" area was reserved for the stage machinery apparatus that provided performances with special effects.

Opposite the entrance to the amphitheatre stands the pre-Romanesque Church of **San Nicolò dei Cordari** (11C). To its right, sits a water tank built by the Romans for collecting water that was used to flood the amphitheatre for performances of *naumachiae* (sea battles re-enactments) and for cleaning the arena after the gory fights pitched by gladiators against wild animals.

Tomba di Archimede – *Visible from the outside only from the corner of via Romagnoli and via Teracati*. At the eastern end of Latomia Intagliatella is the **Grotticelli Necropoglis**. Among the many cavities hollowed out of the rock, one is ornamented with Doric columns (badly damaged), pediment and tympanum. This so-called "Tomb of Archimedes" actually conceals a Roman *columbarium* (a chamber lined with niches for funerary urns).

The limestone quarries

The *latomie*, from the Greek *litos* – a stone – and *temnos* – a cut – are the ancient quarries that supplied blocks of limestone for the construction of public buildings and grand houses. Quarrying was initiated after a suitable site was selected on the grounds that it might yield regular, good-quality blocks of stone. Crevices were made in the bedrock into which wooden wedges were inserted; these were then dampened to make them expand, causing the rock to split.

In the search for layers of compacted rock, the quarrymen would excavate funnel-like tunnels that gradually broadened out the deeper they were dug. Pillars of rock would be left to prop up the ceilings of these hollows. It has been calculated that in such a way, enormous quantities of material could be efficiently quarried. Once the quarry was exhausted, the cavities would be used as prisons, as described by Cicero in his *Speeches against Verres* (or *Verrine Orations*): it is highly probable that the 7 000 Athenian prisoners captured in 413 BC were held in the *latomie*; all of these perished after eight months of incarceration there, save for the few who were lucky enough to be sold as slaves or those who, according to legend, were able to recite verses by Euripides from memory. The caves, it should be noted, would have been very different in those days: they would have been wider, darker and more suited to accommodating large numbers of prisoners; what we see today has been severely affected by falls of rock dislodged, for the most part, by earth tremors. In subsequent eras, the quarries have hosted lengthy funeral rites, have served as refuges and been used as garden allotments. Only recently was it thought appropriate to reassess their historical importance and restore them.

A map situating all the *latomie* (12 have been identified but some are buried below buildings) reveals how they lie in a kind of arc that corresponds to the limestone terrace formation skirting more or less the edge of the two ancient quarters of Neapolis and Tyche.

The most compelling is the **Latomia del Paradiso★★** *(see above)*, located in the Archaeological Park: this, in fact, consists of a series of caves, around which a lovely garden has been landscaped. An overview *(from beside the Greek theatre)* provides a better understanding of how it was engineered, for where the ceiling has collapsed as a result of earth tremors, it is possible to see a number of the stone supports or pit props still in situ.

Continuing along the arc, from west to east, they appear in the following order: **Latomia Intagliatella**, **Latomia di Santa Venera**, **Latomia del Casale** and **Latomia dei Cappuccini**. This last one is perhaps the most majestic and spectacular of them all, on account of its steep limestone walls.

★★MUSEO ARCHEOLOGICO REGIONALE PAOLO ORSI ⊙

The Paolo Orsi Museum nestles in the garden of **Villa Landolina**, virtually hidden from view. Its importance lies in the fact that it provides a fundamental benchmark in the understanding of Sicily's prehistory right up to the period of the colonies of Syracuse.

The museum presents the inception and development of the various cultural phases in chronological order. The three main sections, all extremely well laid out, are provided with a centrally located introductory area, below which, in the basement, is an auditorium where audio-visual presentations are given *(see programme schedule at the entrance)*.

Section A: Prehistory and protohistory – Displays open with a collection of fossils and minerals, skeletons and prehistoric animal remains along with an exhaustive supply of information about the fauna of the island. There follows various human artefacts representing the Palaeolithic and Neolithic eras, followed by specimens dating from successive phases. The majority of artefacts comprise fragments of pottery, including a large red-burnished **vase★** from Pantalica – a simple yet highly sophisticated tall-footed shape.

Finally, a number of hoards are shown alongside groups of bronze objects (spear-heads, belts and buckles) recovered from containers that had been concealed or hidden (underground or in a cavity).

Section B: Greek colonisation – These objects mark and illustrate the foundation and development of Greek colonies in eastern Sicily. The three Ionic colonies included Naxos, Katane and Leontinoi, from where the beautiful headless marble *kouros* (Archaic male figure) came. The two Doric colonies were Megara Hyblaea and Syracuse, both of which are extremely well-represented. The singular limestone figure of the **Mother-goddess**★ nursing twins (6C BC) was recovered from the necropolis at Megara Hyblaea. Seated and headless, the figure powerfully embodies maternity, extending her arms to embrace and contain the two babies which seem to melt into her, as if they were one.

Museo Archeologico, Siracusa/SCALA

The Syracuse collection is vast and includes two famous exhibits

Mother-goddess from Megara Hyblaea (6C BC)

which are often reproduced: a polychrome shallow relief clay panel with a **gorgon** from the Temenos of the Athenaion, and the bronze statuette of a horse, the symbol of the museum, found in the necropolis at Fusco.

At the entrance to this section devoted to Syracuse, is temporarily displayed the splendid headless statue of **Venus Anadyomene**★ or Landolina Venus, after the man who discovered her. This Roman copy of an original by Praxiteles is one of many made in Antiquity (others include the Medici Venus, the Capitoline Venus) graced with soft sinuous lines. The poise with which she holds the drapery is somehow underlined by the very delicate way in which the light fabric falls into folds that echo the perfect shape of a shell.

Section C: Sub-colonies and Hellenised centres – The first part, devoted to the sub-colonies of Syracuse, contains various fine anthropomorphous figures, including a clay *acroterion* representing a **rider on horseback**.

The second part deals with the history of minor centres. Note the tall clay sculpted enthroned figure of **Demeter** or **Kore** dating from the latter half of the 6C BC.

The third and last part of this section is devoted to Agrigento and Gela. The striking painted **Gorgon's mask**, part of a decorative temple frieze, comes from Gela as does the fine Attic red-figure *pelike* (two-handled vase) by Polygnotos.

Three wooden **Archaic statuettes** are rare examples of votive art: although these were probably extremely widespread, in most cases the wood will have perished and disintegrated with time.

FOOTLOOSE IN "TYCHE" AND "AKRADINA"

Museo del Papiro ⊘ – *Viale Teocrito 66.* The rediscovery of papyrus in Syracuse can be attributed to Saverio Landolina who, in the 18C, reassessed the value of the plant which was being used by the local population at that time for decorative purposes. He also succeeded in reinventing the means of making paper (with several examples displayed in the museum).

The material displayed in the museum covers all the possible applications of papyrus. This includes documents from the time of the pharaohs (fragments of the *Book of the Dead*), objects made of rope, fans all made from the same variety of plant, featherweight boats with slightly raised prows and sterns adept for navigating through shallow waters and marshy areas, and still very much in use by hunters and fishermen in Africa. The last section is dedicated to paper, its actual production (reconstruction of a work-bench) as well as the pigments and instruments used by scribes.

★★**Catacombe di San Giovanni** ⊘ – The catacombs are situated in the Akradina area which, until Roman times, was reserved for the cult of the dead. Unlike the Roman catacombs elsewhere in mainland Italy that are excavated from fragile tufa which restricted their size (lest they collapse), these in Siracusa are cut out from a layer of hard limestone and therefore could be extended into considerably larger underground chambers.

Papyrus

Cyperus papyrus is a plant which grows vigorously in Egypt; it has also been known to man in Siracusa, along the banks of the River Ciane *(see Excursions)*, since Antiquity. It consists of a perennial marsh plant which grows in various forms and sizes, and produces a profusion of tall stems ending with ruffs of bracts (inflorescence). In Ancient Egypt, it was used in all kinds of different ways that exploited its amazing versatility: stems were bundled together to build lightweight boats; it was used for making ropes, baskets and trays, for weaving fabric for clothes and wigs, even for making shoes (such as sandals). The ruff at the top was used to make fans and parasols for civil or religious ceremonies and funeral rites. It has even been suggested that the most tender spongy part of the stalk might have been eaten.

The most famous product made from papyrus is paper, although this involves a fairly complex process. The variable factors are the age of the plant, the ablutions applied to strengthen the thin strips sliced from the stalk lengthways, and the stabilising treatment following the bleaching process. The strips are laid in two perpendicular layers one on top of the other, pressed and dried. The resulting sheet has a flat surface (with horizontal fibres) suitable for writing, backed and supported by the vertical fibres.

It is interesting to note that in many languages the word for paper actually comes from the word "papyrus" (French *papier*, German *papier*, Spanish *papel*, English *paper*, Welsh *papur* and so on).

This complex system of catacombs was developed around the tomb of St Marcian, one of the early Christian martyrs (4C-5C). The extensive network of rectilinear tunnels depends upon a central axis that probably followed the lines of an abandoned Greek aqueduct. At right angles to this principal artery lead a series of minor vein-like passageways. The chambers vary in size according to whether it accommodated a single person or a number (maximum 20 people). Interspersed among these large cavities are a number of smaller and shallower hollows for children (at a time when the infant mortality rate was high). At intervals, there appear round or square areas used by the Christians for interring martyrs and saints. The most significant of these is the *Rotonda di Adelfia*, in which a wonderful sarcophagus was found intact, carved with biblical scenes *(awaiting to be displayed, possibly on the second floor of the archaeological museum)*. Note also, beside the main gallery, the Greco-Roman conical cisterns that have later been used as burial chambers.

Cripta di San Marciano – The Crypt of St Marcian, situated near the necropolis, marks the place where the martyr is alleged to have met his death. The Greek-cross chamber lies some 5m/16ft below ground level. The far wall accommodates three semicircular apses: the right one is the altar where St Paul is supposed to have preached on his

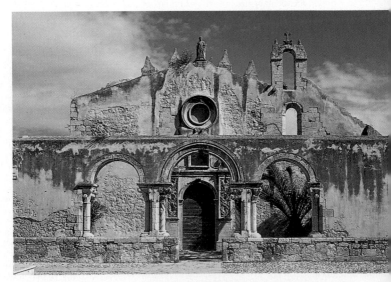

The basilica of San Giovanni

return from Malta in AD 60 (*Acts of the Apostles*, Ch 28 v12); against the right wall of the central apse sits the tomb that is popularly believed to be that of the martyr. The peep-hole inserted on one side was to enable the pilgrims to see the body of the saint and to allow a cloth to be passed over it that might then be considered a special relic-cum-keepsake. The four corners below the central vault are marked with pilasters and Byzantine capitals bearing representations of the Evangelists.

Basilica di San Giovanni Evangelista – The church stands over the crypt of St Marcian. This picturesque ruin, open to the sky, is one of the most atmospheric spots in all Siracusa, especially at sunset, and even more intensely on saint's days and holidays when Mass is celebrated. The basilica was founded in association with the martyr's crypt, for it was usual to mark a sacred burial place with a shrine of some kind. The basilica was destroyed by the Arabs, and restored by the Normans. The main frontage of the Norman church, ornamented with a lovely rose-window, is still visible on the left flank. The main damage was incurred during an earthquake when the roof collapsed, never to be rebuilt. The front portico has been reconstructed using 15C building materials.

The interior, now partly taken over by clumps of tree spurge *(Euphorbia dendroides)*, preserves its original Byzantine.

Basilica di Santa Lucia extra Mœnia ☉ – This basilica faces onto its own piazza: a wide, rectangular area imbued with peace. According to tradition, it was erected to mark the spot where the saint was martyred in 303, as Caravaggio suggests in his painting of the subject *(now in Palazzo Bellomo)*. The original Byzantine church has undergone a considerable number of changes over the years to arrive at its present form in the 15C-16C. The oldest extant parts are the front entrance, the three semicircular apses and the two lower tiers of the bell-tower (12C). The painted wooden ceiling is 17C. Below the church lie the **Catacombs of Santa Lucia** *(closed to the public)*, which by their very existence might substantiate the truth as to whether the saint was indeed martyred here.

Still in the same square, the small octagonal building by Giovanni Vermexio, a 17C architect, contains the tomb of the saint. Her actual relics, however, were transported to Constantinople in the 11C by the Byzantine general George Maniakes, and thence to Venice following the fall of that city during the Fourth Crusade. They are now preserved in the Duomo here.

Santuario della Madonna delle Lacrime ☉ – The rather cumbersome mass of this singular modern conical structure in reinforced concrete (80m/262ft in diameter and 74m/243ft high) dominates the skyline from a long way off. The construction of such an imposing building was prompted by a miraculous event that occurred in 1953 (when an unassuming painting of the Madonna began to shed tears), since when the shrine has attracted large numbers of pilgrims. The architects of this project were the Frenchmen M Andrault and P Parat, and the Italian structural engineer R Morandi. **Inside★**, a dizzy sensation of lofty height is provided and accentuated with the use of vertical windows extending upwards to the apex of the roof.

> ### Santa Lucia
>
> St Lucy, the patron saint of Siracusa, lived here in the 4C, hence the reason why so many local churches are dedicated to her, including the Duomo. The date of 13 December (her *dies natalis*, when the saint's earthly life came to end and her spiritual life began) is celebrated with a procession headed by the silver statue of the saint from the Duomo to the place where she was entombed.

Ginnasio Romano – The so-called Roman Gymnasium, situated on via Elorina just beyond the **Foro Siracusano**, formed with the Forum a part of the market place of ancient Akradina. The description, however, is erroneous. In fact, it was part of a complex building that comprised a *quadroporticus*, with a small theatre – rows of seating are still visible in the *cavea* part – and a small marble temple which served as a stage set.

EPIPOLI – EPIPOLAE

★**Castello Eurialo** ☉ – *9km/5.5mi NW along via Epipoli, in the Belvedere district.* The road up to the fortress gives some idea of the scale of the defensive reinforcements imposed on the city by Dionysius the Elder. In addition to fortifying Ortygia, the able strategist decided to build a wall around the entire settlement, encompassing the districts of Tyche and Neapolis which, until then, had stood outside the city limits and had therefore been easy prey for attack. With this in mind, he ordered the construction of the imposing **Walls of Dionysius** *(mura dionigiane* – 27km/17mi) across the Epipolae high plateau enclosing the north side of the town. The fortification comprised two parallel walls built of rectangular limestone blocks, infilled with rubble. The enclosure reached 10m/33ft in height and 3m/10ft in width; posterns were placed at regular intervals around the perimeter so as to allow traffic to flow freely, and to provide constant surveillance in case of any thought of attack by the enemy. The gates of the castle, being vulnerable, were flanked by defensive towers. One section of the wall is visible along the road up to Belvedere *(on the left)*.

The top of the ridge provided a strategic position for the castle. Its name Euryalus is derived from the headland on which it stood, which vaguely resembles the head of a nail (from the Greek: *euryelos*). The fortress is one of the most impressive Greek defences to have survived from Antiquity. Its heart is ringed with a series of three consecutive ditches linked by a warren of underground passages that prevented garrisons from being controlled as a unit, let alone be supplied centrally with munitions, while at the same time enabling any material fired by the enemy into the ditches to be removed before it incurred any damage. Should the enemy ever succeed in entering the castle precinct, it would have been completely disorientated. The entrance to the archaeological area coincides with the first of these ditches. A little further on, the second deep trench lined with vertical walls may be discerned before, finally, arriving at the third, making this a veritable Chinese-puzzle masterpiece of defensive design. Three tall square piers in the third ditch lead to the assumption that there must have been a drawbridge apparatus providing access to the inner stronghold (or keep). The east side is riddled with a series of communicating passageways; one measuring some 200m/656ft in length led to a pincer-type gateway *(trypilon)* and a way out of the fortress. The west side of the ditch accommodated various underground rooms for storing supplies. Behind stood the square keep, preceded by an impressive series of defensive towers. Within the confines of the keep itself there is an open area with three square cisterns, visible on the right. The far corner provides a fine **view**★ down to *Siracusa (opposite)* and the plain stretching away to the left.

EXCURSIONS

Tempio di Giove Olimpico – *3km/1.8mi out of town along via Elorina, signposted right.*
The Temple of Olympian Zeus, built some time in the 6C BC, occupies a splendid position, slightly raised above the surrounding landscape. Its majestic appearance must have been worthy of the supreme power it represented.

★★**Fonte Ciane** ⊘ – *8km/5mi SE.* The River Ciane, which almost merges with the nearby River Anapo, is the main link with the internal area of Pantalica *(see PANTALICA)*. Its mouth is a favourite starting-point for **boat trips**★★. Shortly after setting off, a splendid view of the Grand Harbour of *Siracusa* opens out before you. The boat then continues in among an area of lush vegetation: predominantly reeds, ancient ash trees, and eucalyptus, before entering a narrow gorge and emerging

Luxuriant clumps of papyrus

in a luxuriant grove of swaying papyrus rising from the water. It was here, according to the myth transcribed by Ovid (*Metamorphoses: The Rape of Proserpine*, Book 5, I 409-437), that the water nymph wooed by Anapus, Cyane, tried to obstruct Pluto from abducting Persephone and, as a result, was transformed into a spring.

Thapsos – *20km/12.5mi NW*. The Magnisi peninsula which separates the Bay of Augusta from the Bay of *Siracusa* is tenuously connected to the mainland by a narrow isthmus of sand. Archaeological findings have now ascertained that in the Middle Bronze Age (15C-13C BC), there grew up one of the most important prehistoric cultures here; this is further underlined by the recovery of Mycenean and Maltese ceramics that suggest Thapsos continued thereafter to be a trading emporium of considerable importance.

Archaeological site ⊘ – Excavation has revealed a number of substantial remains from a settlement, including various round huts from the 15C-14C BC: several of these preserve the holes in which the roof poles were held, and the central hearth. From a subsequent phase (13C-12C BC), there survive traces of a more sophisticated residential complex comprising a series of rectangular chambers arranged around a cobbled courtyard; these concur with Mycenean prototypes. Note also, on a slope to the west of the site, the cisterns for collecting rain water and the small ditch by which it was channelled to the settlement.

Further south along the dirt track edging the area of excavation, on the left, may be seen fragments of the Early Bronze Age fortifications, complete with extant foundations for look-out towers.

A few hundred metres beyond this extends a vast **necropolis** containing some 450 burial chambers. These consist of small man-made hollows preceded by a vestibule, which in most cases consists of a small shaft, *dromos* passageway or tunnel (these are more evident along the sea-shore where the sea has eroded the external wall). The burial chambers are round with conical ceilings; in some, the walls accommodate shallow niches (visible in one tomb where the ceiling has collapsed) in which the grave goods were deposited. These chambers were used for extended groups of people (complete families and dependents), and were designed to serve several generations. Entombment was by inhumation.

Rovine di SOLUNTO ★

Palermo

Michelin map 432 M 22

Solus or Soluntum, one of Sicily's three Punic towns (with Motya and Palermo), enjoys a splendid position on the slopes of the Monte Catalfano headland, with views over the sea beyond Capo Zafferano. It was founded by the Carthaginians in the 4C BC, possibly beside or among the ruins of an old Phoenician town; a century later it succumbed to Roman rule. The name has two origins: one legendary and associated with the evil creature **Soluntus**, who was defeated by Hercules in this very area; the other more plausible explanation links it to the Carthaginian word *Selaim*, meaning crag. The urban layout conforms with the Classical principles upheld by Hippodamus of Miletus, arranged orthogonally around a *decumanus maximus* and perpendicular side streets enclosing *insulae* (blocks); a network of intersecting narrow passages was here inserted to drain away water. The precipitous site required terraces to be built, and for additional living space to be accommodated in tall houses. Although the upper storeys no longer survive, the flights of steps providing access are still visible.

Access ⊘ – *Starting from Bagheria, cross the level crossing near the station and turn down the SS 113 towards Porticello. A minor road forks left towards the hill.* The way up to the ruins passes the **Antiquarium** just inside the gate, which displays artefacts recovered from the site, including a fragment of fresco with a tragic mask.

Baths – *Via delle Terme*. The thermal baths complex preserves the under-floor brick supports which enabled hot air to circulate and heat the rooms from below, and a small room with a mosaic floor which served as a bath.

Via dell'Agorà – The *decumanus maximus* is partly paved in stone and, rather unusually, in terracotta. It bisects the town on a south-west to north-east axis, extending to the *forum*, here designated with the Greek name *agorà*.

Gymnasium – This is the name commonly given to the patrician house with an atrium and a peristyle, from which there remains three Doric columns and part of the entablature, complete with architrave, frieze of metopes and triglyphs and cornice. At the rear, a staircase would have provided access to the floor above.

Via Ippodamo da Mileto – This is a *cardo*: from the bottom, a magnificent **view★★** extends over the bay of Palermo and Monte Pellegrino.

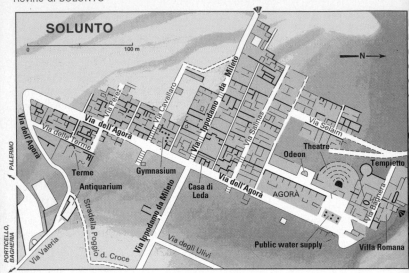

Casa di Leda – This large patrician house is so called because it contains a wall frescoed with Leda and the Swan. The house is arranged around a peristyle (as indicated by the stump of a corner column and cavities for the other columns) with an *impluvium* in which rain water was collected (surrounded by a mosaic cornice with black and white volutes) before being piped to an oval cistern set before and below it. One of the rooms facing out onto the peristyle is frescoed in the fourth Pompeiian style. At the sides of this room, probably a *triclinium*, steps would have lead to the first floor.

Agorà – The square, enclosed on all sides by public buildings, was lined with shops *(at the far end)*. On the east side, there was a large **public tank**: note the bases of the 26 columns that supported the roof.

Theatre – Little survives of the theatre: its shape, however, is still discernible from the air. It was built with rows of seating cut in part from the bedrock – as with the theatre at Segesta. The original building dates from Hellenistic times, although this was substantially altered in Roman times: note how the orchestra is now semi-circular; the Greek orchestra would have been larger and formed almost two-thirds of a circle.

The small round construction on the eastern side probably constituted a **small temple** used for initiation rites associated with the cult of the gods.

Odeon – The small theatre was intended for musical performances or council meetings: the parts still in evidence include the orchestra and a few rows of *cavea* seating.

Villa Romana – This spacious two-storey house was graced with a peristyle. The stairs indicate the way up to the first floor.

From the villa, there is a beautiful view of Capo Zafferano and the little town of **Sant'Elia**. On the right, at the far end of the bay, crowning the tip of the headland, stand the ruins of the **medieval castle of Solanto**.

TAORMINA ★★★

Messina – Population 10 651
Michelin map 432 N 27

Taormina is high up on a rocky plateau 200m/656ft above sea-level, in a fabulous **position**★★★ overlooking the sea, right opposite Mount Etna. Since the 18C it has been a popular destination for travellers, although it has only developed into a substantial tourist resort in the last 30 years. Many foreigners, especially British and German, have decided to build villas in the town and many illustrious personalities have sojourned there, including Emperor William II and King Edward VII, and such famous families as the Rothschilds and the Krupps.

Blessed with a mild climate, this beautiful landscape and serene outlook have made Taormina famous worldwide.

🖪 piazza S Caterina (Palazzo Corvaja), ☎ 0942 23 243; Fax 0942 24 941.

GETTING TO TAORMINA

Trains and buses run to and from Catania (45-90min), Messina (1hr) and Siracusa (2hr 30min). There is also a daily bus service from the town to Fontanarossa airport in Catania (65km/40mi). Taormina-Giardini train station is situated in Villagonia, 3km/1.8mi from the centre. Ths bus station is on via Pirandello.

EXCURSIONS FROM TAORMINA

The CST (Compagnia Siciliana Turismo) bus company offers a number of excursions to places of interest, including Siracusa, Agrigento, Piazza Armerina, Palermo, the Aeolian Islands, the Alcantara gorge and Etna. For further information, contact CST, corso Umberto 101, ☎ 0942 62 60 88, Fax 0942 23 304; www.tin.it./cst

WHERE TO STAY

Hotels are listed in alphabetical order. Visitors are advised to check prices before booking and to book ahead of time. *For further accommodation options, see NAXOS.*

Andromaco – Via Fontana Vecchia, ☎ 0942 23 436, Fax 0942 24 985. Situated approximately 800m/880yd from the old town *(take via Cappuccini)*, this family-run hotel has 20 well-appointed rooms (some with sea views) and a swimming pool on the sun terrace. 200 000L for a double room (including breakfast).

Hotel Isabella – Corso Umberto I 58, ☎ 0942 23 153, Fax 0942 23 155. A recently renovated hotel with 32 comfortable, well-furnished rooms.

Villa Regina – Punta San Giorgio, Castelmola (5km/3mi NW of Taórmina), ☎ 0942 28 289. A guesthouse with 10 simple but well-maintained rooms with delightful views and a small shady garden. 230 000L for a double room (including breakfast).

Villa Sonia – Via Porta Mola 9, Castelmola (5km/3mi NW of Taormina), ☎ 0942 28 082, Fax 0942 28 083. This recently renovated hotel, situated at the entrance to this delightful village, has 30 well-furnished rooms offering fine views.

A TRIP BACK IN TIME

Grand Hotel Timeo – Via Teatro Greco 59, ☎ 0942 23 801, Fax 0942 62 85 01. It was this hotel, with its superb location, which helped to establish Taormina's reputation. The hotel offers incomparable views which can be enjoyed from the terraces or balconies of the individual bedrooms. Modern comforts and impeccable hospitality complement the fine decor of this period residence. Famous guests include Kaiser Wilhelm II, Gide and Guy de Maupassant. Prices reflect the hotel's well-established reputation (approximately 600 000L for a double room).

EATING OUT

Nautilus – Via San Pancrazio 48 *(this street runs alongside the church of the same name)*, ☎ 0942 62 50 24; closed Tues and from 15 Jan to 15 Feb. A simple, elegant restaurant which prides itself on its fine cuisine using the very best ingredients. Approximately 90 000L for a meal.

Porta Messina – Largo Giove Serapide 4, ☎ 0942 23 205. A good restaurant for pizza lovers.

The delicious smell of Sicilian cuisine pervades the districts that lie west of corso Umberto I. This area is teeming with typical local restaurants with outdoor tables on intimate terraces or in secluded gardens.

LEGEND AND HISTORY

Legend relates how the crew aboard a Greek vessel that was sailing along the eastern coast of Sicily had the impudence to be distracted while making a sacrifice to Neptune, the god of the sea. The god, outraged, sent forth such a strong wind that the boat was shipwrecked. Just one of the sailors escaped death and the anger of the god, and succeeded in reaching the beach at Capo Schisò. Fascinated by the area, the lonely survivor Theocles decided to return to Greece to persuade a band of his compatriots to come to Sicily and found a colony: **Nasso**, modern-day Naxos *(see NAXOS)*.

There is a seed of truth in the legend: for a Greek colony was indeed founded here in the 8C BC, and its people prospered quietly until 403 BC when Dionysius, the tyrant of Syracuse, decided to extend his territory by including this part of the island; following their defeat, the colonists were allowed to settle on the plateau of Monte Tauro (200m/656ft above sea-level) which hitherto had been occupied by the Siculi. From that time, records begin to refer to the settlement of *Tauromenion*, modern Taormina. At first the town was allied with Rome, it was then conquered by Octavian; when the Roman Empire fell, it became the capital of Byzantine Sicily. Shortly after the arrival of the Arabs it was destroyed, only to be immediately rebuilt and, in 1079, to be conquered by the Norman Count Roger d'Altavilla, under whom it enjoyed a long period of prosperity.

The open-air theatre

In the centuries that followed, it became a Spanish dominion before succumbing to French and then Bourbon rule, until the Unification of Italy.

SIGHTS

The centre of Taormina, now reserved for pedestrians, radiates from the main thoroughfare corso Umberto I, from which it is possible to reach all, or almost all, the main sights.

★★★ Theatre ⓥ

The theatre was built by the Ancient Greeks (Hellenistic period), and then transformed and enlarged by the Romans. What survives today dates from the 2C AD. The amphitheatre is built in such a way as to exploit the natural lie of the land: several of the *cavea* steps are cut directly from the base rock. The Greek theatre conformed with the correct application of the Classical orders; it included a semicircular *orchestra* section reserved for musicians, chorus and dancers. The Romans removed the lower tier of steps when converting the orchestra into an arena (circular, therefore), a shape better suited to hosting circus games; they also added a corridor to provide access for gladiators and wild animals.

The red of the bricks, the white of the marble columns which still adorn the stage, and the intense blue of the sky above are the predominant colours in this idyllic landscape. From the top of the *cavea* (auditorium), visitors and spectators can absorb the full impact of the glorious **panoramic view★★★** spread before the majestic presence of Mount Etna, its summit often capped with snow, sloping gently down and into the sea which, in turn, silently laps at the undulating coastline below. The magical prospect is extended all along the top of the *cavea* as far as the opposite left-hand corner where the outlook encompasses Taormina itself.

The theatre, which continues to be used, has hosted in the past the *David di Donatello* prize, one of the most prestigious events in the Italian film industry. It now hosts *Taormina Arte*, an international festival of cinema, theatre, ballet and music, which takes place during the summer months.

Sarano/SCOPE

★Corso Umberto I

What a pleasure it is to stroll along this peaceful thoroughfare beginning at **Porta Messina** as it gently climbs up to **Porta Catania**, past its elegant shops, restaurants and cafés. Behind this front, most especially off to the left near the bottom, extends an intricate network of side streets full of unexpected sights and smells (like the sweet scent of marzipan fruits and almond paste wafting up from back-street sweet-shop kitchens). Just beyond Porta Messina, at the entrance to the street, stands the 17C **Chiesa di San Pancrazio**. This is dedicated to St Pancras who, according to legend, was the first Bishop of Taormina. The church, meanwhile, sits among the foundations of a temple dedicated to Zeus Serapis (notice the remains of the old wall incorporated into the building's left flank). The main front is graced with an attractive portal of Taormina stone, framed on each side by niches containing statues of saints.

In the course of the street there are three lovely piazzas.

Piazza Vittorio Emanuele – This square occupies the site of the ancient Roman Forum. Behind the **Chiesa di Santa Caterina** with its fine Baroque pink marble and Taormina stone doorway, vestiges of ancient buildings can be seen. These red brick ruins belong to an **Odeon**, a small covered theatre from the Roman period (1C AD).

Palazzo Corvaja – The main heart of the building, which includes the square tower and the central section overlooking the internal courtyard, dates from the period of Arab domination. The left wing and the staircase up to the first floor were added in the 13C; the right wing dates from the 15C. Having been abandoned and left to become completely dilapidated over the years, it was completely restored after the Second World War. A succession of styles are clearly discernible: the top of the tower is Arab, the two-light windows of the state room (13C) and the elegant front entrance are Catalan Gothic (the stairway before it is ornamented with shallow relief panels depicting scenes from Genesis; alas, badly damaged), the so-called Sala del Parlamento *(in the right wing)* is Norman – it is so called because the Sicilian parliament used to meet here in the 15C.

The offices located off the courtyard, on the right, are in part occupied by APT the Sicilian Tourist Authorities; they also display various typical Sicilian puppets and splendidly ornate Sicilian carts, intricately carved and decorated with wrought-iron fixtures. On close observation, these examples of traditional folk art will reveal a host of minute detail which could pass unnoticed at a single glance.

Naumachie – *In a side-street off to the left.* The name technically refers to the simulated naval battles that the Romans so enjoyed watching. In this case, it relates to a red-brick wall dating from the Roman period that has been reinforced by a system of blind arcading. In fact, it probably served as a supporting wall for a large reservoir of water and formed part of a rectangular building, possibly a gymnasium.

★**Piazza IX Aprile** – This delightful little square overlooks the sea offering wonderful **views**★★ over the bay and across to Mount Etna. It is enclosed on the other three sides by the bare façade of San Giuseppe (17C), San Agostino (now a library) and the Torre dell'Orologio, which sits on an open loggia that provides a through way to the 15C part of the town. The extant building dates from the late 17C, when the clock was added, although it would appear that the foundations date as far back as the 6C AD, when the tower formed an integral part of the town's defences. The piazza serves as a standard meeting-place which means it is often crowded with people happy to while away the time at one of the bars with tables outside.

Piazza Duomo – A splendid Baroque **fountain** in Taormina stone rises from a circular base at the centre of the square. The largest basin facing eastwards at one time served as a drinking-trough. In the middle, raised up, it bears the symbol of the town, a centaur, which in this case takes on a female form with, instead of the usual four legs, two legs and two arms holding an orb and a sceptre, the attributes of power.

Duomo ⊙ – The 13C cathedral is dedicated in honour of St Nicholas of Bari. The front elevation has a starkly simple façade, relieved only by a Renaissance doorway flanked by single-light windows, surmounted by a rose-window. The crenellations along the roof line have earned it the name of "cathedral-fortress". The left lateral wall has a fine entrance set into a pointed arch ornamented along the edge with vines; the rose-window is aligned with the transept.

Interior – The fabric of the building is Gothic; the ground plan is a Latin cross; the nave is separated from the side aisles by an arcade of pointed arches. These spring from column shafts of pink marble. The clerestory above comprises simple one-light windows that light the nave. Over the second altar in the south aisle sits a fine 16C polyptych by Antonello de Saliba.

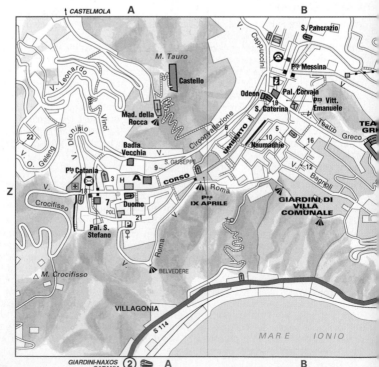

★Taormina's palazzi

The old town centre is dotted with fine *palazzi* which share various features: most are Gothic in style with Arabo-Norman inflections, most are built of black lava stone and white Syracuse stone in a combination to provide geometric patterning and other decorative effects such as articulating arches, arcades and doorways. The application of such simple ideas animate the elevations of Taormina's most interesting town houses.

Palazzo di Santo Stefano – *Turn left up via del Ghetto just before Porta Catania.* This fine building dates from the 15C. It was built for the Dukes of Santo Stefano, who formed part of the De Spuches family whose origins were Spanish. The bold rustication gives it the appearance of a fortified residence. The most effective decorative element is the two-tone (black lava and white Syracuse stone) geometric frieze which runs the length of the upper storey. The two levels which articulate the elevation have two-light windows: those on the second floor are set into elaborate arches.

The palazzo presently accommodates the **Fondazione Mazzullo** ⊙, which hosts permanent exhibitions of sculpture and drawings by the artist Graniti (and the occasional temporary show, notably during Advent when a display of terracotta nativity scenes is arranged). A recurrent theme among the works in lava, granite and bronze, is the expression of pain: this is especially notable in a series of *Executions by Firing Squad* in which crumpled bodies are depicted as mutilated and incomplete, yet powerfully expressive; and in the *Wounded Cat* that is roughly hewn in stone. In contrast, what is striking about the female busts is their impenetrable facial expressions portrayed through features that in some are barely delineated, and in others are perfectly modelled – as in the *Amazon* and *Sappho*.

Badia Vecchia – *Via Dionisio 1.* The name may derive from the false impression that the building had been an abbey. Its solid proportions are reminiscent of the Palazzo di Santo Stefano, as is the two-tone lace-like frieze between the first and second floors. Attractive two-light windows open above the frieze.

Palazzo Ciampoli – *Providing a backdrop to the steps of salita Palazzo Ciampoli, to the right of corso Umberto I, just before piazza Duomo.* Despite its poor condition and an unsightly old discotheque sign (it having closed a few years ago and made way for a hotel), the front of this *palazzo* is composed of two levels separated by a decoratively engraved stone panel. The entrance is set into an elegantly pointed arch, and is surmounted by a shield bearing the date when the palace was built: 1412.

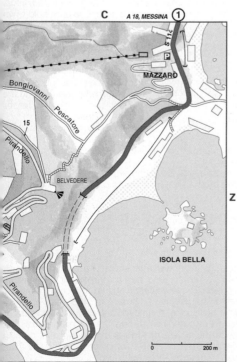

TAORMINA

Traffic restricted in town centre between June and September

Palazzo Ciampoli .... **AZ A**

Palazzo Corvaja – *See above.*

★★I giardini di Villa Comunale – *Via Roma*. The gardens are planted with a huge variety of flowering plants and shrubs ranging from the most common to the exotic. During the times when still under private ownership, a series of follies were erected in various eclectic styles with a touch of the exotic. The most unusual consists of a conglomeration of arches and arcades which, at a glance, might be construed as a beehive, hence the name *(the Beehives)* appropriated to it by its owner, Lady Florence Trevelyan. An enthusiastic ornithologist, she used these follies for bird-watching purposes.

The little road that runs along the seaward edge provides a fine view of Mount Etna and the south coast.

EXCURSIONS

Beaches ⊘ – While Taormina perches high up on its headland, the sea laps gently at the wonderful beaches below. The little bay of **Mazzarò** is enclosed on the south side by **Capo Sant'Andrea**, which is riddled with caves and grottoes, including one known as the Blue Grotto (Grotta Azzurra). The sound of fishermen calling for people to join a boat trip echoes the lengths of all the beaches. Beyond the headland nestles the delightful bay that sweeps round to Isola Bella, which is tenuously linked to the main shore by an extremely narrow strip of land. The longest beaches, **Spisone** and **Mazzeo**, extend north of Mazzarò.

Castello – *4km/2.5mi along the road to Castel Mola; a track turns up to the right*. The castle can also be reached on foot by following the signs for "Salita Castello", up a series of broad steps, from via Circonvallazione *(about 1km/0.6mi there and back)* in Taormina, or by taking Salita Branco, which starts in via Dietro i Cappuccini. Avoid undertaking this walk in the midday sun or at the height of summer!

The **castle** stands isolated on the summit of Monte Tauro (398m/1 305ft). Just below it stands the **Santuario della Madonna della Rocca**: the little terrace before the church offers a fine **view★★** of the Taormina's ancient theatre and town. A footpath continues up to the castle, which consists of a medieval fortress built on the foundations of a former acropolis from Antiquity. Little of the trapezoidal-shaped building survives other than the old walls and the fragments of a tower. From here, yet another splendid **view★★** extends over the theatre and Taormina.

★Castel Mola – *5km/3mi NW*. This little village, occupying a strategic **position★** up behind Taormina, centres around the picturesque little piazzetta del Duomo; from here, an intricate network of tiny paved streets extends outwards. Magnificent glimpses of the surrounding landscape may be snatched from various points, most especially from piazzetta di Sant'Antonino, where the **view★** opens out towards Mount Etna, the north coast and the beaches nestling at the foot of Taormina. The staircase on the right side of this piazza used to lead up from one of the old town gates to the castle; it was moved here when the road was built. The ruined **castle**, of which little remains other than sections of the 16C walls, maintains a good view of Monte Venere (beyond the cemetery) and the lesser Monte Ziretto.

The **Chiesa dell'Annunziata** next to the cemetery, although of Norman foundation, has been completely rebuilt; it preserves an attractive doorway sculpted in white stone.

A regional speciality typical of these parts is almond wine, a potent concoction which, it is claimed, was invented by the local inhabitants of Castel Mola.

A Traditional café

Caffè San Giorgio – *Piazza S Antonio 1*. Founded at the beginning of the 20C, customers of this traditional café have included Rolls and Royce, Rockefeller and the Duke of Aosta.

TERMINI IMERESE

Palermo – Population 27 978
Michelin map 432 N 23

Famous since Antiquity for its hot springs, from which emanates water rich in chloroiodide salts at a temperature of 43°C, Termini also has an important commercial harbour and an extensive industrial estate. The town began acquiring a certain importance after the Carthaginians defeated the people of Himera in 408 BC, forcing a number to flee and settle here near a hot spring. It enjoyed a period of considerable prosperity as a Roman colony, but fortunes declined during the Barbarian invasions until the tide changed once more with the advent of Arab and then Norman rule. In the Middle Ages, it became the principal point of export for buckwheat; in the 16C, it was granted special protection by the Spanish Viceroys.

Today, Termini comprises two sections: the older upper part and a new lower part. It is especially busy at carnival time when allegorical floats process through the streets with groups of revellers in fancy dress – a long-running tradition of which the town is especially proud.

CENTRE

A good place to start exploring the town is piazza Duomo, overlooked by the Palazzo del Comune containing a former Council Chamber decorated with frescoes by Vincenzo La Barbera (1610) depicting the history of the town.

Duomo ⊘ – The cathedral was largely rebuilt in the 17C. Inside, it has a fine marble relief Madonna del Ponte *(fourth chapel on the right)* by Ignazio Marabitti (1842). A lovely wooden statue of the Immacolata by Quattrocchi (1799) adorns the chapel dedicated to the Immaculate Conception, and the chapel of San Bartolomeo is furnished with an interesting Venetian-style Rococo sedan chair once used for taking communion to the sick.

Museo Civico ⊘ – *In via Museo Civico, on the opposite side of the piazza to the Duomo.* The museum is well laid out with helpful information boards; it comprises an archaeological collection and a section dedicated to art. The first rooms display material from Paleolithic and Neolithic times recovered from local caves; excavated artefacts from Himera, including two fine red-figure Attic kraters (5C BC); coinage from the Ancient Greek, Roman and Punic periods. Finally, a large room is dedicated to Hellenistic and Roman pottery: grave goods such as oil-lamps, small receptacles and ointment jars; figurines dressed in togas found in the forum and the so-called House of Stenius (1C AD); portraits including one of Agrippina, the mother of Caligula, which still bears traces of paint; terracotta pipe from the aqueduct of Cornelius and Roman inscriptions.

The chapel of San Michele Arcangelo frescoed by Nicolò da Pettineo leads off the archaeology department. It also contains a *Madonna and Saints* triptych by **Gaspare da Pesaro** (1453), a two-faced marble cross (15C) by followers of the Gagini, and an interesting 15C wooden composition unusual in that it depicts the Trinity as a *Pietà* (with the Holy Spirit personified).

Through the chapel and up to the floor above, the **art gallery** is hung with paintings from the 17C-19C. Notable works include a Flemish *Annunciation* (16C), several pieces by the local painter Vittorio La Barbera (*Crucifixion*, 17C), a *St Sebastian* by Solimena and, in a small room at the far end, a tiny portable Byzantine-style 18C panel triptych.

From behind the Duomo, via Belvedere leads up to a terrace that provides extensive **views** of the coast. A little further on, on the left, is an attractive little church dedicated to **Santa Caterina d'Alessandria** (14C); above the fine pointed arch doorway is set a shallow relief of the saint. Just beyond lies the shaded gardens of **Villa Palmeri**, where the remains of the **Roman Curia** can still be seen. From the park, follow via Anfiteatro down to the ruined **Roman amphitheatre** (1C AD), its ambulatory piers still much in evidence.

Return to piazza Duomo and follow via Mazzini; on the right stands the 17C **Chiesa del Monte**, which was long used as the town's Pantheon (mausoleum for dignitaries).

Città bassa – Return to the car and drive down to the lower part of town along the serpentina Balsamo. A lane leading off a left bend provides a perfect opportunity to stop and take in the lovely view of the pale blue tiled dome of the **Chiesa dell'Annunziata**. **Piazza delle Terme**, at the bottom, is dominated by the Grande Albergo delle Terme, built in the 19C to designs by the architect Damiani Almeyda.

OUTSIDE TOWN

Acquedotto Cornelio – Take the road to Caccamo, and turn left *(yellow sign)*; after some 300m/330yd, on a bend, the Roman aqueduct comes into view on the left, its two tiers of arcades spanning the valley formed by the River Barratina.

Instant refreshment on a hot summer's day...

... try the exquisite home-made ice-creams and water-ices *(granita)* on sale at the Gelateria Cicciuzzu, situated on the Belvedere terrace just behind the Duomo.

EXCURSIONS

Scavi di Himera ⊘ – *18km/11mi E*. Himera was founded in 648 BC by colonists from Zancle (modern Messina). In 480 BC, it was here that the Carthaginians suffered a crushing defeat at the hands of the allied forces of Agrigento and Syracuse. Its demise came in 408 BC, however, when a second wave of invading Carthaginians first conquered, then razed the town to the ground for good.

The ancient town is sited at the top of a hill south of the main Messina-Palermo road. Here, sections of wall and part of the sacred area with three temples have been brought to light. Further along the road up to the site is the **antiquarium** ⊙ used to display artefacts found on site.

The most significant and best-preserved structure, however, is the **Temple of Victory** (5C BC), which stands at the bottom of the hill, on the northern side of the main road. It seems probable that the Greeks forced the Carthaginians to build this temple to celebrate their victory in 480 BC. Possibly dedicated to Athena, it would have been a Doric temple with six columns at the front and 14 down each side; stumpy vestiges of columns, the *cella*, the *pronaos* and the *opisthodomus* are clearly visible. The eaves were marvellously decorated with sculpted lions' heads, now in the archaeological museum in Palermo.

San Nicola l'Arena – *13km/8mi W.* A **castle** with three round towers overlooks the picturesque little harbour of this seaside resort. An old shed on the harbour front still preserves various boats used for tuna fishing.

In the distance (westwards) stands a look-out tower, poignantly situated on Capo Grosso.

TINDARI★

Messina
Michelin map 432 M 27

From the east, Tyndaris appears backed up against a succession of hills that emerge from the sea and rise to form a land mass resembling a great dragon slumbering peacefully; perched high upon its head stands the sanctuary, a discernible landmark from afar. As the road winds down the dragon's back, wonderful **views★** open out over the bay of Patti and the beaches that sweep right round to Capo Milazzo.

The **sanctuary**, a relatively recent addition to the landscape, shelters a Byzantine *Black Virgin* which attracts large bands of pilgrims, notably around the Marian feasts of the Visitation (31 May) and the Nativity (8 September).

At the foot of the rock face nestle the **Laghetti di Marinello** (visible from the terrace before the church) – small rock pools caught when the sea floods the sandy bay, ever-changing and ever a-shimmer with sunshine. According to legend, these rock pools came into being to save a little girl who otherwise would have fallen to her death from the top of the headland because of her faithless mother (unable to believe in a Black Virgin); she was saved when the sea miraculously withdrew to leave a soft landing pad of sand that cushioned her fall. In 1982, one of the rock pools assumed the profile of a veiled woman, identified by the local people as the Madonna of the sanctuary.

These rock pools are accessible on foot from the beaches of Oliveri *(see Golfo di PATTI)*.

Greek foundation – The Greek colony of **Tyndaris**, which occupies a magnificent position, high on its own headland (Capo Tindari), was founded by the tyrant of Syracuse, Dionysius the Elder, in 396 BC to accommodate refugees from Sparta at the end of the Peloponnese War (404 BC). The name may predate the foundation of the settlement as its origins lie with the Dioscuri (Castor and Polydeuces/Pollux), also known as the Tyndaridi, and their earthly father, the mythical hero Tyndareus of Sparta, the husband of Leda and the father of Helen who, according to Homer's *Iliad*, indirectly provoked the War of Troy. The link between the town and the heavenly twins (born out of Leda's alliance with Zeus) is taken up on coins and mosaics.

The new town, occupying a raised, yet naturally defensible position, developed its strategic importance in policing the sea between Messina and the Aeolian Islands. Despite its impressively solid defensive fortifications on the landward side, the town fell into the hands of the Carthaginians. Later, under Roman dominion, it flourished through a period of great prosperity, prompting a range of public buildings such as schools, markets and public baths to be constructed or redeveloped. The theatre, which was built by the Greeks, was modified so as to accommodate the demands of its new audience.

Thereafter, Tyndaris progressively declined: a landslide destroyed part of the city together with its most important features, and further damage was then incurred by the Arab conquest in the 9C.

★ARCHAEOLOGICAL SITE ⊙

Walls – The path up to the top of Capo Tindari passes alongside sections of the defensive walls built during the reign of Dionysius; these were later reinforced and replaced by a double barrier of square stone blocks. The walls were only built around the vulnerable parts of the town, which was laid out on a regular grid system with three wide *decumani* (main thoroughfares) interconnected by perpendicular *cardini*. The natural inclination of the site facilitated an efficient drainage system along the secondary streets.

A small **antiquarium**, just beyond the entrance to the site on the left, displays artefacts recovered from the excavations.

Insula romana – This area comprises an entire block to the south of the main axis or *decumanus superiore*, complete with baths, taverns and houses including a large patrician house which preserves fragments of mosaic.

Basilica – The arcaded remains give some suggestion of the scale and elegance of the original basilica. Even though the ruin has been classified as a basilica or public meeting house, its true function is still uncertain: it may possibly be a part of some monumental *propylaeum* (gateway) for the *agora* or main square of the city. It is built of large square blocks of sandstone, and must have comprised five great arches. The central archway, also the widest, provided access to a barrel-vaulted passage spanning the main road.

Teatro – *Left off the decumanus superiore*. The theatre stands just off the *decumanus superiore* which was probably the settlement's principal thoroughfare (although of the three parallel axes only two have been brought to light so far). The theatre was built by the Greeks (late 4C BC) in such a way as to take full advantage of the natural lie of the land, with the *cavea* (auditorium) facing the sea and the Aeolian Islands. It was adapted in Imperial times for staging gladiator fights.

TRAPANI

Population 69 510
Michelin map 432 M 19

Trapani sits directly opposite the Egadi Islands, providing them with regular communication links with the main island. Besides the ferry traffic, the well-protected harbour handles large consignments of salt gathered in the saltpans just south of the town and tuna fish processed at the important local canning factory.

Trapani, the ancient Drepanum, extends along a curving tongue of land that ends in two horns – one occupied by the Torre di Ligny, the other by a *lazaretto* (a house for the reception of the diseased poor, especially lepers). According to legend, this was formed by the sickle that was dropped by the goddess of agriculture Demeter (Ceres) while she desperately sought her daughter Persephone, who had been carried off to Hades. The inner edge of the sickle *(north)*, sheltered by the Tramontana reef, provides protected anchorages and moorings for fishing-boats. Each morning, on the shore opposite, is held a picturesque fish market *(pescheria)*.

The most exciting time to visit Trapani is undoubtedly over Easter when the old town is thronged with multitudes of people participating in the processions and festivities held during Holy Week. These celebrations culminate in the **Processione dei Misteri** on Good Friday as 20 groups of sculpted figures are borne round and through the streets all day and the following night. At other times, the statues are kept in the **Church of the Purgatorio** (in the town centre, in via San Francesco); made of wood, cloth and glue by local craftsmen, they date from between 1650 and 1720.

The harbour

🛈 piazza Saturno, ☎ 0923 29 00, Fax 0923 24 004.

GETTING TO TRAPANI

Trapani is approximately 150km/94mi from Agrigento and 100km/62mi from Palermo, to which it is connected by both bus and train (3hr 30min and 2hr respectively). The bus and train stations are both situated in piazza Umberto I. For further information and timetables contact the tourist office.

Birgi airport, 15km/9mi south of the town (☎ 0923 84 25 02), operates services from Trapani to Pantelleria.

Services to the Egadi Islands, Pantelleria, Sardinia and Tunisia – Ferry services to the Egadi Islands *(see Isole EGADI)* and Pantelleria leave from Trapani, with sailings operated by Siremar, Agenzia Salvo, corso Italia 52, ☎ 0923 54 54 11, Fax 0923 54 54 44.

For services to Cagliari, consult the Practical Information section of the guide. For information on sailings to Tunisia, contact Tirrenia Navigazione, Agenzia Salvo *(see above)*.

EATING OUT

One of Trapani's most typical dishes is *cuscus di pesce*, a dish brought from North Africa which, according to the locals, is enhanced by the addition of locally caught fish.

Ai Lumi Tavernetta – Corso Vittorio Emanuele 75, ☎ 0923 87 24 18; closed from 15 June to 15 July. A fairly new, attractive restaurant offering meat and fish specialities based on local produce. Approximately 70 000L for a meal.

Taverna Paradiso – Lungomare Dante Alighieri, 22, ☎ 0923 22 303; closed Sun and from 4 to 31 Aug. This atmospheric restaurant serves delicious local cuisine with a particular emphasis on fish. Approximately 70 000L for a meal.

TRAPANI

A

A

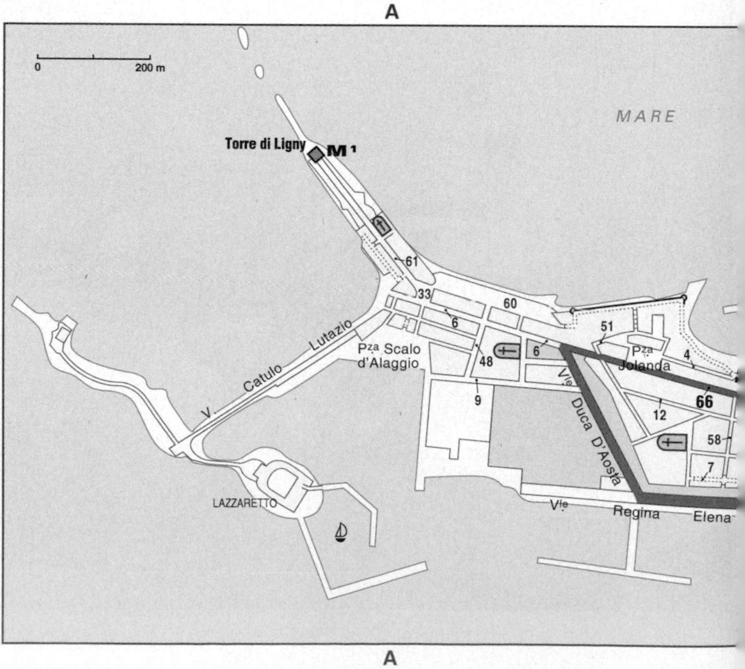

L'ANNUNZIATA

In via Pepoli at the far eastern end of town (in the direction of Palermo) stands the large Carmelite institution known as the Annunziata. The actual church adjoins the former convent which now houses the town's main museum, the Museo Pepoli.

★**Santuario dell'Annunziata** ⊘ – The church, although built in the early 14C, was transformed and enlarged in the course of the 18C. The original front elevation is ornamented with a Chiaramonte Gothic portal, surmounted by an elaborate **rose-window** above.

The **Cappella dei Marinai** (16C) along the left flank, comprises a lovely Renaissance tufa building surmounted by a dome. Inside, it is decorated with a fusion of styles drawn from Eastern and Renaissance sources: recurring elements include the shell which appears in the side niches, pendentives and apse.

The **Cappella della Madonna** extends like a lady chapel from behind the main altar of the church. Access is through a fine Renaissance arch designed by the Gagini (16C) with bronze gates dating from 1591. On the altar sits the delicate figure of the **Madonna of Trapani** (14C), attributed to Nino Pisano. Off the right side of the nave, near the door, lies the **Cappella dei Pescatori** (16C) enclosed with a frescoed octagonal dome.

★**Museo Pepoli** ⊘ – The ex-Carmelite convent beside the Santuario dell'Annunziata provides a magnificent setting for the museum and its fine collections of historic artefacts from prehistoric times to the 19C.

The ground floor is devoted to sculpture. The Gagini family is well represented, with four graceful statues of saints; the most striking is probably the figure of *St James the Greater* by **Antonello Gagini**.

A sumptuous polychrome marble staircase leads up to the first-floor **art gallery**: the most notable paintings are the **Trapani polyptych**★ (15C), a **Pietà**★ by the Neapolitan Roberto di Oderisio (14C) and a lovely *Madonna and Child with Angels* by Pastura (1478-1509). Works from the Neapolitan School include a fine *St Bartholomew* by Ribera.

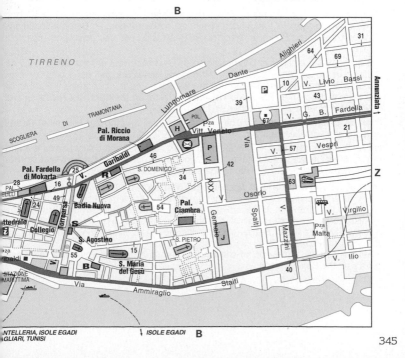

The medium most favoured by the local artists and craftsmen is the Mediterranean red coral (pink coral comes from China). Examples displayed here include liturgical objects and various pieces of jewellery (look out for those made by Matteo Bavera, 17C). There is also a wonderful series of 16 small figurative groups carved of wood and dressed in cloth depicting the *Slaughter of the Innocents* (17C).

The local **pottery** "**industry**" is represented by a pair of fine maiolica panels depicting the **mattanza** (the ritual killing of the tuna fish) and a view of Trapani (17C).

★CENTRO STORICO

The medieval districts of the old part of town are situated on the headland pointing out to sea. The tip was developed by the Spanish in the 14C *(quartiere Palazzo)* and remodelled in the Baroque style later. The oldest section, built in true Moorish fashion around a tight network of interconnecting narrow streets, stretches back along the peninsula; this would originally have been enclosed by walls.

Palazzo Ciambra (della Giudecca) – This fine example of the Plateresque style (16C) has heavy rustication to emphasise the doors and windows, as well as the front of the tower.

Turn down corso Italia.

Santa Maria del Gesù ⊘ – This church with its fine Catalan doorway dates from the beginning of the 16C. Inside the church, the Cappella Staiti (in the right aisle at the back of the church) houses the **Madonna degli Angeli**★ by Andrea della Robbia, underneath a magnificent marble tribune by Antonello Gagini (1521).

Biblioteca Fardelliana ⊘ – The library displays a series of interesting topographical engravings from the Gatto collection, including views of the Trapani area from the 17C-20C.

Sant'Agostino – This church, built by the Knights Templar in the 14C, was badly damaged during the Second World War. The lovely **rose-window**★ and the Gothic doorway are original.

The Fountain of Saturn in front of the church was built in 1342 to commemorate the building of an aqueduct.

Rua Nova – Now named via Garibaldi, the "New Road" was laid in the 13C by the Aragonese. Today, it is lined with fine 18C *palazzi* and churches, including the statue-crested **Palazzo Riccio di Morana**, **Palazzo Milo** and **Badia Nuova** (Santa Maria del Soccorso) ⊘, the interior of which is decorated with Baroque polychrome marble and two elaborate **galleries**★ supported by angels. Palazzo Burgio opposite is graced with a fine 16C doorway.

Via Torrearsa is lined with elegant shops to the left and leads down to the Pescheria (fish market) on the right. Beyond the intersection, via Garibaldi continues as via Libertà, past the splendid **Palazzo Fardello di Mokarta** (the inner courtyard is enclosed within a portico and a round-arch loggia) and Palazzo Melilli with its 16C doorway.

Rua Grande – The second principal thoroughfare constructed in the 13C (the modern corso Vittorio Emanuele) stretches between elegant Baroque buildings such as the Palazzo Berardo Ferro (no 86) and the Sede del Vesvovado (Bishop's Palace).

Cattedrale ⊘ – The cathedral dedicated to St Lawrence was erected in the 17C on the site of an earlier 14C building. The front elevation, put up a century later (1740), is a marvellous expression of the Baroque. Inside, it contains a number of paintings by Flemish artists: a Nativity *(third chapel on the right)*, a Crucifixion and a **Deposition** *(fourth chapel on the left)*.

Chiesa del Collegio dei Gesuiti ⊘ – The 17C church has an imposing Mannerist façade ornamented with pilasters and female caryatid-figures.

Palazzo Senatorio (Cavaretta) – This lovely *palazzo* stands dramatically across the end of the street. Its elaborate façade rises through two orders of columns and statues up to a pair of large clocks. Alongside stands a 13C bell-tower.

Museo della Preistoria e di Archeologia Marina ⊘ – The **Torre di Ligny**, built in 1671 as a defensive bastion on the tip of the "sickle", houses a collection of archaeological artefacts; informative panels complete with illustrations outline the prehistoric era in Sicily. Most of the medieval objects were recovered from the many shipwrecks found nearby. Among the most interesting things on display are the Spanish amphorae.

From the terrace at the top of the tower extends a fine view over the town and across to the Egadi Islands.

USTICA★★

Palermo – Population 1 380
Michelin map 432 K 21

This tiny volcanic island (8.6km²/3.2sq mi), the summit of a large submerged volcano, is the oldest of the Sicilian outer archipelago, having emerged long before the Aeolian Islands. Both the way the volcano was formed and the blackness of its lava have determined the choice of a name derived from the Latin *Ustum*, meaning burnt. Its jagged coastline shelters a series of wonderful caves, bays and creeks. Local residents eke out a living from fishing and tourism; additional income is presently being generated by developing the range of crops grown (vines, vegetables and cereals, especially lentils).

It was inhabited continuously from the late Neolithic until the end of the Classical period, and left to serve as a refuge for pirates. A handful of settlers moved there from Lipari in the Bourbon era. Until the 1950s, it was used as a penal colony. Tourism developed when underwater diving enthusiasts came to explore the surrounding beautifully limpid waters and wonderfully scraggy coastline. In 1987 it was designated a marine national park.

THE ISLAND

★**Ustica** – The small hamlet centres around the largest bay, populating the bowl around the harbour. A single road and various flights of steps, flanked with magnificent hibiscus bushes, lead up to the main town above. A characteristic feature of the houses peculiar to Ustica is the relatively recent practice of painting their exteriors with artistic murals: landscape scenes, *trompe-l'œils*, portraits, still life

Tourist Information – The headquarters of the **Marine National Park** (Riserva Naturale Marina), located in the main square of the town, provides a comprehensive range of information on activities on offer on the island. ☎ 091 84 49 456.

GETTING TO USTICA

Direct services operate out of **Palermo**. Crossings by ferry (2hr 30min) and hydrofoil (1hr 10min) are provided by Siremar, ☎ 091 58 24 03
During the summer season, a hydrofoil service calling at Trapani-Favignana-Ustica-Naples is operated by Ustica Lines, ☎ 0923 22 200. The Ustica-Naples leg takes approx 4hr.

EXPLORING THE ISLAND

Around the island – The standard means of transport available include hired mopeds and a regular minibus service around the island in both directions. Extremely good value bus passes, valid for a week, two weeks or a month, are available from the Town Hall.

A special initiative – Every year, a special week-long sub-aqua course is organised, including theoretical and practical diving lessons (marine archaeology, marine biology, modern recovery techniques for lifting artefacts from the seabed) and guided tours. For further information, apply to the Riserva Marina or to **Archeologia Viva**, ☎ 055 50 62 303.

Rassegna Internazionale delle Attività subacquee – An International Review of Underwater Activities is organised annually during the summer (usually in May, June or September). This gathering includes a range of different events, such as exhibitions and other activities. For detailed information, contact the Azienda di Promozione Turistica in Palermo, ☎ 091 58 38 47.

Underwater equipment – Those who love the sea and enjoy swimming should not forget to bring a mask, snorkel and fins: snorkelling will introduce the visitor to a spectacular underwater world and add a new perspective to their appreciation of the natural beauty of Ustica.

WHERE TO STAY

Pensione Clelia – Via Magazzino 7, ☎ 091 84 49 039, Fax 091 84 49 459. A simple but well-maintained *pensione* with 15 rooms and a lovely outdoor terrace with fine views. 80 000L for a double room (not including breakfast).

EATING OUT

Mamma Lia – Via S Giacomo 2, ☎ 091 84 49 594; open from Mar to Nov. A typical restaurant, located on the first floor of a building in the town centre, serving regional specialities. The decor includes an interesting collection of fishing equipment. Approximately 50 000L for a meal.

paintings, and any other fanciful composition that might spring to mind. The most eye-catching building is the **Torre di Santa Maria** which houses the **Museo Archeologico** ⊙ and its collections of artefacts recovered from the prehistoric village at I Faraglioni and from Hellenistic and Roman tombs found on Capo Falconiera. Note, in particular, the unusual circular fire basket in four sections (and thus transportable) and the lovely tall two-handled cups.

Capo Falconiera – At the far end of the central piazza where the Chiesa Madre is situated, turn right past the Stations of the Cross. From here, a stepped path on the left climbs to the top. The ruins of a Bourbon fortress and a 3C BC rupestrian settlement were positioned up here doubtless because the site could be well-defended and because it surveyed traffic into the only harbour on the island at Cala Santa Maria (still the port today). Naturally restricted by space and inaccessibility, the area was extended by cutting terraces into the rock: as a result, three tiers of housing are stacked one above the other. Many of the cisterns for collecting rainwater are clearly in evidence as is a staircase cut into the rock (right at the top). At the foot of the fortress, remnants of a contemporary hypogeum necropolis have been discovered together with a second necropolis with burial sites (and hypogea) dating from paleo-Christian times (5C-6C AD). From here, a **view**★ stretches from the harbour to the centre of the island, marked with the distinctive profiles of Monte Costa del Fallo and Monte Guardia dei Turchi.

★**Villaggio preistorico** ⊙ – An extensive Bronze Age settlement has been discovered at Colombaia, in the vicinity of **I Faraglioni**. This comprises a collection of foundations for circular huts that were re-used later for square-based constructions of a type similar to a kind of prehistoric house found on the Island of Panarea. The residential area is bisected by a single "high street"; this would indicate that the settlement was developed according to a town plan (albeit fairly basic) with a consideration for public areas, something unusual for the time (usually, the huts were randomly arranged). The village was protected by a strong set of **enclosure walls** (the surviving section suggests it was elliptical in shape) formed by two curtain walls 6m thick at the base, fortified by semicircular towers. The missing sections of curtain walling and the presence of huts founded on base rock, have been read as the rock having been joined at that time to the mainland, and that the collapse (probably caused by an earthquake) provoked the village to be abandoned suddenly.

Coast – The jagged coastline is interrupted by a number of caves which can be explored either by boat (fishermen in the harbour volunteer their services to visitors using boats that are small enough to enter the narrowest caves) or by land. Small beaches (Cala Sidoti, Punta dello Spalmatore, al Faro) succeed lovely rocky bays – including one enclosing the **piscina naturale**★ (a natural pool popular with bathers) along the west coast of the island. Conversely, the east coast shelters the magnificent caves like Grotta Azzurra, Grotta Verde and Grotta delle Barche, which are best-explored with mask and snorkel; the Grotta delle Barche can also be reached on foot by a lovely **path**★ that threads its way through pines and past tall hedges of prickly-pears from Torre di Santa Maria, along the side of the hill, providing marvellous **views**★ of the sea and the coast.

MARINE NATIONAL PARK

The nature reserve was brought into being in 1987 to preserve and protect the huge natural diversity of flora and fauna present in their submarine habitats off Ustica's coastline. The National Park comprises three zones. **Zone A**, classified as **riserva integrale**, extends along the west flank of the island from Cala Sidotti to Caletta and as far as 350m/1148ft offshore (marked with special yellow buoys): swimming is permitted, fishing and boating are prohibited.

Zone B, classified as **riserva generale**, extends beyond Zone A from Punta Cavazzi to Punta Omo Morto (thereby including the entire length of the south-west to the north-east coastline, to a distance of 3 nautical miles offshore): here swimming is permitted as is underwater photography (but not fishing with a speargun), hook-and-line fishing and commercial fishing (on acquisition of a permit from the Commune).

Zone C, classified as a **riserva parziale**, applies to the rest of the coast: here national fishing regulations apply and spear-gun fishing is permitted.

The submerged world – The sea around Ustica is especially clean and pollution-free (lying in the middle of an inward current from the Atlantic Ocean). It therefore provides ideal conditions for multitudes of different species of aquatic flora and fauna to live and proliferate. One striking sight is the vast meadow of *poseidonia oceanica*, a truly effective seaweed, nicknamed the "lungs of the Mediterranean" (because it oxygenates the water), to be found up to a depth of 40m/131ft. Just below the surface, the water often shimmers with passing shoals of white bream, two-banded bream, the dark Ray's bream which emerge from their eggs as piercingly blue fry,

voracious-looking grey mullet (at the worst they only tickle), saddled bream, salpas, and the brilliantly coloured rainbow wrasse. The patches shaded by some over-hanging rock attract groups of cardinal fish; the rock face itself shelters colonies of beautiful orange "flowered" madrepore, which sometimes cover vast sections at a time with colourful sponges (for those unfamiliar with these, sponges come in shades of black, white, yellow and orange, in shapes compact, long, thin and string-like). Little groupers also cower in the shadow of the rocks, but emerge, peeking with curiosity, as anything or anyone approaches. At greater depths lurk the larger fish – notably grey mullet. Here the underwater landscape harbours shy moray eels, lob-sters, mantis prawns and shrimps (in the caves), sea urchins, sea bream, enormous white bream, splendid red gorgonians, and black coral (a pale yellow "living" skin covers the ossified darker interior). With a bit of luck, tuna, ocean sun-fish, turtles and barracuda might also make a brief appearance on the scene.

What's on offer – There are various possibilities both for scuba divers and snorkellers. Those who do not like to get wet can still participate in the under-water world by taking a trip (by day or by night) on the motorised glass-bottomed boat called the *Aquario*, that carries up to 20 passengers.

There are two other reserve centres located at Torre dello Spalmatore (the twin of Torre Santa Maria) – where conferences and other special delegations are hosted – and at Caletta – from where guided tours to the Grotta Segreta start; the **aquarium** ⊙ there reconstitutes 13 different environments corresponding to the various habitats found at different depths.

Guided tours – The west coast, the area designated *riserva integrale* (most highly restricted), harbours the secret and the pink-hued grottoes: **Grotta Segreta** and **Grotta Rosata**, the entrance to which is hidden by rocks whether approaching by land or by sea; its descriptive name effectively sums up the pink marbling of the palest tone to shades of "antique pink" imparted by a distinctive kind of algae.

For those who prefer to enjoy the sea from above or from just below the surface, the reserve authorities lay on **sea-watching** trips (with a commentary) in the *riserva inte-grale*: these involve a guide pointing out the specific organisms and fish as they appear (accustomed as they have become to the presence of man, they appear almost tame).

Scuba-diving – Highlights for any scuba-diving enthusiast include the **Grotta dei Gamberi**, near Punta Gavazzi, where incredibly delicate fan-like red gorgonians thrive (at a depth of approx 42m/138ft), and the **sub-aqua archaeological trail** off the light-house-topped headland Punta Gavazzi (depths of 9m/30ft-17m/56ft, marked by an orange buoy), where many artefacts – anchors and Roman amphorae – can be admired *in situ*.

Another popular haunt is the **Scoglio del Medico**: this consists of an outcrop of basalt riddled with caves and gorges that plunge to great depths, and so provides a spec-tacular underwater **seascape★★**. **Secca di Colombara** (40m/131ft below) is spectacular in a different way, populated as it is by rainbow-coloured arrays of sponges and gorgonians.

Riserva Naturale di VENDICARI★

Siracusa

Michelin map 432 Q 27

The Vendicari Nature Reserve was created in 1984, but did not become operational until 1989. It consists of a narrow strip of marshy coastline covering 574ha/1 418 acres and provides a rare, and now completely protected, habitat for migratory species and a highly peculiar kind of sand-loving Mediterranean vegetation. The large stretch of swamp, a hostile environment in many ways because of high salinity levels, has evolved a very unusual ecosystem which continues to attract vast numbers of birds passing through the area on migration.

During the autumn months, it is common to see a variety of waders: grey heron, little egret, white and black stork, greater flamingo. Later lesser black-backed, slender-billed and Audouin's gulls regularly winter in the area. Between November and March, when the level of the water rises, the swamp attracts many species of wintering duck, including teal, shoveler, pintail, mallard, tufted duck, pochard and red-crested pochard. Among the few species to breed here are black-winged stilt (white body, black wings, long red legs) – adopted as the emblem of Vendicari – as well as Kentish plover, little tern, reed warbler and little bittern.

TOUR ⊙

The reserve is open throughout the year; the best time of day for bird-watching is the early morning or late afternoon. Needless to say, binoculars are vital.

The track briefly skirts the edge of the **Pantano Grande** before leading off towards the so-called **Torre Sveva**, actually erected in the 15C by Peter of Aragon, and the chimney that rises from among the ruins of the **tonnara** (tuna fishery) which functioned until the Second World War. Nearby, set back against the rocks where the waves break over the shore, sit the vestiges of a Hellenistic **fish-processing plant**: the tanks were used to steep the excess fish before salting them *(tarichos)* or using the by-products to make *garum* or fish paste by breaking down the fish gut and offcuts in sea-water – a highly lucrative commodity that was traded right across the Mediterranean from Phoenician to Roman times.

As regards the flora of the area, Vendicari consists essentially of rock and sand: the rocky subsoil mainly found in the north of the reserve, near **Pantano Piccolo**, supports garrigue-type vegetation with cushions of thyme and thorny burnet *(Sarcopoterium spinosum)*. Near **Pantano Roveto**, on the other hand, where sand predominates, sand-loving perennials such as prickly juniper *(Juniperus oxycedrus)* and rosemary grow among the maquis plants.

Capo Passero

The extreme south-eastern tip of Sicily consists of a headland with a lighthouse: to sea, it marks the point at which the Ionian Sea meets the Canale di Sicilia.

The local **tuna fishery** ⊘ flourished during the course of this century, and continues to be owned by the Baron of Belmonte who, only in 1994, took part in a *calata*, when the fishermen go out to lay the nets for catching tuna. The complex comprises a canning works, albeit now unused, where the tuna was put into tins, a house for the *Rais* – the quarter-master responsible for overseeing the *mattanza* (the killing of the tuna) – and a family residence for the owner himself.

A splendid **view★★** stretches across the water to the open horizon, a seascape which changes tirelessly at the whim of the elements.

A natural channel separates the **islet of Capo Passero** from the mainland, this can prove to be an especially strategic place to lay nets when the tuna are running. The islet, meanwhile, has been subject to a compulsory purchase so that the colony of dwarf palms growing there might be protected; this has forced the fish-rearing tanks that were there to be jettisoned at sea, and has decimated tuna fishing in the area. As a result, the place is no longer the centre of activity it used to be.

A curious fact about the mattanza

During the catch, the fishermen used to signal the number of tuna netted in the various chambers: a white and red flag was flown when there were 10; a red flag meant there were 20; a white one meant 30; a red and white one was flown with a white one to signal 40, and so on. If they were unable to estimate the number of fish, they used to wave a sailor's jacket on top of an oar, a gesture known as *u' cappottu*, which meant "we can't count them any more, there are too many".

Portapalo di Capo Passero – This comprises the small, picturesque, archetypal fishing village. Naturally, the hub of activity is the harbour where, between noon and 2pm, the fishing boats return and the quays suddenly throng with curious old men and busy housewives come to purchase the fresh catch straight from the sea.

La VIA DEL SALE
Trapani
Michelin map 432 N 19

The road from Trapani to Marsala skirts round the edge of the lagoon and the island of Mozia *(see MOZIA)* providing fine **views★★** of the local saltworks: panels of mirror-like water, held by thin strips of earth, synchronise to form an irregular and multicoloured scene. In places, the profile of a windmill may be discerned, a reminder of times past when they provided the main means of pumping the water and grinding the salt. The sight is even more striking in summer when the salt is ready to be collected: then, the pinkish hues of the concentrated saline contained in the outer pans vie with those towards the centre of a deeper colour, while the innermost, now dry, sparkle in the sunshine.

Ancient origins – The coastal area between Trapani and Marsala came to be exploited back in the time of the Phoenicians who, realising the extremely favourable conditions available, set about building basins in which to collect salt; this valuable commodity they then exported all over the Mediterranean. So this otherwise barren stretch of land came to be systematically worked: from the shallow water, the searing temperatures and arid winds (which also facilitate evaporation, of course) was born a tough but beneficial industry to produce the precious element, so vital to the survival of man. One of the foremost and fundamental properties of salt is its ability to preserve food,

M. Magni/MICHELIN

a quality with which the earliest peoples were familiar, using it to treat perishables for the lean winter months or simply during transportation. After the Phoenicians, however, there are no reliable references to the saltpans around Trapani until the Norman Era when Frederick II himself alludes to them in the Constitutions of Menfi, making them a Crown monopoly. From this date on, the rise in status of the port of Trapani may be tracked fairly easily. The economic success of the saltpans, meanwhile, shows that major fluctuations in output shadowed the rise and fall in fortunes of the territory as it succumbed to various external events beyond its control. War, epidemic, transitions of government from one dominion to another influenced the production and trading of salt just as it would any other field. On the whole, the area was profitable, as was the commercial activity itself, and that is why it has continued, albeit with fits and starts, until the present day. The salt is still being extracted, although the methods used (and the effort expended) have changed as processes have become mechanised. The picturesque windmills that characterise the landscape are no longer employed and the back-breaking demands on the manual workers have been minimised.

Approx 29km/18mi excursion between Trapani and Marsala along the SP 21: allow a whole day to include a visit to the Island of Mozia.

Trapani – *See TRAPANI.*

From Trapani, follow the coast road *(SP 21)* to Marsala, which provides a succession of fine **views**★★ over the saltpans of Trapani and Paceco and those at Stagnone. The first stop is Nubia.

Nubia – The headquarters of the WWF, formerly the World Wide Fund for Nature *(via Garibaldi 138)*, manages the **Riserva Naturale Salina di Trapani e Paceco** ⊙, a saltwater nature reserve habitat where 170 species of bird – resident and migratory – have been recorded. Indeed, it is not unusual to see migrating flamingos, storks, cranes and herons.

Museo del Sale ⊙ – A small, yet highly interesting salt museum has been set up in a 300-year old saltworker's house: it recounts the different stages involved in collecting salt from the saltpans and displays various specialist tools adapted for its extraction and harvest, including mill gearing, windmill vanes, cog wheels, spikes and sprockets. Additional information about the methods and practices are further clarified by means of explanatory boards and photographs of saltworkers in action.

Le saline – The saltworks in front of the museum successfully demonstrate how and why the different saltpans interact, as well as describing the successive phases in the "cultivation" and extraction of the crystallised salt.

An appropriated canal supplements the two large basins on the outer edge of the complex known as the *fridde* (a corruption of *freddo* meaning cold) because of the temperature of the incoming water. The *Mulino Americano* (literally the American mill – *see Automating the saltworks*) located between these two basins uses an Archimedes screw contraption (of a type displayed in the museum) to transfer water into the *vasu cultivu*, where it blends with the yeast-like residue of the previous crop. The greater the saline concentration (measured in Baum), interestingly enough, the warmer the water. From here, the water is drained to the *ruffiana*, an intermediary stage between the *vasu* and the *caure*, where the water temperature is considerably warmer and the salinity attains 23 Baum. Next in line comes the *sintine*, where the high concentration of salt and the high temperature combine to lend a pinkish tinge to the solution: and so begin the last stages in the process. The water now passes into the salting pans or *caseddri*, where layers of pure salt crystals are allowed to form (27-28 Baum) in preparation for harvest twice a year, usually around mid-July and mid-August. The conical piles of sand,

Automating the saltworks

Mechanisation – The most important individual pieces of machinery used in the cultivation and processing of salt, in the past at least, were the classic Dutch windmill *(see above)*, the American windmill, which was introduced in the early 1950s, and the Archimedes screw. The main difference between the **American windmill** and its smaller Dutch counterpart is its sophistication: it has a massive wheel of 24 iron vanes (instead of six meagre wooden ones) and a greater degree of automation (including a gearing system allowing the roof to regulate itself automatically to catch the wind). The mechanical technology has in most cases been installed inside the pre-existing base of a disused Dutch windmill; the other alteration required involves the mounting of three cogged wheels to the upper wall that must carry the extended sails.

The **Archimedes screw**, the most efficient tool for pumping water from any depth (as it can be activated in a few centimetres of liquid), is powered by hand or by means of a windmill. In simple terms, the screw consists of a rotating shaft with small wooden blades attached to form a continuous spiral. The screw is surrounded by closely fitted staves and bound with metallic strips to make it water tight.

Manpower – Few people were ever fully employed to work the saltpans all year round other than the *curatolo*, the highly trustworthy overseer, and the miller, who was responsible for maintaining the windmill in proper working order. Additional workers were employed on a seasonal basis. The harvest involved the hiring of various labourers. In July, a team would begin by breaking up the crust of salt; other tasks involving creating small channels for the remaining water to be drained away into the *vasu cultivu* (where it was stored until the following year).  Next, the salt was shovelled into small piles in neat rows, thereby allowing any damp residue to dry out. For the actual harvest to begin in earnest, a band of 20 men or *venna* would be hired; they were charged with filling baskets with salt and emptying them on the dyke in much larger piles. In the autumn, the heaps were covered with tiles by the *curatolo*.

E. Kaufmann

aligned the length of the *arione*, are left open to the elements to be rinsed through by the rain, before being covered with "Roman" tiles for protection from heavy downpours and dirt.

From Nubia, return to the main road and continue towards the Stagnone lagoon, where the most spectacular saltpans are located. A sign indicates the way to the Ettore e Infersa saltworks.

Working windmill ⊘ – This 16C (or so) windmill, once indispensable for grinding salt, survives today solely because of the love and attention lavished upon it by its owners (Saline Ettore e Infersa); presently restored to working order, it demonstrates what is involved and inspires a romantic fascination in the practices of yore in the young minds of modern generations.

The **Dutch windmill** comprises a conical building, capped with a conical roof, and six trapezoidal vanes consisting of cloth sails attached to wooden frames that catch the wind and propel a system of mechanical gears. Inside the building, a complex system of interconnected cogs and wheels, shafts and stays allow the circular roof (and, hence, the sails) to be orientated according to the direction of the wind and so exploit the natural resource to grind the salt (in this case) or to pump water (if the windmill is situated between two pans). Should the mill be required to pump water, the gearing is harnessed to an Archimedes screw *(see Automating the saltworks above)*.

The sails can rotate at a speed of 20kph and generate a power equivalent to 120 horsepower (30/40hp are required to activate the grinder in the ground floor rooms alone).

★**Mozia (Motya)** – *See MOZIA.*

The coast road picks its way to Marsala along a most pleasant route, which can be particularly spectacular at sunset.

Marsala – *See MARSALA.*

Admission times and charges

The visiting times marked in the text with the clock-face symbol ⏱ indicate the normal hours of opening and closing. They are listed here in the same order as they appear in the main text. Admission times and charges are liable to alteration without prior notice and so the information given here should merely serve as a guide. It may be preferable to telephone in advance before setting off on visits.

Museums, churches etc may refuse admittance during private functions, religious services or special occasions, and may stop issuing tickets up to an hour before the actual closing time.

When **guided tours** are indicated, the departure time for the last tour of the morning or afternoon will once again be prior to the given closing time.

Most tours are conducted by Italian-speaking guides but in some cases the term "guided tour" may cover group visiting with recorded commentaries. Some of the larger and more frequented museums and monuments offer guided tours in other languages. Enquire at the ticket or book stalls.

The **admission prices** indicated are for single adults benefiting from no special concession; reductions for children, students, the over-60s and parties should be requested on site and be endorsed with proof of ID. In some cases, admission is free (notably Wed, Sun and public holidays). Special conditions for both times and charges are generally granted to groups if arranged beforehand.

Remember to leave a tip if accompanied on a visit by the custodian.

Churches and chapels are usually open from 8am to noon and from 2pm to dusk. Visitors are not admitted during services and so tourists should avoid visiting at that time. As it is the norm for all churches to be open daily, only exceptional conditions are listed here.

Visitors are requested not to wear shorts, miniskirts or low-cut, sleeveless tops when visiting churches. Visitors are not admitted to churches during services. It is advisable to make an early start as some churches may be closed in the afternoon owing to lack of staff. The natural light also offers better visibility in the morning. Machines taking 100L, 200L and 500L coins are sometimes available to illuminate works of art. Although no fee is charged, donations towards maintenance and upkeep are welcome. Contact the local tourist office for details of local festivals which sometimes allow for free entrance to sights.

If facilities for the disabled are available, this is indicated below by the symbol &.

The symbol 🛈 denotes the local tourist office.

Although admission prices are given in Italian Lire (L), visitors should be aware that in January 2002 the Lira will be replaced by the euro, with € equal to approximately 1 900L. See conversion table below.

L	€	€	L
1 000.00	0.52	1	1 936.27
5 000.00	2.58	3	5 808.81
7 000.00	3.62	5	9 681.35
9 000.00	4.65	7	13 553.89
11 000.00	5.68	10	19 362.70
15 000.00	7.75	11	21 298.97
25 000.00	12.91	15	29 044.05
30 000.00	15.49	20	38 725.40

A

ACIREALE 🛈 Corso Umberto 179 – ☎ 095 60 45 21

Duomo – Open 8am-noon and 4.30-8.30pm (winter 3.30-8pm). ☎ 095 60 17 97.

Basilica di San Sebastiano – Open 10am-noon and 4.30-6.30pm. ☎ 095 60 13 13.

Art gallery – Open Mon and Wed only, 9am-12.15pm. No charge. ☎ 095 76 34 516.

Roman Baths of Santa Venera al Pozzo – Open Mon-Sat, 9am-noon, guided tours only (1hr). Book at least two days ahead. No charge. ☎ 095 60 12 50.

Grotta del Presepe di Santa Maria della Neve – Open Sun, 9am-noon. Audio-guided visit (20min). For information, ☎ 095 60 56 33.

Museo dei Pupi dell'Opra – & Open Wed and Sat-Sun, 9am-noon and 5-8pm; the rest of the year, 9am-noon and 3-6pm. 5 000L, 3 000L (child). Guided tour available (30min) by appointment. Audio-visual presentation. ☎ 095 76 48 035.

Aci Castello: Museum – Open May to Sept, Mon-Sat, 9am-1pm and 4.30-8pm; the rest of the year, 3-5pm; Sun open all day. No charge. ☎ 095 73 71 506.

AGRIGENTO

◪ Via Cesare Battisti – **☎** 0922 20 454

Tickets – 8 000L for the Tempio di Giove, the Collina dei Tempi and the Greco-Roman quarter; 4 000L for the Antiquarium di Agrigento Paleocristiana and the Antiquarium iconografico; 10 000L for all the monuments.
12 000L for a combined ticket to the Tempio di Giove, Collina dei Templi, Greco-Roman quarter and Museo Archeologico Regionale.

La Valle dei Templi – Open 8.30am-1hr before dusk. 4 000L; 12 000L combined ticket with the Museo Archeologico Regionale. **☎** 0922 29 702.

Antiquarium di Agrigento Paleocristiana – Open 8.30am-1hr before dusk.

Antiquarium Iconografico della Collina dei Templi – **ර** Open Mon to Sat, 9am-1pm. Closed public holidays. No charge.

Museo Archeologico Regionale – Open daily, 9am-4pm. Opening times are subject to change so it is advisable to telephone for confirmation. 8 000L. **☎** 0922 40 15 65.

Chiesa di San Nicola – Open 9.30am-noon and 3.30-7.30pm.

Oratorio di Falaride – Open 9am-1.30pm. No charge.

Greco-Roman quarter – **ර** Open Mon to Sat, 8.30am-5pm.

San Lorenzo – Closed for restoration at time of going to press.

Abbazia di Santo Spirito – Contact the monastery next door about opening times.

Biblioteca Lucchesiana – Open Fri by appointment only, 9am-1.30pm. **☎** 0922 22 217.

Cathedral – Open 9am-12.30pm and 4.30-7pm.

Excursion

Il Caos: Birthplace of Luigi Pirandello – Open daily, 8am-8pm. 4 000L. Audio-visual presentation. **☎** 0922 44 41 11.

Gole dell'ALCANTÀRA

The gorge – Open May to Oct, 7am-8pm; Nov to Apr, 7am-5pm. 4 000L. Rental of boots and salopettes 13 000L. Charges are subject to change. Bar and restaurant. **☎** 0942 98 50 10.

Castiglione di Sicilia: Chiesa di San Antonio – Closed for restoration at time of going to press. For information, **☎** 0942 98 03 47.

B

BAGHERIA

Villa Palagonìa – Open summer, 9am-12.30pm and 4-7pm; winter, 3-5pm. 5 000L, 2 000L (child under 11). **☎** 091 93 20 88.

Civica Galleria d'Arte Moderna e Contemporanea Renato Guttuso – **ර** Open May to Sept, 10am-8pm; Oct to Apr, 9.30am-7pm. Closed Mon and public holidays. Guided tours (1hr) available. 8 000L. **☎** 091 90 54 38.

Villa Palagonìa, Bagheria

B. Kaufmann

C

CACCAMO

Castle – Guided tours only (1hr) by appointment. Book two days in advance. Tours daily, 9.30am-noon and 4.30-7pm (winter 3.30-6pm). Closed public holidays. No charge. ☎ 091 81 03 245.

Chiesa Madre – For information on admission times, contact the tourist office. ☎ 091 81 03 245.

San Benedetto alla Badia – Same admission times and charges as the castle.

Santa Maria degli Angeli – The church is always open 8am-noon. For afternoon visits contact the tourist office, ☎ 091 81 03 245.

CALTAGIRONE
🛈 Palazzo Libertini – ☎ 0933 53 809

Museo della Ceramica – Open 9am-6.30pm. Guided tours (45min) available. 5 000L. ☎ 0933 21 680.

Museo Civico – Open Tues, Fri and Sat, 9.30am-1.30pm and 4-7pm; Wed and Thur, 9.30am-1.30pm; Sun, 9.30am-12.30pm. Closed Mon. No charge. ☎ 0933 31 590.

Chiesa del Gesù – Open weekdays, 9am-1pm and 3.30-7.30pm. Closed Sun. ☎ 0933 41 812 or 0933 22 707 (Curia).

The piazza, Caltagirone

Santa Maria del Monte – Contact the parish priest. ☎ 0933 21 963.

Santissimo Salvatore – Open Mon-Sat, 9am-1pm and 3.30-7.30pm. Closed Sun. ☎ 0933 41 812 or 0933 22 707.

Chiesa dei Cappuccini – Open 9am (10.15am Sun)-noon and 3-7pm. 2 000L. ☎ 0933 21 753.

CALTANISETTA
🛈 Viale Conte Testasecca – ☎ 0934 21 089

Cathedral – Open Mon-Sat, 8-11.30am and 4-6.30pm (winter 3.30-5pm); Sun 11.15-11.45am and 4-6.30pm (winter 5.30pm). ☎ 0934 21 642.

Sant'Agata al Collegio – Open weekdays, 10-11.30am and 4-5pm. Closed Sat-Sun. ☎ 0934 21 949.

Chiesa di San Domenico – Open 4-5.30pm. ☎ 0934 25 104 or 0934 57 63 63.

Museo Archeologico – ♿ Open 9am-1pm and 3.30-7.30pm. Closed last Mon of each month. 4 000L. ☎ 0934 25 936.

Abbazia di Santo Spirito – Open 10am-12.30pm and 4-7pm. If closed press the bell marked "Parrocchia" on the door. It is advisable to contact the parish priest prior to visiting. ☎ 0934 56 65 96.

CAPO D'ORLANDO
🛈 Via Piave 71 A/B – ☎ 0941 91 27 84

Terme di Bagnoli – Open Apr to Oct, 9am-1hr before dusk; Nov to Mar, 9am-2pm. No charge. ☎ 0941 95 54 01.

Villa Piccolo di Calanovella – Guided tours only (approx 1hr), 9am-noon (year-round) and 5-8pm during the summer months, 3-6pm in autumn and winter and 4-7pm in spring. Closed public holidays. 5 000L. Audio-visual presentation. ☎ 0941 95 70 29.

Excursion inland

Frazzanò: Chiesa di San Lorenzo – Open 9am-noon and 3-6pm. Guided tours only. Book at least five days ahead. ☎ 0941 95 90 37 or 0941 95 90 23.

Convento di San Filippo di Fragalà – Guided tours only, 9am-1pm. Book at least 10 days in advance. For visits on Sat-Sun, contact the local authorities. ☎ 0941 95 90 37.

San Salvatore di Fitalia:

Chiesa di San Salvatore – Open 9am-12.30pm and 3.30-6.30pm (3-5.30pm in winter). ☎ 0941 48 60 14.

Museo Siciliano delle Tradizioni Religiose – &. Open Mon to Fri, 9am-1pm; Sun, by appointment only. Closed public holidays. No charge. ☎ 0941 48 61 72.

Piràino:

Churches – The **Chiesa del Rosario, Chiesa della Catena** and **Chiesa di Santa Caterina d'Alessandria** are open from June to Aug, 10am-noon and 6-8pm; the rest of the year, 10am-noon only. For information or visits at other times contact the tourist office, ☎ 0941 58 14 07.

CARINI

Castle – Guided tours only (1hr), Sat-Sun, 9am-1pm and 4-8pm. No charge. ☎ 091 86 11 349 or 091 86 11 339.

Churches – The churches in Carini are generally open Sat-Sun, 9am-1pm and 4-8pm. For information contact the Ufficio Cultura del Comune. ☎ 091 86 11 341 or 091 86 11 339.

Excursion

Terrasini: Museo Civico – &. Open May to Sept, 9am-12.30pm and 3.30-7.30pm, Sun, 9am-12.30pm only; the rest of the year, 9am-12.30pm, also Sat 3.30-7.30pm. Closed public holidays. Guided tours available. Audio-visual presentation. 2 000L. ☎ 091 86 82 652 (natural history) or 091 86 85 636 (ethno-anthropology).

Villa Romana del CASALE

Tour Open 8am-5.30pm. 8 000L. ☎ 0935 68 00 36.

CASTELBUONO
🛈 Corso Umberto I 69 – ☎ 0921 67 34 67

Museo Civico – Open summer, 9am-1pm and 4-8pm; the rest of the year, 9am-1pm and 3-7pm. Closed Mon afternoon. 1 000L. ☎ 0921 67 34 67.

Madrice Vecchia – Same admission times and charges as Museo Civico.

Cappella Palatina – Same admission times and charges as Museo Civico.

Museo Francesco Minà-Palumbo – Same admission times and charges as Museo Civico.

Chiesa di San Francesco – Open Mon to Sat, 8-9am, Sun and public holidays, 8-10am. ☎ 0921 67 22 94.

Madrice Nuova – Open 9am-noon and 4-6pm.

Golfo di CASTELLAMMARE

Riserva Naturale dello Zingaro – Open dawn-dusk. Guided tours available by written request to Distaccamento Forestale, via Segesta 197, 90014 Castellammare del Golfo. No charge. Audio-visual presentation. ☎ 0924 35 093.

Excursion inland

Alcamo: Chiesa Madre – Open 8am-noon and 4-7.30pm. ☎ 0924 21 578.

CASTELVETRANO
🛈 Piazza Generale Cascino – ☎ 0924 90 91 36

Chiesa Madre – Open 9am-1pm and 3.30-7pm. ☎ 0924 90 91 00.

Museo Selinuntino – Open 9am-1pm and 3.30-7pm. Guided tours available (30min). 5 000L. ☎ 0924 90 49 32 .

Excursion inland

Santa Trinità di Delia – Contact Sig Stefano Saporito for the keys. ☎ 0924 90 42 31.

CASTROREALE

Chiesa Madre – Open daily, 9am-1pm and 4-8pm. ☎ 090 97 46 444 or 090 97 46 036.

Pinacoteca di Santa Maria degli Angeli – &. Open by appointment only. 2 000L. Contact Signor Bilardo, ☎ 090 97 46 036.

357

CASTROREALE

Museo Civico – Open July and Aug, daily, 9am-1pm and 4-8pm; the rest of the year, daily, 9am-1pm and 3-7pm. Closed public holidays and Wed afternoon. No charge. ☏ 090 97 46 444.

Chiesa di Sant'Agata – Guided tours only, 9am-1pm and 3-7pm. Closed Wed afternoon. Book at least two days in advance. ☏ 090 97 46 444 or 090 97 46 036.

CATANIA
🛈 Via Cimarosa 10 – ☏ 095 73 06 211

Duomo – Open 8am-noon and 4-7pm. ☏ 095 32 00 44.

Palazzo Biscari – Guided tours only (20min), weekdays, 9.30am-12.30pm and 4-7pm. By appointment. Closed Aug, Sun and public holidays. 10 000L. No charge on the first Tues of the month. ☏ 095 32 18 18.

Museo Belliniano – Open weekdays, 9am-1pm. Closed public holidays. Guided tours available (45min). No charge. ☏ 095 71 50 535.

Museo Emilio Greco – ♿ Open 9am-1pm; Tues and Thur also open 3-6pm. Closed public holidays. Guided tours available (30min). No charge. ☏ 095 31 76 54.

Teatro Antico – Closed for restoration at the time of going to press. ☏ 095 73 06 211 or 095 53 01 18.

Casa di Verga – Open Mon-Sat, 9am-1pm. 4 000L. ☏ 095 71 50 598.

San Biagio – Open Mon-Sat, 5-7pm; Sun and public holidays, 9am-1pm. ☏ 095 71 59 360.

Orto Botanico – ♿ Open 9am-1pm. Closed Sun, public holidays, and 12 to 15 Aug. No charge. Guided tours available (1hr). Audio-visual presentation. ☏ 095 43 09 01.

San Nicolò l'Arena – Open Mon-Fri, 9am-noon and 3.30-6pm; Sat-Sun, 9am-noon only.

Santa Maria del Gesù – Always open. ☏ 095 43 84 46.

Castello Ursino – Open Tues to Sat, 9am-1pm and 3-6pm (Sun, 9am-1pm only). ☏ 095 34 58 30.

CEFALÀ DIANA

The baths – Open Tues-Sat, 9am-1pm; Sun in summer, 9am-1pm and 3-7pm; the rest of the year, 9am-1pm and 2.30-4.30pm. Closed Mon and 25 Dec. Guided tours available (10min). No charge. ☏ 091 82 01 184.

CEFALÙ
🛈 Corso Ruggero 77 – ☏ 0921 42 10 50

Chiesa del Purgatorio – Open Sun, 10-11am.

Duomo – Open daily, 8am-noon and 3.30-dusk. ☏ 0921 92 20 21.

Museo Mandralisca – Open Apr to Sept, 9.30am-12.30pm and 3.30-7pm; the rest of the year, 9.30am-12.30pm and 3.30-6pm. 8 000L. ☏ 0921 42 15 47; www.museo mandralisca.it

Excursion inland

Santuario di Gibilmanna – Open daily, 7.30am-1pm and 3pm-dusk. ☏ 0921 42 18 35.

COMISO

Museo Civico di Storia Naturale – ♿ Open Tues-Sat, 9.30am-1.30pm and 4-7pm; Sun, 9.30am-1.30pm. Closed Mon and 1 Jan. Guided tours available (40min). No charge. ☏ 0932 72 25 21.

Biblioteca di Bufalino – Open 9am-1pm and 4-8pm. Closed Sat afternoon and Sun. Guided tours available (30min). ☏ 0932 96 26 17.

Chiesa dell'Annunziata – Open daily, 8am-noon and 3.30-7pm (in summer, 5-8pm). It is advisable to book a few days in advance. ☏ 0932 72 25 21.

Chiesa di San Francesco – Open 7am-noon and 4.30-8pm. It is advisable to book a few days in advance. ☏ 0932 72 25 21.

Chiesa dei Cappuccini – It is advisable to book in advance through the Comiso Tourist Office. ☏ 0932 72 25 21.

Excursions

Vittoria:

Museo Civico – ♿ Open 8am-1pm. Guided tours available (45min). Closed Sun, public and local holidays. ☏ 0932 86 59 94.

Museo Storico Italo-Ungherese – Open weekdays, 8.30am-1pm. Closed Sun and public holidays. No charge. ☏ 0932 86 59 94.

Cave di CUSA

Quarry – Open 9am-dusk.

D – E

Castello di DONNAFUGATA

Gardens – Open 8.30am-1.30pm. Closed Mon. No charge. ☎ 0932 61 92 60.

Villa – Closed for restoration at the time of going to press.

Isole EGADI
🔹 Piazza Madrice 8, FAVIGNANA – ☎ 0932 92 16 47

Levanzo: Grotta del Genovese – For opening times contact Sig Castiglione, Via Calvario, Levanzo. ☎ 0923 92 40 32, 0360 63 92 61 or 0339 74 18 800 (mobile).

ENNA
🔹 Via Roma 413 – ☎ 0935 52 82 28

Duomo – Open 9am-1pm and 4-7pm (8pm in summer). ☎ 0935 50 31 65.

Museo Alessi – Open 8am-8pm (10pm in summer). Guided tours available (1hr 30min). 3 000L. ☎ 0935 50 31 65.

Museo Archeologico Varisano – Open 8am-6.30pm. 4 000L. ☎ 0935 24 720.

San Michele Arcangelo – Closed for restoration at the time of going to press. ☎ 0935 50 09 40.

Santa Chiara – For information, ☎ 0935 37 038 or 0935 44 111.

San Giovanni – Open 8.30am-noon and 6-7pm. ☎ 0935 50 09 38.

San Marco – Open mornings only. ☎ 0935 50 10 98.

Castello di Lombardia – Open Apr to Sept, 9am-5pm; the rest of the year 9am-1pm and 3-5pm. No charge. ☎ 0935 40 347.

Santuario del SS Crocifisso di Papardura – Book at least one day in advance. ☎ 0935 26 108.

Assoro: Basilica di San Leone – Contact the parish priest for opening times. ☎ 0935 66 72 78.

Agira: Abbazia San Filippo – Open 8am-11.30am and 5-8pm (4-7pm in winter). It is, however, advisable to contact the parish priest a few days in advance. ☎ 0935 69 10 08 or 0935 69 13 01.

Centùripe: Museo Archeologico – The museum collection has been moved to via SS. Crocifisso 1. For information on admission times and charges, call ☎ 0935 91 94 29 or 0935 91 94 40.

Pietraperzia: Chiesa Madre – Open Mon-Sat, 5-9pm (4.30-8pm in winter), Sun, 9.30-11.30am and 5.30-8.30pm (4.30-7.30pm in winter). ☎ 0943 40 16 83.

Isole EOLIE
🔹 Corso Vittorio Emanuele 202, LIPARI – ☎ 090 98 80 095
🔹 Porto Levante, VULCANO (July to Sept) – ☎ 090 98 52 028

Lipari: Museo Archeologico Eoliano – Open 9am-1.30pm and 3-7pm. 8 000L. ☎ 090 98 80 174; www.museolipari.org

Canneto: White beaches – Contact the fishermen in the harbour for information on how to get to the beaches at the Pomice stone quarries by boat. 10 000L return ticket. Departure times at visitors' request. Alternatively, take the bus from the Marina Piccola and ask to be dropped near the only factory that is still in operation (5min on foot).

Stromboli: Guided tours – Contact the CAI-AGAI authorised guides at Porto di Scari and in piazza San Vincenzo, Stromboli. ☎/fax 090 98 62 63 or 090 98 62 11, 0368 66 49 18 or 0330 96 53 67 (mobile).

ERACLEA MINOA

Ruins – Open daily, 9am-1hr before dusk. 4 000L.

ERICE
🔹 Viale Conte Pepoli 11 – ☎ 0923 86 93 88

Chiesa Matrice – Open daily, 10am-1pm and 3-6pm. ☎ 0923 86 91 23.

Museo Cordici – (♿) Open weekdays, 8am-2pm (also 2.30-5.30pm Mon and Thur). Closed Sat-Sun, and local and public holidays. No charge. ☎ 0923 86 00 48.

Santa Orsola – Open May to Oct, 9am-1pm and 3-6pm; during Easter and Christmas holidays, 9am-5pm; the rest of the year by appointment only. ☎ 0923 86 91 71.

Excursion

Tonnara di Bonagìa: Museo della Tonnara – Guided tours only (30min), 10am-noon and 4-6pm (20 Octto 31 Mar, mornings only). Book at Hotel Tonnara. No charge. ☎ 0923 43 11 11.

Ascent from the south side – Excursions run from the week before Easter to 31 Oct(depending on snow conditions). Duration: approx 3hr. 70 000L including insurance and guide. For more details and information on tours by night contact the Gruppo Guide Alpine Etna Sud, via Etnea 49, Nicolosi ☎ 095 79 14 755 or Funivie dell'Etna, piazza V Emanuele 45, Nicolosi. ☎ 095 91 11 58 or 095 91 41 41. The Gruppo Guide Alpine also organises trekking and skiing trips, as well as visits to the lava caves, by appointment.

Linguaglossa: Chiesa Madre – Contact the Pro Loco for admission times. ☎ 095 64 30 94.

Ascent up the north flank – Excursions May to Oct departing from Piano Provenzana. Duration: approx 3hr. 65 000L including guide. For more details and information on tours at dawn and by night contact S.T.A.R. via Santangelo Fulci 40, Linguaglossa ☎ 095 37 13 33, Catania, or Le Betulle hotel in Piano Provenzana, Linguaglossa ☎ 095 64 34 30.

Sant'Alfio: Castagno dei 100 cavalli – Open Sat-Sun, 10am-12.30pm and 3.30-6.30pm. Contact the Pro Loco for weekday admission times and details of guided tours (15min). ☎ 095 96 87 72.

Misterbianco: Santa Maria delle Grazie – Guided tours only, Mon-Sat, 8am-noon and 3-8pm. ☎ 095 30 14 83.

Adrano: Castle – Open 9am-1pm and 4-7pm (winter 3-6pm). No charge. ☎ 095 76 92 660.

Climbing up Etna

Castello di Nelson – Open 9am-1pm and 2.30-7.30pm (Oct to Mar, 2-4.30pm). Closed Mon, 20 Janand penultimate Sun in May. Guided tours available (45min). 5 000L; 2 000L (child). ☎ 095 69 00 18.

Riserva naturale del fiume Fiumefreddo – Open May to Sept, 9am-6pm; the rest of the year, 8.30am-4.30pm. Closed Mon. No charge. Guided tours available (1-2hr). Audio-visual presentation. Bar and restaurant. ☎ 095 64 62 77, Fax 095 64 95 34.

Riposto: Santuario della Madonna della Lettera – Guided tours only. Open Mon-Fri, 9.30-11.30am and 4.30pm-dusk. Closed the week before 15 Aug. Book at least one day in advance. ☎ 095 93 35 27 or 095 93 11 87.

G

GANGI
🇮 Corso Fedele Vitali 54 – ☎ 0921 50 20 17

Visitors wishing to visit the church are advised to contact the tourist office in advance.

Palazzo Bongiorno – Open Tues-Sun, 9am-6pm.

Chiesa Madrice – Open 10am-8pm.

Museum – Open Tues-Sun, 9am-6pm.

Chiesa del Santissimo Salvatore – Open Sun, 9am-7.30pm; Mon-Sat in July and Aug, 5-7.30pm; the rest of the year, 3.30-7.30pm.

Chiesa di Santa Maria di Gesù – Open 8am-7pm; Sun in July and Aug, 4-7pm.

Santuario dello Spirito Santo – Open 9am-7pm.

GELA
🖬 Via Giacomo Navarra Bresmes 48 · ☎ 0933 91 14 23

Museo Archeologico – ♿ Open daily, 9am-1pm and 3-7pm. Closed last Mon of the month. 6 000L. Audio-visual presentation. ☎ 0933 91 26 26.

Fortifications – ♿ Open 9am-1hr before dusk. 4 000L. ☎ 0933 93 09 75.

Complesso termale – ♿ Open 9am-1pm and 3-5pm by appointment. No charge. ☎ 0933 91 26 26.

I

Gli IBLEI

Buscemi: I Luoghi del Lavoro Contadino – Guided tours only (approx 2hr), 9am-1pm. 6 000L; 3 000L (child). Audio-visual presentation. ☎ 0931 87 85 28.

Vizzini: Chiesa di Santa Maria di Gesù – Open by appointment only through the Pro Loco in Vizzini. Book a few days in advance. ☎ 0933 96 59 05.

Grammichele: Museum – Open 9am-1pm; Tues and Thur also open 4-6pm. Closed Mon, Easter and 25 Dec. No charge. ☎ 0933 85 92 09.

Santuario di Gulfi – Open 9am-noon and 3.30-6.30pm (July to Sept, 4-7.30pm). ☎ 0932 92 22 46.

Monterosso Almo: Chiesa di San Giovanni – Open 8-10am (noon Sun) and 4-8pm. ☎ 0932 97 72 30.

Cava d'ISPICA

Tour of the gorge – Open summer, 9am-7pm; the rest of the year, 9am-1.30pm. Guided tours available. 4 000L. ☎ 0932 77 16 67.

Parco della Forza – Open 9am-dusk. No charge.

Santa Maria Maggiore – Open 6.30am-noon and 4-8pm (closed during church services). ☎ 0932 95 11 32.

Chiesa dell'Annunziata – Closed for restoration at the time of going to press.

J – K – L

Scavi del Monte JATO

Excavations – Open 8am-6pm (Nov to Mar 2-6pm). No charge. ☎ 091 85 72 976.

Excursion

San Cipirello: Museo Civico – (♿) Open Mon to Sat, 9am-1pm and 3-7pm (10pm in summer and on the patron saint's feast day); Sun and public holidays, 9am-noon and 3-6.10pm. No charge. ☎ 091 85 73 083.

Monte KRONIO

Stufe di San Calogero – ♿ Guided tours only (15min). Open Mon-Sat, 8am-1pm. Closed Sun, public holidays and from 16 Dec to 16 Jan. 2 000L. Audio-visual presentation. ☎ 167 88 10 79 (freephone).

Antiquarium – Open Wed, Fri and Sat, 9am-1pm and 3-7pm; Sun, 9am-1pm only. No charge. ☎ 0925 28 989.

LAMPEDUSA

Centro studi sulle tartarughe marine – (♿) Open 15 June to 15 Sept, 10am-noon and 5-7pm. Guided tours available (1hr). No charge. For information contact the Hydrosphera in Rome. ☎ 06 37 51 37 20.

LEONTINOI

Chiesa Madre – Open 8.30am-noon; also 5-6pm from Apr to Oct. ☎ 095 94 17 34.

Archaeological museum – Closed for restoration at the time of going to press.

LEONTINOI

Ancient town – Open summer, 9am-8pm; the rest of the year 9am-1pm. ☎ 095 78 32 962.

Excursion

Case del Biviere – Garden open by appointment. Telephone or fax at least a fortnight in advance. Meals and drinks can be booked for groups. 10 000L. ☎ 095 78 31 449, Fax 095 78 35 575.

M

MADONIE e NEBRODI

Geraci Siculo: Chiesa Madre – Open 8.30am-1pm and 4-7pm. ☎ 0921 64 35 29 or 0921 64 36 07.

Petralia Soprana: Churches – Book a few days in advance through the Polizia Municipale. ☎ 0921 64 10 88.

Petralia Sottana:

San Francesco – Open by appointment only.

Chiesa Madre – Open 8am-12.30pm and 3.30-7pm.

Chiesa della Trinità – Open by appointment only.

Polizzi Generosa:

Museo Ambientalistico Madonita – Guided tours only (30min). Open Sun and holidays, 10am-1pm and 5-7pm (Oct to Apr, 4-6pm); Mon-Sat by appointment only. 5 000L; 3 000L (child). Audio-visual presentation. ☎ 0921 64 94 78.

Chiesa Madre – Under restoration at time of going to press. For information contact the tourist office. ☎ 0921 64 90 18.

Caltavuturo: Chiesa Madre – Guided tours only by appointment three days in advance. Open 10am-12.30pm and 3-6pm; Sun 2.30-5.30pm only. ☎ 0921 54 11 59.

Sclàfani Bagni: Chiesa Madre – Open 9am-noon and 4-7pm (8pm in summer). ☎ 0921 54 06 80.

Sperlinga: Castle-fortress – Open 9am-1pm and 4.30-7pm. ☎ 0935 64 31 98.

San Mauro Castelverde: Chiesa di Santa Maria dei Franchi – Open 10am-5pm. Contact the Ufficio Relazioni del Comune a few days in advance. ☎ 0921 67 40 83.

Pollina: Chiesa Madre – Open 8am-noon and 4-7pm.

Halaesa: Excavations – Open 9am-2hr before dusk. 4 000L. ☎ 0921 33 45 31.

MARSALA   🛈 Via XI Maggio 100 – ☎ 0923 71 40 97

Chiesa Madre – Open Mon-Sat, 10am-noon and 3-6pm.

Museo degli Arazzi – Guided tours only (20min), 9am-1pm and 4-6pm. Closed Mon. 2 000L. ☎ 0923 71 29 03.

Wineries:

Florio – Guided tours only (1hr). Book five days in advance July to Sept and 10 days in advance the rest of the year. Open Mon-Fri morning. Closed public holidays and Aug. No charge. ☎ 0923 78 11 11, Fax 0923 98 23 80; www.cantineflorio.com

Pellegrino – ♿ Guided tours only (30min). Open Mon-Sat, 9am-12.30pm and 2-6pm (9am-1pm only Sat in winter). It is advisable to book. Closed Sun and public holidays. Audio-visual presentation available. ☎ 0923 95 13 65, Fax 0923 95 35 42.

Marco De Bartoli – Guided tours only (1hr). Book one day in advance. ☎ 0923 96 20 93, Fax 0923 96 29 10.

Museo Archeologico di Baglio Anselmi – ♿ Open 9am-2pm and 4-7pm (Mon, Tues and Thur, morning only). 4 000L. Audio-visual presentation. ☎ 0923 95 25 35.

Insula di Capo Boeo – ♿ Open Mon-Sat, 8am-1pm and 2-7pm. Closed Sun. No charge. ☎ 0923 95 25 35 or 0923 80 81 11.

Chiesa di San Giovanni al Boeo – Guided tours only by appointment with the tourist office.

MAZARA DEL VALLO

San Nicolò Regale – Open 9am-1pm. Closed Sun. ☎ 0923 90 94 31.

Museum – Open 8.30am-1.30pm, also 3.15-5.45pm Tues and Fri. No charge. ☎ 0923 94 95 93.

Sala Consagra – Closed until 2001. For information, call ☎ 0923 94 95 93.

Cathedral – Open 8am-7pm. ☎ 0923 94 19 19.

Museo Diocesano – Open Mon-Sat, 9am-1pm. ☎ 0923 90 94 31.

MEGARA HYBLAEA

Excavations – Open Apr to Oct, 9am-6pm; the rest of the year 9am-4pm. No charge.
☎ 0931 48 11 11.

MESSINA
🄴 Via Calabria isol 301b – ☎ 090 67 42 36

Museo Regionale – 㐂 Open 9am-1.30pm (12.30pm Sun), also Tues, Thur and Sat,
3-6.30pm (5.30pm winter). Guided and audio-guided tours available. 8 000L. Audio-
visual presentation. ☎ 090 36 12 92.

Duomo – Open Mon-Sat, 9.30am-5pm, Sun 10.15-11am and 4-5pm; closes at 6pm
in summer. ☎ 090 77 48 95.

Treasury – Open Mar to Oct, 9am-1pm and 3-7pm; the rest of the year, 9am-1pm (also
Sun 4-6.30pm). Closed public holidays. Guided tours available (45min). 5 000L.
☎ 090 67 51 75.

Monastero di San Placido Calonerò – Open weekdays, 4-7pm; Sat-Sun, 3-6pm.
Closed Aug and during Easter and Christmas holidays. It is advisable to contact the
Istituto Agrario several days in advance. ☎ 090 82 11 07, Fax 090 82 12 34.

Scaletta Zanclea: Museo Civico – Open summer only, 9am-1pm and 4-8pm. Closed Sun.
Guided tours available (45min) by appointment: contact the town hall several days in
advance. No charge. ☎ 090 95 10 10.

Itala: San Pietro e San Paolo – Open Sun, 11-11.30am.

Savoca: Convento dei Cappuccini – Open Apr to Sept, 9am-1pm and 4-7pm; the rest of
the year, 9am-noon and 3-5pm. Closed Mon. Guided tours available (15min). Donations welcome.

Casalvecchio:

Chiesa Madre di Sant'Onofrio – Contact Sig. Carmelo Crisafuli at the town hall for information. ☎ 0942 76 11 22 or 0942 76 10 08.

Museo Parrocchiale – Same admission times as Chiesa Madre.

Chiesa dei Santi Pietro e Paolo d'Agrò – Open 8.30am-5.30pm. ☎ 0942 76 11 50.

MILAZZO
🄴 Piazza Caio Duilio 20 – ☎ 090 92 22 865

Santuario di San Francesco di Paola – Open 9am-12.30pm and 4-8pm (6.30pm in
winter). ☎ 090 92 81 337.

Chiesa della Madonna del Rosario – Open weekdays, 5-7pm; Sat, 7-9am and 4.30-
7pm; Sun, 9-11.30am and 5-7pm. For visits at other times or guided tours, contact
Signor Neri. ☎ 0347 50 76 911.

Citadel and castle – Guided tours only (1hr 30min), 10am-2hr before dusk. Closed
Mon and the day after a public holiday. 5 000L; 2 500L (child). For further information on opening hours, contact ☎ 090 92 21 291.

Duomo Nuovo – Open 9am-noon and 5-7pm. ☎ 090 92 81 857.

Excursions inland

Santa Lucia del Mela: Santuario della Madonna della Neve – Open 8.30am-noon and
3-6pm. ☎ 090 93 52 62.

Roccavaldina: pharmacy – Guided tours only (15min), Mon-Sat, 8am-2pm. 5 000L. For
visits at other times, ☎ 090 99 78 302 or 090 99 77 542.

MILITELLO IN VAL DI CATANIA

Monastero Benedettino – Open Sat, 10am-noon and 4-6pm; Sun, 9-11am and
4-6pm. It is advisable to contact the Presidio Turistico at via Porta della Terra 21 several days in advance. ☎ 095 65 52 02 or 095 81 16 66.

Museo di San Nicolò – Open 9am-1pm and 4-7pm (8pm in summer). Closed Tues.
4 000L. ☎ 095 81 12 51.

Santa Maria alla Catena – Same admission times and charges as Museo di San Nicolò.

Maria Santissima della Stella – Open Mon-Sat, 4.30-9pm; Sun, 8am-9pm. ☎ 095
65 52 02. For information on visiting the **treasury**, ☎ 095 65 53 29.

Chiesa dei Santissimi Angeli Custodi – Guided tours only. Book at least one day in
advance. ☎ 095 65 53 29.

San Giorgio – Open 8am-8pm.

Pinacoteca Comunale – Open 9am-1pm.

Casa Natale di Salvatore Quasimodo – Open 10am-1pm and 3.30-6.30pm. For information contact the Cooperativa Etnos. ☎ 0932 75 27 47.

In the company of angels

Chiesa Rupestre di San Nicola Inferiore – Same admission times and charges as Casa Natale di Salvatore Quasimodo.

Museo Civico – Open 9am-1pm.

Museo delle Arti e Tradizioni Popolari – Open 10am-1pm and 3.30-6.30pm. 4 000L. ☎ 0932 75 27 47.

Santa Maria di Betlem – Open 9am-1pm and 3.30-7.30pm. ☎ 0932 75 27 47.

MONREALE

Duomo – Open 8am-6.30pm. Treasury in **Cappella del Crocifisso** open 9.30-11.45am and 3.30-5.45pm; 4 000L. **Ascent to the terraces** from 9.30-11.45am and 3.30-5.45pm; 3 000L. ☎ 091 64 02 424 or 091 64 04 413.

Cloisters – Open daily, 9am-6.30pm (1pm Sun). 8 000L; 15 000L (combined ticket with the cloisters of San Giovanni degli Eremiti, La Cuba and La Zisa in Palermo, valid for two days). ☎ 091 64 04 403.

Excursion

San Martino delle Scale – Open by appointment Mon-Sat, 9am-12.30pm and 4.30-7pm. For information, contact Don Bernardo. ☎ 091 41 81 04.

MOZIA

Access to the island and museum – ♿ 9am-1pm and 3-6pm. 5 000L (boat crossing); 8 000L (museum). ☎ 0923 71 25 98.

N

NARO

Chiesa di Santa Caterina – For information contact the parish priest for the Chiesa Madre at least two days in advance. ☎ 0922 95 63 59.

Chiesa Madre – For information contact the parish priest at least two days in advance. ☎ 0922 95 63 59.

Santuario di San Calogero – Open 7am-noon and 2.30-8pm. If the Sanctuary is closed ask at the building next door. ☎ 0922 95 60 28.

NAXOS

Excavations – Open 9am-2hr before dusk. 4 000L. Audio-visual presentation. ☎ 0942 51 001.

Archaeological museum – ♿ Open 9am-1hr before dusk. 4 000L. Audio-visual presentation. ☎ 0942 51 001.

NICOSIA

Cattedrale di San Nicolò – Open summer, 7.30am-noon and 4.30-8pm; in winter, 7.30am-noon and 4-7pm.

Chapter-house – Open 8.30am-noon and 4.30-7.30pm. ☎ 0935 64 67 92.

Chiesa di San Vincenzo Ferreri – Open 10am-noon and 3-7pm; Sun, 11.30am-12.30pm and 3-8pm; closes at 5pm daily in winter. ☎ 0935 63 90 15.

Santa Maria Maggiore – Same admission times as Chiesa di San Vincenzo Ferreri.

Chiesa dei Cappuccini – Open by appointment only. ☎ 0935 64 62 70.

NOTO
🛈 Piazza XVI Maggio 16 – ☎ 0931 83 67 44

San Francesco all'Immacolata – Open 8am-noon and 4-6pm (7pm summer). ☎ 0931 83 50 05.

Chiesa di San Domenico – For information contact the Allakatalla office. ☎ 0931 83 50 05.

Chiesa del Santissimo Crocefisso – Closed for restoration at the time of going to press.

Excursion

Villa Romana del Tellaro – Open Apr to Oct, Mon-Sat, 9am-6pm; the rest of the year, 9am-4pm; Sun, 9am-2pm. No charge. ☎ 0931 48 11 11.

P

PALAZZOLO ACREIDE

Ancient town of Akrai – Open Apr to Sept, daily, 9am-6pm; the rest of the year, 9am-4pm. 4 000L. ☎ 0931 48 11 11.

Chiesa dell'Immacolata – Contact the custodian.

Casa-Museo dell'etologo Antonino Uccello – Open 9am-1pm. No charge. ☎ 0931 88 14 99.

PALERMO
🛈 Piazza Castelnuovo 34 – ☎ 091 58 38 47

There are a number of combined tickets available, valid for two days:
Galleria Regionale di Palazzo Abatellis, Museo Archeologico Regionale and Palazzo Mirto, 15 000L; the two museums, 12 000L; Palazzo Mirto and one museum, 10 000L. Monreale cloisters, La Cuba, La Zisa and San Giovanni degli Eremiti cloisters, 15 000L.

Cappella Palatina – Open 9am-noon and 3-5pm; Sun, 9-10am and noon-1pm (last entry 30min before closing time). Closed Sat and Sun afternoon, public holidays and Easter Mon. No charge. ☎ 091 70 54 879.

Royal Apartments – Guided tours only (30min), Mon, Fri and Sat, 9am-noon. For group visits, fax ☎ 091 705 47 37.

Osservatorio Astronomico – Guided tours only (1hr). Book one month in advance. ☎ 091 23 34 43.

San Giovanni degli Eremiti – Open 9am-6.30pm (1pm Sun). 8 000L. ☎ 091 65 15 019.

Cathedral – Open Mon-Sat, 7am-7pm; Sun, 8am-1pm and 4-7pm. ☎ 091 33 43 76.
Treasury – Open Mon-Sat only, 9.30am-5.30pm. 2 000L.

Chiesa del Santissimo Salvatore – Open daily, except Tues, 9am-12.30pm. Contact the custodian about afternoon visits. ☎ 091 32 33 92.

San Matteo – Open 9am-5pm; Sun, 10-11am. ☎ 091 33 48 33.

Palazzo Pretorio – Open 9am-8pm; Sun, 9am-1pm. No charge. ☎ 091 74 02 249.

San Giuseppe ai Teatini – Open 8.30am-noon and 6-8pm. ☎ 091 33 12 39.

La Martorana – Open Mon-Sat, 8am-1pm and 3.30-7pm (5.30pm winter); Sun, 9.30am-1pm only. ☎ 091 61 61 692.

San Cataldo – Open 9am-3.30pm (12.30pm Sat-Sun). For information contact the Chiesa della Martorana.

Palazzo Marchesi – Open Mon to Fri, 8am-3.30pm. No charge. ☎ 091 74 06 035 (town council – *assessorato* – in the old town).

Sant'Orsola – For admission times, ☎ 091 74 06 035.

Palazzo Comitini – Guided tours only (1hr), available in a number of languages, 9am-1pm. Closed Sat-Sun. ☎ 091 66 28 260 or 091 66 28 892.

Chiesa del Gesù – Open 7am-noon and 5-6.30pm; mornings only in Aug. ☎ 091 60 76 111.

Chiesa del Carmine – Open 8.30am-noon. ☎ 091 65 12 018.

Galleria Regionale di Sicilia – Open 9am-1.30pm (12.30pm Sun); Tues and Thur, also 3-7.30pm. 8 000L. ☎ 091 62 30 011.

Porta Nuova, Palermo

La Gancia – Open 9.30am-12.30pm and 3-5pm; Sat, 8.30am-12.30pm. Closed Sun. ☎ 091 61 65 221.

La Magione – Open 9am-6.30pm (the church is closed during services).

San Francesco d'Assisi – Open daily, except Sun, 10am-4pm (noon Sat). It is advisable to contact the parish priest a few days in advance. ☎ 091 58 23 70.

Oratorio di San Lorenzo – Open daily, 9am-4pm.

Palazzo Mirto – Open 9am-6.30pm (1pm Sun and public holidays). 5 000L. ☎ 091 61 64 751.

Museo Internazionale delle Marionette – Open 9am-1pm and 4-7pm; Sat, 9am-1pm only. Closed Sun, public holidays and during the week of 15 Aug. 5 000L. Audio-visual presentation. ☎ 091 32 80 60.

Santa Maria della Catena – Open 9am-1pm. Closed Sat and during Aug. ☎ 091 60 67 111.

San Domenico – Open 9am-noon, also Sat-Sun, 5-7pm. ☎ 091 32 95 88.

Oratorio del Rosario di San Domenico – Closed for restoration at the time of going to press.

Santa Maria di Valverde – Open Mon, Wed and Fri, 11am-1pm (also 3.30-5pm Wed). ☎ 091 74 06 035.

Santa Cita – Open 8am-1pm and 3-6pm. If **crypt** in the Cappella Lanza is closed, contact the nuns. ☎ 091 33 27 79.

Oratorio del Rosario di Santa Cita – Open 9am-1pm and 3-5pm; Sun, contact the nuns at the nearby Istituto del Sacro Cuore. Donation welcome. ☎ 091 33 27 79.

San Giorgio dei Genovesi – Open for exhibitions only.

Museo Archeologico Regionale – (&) Open 9am-1.45pm (1.15pm Sun and public holidays); Tues and Fri, also 3-6.45pm. 8 000L. Audio-visual presentation. ☎ 091 61 16 805.

Sant'Ignazio all'Olivella – Open Mon-Sat, 8.30-10.30am and 5.30-6.30pm. ☎ 091 58 68 67.

Oratorio di San Filippo Neri – Open weekdays only, 8.30am-5.30pm. ☎ 091 58 68 67.

Oratorio di Santa Caterina d'Alessandria – Open Thur only, 12.30-2.45pm. ☎ 091 87 28 047.

Chiesa di Sant'Agostino – Open 8am-noon and 4-6pm; Sun and public holidays, 8am-noon only. ☎ 091 58 46 32.

Galleria d'Arte Moderna Empedocle Restivo – Open 9am-8pm (1pm Sun and public holidays). Closed Mon. Guided tours available (1hr). 6 000L. ☎ 091 58 89 51.

Villa Malfitano – Guided tours only (30min), 9am-1pm. Closed Sun, public holidays and 15 July. 5 000L. ☎ 091 68 20 52.

Museo della Fondazione Mormino – ♿ Open 9am-1pm and 3-5pm. Closed Sat afternoon, Sun and national holidays. No charge. ☎ 091 62 59 519; www.aesnet.it/fondasicilia

Orto Botanico – Open Mon-Fri, 9am-5pm; Sat-Sun, 9am-1pm. Closed public holidays. 6 000L. ☎ 091 62 38 241.

San Giovanni dei Lebbrosi – Open Mon-Sat, 9.30-11am and 4-5pm; Sun 9am-noon. ☎ 091 47 50 24.

Chiesa di Santo Spirito o dei Vespri – Open 9am-noon. ☎ 091 42 26 91.

Santuario di Santa Maria di Gesù – The church is part of the "100 open churches" initiative. For information, ☎ 091 74 06 035.

Catacombe dei Cappuccini – Open 9am-noon and 3-5pm. 2 500L. ☎ 091 21 21 17.

Museo Etnografico Pitré – ♿ Open 8.30am-8pm. Closed Fri and public holidays. 6 000L. Guided tours available (45min) by appointment. ☎ 091 74 04 893.

La Zisa – Open 9am-6.30pm (1pm Sun). 5 000L. ☎ 091 65 20 269.

La Cuba – Open 9am-6.30pm (1pm Sun). 5 000L. ☎ 091 52 02 99.

Excursion

Grotte dell'Addaura – The caves are closed at the time of going to press. For information, contact the government office (Soprintendenza di Palermo), ☎ 091 69 61 319, Fax 091 67 02 070.

PANTALICA

Archaeological site – Always open. No charge. ☎ 0931 48 11 11.

Protected natural area – Open May to Oct, 8am-7.30pm; the rest of the year 8am-5pm. Guided tours available (approx 2hr). No charge. ☎ 0931 95 36 95 or 0931 46 24 52.

Excursions

Ferla: Chiesa di San Antonio – Guided tours only, Mon-Sat, 4-6pm; Sun, 10-11.30am and 4-6.30pm. Book three days in advance. ☎ 0931 87 00 81.

Sortino:

Chiesa Madre – Open 5.30-6.30pm, also 9.30-11am Sun.

Museo dell'Opra dei Pupi – Open 10am-12.30pm and 3.30-5.30pm. Closed public holidays and 10 Sept. Guided tours available (30min). No charge. ☎ 0931 91 74 33.

Golfo di PATTI

Patti: Cathedral – Open Mon-Sat, 9am-noon and 3.30-5pm; Sun, mornings only.

Villa Romana di Patti – ♿ Open 9am-2hr before dusk. 4 000L; 6 000L (combined ticket with Tindari archaeological site). ☎ 0941 36 15 93.

Villa Romana di Terme Vigliatore – ♿ Open 9am-2hr before dusk. 4 000L. ☎ 090 97 40 488.

Excursion inland

Montalbano Elicona: Castle – Open Apr to Sept, 9am-1pm and 3-7pm; Oct and Nov, 9am-1pm and 3-5.30pm; the rest of the year by appointment. No charge. ☎ 0941 99 38.

PIANA DEGLI ALBANESI

Excursion

Palazzo Reale – Open summer, 9.30am-1.30pm and 3.30-7.30pm; the rest of the year, 10am-1pm and 2-5pm. For information on trips into the forest, contact the Centro di Recupero della Fauna Selvatica (same admission times as the palace). ☎ 091 84 60 107.

PIAZZA ARMERINA   🛈 Via Cavour 15 – ☎ 0935 68 02 01

Duomo – Open 8am-12.30pm and 3.30-6.30pm. ☎ 0935 68 02 14.

Excursions

Aidone: Museo Archeologico Regionale – Open 9am-7pm. 6 000L. ☎ 0935 87 307.

Scavi di Morgantina: Site – Open 9am-1hr before dusk. 6 000L. ☎ 0935 87 955.

R

RAGUSA

🏛 Via Capitano Bocchieri 33, IBLA – ☎ 0932 62 14 21

Santa Maria delle Scale – Open 10am-noon and 5-7pm.

Santa Maria dell'Itria – Open 10am-noon and 5-7pm.

Duomo di San Giorgio – Open 9am-noon and 4-6pm.

San Giuseppe – Open 9am-noon and 3.30-5pm (visitors are requested to keep silent during church services).

San Giacomo – Open 10am-noon and 5-7pm.

Chiesa dei Cappuccini – Open 10am-noon and 5-7pm.

Cattedrale di San Giovanni – Open 7.30am-noon and 4-7.30pm. ☎ 0932 62 15 99.

Museo Archeologico Ibleo – Open daily, 9am-6.30pm. 4 000L. ☎ 0932 62 29 63.

Camarina:

Excavations – Open 9am-dusk. No charge. ☎ 0932 82 60 04.

Museo Archeologico Regionale – ♿ Open 9am-2pm and 3.30-6pm. 5 000L; 6 000L (combined ticket with the Parco Archeologico di Kaucana). ☎ 0932 82 60 04.

Parco Archeologico di Kaucana – Open 9am-6pm. 4 000L; 6 000L (combined ticket with the Museo Archeologico Regionale di Camarina). ☎ 0932 91 61 42.

RANDAZZO

Chiesa di San Martino – Open 8.30am-12.30pm (10am Sun) and 4-6.30pm. ☎ 095 92 22 79.

S

SALEMI

Museo Civico – Open Tues-Sun, 9.30am-12.50pm and 4-7.30pm. No charge. ☎ 0923 99 13 20.

SAN MARCO D'ALUNZIO

San Teodoro – Guided tours only by appointment, 9am-1pm and 3-7pm. ☎ 0941 79 73 39.

Monastero delle Monache Benedettine: museum – Guided tours only, 9am-1pm and 3-7pm. Closed Mon. 3 000L. ☎ 0941 79 73 39.

San Giuseppe: Museo parrocchiale – Guided tours only, 10am-1pm and 4-7pm; winter, Sat-Sun. 3 000L. ☎ 0941 79 70 45.

Santa Maria delle Grazie – Guided tours only, 9am-1pm and 3-7pm. ☎ 0941 79 73 39.

Church of Ara Coeli – Same admission times and charges as Santa Maria delle Grazie.

San Salvatore – Same admission times and charges as Santa Maria delle Grazie.

SANTO STEFANO DI CAMASTRA

Museo della Ceramica – Open summer, 9am-1pm and 4-9pm; the rest of the year, 9am-1pm and 3.30-7.30pm. Closed 25 Dec. No charge. Audio-visual presentation. ☎ 0921 33 11 10.

Mistretta: Chiesa Madre – Open 8am-noon and 2.30-7pm. ☎ 0921 38 12 18.

San Fratello: Chiesa Normanna dei Santi Alfio, Filadelfo e Cirino – Open 9am-1pm; Sun by appointment only. ☎ 0941 79 43 64.

Sant'Agata di Militello: Museo Etnoantropologico dei Nebrodi – Open 8.30am-12.30pm. Closed Sat-Sun. No charge. ☎ 0941 72 23 08.

SCIACCA

🏛 Corso Vittorio Emanuele 84 – ☎ 0925 21 182

Duomo – Open 7.30am-noon and 4.30-7.30pm. It is advisable to book several days in advance. ☎ 0925 21 693.

Palazzo Scaglione – Open Mon, 9am-1pm, Tues and Thur, 9am-1pm and 3-7pm (9am-1pm only during public holidays). No charge. ☎ 0925 28 025.

Convento di San Francesco – ♿ Open 9am-12.30pm. Closed Sun and public holidays. No charge. ☎ 0925 21 431.

San Nicolò la Latina – Contact the parish priest a few days in advance. ☎ 0925 21 315.

San Michele Arcangelo – Open 8.30-11am and 4.30-7.30pm.

Santa Margherita – Open weekdays, 8am-2pm. ☎ 0925 20 478.

Nuovo Stabilimento Termale – ♿ Guided tours only (30min), 8am-1pm. Closed Sun, public holidays and 16 Decto 16 Jan. No charge. Audio-visual presentation. ☎ 1678 81 079 (freephone).

Castello Incantato – ♿. Open May to Sept, daily except Mon, 10am-noon and 4-8pm; Oct to Apr, daily except Mon, 9am-1pm and 3-5pm. Donations welcome. ☎ 0925 99 30 44.

Scavi di Monte Adranone – Open 8.30am-1hr before dusk. 4 000L. ☎ 0925 28 989.

SCICLI
🚹 Piazza Municipio – ☎ 0932 93 16 52.

Churches – The churches in Scicli are generally open 10.30am-12.30pm and 5-7.30pm. For information contact the Cooperativa Etnos di Modica. ☎ 0932 75 27 47.

Santa Teresa – Open 9am-1pm and 3.30-7.30pm. ☎ 0932 75 27 47.

SEGESTA

Excavations – Temple open 9am-1hr before dusk. 8 000L. There is a shuttle service to the theatre. 2 000L round trip. Bar and restaurant. ☎ 0924 95 23 56.

Antica città di SELINUNTE

Ruins – ♿ Audio-guided tour, 9am-3hr before dusk. 8 000L. ☎ 0924 46 277.

SIRACUSA
🚹 Via Maestranza 33   ☎ 0931 46 42 55

There are a number of combined tickets available, valid for two days: Museo Archeologico Regionale Paolo Orsi and Galleria Regionale di Palazzo Bellomo, 12 000L; Museo Archeologico Regionale Paolo Orsi and Parco Archeologico della Neapolis, 12 000L; Museo Archeologico Regionale Paolo Orsi, Galleria Regionale di Palazzo Bellomo and Parco Archeologico della Neapolis, 15 000L; Parco Archeologico della Neapolis, Castello Eurialo and the archaeological sites of Megara Hyblea, Palazzolo Acreide and Lentini, 15 000L.

Siracusa by sea – Trips aboard the *Selene* and *Linea d'Ombra*, Mar to Nov; the rest of the year, weather permitting. Booking required. ☎ 0931 62 776 or 0368 66 67 21 (mobile).

Duomo – Open 8am-noon and 4-8pm (6.30pm during winter). Opening times given as a guideline only.

Galleria Civica di Arte Contemporanea – ♿ Open 9am-1pm and 5-9pm. Closed Mon. No charge. ☎ 0931 46 46 57.

Galleria Regionale di Palazzo Bellomo – Open daily, 9am-1.30pm (also 2.30-6pm Wed and Fri). 5 000L. ☎ 0931 69 511.

Selinunte

Chiesa di San Benedetto – Closed for restoration at the time of going to press. For information contact the parish priest. ☎ 0931 24 285.

Parco Archeologico della Neapolis – ♿ Open 9am-2hr before dusk. 8 000L. ☎ 0931 48 11 42.

Museo Archeologico Regionale Paolo Orsi – ♿ Open 9am-1pm, also Mon, Wed and Sat, 3.30-6.30pm. Closed Mon morning and second and fourth Sun of the month. 8 000L. Audio-visual presentation. ☎ 0931 46 40 22.

Museo del Papiro – ♿ Open 9am-1pm. Closed Mon. Audio-visual presentation. No charge. ☎ 0931 61 616.

Catacombe di San Giovanni – Open 9am-1pm and 2-5pm. Closed Tues. 4 000L. ☎ 0931 67 955.

Basilica di Santa Lucia extra Moenia – Open 8-11.30am and 4-7pm, except Thur morning and during religious services. For information contact the parish priest. ☎ 0931 67 946.

Santuario della Madonna delle Lacrime – Open 7am-1pm and 3-8pm. ☎ 0931 21 446.

Castello Eurialo – Open 9am-2hr before dusk. No charge. ☎ 0931 71 17 73.

Excursions

Fonte Ciane – Contact Sig. Vella for an appointment. ☎ 0931 69 076 or 0368 31 68 199 (mobile).

Thapsos: Archaeological site – Contact the Soprintendenza in Siracusa at least one week in advance. No charge. ☎ 0931 48 11 11.

Rovine di SOLUNTO

Access and tour – Open Mon-Sat, 9am-1hr before dusk; Sun, 9am-12.30pm. 4 000L. ☎ 091 90 45 57.

T

TAORMINA   🚹 Palazzo Corvaja, Piazza S Caterina – ☎ 0942 23 243.

Theatre – ♿ Open 9am-2hr before dusk. 8 000L. ☎ 0942 23 220.

Duomo – Open 8.30-11.30am and 4-6pm. ☎ 0942 23 123.

Fondazione Mazzullo – Open 8.30am-12.30pm and 3-8pm. No charge.

Excursions

Beaches – To get to the beaches take the cable-car that connects Taormina (via Pirandello) with Mazzarò. From Mazzarò there is a bus, called the Funibus, to the beaches; the ticket covers both cable-car and bus. 3 000L, 5 000L return ticket (round trip). Every 15min (cable-car) and 30min (bus).

TERMINI IMERESE   🚹 Palazzo Civico, Piazza Duomo – ☎ 091 81 41 700

Duomo – Open 8.30am-12.30pm and 4-8pm. Closed Thur morning. ☎ 091 81 41 291.

Museo Civico – Open 9am-1.30pm and 3.30-6.30pm (5.30pm Oct to Feb), Tues and Fri morning only. Closed Mon and public holidays. Guided tours available (1hr 30min) No charge. ☎ 091 81 28 279.

Excursions

Scavi di Himera – Open 9am-5.30pm (1pm Sun). No charge. ☎ 091 81 40 128.

Antiquarium – The Antiquarium is scheduled to re-open in February 2001. ☎ 091 81 40 128.

TINDARI

Archaeological site – Open 9am-2hr before dusk. 4 000L; 6 000L combined ticket with Villa Romana di Patti. ☎ 0941 36 90 23.

TRAPANI   🚹 Piazza Saturno – ☎ 0923 29 00

Santuario dell'Annunziata – Open daily, 7am-noon and 4-7pm (8pm summer). It i advisable to contact the parish priest a few days in advance. ☎ 0923 53 91 84.

Museo Pepoli – ♿ Open 9am-1.30pm (12.30pm Sun), also 3-6.30pm Tues and Thur 5 000L. Audio-visual presentation. ☎ 0923 55 12 42.

Santa Maria del Gesù – Under restoration at time of going to press. For information, ☏ 0923 87 20 21.

Biblioteca Fardelliana – Open July to Sept, 9am-1pm; the rest of the year, 9am-1.30pm and 3-7.30pm, Sat, morning only. Closed Sun, public holidays and 7 Aug. No charge. ☏ 0923 21 506.

Badia Nuova – Open 8.15am-1pm.

Cattedrale – Open weekdays only, 9am-noon and 5-6pm. ☏ 0923 23 362.

Chiesa del Collegio dei Gesuiti – Closed for restoration.

Museo della Preistoria e di Archeologia Marina – Closed for restoration at the time of going to press. ☏ 0923 22 300.

U – V

USTICA   🗗 Riserva Naturale Marina – ☏ 091 84 49 456

Museo Archeologico – Open summer only, daily (except Mon), 4-10pm. 5 000L. For information contact the Riserva Naturale Marina.

Villaggio preistorico – The village can always be seen through the fence. For a more detailed visit contact the Riserva Naturale Marina.

Aquarium – Open summer, daily (except Mon), 10am-1pm and 3-6pm; the rest of the year, daily (except Mon), 10am-1pm only. 5 000L. ☏ 091 84 49 456.

Riserva Naturale di VENDICARI

Tour – Open 9am-dusk. Guided tours available (2hr). No charge. Authorisation from the Ispettorato Foreste required. ☏ 0931 46 24 52 or 0931 46 25 53.

Capo Passero: Tuna fishery – By appointment only. ☏ 0931 84 20 18 or 0931 84 62 99 (mealtimes).

VIA DEL SALE

Nubia:

Riserva Naturale Saline di Trapani e Paceco – ♿. Open 18 Apr to Sept, 9am-5pm. Closed public holidays. Some visits are guided and must be booked in advance. ☏ 0923 86 77 00.

Museo del Sale – ♿ Open 9am-1pm and 3-5pm; Sun, mornings only. 2 000L; 1 000L (child). Guided tours available (30min). Audio-visual presentation. ☏ 0923 86 71 42.

Working windmill – Wind permitting, the mill is put into operation in summer, Wed and Sat from 4pm to 6pm and in winter Sat-Sun by appointment. For information contact Saline Ettore e Infersa. ☏ 0923 96 69 36.

Index

Palermo .... Building, monument, street or place
Gagini, Antonello .... Famous or historical figure, term covered by an explanatory
note

Isolated sights are listed under their proper name.

Q – R

S

Notes

Please write to us !
Your input will help us to improve our guides.

Please send this questionnaire to the following address:
**MICHELIN TRAVEL PUBLICATIONS, The Edward Hyde Building
38 Clarendon Road Watford Herts WD1 1SX**

1. Is this the first time you have purchased THE GREEN GUIDE? yes ☐ no ☐

2. Which title did you buy? : _____

3. What influenced your decision to purchase this guide?

	Not important at all	Somewhat important	Important	Very important
Cover	☐	☐	☐	☐
Clear, attractive layout	☐	☐	☐	☐
Structure	☐	☐	☐	☐
Cultural information	☐	☐	☐	☐
Practical information	☐	☐	☐	☐
Maps and plans	☐	☐	☐	☐
Michelin quality	☐	☐	☐	☐
Loyalty to THE GREEN GUIDE collection	☐	☐	☐	☐

Your comments : _____

4. How would you rate the following aspects of THE GREEN GUIDE?

	Poor	Average	Good	Excellent
Maps at the beginning of the guide	☐	☐	☐	☐
Maps and plans throughout the guide	☐	☐	☐	☐
Description of the sites (style, detail...)	☐	☐	☐	☐
Depth of cultural information	☐	☐	☐	☐
Amount of practical information	☐	☐	☐	
Format	☐	☐	☐	

...ase comment if you have responded poor or average on any of the

5. What do you think about the establishments provided in the guide?

HOTELS :	Not Enough	Sufficient	Too ma
All categories			
"Budget"			
"Moderate"			
"Expensive"			
RESTAURANTS :	**Not Enough**	**Sufficient**	**Too ma**
All categories			
"Budget"			
"Moderate"			
"Expensive"			

Your comments: ______________________________

6. On a scale of 1-20, please rate THE GREEN GUIDE (1 being the lowest, 20 bei the highest): ______________________________

How would you suggest we improve these guides?

1. Maps and Plans: ______________________________

2. Sights: ______________________________

3. Establishments: ______________________________

4. Practical Information: ______________________________

…er: ______________________________

…ographic information: (optional)

…ale ☐ Female ☐ Age ______

above:

383

…avel Publications for internal purposes only and not for re